MARRIAGE and DEATH NOTICES
from
THE (CHARLESTON) TIMES
1800-1821

Compiled by

Brent H. Holcomb, CAIS

CLEARFIELD

Copyright © 1979
Genealogical Publishing Co., Inc.
Baltimore, Maryland
All Rights Reserved.

Library of Congress Catalogue Card Number 79-53896

Reprinted for Clearfield Company by
Genealogical Publishing Company
Baltimore, Maryland
2012

ISBN 978-0-8063-1919-3

Made in the United States of America

INTRODUCTION

The (Charleston) Times has been largely overlooked as a source for marriage and death notices. This is unfortunate, since this newspaper contains notices not appearing in other Charleston newspapers of the period. This is an early daily newspaper (Sunday excepted), thereby having more space for such notices than a weekly publication. The Times was the official newspaper of the Charleston City Council. This fact may account for the notices of minor officials all over South Carolina.

The compiler was pleasantly surprised by the number of up-country notices, especially from the districts of Abbeville and Pendleton; but of equal importance are the notices from the parishes of such "burned" districts as Beaufort and Colleton (Prince William's, St. Paul's, St. Bartholomew's, etc.). The close contact between Charleston and the islands of St. Domingo and Jamaica is evidenced by the number of notices from those places. The completeness of the files for the early years (1800-1813) helps to fill in gaps in the Georgetown newspapers, and gives a new source for early notices from the Camden area. (Although Camden had a newspaper as early as 1802, no significant file is extant before 1816). Also some gaps in the *Pendleton Messenger* notices (beginning 1807) are filled in by this publication. Newspapers of this time period often copied notices from one another without giving credit. Therefore we may have notices in the *Times* from newspapers about which we know little or nothing, such as the Edgefield newspapers of the 1810s.

The exact date of the demise of the *Times* is unknown. This volume covers the entire extant run of the newspaper from microfilm files at the South Caroliniana Library. Fortunately for the compiler, this microfilm represents collections of all known institutions holding any files of this publication. The cooperation of the South Caroliniana Library is greatly appreciated.

Brent H. Holcomb, C.A.L.S.
Columbia, South Carolina
May 7, 1979

Issue of October 7, 1800 (Vol. I, #2)

Married, last evening, by the Reverend Mr. Mathews, Doctor William De Bow to Mrs. Hannah Hunt, both of this place.

Issue of October 10, 1800

Married, last evening by the Rev. Dr. Buist, Mr. John Coburn, to Miss Ann Pendarvis, both of this city.

Issue of October 14, 1800

Married, last evening, by the Rev. Mr. Munds, Mr. Charles Aikman, to Miss Leonora Mills.

Issue of October 15, 1800

Died, on Sunday last, in the 53d year of her age, Madame Guerin, widow of the late Mons. Guerin, confectioner.

Issue of October 16, 1800

Died, at New-York, on the 27th ult., in the 21st year of his age, Mr. Thomas Cooper, late a merchant of this city- a young man, whose virtues and integrity justly endeared him to all his acquaintances.

Issue of October 18, 1800

Married on Thursday evening last, by the Rev. Mr. Munds, Mr. William Haughton, to Miss Mary Leslie.

Issue of October 21, 1800

Married, on Saturday evening, by the Rev. Mr. Jenkins, David Deas, Esq. to Miss Mary Sommers.
Died on Saturday morning, the 18th inst., George Taylor, Esq., Attorney at Law, a native of the county of Kent, in England. He has resided upwards of 17 years in this country, during which time he practiced at the bar with strict integrity, and for several years past filled the office of Register in the Court of Equity. His friends have to regret in him, the loss of a cheerful member of society and the country a firm supporter of the federal government.
Died, on Wednesday the 15th October, 1800, Mr. Adam Culiatt, of Jacksonborough, in the thirty-first year of his age. His death was occasioned by his horse running away with him, and violently rushing him against a cotton scaffold; he languished about two hours, and was sensible to his end. His funeral was attended by a number of respectable inhabitants, and a detachment of the Pon-Pon troop of horse, to which he belonged and was by them buried, with the honors of war, at the burial-ground of his ancestors on Pon-Pon creek.

Issue of October 31, 1800

Died yesterday, after an illness of two days, Mr. Stephen Toussiger, truly and justly lamented by all who had the pleasure of his acquaintance; whose affable and engaging manners endeared him to all who knew him.

Issue of November 1, 1800

Married on Thursday, the 23d ult. at Camden, by the Rev. Mr. Smith, Mr. William Adamson, merchant, only son of John Adamson, Esq., to Miss Amelia Alexander, only daughter of Dr. Isaac Alexander, both of that place.

Married on Thursday evening last, by the Rev. Mr. J. C. Faber, Mr. John Spring, to Miss Catherine Reader, both of this city.

Married, on Thursday evening last, by the Rev. Mr. Furman, Capt. Benjamin Pearson, to the amiable and accomplished Miss Frances Ann Adely, both of this city.

Died, at Camden, on Friday morning, the 24th ult., Mr. William Layten, formerly a merchant of this city.

Died, on Thursday last, after a few days illness, Mr. William Hicks, native of Boston. He was a promising young man, and of modest deportment.

Issue of November 3, 1800

Died, on the 10th October, at Cheshire, in Connecticut, Edward Trescot, jun. son of E. Trescot, esq. of this city. Whilst himself with three of his school-mates, were amusing themselves in a cyder-mill, a piece of timber gave way, and with such violence struck him, as to put a period to his life in 24 hours. (eulogy)

Issue of November 4, 1800

Died, at Philadelphia, on the 20th October last, after a long illness, Miss Eliza Paterson--in hopes the change of climate might prove beneficial to her health, this young lady spent the last winter in this city, during which short stay, her amiable disposition and agreeable manners endeared her to a large and respectable circle of acquaintances.

Issue of November 6, 1800

Died on Monday the 3d inst., in the 27th year of her age, after a long and painful illness...Mrs. Margaret Ann Hrabowski, the amiable consort of Mr. John S. Hrabowski, of this city, late merchant. In the dissolution of this amiable woman, Mr. H. has, with three children, to weep the irreparable loss of an obedient wife.... Her remains were on the day following interred in St. Philip's Church-yard, attended by a very respectable number of friends and relations.

Issue of November 7, 1800

Married last evening, by the Rev. Mr. Munde, Captain Joshua Jones, to the amiable and accomplished Miss Maria Ann Gibbs.

Issue of November 8, 1800

Died, at his father's house, in Darlington district, after a tedious and distressing illness, Capt. John Augustus Benton, eldest son of Col. Lamuel Benton, aged 25 years....

Issue of November 10, 1800

Married, last evening, by the Rev. Doctor Buist, Mr. John Anthony Woodle, to the amiable Miss Susanna Sansom, both of this city.

Issue of November 11, 1800

Married, on Saturday evening, the 1st inst., by the Rev. Dr. Buist, Mr. James Turnbull, to Miss Emma Whitaker, both of this city.

Issue of November 12, 1800

Married on the 3d of October last, in St. Bartholomew's Parish, by the Rev. Mr. Gourlay, Mr. John Witsell to Miss Mary Oswald.
Married on Sunday evening last, by the Rev. J. C. Faber, Mr. J. J. Scroter, to Miss Elizabeth R. Dubbert, youngest daughter of the late Rev. Mr. Dubbert, of the German church in this city.
Married on Saturday evening, by the Rev. Mr. Frost, Mr. William Hutson, to Miss Mary Ann Miller, both of this city.

Issue of November 13, 1800

Married, on Tuesday last, by the Rev. Mr. Keith, Daniel Boyle, Esq. to Mrs. Jane Slann, both of St. Paul's parish.

Issue of November 18, 1800

Died, this morning, Mr. John Burch, aged 19 years, a native of the Island of Bermuda, after a short illness.

Issue of November 19, 1800

Married on Sunday evening, the 9th inst., by the reverend Mr. Gourley, William Youngblood, Esq., to Miss Elizabeth Singellton, both of St. Bartholomew's parish.

Issue of November 20, 1800

Married on Sunday, the 2d instant, by the Rev. Mr. Gourley, Thomas G. Scot, Esq. to Miss Mary Stevens, both of Prince William's parish, Beaufort District.

Issue of November 24, 1800

Married on Thursday evening, by the Rev. Mr. Frost, Timothy Ford, Esq. to Miss Mary Prioleau.
Married at Beaufort on Tuesday the 18th inst., Mr. James Mair, of this city, merchant, to Miss Ann Graham, daughter of the Rev. W. E. Graham deceased.
Married in St. Thomas's parish, last Thursday evening, by the rev. Bishop Smith, capt. Robert Wilson, to Miss Catharine Latham, daughter of Mr. Daniel Latham, both of this city.
Married on Thursday evening, by the rev. Mr. Jenkins, Mr. John Hanahan, jun. to the amiable and accomplished Miss Ann Godfrey, both of this city.
Married on Saturday evening last, by the rev. Mr. Keith, Mr. Sylvester Arms, to Miss Elizabeth Oliver, both of this city.

Issue of November 25, 1800

Married on Tuesday the 18th inst., at Black Mingo, Mr. James Davidson, to the amiable Miss Sarah Dickey.
Married on Saturday evening, by the rev. Mr. Mathews, capt. Ebenezer Platt to Miss Jane Clarke, both of this place.
Died, on Monday the 17th instant, John M'Call, sen, esq. after a long and painful illness... His amiable virtues render his

loss truly irreparable to his afflicted family and friends.

Issue of November 27, 1800

Married, last evening, by the Rev. Mr. Mathews, Mr. Michael Jordain, to Miss Eliza Smith, both of this city.
Died on Sunday, the 23d instant, of a lingering illness, Mr. Thomas Vernon, aged 23 years, a young man much regretted by all who had the pleasure of his acquaintance.

Issue of November 29, 1800

Died, in this city, on the 24th instant, aged 85 years, Benjamin Mazyck, esquire, a native of this state, and a respectable inhabitant of the parish of Goose-creek, for near seventy years.

Issue of December 3, 1800

Married, on Tuesday evening, by the Rev. Mr. Mathews, Mr. Robert Lebby to Mrs. Catharine Ecklin Lees, both of this city.

Issue of December 11, 1800

Died, last evening, after a long and painful illness, which he born with Christian fortitude and perfect resignation, Mr. William Long, aged 19 years, son of Mr. Wm. Long, deceased, late of this city.

Issue of December 13, 1800

Married, on Thursday last, Mr. Archibald Gilben, to the most admirable Mrs. Margaret Pickam, both of this city.
Died, on the 11th instant, after a short illness, Mr. James Morrison, much lamented by his relations and friends.

Issue of December 17, 1800

Married, on Thursday evening last, by the Rev. Bishop Smith, Stephen Ravenel esq. to Miss Catharine Mazyck, second daughter of William Mazyck, esq. deceased.

Issue of December 18, 1800

Married, by the Rev. Dr. George Buist, John Champneys, Esq., to Mrs. Amarintha Saunders, widow of the late Roger Parker Saunders, Esq. and eldest daughter of the late Rawlins Lowndes, Esq.
Married on Sunday evening last, by the Rev. Mr. Mathews, Mr. Morang, to Mrs. Lane, widow of Mr. Lane.
Married on Tuesday last, by the Rev. Mr. Mathews, Mr. Thomas Darrell of Goose-creek, to Miss Jane Cook, of the same place.
Died on Saturday last, Mr. James Davison, grocer.
Died on Monday evening last, in the 60th year of her age, Mrs. Sarah Williams, relict of the late Mr. John Mortimer Williams, of this city.

Issue of December 19, 1800

Married, last evening, by the Rev. Mr. Jenkins, Mr. John Turnbull, merchant, of Savannah, to Miss Henrietta Guerin, of this city.
Married, last evening, by the Rev. Mr. Jenkins, Mr. William C. Marlen, to the agreeable Miss Margaret Davis, both of this city.

Died, on Wednesday evening, the 17th inst., James Alexander Wright, Esq., eldest son of the late Alexander Wright, Esq., of the island of Jamaica, and formerly of this state. (eulogy)

Issue of December 20, 1800

Married on Tuesday evening by the Rev. Doctor Keith, Mr. John Stent, to Miss Elizabeth North.

Died on Thursday the 11th inst., in Clarendon county, in the 35th year of her age, Mrs. Agnes Colclough, wife of Colonel Alexander Colclough, suddenly cut off, while there was to her affectionate husband and a rising family of children, a prospect of lengthened happiness and pleasure, this event is indeed greatly afflictive....

Issue of December 22, 1800

Married on Tuesday evening last, by the Rev. Mr. Frost, Mr. David Johnston, to Miss Eleanor Clement, youngest daughter of Mr. John Clement.

Married on Saturday evening last, by the Rev. Mr. Frost, Dr. Isaac Chanler, to Mrs. Catharine M'Cord, relict of the late William M'Cord, Esq.

Issue of December 23, 1800

Married, last evening, by the Rev. Mr. Furman, Mr. John C. W. Cox, of this city, to Miss Eleanor Screven, of Goose-creek.

Issue of December 24, 1800

Married last evening, by the rev. Mr. Munds, Mr. James Hinton to Miss Charlotte Dunscomb.

Married on Sunday evening last, by the rev. Mr. Furman, Mr. Bordman Estel to Mrs. Sarah Huff, both of this city.

Departed this life on Monday last, Colonel Benjamin Postell, of St. Bartholomew's Parish, in the 42nd year of his age. At the commencement of the late revolution, he took an active and decided part in favor of his country, by receiving a commission as a lieutenant of the first continental regiment which was raised in this county, and continued stedfast in his duty until the surrender of Charleston...(eulogy)

Issue of December 27, 1800

Married on Wednesday evening last, by the Rev. Mr. Matthews, Mr. James M'Heath, to the amiable and accomplished Miss Anne M'Herron, both of this city.

Died on Thursday, the 18th December, John Charles Joyeux, aged 80 years. He was a native of Bourdeaux in France, and for near 50 years a resident in Cape Francois: during which period he transacted the greatest part of the mercantile concerns of the U. S. in that place....As a husband and father, he was beloved and respected....

Issue of December 29, 1800

Married on Thursday evening, by the rev. Dr. Furman, Mr. Wood Furman, to Miss Hanan Bowers, daughter of captain David Bowers, both of this city.

Married on Thursday evening, by the rev. Dr. Hollinshead, Andrew Burnet, esq. of Combahee, to Miss Eliza Washington Desaussure, of this city.

Issue of December 31, 1800

Married, on Tuesday evening, by the Right Rev. Bishop Smith, Major James Simons, Collector of the Customs for this Port, to Miss Sarah Tucker Harris, daughter of Doctor Tucker Harris.

Died in this city, on Wednesday morning last, aged 24 years, Miss Sarah Bruce Rhind, eldest daughter of the late David Rhind, esq. (eulogy)

Issue of January 3, 1801

Married last Wednesday evening, by the Rev. Doctor Gallaghar, Mr. Nicholas Fitzpatrick, store-keeper of this city, to the amiable Miss Eleanor Haly, late from Ireland.

Married on Wednesday evening last, by the Rev. Mr. Furman, Mr. Henry Bowering, to Miss Martha Adams, both of this city.

Married on Thursday evening last, by the Rev. Dr. Buist, Mr. Alexander Douglas, to Miss Eleanor Carew, both of this city.

Issue of January 5, 1801

Married on Wednesday evening last, by the rev. Mr. Munds, Capt. Joshua Clark, to the amiable and accomplished Miss Charlotte Harper.

Issue of January 8, 1801

Married, on Tuesday evening last, by the Rev. Dr. Jenkins, Mr. Benjamin Leefe, merchant, to Miss Harriet Sophia Bentham, daughter of James Bentham, esq.

Issue of January 9, 1801

Married, last evening, by the Rev. Dr. Keith, Mr. John You, to Miss Antoinette Tarduie, daughter of the late Mons. Louis Tarduie, of St. Domingo.

Died, last evening, after a short illness, Mr. James Muirhead, merchant, of this city.

Issue of January 12, 1801

Married, on Saturday evening last, by the Rev. Dr. Hollinshead, Mr. Joseph Hargreaves, merchant, to Mrs. Elizabeth B. Cantey, widow of the late James Cantey, Esq. of Georgia.

Died, on the 18th of last month, Mr. Ralph Atmar, in the 81st year of his age, after a residence of 53 years in this city. He was a native of Hull, in England, and bred a shipwright. In early life he went to Boston, N. E. and worked at his trade in the first shipyard established in that place. In the year 1747 he settled in Charleston...steady attachment to the cause of American Independence, after the surrender of Charleston, the British banished him from South-Carolina....(eulogy)

Issue of January 14, 1801

Married, at Beaufort, on Tuesday evening, last, by the rev. Mr. Cook, Mr. Robert Guerard, to Miss Harriott L. DeTreville, daughter of the late Capt. John L. DeTreville.

Same day, Mr. Robert L. DeTreville, to Miss Sarah Ellis, youngest daughter of Richard Ellis, esq. planter.

On Wednesday, the 7th instant, departed this life, at Pon Pon in the 36th year of his age, George Savage, esq. whose urbanity of manners, cheerfulness of disposition and benevolence of heart, whose unbounded hospitality to all, and whose kind, affectionate, and endearing conduct to his immediate family and friends, make him to be sincerely mourned and regretted.

Issue of January 15, 1801

Married last evening, by the Rev. Mr. Jenkins, Mr. Gilbert Davidson, merchant, to Mrs. Eliza Hahnbaum, relict of Dr. G. F. Hahnbaum.

Married, last evening, by the Rev. Mr. Jenkins, Mr. Angus Bethune, merchant, to Miss Margaret Williman, daughter of Christopher Williman, Esq.

Married on Monday the 12th inst., in St. Bartholomew's parish, by the Rev. Mr. Thompson, Mr. Richard M'Ginney, to Miss Jane Wasson, both of said parish.

Died on Saturday evening last, after a short and painfull illness, which he bore with fortutude and patience, Mr. John Clark, aged 39 years, leaving a disconsolate wife and children....

Issue of January 16, 1801

Married, last evening, by the Rev. Mr. Fabre, Mr. Lewis Strobel to Miss Jane Stent Austen.

Married on the Wateree, on Sunday the 4th instant, Mr. Austin F. Peay, merchant of Camden, to the agreeable Miss Mary English, daughter of Joshua English, esq. deceased.

Issue of January 17, 1801

Married on Thursday evening last, by the Rev. Dr. Purcell, The Rev. Edmund Matthews, to Miss Eliza Ward, youngest daughter of Joshua Ward, esq.

Issue of January 22, 1801

Married, on the 8th instant, in Prince William's Parish, by the Rev. Mr. Gourlay, Mr. John Wilkins, to Miss Mary Eliza Broughton, both of that place.

Issue of January 23, 1801

Married, on Sunday evening last, by the rev. Mr. Faber, Mr. John R. Switzer, sadler, to Mrs. Mary Hahnbaum, widow of the late Dr. Christian Hahnbaum, of this city.

Married on Wednesday the 14th instant, at the Hills, by the reverend Mr. Roberts, James S. Guignard esq. to Miss Carolina Richardson.

Died on Monday, 19th instant, Mrs. Margaret Gordon, wife of Mr. James Gordon, a native of Camden in this state, after a lingering illness of five months, which she born with christian fortitude.

Died, in the 34th year of his age, Dr. Duncan, a respectable physician, born and educated in Scotland, who had practiced physix, for 12 years in Tobago...since the winter season, commenced in Charleston...remains to the Presbyterian church, in the yard of which he is to be interred this afternoon.

Issue of January 24, 1801

Married, on Thursday evening last, by the rev. Dr. Buist, Mr. Park Avery, to Mrs. Mary Macomb, widow of Mr. James Macomb, formerly of this city.

Issue of January 26, 1801

Married, at Beaufort, on Thursday the 15th inst., by the rev. Dr. Cook, Mr. John Burton, to Miss Sarah Oliver Joyner, eldest daughter of J. Joyner, esq. of same place.

Married, at Beaufort, on Sunday evening, the 18th inst., by the Rev. Mr. Cook, Mr. Samuel Lawrence, merchant, to Mrs. Elizabeth Givens, widow of Mr. John Givens, deceased.

Married by the rev. Dr. Buist, on Thursday evening, Captain William B. Brown to Miss Ann Denoon.

Married by the rev. Dr. Buist, on Saturday evening last, Captain James Baird, to Miss Margaret Bonner, of this city.

Issue of January 27, 1801

Married, on James Island, on **Thursday the 17th** of **December**, by the rev. G. H. Price, Mr. William Stone to Mrs. Frances Holmes(?).

Married, **on James Island**, on **Tuesday** the 23d of December by the rev. G. H. Price, Mr. Mallory Rivers to Miss Lois Burchell, eldest daughter of Mr. Thomas Burchell.

Issue of January 28, 1801

Died, on the 1st instant, after a short but painful illness in the 35th year of her age, much lamented by many friends, Mrs. Mary Dubose, consort of Samuel Dubose, Esq. of St. Stephen's parish.

Washington
Died on Monday, in this city, in his 32d year, James Jones, of Georgia, a member of the House of Representatives of the United States...(eulogy)

Issue of January 30, 1801

Married, last evening, by the Rev. Doctor Isaac S. Keith, Mr. William Alexander, to Miss Mary Witter, of John's Island.

Married, on Sunday evening, the 28th of December last, Joseph Gist, esq. to Miss Sarah M'Daniel, both of Union county.

Married on Tuesday last, by the rev. Edward Jenkins, T. R. Wilmer, esq. late of Maryland, to Miss Sarah R. Gibbes, daughter of the deceased Robert Gibbes, esq.

Died, this morning, Mrs. Rachael Monk, wife of James Monk, silver-smith, a native of England, aged 35 years.

Died at Pon Pon, on Sunday the 25th instant, Mr. David Culliatt, after a short and painful illness...His loss is irreparable to his disconsolate widow and infant....

Issue of January 31, 1801

Married on Thursday last, by the rev. Mr. Geo. Buist, Mr. John Hughes to the amiable Miss Bulah Lawton, of this city.

Died, on Thursday the 29th inst. of a deep decline, Mr. Robert Shedden, a native of Bristol in England...at the age of 21.

Issue of February 4, 1801

Married, last evening, by the Rev. Mr. Croft, Captain James Johnson, to the amiable Mrs. Will, relict of doctor John Will, deceased.

Issue of February 6, 1801

Died suddenly, on the 29th ult at Beaufort, Mr. John Wilson Hext, a young man of an amiable character, whose loss is much lamented by all his friends and acquaintances; his exit was caused by an unfortunate fall from a building.

Issue of February 7, 1801

Married on Wednesday evening last, by the Rev. Mr. Frost, James Gregorie jun. Esq. to Miss Ann Ladson, second daughter of Major James Ladson.

Married on Thursday evening by the Rev. Mr. Holinshead, Mr. Alexander Thompson to Miss Susannah Rose, daughter of Mr. Jeremiah Rose, both of this city.

Died on Sunday evening, the 4th of January, 1801, at the house of Robert Wilson, Esq. in East Windsor township, Middlesex county, N. J., Ann Hutchinson, widow of William Hutchinson, esq. late of said county, aged 101 years, 9 months, and 7 days. She was the mother of 7 children, and grand mother, and great-grandmother, and great great grandmother to the amount, as is known of 375 persons, and a number of them of the 5th generation.

Issue of February 10, 1801

Married on Saturday evening the 7th instant, by the rev. J. C. Faber, Mr. Julien Henry to Miss Mary Coburn, both of this city.

Issue of February 11, 1801

Died, on Saturday morning, the 7th instant, Mr. Godfrey Dubbert, cabinet maker, aged 26 years, a native of this place. At an early period in life consumptive symptoms appeared, which gradually increased, baffling the art and the power of medicine. During the last summer, he travelled through the back parts of this state, North-Carolina, Virginia, and Tennessee, hoping to find that relief in a change of climate....

Issue of February 14, 1801

Married, last evening, by the Rev. Mr. Munds, Mr. John Hosley to Miss Isabella Avery, both of this city.

Georgetown, February 11
Died on Saturday evening last, Mrs. Mary Capers, the amiable consort of Mr. William Capers. Her exit is much lamented by her friends and severely felt by her relatives.

Issue of February 17, 1801

Departed this life on Saturday morning last, Mr. William Prosser, a worthy member of society. His remains were yesterday interred in St. Philip's church yard, attended by a number of masonic brethren and one of the military corps, who performed the customary funeral honors over him.

Issue of February 18, 1801

Died, last night, Mr. John Kennedy, innkeeper.

Issue of February 19, 1801

Died, last night, Mr. John Roberts, Taylor.

Issue of February 20, 1801

Married on Tuesday evening, the 17th instant by the rev. Dr. Gallagher, John Grochan, Esq. to the amiable Miss Adelle DeGrasse daughter of the late count DeGrasse, lieut. general of the naval army of the late king of France.

Married, on Thursday evening, by the Rev. Dr. Keith, Mr. Thomas Bennett jun. lumber-merchant, to Miss Mary Lightbourn Stone, daughter of captain Benj. Stone, deceased, both of this city.

Died on Wednesday last, at his plantation on John's island, Benjamin Mathews, Esq.

Issue of February 21, 1801

Married on Thursday evening by the right rev. Bishop Smith, Samuel Wragg, esq. to Miss Mary Ashby Pon.

Died at Philadelphia, on the 3d inst., Mr. James Carey, printer, formerly one of the editors of the Star and afterwards of the Telegraphe, in this city.

Died on Tuesday the 14th instant, Mr. John Kennedy, an old and respectable inhabitant of this city. He was an affectionate husband, a kind father, and indulgent master.

Died on the 27th of Dec. at Port Republica, Mr. Samuel Smith Ramadge, aged 22 years, only son of Mrs. Ramadge, of this city.

Issue of February 28, 1801

Married, at Albany (New York) Joseph Alston, esq. of this city, to Miss Theodosia Burr, only child of Mr. Burr, candidate for President of the U. S.

Married on Thursday evening last, by the Rev. Dr. Hollingshead, Mr. George Smith, jun. of Charleston, carpenter, to Mrs. Ester Channer, relict of the late Benjamin Channer, deceased, from London.

Married on Thursday evening, by the Rev. Mr. Buist, captain Moses Hoyt, of Norwich, Connecticut, to Miss Nancy Ellis, of N. York.

Issue of March 2, 1801

Married, on Saturday evening last, by the Rev. Mr. Furman, Mr. John Eddy of this city, to Miss Sarah Rodman, of Pennsylvania.

Issue of March 3, 1801

Married, last evening, by the rev. Mr. Jenkins, Mr. Joseph B. Seabrook of Edisto-Island, to Miss Margaret Austin, of this city.

Issue of March 4, 1801

Died, on Sunday, 22d February, Mrs. Anna Barbary Trair, a native of Epfingen, in Wirtemberg, aged 85 years and one month-- a respectable inhabitant of this state upwards of 47 years.

Issue of March 5, 1801

Married, on Monday last, by the rev. Mr. Gallaghar, Mr. Peter Benoitte Honoteau to Miss Theresa Victoria du Mouchel Benoitte, both of Europe.

Issue of March 6, 1801

Married, on Tuesday evening last, by the rev. Dr. Isaac S. Keith, William Simmons, esq. to Miss Sarah Yonge, daughter of Francis Yonge esq. deceased.
Died, on Sunday, the 1st instant, Mrs. Anne Keily, aged 72 years, relict of the late Mr. James Keily, architect and mason, of this city.... An only daughter is left to mourn the irreparable loss of a tender mother.

Issue of March 9, 1801

Married at the Round O, last Thursday evening, by the Rev. Mr. Bladen, Alexander Cochran, Esq. to the amiable Miss Eliza Snipes.

Issue of March 11, 1801

Married on Tuesday evening, by the Rev. Dr. Buist, Mr. William Walk er to Mrs. Jane Reid, relict of the late Mr. Joseph Reid.

Issue of March 13, 1801

Married, in Savannah, on the 4th of February last, Mr. Thomas Harvey Miller merchant, to Miss Mary S. Jackson, both of that city.

Issue of March 16, 1801

Died, on Friday night, in the bloom of life, after a short illness of 19 hours, Miss Elizabeth Foissin, a native of Georgetown, in this state.
Died on Saturday last, much regretted, Mr. Thomas Tims.

Issue of March 18, 1801

Married, at Havanna, on the 22d February, by the Rev. Mr. Flannery, Capt. William Laughton, to Miss Elizabeth Cammel, of Baltimore.
Died on the 22d ultimo, Major Daniel Jenkins, of Edisto-Island, in the parish of St. John's, Colleton. He was one of the patriots of 1776...(eulogy)

Issue of March 20, 1801

Died, on Tuesday last, in the 77th year of his age, Captain Roger Browne, an old and respectable inhabitant of this city. His remains were interred the following evening, in the burial ground of the Independent Church.

Issue of March 23, 1801

Married, on Saturday evening last, by the rev. Dr. Keith, Mr. Joseph Gladding, to Miss Martha Wilkins, both of this city.

Issue of March 24, 1801

Died at Inglefield Green, nearLondon, on the 26th December last, Mrs. Robinson (the celebrated Perdita) authoress of several literary pieces of considerable merit, and formerly a shining character in the fashionable world.

At Edinburgh, on the 27th Dec., at a very advanced age, the Rev. Hugh Blair, D. D., Professor of Rhetoric and Belles Lettres in the University of Edinburg, one of the Ministers of the High Church, and author of the Sermons which have been so greatly admired.

Issue of March 25, 1801

Died yesterday, Mr. John Filley, merchant.
Mr. John Williams, tavern keeper.
Mr. Daniel Spiesseger, baker.

Issue of March 27, 1801

Departed this life on the 22d inst., and in the 69th year of her age, Mrs Elizabeth Branford, who was universally respected and beloved, and whose death is generally lamented by her numerous friends and connections.

Issue of April 1, 1801

Married on Thursday evening last, at Prince William's parish, ___ Alston esq. second son of William Alston to Miss Sarah M'Pherson, daughter of ___ M'Pherson, esq. deceased.

Issue of April 2, 1801

Married on the 6th inst., in St. Paul's parish, by the Rev. Mr. Bladen, Mr. John Williams, of St. Bartholomew's Parish, to Miss Mary Chapman, of this city.

Yesterday departed this life at the age of 55 years, Dr. Thomas Collins Flagg, an eminent physician and inhabitant of this city, and a member of the Cincinnati--a native of Rhode Island, but had long resided in this state. In the late contest with Great Britain, he took an active and decided part with his countrymen, and accepted the appointment of surgeon to the First South-Carolina Continental Regiment....(eulogy)

Issue of April 7, 1801

Married on Saturday by the Rev. Mr. Thompson,Mr. John Stoney, merchant, to Miss Harriet E. Wells, both of this city.

Issue of April 8, 1801

Died on the 1st instant, at his mother's house in this city, captain John Lyons, aged 26 years; of this young man, it may be truly said, that in him were united the relative duties annexed to Son, Brother and Friend.

Died on Saturday morning last, greatly lamented in the 78th year of her age, Mrs. Jane Stevenson. She was a pious and good christian, respected through life and regretted in death.

Issue of April 11, 1801

Married on Thursday, the 9th instant, by the Rev. James Gourlay, Mr. Abraham Huguinan, to Miss Anna Maria Gillison, daughter of Derry Gillison, Esq. of St. Luke's parish.

Issue of April 14, 1801

Married on Saturday evening last, by the rev. Mr. Harper, Mr. Daniel Collins, to Mrs. Jane Foutain, both of this city.
Departed this life, on the 11th inst., Mr. George White, of Christ-Church Parish, planter, aged 62 years and 7 months. In him the wife has lost an affectionate husband, and the child an indulgent and fond parent....

Issue of April 20, 1801

Married on Saturday evening, last, by the rev. Dr. Frost, Mr. David Oswald, taylor, to Miss Elizabeth Oliphant, both of this city.

Issue of April 21, 1801

Married, on Saturday last, by the Rev. Mr. Jenkins, Mr. William Allan, merchant, to Miss Sarah Haig, daughter of the late Dr. George Haig.
Married, at Portland, Edward Prebble, esq. capt. of the U. S. frigate Essex, to Miss Maria Deering.

Issue of April 22, 1801

Married on Monday evening last, by the rev. Dr. Buist, Mr. James Duddel, to the agreeable Miss Ann Meadows, both of this city.
Died at Philadelphia, on Thursday the 19th ult., Dr. William Sheed, a native of this city, after a short illness....his remains were interred in Christ Church burial ground on Sunday, attended by relations and friends to lament his loss.
Died, in Christ Church Parish, on the 10th inst., Mrs. Elizabeth Player, relict of the late Mr. Thomas Player, of said parish....

Issue of April 23, 1801

Died at his house in Slough Lane, near Windsor (England) on Sunday the 1st of March, Dr. Herschel, the celebrated astronomer, and discovered of the new planet Georgium Sidus.

Issue of April 28, 1801

Died, on the 18th inst., in Christ Church Parish, Mr. James Evans, aged 59 years and 2 months.

Issue of April 29, 1801

Married on Sunday evening last, by the Rev. Dr. Frost, Mr. John Hasell, to Miss Mary Shelback, both of this city.
Married on Monday evening last, by the Rev. Dr. Purcell, Mr. John Bride, merchant, to Mrs. Elizabeth Sargeant, relict of the late Mr. John P. Sargeant.
Married last evening by the Rev. Dr. Furman, Mr. Thomas Blackwood, merchant, to Miss Harriot Quelch, both of this city.

Issue of April 30, 1801

Died, on Monday evening, Mr. John Robinson, of the house of Robinson & Pendall, aged 25 years....

Issue of May 1, 1801

Married last evening, by the Rev. Mr. Furman, Mr. Thomas P. Shaw, of this city, Insurance broker, to Miss Mary P. Adams, of St. Helena Island.

Married on Tuesday evening, by the Rev. Dr. Buist, Mr. George Kenan, Grocer, to Miss Montgomery, lately from Europe.

Issue of May 2, 1801

Married at Coosawhatchie, on Thursday, 23d April, Mr. Charles Scrimzeour, merchant, of this city, to Miss Susan Morgandollar, daughter of John Morgandollar, Esq. of St. Luke's parish.

Issue of May 4, 1801

Married, last evening, by the Rev. Mr. Muns, Captain Stephen Anthony to Miss Maria Russell.

Issue of May 5, 1801

Died, on Thursday, the 30th of April, in the 27th year of her age, Mrs. Mary Spidel, wife of Mr. Eberhart Spidel, and only daughter of Mr. John Gerley, of this city. (eulogy)

Issue of May 6, 1801

Married last evening by the rev. Dr. Hollinshead, Mr. John Calhoun, to Miss Sarah Stevens, both of this city.

Issue of May 7, 1801

Died this morning, John M'Iver, Esq., Printer, joint proprietor of the City Gazette.

Died at Woolwich, in England, lately Mr. Barlett, aged 74 who had confined himself to his room for 23 years....

Issue of May 9, 1801

Married, on Thursday evening last, by the Rev. Daniel M'Calla, Mr. Samuel Jones, of this city, to Miss Mary Legare, daughter of Joseph Legare, Esq. St. James, Santee.

Issue of May 11, 1801

Died on Thursday morning last, in the neighbourhood of this city, aged 37 years, John M'Iver, Esq., one of the proprietors and editors of the City Gazette, and by whom it was established in the year 1785.

Issue of May 12, 1801

Married, on Friday evening last, by the rev. Mr. Mathews, Thomas Bannatyne, to Miss Susanna Rose, both of this city.

The following melancholy accident happened last Thursday afternoon, at the mills of Mr. Daniel Cannon....a son of Mr. John Combe, about 11 years of age, had got into a small canoe, and attempted to pass through the flood-gate at the time of the tide's flowing in. We learn from a younger brother, who was the only person near the place, the the boat struck the tongue of gate...The body was found a few hours after....

Issue of May 14, 1801

Married, on the 6th instant, by the Rev. Dr. Parker, John Paul Thompson, Esq. to the amiable Miss Caroline Theus of Santee.

Issue of May 15, 1801

Died yesterday, Mr. Theodore Trezevant, in the 80th year of his age. He was descended from respectable ancestors, who being exiled from France in consequence of the revocation of the edict of Nantz, settled in St. Thomas's parish in the infancy of South-Carolina...He brought up a large family....

Issue of May 16, 1801

Married, at Camden, on Wednesday evening, the 13th inst., by the Rev. J. M. Roberts, Mr. _____ Reese of the High Hills of Santee, planter, to Miss Elizabeth Adamson, daughter of John Adamson, Esq. merchant, of said place.

Issue of May 20, 1801

Died, on the 16th instant, Dr. James Clitherall, in the 57th year of his age, after a long and painful illness.
Died on the 18th instant, Mr. John Lahiffe, who through life supported the character of a sincere friend, and an honest man.

Issue of May 21, 1801

Departed this life, on the 19th instant, Mrs. Mary Pritchard, aged 28 years. She has left six young children and a disconsolate husband....The next day her remains were decently interred at the family burial ground, at Hobcaw.

Issue of May 22, 1801

Married, last evening, by the Rev. Mr. Munds, capt. Robert Sherlock, to the amiable Miss Mary Power.
Died, lately, in Laurens district, Major John Moore, a member of the house of representatives from that place.

Issue of May 23, 1801

Married on the 7th inst., at the city of Anapolis, by Bishop Corroll, the Hon. Robert G. Harper, late Member of Congress from South Carolina, to Miss Carroll, daughter of the hon Charles Carroll, of Carrollton.

Issue of May 28, 1801

Died in this city, on the 12st instant, after a few days illness, Mr. Nicholas Fitzpatrick, grocer. He has left a disconsolate widow....

Issue of May 29, 1801

Married last evening by the Rev. Dr. Jenkins, Mr. Acey Hill, of Boston, to the agreeable Mrs. Jane Thorney, of this city, and relict of the late William Thorney.

Issue of June 1, 1801

Married last evening by the Rev. J. C. Fabre, Mr. Sampson Rogers, to Mrs. Elizabeth Martin, relict of the late John Christian Martin.

Issue of June 2, 1801

Died, on Thursday last, in the 19th year of her age, Mrs. Elizabeth Verree. (eulogy)

Departed this life on the 6th May last, aged 66 years, Mrs. Sarah De Tollenare, much lamented by all her friends and acquaintances.

And on the next day, Charles De Tollenare, jun. in the 23d year of his age... Mrs. De Tollenare had expressed a wish to be buried in the country, without pomp, by her father's side, in a family burial ground; her son, anxious to obey the last dictate of a dying parent, bids an affectionate adieu to his disconsolate sister, embarks in a boat, with his mother's corpse....

Issue of June 3, 1801

Married on Tuesday the 26th ult., by the Rev. Mr. Jenkins, Mr. John Muncreef to Mrs. Sarah Clarke Schepeler, relict of the late Mr. George Schepeler, merchant, deceased.

Married, on the 1st inst., by the Rev. Daniel M'Calla, Mr. George Edwards of Spring Island, to Miss Elizabeth Barksdale, daughter of Thomas Barksdale, deceased, of Christ-Church parish.

Issue of June 4, 1801

Died on the 27th ult., in the 34th year of her age...Mrs. Mary Wilson, wife of Dr. Samuel Wilson, of this city. left a large family of children....

Issue of June 5, 1801

Married last evening, by the Rev. Dr. Keith, Mr. Lewis Griffin, of this city, to the amiable Miss Susannah Davidson, of Jacksonborough.

Issue of June 8, 1801

Died, in Ireland, Miss Sarah Thursting, aged 27....

Issue of June 9, 1801

Philadelphia, May 26.
Died on the 11th inst., at Bermuda, whither she had retired for the restoration of her health, Mrs. Bingham, consort of the hon. William Bingham, of this city.

Issue of June 10, 1801

Married on Saturday evening last, by the Rev. Dr. Gallagher, Peter Desiree Chevard, Esq. of Chartres in France, to the amiable and accomplished Miss Maria Rose Antoinette De Michel, daughter of the late John Baptiste Ignace De Michel, Esq., planter, of St. Domingo.

Issue of June 11, 1801

Married on Thursday last, the 4th instant, by the Rev. Dr. Gallagher, Mr. Joseph Jahan, late of St. Domingo, to Mrs. Mary Terasson, relict of Jean Jaques Chartier.

Issue of June 15, 1801

Married on Saturday evening last, by the Rev. Mr. Thompson, at the eight mile Green Grove, Mr. John Hunter, to the amiable Mrs. Mary Watson, both of this city.
Married, last evening, by the Rev. Dr. Pursell, capt. John Morrison, to Miss Elizabeth Watson, both of this city.

Issue of June 22, 1801

Died at Lancaster (Penn.) on the 4th inst. Frederick Augustus Muhlenberg, receiver general of the land-office.

Issue of June 27, 1801

Married, at South Amboy (N. J.), on the 15th ult., Mr. Joseph Hall, aged 96, to Miss Patience Gulick, aged 90.

Issue of July 2, 1801

Married on Thursday the 18th June by the Rev. Moses Waddel, John S. Newby, Esq. to Miss Lucy Bickley, both of Southampton.
Died suddenly, on the 30th ult., Mrs. Catharine Hahnbaum, widow of the late Dr. George Hahnbaum. (eulogy)

Issue of July 3, 1801

Departed this life on Tuesday morning, Dr. Thomas Marshall, of this city, aged 36 years, much lamented by all his friends and acquaintances.

Issue of July 10, 1801

Died at Woodstock (Con.) Mrs. Morse, aged 99, grandmother of the Rev. Dr. Morse, of Charlestown. Her posterity is very numerous; she was the mother of 10 children, and grandmother of 72; 210 of the 4th generations, and 14 of the 5th, total 315.

Issue of July 17, 1801

Married, a few days since, Col. Wade Hampton, of Richland District, to Miss Polly Cantey, daughter of the late John Caytey, esq. deceased of Santee.
On Tuesday, the 14th inst., departed this life, Mrs. Elizabeth Rivers, widow of Mr. John Rivers, late of St. Andrew's parish, deceased. (eulogy)

Issue of July 18, 1801

Departed this life yesterday morning, in the 23d year of her age, Mrs. Mary Cape, consort of Mr. Thomas Cape, and youngest daughter of Nathaniel Adams, Esq. of Edisto Island, deceased. (eulogy and poem).

Issue of July 20, 1801

Died, yesterday morning, after a lingering and painful illness, Mrs. Cornelia Emerentia Richardson, she was an affectionate wife, a tender mother....

Issue of July 21, 1801

Died, on Wadmelaw Island, the 11th inst., Edward Delegall Campbell, Esq. an irreparable loss to his numerous friends and acquaintances. He was an affectionate husband and brother....

Issue of July 22, 1801

Died, last evening, after a short illness, Mr. William Milligan, grocer.
Died, yesterday morning, master Lambert Lance, eldest son of major Lance, in the 17th year of his age (eulogy)

Issue of July 27, 1801

Died, on Saturday evening, the 25th inst., in the 28th year of his age, Mr. Elisha H. Waldo, printer, a native of Connecticut--regretted by all those who had the pleasure of his acquaintance.

Issue of July 28, 1801

Departed this life, on Sunday the 26th inst., Mr. William Axson, in the 34th year of his age.

Issue of July 29, 1801

Died, yesterday afternoon, of a severe and tedious illness, Mrs. Sarah House, wife of Samuel House. She was an affecionate wife, a dutiful daughter, a tender and indulgent parent. She has left a husband and five young children....

Issue of July 30, 1801

...death of Master David Gaillard, youngest son of Theodore Gaillard sen. esq. who but a month past had completed his 15th year. (account and eulogy)

Issue of August 1, 1801

Died, on Sunday the 3d May, at Edinburgh, in consequence of a fall from his horse, Mr. H. Mackenzie, Comptroller-general of Taxes for Scotland, better known as the autor of "The Man of Feeling," "The Mirror," and other ingenious performances.

Issue of August 4, 1801

Departed This life, at Lamlash, in the Isle of Avon, on the 15th of April last, and in the 15th year of his age, Master Thomas Edward Foster, eldest son of Mr. Thomas Foster of this city. (eulogy and poem)

Issue of August 5, 1801

Died, on Sunday evening last, after an illness of 6 days, Mr. John Oswald in the 25th year of his age. (eulogy)

Issue of August 6, 1801

This morning departed this terrestial abode, for the celestial mansions of bliss, James Howard, a native of this city, in the 18th year of his age. (eulogy)
Died on Edisto Island, the 24th of June last, in the 25th year of his age, Henry Hailey Seabrook, son of Joseph Seabrook, esq. of that place. (eulogy)

Issue of August 7, 1801

Died, yesterday morning, in this city, after a lingering illness, in the 56th year of his age, Mr. Daniel Sinclair, late of St. James's parish, Santee.

Issue of August 8, 1801

Died this morning, Miss Catharine Desel, in the 17th year of her age, eldest daughter of Mr. Charles Desel, of this city. (poem)
Departed this life in the bloom of youth, on Wednesday, the 5th instant, in the 15th year of her age, Miss Sarah Folker, much lamented by those of her acquaintence, more so, by her affectionate parents and relatives. (lines)

Issue of August 11, 1801

Married, on Tuesday the 4th instant, by the Rev. Mr. Bladen, Mr. Philip B. Martain, to Mrs. Ann Cullait, both of St. Paul's Parish.

Issue of August 12, 1801

Died, in Edinburgh, on the 8th ult., Mr. Isaac B. Chanler, student of medicine, son of Dr. Chanler, of this city.

Issue of August 14, 1801

Married last evening, by the Rev. Dr. Purcell, Lieut William smith, of the frigate John Adams, to Miss Harriet Valk.
Died on Saturday the 1st instant, in the 77th year of his age, Mr. Nicholes Power, a native of Waterford, in Ireland....

Issue of August 15, 1801

Died on Monday the 10th of August, in the 74th year of her age, Mrs. Charlotte Izard, widow of Henry Izard, esq.

Issue of August 18, 1801

Married on the 28th July last, at Providence, Rhode-Island, by the Rev. Mr. Clark, of Bristol, Thomas Redcliffe jun. Esq. of this city, to Miss W. F. Tracey, youngest daughter of the late Col. Tracey, of the island of Jamaica.

Issue of August 21, 1801

Departed this life, on Friday the 14th inst., Mrs. Jane Oliphant, widow of the late James Oliphant, in the 66th year of her age.

Issue of August 22, 1801

Died yesterday evening, at his lodging in Tradd Street, Mr. Charles Maylie, in the 22d year of his age, a native of Italy, who arrived here a few days since, in the Horizon, from London.
Died this morning, in the 22d year of his age, Thomas D. Scott, son of Mr. William Scott, of Ninety Six District, after an illness of six days--his loss is much regretted by his friends and acquaintance.

Issue of August 24, 1801

Died, this morning, Alexander Shivas, Esq. merchant.
Died on Friday morning last, after a few days illness, Mrs. Margaret Buckle, widow of the late capt. Thomas Buckle, in the 80th year of her age.
Died on Wednesday evening the 18th inst., Mr. Joseph Dill, in the 35th(?) year of his age...an affectionate and indulgent husband, a kind parents, and a dutiful son. (eulogy)

Issue of August 25, 1801

Died this morning, in the 20th year of his age, Mr. John Rugan, merchant, a native of Philadelphia....
Died on the 21st instant, in the 80th year of her age, Mrs. Margaret Buckle, widow of the late Capt. Thomas Buckle. She was a native of Switzerland, in Germany, and had resided in this country, over 60 years....
Died on Sunday last, in the 21st year of his age, Mr. John Logan, for some time past a resident of this city....
Died on Thursday morning last, Mr. Zebulon Fields, lately from the northward, aged 23 years....

Issue of August 26, 1801

Died on board the ship Mary, of Kennebunk, after three days illness, Mr. William Moody, a respectable young man, beloved by all that knew him.
Died, on Saturday morning, the 22d inst., Miss Jane Mecomb, in the 19th year of her age, eldest daughter of Robert Mecomb, of North Carolina.
Died at his plantation, near Montego-Bay, in the island of Jamaica, on the 5th day of May last, in the 69th year of his age, John Stevens, esq. formerly of this city...an affectionate husband, a kind father....left a widow and six young children....

Issue of August 28, 1801

Died, last night, Mr. Phineas Parmele, aged 19, a native of Windsor, Fermont.
Died, at Havannah, the 25th ult., Mr. Arthur Otis, aged 16 years and 7 months, son of Joseph Otis, Esq. Massachusetts. (eulogy)
Died on the 11th ult., in Burke county, North Carolina, of an apoplectic stroke, Gen. Joseph M'Dowell, late a member of the House of Representative of the U. S. from that state.

Issue of August 29, 1801

Died, suddenly, on his passage for Norfolk, Mr. John Tool., taylor, of this city.
Died, yesterday morning, Mr. Benjamin Citchfield, a native of Kennebunk, Massachusetts.

Georgetown (S. C.) August 22

Departed this life on Thursday evening last, Miss Mary Hutchinson, daughter of Thomas Hutchinson, Esq. (lines)

Died yesterday morning, after a short illness, Thomas Hutchinson, esq. His remains were interred in the evening with military honors....

Issue of August 31, 1801

Died, on Friday the 28th instant, of a decline, in her 19th year, the amiable and accomplished Miss Mary Cape, only daughter of Brian Cape, Esq. of this city. (eulogy)

Died on board the ship Mary, of Kennebunk
  Smith Bradbury, master
  William Moody
  Benjamin Littlefield
  Ebenezer Borton
  Thomas Lord.

Died on Saturday last, on board the ship Mary, Capt. Hutchins, Edmund Hill, a native of Biddeford, Massachusetts.

Issue of September 1, 1801

Died, yesterday morning, in the 19th year of his age, John George Winter, a native of Bremen....

Issue of September 2, 1801

Married, on Thursday evening, the 27th ult., by the Rev. Moses Waddle, Mr. Zachariah Bowman, to Miss Nancy Goodman, both of Vienna, S. C.

Died, on Friday the 28th ult., after a few days illness, in the prime of life, Mr. John Stephen, a native of Aberdeen, in Scotland. This young gentleman arrived in this city in October last...The only hope of a widowed mother. In the evening of the same day his body was deposited in the Presbyterian churchyard, and a suitable and pathetic discourse delivered by the Rev. Dr. Buist.

Died, on Sunday last, on Sullivan's Island, Mr. George Tait, in the 22d year of his age, a native of Fifeshire, in Scotland, justly regretted by his friends and acquaintances.

Issue of September 3, 1801

Died on the night of the 31st ult., Mr. John Travers, of Fayetteville, North Carolina, in the 22d year of his age...left an aged mother and only brother (now in Fayetteville)....

Died at M'Cord's Ferry, Mr. John Brown, son of Capt. Richard Brown, of Richland District, on the 18th ult. (eulogy)

Issue of September 4, 1801

Married, last evening, by the Rev. Mr. Mathews, the Rev. Israel Munds, to Mrs. Charlotte D. Mayer, both of this place.

Married, last evening, by the Rev. Mr. Jenkins, Mr. Laurence Quackinbush, to Miss Mary Pringle, both of this city.

Married on Monday evening last, by the Rev. Dr. George Buist, Mr. John Paton to the agreeable Miss Sarah Dobel, both of this city.

Died, last evening, Mr. Benjamin Dupont.

Issue of September 7, 1801

Died on Saturday the 5th inst., Mr. John Gillespy, a native of Ireland. (eulogy)

Issue of September 8, 1801

Married last evening, by the Rev. Mr. Munds, Capt. Jonathan Bogle, to the amiable Miss Mary Easter.

Married on the evening of the 1st instant, in Barnwell district, Mr. James Furse, to the truly amiable and accomplished Miss Martha Wyal.

Died, yesterday morning, Mr. Henry Ellison, plaisterer, a native of Yorkshire (England)

Died on Sullivan's Island, on Saturday the 5th inst., Mr. John Mac Errocher, a native of Scotland. (eulogy)

Died, on Friday, on board the brig Enterprise, capt. Arnold, of Baltimore, Mr. John M'Keever, a native of Ireland.

Issue of September 9, 1801

Married at Smithfield (mass.) capt Peter Warren, to Miss ann Shrine, of Georgetown, S. C.

Departed this life on Monday the 7th inst., in Christ-church parish, John Jonah Murrel, Esq. planter. A disconsolate widow is left to bemoan his irreparable loss. (eulogy)

Died on Friday, the 4th inst., Mr. Alexander M'Bride, a native of Ireland.

Issue of September 10, 1801

Died the 8th instant, Mr. Archibald Anderson, a Plaisterer, a native of East Lothian (Scotland)...He has left a disconsolate widow and infant child to deplore their loss.

Died, this morning, Mr. Joshua Clark, a native of Milford, (Del.)....

Issue of September 12, 1801

Died yesterday, in the 19th year of his age, Mr. Edward Lawrence, a native of Ireland. (eulogy)

Departed this life, on Sunday last, Rippon Sams Hamilton Hanahan, youngest son of William Hanahan, esq. of Edisto Island, sincerely regretted by a number of friends and relatives.

Died, on Tuesday morning the 1st instant, Mr. John Screven, in the 51st year of his age...loss of a disconsolate wife and 8 children.... As a patriot, Mr. John Screven early took arms in the defence of political liberty....

Died on Wednesday the 8th inst., after 4 days illness, Mr. William Bean, Coach-maker, late from Wrentham in the state of Massachusetts. (eulogy)

Issue of September 14, 1801

Died, on Thursday last, in the 18th year of his age Mr. James Dealy, a native of England, much lamented by those who had the pleasure of his acquaintance.

Died on the 11th inst., Mr. James Coleclough, of the city of Dublin, merchant....

Issue of September 15, 1801

Died, on Friday last, in the 19th year of his age, Mr. William Keanon, a native of Ireland.

Issue of September 16, 1801

Died, on Monday last, in the 18th year of his age, Mr. John Croskey M'Cants, eldest son of William M'Cants, esq. of St. Bartholomew's parish.... (poem)

Issue of September 18, 1801

Died, this morning, Seth Paine, Esq., Printer.

Issue of September 21, 1801

Died, yesterday morning, in the 10th year of her age, Miss Amelia Scottowe. Ere five weeks had elapsed, two tender children, in whom were placed the future happiness of a fond mother, are torn from her embrace....
Died, on Saturday the 19th inst., Mr. Henry Colwell, jun. He has left a wife and four children....

Issue of September 22, 1801

Married on the 15th instant, by the Rev. Mr. Bladen, in St. Paul's parish, Mr. Hardy Pitman, to Mrs. Avey Culliatt, of Jacksonborough.
Married, last evening, by the Rev. Mr. Munds, Mr. Joseph Sharp, to Miss Sarah Fields.
Died in Savannah, on the morning of the 15th instant, aged 13 years and 11 months. Master Barnaby Bull Bellinger, only son of Barnaby B. Bellinger, Esq. of this state....(eulogy)
Died, on Sunday the 20th instant, Miss Eliza R. Whaley, aged 15 years, only daughter of Thomas Whaley, Esq. of Charleston.... (poem)
Died, on Saturday last, Edward B. Nowell, Esq. in the 33d year of his age...left a disconsolate widow and four infant children....
Died the 13th August, at Newcastle, in the state of Delaware, in the 41st year of his age, Mr. George Henry Myers, a respectable inhabitant of this city. He has left a wife and two small children; a member of the Methodist Church.
Departed this life on the 7th inst., in the 36th year of his age, Mr. Arthur M'Cormick, a native of the county of Roscommon, Ireland. (eulogy)

Issue of September 23, 1801

Died, on the 29th ult., aged 26 years, Mr. William Pilsburg, son of Samuel Pilsbury, of this city. This young gentleman had resided but a few months in Charleston, previous to his death.... (long account)
Died, at Ashepoo, on the 5th inst., Mrs. Bellinger, the amiable consort of Joseph Bellinger, esq. Her remains were deposited with her infant in her arms, in Dorchester church-yard, by the side of her father and grand-father. (eulogy)

Issue of September 26, 1801

Died, in All Saints Parish, on the 12th instant, Mrs. Mary G. Allston, wife of Benjamin Allston, sen. Esq.

Issue of October 1, 1801

Married on the 27th September by the Rev. Moses Waddle, Mr. Sterling Dixon, to Mrs. Mary Ann Noble, both of Abbeville district.

Issue of October 2, 1801

Died on Monday last, in the 58th year of his age, Mr. John Clement, an inhabitant of this city. (eulogy)
Died, in four days illness, in the 46th yearof her age, Mrs. Honoria Mills, wife of the Rev. Thomas Mills, after a late arrival from England. (poem)

Issue of October 5, 1801

Died, October 1st, after a lingering illness, Mrs. Jane Ross. She had arrived only four days from New York, to which place she went in quest of health, but got worse...left two children.

Issue of October 7, 1801

Married on Thursday the 17th instant, in Kichmond, Virginia, Col. Douglass Starke of South Carolina, to Miss Lucy Starke, daughter of Mrs. Elizabeth Starke, of Hanover.

Issue of October 8, 1801

Married, at Sullivan's Island, on Monday last, the 5th instant, by the Rev. Mr. Spierin, Capt. Israel G. Collins, to Miss Mary Ann Allan.
Died on Saturday evening last, the 5th instant, of a short illness, Mrs. Martha Sommers, relict of the late John Sommers, Esq. deceased...left five children. (eulogy)

Issue of October 9, 1801

Married, last evening, by the Right Rev. Bishop Smith, Mr. Andrew Smylie, to Mrs. Sarah Bruce.
Married, last evening, by the Rev. Dr. Holingshead, Mr. John Cummings, merchant, to Miss Elizabeth Airs, both of this city.
Departed this life, on the 3d inst., Mrs. Sarah Hopton, aged 90 years. She was a native of Cheshire in the kingdom of Great Britain, but resided 71 years in this city....

Issue of October 10, 1801

Died, in this city, on the 8th inst., Master Paul Walter, the only son of Major Paul Walter, of St. Bartholomew's Parish, aged 15 years....

Issue of October 14, 1801

Died, on Sunday last, after a short but painful illness, in the 35th year of her age, Mrs. Sarah Guy, a native of this place, and wife of Mr. James Guy, taylor.

Issue of October 16, 1801

Married on Tuesday evening, by the Rev. Mr. Abraham Azuby, of the Hebrew congregation, Mr. Cherry Moise, of St. Domingo, to the amiable Miss Esther Moses, daughter of the late Myer Moses, merchant of this city.

On Wednesday, the 30th of September, departed this life, at the Waxhaws, Lancaster district, in the meridian of life, Mr. James Cowsar, merchant...left a disconsolate widow and one child. (eulogy)

Issue of October 22, 1801

Married on the 26th of August, at St. Augustine, William Gibson, esq. merchant, of St. Mary's, to Miss Mary Fatio, daughter of Lewis Fatio, esq. deceased.

Issue of October 23, 1801

Died, on Wednesday morning, in this city, James Kincaid, esq. member of the house of representatives of this state, from Fairfield district--a man universally esteemed by all his acquaintances.

Issue of October 24, 1801

Married, on Thursday evening last, by the Rev. Mr. Mathews, Mr. William Langley, equestrian, to the amiable and accomplished Miss Jane M'Hugo.

Issue of October 27, 1801

Died, at Georgetown, on Thursday last, Mr. John Burd, printer, editor and proprietor of the "Georgetown Gazette."

Issue of October 29, 1801

Died, yesterday afternoon, after a short illness, the Right Reverend Robert Smith, Bishop of South-Carolina, in the 73d year of his age, 47 of which he has performed the duties of minister of St. Philip's Church.

Issue of October 30, 1801

Married last evening, by the Rev. Mr. Munds, John Mulligan, to Miss Catharine Merry.
Died, on the 15th inst., at Mrs. Ann Postell's in St. Bartholomew's parish, Master James Day, 6 years of age, after a short illness.
Died, at Philadelphia, on the 19th instant, in the 88th year of her age, Mrs. Susannah Budden, the relict of Capt. Richard Budden, a native of Old England...buried in Christ Church burying ground. (interesting account)

Issue of November 3, 1801

Married, on Sunday evening, by the Rev. Mr. Jenkins, Dr. Henry Richardson, to Miss Mary Fraser, daughter of James Fraser, Esq. of Daufusky island.
Married, on Sunday last, by the Rev. Mr. Azuby, Mr. Solomon Alexander, to Mrs. Celice Cohen, relict of the late Mr. Abraham Cohen.

Issue of November 5, 1801

Married, last evening, by the Rev. Dr. Jenkins, Mr. George Arthur, to Miss Ann Mary Scot, both of this city.
Married on the 22d ult., by the Rev. Moses Waddle, Mr. Jesse Babbs(?) to Miss Mary Rogers, both of Abbeville district.

Died, on the 31st last month, Mr. John Levy, aged 33 years, a native of the Isle of Man. He arrived in this city in May last.

Issue of November 7, 1801

Married on Thursday evening, by the Rev. Dr. Hollinshead, Mr. James Oliver, Bricklayer, to Miss Eliza Limehouse, both of this city.

Died, at Georgetown, S. C., on Thursday morning, the 5th instant, Mr. John M'Culloch, a partner of the house of M'Farlane & Co. (eulogy)

Issue of November 10, 1801

Married, on Saturday evening by the Rev. Dr. Purcell, Capt. Samuel Kerrison, to Mrs. Elizabeth M'Giveran.

Died, this morning, Captain Luke Swaine, Pilot.

Issue of November 11, 1801

Died last evening, in the 31st year of his age, Edward Darrel, Esq. Lieut Col. Commandant of Artillery.

Died, on the 6th instant, at North Santee, Francis Huger, Esquire.

Issue of November 12, 1801

Married, on Sunday evening last, by the Rev. Dr. Keith, Mr. Joseph N. Warnock, to Miss Sarah Harvey, both of this city.

Married, last evening by the Rev. Dr. Frost, Mr. William Akin, merchant, to the amiable and accomplished Miss Henrietta Wyatt.

Issue of November 13, 1801

Married, on the 5th inst., William Doughty jun. Esq. Planter, to Miss Mary Ann Tock, both of St. John's parish.

Issue of November 14, 1801

Married, at Providence, R. I. on the 23d of October, by the Rev. Dr. Gano, Charles James Air, esq. of Christ Church Parish, to Miss Rebecca Power, youngest daughter of Captain Nicholas Power, of that place.

Issue of November 17, 1801

Married, last evening, by the Rev. Dr. Buist, Mr. Patrick Mair, merchant, to Miss Martha Begelow.

Departed this life on Saturday evening last, Miss Henrietta Raven Toomer, youngest daughter of the late Major Anthony Toomer, deceased, in the 16th year of her age...left aged mother....

Issue of November 20, 1801

Married on Sunday the 8th instant, by the Rev. Dr. Hollinshead, captain Millen, to Mrs. Humphreys.

Married on Wednesday evening, by the Rev. Dr. Buist, Mr. Charles Shelback, baker of this city to Mrs. Sarah Watkins, widow, daughter of Mr. Roger Champneys deceased.

Died on Wednesday last, Mrs. Sarah Harvey, aged 68 years....

Issue of November 23, 1801

Married on Tuesday evening last, by the Rev. Dr. Holinshead, Mr. Samuel Fickling, of Edisto Island, to Miss Ann Eliza Wilkie, only daughter of Major Wilkie.

Married on Wednesday evening last, by the Rev. Mr. Jenkins, at Sandy Hill, James H. Ancrum, Esq. to Miss Jane Washington, daughter of Hon. Gen. Washington.

Died on Monday last, the 16th inst., at his residence in St. Stephen's parish, Santee, O'Neal Gough Stevens, esq. aged 34 years. He was sometime since a representative of that parish in the legislature...left a widow and five young children.

Died, on Saturday night last, Mr. John Christian Smith, in the 50th year of his age. This gentlemen was a native of Wirtemburg, and has resided in this county 30 years...

On Thursday last, departed this life, Miss Elizabeth Mylne, youngest daughter of James Mylne, in the 18th year of her age (eulogy)

Issue of November 24, 1801

Married on Saturday evening last, by the Rev. Mr. Munds, Mr. Lewis J. Harper, to Miss Caroline Raynoldes.

Married last evening by the Rev. Mr. Munds, Mr. Robert Foster, to Miss Louisa Gillman.

Married on Sunday, the 15th inst., by the Rev. Mr. Jenkins, Mr. George Perman, to Miss Isabella Fell.

Died on Saturday night last, in the 77th year of her age, Mrs. Ann Maria Mintzeng, widow of the late Mr. John P. Mintzeng, blacksmith. This lady was a native of Wirtemburg, and resided in Charleston upwards of 50 years...left an only grandson to lament her loss.

Issue of November 25, 1801

Married on Saturday evening last, by the Rev. Mr. Holinshead, Mr. Samuel Henwood, to Miss Mary Perry.

Married on Saturday evening last, by the Rev. Mr. Faber, Mr. John Brown, to Mrs. Ann Ward, both of this city.

Issue of November 26, 1801

Died on Sunday the 15th inst., in the 53d year of his age, Mr. Nathaniel Black, house carpenter, a native of this city.

On Saturday, the 21st inst., departed this life, Mrs. Catharine Dickinson, amiable consort of capt. Joseph Dickinson, and eldest daughter of Mr. Nathaniel Cudworth, in the 26th year of her age....

Died at his plantation in St. Peter's parish, on the 20th inst., Thomas Coachman, Esq. in the 29th year of his age....

Issue of November 27, 1801

Died, on the 9th of September last, at Balstown Springs, in the state of New-york, Mrs. Mary Peyre, wife of Mr. John Peyre, of St. Stephen's parish....

Issue of November 28, 1801

Married on Thursday evening, by the Rev. Dr. Gallagher, Mr. Daniel Remoussin, planter, of the island of St. Domingo, Mrs. Mary Snipes.

Died in this city on Wednesday last in the 28th year of her age, Mrs. Mary Ehney, wife of Mr. Jacob Ehney....

Departed this life, the 26th instant, on Wadmalaw Island, Richard Muncreef, esq. in the 47th year of his age....had just returned from the Sweet Springs in Virgia....

Issue of November 30, 1801

Married on Wednesday evening last, by the Rev. Mr. Bladen, Richard Singleton junior, Esq. to Miss June Eliza Postell, daughter of Major John Postell, deceased, of the Round O.

Died on the 8th inst., at Silver Bluff, Edgefield District, aged 35 years, the hon. Ephraim Ramsdy, one of the Associate Judges of South-Carolina. (eulogy)

Issue of December 1, 1801

Died in the prime of life, in St. John's Parish, on the 22d ult., of the quinsey, in the last month of pregnancy, Mrs. Margaret E. Solan....

Died, on the 29th ult., in the 16th year of his age, Thomas Hall, jun., eldest son of Capt. W. Hall, of this city. (poem)

Issue of December 5, 1801

Married, on Wednesday evening last, by the rev. Dr. Parker, William Pritchard, sen. esq. to the agreeable and accomplished Miss Eliza Latham, daughter of Daniel Latham, esq. of this city.

Issue of December 7, 1801

Married, on Sunday evening, by the Rev. Mr. Frost, Mr. Samuel Richards, broker, to Miss Mary Singleton, only daughter of Daniel Singleton, esquire, deceased.

Issue of December 8, 1801

Married, near Statesburg, on the evening of the 5th instant, by the Rev. I. M. Roberts, Col. Colclough, of Santee, to the amiable Mrs. Elizabeth Wright.

Married on Sunday evening, by the rev. Dr. Purcell, Mr. Samuel Dubose of St. Stephens parish, to Mrs. Martha White, of this city.

Died on the 30th October, in St. Bartholomew's Parish, Mr. Samuel Brown, of a short illness....

Issue of December 10, 1801

Died, at Beaufort, Port Republic, on the night of the 4th instant, in the 80th year of her age, Mrs. Mary Barnwell, relict of Col. Nathaniel Barnwell, deceased. (eulogy)

Issue of December 11, 1801

Married, last evening, by the rev. Mr. Munds, Mr. Thomas Appleton, to Mrs. Mary Piercy.

Issue of December 12, 1801

Married, on Thursday evening, by the Rev. Mr. Hollinshead, Mr. Joseph Prince, to Miss Eliza Cudworth, both of this city.

Issue of December 14, 1801

Married, on Saturday evening last, by the rev. Dr. Keith, Mr. William Butler Minott, to Miss Jane Field Smith, both of this city
Married, last evening, by the rev. Mr. Furman, Mr. Samuel Rain, pilot, to the amiable Miss Hester Nelson, both of this city.

Issue of December 15, 1801

Died at his plantation in St. John's parish, Berkley, on Tuesday last, of a pleuritic complaint, James Gray Wiare, esq. He has left a wife and three small children... In his parish, his services will be long remembered as those of an active and upright magistrate.

Issue of December 17, 1801

Departed this life, on the 13th inst., Mrs. Mary Besselleu, second daughter of Mr. John Riley senior, and wife of Mr. Charles Besselleu, of Jacksonborough, in the 18th year of her age...(poem)

Issue of December 18, 1801

Married, on last evening, by the Rev. Mr. Best, Dr. T. Reilly, to Miss Eliza Hayward Maybery, both of this city.

Issue of December 19, 1801

Married, on Thursday evening, the 10th inst., by the Rev. Dr. Keith, Mr. Henry W. Paxton, to Miss Eliza Ann Yeadon, both of this city.

Issue of December 24, 1801

Died, on the 22d instant, in the 30th year of his age, James Horne, esq. attorney at law...
Died, lately, at Goose-creek, aged 47, Mr. Daniel Weatherby, botanist.

Issue of December 26, 1801

Married, on Wednesday evening, by the Rev. Dr. Keith, Capt. Jared Bunce, of Weathersfield Conn. to Miss Mary Ann Dickenson, of Charleston.
Married, last evening, by the Rev. Mr. Mathews, Mr. Samuel Redmann to Mrs. Sarah Andrews, late relict of Mitchel Andrews, both of this place
Died, on the 17th instant, in the 48th year of his age, Mr. James Andrews, a native of Norwich (Eng.) He was for many years a successful English teacher in this city.
Died, on the evening of the 23d instant, at Howe-hall, Goose-creek, in the 37th year of her age, Mrs. Esther Smith, the wife of Mr. Thomas Smith. Her remains were deposited last evening, in the family vault, near the chapel. (eulogy)

Issue of December 28, 1801

Died, on Friday last, in the 57th year of his age, Mr. John Grantt, a native of Scotland, and for 30 years an inhabitant of this city.

Issue of December 31, 1801

Married on Wednesday evening, the 23d inst., by the Rev. Mr. Hollingshead, Mr. G. Petre, of Charleston, to Mrs. Esther Randal, of Bermuda.

Issue of January 2, 1802

Married on Sunday evening, by the Rev. Mr. Da Wega, Mr. Elizer Levy, of this city, to Miss Anna Abrahams, of New-Jersey.

Died on Christmas day, at his residence on the Congaree, Jacob Geiger, Esq. a member of the state legislature, from Saxe Gotha district.

Issue of January 4, 1802

Married, on the 24th ult., in the parish of St. James, Santee, by the Rev. Dr. Fraser, Mr. Abraham Michau, planter, to Mrs. Mary S. Dupre.

Married on Thursday evening, the 31st ult., by the Rev. Dr. Holinshead, Mr. John Whitesides, to Miss Harriet Ann Anderson, both of this city.

Married, on Thursday night, Joshua Player, Esq. to Miss Charlotte Elizabeth Thompson, daughter of the late Mr. James H. Thompson.

Died, at his plantation near Columbia, lieut. col. William Goodwin, commandant of the 34th regiment of militia of this state.

Died, on the 25th Dec. last at his plantation in Christ Church parish, Nathaniel Legare, Esq.

Issue of January 5, 1802

Married on Thursday evening, the 31st ult. by the Rev. Dr. Furman, Mr. Samuel Yates, to Miss Ann Hanahan, both of this city.

Married on Sunday evening, by the Rev. Mr. Munds, Mr. William Taylor, to Miss Elizabeth Fordyce, both of this place.

Died, on Monday, the 14th of December last, at his plantation in St. Mathew's parish, universally regretted, William Heatly Esq. He served for many years as representative of that parish--during the revolutionary war, in which station he was distinguished with the highest confidence of Gen. Green....

Issue of January 6, 1802

Married on Sunday evening, by the Rev. Mr.Hollinshead, Mr. Lewis Monuar, to Mrs. Mary Smith.

Married last evening, by the rev. Mr. Munds, Mr. James Cross to Miss Margaret Meek.

Died, on the 31st ult., in the 32d year of his age, Mr. Jacob Strobel(?), of Indian Field....

Died, on the 26th ult., in the 52d year of his age, Mr. Nicholas Silbery, a native of Sweden, and for many years an inhabitant of this city.

Died, on Ponpon Neck, in St. Bartholomew's parish, Mr. John Croll, aged 73 years, upwards of 40 of which he had spent on that spot, so generally reputed to be unhealthy. He was a native of this state and sprung from a respectable family of the first settlers....

Issue of January 8, 1802

Died, on Tuesday, the 5th instant, Mrs. Christian Dawson, a native of Scotland, and relict of the late Rev. William Dawson, in the 82d year of her age, 35 of which she passed in this state and city....

Died, at Kingston in Massachusetts, Mr. Ebenezer Cobb, aged 107 years, 8 months and 6 days, having lived in three centuries.

Issue of January 9, 1802

Died on the 21st Dec. in Caroline county, Maryland, Mrs. Mary Beauchamp, at the very advanced age of 119 years....

Died at Kingston in Massachusetts, Mr. Ebenezer Cobb, aged 107 years, 8 months and 6 days...born in Plymouth, 22 March 1694...(long account)

Issue of January 11, 1802

Married on Thursday last, by the Rev. Doctor Frost, Paul Trapier, esq. to Miss Sarah Shubrick, eldest daughter of Col. Shubrick, of Belvedere.

Married on Thursday evening, by the rev. Dr. Purcell, capt. Benjamin Fernald, of Portsmouth, New Hampshire, to Miss Eleaner Crowley, eldest daughter of Mr. Charles Crowley, merchant, of this city.

Issue of January 13, 1802

Died on the 8th inst., after a lingering and painful sickness, in the 24th year of her age, Mrs. Mary Wall, widow of Mr. Richard Gilbert Wall, merchant.

Issue of January 15, 1802

Married, last evening, by the Rev. Dr. Keith, Archibald Scott, esq. of James Island, to Miss Elizabeth Rivers Stone, daughter of the late capt. Benjamin Stone, of James Island.

Issue of January 16, 1802

Married on Saturday the 2d instant, by the Rev. Mr. Furman, Mr. Boudet, miniature-painter and drawing master, to the amiable Miss Margaret M'Gill, both of this city.

Married, on Tuesday night, by the Rev. Mr. Hollinshead, Mr. Jonathan Cape, to Miss Letitia Roulain, daughter of Daniel Roulain, deceased, both of this city.

Issue of January 19, 1802

Died, on the 7th instant, Mrs. Elizabeth Moles, wife of Mr. James Moles, of this city....left husband and four small children.

Issue of January 20, 1802

Married on Sunday evening last, by the Rev. Mr. John Garvin, Mr. James C. Donnon, merchant, to Miss Maria Wells, daughter of the late Mr. Edgar Wells, of this city.

Issue of January 23, 1802

Married on Thursday evening last, in the village of Washington, by the Rev. Mr. Frost, Mr. Joseph Borohay, to Miss Charlotte Jarman.
Died on the 3d instant, in St. George's parish, Mrs. Henrietta Wragg, widow of the late William Wragg, esq.
Died on the 30th ult., at Providence, Rhode-Island, in the 40th year of her age, Mrs. Anna E. Mitchell, relict of the late Edward Mitchell, esq. of Georgetown, S. C. and daughter of Dr. Ephraim Bowen, of Providence, R. I. She has left two small orphan children....(eulogy)

Issue of January 27, 1802

Died on Sunday last, the 24th inst., Mr. Gershon Cohen, many years a respectable citizen and residence of this city...left a wife and nine children...member of the Hebrew Society, he was selected as one of their trustees. (eulogy)

Issue of January 28, 1802

Columbia, January 22.
Died on Saturday night last,John Malone, esq. much and deservedly esteemed and greatly lamented by all who knew him.

Issue of January 29, 1802

Married on Saturday evening, the 23d instant, Mr. John G. Happoldt, to Miss Mary Elizabeth Strobel, of this city.

Issue of February 1, 1802

Married on Saturday evening, by the Rev. Mr. Frost, Mr. George W. Brown, to Miss Mary-Ann Bouchonneau, both of this city.
Married, Oct. 1, 1801, by the Rev. Mr. Munds, Mr. Le Roy, merchant in Savannah, to Mrs. Jane Belzons.

Issue of February 2, 1802

Married on Thursday evening last, by the Rev. James S. Adams, Mr. Samuel Prior, of St. George's parish, to Miss Elizabeth D. Eckely, daughter of William Eckely, esq. of St. Paul's parish.

Issue of February 3, 1802

On Friday morning last, departed this life, in the 18th year of his age, Mr. Abraham Markley jun...left with an aged father and mother, three sisters and a younger brother. (eulogy)

Issue of February 5, 1802

Married, on Tuesday evening last, by the Rev. Mr. Jenkins, Doctor James Henry Air, to Miss Harriet Atkinson, daughter of the honorable Joseph Atkinson, deceased.
Married on Wednesday evening last,by the Rev. Mr. Jenkins, Capt. Charles Bishop, to Miss Jane Stewart, both of this city.
Died at Ashepoo, on the 15th inst., Mr. William Bohun Baker, (eulogy)
Died on Wednesday last, after 6 days illness of a pleuratic complaint, Mrs. Mary Chouler, wife of Dr. Chouler, of this city. (eulogy)

Issue of February 9, 1802

Died, on Saturday last, Miss Rebecca Holmes eldest daughter of John Bee Holmes, Esq. in the 16th year of her age....

Issue of February 10, 1802

Married, last evening, by the Rev. Dr. Buist, Mr. David Kinmont, to Mrs. Jannet Murdoch, widow of the late Mr. Archibald Murdoch, blacksmith, both of this city.

Issue of February 11, 1802

Married, on Tuesday last, by the Rev. Doctor Faber, Mr. J. M. Happolt, to the amiable Miss Catharine Feffcken, daughter of Mr. Henry Geffcken, of this city.

Issue of February 12, 1802

Married, on Tuesday evening, by the Rev. Edmund Matthews, Benjamin Stiles, esq. to Miss Massey.
Married, last evening, by the Rev. Mr. Jenkins, Mr. John Hearne Stent, to Miss Annis Alexander, both of this city.
Married, last evening by the Rev. Mr. Munds, Mr. Charles Gren, to Mrs. Sarah Berry, both of this place.

Issue of February 13, 1802

Died, on the 22d ult., in All Saints parish, Mr. Thomas Todd, aged upwards of 91 years, a number of years a resident in that district, and universally respected.

Issue of February 19, 1802

Married, last evening, by the Rev. Dr. Frost, Mr. John Smith, to Mrs. Elizabeth Reynolds, both of this city.
Married on Thursday evening, the 11th inst., by the Rev. Dr. Hollinshead, Mr. William Bedford, to Miss Mary Lacy.
On Wednesday last, departed this life, Mr. William Kelsey, aged 74 years. He was born in the county of Hampshire, England, but had resided in this state upwards of 56 years....

Issue of February 20, 1802

Died, on the 16th instant, in St. Thomas's parish, in the 60th year of her age, Mrs. Elizabeth Deas, widow of John Deas, esq. deceased.
Died, at his seat on Fairforest, Union district, on the 5th instant, General Thomas Brandon, aged 60 years, after a lingering and agonizing complaint of 60 days.

Issue of February 22, 1802

Married, on the 9th instant, by the Rev. Mr. Brown, Dr. William Hunter, of Pendleton, to Miss Anne Anderson, second daughter of general Robert Anderson.
Died, yesterday morning, Mrs. T. Tunno, much and deservedly regretted...
Departed this life on Tuesday the 9th inst., at Edgefield court-house, S. C., captain William Simkins, second son of Arthur Simkins, esq.

Issue of February 24, 1802

Married, on Saturday evening the 20th inst., by the Rev. Dr. Matthews, Mr. James Custer, factor, to Miss Mary Vionnay, from Lyons in France.

Died on Sunday morning last, in the 28th year of her age, Mrs. Judith Wrainch, wife of Mr. John Wrainch.

Died, yesterday, in the 38th year of his age, Mr. Robert Smith Timothy, eldest son of the late Peter Timothy, esq., printer.

Issue of February 25, 1802

Married, on Wednesday evening, by the Rev. Dr. Keith, Mr. Samuel Welch, to Mrs. Elizabeth Gordon, both of this city.

Issue of February 26, 1802

Married, last evening, by the Rev. Dr. Frost, Mr. Richard F. Howard, to Miss Elizabeth Gratten, both of this city.

Died on the 13th inst., at his residence in Cannonsville, in the 67th year of his age, John Parker, esq. of St. James, Goose-creek. He served that parish, of which he was a native, for many years as a representative in the legislature.

Died on the 24th inst., in the 72d year of her age, in St. Stephen's parish, Santee, Mrs. Dorcas Harvey, widow of Mr. Maurice Harvey. She was the only surviving sister of the late John Parker, Esq.

Departed this life, on Wednesday the 23d inst., in the 32d year of his age, Mr. James Killan, a native of Ireland.... professor of classical languages.

Died, at his residence in York district, on Wednesday the 3d inst., the Rev. James Fowler, in the 61st year of his age... as a pastor in the Baptist Church. (eulogy)

Issue of February 27, 1802

Died on Tuesday evening, the 26th ult., aged 17 years, Miss Mary Hume, eldest daughter of John Hume, Esq.

Issue of March 2, 1802

Died, on Sunday morning last, Mr. Francis Bonneau, aged 47 years and 7 months, a respectable inhabitant of this city. His remains wre interred yesterday in St. Philip's church-yard....

Died on the night of the 10th ult., in Georgetown (Potomack) Mrs. Rebecca Stoddert, wife of Major Benjamin Stoddert, late Secretary of the Navy of the U. S.

Issue of March 3, 1802

Died on the 23d of Feb., in the 36th year of her age, Mrs. Elizabeth Morgan, wife of Mr. Charles Morgan. (eulogy)

Issue of March 5, 1802

Died, at his seat in Massachusetts, the Hon. Samuel Phillips, Esq., lt. gov. of that Commonwealth, aged 50 years.

Issue of March 7, 1802

Married on Monday evening last, by the Rev. Mr. Frost, Mr. William Woolcock, of this city, to Mrs. Anne Taylor, late of

Nassau, N. P.
   Died in this city, on the 2d inst., Mrs. Frances Paulin Josephine De Stack, born at Sarguemine, in the German Loraine, widow of the late John Philip De Petiot, capt. in the French army...arrived in this city about 6 years ago....

Issue of March 8, 1802

   Married, on Saturday evening last, by the Rev. Dr. J. C. Faber, Mr. Samuel Seyle, to Miss Mary Susanna Wesner.
   Died, lately, in the South Western Territory, Mr. Minor Winn, jun. eldest son of Major General Winn, lt. gov. of this state.
   Died in this city, on Wednesday last, in an old age, Mrs. Christiana Warley, widow of the late Mr. Melchor Warley, of this city.
   Died, yesterday, capt. Benjamin Fernald, a native of Portsmouth, N. H. aged 34 years....

Issue of March 9, 1802

   Died on the 15th ult., at his plantation in Orangeburgh district, Samuel Rowe, esq. in the 58th year of his age, a native of that place, who for several years acted as representative and magistrate for that district....

Issue of March 15, 1802

   Married, at Beaufort, on the 4th inst., by the Rev. Andrew M'Culley, Mrs. John Cross jun. to Miss Ann Watson, lately from London.
   Married, last evening, by the rev. Dr. Gallagher, Mr. John Kenny, merchant, from Dublin, to Mrs. Mary Sutton, of this city.

Issue of March 18, 1802

   Died on Edisto Island, on Tuesday, the 9th inst., Mr. William Crawford. (lines)

Issue of March 19, 1802

   Married on Thursday evening last, by the Rev. Dr. Hollinshead, Mr. John Theophilus Elsworth, of this city, to Mrs. Ann Elizabeth Boulger, of Christ Church parish.
   Married last evening, by the Rev. Mr. Munds, Mr. Maran Grado, to Mrs. Sarah Drath.
   Married, last evening, by the rev. Mr. Munds, Mr. George Broker, to Miss Eliza Carlton.

Issue of March 20, 1802

   Married on the 19th inst., by the Rev. Mr. Thompson, Dr. Thomas Lynch Dart, to Miss Mary Muncreeff, daughter of Richard Muncreef, deceased, late of Wadmelaw island.

Issue of March 22, 1802

   Died, on Friday morning last, at an early period of life, William M'Kenzie Parker, esq., attorney at law (eulogy)

                                        Savannah, March 18
Married in Liberty County, on the 10th instant, Mr. Adam Alexander, to Miss Rachel Schmidt; on the 11th, Dr. Edward North to Mrs. Parker, widow of Ferguson Parker, Esq.

Issue of March 24, 1802

Married, in New Kent county (Petersburgh, Virginia), on the 18th February last, Mr. Michael Sherman, aged 97 years and 4 days, to the amiable and accomplished Miss Eliza Poindexter, aged 14

Issue of March 25, 1802

Married on Tuesday evening, by the Rev. Dr. Hollinshead, Mr. Edward W. Bounetheau, of this city, to Miss Martha Glen, of Daniel's Island.
Married on Thursday the 11th March, by Samuel Linton, esq., Mr. William P. Raiford, to Miss Susannah Montague, both of Abbeville District.

Issue of March 26, 1802

Married on Wednesday evening last, Mr. William Thynnes, to the amiable Mrs. Tracy, both of this city.
Married on Thursday evening, by the Rev. Mr. Jenkins, Doctor Edward Brailsford, to the amiable Miss Eliza Charlotte Moultrie, only daughter of William Moultire, Esq. deceased.
Died on Tuesday evening last, captain John Fordon Torrans. On Wednesday Mr. Nathaniel Lebby sen. an old and respectable inhabitant of this city.
Died on Wednesday evening, in the 63d year of his age, the Rev. Henry Purcell, D. D. and one of the resident ministers, of St. Michael's church, in this city.

Issue of March 29, 1802

Died, last evening, John Brown Williamson, one of the managers of the Charleston Theatre. He has left a large family....

Issue of April 1, 1802

Died at his plantation on Edisto Island, on the 9th inst., William Crawford, esq. aged about 40 years....a widow and four children. (eulogy)

Issue of April 2, 1802

Died, on Tuesday the 30th day of March in the 59th year of his age, the hon. Aedamus Burke, one of the chancellors of this state. He was a native of Galway, in Ireland.(long account and eulogy)

Issue of April 3, 1802

Married on Thursday evening, by the Rev. Dr. Hollinshead, Mr. John Revel, to Miss Rachel Kimmel.

Issue of April 5, 1802

Departed this life on the 2d inst., in the 56th year of his age, Mr. William Mills. He was a native of Dundee in Scotland, but most of his life a resident in this city....
Died on Friday afternoon, the 2d inst., Doctor Isaac Chanler...

Issue of April 9, 1802

Married, on Thursday morning, the 1st instant, by the rev. Mr. Faber, Mr. Joseph Yates, to Miss Elizabeth A. Sailor, both of this city.

Issue of April 10, 1802

Georgetown (S. C.) April 3
Died in Marion district on Saturday the 27th ult., Col. Hugh Giles, aged about 50 years....

Issue of April 13, 1802

Married on Wednesday the 7th instant, by the rev. Mr. Thomas Mills, rector of St. Andrew's parish, Mr. Joseph M'Innes to Mrs. D. Grigson, both of St. Andrew's parish.
Married on Wednesday morning, Mr. Morris Clayton, ship broker, aged 33 years, a native of Shropshire in England. He resided in this city about 5 years....

Issue of April 14, 1802

Died, on Saturday last, after a lingering and painful illness, Miss Anna Maria Hall, only daughter of captain William Hall.
Died, in this city, Mrs. Mary Rowand, wife of Robert Rowand, esq.

Issue of April 15, 1802

Died, this morning, Mrs. Ann Mair, wife of Mr. James Mair, of this city, merchant.
Died, at Philadelphia, on Wednesday, 17th ult., one of the Indian Chiefs of the Shawnee Tribe....

Issue of April 17, 1802

Died, at Georgetown, on Saturday last, Mr. William Davidson, late keeper of Georgetown gaol.

Issue of April 20, 1802

Married at Georgetown, on Thursday evening last, by the Rev. Mr. Hammet, Mr. Levi Durant, Merchant, to Miss Carlotte Holmes, both of said place.

Issue of April 21, 1802

Married, last evening, by the Rev. Mr. Jenkins, Mr. Joseph Price Pritchard, to Miss Claudia K. Hornby, both of this city.

Issue of April 22, 1802

Married on Tuesday evening, by the Rev. Dr. Buist, Mr. John Cox, of Savannah, mathematician, to the agreeable Miss Jane Wylie, of this place.

Issue of April 24, 1802

Married last evening, by the Rev. Mr. Munds, Mr. John Corry, to Madam Anville(?) Delacroix.
On Wednesday the 14th inst., departed this life at Halifax, N. C., Mrs. Davie, consort of Gen. William Richardson Davie....

Issue of May 3, 1802

Departed this life on Monday the 26th ult., Mrs. Sarah Ehney, wife of Mr. William Ehney...left husband, mother and sisters....

Issue of May 4, 1802

Married on Sunday evening the 2d inst., by the Rev. Dr. Buist, Mr. Rene Bernard to the amiable Miss Maria Louisa Giroy, late of St. Domingo.

Married on Sunday evening last, by the Rev. Dr. Gallagher, Mr. William Keating to Mrs. Eliza Crowley, both of this city.

Married at Cumberland Island, on the 22d ult., Mr. Peyton Skipwith, junr. son of Sir Peyton Skipwith, of Virginia, to Miss Cornelia L. Greene, second daughter of the late Major-Gen. Greene.

Departed this life on Sunday last, capt. Thomas M'Intire, aged 28 years.

Died on the 1st instant, at his plantation in Laurens district, William Hunter, esq. aged 40 years.

Issue of May 5, 1802

Married, near Dorchester, on the 28th ult., by the rev. Mr. Adams, Mr. Daniel Cahill, of Jacksonborough, to Mrs. Eliza Coburn, relict of Mr. James Coburn, late of Sandy-Hill.

Issue of May 6, 1802

Married by the Rev. Mr. M'Calla, at Christ Church parish, on Thursday evening, Mr. Joseph Cocke, to Miss Mary Logan.

Died, at Washington, on the 11th ult., Joshua Johnson, Esq. commissioner of stamps, and formerly American consul at London.

Issue of May 7, 1802

Married on Tuesday evening last, by the rev. Mr. Jenkins, William Blacklock, esq. to Miss Mary Freer, of John's Island.

Died on the 4th instant, in the 60th year of her age, Mrs. Sarah Ruberry, relict of the late Mr. John Ruberry, of this city.

Issue of May 8, 1802

Married on Friday evening last, by the Rev. Mr. Munds, Mr. John Hort M'Call, of this city, to Miss Sarah Perritt, daughter of Abraham Perritt, esq. deceased, planter, of Santee.

Married on Thursday evening, by the Rev. Mr. Hollinshead, Capt. Thomas H. Jervey to Miss Floride Taylor, both of this city.

Issue of May 10, 1802

Married, on Thursday evening last, by the Rev. Dr. Hollinshead, Mr. Thomas Burnham, to Miss Mary Bennet, both of this city.

Died on the 4th instant, Mr. Benjamin Simons, aged 26 years....

Issue of May 12, 1802

Married on Saturday the 8th instant, by the rev. Mr. Jenkins, Isaac Porcher, esq. planter, to Miss Mary Jennett Weston, only daughter of Plowden Weston, Esq.

Died on Sunday evening last, Miss Elizabeth Timothy, only daughter of Mr. Benjamin Franklin Timothy, printer, aged 6 years

and 10 months.
Died, yesterday, in the 13th year of her age, Miss Grace Young, second daughter of Mr. William Price Young, bookseller.
Died on Tuesday the 27th ult., at Trenton, Richard Howel, Esq., late Gov. of New Jersey.

Issue of May 13, 1802

Died, in Ireland, the rev. William Knox, aged 95 years, 45 years a preacher of the gospel in the parish of Dunbar....

Issue of May 17, 1802

Married, at Augusta, on Sunday evening, 9th inst., by the Rev. Mr. Hull, Maj. James Goodwin, of South-Carolina, to Mrs. Jane Green, widow of Mr. John Green, deceased.
Died in Effingham county, on the 26 ult., Mrs. Hannah Noble, aged 111 years.
at Varniszobus, in South Carolina, master William Henry Roberts, son of Capt. H. Roberts, of that place, aged 5 years.

Issue of May 18, 1802

Married on Thursday evening last, by the Rev. Mr. Parker, Mr. Charles Mouzon, to Miss Susannah McClalen, both of this city.
Died on the 7th inst., Mr. Charles Snetter, rope-maker, aged 42 years.
Died on Saturday last, Mr. Daniel Loper, in the 28th year of his age (long account)

Issue of May 21, 1802

Died on Tuesday the 11th inst., Miss Henrietta Claude Bigrel de Grand Clos, daughter of the late Mr. Bigrel de Grand Clois, when living, recorder of the tribunal of St. March, in St. Domingo....

Issue of May 22, 1802

Died on the 9th instant, capt. John B. Foster, a native of Yorkshire, England.

Issue of May 24, 1802

Married, on Thursday evening last, by the Rev. Mr. Hammet, capt. William Hunter Torrans, attorney at law, to Miss Mary Christian, both of this city.

Issue of May 27, 1802

Married, at Beaufort, on Sunday evening last, by the Rev. Mr. Cook, Mr. Moses Foster, to Mrs. Fripp, widow of Thomas Fripp, late of St. Helena Island, planter.
Died on Sunday evening last, Mr. William Miller, factor.

Issue of May 28, 1802

Died on Wednesday, the 28th instant, in the 37th year of his age, Mr. John Moore, a native of Ireland, who had resided in this city many years...left widow with three young children....

Issue of June 1, 1802

Married on Saturday evening last, by the Rev. Mr. Munds, Mr. John Vidler, to Miss Charlotte Floyd, both of this place.

Married, Sunday evening, by the rev. Mr. Munds, Mr. Joseph Young, to Miss Frances Miller, both of this place.

Issue of June 2, 1802

Married on the 30th inst., by the Rev. Mr. O'Farrell, Turner Starke, Esq. of Camden to Miss Charlotte Richardson of Clarendon.

Issue of June 3, 1802

Married at Ashepoo, on the 25th ult., by the Rev. Mr. Bladen, John H. Girardeau, esq. to Miss Emily Bay.

Married in Abbeville district, on the 8th ult., by the Rev. Robert Wilson, Dr. Jesse C. Bouchell, to the very amiable and accomplished Miss Rebecca Catharine Cummins, eldest daughter of Rev. Francis Cummins.

Married on the 16th ult., by the Rev. Moses Waddel, Gen. John Martin, to Mrs. Mary Ann Barksdale, relict of Richard Barksdale, esq. of Abbeville district.

Married on the 25th ult., by the Rev. Moses Waddel, Col. Joseph Colhoun, to the amiable Miss Patsey Mosely, both of Abbeville

Died at Camden, on Wednesday the 26th ult., Mrs. Elizabeth Rees, wife of William Rees, jun. esq, near Statesburg, and daughter of John Adamson, Esq. of Camden.

Issue of June 4, 1802

Died in May last, Miss Sarah Levy, aged 8 years.

Died at Mount Vernon, on the 23d ultimo, Mrs. Martha Washington, relict of the late Gen. George Washington, aged 71.

                        Wash. Fed.

Issue of June 7, 1802

Married on Saturday evening, by the Rev. Dr. Buist, Mr. William Hall, merchant, to Miss Hannah Jacks, both of this city.

Died on Saturday last, William Logan, Esq. a native of this state, aged 75 years and 6 months...grandson of George Logan, Esq. one of the first settlers in this state, who came from Aberdeen, Scotland, in the year 1690, a colonel in the British army then stationed in Charleston. (eulogy)

Issue of June 8, 1802

Died, on Sunday last, Master Thomas Hall, son of Capt. William Hall, the third child this unfortunate family have lost within a few months.

Issue of June 9, 1802

Married, last evening by the Rev. Dr. Keith, Capt. George Anderson, to the agreeable Miss Catherine Roope.

Died, a few days since at Camden, Mrs. Rebecca Brevard, wife of the hon. Judge Brevard.

Issue of June 10, 1802

Married on Thursday the 3d instant, by the Rev. Mr. Gourley, of Prince William's Parish, Mr. William Black, of the Eutaw, to Miss Sarah H. Reid, daughter of Robert Reid, Esq.

Issue of June 11, 1802

Married last evening, by the Rev. Dr. Hollinshead, Mr. Thomas Whitesides, of Christ Church Parish, to Miss Jane Humphreys, of Johns Island.
Married on the 6th inst., by the Rev. Mr. Dunlap, Charles Williamson, esq. to Miss Nancy Coleman, both of Columbia.
Married in New York, on the 23d ult., Mr. David D. Burger, of this city, to Miss Jane Burger, of New-York.
Departed this life on Monday, the 31st of May, at Orangeburgh, in her 20th year, Mrs. Mary Eliza Ward, wife of the hon. Henry Dana Ward, of that place. (eulogy)

Issue of June 12, 1802

Married, on Thursday evening, by the Rev. Dr. Gallagher, Mr. Thomas Cormick, to Miss Tobin, both of this city.
Died, of a dysentery, on board the schooner Mary on her passage from Port-au-prince, to this port, captain Atcheson Anderson, of North-Carolina....

Issue of June 14, 1802

Married, on Saturday evening last, by the Rev. Mr. Frost, Mr. Charles Bradley, to Miss Elizabeth Harvey, both of this city.

Issue of June 15, 1802

Married on the 26th May, by the Rev. Moses Waddel, the hon. Col. Joseph Colhoun, to Miss Patsey Moseley, daughter of William Moseley, esq. late of Virginia.
Married on the 3d of June, by the Rev. Moses Waddel, James Colhoun, jun. esq. merchant of Vienna (S. C.) to the amiable and well accomplished Miss Sarah C. Martin, of Abbeville District.
Departed this life on Tuesday the 8th instant, in this city, Mrs. Amelia Munro, in the 45th year of her age, widow...left an only daughter....

Issue of June 16, 1802

Died, in Effingham county, (Virginia) on the 26th ult., Mrs. Hannah Moore, aged 111 years.
Died in England, on Sunday morning, the 18th of April, at the Priory, near Derby, Dr. Darwin, without the least previous indisposition....

Issue of June 17, 1802

Yesterday morning, departed this life, Mr. Isaac Motta, auctioneer, of this city, in the 30th year of his age...left wife and three infants....

Issue of June 19, 1802

Married, on Thursday evening last, by the Rev. Dr. Buist, Mr. George Kenan, to the amiable Miss Elizabeth Reside, both of this city.

Issue of June 22, 1802

Married, on Thursday last, Mr. Thomas Way, to Miss Barbara Muckinfuss, both of St. George's parish.

Issue of June 23, 1802

Married on Tuesday evening, by the Rev. Dr. Buist, Mr. Lewis T. Raynal, to the amiable and well accomplished Miss Martha M. Rouse, both of this city.

Issue of June 29, 1802

Married, on the 21st inst., by the Rev. Moses Waddle, Dr. Richard M. L. Allen, to the amiable and accomplished Miss Lettice Winn, daughter of Thomas Winn, esq. both of Abbeville district.
Married on Sunday evening, the 20th instant, by the rev. Mr. Munds, Mr. John Kelly, pilot, to Mrs. Margaret Norman, relict of Mr. Robert Norman, both of this city.

Issue of June 30, 1802

Died, in April last, in Great Pultney-street, Bath, in the 79th year of his age, the Rev. E. Nelson, Rector of Burnham Thorpe, Norfolk, and father of Lord Viscount Nelson.

Issue of July 2, 1802

Died, on Friday, the 25th ult., near Lancaster Court-House, Mr. James Barr, second son of Nathan Barr, esq. of that place.

Issue of July 9, 1802

Died, on Tuesday evening, Master Thomas Simons, the only son of Thomas Simon, esq. an amiable boy of 6 years old....

Issue of July 13, 1802

Married on Tuesday the 29th ult., in M'Intosh county, (Georgia), Josias Heyward, esq. of Prince William's parish, S. C. to Miss Ann H. Gingiliatt, of that county.

Issue of July 15, 1802

Married, at Newport, R. I., Mr. John A. Shaw, to Miss Elizabeth Muchmore.

Issue of July 17, 1802

Died, on Edisto Island, on Tuesday the 13th inst., Mr. William Evans. He was a tender husband, an indulgent parent, and a kind master....

Issue of July 19, 1802

Died on the 9th instant, in the 6th year of her age, Miss Leah Cardose, daughter of Mr. David Cardosa....
Died at New-York, on the 4th inst., in the 78th year of his age, Mr. James Rivington, an old and truly respectable inhabitant of that city, a native of Great Britain, but many years an eminent printer and book seller of New York....

Issue of July 20, 1802

Yesterday departed this life, Miss Mary Newman, a native of England, but long resident in this state....

Issue of July 21, 1802

Died, yesterday, Mr. Isaac Dacosta, an old and respectable inhabitant of this city....

Issue of July 23, 1802

Married, last evening, by the Rev. Dr. Frost, Mr. Thomas Hall, to Miss Sarah Howard, both of this city.
Died on the 21st instant, Mrs. Esther Dunlop, the amiable consort of Dr. Rt. Dunlop, of this city, being in the 29th year of her age.

Issue of July 24, 1802

Married last evening, by the Rev. Mr. Mund, Mr. Samuel Sewell, to Miss Elizabeth C. Cleark, both of this place.
Died, on Wednesday last, Mrs. Esther Dunlop, wife of Dr. Robert Dunlop of this city, at the early age of 29 years. This amiable lady with her infant child, were passengers on board the brig Echo, on the 22d of Feb. last, was wrecked on Staten Island....

Issue of July 26, 1802

Married, on Sunday evening last, by the Rev. Mr. Frost, Mr. Edward Thwing, to Mrs. Margaret Wolf, both of this city.
Died, lately, at Halifax, capital of Nova-Scotia, Mr. Edward Phoelon, aged 78; also Mrs. Eliza Story, in the bloom of life, leaving several young children--and being the uncle and sister of Major Edward Phoelon, planter, of this state.

Issue of July 30, 1802

Died, at Amboy, on the 14th instant, Nicholas Gouvernuer, Esq. President of the Bank of New-York.

Issue of August 2, 1802

Married last evening, by the Rev. Dr. Hollinshead, Mr. Elias Jones, carver and gilder, to Miss Tabitha Johnson, both of this city.
Died, on Thursday last, in the 62d year of his age, Mr. Jeremiah Clarke, a native of Cork, in Ireland, and for many years a resident of this city....

Issue of August 4, 1802

Married on Saturday evening last, by the Rev. Mr. Jenkins, Samuel Ker, esq. to Mrs. M. Harrison, and capt. M'Neil of the house of Sherman & M'Neil to Miss Mary Lightburn.
Married on Sunday evening last, on James Island, by the Rev. Mr. Price, Mr. William Turner, to Miss Martha S. Burchall.
Died, on Black Swamp, the 31st ult., in the 17th year of her age, Miss Esther Hutchinson, daughter of Mr. John Hutchinson, of that place....

Issue of August 7, 1802

Married on Monday evening last, by the Rev. Mr. Munds, Mr. Jonathan Stevens, to Miss Sarah Smith, both of this place.
Married, on Wednesday evening last, by the Rev. Mr. Munds, Mr. James Bell to Miss Frances Harrison, both of this place.

Issue of August 9, 1802

Married on the 3d inst., by the rev. Mr. Gallagher, Mr. Paul Jacinthe Perrault De la Gorce, to Miss Lise Emeline Delezay, both residing in this place.
Drowned, on the 17th of July, Mr. Samuel Levy, of this city, merchant...on his passage when about 40 miles of New-York....left wife and two small children....

Issue of August 11, 1802

Married on Sunday evening last,by the Rev. Dr. Buist, Mr. Thomas Kenan, to Miss Hester Kay, both of this city.
Died at Georgetown, on Tuesday last, Mr. Moses Carter, a native of Philadelphia.

Issue of August 14, 1802

Married, on Saturday evening, the 7th instant, by the rev. Mr. Hammet, Mr. William Millar, baker, to Miss Jane Shaw, both of this city.

Issue of August 16, 1802

Augusta, August 7
Died, last Monday, at the house of Col. Thomas Murray, in Lincoln County, Peter L. Van Allen, Esq. of a wound he received in a fight with William H. Crawford, Esq. on Saturday last, in South-Carolina.

Issue of August 18, 1802

Mrs. Tunno was safely delivered of a daughter early this morning.

Issue of August 19, 1802

Died,yesterday, in this city, John Bull, of St. Luke's parish, formerly a delegate from this state in the old congress, many years a member of the legislature of this state, and deputy secretary of the province, some time prior to the revolution.
Died, on Monday last, Miss Ann Dimes, a maiden lady....

Issue of August 20, 1802

Died, at Marseilles, on the 23d of April last, Mr. Peter C. Graaf, late a merchant in this city, and at the time of his death, supercargo of the brig Daniel and Frederick, belonging to Mr. J. F. Kern, of this city. Mr. Graaf had resided 18 years in this city; he has left a widow and many friends.
Died, on Saturday, the 7th inst., at Mount Eagle, near Cameron, the right honourable and Rev. Brian Lord Fairfax, aged nearly 76 years....

Issue of August 21, 1802

Married, at Camden, on the 26th of July, William Ancrum, jun. esq. planter, to Miss Elizabeth Brisbane, eldest daughter of Col. Brisbane, deceased.

Died in England, Dr. Hoare, aged 90. This divine married the proxy of George III to his present queen in 1761....

Died in England, the Earl of Lonsdale....

Died at Erome (England), Mrs. Ann Whitehead, aged 100. her grandfather built the first house at Isleworth, near London.

Died, in Russia, Admiral Kutusoff....

Issue of August 25, 1802

Married at Stoughton (Mass.) Mr. Sardo Darke to Miss Polly Dregs. (lines)

Died in Boston, the 6th inst., in the 75th year of his age, Arnold Welles, Esq. President of the Branch Bank of the U. S.

Issue of August 27, 1802

Married on Wednesday evening, by the Rev. Mr. Munds, Capt. Stephen Douglas, to the amiable Miss Eliza Stewart.

Married at Cambridge, S. C. on the 8th instant, by the Rev. Mr. Lilley, Mr. James Crawford, merchant, to Miss Tirza Hagood.

Issue of August 30, 1802

On Friday, departed this life in the 48th year of his age, Richard Wainwright, esq. of this city....

Died on Friday last, on Sullivan's Island, Mrs. Elizabeth Simons, the consort of Thomas Simons, esq...Her remains were interred Saturday last, in the family burial ground in Christ Church parish.

Died, on Friday morning last, Mr. Abraham Depass, aged 35 years, son of Mr. Ralph Depass of this city....

Died, on Saturday the 21st instant, Mrs. Eleanor Perry, in the 46th year of her age.

Issue of September 1, 1802

Married, on Saturday evening last, by the Rev. Dr. Furman, Mr. George Hamilton, of New-York, to Mrs. Margaret Ferguson, of Wilmington, North-Carolina.

Issue of September 2, 1802

Died, this morning, Mr. John Smith, in the 25th year of his age.

Died at Columbia, on the 26th ult., Mr. Bartlee Smyth, of the town.

Issue of September 4, 1802

Married, at Lynch's Creek, on Tuesday the 24th ult., Mr. George Myers, to Miss Mary Harrell.

At Georgetown, on the 26th ult., Mr. James M. Grier, to Miss Martha Gamble.

At Savannah, a few days ago, Mr. Samuel Comb, to Miss Sarah Ruffhead.

Died on Thursday last, in the 38th yearof his age, Mr. George Paul, merchant, a native of Kircudbright, in Scotland.

Issue of September 6, 1802

Died on Thursday last, in the 28th year of his age, Mr. George Paul, merchant....

Issue of September 8, 1802

Died on the 6th inst., Mrs. Ann Hawthorn, of the present prevailing fever....

Issue of September 11, 1802

Married, at Scarboro' (Mass.) Mr William Larrabee, aged 77, to Mrs. Tabitha Whitmore.
Married on Thursday last, by the Rev. Mr. Munds, Mr. John Fornew, to Mrs. Ann Young.
Married on Monday last, by the Rev. Mr. Munds, Mr. Isaac Muller, to Miss Elizabeth Charles, both of this place.
Died on the 11th ult., in Lancaster district, in the 25th year of his age, Mr. Nathan Barr, jun. youngest son of Nathan Barr, esq. of that place.
Died, on the 28th ult., in Orangeburgh district, of an apoplectic fit, John Fitts, sen. aged 72.

Issue of September 14, 1802

Married on Tuesday evening the 7th instant, on James-Island, by the rev. Mr. Price, Mr. John Smiley, planter, to Miss Martha Whitter.
Married on Thursday last, by the rev. Mr. Frost, Mr. John Baptiste Henneguin, confectioner, to Mrs. Olman, widow of the late Joseph Olman.
Died, Mr. John Jones, after two and a half days sickness....

Issue of September 15, 1802

On Sunday evening last, departed this life, capt. William Ormond, after a short illness....

Issue of September 16, 1802

Died, on Monday last, in the 47th year of her age, Mrs. Mary-Magdalen Poyas, wife of Mr. John-Lewis Poyas.
Died on the 7th inst., Miss Prisgy Saunders, a niece and ward of Mr. William Mason, in the 12th year of her age.

Issue of September 17, 1802

Married on Wednesday the 1st inst., at the Round O., by the rev. Thomas D. Bladen, James Ladson junr. esq. to Miss Elizabeth Day, daughter of capt. William Day, deceased.
Died, yesterday morning, after three days illness, Mr. Samuel Hart, printer, a native of New-England, and about 10 months a resident of this city.

Issue of September 18, 1802

Married on Thursday last, at Moultrieville, on Sullivan's Island, by the rev. Mr. Frost, William Lowndes, esq. to Miss Pinckney, eldest daughter of Thomas Pinckney, Esq.
Died, this morning, in the 28th year of his age, Mr. John Wallis, merchant, a native of Ireland....

Died, last Wednesday night, Mr. Michael Makahaly, from the North of Ireland, but a few months a resident in this city.

Issue of September 20, 1802

Died on ___ last, the 17th inst., Mr. James Thomson, a native of Perthshire, in Scotland, and six years a resident in this city. ...

Issue of September 21, 1802

Married, at St. Bartholomews' Parish, on the 9th inst., by the Rev. T. D. Bladen, John Williams, esq. to Mrs. Mary Estes and At the parsonage, in the aforesaid parish, on Sunday, the 12th instant, Mr. Vinson Jones, to Miss Sarah Margaret M'Collough.
Died, at Chehaw, the 15th instant, in the 78th year of her age, Mrs. Susannah Hughes, relict of the late Mr. John Hughes.

Issue of September 23, 1802

Died, on Tuesday morning last, Miss Catharine Ashby, in the 13th year of her age....

Issue of September 24, 1802

Died on the 18th instant, at his plantation in St. John's parish, in the 40th year of his age, Mr. Andrew Kennedy....

Issue of September 25, 1802

Died yesterday morning of the prevailing fever, in the 17th year of her age, Miss Maria Louisa Victoria de Cottes, only daughter of Madame de Cottes, of St. Domingo....

Issue of September 28, 1802

Married on Tuesday evening last, by the Rev. Dr. Buist, Mr. Frederick Smith, to Miss Eliza Ker, both of this city.
Departed this life, Mrs. Sebellow Shaw, wife of William Shaw, esq. attorney at law.
Died, on the 10th instant, in the 21st year of her age, Mrs. Eliza Mathewes, wife of the Rev. Edmund Mathewes....
Died on Saturday night last, Miss Judith Isaacks, aged 79 years, a native of New-York, and lately from Newport, Rhode-Island.

Issue of September 29, 1802

Departed this life on Sunday evening, the 26th instant, in the 51st year of her age, Mrs. Sarah Stoll, of this city.
Died, at New-York, on the 12th inst., Mrs. Mary Mathews, wife of Thomas Mathews, Esq. of South Carolina.

Issue of October 2, 1802

Married, on Tuesday the 14th ult., Mr. Jesse Goodlett, of Greenville, South-Carolina, to Miss Elizabeth Johnson, daughter of Lawyer Johnson, of Rutherford County, North-Carolina.
Died, yesterday, Mr. Thomas Annesley, a native of Ireland....
Died on the 10th ult., Mrs. O'Connor; on the 21st ult., Mr. Thomas O'Connor; and on the 28th ult. Mr. Daniel O'Connor--the mother, father and son....

Issue of October 4, 1802

Died, at Stono Ferry, on Thursday last, aged 21 years, Mrs. Mary Frierson, wife of Mr. John Frierson, of this city.... (lines)

Issue of October 6, 1802

Married last evening, by the Rev. Mr. Jenkins, Mr. James Cox, merchant, to Miss Bonneau; and Doctor Joseph Johnson, to Miss C. Conneau.
Died on Monday last, the 4th inst., Daniel Cannon, esq., aged 76 years and 8 months. His remains were interred in St. Philip's church yard on the day following....

Issue of October 7, 1802

Died, yesterday evening, Mr. Jacob Stol, tinman. He has left a wife and several small children....

Issue of October 8, 1802

Died, in Christ Church Parish, on the 2d inst., in the 59th year of his age, Gabriel Capers, Esq. (eulogy)
Departed this life on Wednesday the 6th inst., Miss Margaret Weaver, in the 15th year of her age.

Issue of October 9, 1802

Died at Statesburg, on the 1st inst., Mrs. Sarah Caroline Heriot, the amiable consort of Robert Heriot, esq. ...

Issue of October 11, 1802

Died on the 5th instant, in the 55th year of her age, Mrs. Rosetta Vaughan, late an inhabitant of St. Paul's parish.
Died on Wednesday last, Miss Margaret Weaver, in the 15th year of her age. (eulogy)

Issue of October 13, 1802

Died on Saturday night last, in the 47th year of her age, Mrs. Susan Mason, relict of the late William Mason....
Died on Sunday last, Mrs. Rebecca Gell...a fond wife and tender parent.
On Sunday morning last, departed this life, in the 35th year of his age, Mr. Abraham Joy, ship-joiner...left widow and two small children...
Died on the 20th of July last, at the Isle de Los, Capt. Isaac Barre Hichborne, master of the brig Hope of this port, in the 34th year of his age...left a widow and ond child in this city....

Issue of October 15, 1802

Married, yesterday evening, by the Rev. Mr. Frost, Mr. John J. Baker, to Mrs. Susannah Kennedy, both of this city.
Married on Tuesday 1st, by the Rev. Mr. Munds, Mr. James Smith, to Mrs. Hannah Jones, both of this place.
Married on Monday last, by the Rev. Mr. Munds, captain Charles Young, to Miss Mary Caroline Baker, both of this place.
Married last evening, by the Rev. Dr. Buist, Capt. James Messroon, to Miss Margaret M'Bride, both of this city.

48

Died on Saturday morning, the 9th inst., Mr. John Michael Row, in the 55th year of his age.

Issue of October 16, 1802

Married, at Savannah, on the 22d June last, Mr. Charles Gharnock, to Miss Joanna Tredwell.

Issue of October 18, 1802

Married on Saturday last, by the Rev. Mr. Forst, Peter Anthony Poincignon, to Mrs. Jane Poincignon, both of this city.
Died, at Beaufort, on Saturday the 9th inst., Mr. John Johnson, an old and respectable inhabitant, in the 61st year of his age.

Issue of October 19, 1802

Married on Sunday evening last, by the Rev. Mr. Munds, capt. John Sewall to Miss Susannah Charles.

Issue of October 20, 1802

Died on Sunday evening, the 17th inst., at Islington, in the vicinity of Charleston, Mr. Isaac Parker, aged 35 years--left a widow and one children....
Died on Sunday, the 17th inst., in the 35th year of her age, Mrs. Gibbes, wife of John Gibbes, esq.....

Issue of October 21, 1802

Died on the 20th inst., Mrs. Mary Williamson (relict of the late J. B. Williamson) in the 32d year of her age...left three orphans....

Issue of October 22, 1802

Died, at his plantation on Colonel's Island, in the State of Georgia, on the 11th instant, Robert Lithgow, esq., many years an inhabitant of this state, and one of the commissioners for disposing of the lots in the town of Columbia....
Departed this life on Thursday morning, the 21st inst., in the 64th year of her age, Mrs. Rebecca Isaacks, the relict of the late Mr. Jacob Isaacks, of Newport, Rhode Island....

Issue of October 25, 1802

Married on the 5th inst., Mr. Samuel Maverick, of this city, to Miss Elizabeth Anderson, daughter of Gen. Anderson, of Pendleton District.
Died, on Monday, the 17th inst., Mr. John Low, a native of Scotland, well known as a dealer and an honest man.

Issue of October 26, 1802

Married on the 28th ult., Mr. William Wallace, to the amiable and accomplished Miss Jane Winters, both of Union district.
Died, yesterday morning, Miss Johebed Isaacks, aged 35 years, daughter of the late Mr. Jacob Isaacks, of New-Port, Rhode-Island, and daughter of the lady whose death was announced a few days ago.

Issue of October 30, 1802

Married on Thursday evening last, by the Rev. Mr. Hammet, Mr. Zachariah Wheeler, of this city, to the amiable Miss Eleanor Davis, late of New-York.
Married on Thursday evening, by the Rev. Mr. Munds, Mr. John Tofet, confectioner, to Miss Catherine Frish.
Married on Thursday evening, by the Rev. Mr. Munds, Mr. Henry Hopkins, to Mrs. Rebecca Holmes.
Died on Wednesday the 27th inst., Mrs. Elizabeth Libert, aged 38 years.
Departed this life on Tuesday 26th inst., in the 19th year of his age, Mr. Edward C. Smith, from the island of Bermuda....
Died, in this city, on Tuesday evening last, in the 58th year of his age, the hon. John Mathews, esq. formerly gov. of this state...(account and eulogy)

Issue of November 1, 1802

Married on Sunday evening, by the Rev. Mr. Faber, Mr. L. Wright, plaisterer, to the amiable and accomplished Miss Susannah Louise Bell.
Died, at Savannah, Mr. Nicholas Johnson, Printer, and one of the Proprietors of the Georgia Gazette....

Issue of November 2, 1802

Married, on Sunday evening last, by the Rev. Mr. Jenkins, Doctor Benjamin B. Simons, to Miss Maria Vanderhorst, second daughter of Gen. Vanderhorst.

Issue of November 3, 1802

Married on Sunday evening last, at Mr. M'Nair's plantation by the Rev. J. B. Cook, of Beaufort, the Rev. J. M. Roberts, Minister of the Baptist Church, and Master of the Academy near Statesburg, to the amiable Miss Martha A. G. Miller, of said place.
Departed this life, on the 31st October, Mr. William Gist, merchant, in the 63d year of his age.

Issue of November 4, 1802

Married, on Tuesday, 12th October, Mr. Frederick Foster, to the amiable Miss Ann Tinch, daughter of Edward Tinch, esq., both of Newbury District.
Married yesterday morning, by the rev. Mr. Jenkins, Levi Durand Wigfall, esq. of St. James, Santee, to Miss Eliza Thompson, second daughter of Mr. James. H. Thompson, deceased, of this city.
Married by the Rev. Mr. Azuby, yesterday afternoon, Mr. Isaac C. Moses, youngest son of the late worthy Meyer Moses, to the amiable Miss Hannah Lazarus, both of this city.

Issue of November 5, 1802

Died, on Wednesday last, the 3d instant, in the 21st year of her age, Mrs. Floride Jervey, amialbe consort of Capt. Thomas H. Jervey, of this place.... (lines)

Issue of November 6, 1802

Married on Thursday evening last, on James Island, by the Rev. Mr. Price, Mr. John James Calvert, to Miss Eliza Thompson.

Issue of November 8, 1802

Died on Thursday last, at his plantation on Santee, Thomas N. Johnson, esq. in the 33d year of his age...left wife and child...

On Friday the 5th inst., departed this life, in the 63d year of her age, Mrs. Elizabeth Horlbeck, wife of John Horlbeck, sen... left two sons.

Died, on Thursday morning last, at the four mile house, Mr. Thomas Tapper, in the 24th year of his age, a native of England... buried in St. Philips church yard....

Issue of November 9, 1802

Married on the 30th of October last, by the Rev. Doctor Gallagher, Mr. Andrew Leonvalle, of St. Domingo, to Miss Rose Vigree, of Bourdeaux.

Married on Saturday evening last, Mr. Antcine Goudrand, to Mrs. Jane Elizabeth Boillas, both of this city.

Died, a few days ago, at his plantation, at the Horse Shoe, in Colleton district, Thomas Gough, esq.

Died at his seat in Pendleton district, on the 26th ult., in the 53d year of his age, John Ewing Colhoun, esq. Senator from this state in Congress...left widow and three small children....

Issue of November 10, 1802

Died, on Monday evening, the 8th instant, in the 31st year of his age, Mr. Robert Willington, a native of the Isle of Wight, in the county of Hampshire, England....

Issue of November 12, 1802

Married on Wednesday evening last, by the Rev. Mr. Faber, Mr. Michael Muckinfuss, to Miss Elizabeth Custer, eldest daughter of Mr. James Custer, factor, all of this city.

Married last evening, by the Rev. Dr. Jenkins, Edward Croft, Esq. Barrister at Law, to Miss Florida Lydia Gaillard, daughter of John Gaillard, Esq., deceased.

death of Mr. Alexander McKenzie, merchant, on his passage from this port to Glasgow, in the ship Montezuma....

Died on Monday, the 1st inst., in the 22d year of her age, Mrs. Mary Ann Doughty, wife of William Doughty, jun....

Issue of November 13, 1802

Married, on Tuesday evening last, by the Rev. Dr. Hollinshead, Doctor Edward D. Smith, to Miss Sarah North, eldest daughter of the late capt. Edward North.

Died this morning, Mr. John Borrow, a native of England, in the 28th year of his age...funeral at the house of Mr. Newton, in Hampstead village.

Issue of November 15, 1802

Married, yesterday evening, by the Rev. Dr. Jenkins, capt. John Luscombe, to Miss Dorothea M. l'Ans, both of this city.

Married, the 2d inst., Mr. Simon T. Sherman, of this place, to Miss Esther Lindsey, second daughter of capt. Samuel Lindsey, of Newberry District.

Married on the 28th ult, in the County of Newcastle, by the Rev. Mr. Wallace, Dr. George Logan, of S. C. to Miss Margaret White Poalk, of that state.

Issue of November 16, 1802

Married, on Sunday evening last, by the Rev. Dr. Buist, Capt. James Lamont, to Miss Ellen Hunter, of this city.

Issue of November 17, 1802

Married, last evening, by the Rev. Mr. Jenkins, Mr. Henry Mills, to Miss Mary Phelps.
Died, in the night of the 15th inst., aged 79, Mrs. Judith Pringle, relict of the hon. Robert Pringle, and a native of this state....

Issue of November 18, 1802

Departed this life on the 24th ult., at his residence in Chester district, after a long and very painful illness, Mr. John Walker, in the 75th year of his age....

Issue of November 19, 1802

Married, on Tuesday evening last, by the Rev. Mr. Jenkins, Mr. Henry Mills, to Miss Mary Philp Phillips, both of this city.
Married on Wednesday last, by the Rev. Mr. Azuby, Mr. Morriss Goldsmith, to Miss Sarah Levy.
Married in Philadelphia, on the 2d inst., by the Rev. Mr. Linn, Mr. Jacob Lippincott, of Cloucester county, New Jersey, to Miss Jane Ann Sikes, of this city.

Issue of November 20, 1802

Died, at his seat, Montpelier, St. Luke's parish, on the 14th inst., George Hipp, esq. a native of Germany, in the 66th year of his age. At an early period of life, he removed to this country....

Issue of November 23, 1802

Died on Toodondoo, St. Paul's parish, on the 18th inst., Mr. Andrew Smindersine, in the 40th year of his age...two orphan children, for years without a mother-...
Died, on Saturday morning last, Mr. George Rout, a native of Portsmouth, England, for many years a worthy member of this community....
Died on Thursday the 18th inst., Mr. Caleb Smith, a native of the island of Pomona Orkney, North-Britian, aged 47 years. He left a widow, two children and relations....

Issue of November 25, 1802

Married on Sunday last, on Edisto Island, by the Rev. Mr. Donald M'Leod, Mr. Thomas Maxy, of St. Augustine, to Miss Frances Cowen, of Edisto Island.
On Sunday evening last, departed this life in the 43d year of her age, Mrs. Mary Burger, wife of Mr. David Burger.(poem)

Issue of November 27, 1802

Georgetown (S. C.) November 20 On the 10th instant we announced the condemnation of John Smithart, for the murder of his wife--we are sorry to add, that on the night of the 26th ult.,he made his escape from Gaol....

November 24

Died on the 4th instant, near Statesburg, where she had resided for some years, in the 67th year of her age, Mrs. Ann Isabella Kinloch, relict of Francis Kinloch, Esq. deceased.

Died, on Saturday night last, Mr. Robert Smith, a native of Yorkshire, in England.

Died on Monday night last, Mr. Peter Gilbo, a native of the Department of Nantes, aged 62 years....

Issue of November 29, 1802

Died on Friday evening last, Mrs. Elizabeth Parks, in the 58th year of her age.

Died on Saturday evening the 27th inst., Mr. George Tunno, much and deservedly regretted by his relations and friends.

Issue of December 3, 1802

Married on Wednesday evening last, by the Rev. Mr. Munds, Capt. Richard Young, to Miss Eliza Kelly.

Married, last evening, by the Rev. Mr. Munds, Mr. Thomas Holwell (Rolwell?), to Miss Mary Webb.

Died, yesterday, Mr. George Stewart, coachmaker, a native of Scotland. This gentleman had resided in this city six years ....

Issue of December 4, 1802

Married on Thursday evening last, in St. Andrew's Parish, by the Rev. Mr. Mills, Francis Rose, esq. to Miss Martha Fuller, youngest daughter of the late Col. Thomas Fuller.

Married on Thursday evening last, on James Island, by the Rev. Mr. Price, Mr. Joseph H. Livingston, printer, of this city, to Miss Mary Stent, of James Island.

Married at St. Helena, on Saturday evening last, by the Rev. Mr. Cooke, Mr. Garret De Bow, to Miss Mary Norton, eldest daughter of William Norton, esq. of said place.

Issue of December 6, 1802

Died on the 17th ult. at the plantation of John Course, Esq. in the state of Georgia, Jack Wright, a negro and African born. From his own account...he was about 109 years old. He was servant to captain, afterward, Lord Anson...(account)

Issue of December 7, 1802

Married, in Boston, on the 11th ult., John Depont, esq. of Goose-creek, to Mrs. Mary C. Stent, of this city.

Issue of December 8, 1802

Married, on Saturday evening, Mr. William Buntin, shoemaker, to Mrs. S. M----.

Issue of December 10, 1802

Departed this life, on Wednesday night last, in the 44th year of her age, Mrs. Agnew Stewart, a native of Argyleshire in in Scotland, and wife of Mr. Alexander Stewart, of this city, leaving an affectionate husband and six children, three of whom are yet helpless infants....

Issue of December 13, 1802

Died, at Savannah, on the 3d inst.,Mrs. H. Tattnall, consort of Josiah Tattnall, jun. Esq. late governor of Georgia.

Issue of December 14, 1802

Departed this life at Savannah, the 9th inst., William Neyle, of Hutchinson's Island....

Issue of December 15, 1802

Died, on John's Island, on Saturday last, Mrs. Jane Watter, aged 60 years....

Issue of December 17, 1802

Married, last evening, by the Rev. Mr. Munds, Capt. Ebenezer Hopkins, to Miss Catherine Frances Harvey, of Georgetown.
Married in November last, Charles Hagety, esq. merchant, to the amiable and well accomplished Miss Effey Hagan, both of Sumter district.

Issue of December 18, 1802

Died at his plantation on James Island, on Wednesday last, the 15th inst., Archibald Henry Scott, Esq., aged 25 years, who has left a wife, mother and many friends....

Issue of December 21, 1802

Died, on the 18th instant, Mrs. Ann Gray. She was born 3d December 1721, on James Island...She has had 12 children, 40 grandchildren, and 12 great grandchildren....
Died at Goree, on the 26th July last, in the 43d year of his age, captain William Richards, of this city....

Issue of December 23, 1802

Died, on Friday the 17th inst., Mr. Rettier Whittimore, aged 44 years...left a widow.

Issue of December 24, 1802

Married, last evening, by the Rev. Mr. Frost, Mr. James Gabeau, to Miss Dorothy Smith, daughter of captain Peter Smith, factor.
Married, last evening by the Rev. Mr. Jenkins, Dr. William Ioor, of St. George, Dorchester, to Miss Ann Mathewes, daughter of George Mathewes, Esq. of this city.
Married on Sunday evening last,by the Rev. Mr. Furman, Mr. John M'Clain, pilot, to Miss Mary Ann Rankin, both of this city.
Married on Tuesday evening last, at Pine-Grove, Christ-Church parish, by the Rev. Dr. Hollinshead, Dr. John R. Witherspoon, of Williamsburgh, to Miss Jane Harrison, M'Calla, daughter of Rev. Dr. Daniel M'Calla.
Married on Tuesday the 21st inst., by the Rev. Philip Matthews, of Christ Church parish, Mr. Richard Fowler, to Miss Mary Smith, both of the same place.
Married by the Rev. Mr. Munds, Mr. J. W. Brandt, merchant, to Mrs. Hannah A. Legare, of Christ Church Parish.

Issue of December 27, 1802

Married on Saturday last, by the Rev. Mr. Munds, Mr. Neal M'Gregor, to Mrs. Jane Phipps.

Issue of December 29, 1802

Died on the 10th inst., on his passage from Jamaica to this place, in the 22d year of his age, Mr. John Revell...left wife and connexions....

Issue of December 30, 1802

Married, last evening, by the Rev. Dr. Frost, William Dawson, Esq. to Miss Caroline Prioleau, daughter of Samuel Prioleau, Esq.
Married last evening, by the Rev. Mr. Azuby, Mr. David Mordecai, to the amiable Miss Rina Cohen.

Issue of December 31, 1802

Married, on the 23d inst., by the Rev. Mr. Jenkins, Benjamin Foissin Trapier, esq. to Miss Hannah Shubrick Heyward, eldest daughter of the late William Heyward, esq.

Issue of January 5, 1803

Married in Christ Church Parish, on the 29th ult., by the Rev. Philip Matthews, Mr. Samuel Boya, to Mrs. Calhoun, of this city.
Died, on the 27th ult., Mr. Richard Holmes Cheevers, a native of Ireland.
Died on Wednesday the 29th ult., in the 55th year of his age, Mr. Samuel Pelot, of St. Luke's parish.
Died on the 29th ult., in the 59th year of her age, Miss Susannah Poinsett, only sister of Doctor E. Poinsett, of this city.

Issue of January 11, 1803

Married in St. James's Santee, by the Rev. Mr. O'Daniel, Thomas Smith, esq. of St. James's, Goose-Creek, to the amiable Miss Mary Buchanan, eldest daughter of Dr. John Buchanan, decd.

Issue of January 13, 1803

Married, last evening, by the Rev. Mr. Azuby, Mr. Abraham Sasportas, merchant, to Miss Charlotte Canter.
Married, last evening, by the Rev. Dr. Keith, captain Francis Stiles Lightbourn, of this city, to Mrs. Eliza B. Edings, of Wadmalaw.
Married, last evening, by the Rev. Dr. Buist, John Sanders, esq., to Miss Eliza O'Hear, daughter of James O'Hear, esq.

Issue of January 15, 1803

Died on the 13th instant, in the 30th year of her age, Mrs. Jane Pogson White, wife of John White, esq....
Died on the 26th December last, at his plantation on Pedee river, Darlington district, in the 71st year of his age, the Rev. Evan Pugh, A. M. pastor of the Baptist Church at Mount Pleasant...a native of Pennsylvania, and educated in the principles of the Quakers...(eulogy and account)

Issue of January 18, 1803

Died on the 15th instant, Mr. Peter Buyck, a native of Ghent in Flanders, aged 87 years.

Issue of January 19, 1803

Married on Edisto Island, on Tuesday the 4th inst., by the Rev. Mr. M'Cleod, Ephraim Mitchel, Esq. of said island, to Miss Providence Jenkins, of this city, second daughter of Isaac Jenkins, Esq. deceased.

Issue of January 21, 1803

Married last Sunday evening, at Statesburg, by Rev. J. M. Roberts, Mr. John Monk, of this city, to Miss Rachael Haynesworth, daughter of Henry Haynsworth, near Statesburgh.
Married on Thursday evening last, by the Rev. Mr. Hollinshead, capt. S. Patterson, to Miss Mary Parinchief, of this city.
Married, last evening, by the Rev. Dr. Hollinshead, Doctor J. P. Gough, to Miss E. Lightwood, both of this city.

Issue of January 24, 1803

Married, on Saturday evening last, by the Rev. Mr. Bowen, Mr. Joseph Cook, of St. Pauls Parish, to Mrs. Susannah Heileger, of this city.

Issue of January 25, 1803

Married, on Saturday evening last, by the Rev. Mr. Faber, Mr. James Smith, of this city, to Miss Sarah Davison, of Jacksonborough.
Married, last Saturday, by the Rev. Mr. Bowen, Mr. Joseph Cook, of St. Pauls Parish, to Miss Susannah Bennett, of Charleston.

Issue of January 26, 1803

Married on Sunday evening last, by the Rev. Doctor Gallagher, Mr. James Guy, to Mrs. Grace Ingram, both of this city.
Married, last night, Mr. Christian M. Logan, to Miss Sarah White Chanler, youngest daughter of the late Doctor Isaac Chanler.
Died in the parish of St. George, Dorchester, in the 26th year of his age, Major M. Henry.
Died in St. Paul's Parish, William Flack, Esq. an honest, industrious man....
Died on Monday last, Miss Catherine Poppenheim, aged 14 years and 3 months...daughter of Mr. Lewis Poppenheim, of St. Georges, Dorchester, and had lately come to Charleston, in order to finish her education....

Issue of January 28, 1803

Married, last evening, by the Rev. Mr. Frost, Mr. Daniel B. Mazyck, to Miss ---- Harris.

Issue of January 29, 1803

Married on the 23d inst., by the Rev. Mr. Fraser, Benjamin Allston, sen. Esq. to Mrs. Singleton, of Pee Dee.

Married on Tuesday evening, the 25th instant, by the Rev. Dr. Gallagher, Mr. John Adrien Desjardin, to Miss Margueritte Carmand, daughter of Mr. Peter Carmand, taylor of this city.

Issue of January 31, 1803

Married, last evening, by the Rev. Mr. Furman, Mr. Thomas Pritchard, to Miss Elizabeth Capers, both of St. Helena.

Died, on board the ship Columbian Packet, on the 11th inst., on his passage from Jamaica, Captain Frederick Swain, son of capt. Barnabas Swaine, of Nantucket, aged 22 years, and late master of the schooner Dispatch, of Wilmington, N. C....

Issue of February 1, 1803

Married, on Thursday, 20th Jan. last, Mr. George Verree, of this city, merchant, to Miss Rebecca Jerman, daughter of the late Edward Jerman, esq. of St. James's, Santee.

Departed this life on the 27th inst., on James Island, Mr. Jonathan Evans, aged 24 years....

Issue of February 2, 1803

Died, this morning, Thomas Bourke, Esq. formerly an eminent merchant in this city, but late a planter of Georgia.

Issue of February 5, 1803

Departed this life, on the 19th ult., and in the 58th year of her age, Mrs. Lydia Anderson, consort of Gen. Anderson, of Pendleton district....

Died on Wednesday morning the 2d instant, Mr. John Otto, in the 55th year of his age...left a wife and three children....

Issue of February 8, 1803

Married, in Clarendon county, on Thursday the 20th ult., by the Rev. John M. Roberts, David Dubose, esq. to Miss Clarissa James, youngest daughter of the late col. John James, of said place.

Died in this city, on Sunday last, Richard Beresford, esq. Died this morning, Mrs. Harriet Lee, wife of Mr. William Lee, merchant, of this place.

Issue of February 9, 1803

Died, yesterday morning, Mrs. Sarah Williams, wife of Mr. David R. Williams one of the proprietors of the City Gazette, and daugher of Nicholas Power, Esq. of Providence, R. I.

Issue of February 10, 1803

Departed this life on Monday the 31st January, aged 39 years, Mrs. Elizabeth Negrin, and on Tuesday following was interred in the burial ground of the Independent Congregational Church...

Died this morning, Mrs. Amelia Dart, aged 70 years and 8 months, the relict of Benjamin Dart, senior, esq.

Issue of February 12, 1803

Married on Thursday evening last, by the Rev. Dr. Frost, Mr. Paul Pritchard, jun. to Miss Catherine Hamilton, both of this city.

Married on the 10th of December last, by the Rev. Dr. Buist, James Scott, Esq. planter, St. Andrew's parish, to the amiable and accomplished Mrs. Elizabeth Davis, of th same place

Died, on the 7th inst., Mrs. Anne Motte, aged 73 years... relict of Hon. Jacob Motte, sen. formerly the Treasurer of the King, in this then Province.

Issue of February 14, 1803

Died on the 8th inst., in St. John's Parish, Berkley, Mrs. Catherine Ravenel, wife of Stephen Ravenel, esq....

Issue of February 17, 1803

Died, yesterday morning, in the 68th year of his age, Capt. Alexander Tweed....

Issue of February 18, 1803

Married on Tuesday evening last, by the Rev. Mr. Bowen, Dr. Foissin to Miss Fayssoux, eldest daughter of the late Dr. Peter Fayssoux.

Married, yesterday evening, Mr. Christopher Wagoner, to the amiable Mrs. Mary Critesburg.

Married on Sunday, the 13th instant, Mr. George Medowes, to Miss Ann Margaret Attiner, both of this city.

Died on Wednesday the 16th inst., Peter A. R. Neil, esq. planter, of St. Domingo, and a native of that Island....

Died on Wednesday the 16th inst., Mrs. Ann Duncan, wife of Mr. John Duncan, aged 48 years....

Issue of February 19, 1803

Married on Wednesday evening last, by the Rev. Mr. Jenkins, Doctor Samuel Thomas, of Georgetown, to Miss Mary Gaillard, daughter of the late John Gaillard, esq.

Departed this life on the 8th inst., Mrs. Harriot Lee, the amiable consort of Mr. William Lee, merchant, of this city....

Died, on Sunday, 13th inst., on James Island, Mr. Mallory Rivers, in the 38th year of his age. He has left a family....

Issue of February 22, 1803

Married on Sunday evening last, Mr. Robert Paterson to Miss Ann Hampton, both of this city.

Died on the 20th instant, Mrs. Martha Ruberry, wife of Mr. John Ruberry, aged 30 years.

Died on Friday last, the 18th inst., Mr. Sebbe Sebbin, a native of Sanstodt, Germany, aged 43 years...an inhabitant here for many years.

Died on Saturday evening last, Mr. John Eddy, a native of Providence, AE 27 years; left a widow...

Died on Saturday, the 19th inst., Mrs. H. Smith, the amiable relict of Captain W. Smith, and daughter of Jacob Valk, formerly merchant of this city.

Issue of February 23, 1803

Married last evening by the Rev. Mr. Jenkins, William Lee, jun. Esq. Attorney at Law, to Miss Elizabeth Markley, daughter of Mr. Abraham Markley, merchant, of this city.

Departed this life, on Monday the 22d inst., John Logan, esq., planter of the Round O.

Died, yesterday, Mr. John Calder Whaley.
Died on Monday last, Mr. Jeremiah Rose, of James Island, planter, formerly of this city.

Issue of February 24, 1803

Married, on the 9th instant, by the Rev. Dr. ___, Mr. James Dorrill, of Christ Church parish, to Miss Ann Dorrill, of the same place.
Married on Tuesday evening last, by the Rev. Hollinshead, Mr. John Lequeux, factor to Martha Darrell, second daughter of Edward Darrell, esq. merchant, deceased.

Issue of February 25, 1803

Died, on Friday the 18th instant, Mr. Daniel Seiller, aged 37 years...left a wife and aged father, two brothers....
Died on the 22d instant, in the 20th year of his age, Mr. John Calder Whaley, planter, of St. John's Island, son of Thomas Whaley, Esq. of Charleston....

Issue of March 2, 1803

Died on Sunday last, in the 43d year of his age, Joshua Hargreaves, Esq. a native of England, and many years a respectable merchant of this city.

Issue of March 4, 1803

Married on Tuesday the 1st instant, at Beaufort, by the Rev. Mr. Cock, Dr. James Perry, of St. Bartholomew's Parish, to Mrs. Catharine Sams, of Beaufort.
Died on the 2d instant, in the 27th year of her age, Mrs. Elizabeth Stanyarne Flud, consort of Daniel Flud, esq...affectionate wife, tender mother....

Issue of March 8, 1803

Died on the 11th ult.,in Barnwell district, John M'Ilhenny... left wife and four children.
Died, yesterday, Mrs. Mary Byrne, wife of Mr. P. Byrne.... funeral at No. 38 Hasell-street.

Issue of March 12, 1803

On Wednesday the 9th inst., departed this life, Mrs. Elizabeth Horlbeck, wife of Mr. John Horlbeck, jun., aged 23 years and 7 months...

Issue of March 14, 1803

On Thursday the 3d of March, Mr. Thomas Harrell, left Charleston on horseback. At four o'clock of the same day, he was seen at the Four Mile House....his body was found, on the 12th inst ...On the 13th of Feb. he received 580 dollars, for work lately done on Mr. Gaillard's farm, near Clement's ferry....He had announced his intention of visiting his father at the High Hills of Santee.
Married, last evening, by the Rev. J. C. Faber, Mr. Jacob Belser, to Miss Martha Clark, both of this city.

Issue of March 16, 1803

Married last evening, in this city, Mr. Robert May, of St. Bartholomew's parish, planter, and Mrs. Margaret Hall, of said parish.

Died, at Georgetown, on Sunday last, Mr. John Hardwick, surveyor, a native of England.

Died near Fort Wilkinson, on the frontiers of Georgia, Mr. William Skrine, of this city. He had been at West Florida, and was on his way returning to his family...on the 15th Nov. last, in the 49th year of his age.

Issue of March 18, 1803

Married on Saturday evening last, by the Rev. Mr. Frost, Mr. Archibald Smith, jun. to Mrs. Ann Chevers, widow of the late Mr. Richard Holmes Chevers, both of this city.

Died, last night, Mrs. Frances Moon, of Christ Church parish.

Issue of March 19, 1803

Died, at his plantation in St. George's Parish, Dorchester, on Wednesday last, Mr. Henry Markley.... left a wife and three children...in the 42d year of his age.

Issue of March 21, 1803

Married on Thursday evening last, Mr. Joseph Huggins, to Miss Ann Huger, daughter of Gen. Huger, both of Prince George's, Santee.

Issue of March 22, 1803

Died, on the 16th instant, Mr. Lewis A Graeser, merchant of this city.

Died on Friday last, the 18th inst., in the 43d year of his age, Mr. Isaac Donaven; he has left a widow and four children....

Died, at Philadelphia, on the 28th ult., Godfrey Wellser, senior, aged about 98 years....

Issue of March 25, 1803

Married last evening, by the Rev. J. C. Faber, Edward Penington, lieutenant in the revenue department of the U. S., to Mrs. Ann Elizabeth Goring, both of this city.

Issue of March 28, 1803

Died on Wednesday the 23d inst., Mr. William Gray, Silver Smith, aged 31 years.

Issue of March 29, 1803

Departed this life, on Wednesday the 16th inst., Gabriel Gignilliat, esq. one of the Representatives in the state Legislature, for the Parish of St. John's in the 24th year of his age ....

Issue of April 5, 1803

Married on Saturday evening last, the 2d inst., by the Rev. Mr. Furman, Mr. Joseph Champlin, to the agreeable Miss Jane Carr, both of this city.

Died at Hillsborough, Mr. Wm. Jones, aged 78. He has left a wife, with whom he lived 53 years, with a numerous posterity. They had 12 children, 8 of whom are now living, 82 grandchildren, 74 of which are still living, 54 greatgrandchildren, 53 of whom yet survive. Three of the grandsons are removed to a great distance...His two last children were twins, both daughters; they married two brothers who were twins; one of them has had three daughters at a birth! two of which are living. Salem paper

Issue of April 6, 1803

Died on the 9th of March last, at Northampton, Mass., in the 30th year of her age, Mrs. M. M. Seiger, wife of Dr. Charles L. Seiger, and eldest daughter of Daniel Strobel, senior, of this city....

Issue of April 12, 1803

Married, on Sunday evening last, by the Rev. Mr. Frost, Mr. George Revell, to Miss Margaret Timmons.
Married, on Sunday evening last, by the Rev. Mr. Munds, Mr. Richard Hancock, to Miss Polly Stack, both of this city.

Issue of April 13, 1803

Death. On Monday last, was consigned to the silence of the grave, Mrs. Phoebe Wells, widow of the late Mr. Edgar Wells, of this city.... (poem)

Issue of April 15, 1803

Died at the City of Washington, Gen. Donald Campbell. The disinterested part Gen. Campbell took in our revolutionary war, in resigning his commission in the British army, and accepting one in the American....

Issue of April 25, 1803

Married, on Saturday evening last, by the Rev. Dr. Hollinshead, Captain Orlando Denny, to the amiable Miss Clarissa Woodworth, late of Philadelphia, and now of this city.
Married on Saturday evening last, by the Rev. Dr. Hollinshead, Mr. Thomas Hamett, to Miss Caroline Myrtilda Singleton.
Married, on the 21st instant, in St. James's Parish, at the seat of Thomas Boone, Esq., Doctor Sims White, of St. John's Parish, to Miss Mary Ford Boone, daughter of Robert Boone, Esq., deceased.

Issue of April 26, 1803

Married on the 14th instant, by the Rev. Mr. M. Roberts, at Santee, Robert Brailsford, Esq. of Charleston, to Miss Eliza L. James, of that place.
Married on Tuesday the 22nd March, Mr. William Hamilton, to Miss Ann Childs, both of Abbeville district.
Married on Thursday, 24th March, Mr. William Bass, of Virginia, to Miss Mary Baker, of Abbeville district.

Issue of April 27, 1803

Died Sunday, the 24th inst., departed this life, John C. Martin, aged 60 years and 7 months....

Issue of April 28, 1803

Died on Tuesday last, Mr. Lewis Timmons, for many years past, Cryer of the Superior Courts in this city....

Issue of April 29, 1803

Died, on Thursday the 21st April, at his seat in Manchester on the High Hills of Santee, Isham Moore, Esq....left a large family.

Died, on the 26th instant, Miss Mary Skrine, of this city, aged 30....

Issue of April 30, 1803

Died, on Wednesday the 27th instant, Mrs. Elizabeth Godfrey, of this city, aged 66 years, daughter of Mr. William Chapman, of James Island.... (lines)

Issue of May 2, 1803

Married last evening, Mr. James Hunter to Miss Louisa Provost, of St. Domingo.

Married on Saturday evening last, by the Rev. Mr. Munds, Mr. George Harper, to Miss Eliza Harriett, both of this place.

Married on Saturday evening last, by the Rev. Mr. Munds, Mr. John Kimbal, to Miss Elizabeth Leger, both of this place.

Issue of May 3, 1803

Married on the 31st March last, at Rocky Point, Prince William's parish, John Marsden Pintard, esq. late Consul at Madeira, to Miss Eliza Smith, eldest daughter of the Rev. Dr. Smith, president of the college at Princeton, New-Jersey.

Died on the 30th ult., in the 45th year of his age, Mr. John Nivison, a native of Scotland....

Issue of May 4, 1803

Died, on the 30th ult., in the 21st year of her age, Mrs. Martha Mair, wife of Mr. Patrick Mair, merchant of this city....

Issue of May 6, 1803

Died, in London, Mr. Daniel M'Guerton, shoemaker....

Issue of May 7, 1803

Married, on Thursday evening last, Mr. Fasthender, to Mrs. Catherine Grose, both of this city.

Died, at St. Mary's Georgia, on the 18th ult.,in the 30th year of her age, Mrs. Margaret Pearis, wife of Richard Pearis, and daughter of Gen. Robert Cunningham, formerly of this state.

Issue of May 11, 1803

Married, last evening, by the Rev. Mr. Jenkins, Mr. John Howard, to Miss Mary Elfe.

Issue of May 12, 1803

Married on Tuesday last, by Mr. Azuby, Mr. Aaron Lazarus, merchant, to Miss Hetty Cohen, second daughter of the late Mr.

Gershom Cohen.

Issue of May 14, 1803

Died on the 12th inst., Mr. Jonathan Cape, in his 24th year, youngest son of Brian Cape, esq. of this city...left aged parents, widow and an infant son....

Issue of May 16, 1803

Married on the 3d inst., by the Rev. Mr. Pogson, Mr. John Kennedy, of St. John's parish, to Miss Mary Coon Russ, of St. Stephen's parish.

Died on Saturday evening last, the Rev. Mr. Hammet, of Trinity Church...aged 47 years; he was in the Ministry twenty years the day he died....

Issue of May 17, 1803

Died on Monday last in the 21st year of her age, Mrs. Catherine Williams, wife of Mr. William Williams of this city, portrait painter, and daughter of James Simpson, esq. of Georgetown....left two infant children and husband.

Issue of May 18, 1803

Married on Wednesday the 11th inst., at Chehaw, by the Rev. Mr. Bladen, Mr. Edward Kennedy, of this city, to Miss Elizabeth Hutchinson, of that place.

Married on Sunday last, by the Rev. Mr. Frost, Mr. John Anderson, to Miss Elizabeth S. Clark, both of this city.

Married on Tuesday evening, by the Rev. Mr. Frost, Mr. William Shite of St. John's parish, to Miss Ann Maromet, of this city.

Died, this morning, Mr. Nathaniel Darrell...funeral at the house of Mr. Muckinfuss, in Wentworth-street....

Issue of May 20, 1803

Married, last evening, by the Rev. Dr. Hollinshead, Mr. Stephen Gordon, to Miss Jane Hayes, both of this city.

Issue of May 21, 1803

Married on Thursday the 19th inst., by the Rev. Dr. Hollinshead, Mr. Joseph Chapman, to Miss Jane Flemming, both of this city.

Died, this morning, Mr. James C. Green, in the 31st year of his age...funeral at his late residence, No. 98 Church-st....

Died at Philadelphia, on the 9th inst., Gen. Stephens Thomson Mason, one of the Senators of the state of Virginia in the Congress....

Issue of May 23, 1803

Died, this forenoon, Mr. James M'Bride....

Issue of May 24, 1803

Departed this life, on the 18th inst., in the 32d year of his age, Benjamin Snipes, esq....

Issue of May 27, 1803

Married, at Wexford, on the 19th ult., Mr. Prater Gander, to Miss Susannah Goose.

Issue of May 30, 1803

Died on Wednesday the 25th inst., Mr. William Lenox, aged 74 years, an old and respectable inhabitnat and merchant of this city...lived upwards of 50 years in S. C., and the greatest part of that time in Charleston.

Died in Curracoa, on the 14th of last March, in the 47th year of his age, Benjamin Hammett Phillips, Esq. Consul for the U. S. at that Island.

Issue of May 31, 1803

Died, at Georgetown, on Tuesday last, Mr. Elisha Bowles, Printer of the Georgetown Gazette.

Died in London, on the 7th April, at his house in Picadilly in the 74th year of his age, the R. H. Sir William Hamilton, K. B. &c....

Issue of June 1, 1803

Married, on Monday evening, the 30th ult., Charles Robiou, esq. to Miss Melanie Niel, both of St. Domingo.

Married, on Thursday evening, the 19th inst., at Savannah, by the Rev. Mr. Holcombe, Judge Trezevant, of South Carolina, to Mrs. Henrietta Morel, relict of the late Hon. John Morel.

Married at Georgetown (S.C.), on Thursday the 26th inst., Thamas Mitchell, esq. to the amiable Miss Charlotte Mitchell, of that place.

Issue of June 2, 1803

Died, yesterday, Mrs. Susanna Skrine, aged 43 years....

Issue of June 3, 1803

Married, on the 26th ult., Mr. John Johnson, jun., of this city, to Miss De Bernier, of North-Carolina.

Issue of June 9, 1803

Married, on Sunday evening last, by the Rev. Dr. Hollinshead, Mr. James Stafford, to Miss Elizabeth Ivey, both of this city.

Issue of June 10, 1803

Married on Tuesday evening last, by the Rev. Mr. Frost, Andrew Norris, esq. attorney at law, of Abbeville district, to Miss Ann Eliza Wrainch, of this city.

Issue of June 11, 1803

Died, on the 9th inst., in the 53d year of his age, Caspar C. Schutt, Esq...18 years residence therein....

Issue of June 13, 1803

Married, on Saturday evening last, by the Rev. Mr. Frost, captain John Lawson, to Miss Mary Danford, both of this place.

Married on Sunday evening last, by the Rev. Mr. Frost, Mr. Arthur Honywood, to Miss Susannah Mills, youngest daughter of the Rev. Thomas Mills.

Departed this life, on Friday evening, the 10th inst., Mrs. Rachel Alexander, relict of Mr. Alexander Alexander...interred in St. Philip's Church yard....

On Thursday morning last departed this life, Mrs. Harriet E. Stoney, consort of Mr. John Stoney, merchant, of this city....

Issue of June 14, 1803

On Saturday last departed this life, in the 47th year of her age, Mrs. Susanna Bulleine Bee, consort of Judge Bee....

Died on the morning of the 12th inst., John M'Crady, Esq., in the 28th year of his age. (long eulogy)

Issue of June 16, 1803

Married at Washington, on the 31st ult., Lieutenant James Thompson, Paymaster of the Marine Corps, to Miss Burrows, daughter of Col. Burrows, commandant of the Marines, all of Washington.

Died on the 6th ultimo, at his seat (Belville) near Nashville, in the state of Tennessee, Capt. Edward Butler, of the 2d regt. of Infantry in the army of the U. S. (long account)

Issue of June 17, 1803

Married, on the 2d instant, by the Rev. Mr. Rattoone, Humphrey Minchen, Esq. of Charleston, S. C. to Miss Margaret Gudirow, of this city.   **Baltimore paper.**

Issue of June 18, 1803

Married at Philadelphia, on the 6th inst., Mr. George Izard, of this city, to Mrs. Elizabeth Carter Shippen, of Farley, Bucks co., Pa.

Died last night, Mr. Owen M'Mahon, in the 76th year of his age, for many years a resident in this city, and an officer of the Customes....

Issue of June 20, 1803

Married, at his plantation, in St. Andrew's Parish, by the Rev. Mr. Mills, Dr. Joseph Chouler, to Mrs. Mary Brune, widow of the late D. I. Brune, esq., merchant, of New-York.

Married, last evening, by the Rev. Dr. Keith, Mr. William Noel, of the Island of St. Domingo, to Miss Sarah Ann Rain, of this city.

Married, at Wadmalaw, on Wednesday the 15th inst., by the Rev. Edmund Mathews, William Reynolds, esq. of St. Helena, to Miss Sarah Adams, daughter of Bernard Adams, esq. of Wadmalaw.

Issue of June 21, 1803

Savannah, June 18

On Wednesday the 15th inst.,departed this life, Mrs. Elizabeth Wayne, wife of Richard Wayne, Esq. of this city, aged 52 years. (eulogy)

Issue of June 22, 1803

Married, on Sunday last, by the Rev. Dr. Buist, Captain Tousset, to Miss Anna Ker, both of this city.
Died, on Sunday evening last, in the 42d year of her age, Mrs. Ann Bensley Kennedy, consort of Capt. James Kennedy, and daughter of Dr. Lionel Chalmers, deceased....(lines)

Issue of June 23, 1803

Married, on Tuesday evening last, by the Rev. Dr. Keith, Citizen Simon Jude Chancognie, Commissary of the Commercial Relations of the French Republic, at Charleston, to Miss Maria Susannah Delaire, only daughter of James Delaire, esq. formerly of St. Domingo, now of this city, merchant.

Issue of June 27, 1803

Died, on the 23d instant, Joseph Kirkland, jun., youngest son of Doctor Joseph Kirkland, of Charleston, in the 5th year of his age.

Issue of June 25, 1803

Departed this life, on the evening of the 21st inst., in the 33d year of his age, Mr. William Smith, of this city....(lines)

Issue of June 30, 1803

Married, last Thursday evening, by the Rev. Mr. Munds, Mr. Samuel Williams, jun., to the amiable Mrs. Eliza Eddington, both of this city.

Issue of July 1, 1803

Married, on Wednesday evening, 29th of June, by the Rev. Dr. Keith, Mr. Thomas Hinson, of John's Island, to Miss Mary Sicile Vanderherchen, eldest daughter of Andrew Vanderherchen, of this city.
Died at his seat at Bunbury, Cheshire...the scientific Pig! London paper

Issue of July 2, 1803

Married on Thursday evening last, by the Rev. Dr. Keith, Mr. William Motte, to Miss Elizabeth Davidson, both of this city.

Issue of July 8, 1803

Married, on Tuesday evening last, by the Rev. John C. Faber, Mr. John Love, of this city, to Miss Eleanor Eden, of Christ Church Parish.

Issue of July 9, 1803

Died in Georgia, on the 22d ult., John Cunningham, Esq., late of Naffan, New-Providence.

Issue of July 11, 1803

Married in Christ Church parish, on Thursday the 7th inst., by the Rev. Dr. M'Calla, Mr. Charles Whitesides, to Miss Rebecca Dorrell, both of said parish.

Issue of July 12, 1803

Married on Saturday evening last, by the Rev. Mr. Frost, Mr. Joseph Assalit, late planter of St. Domingo, to Miss Magdalen Gosselin, of Bordeaux.

Issue of July 15, 1803

Married, last evening, by the Rev. Dr. Buist, Mr. George M'Kay, of St. Paul's Parish, to Mrs. Susanna Cheves, of this city.

Issue of July 19, 1803

Died, on the 15th instant, Miss Penelope Ann Kempton, aged 20 months and 15 days. (lines)

Issue of July 21, 1803

Married, at Columbia, on the 12th inst., by the Rev. Mr. Dunlap, Mr. Robert Clark, of this city, merchant, to Miss Sally Tillinghast, of that town.
Died, at Wilmington, N. C., on the 11th inst., Mr. William Harp, aged 102 years.

Issue of July 22, 1803

Died, yesterday evening, in the 34th year of his age, Mr. Edward L. Woodrouffe, of this city, merchant.
Departed this life, on the 14th ult., Miss Eliza Hilton, aged 15 years, daughter of Mr. Jess Hilton, of Clarendon County. (lines)

Issue of July 23, 1803

Died, on Wednesday last, Mr. Joseph Hazlewood. He has resided in this city for many years....

Issue of July 25, 1803

Died, on the 30th ult., at his plantation near Statesburgh, High Hills of Santee, Mr. John Matthew Langstaff, planter, in the 29th year of his age.

Issue of July 29, 1803

Married on Thursday evening last, by the Rev. Mr. Milward Posson, Mr. Claudius Nicolas Samory, merchant, to Miss Mary Magdeline Antoinette Dupont Delorme, both of St. Domingo.

Issue of August 2, 1803

Died at Mount Gorton Castle(?) on the 16th April, in the 27th year of his age, Rev. William Connor, A. M., brother to the Rev. James Connor, of South Carolina....

Issue of August 6, 1803

Departed this life, on Wednesday evening last, in the 27th year of her age, Miss Mary Ann Jefferys...leaves an aged mother. (lines)

Issue of August 9, 1803

Died, on Saturday morning last, William Wragg, esq.
Died on Sunday morning, Mr. Francis Blakeley.

Issue of August 11, 1803

Died, on Tuesday evening last, Mrs. Mary Rivers, aged 87 years.

Issue of August 15, 1803

Died, at White Hall, in Fairfield County, on the 30th of July, in the 26th year of her age, Mrs. Jane Wilson Rogers, wife of the Rev. James Rogers.

Issue of August 16, 1803

Departed this life, on the 23d July last, at the Waxhaws, Lancaster district, James Simpson, esq., in the 68th year of his age....

Issue of August 22, 1803

Died yesterday, Mrs. Mary Dealy, of this city, aged 55 years.

Issue of August 24, 1803

Died, at New-Haven, Samuel Bishop, Esq. Collector of the District of New-Haven, aged 80.

Issue of September 2, 1803

Married, last evening, by the Rev. Dr. Dwyer, Mr. Robert Blakely, to Miss Lisle Niel, both of this city.

Issue of September 3, 1803

Died, in London, William Blake, esq. of South-Carolina.

Issue of September 5, 1803

Died, on the 28th ultimo, at Edisto Island, in the 19th year of her age, Mrs. Ann Eliza Fickling, wife of Mr. Samuel Fickling, junior, planter, of that island.

Issue of September 8, 1803

Columbia (S.C.) September 2
Married on Sunday evening last, in the village of Granby, by the Rev. Mr. Dunlap, Lieutenant Peter Lampkin, to Miss Charlotte Caroline Seibels, daughter of Mr. Jacob Seibels, of that place.

Issue of September 9, 1803

Departed this life on the 6th inst., in the 38th year of his age, Mr. Thomas Boone, house carpenter, of this city.

Issue of September 10, 1803

Died, on Sunday evening, in the 18th year of his age, Doctor James Fraser, of Dawfuskie.

Issue of September 13, 1803

Married, at Jacksonborough, on Saturday 20th ult., by the Rev. Mr. Bladen, Thomas Taylor, esq., late of the Royal Navy, to Mrs. Mary Elliot, relict of Capt. John Elliot, a native of Massachusetts, and many years a worthy citizen of the above place.

Issue of September 14, 1803

Died at Albany (N. Y.) the 15th ult., Mr. Thomas Otis, of Barnstable, Mass...interred in the new cemetery of the Presbyterian church....

Issue of September 15, 1803

Died, at Saluda, on the 10th ult., Captain John Swigard, in the 47th year of his age.

Issue of September 16, 1803

Married, on Wednesday evening last, Mr. Robert Foster, merchant, to Miss Jane Boswell Bentham, daughter of James Bentham, esq.

Issue of September 17, 1803

Married at Alexandria, on the 6th inst., by the Rev. Mr. Mair, Mr. Daniel C. Puppo. of Charleston, S. C. to Miss Elizabeth Strowman, of that town.
Departed this life on the 12th inst., Mrs. Mary Hughes, in the 62d year of her age....(lines)

Issue of September 19, 1803

Died this morning in the 66th year of her age, Mrs. Susannah Cox. By her children her loss is severely felt....

Issue of September 20, 1803

Died, in this city, on Tuesday the 13th inst., Mr. Richard Lord, in the 30th year of his age....

Issue of September 22, 1803

Died at the village of Athens, in the town of Catskill and state of New-York, on the 3d inst., Mr. Thomas Clarendon Villiers, in the 29th year of his age....native of London, and had distinguished himself as acting manager of the Theatre in Charleston.
New-York paper.

Issue of September 23, 1803

Died, at Beaufort, on the 16th inst., in the 49th year of his age, Col. Thomas Talbird....
Died, yesterday, Mr. William Lenox, merchant of this city, in the 36th year of his age.
Died, yesterday afternoon, Miss Rachael Isaacks, in the 22d year of her age. (lines)

Issue of September 24, 1803

Died, in Saint Andrew's Parish, on last Tuesday morning, John Ladson Fraser, Esq. in the 27th year of his age...represented his parish in the State Legislature....
Died in Philadelphia, on the 13th inst., Commodore Barry.

Issue of September 28, 1803

Account of Commodore John Barry....

Issue of September 30, 1803

Died at Boston, on Sunday the 18th inst., Dr. Elisha Poinsett, in the 66th year of his age....
Departed this life on Thursday the 22d inst., Capt. George Luscombe, in the 47th year of his age....

Issue of October 1, 1803

Married on Sullivan's Island, on Thursday last, the 29th Sept., by the Rev. Mr. Speirin, Mr. Lewis Faust, to Mrs. Mary Roddom; both of this city.
Married on Tuesday evening last, by the Rev. Mr. Munds, Capt. George Harper to Mrs. Catharine M'Vere.
Married, on Thursday evening last, by the Rev. Mr. Munds, William Piercey, to Miss Mary Slowman.

Issue of October 3, 1803

Married at Columbia, on the 8th of Sept., Mr. Nathaniel G. Welch, of this city, to Miss Elizabeth Todd, of Columbia.

Issue of October 4, 1803

Died, at Edisto Island, on the 22d ult., Doctor Griffith, formerly a Physician at Fort Johnson.

Issue of October 5, 1803

Died, at Litchfield, Connecticut, Mrs. Mary Adams, widow of the late Samuel Adams, esq. in the 106th year of her age... She was born at Stratford, May 7th, 1698.

Issue of October 10, 1803

Married, last evening, by the Rev. Mr. Datley, Mr. John Furchane, to Miss Elizabeth Smith, both of this city.
Married, on the 9th inst., by the Rev. Mr. Brazier, captain Joseph Vesey, to Mrs. Blair, both of this city.

Issue of October 13, 1803

Married at Islington, on Tuesday evening last, by the Rev. Mr. Mills, Mr. P. Mooney, to Miss Mary Williamson.
Married, at Newport, R. I. by the Rev. Mr. Dehon, Dr. Edmond T. Waring, to Miss Freelove Sophia Malbone, daughter of Francis Malbone, Esq.
Died at Providence, R. I., the Hon. John Brown, in the 68th year of his age.

Issue of October 14, 1803

Married in Pendleton district, on the 13th ult., by the Rev. Mr. Crowther, Henry Ledbetter, esq. to Miss Patience Brown, eldest daughter of Elijah Browne, Q. U.

Married on Sunday evening last, by the Rev. Mr. Poyer, Mr. David Cameron, to Mrs. Marie Elizabeth Fauche, both of this city.

Yesterday died, Mr. Morton Brailsford.

Died, yesterday morning, Mr. James Barron, merchant, of this city.

Died, on the 8th instant, Mr. Joseph G. Taylor, a native of London.

Providence, October 1.

Died, at Providence, R. I., the Hon. John Brown, in the 68th year of his age....

Issue of October 15, 1803

Died, at his plantation, on Pudding Swamp, in the lower part of Clarendon county, adjoining the county of Williamsburgh, on the 2d instant, Mr. John Burgess, planter, in the 85th year of his age...native of county of Down in Ireland, and came into this state about 1750. (eulogy)

Issue of October 18, 1803

Married last evening, by the Rev. Mr. Munds, Mr. Richard Blan, to Mrs. Margaret Kissick.

Died on Friday last, Mr. Maurice Hearn, carpenter....

Died, on his passage from Boston, Mr. James Bilgin, merchant, of this city.

Departed this life at Boston on the 3d inst., in the 81st year of his age, the hon. Samuel Adams, late Gov. of Massachusetts....

Issue of October 19, 1803

Died, on Edisto-Island, the 14th inst., Josiah Mikell, Esq. (eulogy)

Died on the 1st inst.,in the 47th year of her age, Mrs. Elizabeth Andrews.

Issue of October 20, 1803

Died, on the 10th inst, in St. George's Parish, in the 73d year of her age, Mrs. Mary Waring, relict of Joseph Waring, Esq.

Issue of October 21, 1803

Departed this life on the 13th inst.,in the 20th year of her age, Mrs. Frances Milhouse, the consort of Mr. Daniel Milhouse, of St. George's Parish....

Died, at Columbia, on the 11th inst., in the 23d year of her age, Mrs. Nelly, consort of Mr. Thomas Parker, merchant of Charleston, late of Sheffield in England. Mr. Parker, who was married but a few months ago in Baltimore, reached that place with his family last Monday fortnight....

Issue of October 22, 1803

Died, on Edisto-Island, on Monday evening, the 10th inst., in the 27th year of her age, Mrs. Ann M'Kay, wife of Mr. M. M'Kay, and daughter of Alexander Chisolm, esq. of this city.

Issue of October 27, 1803

Married, on Tuesday evening, by the Rev. Mr. Jenkins, Thomas Simons, Esq. to Miss Ann Simons, only daughter of Keating Simons, Esq.

Issue of November 2, 1803

Died on the 10th August last, at sea, Doctor Thomas Reilly, late of this city....
Died, at New-York, on the 19th ult., Col. Sebastian Bauman, Postmaster of that city, in the 64th year of his age.

Issue of November 5, 1803

Died, at Statesville, N. C. on the 22d ult., Mr. James Woods, in the 86th year of his age.

Issue of November 7, 1803

Married, on Thursday evening last, by the Rev. Dr. Frost, Mr. Nathaniel Lebby, to Mrs. Eleanor Man, both of this place.

Issue of November 8, 1803

Died, last evening, Mr. Jonas Girdeer, a native of Marble=head, mate of the ship Volant, of that port.

Issue of November 9, 1803

Married, on the 8th inst., by the Rev. Mr. Faber, Mr. Christian Henry Faber, to Miss Catharine Landauer, both of this city.
Married, at Providence (R. I.) by the Rev. Dr. Mills, Mr. David Chalmers, of this city, to Mrs. Margaretta Pinkerton, widow of David Pinkerton, merchant, of Philadelphia.
Died in this city, on Friday the 4th inst., in the 72d year on her age, Mrs. Sarah Dill, of James Island....
Died, on Monday evening, in the 23d year of his age, Henry Laurens Gervais, son of the late John Lewis Gervais, esq. decd.
Died, on the 20th ult., at Cheraws, Mr. Laurence Campbell, late of this city.

Issue of November 11, 1803

Married on Tuesday evening last, by the Rev. Mr. Frost, William Cattell, Esq. to Miss Mary Ladson, daughter of Major Ladson.
Married, last evening, by the Rev. Dr. Hollinshead, Mr. Joshua Lockwood, jun., merchant, to Miss Caroline Dorothea Lee, eldest daughter of Major Stephen Lee, all of this city.

Issue of November 12, 1803

Died, on Tuesday last, in the 65th year of his age, Thomas Cochran, Esq....
On Tuesday morning, the 1st inst., departed this life, in the 43rd year of his age, Dr. William Montgomery, of Columbia. He was a native of Carlisle in the state of Pennsylvania....

Issue of November 14, 1803

Died, on Friday morning, Mr. Archibald Gillon, in the 41st year of his age, a native of Ireland...left a wife....

Issue of November 17, 1803

Married, at Philadelphia, on the 2d inst., by the Rev. J. Cohen, Mr. Myer Moses, of Charleston, S. C., to Miss Phillips, daughter of the late Mr. Jonas Phillips, of that city.

Married, on the 8th Oct. last, Mr. Andrew Mitchell, plaisterer, of Charleston, to Miss Ann Jacques, late wife of William Jacques, shoe-maker of Philadelphia.

Died on Wednesday evening last, Mr. Alexander Alexander, the eldest son of the late Alexander Alexander, esq.

Departed this life on Sunday the 13th inst., in the 31st year of his age, Mr. Ettsel Lawrence, formerly of this city, but late of Wadmalaw Island.

Issue of November 18, 1803

Married on Tuesday evening last, by the Rev. Mr. Frost, Dr. Thomas Denny, to Miss Mary Lee Gowdey, both of this city.

Died on the 1st inst., at the house of Mr. Esau Sailor, on the Congaree, Mr. John Liber, in the 49th year of his age... left four children

Issue of November 19, 1803

Died, last night, Herman Davis, esq. Captain of the City Guard, which office he had sustained for 20 years.

Issue of November 21, 1803

Married, on Thursday evening last, by the Rev. John Thompson, Mr. Alexander Doll, to Mrs. Debora Willingham, both of this city.

Died on the 11th inst., Mrs. Mary Bee, wife of Mr. John Bee, and daughter of Mrs. Sarah Freazer....

Issue of November 25, 1803

Married on the 10th instant, by the Rev. Dr. Hollinshead, Daniel Flud, esq. to Miss Mary Stanyarne.

Married, last evening, by the Rev. Dr. Hollinshead, Mr. Isaac Morgan, and Miss Judith Warnock, both of this city.

Married, last evening by the Rev. Dr. Keith, Charles Clifford, esq. to Miss Ceserea Tardieu, daughter of the late Mr. Louis Tardieu, of the Island of St. Domingo.

Departed this life on Saturday the 21st inst., at his place on Wadmalaw Island, Mr. Barnard Adams, in the 45th year of his age.

Died, on Friday, the 18th inst., Mrs. Mary Lee, wife of Mr. Wm. Lee, aged 43 years. And on Saturday the 19th inst., her husband, William Lee, aged 28 years...burial ground of St. Philip's Church....

Issue of November 26, 1803

Died, on the 24th inst., Dr. Joseph Hall Ramsay, in the 41st year of his age. served in the revolutionary war as a junior surgeon....

Issue of December 2, 1803

Married, on Tuesday evening, the 29th ult., by the Rev. Dr. Keith, captain James Jones, to the amiable Miss Mary Davison, both of this city.

Issue of December 3, 1803

Married, on Friday evening, by the Rev. Mr. Holinshead, Mr. Bernard Hay, to Mrs. Ann English.
Died on the 29th Nov., aged 57 years, William Lee, esq. Col. of the 28th regt. of Militia in this State...in the Revolutionary struggle....

Issue of December 5, 1803

Married on Sunday the 27th November, at Grove-Hill, near Statesburgh, Mr. James Wilson Lang, planter, to Miss Elizabeth Hughes Murray, daughter of John Murray, esq., planter, of said place.
Died, near Kingston, Jamaica, in the 32d year of his age, Mr. Israel Moses, a native of Charleston, and eldest son of the late worthy Myer Moses.
Columbia, S. C. November 20
Died, on Sunday night last, Mr. John Calvert, an old and respectable inhabitant of this place.

Issue of December 6, 1803

Married at Savannah, on Thursday, the 1st inst., by the Rev. Mr. Clarkson, Mr. George H. Davidson, merchant, to Miss Sarah C. Bellinger, eldest daughter of B. B. Bellinger, Esq. of South-Carolina.

Issue of December 7, 1803

Married on Saturday evening, by the Rev. Mr. Frost, Mr. Daniel Henderson, to the amiable widow Kirkwood, relict of the late John Kirkwood, of this city.

Issue of December 12, 1803

Married on Saturday evening, by the Rev. Mr. Bowen, William B. Johnston, Esq. of Beaufort, Attorney, to Miss Henrietta Hornby, of this city.
Departed this life on Friday morning last, in the 22d year of her age, Miss Elizabeth Edwards, youngest daughter of the late John Edwards, Esq. merchant of this city.(eulogy)

Issue of December 14, 1803

Married on Thursday evening last, by the Rev. Mr. Frost, William Drayton, Esq., Counsellor at Law, to Miss Ann Gadsden, daughter of the late T. Gadsden, Esq.
On Sunday the 11th inst., died Mrs. Elizabeth Pyeatt, aged 65 years, wife of Mr. Peter Pyeatt....

Issue of December 15, 1803

Married on Tuesday evening last, by the Rev. Mr. Mills, Mr. William Edward Gordon, of the Round O, to Miss Catharine Ann Belser, of this city.

Issue of December 16, 1803

Married last evening, by the Rev. Mr. Munds, Capt. Isaiah Stiles, of the State of Pennsylvania, to Mrs. Mary S. Wilkinson, widow of the late captain Thomas Wilkinson, formerly of Bermuda.

Issue of December 20, 1803

Married on Thursday evening last, by the Rev. Dr. Hollinshead, Mr. William Zuill, of Willton, to Miss Mary Ann M'Claren, of this city.

Issue of December 27, 1803

Married on Sunday evening, the 25th inst.,by the Rev. Mr. Frost, Mr. Henry Jocelin, to Miss Mary Breedlove, both of this city.

Issue of December 28, 1803

Married on Wednesday the 22d inst., by the Rev. Dr. Hollinshead, Mr. Lawrence Benson,to Mrs. Mary Ann Ingraham, both of this place.

Issue of December 30, 1803

Married, at James's Santee, on Thursday the 22d inst., by the Rev. Mr. Frazer, Mr. Charles John Steedman, to Miss Mary Blake, daughter of the late capt. John Blake, of said Parish.
Married on Monday last, by the Rev. Dr. Furman, Mr. John L. Hobbs to Miss Elizabeth James, both of this city.
Died on the 5th last month, on his passage in the ship Cornelia, Mr. Charles Scrimzeous, merchant of this city.

Issue of December 31, 1803

Died in Pendleton district, on the 22d August, in consequence of a fall from his horse, Mr. William Orr, merchant, a native of country Managhan, in Ireland.
Died on Thursday the 22d inst., Mrs. Mary Pritchard, wife of Mr. Paul Pritchard, of this city, aged 28 years.

Issue of January 3, 1804

Married on Saturday evening last, by the Rev. George Buist, Mr. Rupert Kirk, of Charleston, to Miss Jane Newby, of New-York state.
Married on Sunday evening, by the Rev. Mr. Frost, Mr. John Simpson, merchant, formerly of Boston, to Miss Mary Goddfrey, only daughter of Mr. Thomas Goddfrey.
Married on Tuesday evening last, by the Rev. Dr. Hollinshead, Mr. Thomas Gould, to Mrs. Sarah Evans, both of this city.
Married, yesterday evening, at Mazyckborough, by the Rev. Dr. Gallagher, Mr. B. Mulligan, to Miss Maria Merry.

Issue of January 4, 1804

Married on the 22d December last, Mr. Frederick Decker, to Mrs. Mary Hippers, both of this city.
Married on the 27th ult., in St. Andrew's parish, by the Rev. Mr. Mills, Thomas Pinckney, jun. Esq. to Miss Eliza Izard, daughter of Ralph Izard, jun. Esq.
Died on Friday the 29th ult., Mr. James Quin, an old and respectable inhabitant, aged 44 years....

Issue of January 5, 1804

Married, last evening, by the Rev. Mr. Generick, Mr. Daniel Benoist, Bricklayer, to Miss Eliza Bolds, both of this state.

Married, on Tuesday evening last, by the Rev. Dr. Furman, Mr. Isaac Gill, to Miss Ann B. Evans, both of this city.

Issue of January 6, 1804

Married, on Tuesday evening, by the Rev. Dr. Gallagher, Mr. Francis M'Hugh, house carpenter, of Charleston, to Miss Mary Quimlan, of the city of Limerick, Ireland.

Died on Friday, the 23d December last, Mrs. Maria Anderson, a native of England, widow of the Rev. John Anderson. She has left five orphan children....

Departed this life on Sunday the 1st inst.,Mr. John Morrison, a native of the state of New-York, aged 26 years.

Died, on the 1st inst., Miss Ann Elliott, aged 53 years....

Issue of January 10, 1804

Married at Baltimore, on the 24th ult., by the Rev. Bishop Carroll, Mr. Jerome Bonaparte, youngest brother of the First Consul of the French Republic, to Miss Elizabeth Patterson, eldest daughter of Mr. William Patterson, merchant of that city.

Issue of January 11, 1804

Married, last evening, by the Rev. Doctor Buist, Mr. Samuel Robertson, to Miss Ann Thomas, youngest daughter of Mr. Stephen Thomas, all of this city.

Issue of January 12, 1804

On Tuesday afternoon, as seven persons were going on shore at Caper's Island, in the skiff of the pilot-boat Virginia, belonging to this port, she unfortunately upset and four of the number were dorwned, viz--Captain Richard Lewis, William Keeling, branch pilot, John Brown, and David Moffat. The persons saved were Mr. Cuckow, branch pilot, Thomas Cartwright, and James Redman. The bodies have been found and were brought up to town this evening. Capt. Lewis has left a wife and three small children, and Mr. Brown a wife and child.   Courier.

Issue of January 13, 1804

Departed this life on the 8th inst., on James Island, Mr. Jonah Rivers, in the 39th year of his age...left widow and five children.

Issue of January 16, 1804

Married, at Philadelphia, on Thursday evening, the 29th ult., by the Rev. Bishop White, Thomas Manners, Esq. captain in his Britannic Majesty's 49th regiment of foot, to Miss Mary Ruth, daughter of Dr. Rush, of that city.

Issue of January 17, 1804

Died, on Saturday morning last, in this city, Captain John Doar, aged 41 years.

Issue of January 18, 1804

Married, on Tuesday evening last, by the Rev. Dr. Keith, Mr. Bethel Threadcraft, to Miss Sarah Yates, both of this city.

Issue of January 19, 1804

Died, suddenly, on the 6th inst., at Newberry Court-House, in the 22d year of his age, Mr. Lewis M'Creless. (eulogy)

Issue of January 20, 1804

Married, at Boston, on the 7th ult., by the Rev. Dr. West, Capt. Peter Geyer, aged 62, to Miss Polly Sancry, aged 17.

Issue of January 21, 1804

Married, last evening, by the Rev. Mr. Frost, Captain Lewis Forgartie, to Miss Susannah Martha Lee, daughter of the late Col. William Lee.

Issue of January 24, 1804

Married on Saturday evening last, by the Rev. Dr. Hollinshead, Mr. Samuel Colhoun, to Miss Isabella Rogers.
Died on the 21st inst., Mr. Robert Marshall, a native of Scotland, and many years a respectable merchant of the state of New York.
Died, on the 22d inst., Mrs. Sarah Delany, wife of Mr. Michael Delany, pilot, aged 26 years...left husband and a numerous train of relatives.

Issue of January 26, 1804

Died on the 24th inst., in the 71st year of his age, Charles Johnston, Esq. long a respectable inhabitant of this city.
Died, on Saturday last, in the 57th year of his age, Mr. Charles Bouchenneau, for many years past an officer in the Branch Bank of the U. S....left widow and children.

Issue of January 27, 1804

Died, at his house in this city, on Sunday last, in the 63d year of his age, John Huger, esquire....

Issue of January 30, 1804

Died, on Thursday morning last, Mrs. Mary Seymour, aged 49 years, wife of Capt. Isaac Seymour, sen. of this city....

Issue of February 2, 1804

Died in Prince William's Parish, on the 26th ult., in the 31st year of his age, Mr. James Edward Forshaw, son of Mr. Edward Forshaw, of James Island...left a widow and five children.
Died, yesterday afternoon, Brian Cape, esq. aged 65 years....

Issue of February 8, 1804

Married, by the Rev. T. D. Bladen, at Ashepoo, on the first instant, Francis Fishburn, Esq., to Miss Mary C. Bellenger, the youngest daughter of the late Edward Bellenger, Esq.

Died on Tuesday the 25th January last, by a paralytic fit, Mrs. S. Jacobs, wife of Mr. Abraham Jacobs of this city...left a husband and five daughters.

Died on Friday evening last, in the 46th year of his age, Mr. John Parker, a native of Delaware, and several years a respectable inhabitant of this state....

Issue of February 13, 1804

Died, on Wednesday the 9th inst., in the 46th year of his age, Mr. Thomas Godfrey, eldest son of the late Mrs. Elizabeth Godfrey, of this city.

Issue of February 15, 1804

Died, at Carlisle, in Pennsylvania, on Wednesday the 18th inst., at an advanced age, the Rev. Charles Nesbit, D. D. Principal of Dickinson College.

Issue of February 17, 1804

Died, on the 2d inst., at his seat near Augusta, in the 55th year of his age, the Hon. George Walton, one of the Judges of the Superior Court of Georgia.

Issue of February 18, 1804

Married, on Thursday evening last, by the Rev. Dr. Jenkins, Mr. Matthew Knox, to Miss Jane Whorry, both of this city.

Issue of February 20, 1804

Died, at James Island, on Thursday last, in the 69th year of her age, Mrs. Margaret Hearn, relict of Mr. John Hearn....

Issue of February 24, 1804

Married, last evening, by the Rev. Mr. Frost, Mr. Thomas Smith Nowell, to Mrs. Rachel Watson, both of this city.

Married, at Smithfield, on the last day of December, Mr. Samuel Sanders, a widower, to Miss Susannah Bollard, both well stricken in years....both blind.

Died in the town of Salem (Mass.) on the 3d inst., the widow Lydia Beckford, aged 100 years and 5 months....

Issue of February 27, 1804

Died, on Thursday the 9th inst., Mr. Elias Houser, in the 63d year of his age...a respectable inhabitant of this state for upwards of fifty years....

Issue of March 1, 1804

Married at Newport, the 11th inst., by the Rev. Mr. Eddy, Mr. Andrew Vos, Merchant, of this city, to Miss Ruth Attwood, daughter of Mr. Sheffield Attwood, of Newport.

Died, on Tuesday last, Mrs. Sarah Jones, widow of the late Rev. Thomas Jones.

Issue of March 5, 1804

Married on Wednesday evening last, by the Rev. Mr. Fraser, Mr. Samuel Campbell, of Baltimore, to Miss Ann Buford, of this city.

Married on the 17th ult., Mr. John Henry Margart, to Miss Elizabeth Nietheimer, both of this city.

Married, on Saturday evening last, by the Rev. Mr. Jenkins, captain Aaron Oakford, of the state of Pennsylvania, to Miss Mary M'Gillivray, of this city, only daughter of William M'Gillivray, esq. deceased, planter.

Issue of March 6, 1804

Married on Thursday evening, by the Rev. Mr. Bowen, Daniel Huger, esq. to Miss Sarah L. Lance, daughter of colonel Lambert Lance, both of this city.

Issue of March 7, 1804

Married, at the High Hills of Santee, on Thursday last, by the Rev. John M. Roberts, Mr. Merry Bracey, to Miss Elsey Moore, both of that place.

Married on Sunday evening last, by the Rev. Dr. Hollinshead, Mr. Charles Benoist, to Miss Mary Arms, both of this city.

Died, at Jacksonborough, on the 23d ult., Mr. John Riley, sen. aged 53....

Issue of March 13, 1804

Died, at the High Hills of Santee, on the 25th of February, Mrs. Harriot Richardson, wife of William G. Richardson, esq. of Sumter District....

Issue of March 15, 1804

Died, on the 11th inst., at Doctor Haig's plantation, Stono, Mr. William Young, lately from Glasgow.

Issue of March 19, 1804

Departed this life, on Thursday the 15th inst., Miss Mary Hodgson, in the 76th year of his age. (lines)

Died, on the 10th inst., Kendal Coles, of Waterford, Gloucester County, New-Jersey, aged 80 years and upwards, left a widow with whom he had lived in wedlock 59 years....

Issue of March 20, 1804

Married, on the 8th inst., by the Rev. Mr. Mills, Mr. Angelo Santi, Merchant Confectioner, in this city, to Madama Louise Francois Judet Letant, Widow Gilleron, native of Rochelle, late an inhabitant of St. Domingo.

Married, on Friday evening last, by the Rev. Mr. Munds, captain John Hill, of the state of New-York, to Miss Elizabeth Dorrey, of this place.

Married on Thursday evening last, by the Rev. Mr. Munds, Mr. Joshua Campbell, to Miss Maria Harth, both of this place.

Died, on Tuesday morning last, Mr. Archibald Duncan....

Issue of March 21, 1804

On Saturday evening, 17th inst., departed this life, Mrs. Ann Black, aged 49 years.

Issue of March 23, 1804

Married, on Tuesday night last, by the Rev. Daniel M'Cala, Carleton Walker, esq. of Wilmington, N. C., to Miss Sabina T. Legare, eldest daughter of the late Nathan Legare, esq. of Christ Church parish.

Issue of March 27, 1804

Died, at Georgetown, S. C. on Wednesday last, in the 32d year of his age, Thomas Young, Esq., a senator from All Saints' Parish, in the legislature of this state.

Issue of March 28, 1804

Married, on Saturday evening, the 17th inst., by the Rev. Mr. Brazier, capt. Joseph Purcell, to Mrs. Arabella Ormond.
Died, on the 26th of December last, Mr. William Bonneau, of the Round O, an old and respectable inhabitant of that place, aged 93 years and four months. He has left an aged wife and six children....

Issue of March 29, 1804

Died on the 28th inst., Mr. Robert Anderson, a native of Sterlinshire, North Britain, and for many years a respectable merchant of this city.

Issue of April 3, 1804

Married, on Saturday evening last, by the Rev. Mr. Waters, Mr. John Walter Gibbs, to Miss Statira Davidson, youngest daughter of capt. William Davidson, of Georgetown, deceased.
Died, in Syracuse, on the 26th November, Mr. James S. Deblots, of the U. S. frigate Constitution.

Issue of April 4, 1804

Married, on Monday evening last, by the Rev. Dr. Furman, Mr. John Ruberry, to Miss Elizabeth Walker.

Issue of April 5, 1804

Departed this life, on Thursday the 16th ult., in the 25th year of his age, Mr. William Adams, late of Wadmalaw Island.

Issue of April 6, 1804

Died, on the 28th ult., Mrs. Elizabeth Spierin, wife of Mr. Thomas P. Spierin, of this city, in the 41st year of her age.
Died, at Sierre Leone, on the 12th December, in the 30th year of his age, Mr. Alexander M'Farlane, an inhabitant of this city...left wife and five children.
Died, on the 7th of January last, at Aberfeldy, England, John Stewart, commonly known by the name of the Colonel of the Tinkers....

Issue of April 9, 1804

Died, on Thursday last, Miss Eliza Hardy Reid, in the 4th year of George Reid, Esq. (lines)

Issue of April 10, 1804

On Thursday last departed from this transitory abode, in the 22d year of his age, Mr. William Keckeley, of St. James Parish, Goose-Creek....

Issue of April 11, 1804

Married, last evening, by the Rev. Mr. Brazier, Mr. Thomas Holmes, carpenter, to Miss Sarah Roberts, both of this city.

Issue of April 13, 1804

Married, last evening, by the Rev. Dr. Isaac S. Keith, Benjamin Stiles, jun. Esq. of Wadmalaw Island, to Miss Rebecca Theus, eldest daughter of Major Simeon Theus, of this city.
Died, on Sunday last, capt. Thomas Keen, for many years past in the trade between this city and Savannah....

Issue of April 14, 1804

Married, on the 10th inst., by the Rev. Mr. Botsford, John Presley, esq. of Black Mingo, to Miss Mary Brockinton, daughter of the late Capt. John Brockinton, all of that place.

Issue of April 16, 1804

Married, last evening, by the Rev. Dr. Jenkins, Mr. Philip Frazer, to Miss Sarah C. Weatherley, eldest daughter of the late Capt. Isaac Weatherley, of this city.
Married, last evening, by the Rev. Mr. Munds, Mr. John Speissegger, of this place, to Miss Wilhelmina Christiana Heinrichs, of Delmenhorst near Bremen.
Died, at Stratford, Eng., Mrs. Ann Robinson, aged 67; she was the only remaining daughter of the celebrated author of Pamela, Sir Charles Grandison, Clarissa, &c.

Issue of April 18, 1804

Married last evening, by the Rev. Dr. Furman, Mr. Richard Brenan, merchant, to Miss Eliza M'Cormick, both of this city.
Died, on the 1st instant, at the Four Holes, St. James's Parish, Mr. Ephraim Bunche, aged 114 years, a respectable inhabitant of that place.

Issue of April 23, 1804

Died, on the 11th of March, in the Island of St. Domingo, whither he had gone for the benefit of his health, Dr. Robert Dunlop, of this city....

Issue of April 24, 1804

Married, on Sunday night last, in Jacksonborough, by the Rev. Thomas D. Bladen, Mr. Joseph Dilgar, to Miss Martha Catherine Bessellue.
Died, on Friday night last, in the 9th year of his age, Master John Wesley Parker, son of Mr. Thomas C. Parker. (lines)

Issue of April 26, 1804

Died, on Tuesday morning last, Miss Mary Swain, aged 9 years.

Issue of April 27, 1804

Married, last evening, by the Rev. Dr. Furman, Mr. John G. Stevenson, of this city, to Miss Lucinda Christian, of Georgetown, S. C.

Married, on Saturday evening last, by the Rev. Mr. Malcomson, Mr. Robert Gordon, merchant, of Philadelphia, to Miss Nancy Fleming, of this city.

Married on Thursday evening, the 26th inst., by the Rev. Mr. J. Munds, Mr. Thomas Fitzgerald Quin, to Mrs. Eliza Lesesne, both of this city.

Married, last evening, by the Rev. Mr. Munds, Mr. David Ross, to Miss Susannah Fowler Robinson, both of this place.

Married last evening, by the Rev. Mr. Munds, Mr. Laben Slade, to Mrs. Mary Ann Coalfoard, both of this place.

Departed this life on the 23d inst., Mr. Stephen Wood, taylor, of Dorchester, aged 28 years...left an aged mother.

Issue of April 30, 1804

Married, on Thursday evening, the 26th inst.,by the Rev. Dr. Frost, Mr. Thomas Cordray, to Mrs. Ave Pittman, both of this place.

Issue of May 4, 1804

Married, at Goose-creek, on the 1st inst., Captain James Kennedy, to Miss Eliza Glover, eldest daughter of Sanders Glover, esq.

decease of Thomas Radcliffe, Jun. esq...on his return with his family from the Island of Jamaica.

Issue of May 7, 1804

Married on the 5th inst., by the Rev. Doctor Buist, Mr. James Macadam, merchant, of this place, to Miss Mary Graham, of Glasgow.

Issue of May 8, 1804

Married, last evening, by the Rev. Dr. Frost, Mr. John Query, to Miss Honoria Mills, second daughter of the Rev. Dr. Mills.

On Saturday morning the 5th inst., at Coosawhatchie, Beaufort District, departed this life in the 33d year of his age, Samuel Hay, Esq....

Issue of May 10, 1804

Married, on Friday evening last, by the Rev. Mr. Pogson, Robert Brown, Esq., Attorney at Law, to Miss Harriet Singleton, daughter of John Singleton, Esq. of Santee.

Issue of May 17, 1804

Married, on Tuesday last, by the Rev. Mr. Levrier, Mr. Louis Lenud(?), to Mrs. Catherine Floriutiu, both of France.

Issue of May 21, 1804

Died, at his house in this city, on Monday the 14th inst., in the 64th year of his age, Col. Thomas Screven...descended from some of the first of the European settlers of this state. His paternal progenitor, the Rev. William Screven, the first minister of the Baptist Church in this city, and his maternal, Landgrave Smith....

Issue of May 23, 1804

Married, at New York, on the 8th instant, by the Rev. Mr. M'Knight, Mr. George Hopson, jun. of that city, merchant, to Mrs. Mary Lamb, daughter of Mr. JOhn Moncrieffe, of this city.

Issue of May 24, 1804

Died at Boston, Hans Grame, Esq. formerly of Copenhagen, Denmark....

Issue of May 25, 1804

Died on Wednesday night last, Mrs. Catharine Beard, in the 65th year of her age, relict of the late Col. Jonas Beard.

Issue of May 26, 1804

Married, on Sunday evening, 13th inst., by the Rev. Dr. Mathews, Mr. John Vesey, to Miss Mary Maddon, both of this city.

Issue of May 28, 1804

Married on Sunday the 27th inst., by the Rev. Mr. Solomon Hart, Mr. Solomon Levy, Merchant, to Mrs. Hannah Levy, relict of the late Mr. Samuel Levy, both of this city.

Issue of May 29, 1804

Married, at Paris, Citizen Bouguier, aged 86, to Mademoselle (sic) Vervier, aged 16, grand niece to his first wife, after whose death he lived a widower 50 years....
Died in the Island of Goree, on the 26th January, Mrs. Andrew Gow, late merchant of this city.

Issue of May 30, 1804

Died, on Friday last, in the 67th year of her age, Mrs. Mary Morrill, much lamented....

Issue of May 31, 1804

Mr. Richard Johnston, planter, of St. Paul's Parish, was shot dead, on the 27th inst...left a wife and five children....
Yesterday, at 3 o'clock in the afternoon, departed this life, at the age of 62, the Hon. Ralph Izard, Esq. for many years a member of the Legislature of South-Carolina, and of the Old Continental Congress....
Died, on the 30th inst., Mr. T. C. Fricre, formerly a major in the service of the United Provinces of Holland....

Issue of June 1, 1804

Married last evening, by the Rev. Mr. Malcomson, Mr. William Simms, merchant, to Miss Harriet Singleton, both of this place.
Married, on Wednesday last, by the Rev. Mr. Asuby, Mr. Harris Motta, to Miss Sarah Azevado.

Issue of June 4, 1804

Died on Friday the 1st inst.,on Sullivan's Island, in the 49th year of her age, Mrs. Mary Williman, wife of Christopher Williman, Esq. of this city.
Died at his house, in Mazyck-street, on Saturday, the 2d instant, Mr. Terence Riley, aged 42 years.

Issue of June 5, 1804

Died, on Sunday night, the 3d inst., Mrs. Miller, wife of Captain Miller, and daughter of the deceased Dr. John Budd....

Issue of June 6, 1804

Married, yesterday, in St. Phillip's parish, by the Rev. John Thompson, Mr. John Withers, jur. to Miss Mary Bowen, only daughter of John Bowen, esq., of Goose Creek, planter.
Departed this life on the 19th ult., at his residence in Spartanburgh District, James Jordan, Esq. formerly a Senator in the Legislature of this State from that District.

Issue of June 7, 1804

Died on Tuesday morning, Miss Harriet Mackey, daughter of the late Doctor Mackey, formerly of Georgetown...(eulogy)

Issue of June 11, 1804

Married on the 22d ult., by the Rev. Mr. Pogson, Mr. John Dubose, of Camden, to Miss Ann S. Cantey, of St. Stephen's Parish.

Issue of June 12, 1804

Died on Saturday last, aged 71 years, Mr. Israel Joseph, formerly a merchant in this city, and for many years president of the Hebrew Congregation, to which he contributed very amply.

Issue of June 14, 1804

Died on the 12th inst., Mr. Edward Bonneau Legge, aged 27 years, attorney at Law....
Died at Granby, on the 6th inst., in the 23d year of his age, John Gist, esq. attorney at law... He was on his way to the upper country in hopes to recover his health....

Issue of June 15, 1804

Died, the 11th inst., Miss Elizabeth Ross, a native of New-Jersey, in the 64th year of her age. She resided for 40 years past in this city....

Issue of June 16, 1804

Died on Tuesday the 12th inst., Mr. John Frederick Schmidt, merchant, of this city, aged 38 years and 7 months.
Died on the 13th inst., Mr. Donald Sandison, in the 25th year of his age....

Issue of June 19, 1804

Married, on Thursday evening last, at Givhan's Ferry, by the Rev. Mr. Palmer, Mr. James Maull, merchant, of Jacksonborough, to Miss Mary Givhan, youngest daughter of Philip Givhan.
Married at Rumney, on the 17th inst., by the Rev. Dr. Keith, Henry Kennon, Esq. to Mrs. Rebecca Mege, relict of Francis Mege, Esq., formerly of St. Domingo.
Married, last evening, by the Rev. Dr. Hollinshead, Rev. Dr. Isaac S. Keith, to Miss Jane Hunham.
Died on the 18th instant, Mr. James Patterson, lately from the Island of Jamaica.
Died on Saturday morning last, in the 21st year of her age, Mrs Johannes M. Purdie, third daughter of Mr. Philip A. Besselieu, late of this city, deceased....

Issue of June 23, 1804

Married, on Saturday, the 16th inst., by the Rev. Dr. Buist, Mr. James Sutherland, to Miss Margaret Calqohoun (sic) both of this city.
Died, at Hampstead, yesterday morning, Mr. Bailey Forrester, merchant, of Prince William's parish....

Issue of June 25, 1804

Married, at the High Hills of Santee, on Thursday the 14th instant, by the Rev. John M. Roberts, Mr. Charles A. Lynch, of Kentuckey, to Miss Ephatha M. Bracey, youngest daughter of William Bracey, Esq.

Issue of June 27, 1804

Died, on Thursday morning, the 11th of April, of a cancer in his throat, Mr. Charles Bennett, upwards of 40 years an organist of Truto Church. The gentleman was respectably descended; but being in childhood deprived of his sight by the bursting of a wooden gun, he was put under the tuition of that celebrated organist, Stanley, with whom he continued seven years. He was soon after appointed organist of Truto, and during the earliest part of his life, taught his professional science through a great part of his native county. His sprightly wit and convivial temper made him a welcom visitor wherever he went, and often has he "set the table in a roar." Although blind, he delighted in amusements which would appear to give pleasure chiefly to the sight. He was partial to horticulture; and so exquisite was his touch that he could distinguish and describe all his flowers, and even the different weeds which occasionally mixed with them. ... He was author of many musical compositions. Having a son a Lieutenant in the Navy, who was with Captain Sir Edward Pellew and and Carthew Reynolds in several of their engagements....
London paper.

Issue of July 3, 1804

Died on Sunday morning last, the 1st instant, Miss Elizabeth Teasdale, aged 15 years and 10 months, second daughter of Mr. Isaac Teasdale, of this city.
Died, at Savannah, on the 23d ult.,Mr. Robert Brisbane, of South Carolina, aged 37 years....

Issue of July 7, 1804

Died suddenly, on Wednesday last, Mr. Charles B. Bowens, a native of Germany...interred in the Dutch church-yard, by the company of German Fusilliers....
Died, last evening, Mr. John Edwards, Student at Law, in the 20th year of his age...returned but a few months from Yale College....

Issue of July 9, 1804

Departed this life, on Friday the 6th inst., Mrs. Rachel Delozeuir, wife of Mr. Asa Delozeuir, in the 35th year of her age....

Issue of July 11, 1804

On the 28th ult., as Mr. James Harkness, of the High Hills of Santee, was asleep in his bed, his own negro, named Buck...shot his master through the body....

Issue of July 13, 1804

Married on Tuesday evening last, by the Rev. Dr. Hollinshead, Mr. Seats Hubble, to Miss Charlotte Henrietta Broeskie, both of this city.

Issue of July 14, 1804

Married on the 16th ult., by the Rev. Mr. Mitchell, William Hudson Wigg, Esq. only son of the late Major Wigg, of Beaufort, S. C. to Miss Sarah G. Martin, only daughter of Dr. George Martin, of Fincastle, Botetourt County, Virginia.
Died this morning, Master James Rout, son of the late Mr. George Rout.

Issue of July 16, 1804

On Saturday last departed this life, Mr. Warham Woodward, a respectable merchant of this city, in the 39th year of his age....

Issue of July 17, 1804

Died, on Sunday last, John Loveday, esq. At the commencement of the American Revolution, Mr. Loveday entered into the service of this state....
Died at New-York, on the 29th ult., Miss Susannah Saltus, of this state, after a lingering illness.

Issue of July 18, 1804

Died on Saturday last, the 14th inst., Mrs. Rachel Robison, relict of the late Septimus Robinson, aged 52 years and 6 months.

Issue of July 19, 1804

   Died, on Friday last, Mr. Jeremiah Brower, a native of New-York, in the 54th year of his age....

Issue of July 20, 1804

   decease of the Rev. Thomas Frost, rector of St. Philip's Church...born in County of Norfolk, in the kingdom of Great Britain, came to this country in the year 1785. (long account)
   Died, at Beaufort, on the 18th inst., John Bold, Esq., late merchant of this city.
   Married, on the 7th inst., Mr. Benjamin Witter, to Miss Mary Rivers, daughter of Mr. Francis Rivers, sen. planter, --all of St. Andrew's parish.

Issue of July 21, 1804

   Married on Tuesday evening last, the 17th inst.,by the Rev. Mr. Malcomson, Mr. Moses Sandford, to Miss Margaret Welsh.
   Died in this city, on the 7th inst., Mr. William Anderson, formerly of Santee, aged 75 years.
   Died in England, Mrs. Morrel, aged 44, a woman well known throughout Great-Britain...having been born without arms....

Issue of July 24, 1804

   Died, at Georgetown, on Friday last, Capt. John Addison, in the 57th year of his age, many years a respectable inhabitant of that town....

Issue of July 25, 1804

   Married, last evening, by the Rev. Dr. Hollinshead, Mr. Daniel Anderson, of St. Thomas's Parish, to Miss Carlisle Dubois, of this city.
   Died on the 23d inst., Captain Jeremiah Dickinson, aged 64 years--forty of which he lived an harmless inhabitant of this city.

Issue of July 26, 1804

   Died, on Thursday the 19th inst., in the 21st year of his age, Mr. Joshua Lee, who had resided in this city about 8 months, and was to have left it for the neighbourhood of Statesburg, the place of his nativity, the day succeeding....
   Departed this life on the 23d inst., Mr. William Miller, son of John Miller of Glasgow....
   Died at Kingston (Jam.) about five weeks since, Capt. Charles Prince, late commander of the ship Richard Caton, of this port.
   Died, at Cape-Francois, on the 15th ult., of yellow fever, Mr. Edward Moulson, of Norfolk, Virginia.

Issue of July 27, 1804

   Died, at Major Hazzard's plantation, on the 10th inst., Mr. Angus M'Alpin, late merchant of this city.
   Died on Sunday morning last, in this city, Miss Ann R. M'Clellan, late of St. James's, Santee in the 25th year of her age....
   Died on Monday last, Mr. Michael M'Lean, aged 30 years....
   Died on Thursday the 19th inst., Master Joseph Spencer Smith, son of Mr. William Smith, jun. of this city, aged 8 years, 9 months.

Issue of July 28, 1804

Died on Thursday last, Mr. David Cruger, long a respectable inhabitant of this city....

Issue of July 30, 1804

Married, on Saturday evening last, by the Rev. Dr. Hollinshead, Mr. Joseph Lesesne, of Georgetown, to Miss Ann Fowler, of this city.

Issue of July 31, 1804

Died of an apoplectic fit, on Monday the 23d inst.,John Drummond, aged 39 years, a native of Alloa in Scotland, and many years a useful citizen of Charleston....
Died on Saturday last, Mr. George Egleston, aged 25 years, a native of Hartford in Connecticut.

Issue of August 3, 1804

Died, at his house in this city, on Sunday last, John Neufville, Esq. Commissioner of the Continental Loan office of this state. (long account)

Issue of August 6, 1804

Died in New-York, on the 20th ult., Miss Susan Poinsett, daughter of the late Dr. Elisha Poinsett of this city.
Died, on Sunday the 22d ult., in St. Stephen's parish, Master James Sinkler, youngest son of Mr. James Sinklin of that place....

Issue of August 8, 1804

Married on Thursday evening last, by the Rev. Mr. Munds, Mr. Wm. W. Norton of Rhode-Island, to Miss Mary Salter, of this city, late of Philadelphia.

Issue of August 9, 1804

Died on the 7th inst, Mr. John Pressley, aged 22 years.
Died on the 2d inst., ated 41 years, Mrs. Elizabeth Swain, the wife of captain Joseph Swan, one of the branch pilots...left two children.

Issue of August 11, 1804

On Friday, the 10th inst., died in this city, the Rev. Nicholson Waters, aged 65 years, a minister in the Methodist Episcopal Church for near 30 years....

Issue of August 14, 1804

Died in this city, on the 11th inst., in the 22d year of his age, Mr. Alexander Kincaid, a native of Falkirk in Scotland....
death of John B. Barnwell, Esq. of Beaufort, on Monday, the 6th inst., at the Rice-creek springs, about 15 miles about this place....left widow and four children. Columbia paper.

Issue of August 15, 1804

Married at Norfolk, on the 1st inst., by the Rev. James Whitehead, Mr. N. Smith, who was lately tried at the Borough court of that place, on suspicion of being concerned in the murder of Lewis L'Orient, to the widow of said L'Orient.

Died at Philadelphia, on the 29th ult., Maj. Gen. William Irvine, an active officer during the whole of our revolution....

Died in Cambridge, Mass. on Monday, 23d ult., Stephen Sewall, esq. F. A. A. and formerly Hancock professor of Hebrew...born at York, in the district of Maine, in April, 1734....in his 71st year. His only child died in infancy.

Issue of August 16, 1804

Died, at Dr. Chouler's, Broad-street, aged 14 years, Master Edward Whitlock, son of the respectable Actor and Actress of that name....

Died on Monday morning last, in the 21st year of his age, Mr. Abraham Wilkinson....

Issue of August 18, 1804

Married on Tuesday evening last, by the Rev. Mr. Kenrick, Mr. Isaac Weatherly, to Miss Rachel Rambert, both of this city.

Died in this city, yesterday morning, Mr. John Ross, aged 27 years....

Died on the 8th inst., Mr. Henry Hall, aged 21 years....

Died lately, at Nassan, New-Providence, Mr. John Fray, of Glasgow....

Issue of August 20, 1804

Died in this city, on the 30th ult., in the 23d year of his age, Mr. James M'Gain, Musician, a native of Edinburgh, in Scotland....

Died on Thursday last, Mr. Robert Murdoch, of this city....

Died, lately, at the Euhaw, in the 48th year of her age, Mrs. Catharine Broughton, wife of Mr. Richard Broughton.

Died in Boston, suddenly, Mr. Peregrine White, of Westmoreland, N. H., aged 35...descendant of and bore the name of the first white child born in America.

Died on Thursday evening, at Mr. Baker's, East-Bay, Mr. Brice M'Kie, a native of Ireland, and late from New-York...

Issue of August 23, 1804

Died this morning, Dr. Joseph Chouler, in the 45th year of his age, a native of England, and long a respectable inhabitant of this city.

Issue of August 25, 1804

Died yesterday morning, in the 23d year of her age, Mrs. Eleanor Cormick, consort of Mr. Thomas Cormick of this city... interred in the cemetery of the Roman Catholic Church, where her infant firstborn child, only about 3 weeks old, had been deposited the day before....

Issue of August 27, 1804

Died on Wednesday the 22d inst., Mrs. Mary Pinckney, relict of the late Hopson Pinckney....

Died on Sunday last, the 19th inst., Mr. Hugh Grant, in the 34th year of his age, a native of Pennsylvania....

Issue of August 28, 1804

Married on the 2d inst., in Laurens County, by the Rev. Dr. Kennedy, John Bowen, Esq. of Goose-creek, planter, to Miss Rebeca Withers, daughter of John Withers, Esq. of Laurens County.

Death of Mr. George H. Speirin, eldest son of the Rev. Mr. Speirin, of this city, aged 16 years and 8 months...

Died at sea, on his passage from Alexandria to this port, Mr. John Atkinson, a native of Dublin, on the 25th inst....

Died on Friday the 24th inst., at her plantation in Christ Church parish, Mrs. Sarah Townshend, aged 52 years, widow of the late Stephen Townshend....

Died in this city, on Saturday the 25th inst., Mr. Thomas Davis, aged 49 years--born in Kent (Eng.) and has been a respectable citizen of this place 32 years.

Issue of August 29, 1804

Married, last evening, by the Rev. Dr. Keith, Mr. Alexander Thompson, to Miss Martha A. Miller, both of this city.

Issue of September 3, 1804

Died on the 17th ult., at Augusta, Miss Eliza House, daughter of Samuel House, Esq. of this city, aged 15 years and 10 months.

Died in this city, on the 1st inst., Mr. James M'Credie, a native of Strantawer, in the shier of Galloway, Scotland, aged 19 years....

Departed this transitory life, on Saturday last, Mr. William O'Neal, a native of Statesburgh, in the 21st year of his age....

Issue of September 5, 1804

Died on the 27th ult., Mr. James Forsyth, a native of Scotland, younger brother of Mr. Walter Forsyth, of this city.

Died on Monday morning, in the 30th year of his age, Mr. John Gaven, a native of Ireland....

Died in this city, on the 4th inst., Mr. Frederick Boykin, of Virginia, late from Norfolk.

On Monday last departed this life, in the 23d year of her age, Mrs. Charlotte Van Alstyne, of Monmouth county, New-Jersey. ...

Died on the 3d inst., in the 25th year of his age, Mr. John O'Leary, a native of the county of Cork, Ireland....

Issue of September 7, 1804

Married on Sunday last, by the Rev. Dr. Keith, Mr. Thomas A. Vardell, to Miss Margaret D. Webb.

Died at Philadelphia, on the 15th ult.,in the 2d year of her age, Miss Mary B. Fayssoux, eldest daughter of Mrs. Ann Fayssoux.

Departed this life on the 6th inst., Mrs. Mary Ann Benson, in the 24th year of her age....

Died on the 1st inst., in St. Bartholomew's parish, Mr. James Henry Bowler...left an aged mother, an only daughter, and four sisters....

Issue of September 8, 1804

Died on the 4th inst., Mr. Charles D'Arcey, a native of Limerick, in Ireland....

Issue of September 11, 1804

Died, on Sunday, the 9th inst., Doctor Jacob Williman, eldest son of Christopher Williman, Esq.

Issue of September 13, 1804

Married, on Tuesday evening, by the Rev. Dr. Keith, Dr. Joseph Glover, to Miss Eliza Yonge.
Departed this life on Tuesday evening last, in the 52d year of his age, Mr. John Parks....
Died on Tuesday last, in the 30th year of his age, Mr. Bernard Hoey, a native of Ireland.
Died, last night, in the 30th year of his age, Mr. Michael Cahill, a native of Ireland...buried in the Cemetery of the Roman Catholic Church....

Issue of September 14, 1804

Married, last evening, by the Rev. Mr. Israel Munds, Mr. Louis Cuigno, to Miss Jane Celest Gauvin, both of this city.
Died in this city, yesterday evening, Mrs. Brett, of the Charleston Theatre.
Died, in Savannah, on Wednesday the 5th inst., Mr. Peter Johonot Seaver, in the 34th year of his age...a native of Mass., and removed to Savannah about 14 years since....
Died in Barnstable (Mass.) Mr. Thomas Davis, aged 78, 70 of which he lived with his mother, who died at 98, the last seven he resided with his sister...father died in 1732.

Issue of September 15, 1804

Married on Sunday, September 2d, by the Rev. Doctor Furman, Mr. John L. Poyas, sen. to Miss Elizabeth Ball--both of this city.
Died of Wednesday evening last, Mr. Joseph Bolter, aged 26 years, formerly of Boston, Mass.
Died at Pocotaligo, on the 10th inst.,Mr. Henry Ellison, a native of Willshire, England, and late a merchant of this place, aged 54 years.

Issue of September 17, 1804

Died yesterday, Mr. Wm. M'Clure, Jun.
Died on Saturday last, Mr. Gilbert M'Lean, taylor, aged 25 years, a native of Scotland.
Died at Columbia, on the morning of the 10th inst., Mrs. Susannah Dunlap, wife of the Rev. David E. Dunlap, aged 30 years. Also on the evening of the same day, the Rev. David E. Dunlap....
Died at New-York, on Sunday morning, the 2d inst., Commodore John Nicholson of this city....

Issue of September 18, 1804

Died on Sunday evening last, in the 38th year of her age, Mrs. Sarah Parks, widow of the late Mr. John Parks....
Died on the 16th inst., Mr. John Woodman, mate of the schooner, Theoda, of Salem, a native of Providence, R. I.

Died on the 10th inst., in the 20th year of his age, Alexander Sutherland, a native of Caithness, in Scotland....arrived on the 2nd inst., from Wilmington, N. C. to obtain a passage to Baltimore, where he had relations.

Died at Savannah, on the 13th inst., John Walliace, Esq. British Vice-Consul, for the State of Georgia.

Issue of September 19, 1804

Married on Saturday evening last, by the Rev. Dr. Furman, Mr. James Tomlins, to Mrs. Letitia Cape, both of this city.

Died on the 16th inst., Mr. Charles Myers, in the 27th year of his age, a native of Virginia.

Died on Monday evening, the 17th inst., Mrs. Sarah Secut, wife of Doctor John L. E. W. Secut, aged 29 years and 15 days....

Issue of September 20, 1804

Died, on Saturday morning last, Mrs. Amey Reeves, wife of Capt. Enos Reeves, and daughter of Daniel Legare, jun. esq. deceased, in the 45th year of her age....husband and young family.

Died, at Wilmington, N. C., capt. John M'Ilhenny.

Issue of September 21, 1804

Married on Sunday evening the 16th inst., by the Rev. Dr. Hollinshead, Mr. John Evans, to Miss Mary Wilson, both of this city.

Issue of September 22, 1804

Married on Thursday evening, the 20th inst., by the Rev. Dr. Jenkins, Mr. Richard N. Lechmire, to Miss Maria Ingraham, both of this city.

Died on the 13th inst., at Sullivan's Island, Mr. Alexander Leith, a native of Scotland, in the 29th year of his age.

Died this morning, Mr. John Fallon, in the 23d year of his age, a native of Ireland....

Issue of September 25, 1804

Departed this life on the 18th instant, Mrs. Christian Livingston, wife of Capt. Wm. Livingston....

Issue of September 26, 1804

Died, yesterday, the Rev. James Malcomson, a native of Ireland, for many years resident in this country...left wife, a large family and many friends....

On Saturday the 22d inst., died, in this city, Master James Courtney, son of Mr. Humphry Courtney, merchant, aged 5 years and 3 months; also, on the 22d following, Miss Eliza M. Courtney, daughter of Mr. H. Courtney, aged 10 years and 2 weeks....

Issue of September 27, 1804

Died on the 24th inst., Mr. David Burger, a native of New-York, but had resided in this city upwards of 30 years....

Issue of September 29, 1804

Married, in St. Stephen's Parish, Mr. Bernard Taylor, of this city, to Miss Esther Boineau.

Departed this life on the 14th inst., Mrs. Ann Mackgivrin, aged 35 years, a native of London, and a resident of this city 12 years. She has left a daughter four years old....

Issue of October 1, 1804

Died, yesterday morning, Mr. Park Avery, aged 28 years, a native of Connecticut.

Issue of October 2, 1804

Died on Saturday morning last, the 29th inst., Mr. John Desbeaux...left a widow....

Issue of October 4, 1804

Died, at Romney, on Monday, the 1st inst., Mr. Henry Kenan, in the 48th year of his age...a native of Charleston, and took an early part in the American Revolution....

Issue of October 5, 1804

Married, last evening, Mr Henry Barnstine, to Mrs. C. Wyatt, both of this city.

Married, last evening, by the Rev. Mr. Mills, Mr. Daniel Boyden, to Miss Mary Henry, both of this city.

Married at New-York, on the 18th ult., by the Rev. Dr. Roe, Mr. Thomas Tait, merchant, of this city, to Miss Elizabeth Noble, of New-York.

Died on the 2d inst., Mr. Crafts Mackey, Watch-Maker, in the 49th year of his age, a native of Scotland, and for 15 years past an inhabitant of this city...left a wife and three small children.

Issue of October 6, 1804

Died in England, at the Grotto House, Margaret, in the 16th year of his age, Mr. R. P. Oldfield....

Issue of October 8, 1804

Married, on Thursday last, by the Rev. Dr. M'Calla, Mr. William Ehney, of this city, to Miss Mary Cole, of Christ Church Parish.

Issue of October 9, 1804

Died, the 7th Sept. last, in the 67th year of his age, Claudius Alexander Feraud, a native of Provence, in France...resided in Charleston 15 years....left wife and four children.

Departed this life on Saturday last, in the Country, Mr. George James Man.

Died on Sunday morning, in the 19th year of her age, Mrs. Eliza Welch...left an infant....

Issue of October 11, 1804

Died, on Monday morning last, Mrs. Susannah Scottowe, aged 52 years, widow of the late Mr. Samuel Scottowe.

Died at New-Orleans, on the 19th of August, Mr. Zachariah Shaw, brother of the late Mr. James Shaw, who was shot in this city on the 20th of the same month....

Issue of October 12, 1804

Died on the 10th inst.,Miss Eliza Jessop, aged 8 years and 2 months....

Died in this city, on the 5th inst., Mrs. Jane Ball, wife of Mr. John Ball, of St. John's Parish.

Issue of October 13, 1804

Married on Wednesday evening last, by the Rev. Mr. Mathews, Mr. George Welsh, to Mrs. Christiana Smith, both of this city.

Departed this life on Tuesday the 9th inst., Mr. Archibald Smith Jun. aged 47 years, a native of North-Britain, and a resident in this city 21 years....

Died yesterday afternoon, at her residence in Ball-street, Harleston's Green, Mrs. Catharine Snipes, aged 58 years....

Issue of October 15, 1804

Married on Saturday last, the 13th inst., by the Rev. Dr. Munds, Mr. John Gray Green, to Mrs. Mary Susanna Austin, both of this city.

Married, on Thursday last, Mr. Thomas Lesesne to Miss Ann Broun, both of this city.

Married on the 20th ult., by Charles Griffin, Esq., Mr. Isaac Waldrop, to Miss Jenny Davidson, both of Newberry district.

Died on the 29th of August last, at New-Orleans, H. B. Trist, Esq., superintendant-general of the revenue of Louisiana....

Died at Baton Rouge, West-Florida, in August last,Mr. Donnald M'Murrich, late a merchant of this city.

Issue of October 16, 1804

Married on the 12th inst., Mr. James Allwood, of this city, to Miss Elizabeth Allwrong, of St. Stephen's Parish.

Issue of October 19, 1804

Died in England, J. Savage Esq....a naitve of Bermuda (eulogy)

Issue of October 24, 1804

Died on the 27th ultimo, at his seat near Port Tobacco, Maryland, Dr. Gustavus R. Brown....attended Gen. Washington in his last illness.

Issue of October 26, 1804

Married, last evening, by the Rev. Dr. Buist, Mr. Edward Beattie, merchant, to Miss Margaret Sanders, both of this city.

Married, at Philadelphia, Mr. William Moon, to Miss Mary Star.

Died, in Savannah, on the 17th inst., in the 25th year of her age, Mrs. Selina Hueston, wife of Mr. Samuel Hueston, and daughter of Rev. William Best. (eulogy)

Issue of October 29, 1804

Married on Saturday evening last,by the Rev. Dr. Jenkins, Mr. Roger Sanders, of Christ Church Parish, to Mrs. Mary Chandler, of this city.

Issue of October 30, 1804

Died on the 18th inst., Mrs. Catharine Hillegas, in the 73d year of her age, an old and respectable inhabitant of this city.
Died on Saturday the 6th of October, Miss Peggy Richards, aged 32 years, sister of Mr. William Richards, merchant of Pendleton district.
Died in child bed, on the 27th inst., in the 28th year of her age, Mrs. Catharine Faber, wife of Mr. Christian Henry Faber....

Issue of October 31, 1804

Died, at Georgetown, on Tuesday the 23d inst., Mrs. Anna Myers, consort of Moses Myers, Esq.
Died at Port-au-Prince, Capt. Charles Winter,late commander, of the ship Nancy, of this port.
Died, lately in Germany,Mr. Tagek Talpier, aged 120. He had buried ten wives, his last, the 11th who is now living, is but 26 years of age. By her had five children....By his other wives he had 31 children....

Issue of November 1, 1804

Married last evening, by the Rev. Dr. Keith, Thomas Ogier, esq., merchant, to Miss Sarah Henley.
Died in this city, on Monday morning, in the 29th year of his age, Mr. Robert Reily, formerly of Santee.
Died on the 27th ult., Mr. George Bonnor, Engraver, a native of Wales, England.

Issue of November 2, 1804

Married on Thursday evening at St. Andrew's Parish, by the Rev. Dr. Price, Mr. John Thomas Smart, of this city, to Miss Mary Allson Rivers, of said Parish, youngest daughter of Joseph Rivers, esq. planter, deceased.
Married last evening, by the Rev. Dr. Hollinshead, Mr. Jacint Laval, esq. to Miss Frances Susanna Rivers, both of this place.
Married, last evening, by the Rev. Mr. Bowen, Mr. George Phillippi Bechen, merchant of Leghorn,to Miss Sarah Bradford, of this city.

Issue of November 3, 1804

Died, on Thursday, the 1st inst.,Mrs. Elizabeth Benoist, wife of Mr. Daniel Benois, aged 17 years, 4 months and 4 days.... left a husband and an infant a few hours old. (poem)

Issue of November 5, 1804

Married, on Sunday evening, the 28th ult., by the Rev. Mr. Pugson, Major Joshua Houghton, of Greensborough, to Mrs. Mary Richards, of this place.
Died in Tattnal county, state of Georgia, the 11th day of April last, James Thomas, in the 134th year of his age....
                                              Augusta Chronicle

Issue of November 9, 1804

Died, at Frederick-town, Maryland, on the 12th ult., Mr. John D. Carey, Printer.

Died, at New-Orleans, on the 16th Sept., Joseph Briggs, Esq., Private Secretary to his Excellency the Gov. Gen. of La....

Issue of November 10, 1804

Married on the 21st Aug., Lord Viscount Ranelagh, nephew to the brave Gen. Montgomery, who fell at Quebeck, to Miss Stephens, daughter of Sir Philip Stephens....performed by the Bishop of London....

Departed this life on Thursday the 8th inst., Mr. James L. Culliatt, aged 35 years...left wife and two infant children.

Died, at Exmouth (Eng.), Mrs. Rebecca Carson, wife of William Carson, Esq. of South-Carolina.

Issue of November 12, 1804

Died, lately at Beaufort, Richard Ellis, Esq. planter....

Issue of November 13, 1804

Married, at Augusta, on the 5th inst., Mr. Isaac Fare, to Miss Lucilla Pardue, both of South-Carolina.

Issue of November 14, 1804

Married, last evening, by the Rev. Dr. Jenkins, Mr. N. Bixby, merchant of Miss Foissin, both of this city.

Married at Philadelphia, on the 27th ult., by the Rev. Mr. Abercrombie, Capt. Henry Chew, of the brig Charleston Packet, to Miss Mary Curtis, of New-Jersey.

Issue of November 15, 1804

Married, on Saturday evening last, Mr. Simeon Bevens, to Miss Elizabeth Folker, both of this city.

Died, on Thursday night last, the 8th inst., at the seat of his excellency Gov. Richardson, near Jamesville, Master James Burchill Richardson, only son of the Gov....

Issue of November 16, 1804

Married on Wednesday evening last, by the Rev. Dr. Hollinshead, Mr. George K. White to Miss Rebecca Chambers, both of this city.

Departed this life, on the 13th inst., in the 20th year of her age, Mr. Elizabeth Pooser...an affectionate wife.

Issue of November 17, 1804

Married on Tuesday evening last, by the Rev. Dr. Jenkins, Mr. George Jouve, Planter, to Miss Susanna D. Schutt, daughter of the late Caspar C. Schutt, esq. of this city, merchant.

Died on Sunday, 11th inst., Duncan Love, aged 43 years and 10 months...left a disconsolate widow....

Issue of November 19, 1804

Married at Pickensville, on the 6th inst., Mr. Thomas Lorton to Mrs. Fanny Smith, widow of the late Mr. Michael Smith, decd.

Died at Sterling (Mass.) Mrs. Elizabeth Putnam, wife of William Putnam, Esq. formerly of Danvers, aged 77 years. Mr. Putnam lived with his wife 52 years. The average number of his family has been from 10 to 15 persons....

Issue of November 20, 1804

Married last evening, at Toogado, Mr. James Swinton, factor, to Miss Eliza Bailey.

Issue of November 21, 1804

Died at New-Orleans, on the 22d ult., Lieut. John Floyd Powell, of the Corps of Artillerists at that place.

Issue of November 23, 1804

Died, on Monday the 19th inst., Thomas Manuel Julius Morphy, youngest son of Don Diego Morphy, His Catholic Majesty's Consul for the States of South and North Carolina and Georgia, resident in this city....

Issue of November 24, 1804

Married on Thursday last, by the Rev. Dr. Jenkins, Dr. Edward G. Thomas of Georgetown, to Miss Emma Martha Wakefield, of this city.
Departed this life on Thursday morning last, Miss Sarah Bigelow, aged 26 years and 3 months.... (lines)

Issue of November 27, 1804

Died on the 14th inst., at Campbellton, in this state, Mr. Thomas Garrett, late merchant of that place....
Died in Washington county, near Sandersville, on the 6th of October last, Mr. John Robinson, aged 81 years and 5 months, a native of Virginia, but had spent the last 20 years of his life where he deceased...10 children, 96 grandchildren, and 47 great-grandchildren.

Issue of November 29, 1804

Married on Tuesday evening, the 20th inst., by the Rev. Dr. Hollinshead, Mr. John Mikell of Edisto Island, to Miss Sarah D. Wilkinson, eldest daughter of capt. Joseph Wilkinson, planter, of Georgia.
Departed this life on Sunday the 25th inst., Mrs. Elizabeth Warnock, aged 55 years, of this city....(lines)

Issue of November 30, 1804

Died, on Tuesday the 27th inst., Mr. Duncan Littlejohn, a native of Stirling, in Scotland, aged 55 years.
Died, in Norfolk, on the 16th inst., captain William Drummond.

Issue of December 1, 1804

Married at Wilmington (N. C.) on the 24th inst., by the Rev. Mr. Holland, Mr. Nehemiah Harris, of Wilmington, to Mrs. Catharine Pendleton, of this place.
Died, on board the ship Ruby, capt. Shaw, Master George Fraser, son of the late Mr. Hugh Fraser of this place...left mother, sis-

ter and brothers.

Issue of December 3, 1804

Married on the 10th inst., by the Rev. Mr. Walker, John Taylor, Esq. of Pendleton district, to Miss Mary Margaret Smith, daughter of William Smith, of York district.

Issue of December 4, 1804

Died, in this city, on the 20th ult., Mr. Joseph Meyer, late of St. Paul's Parish, planter, aged 57 years....

Issue of December 6, 1804

Married last evening, by the Rev. Dr. Keith, Mr. Robert Maxwell, Factor, to Miss Mary Huxham, both of this city.

Issue of December 8, 1804

Died, on the 12th October, at Camp Claiborne, (New-Orleans) captain Aaron Gregg, of the 2d Regiment of Infantry....

Issue of December 10, 1804

Died, on Thursday the 6th inst., Mr. Frederick S. Shultze, aged 24 years, 6 months and 24 days, leaving an aged mother....

Issue of December 14, 1804

Married, last evening, by the Rev. Mr. M'Culloch, Mr. William Presly, to Miss Eliza Aleanor Adams, daughter of Mr. David Adams, Factor.
Married, on Sunday evening last, by the Rev. Mr. Munds, Mr. Elisha Catlett, to Mrs. Margaret Jennings.
Married, last evening, by the Rev. Mr. Munds, Mr. George Jones, to Miss Elizabeth Murdoch, both of this place.

Issue of December 15, 1804

Married at Cambridge, Abbeville District on the 6th inst., Mr. James M'Crackan, merchant, to Miss Elizabeth Wilson, eldest daughter of Mr. James Wilson, of the same place.

Issue of December 21, 1804

Married on Wednesday evening last, by the Rev. Mr. Keith, Mr. James Graves of St. Bartholomew's Parish, to Miss Sarah Minott, of this city.
Departed this life, on the 19th inst., in the 34th year of her age, Mrs. Jane Bacot, wife of Thomas W. Bacot, Esq., and eldest daughter of the late Henry Desaussure, Esq. deceased....

Issue of December 24, 1804

Died, on Wednesday morning, the 19th inst., Mrs. Elizabeth Sharp, wife of Mr. John Sharp, aged 23 years and 5 months. (poem)
Savannah, September 19
Died in the 64th year of his age, the Hon. Joseph Clay, Esq... a native of England. (account of Rev. War service)

Issue of December 26, 1804

Married at Santee, on Thursday, the 13th inst., Mr. John C. Schultz, merchant, of Columbia, to Miss Sarah Flud Canty.
Died at Boston, on the 6th inst., the Right Rev. Samuel Parker, D. D. Bishop of the Protestant Episcopal Church in Mass., in the 60th year of his age.
Died in London, on the 6th of October, Mr. Thomas Whittington of Hillingden, at the advanced age of 104....

Issue of December 27, 1804

Married on Sunday evening last, by the Rev. Dr. Buist, Mr. Daniel Stewart, to Mrs. Sarah Mallison, both of this city.
Married at Canterbury (Eng.) on the 20th Sept. last, Mr. Tyrall, aged 73 to Miss Lumberton, aged 26....

Issue of December 28, 1804

Married on the 20th inst., in St. John's Parish, by the Rev. Mr. Pogson, Dr. Philip G. Prioleau, to Miss Catharine Cordes.
Married, last evening, by the Rev. Mr. Munds, Mr. Joseph Mulligan, to Miss Jane Simms, both of this city.
Married at New-York, on Saturday evening, the 8th inst., by the Rev. Mr. Miller, Mr. George Edward Charles Frederick Meredith Rose Reynolds, to Miss Ellen Hageman, daughter of Mr. Jacob Hageman, of Baltimore.
Died on Thursday the 20th inst., at his residence in Sumter District, Laurence Manning, Esq., Adjutant General of S. C., in the 28th year of his age. (long account)
Died in Sumter District, on Sunday the 9th inst., Capt. Richard Singleton, a firm patriot...During the American Revolution....
Died in New-York on the 10th inst., at the advanced age of 102 years, Mrs. Jane Le Portevine, a native of France, who has resided in this country upwards of half a century.

Issue of January 2, 1805

Married last evening, by the Rev. Dr. Furman, Mr. David Kettleband, to Miss Margaret Huseey, both of this city.
Married last evening, by the Rev. Dr. Jenkins, Mr. John Dougherty, to the amiable Miss Margaret Borrow, both of this city.
Married on Monday evening last, by the Rev. Dr. Keith, Mr. John S. Bennett, to Miss Ann B. Keith.
Married on Tuesday evening, by the Rev. Dr. Hollinshead, Mr. Josiah Rhodus, of Wadmalaw, to Mrs. Rebecca Humphreys, of John's Island.
Married on the 25th December last, by the Rev. Dr. O'Farrell, Mr. George Robertson, of this city, to Miss Mary Mis-Campbell, daughter of James Mis-Campbell, of Santee.
Married on Thursday, the 27th Dec., by the Rev. Mr. Darley, Benjamin Risher, Esq. to Miss Mary Koger, eldest daughter of Capt. Joseph Koger, of St. Bartholomew's.
Died on the 19th December last, Mrs. Sarah Hasell, in the 75th year of her age, an old and respectable inhabitant of St. Thomas's Parish.

Issue of January 3, 1805

Married on Tuesday last, by the Rev. Dr. Gallagher, Mr. James M'Kiernan, to Mrs. Ann Desbeaux, both of this city.

Issue of January 4, 1805

Married last evening, by the Rev. Dr. Hollinshead, Mr. Thomas Sheppard, one of the Editors of this paper to Miss Christiana Coates.

Married on Sunday evening, by the Rev. Mr. Munds, Mr. George Dunscombe, to Miss Sarah Campbell, both of this place.

Married last evening, by the Rev. Mr. Munds, Mr. William Lindo, to Miss Harriet Fair, both of this place.

Married on Thursday evening last, by the Rev. Mr. Price, Mr. Charles Holmes, to Miss Eliza Margaret Harvey, daughter of Capt. Benjamin Harvey, of this city.

Married on the 18th ult., at St. Bartholomew's parish, by the Rev. Mr. Floyd, Dr. John Oswald, to Miss Keziah Walter, daughter of Jacob Walter, Esq.

Died on Saturday the 29th ult., Capt. Zenas Hubbard, who served during our revolutionary war.... Georgetown Gazette

Issue of January 5, 1805

Married on Friday evening last, by the Rev. Dr. Jenkins, Mr. Nathaniel Pike, to Miss Mary Turner, both of this city.

Died on the night of the 4th inst., Mrs. Elizabeth Harleston, relict of the late Col. John Harleston, of St. John's parish....

Issue of January 7, 1805

Married last evening, by the Rev. Dr. Buist, Mr. Archibald Brebner, to Miss Margaret D. Rowland, both of this city.

Married, on the 13th of Nov. last, by the Rev. Mr. M'Culler, Mr. George Washington Chinners, of this city, to Miss Sarah Ann Elizabeth Chinners, of St. John's Berkeley county.

Died on Saturday the 5th inst., on Sullivan's Island, where he had resided for many years, Capt. Simon Tufts, in the 82d year of his age. He was one of the first naval officers appointed in this state, in the late revolution....

Issue of January 8, 1805

Married on Sunday evening last, by the Rev. Mr. Mathews, Mr. John M'Neall, to Mrs. Susannah Allison, widow of the late William allison.

Died last evening, Mrs. Ann Roberts, relict of Col. Roberts, a brave and distinguished officer in the American army, who was killed in the battle at Stono-Ferry in June '79....

Died on Thursday the 27th ult., Mrs. Elizabeth Torrance, in the 23d year of her age...left husband an infant child...

Issue of January 9, 1805

Married last evening, by the Rev. Dr. Jenkins, Thomas Hunt, Esq. to Miss Gaillard, daughter of John Gaillard, esq. decd.

Married at Liberty Hill, Newberry district, on Friday, the 28th Dec., Mr. John Blair, of this city, merchant, to Miss Sarah C. Ewell, daughter of Mr. James Ewell, late of Lancaster County, Virginia.

Died on Saturday last, Mr. Isaac D'Azevedo, aged 46 years....

Issue of January 10, 1805

Died on Saturday the 29th Dec. last, on his way to this city, Captain Adrain Provoux, in the 53d year of his age...a native of Cape Francois, in the island of St. Domingo...Rev. War. service.

Died, on Monday last, Mrs. Dorothy Davis, widow of the late Captain Harman Davis, aged 40 years.

Issue of January 11, 1805

Married at Georgetown on Tuesday the 1st inst., by the Rev. Mr. Botsford, Mr. George Washington Heriot, to Miss Eliza Fuchey, both of that town.

Issue of January 14, 1805

Departed this life on Wednesday last, Miss Mary Magdalene Combe, of this city, in the 84th year of her age. (poem)

Issue of January 15, 1805

Married onSunday evening, on Edisto Island, by the Rev. Donald M'Leod, Mr. James Mair, of this city, to Miss Martha Graham, youngest daughter of the Rev. Wm. E. Graham, deceased.

Savannah, January 12
Died at a very advanced age, on the 9th inst., Dr. Nuble Wimberly Jones; this gentleman's family were the neighbours of Gen. Oglethorpe, in England, and came to Georgia with its founder...(long account)

Issue of January 17, 1805

Married on the 20th ult., by the Rev. Mr. M'Whorter, Mr. David Shaw, to Miss Rebecca M'Bride, of Salem County.
Died on Monday last, at the Euhaws, Mr. James Heyward, youngest son of the late William Heyward, esq....
departed this life on the 11th inst., Thomas Doughty, junior (second son of Mr. William Doughty) in the 21st year of his age ....

Issue of January 18, 1805

Married on the 1st inst.,Mr. Peter Gaillard, jun. of St. Stephen's Parish, to Miss Elizabeth Gourdin, eldest daughter of Theodore Gourdin, Esq.
Died on Sunday evening last,the 13th inst., at his plantation, on Wadmalaw Island, Benjamin Stiles, Jun. esq. aged 35 years.

Issue of January 19, 1805

Died on Thursday last, in the 36th yearof his age, Mr. James Hughes, Ship-Joiner.
Died at Norwich (Con.) Mr. Samuel Brown, aged 90 years....

Issue of January 22, 1805

Died on Sunday last, William Freeman, Esq. one of the Tellers, of the National Branch Bank....

Savannah, January 19
Died in this city, on the 12th inst., John Miller, Esq., aged 55 years, late Sheriff of Beaufort district, South-Carolina.
Died on the 14th inst., Richard Stuart, a native of Ireland.
Died on the 15th inst., Mr. Adam M'Kay, aged 53 years.
Died on the 16th inst.,Capt. Benj. Webley, commander of the U. S. Revenue Cutter, stationed here....

Issue of January 24, 1805

Died on Saturday last, Mr. David Denoon, for upwards of 20 years, a respectable inhabitant of this place.

Issue of January 25, 1805

Married last evening, by the Rev. Dr. Hollinshead, Mr. Robert Washington Cleary, to Miss Eliza Bee, daughter of Mr. Joseph Bee, deceased.
Married on Thursday the 24th inst., by the Rev. P. Mathews, John Allman, Esq. to the amiable MissSarah Heartman, of Christ Church parish.
Married, on Edisto, the 21st inst.,by the Rev. Donald M'Leod, Mr. Hugh Wilson Jun. to Miss Ann Jenkins, daughter of Col. Joseph Jenkins, decd.
Died at Washington, on Friday morning the 11th inst., Col. James Gillespie, a representative fromN. C....
Died on the 8th inst., at Middleton Township, (Pennsylvania) a Negro Man named Jack aged about 116 years, the property of Col. William Chambers, of said township.

Issue of January 26, 1805

Died on Wednesday last, Miss Mary Keen, aged 20 years and 3 months, the only child of Capt. Thomas Keen, decd., an old inhabitant of Charleston....

Issue of January 28, 1805

Married on Sunday last, by the Rev. Mr. Mathews, Mr. John Johnston, to Mrs. Ann Smith, widow of Archibald Smith, jun. both of this city.
Departed this transitory life, on the 21st inst.,Mrs. Elizabeth Egleston, a native of Philadelphia, in the 28th year of her age...left aged father and mother, a tender husband and a promising son....
Died on the 6th inst., of the small-pox, on his passage from Guadeloupe for this port, Mr. Thomas Langfitt, mate of the brig Maria, Silvanus Rich, master, belonging to Charleston.
Died at Grand Ecore on Red River, on the 8th of Nov. last, John Miller, aged 96 years...born in German, and in 1757, was a soldier in the French army in Canada (long account)
Drowned on the 29th ult., between Williams Island and Hancock's wharf, in the port of Boston, Mr. Henry Davis, of Boston, aged 33....

Issue of January 29, 1805

Died on Saturday morning, the 26th inst., in the 18th year of her age, Miss Elizabeth Darby, youngest daughter of the late William Darby, Merchant, of Union District.

Issue of January 30, 1805

Married last evening, by the Rev. Mr. Bowen, Mr. Charles Kiddell, to Miss Rachel Alexander, both of this city.
Died on Saturday morning last, in the 19th year of her age, Miss Elizabeth Harvey Roper, only daughter of Major Thomas Roper....

Issue of January 31, 1805

Died on the 24th Oct. last, in the River Gambia, Africa, Mr. William Verree, late of this city....

Issue of February 2, 1805

Married on Wednesday the 23d ult., on Edisto Island, by the Rev. Mr. M'Leod, Henry John Jones, Esq. to Miss Mary Ann Miot, both of this city.
                            Pendleton, January 17
This morning, departed this life, in Child-bed, Mrs. Jane Shaw, the wife of William Shaw, Esq. and second daughter of Gen. Anderson....family burying ground of Gen. Anderson....

Issue of February 4, 1805

Died at Richmond, (V.) on Sunday the 20th ult., Mrs. West, Jun. (Formerly Mrs. Bignall) the most distinguished ornament of the Virginia Stage.
Married on Sunday evening last, by the Rev. Mr. Pilmore, Mr. William Earley, to Miss Hope Hugg, both of Gloucester County, New-Jersey.
At Lancaster, on the 9th inst., by the Rev. Mr. Latta, Mr. Charles S. Sewell, of the Eastern Shore of Maryland, to Miss Ann Catharine Keagg of Lancaster (Penn.)
At Amity, on the 10th ult., by Joshua Wells, Esq. Mr. Garret Decker, of Brimstone-Hill to Miss Eliza Gardenhouse, of Mares Point, both near Skunk's Misery, in the village of Jount Eve.
                                                Orange Eagle

Issue of February 7, 1805

Died at Gloves, near Athenry (Eng.) Mr. Dems Doorobee, of Billinchangin, aged 117....
Died lately in the work-house of Yarmouth (England) Martha Stannought, aged 70....

Issue of February 8, 1805

Married last evening, by the Rev. Mr. Bowen, Mr. Laurence Bradson, Ship-Wright, to the amiable Miss Elizabeth M'Guire, both of this city.
Married, last evening, by the Rev. Mr. James H. Mellard, Doctor John L. E. W. Shecut, of this city, to Miss Susanna Hallard, of Georgetown.

Issue of February 9, 1805

Married, on Thursday evening last, by the Rev. Dr. Jenkins, the Rev. Nathaniel Bowen, Rector of St. Michael's Church, to Miss Margaret Blake, daughter of John Blake, Esq.
Died at New-York, Mr. Thomas Gardner...
Died in England, Mrs. Lewis, wife of Mr. D. Lewis, butcher....
Died at Shirley (Mass.) on the 27th Dec., Mrs. Sophia Parker, aged 21...oldest daughter of Dr. Benjamin Hartwell....

Issue of February 11, 1805

Married on Saturday evening last, by the Rev. Dr. Buist, Mr. James Carmichael, of this city, to Mrs. Eliza Evans Johnston, of Savannah.

Died yesterday morning, at his house, in the 67th year of his age, Rev. Mr. Abraham Azuby, Minister of the Hebrew Congregation upwards of 20 years, a native of Amsterdam....

Issue of February 13, 1805

Married on Monday evening last, by the Rev. Dr. Hollinshead, Col. Morton A. Waring, to Miss Rebecca Hamilton, daughter of his Excellency Paul Hamilton, Esq.

Died in Baltimore, on the 19th ult., in the 60th year of her age, Mrs. Frances Presstman, consort of George Presstman, esq. of that city...remains were deposited in the Baptist burial ground....

Issue of February 14, 1805

Married on Thursday last, by the Rev. N. Bowen, the Rev. Milward Pogson, to Miss Henrietta Wragg, eldest daughter of the late William Wragg, Esq. of Ashley Barony.

Died on the 28th of Jan. last,in Pendleton district, Mr. Peter Engevin, aged 78 years...a native of France , but a resident in this state for 40 years.

Died at Otaheite, Pomarry, King of that Island....

Issue of February 15, 1805

Died, at Long Island, on the 15th of Nov., in the 60th year of his age, M. Peries, a French Gentlemen....(long account)

Issue of February 18, 1805

Died at Kingston (Plymouth county, State of Mass.)Mrs. Thankful Adams, wife of Mr. J. Adams, aged 89. She had lived with her present husband about 70 years, and has left him aged 91....

Died at Boston, on the 24th ult., Thomas Macdonough, Esq. Consul of his Brittanic Majesty for the Eastern Department of the U. S., aged 65.

On the 24th ult., were entombed at Boston, the remains of Hon. Thomas Davis....

Issue of February 19, 1805

Married this forenoon, at St. Philip's Church, by the Rev. Dr. Percy, William Turnbull, Esq. to Miss Eliza Catharine Percy, both of this city.

Issue of February 20, 1805

Married, last evening, by the Rev. Dr. Bowen, Col. William Fishburne, to Miss Mary C. Snipes.

Died on the 14th inst., Mr. William Mason, in the 36th year of his age...native of Salem, Mass., and for the last 15 years resided in this city...

Died at Wambaw, on the 11th inst., in the 37th year of his age, Mr. John Burford Halsall....

Died at his seat at Coombe, in Surry (Eng.) on Saturday the 3d of November last, James Bourdieu. Esq. of the House of Bourdieu, Cholet and Bourdieus, in the 90th year of his age.

Issue of February 21, 1805

Married last evening, by the Rev. Dr. Hollinshead, Mr. James Freeman, of Wadmalaw Island, to Mrs. Rachael E. Ravell, relict of the late Mr. John Ravell, of this city.

Issue of February 22, 1805

Married on Tuesday evening last, by the Rev. Mr. Bowen, Col. William Fishburne, to Miss Mary C. Snipes.
Married last evening, by the Rev. Mr. Hollinshead, Mr. William Godber, of Charleston, to Mrs. Martha Hinson, of James Island.

Issue of February 26, 1805

Died on Wednesday the 20th inst., Mr. John Anthony Woodill, in the 27th year of his age....
Died on Saturday the 23d inst., at the plantation of Jo-nson Hagood, esq. Parker's Ferry, Mr. Gates O'Hear, eldest son of Mr. James O'Hear, of this city....lost a daughter aged 14 years....

Issue of February 28, 1805

Died, at Spartanburgh district, on the 31st of December last, Mr. Charles Moore (the father of General Moore.)...(eulogy) raised 10 children, three sons and seven daughters....

Issue of March 1, 1805

Died, on Tuesday last, in the 38th year of her age, Mrs.Ann Mazyck, wife of Stephen Mazyck, Esq. of Woodboo, St. John's Parish, and second daughter of Dr. Robert wilson, of this city....

Issue of March 4, 1805

Married, last evening, by the Rev. Mr. Levrier, Mr. John Schirer, to Miss Eliza Galler.

Issue of March 8, 1805

Married on Tuesday evening last, by the Rev. Mr. Tyson, Mr. Winborn Lawton jun. to Miss Margaret Frampton, daughter of John Frampton, Esq., Pocotaligo.

Issue of March 9, 1805

Died in this city, on the 6th inst., Mrs.Susannah Wadsworth, aged 72 years, mother to the late Thomas Wadsworth, Esq. formerly of Boston, Mass.

Issue of March 11, 1805

Married on Friday evening last, Mr. J. H. Fasbender, to Miss Margaret M'La Henderson, both of Delemhorst, Germany.(see below)

Issue of March 12, 1805

Married on Saturday last, by the Rev. Israel Munds, Mr. John H. Fasbender, to Miss Margareta Magdalena Neinerichs, of Delmenhorst, Germany.
Died on the 19th Nov. at Parish, aged 88, M. F. Tanois, clerk in the French treasury...left no less than 10 widows....

Issue of March 13, 1805

Married on Thursday evening, last, in Statesburgh, by the

Rev. Mr. Jones, Mr. James Monk, Silversmith and Watch-maker, of this city to Miss Jane Campbell, of Statesburgh.

Issue of March 14, 1805

Married, on Tuesday the 12th inst., by the Rev. Philip Mathews, Francis Marion Bennett, Esq. of St. James's Santee, to Miss Ann Elizabeth Brown, of St. James'Goose-creek.

Issue of March 16, 1805

Married on Sunday evening last, by the Rev. Mr. Mills, Mr. Henry Monpoey, Merchant, to Miss Margaret Brown, of Tooboodoo.

Issue of March 18, 1805

Married on Sunday evening last, by the Rev. Dr. Jenkins, Mr. Richard Hagen, to Miss Henrietta Donnavan, both of this city.

Issue of March 19, 1805

Departed this life on Saturday evening last, Mr. George Verree, a native of this city, in the 32d year of his age....

Issue of March 21, 1805

Died in this city on Tuesday last, Mr. Solomon Harby, a native of England, in the 43d year of his age....

Issue of March 22, 1805

Married on Tuesday last, by the Rev. Israel Munds, Mr. William Lewis, to Mrs. Barbara Amelia Thompson, residing near Jacksonborough, St. Bartholomew's Parish.

Died at Beaufort on Wednesday morning last, Mr. Patrick Mair, late merchant of this city....

Died in this city, on the 19th inst., Mr. Conrad Hook, a native of Baltimore, in the 28th year of his age...left a widow and two daughters....

Died on the 6th inst., in the City of Washington, Col. William W. Burrows, late Col. Commandant of the Marine Corps....

Issue of March 23, 1805

Suicide. On Thursday evening at 8 o'clock, Captain Matthias Rider, of the schooner Clarissa & Eliza, shot himself on board his vessell...formerly resided in Wellstreet (Mass.) and has a wife and family in Buckstown, Maine.

Died at Beaufort, on the 9th inst., Mr. Thomas Witter, who was a native of this state....

Died on the island of St. Vincent, on the 19th Dec. last, the Hon. David Miller, Esq. Speaker of the Hon. House of Assembly and Assistant Judge of the Court of King's Bench....

Issue of March 25, 1805

Died at Gloves near Athenry (Eng.) Mr. Dems Goorobee, aged 117....his own youngest son is about 18 years old.

Issue of March 26, 1805

Died in this city, Mr. Nathan Riley, aged 20, a native of Middletown, Con. and mate of the ship Anna, of New-York.

Died, on the morning of the 22d inst., Mr. Mathias Woolfe, butcher, in the 66th year of his age...born in dukedom of Wirtemburg....

Issue of March 27, 1805

Married on Thursday evening last, by the Rev. Dr. Hollinshead, Mr. Mathew Miller to Miss Rose Ann May.
Married on Sunday evening, by the Rev. Dr. Furman, Doctor S. N. Niderburgh, to Mrs. Mary Reynolds.

Issue of March 28, 1805

Died at Boston, the Hon. Peleg Coffin, in the 49th year of his age.

Issue of March 29, 1805

Married on Sunday evening last, by the Rev. Doctor Jenkins, Mr. James King to Mrs. Rase Love, widow of the late Duncan Love, both of this city.

Issue of March 30, 1805

Died on the 27th inst., Mr. Samuel Robinson, in the 35th yearof his age...left father and mother who reside at Portland (Mass.).

Issue of April 1, 1805

Married last evening, by the Rev. Dr. Buist, Mr. James Pennall, merchant, to Miss Catherine Eliza Smith, only daughter of the late Mr. Andrew Smith, both of this city.

Issue of April 2, 1805

Died on Sunday morning last, Mrs. Frances Rodgamon, in the 70th year of her age...a native of Maryland, and 50 years an inhabitant of Carolina...mother, widow, grandmother, great-grandmother....

Issue of April 3, 1805

Married, at Georgetown, on Thursday evening, the 28th ult., by the Rev. Mr. Fraser, John B. White, Esq. of this city, to Miss Eliza Allston, of Georgetown.

Issue of April 4, 1805

Married, on Thursday last, by the Rev. Dr. Hollinshead, John Geddes, Esq. Attorney at Law, to Miss Ann Chalmers, both of this city.
Married last evening, by Mr. E. D. L. Motta, Mr. Aaron Moise, to Miss Philah Cohen, both of this city.
Married last evening, by the Rev. Mr. Munds, Captain Joshua Fisher, to Miss Rosanna Fairley.
Married last evening, by the Rev. Mr. Munds, Mr. James Thompson, to Mrs. Elizabeth Robinson, both of this place.
On Wed. the 27th ult., departed this life in the 60th year of his age, Mr. James Mylne, a native of Dundee in Scotland, resided in this city 40 years....
Departed this life on Thursday the 28th March last, at Ashley River, Mrs. Mary Freazer, relict of John Ladson Frezer,

Esq. in the 26th year of her age....
    Died in the parish of St. Elizabeth (jamaica) Rebecca Mills, aged upwards of 113 years....

Issue of April 5, 1805

Married, last evening, by the Rev. Dr. Hollinshead, Mr. James Hasell, to Miss Margaret Dawes, both of this place.
    Married on Wednesday evening last, by Mr. Solomon Hyams, Mr. Samuel Jacobs, to Miss Catherine Hyams, both of this city.
    Died at his plantation in St. James's parish, Santee, on Tuesday, 2d instant, in the 39th year of his age, Samuel Wigfall, Esq.
    Died at the Euhaw, on the 18th of last month, The Rev. Aaron Tison, pastor of the Baptist Church at that place...He had been several years Pastor of the Baptist Church at Coosawhatchie....
(long account)

Issue of April 10, 1805

Died on Tuesday the 2d instant, on Pee Dee, Dr. James Wilson, a native of Scotland, in the 52d year of his age....twenty of which he resided in this state.
    Died in the city of Richmond, on the 27th ult., General Robert Lawson, an officer in the Rev. war....

Issue of April 12, 1805

Married on Tuesday evening last, by the Rev. Mr. Jenkins, Captain Charles Taylor, of Alexandria, to Miss Sophia George, daughter of Captain James George, of this city.
    Died on Sunday evening, the 31st of March, at his house in Ellery-street, Mr. William Brown Fields, in the 32d year of his age...interred in St. Philip's Church yard, of which Church he was clerk for near six years past.

Issue of April 16, 1805

Married at Nassau, N. P., on the 2d inst., Robert Anderson, Esq. of this city, to Miss Maria Thomas, daughter of George Thomas, esq. late Capt. in his Majesty's 6th West-India regiment.

Issue of April 17, 1805

Married in London, Mr. Ebenezer Manson, aged 19 a private in the Suffolk militia, to Mrs. Scholfield, aged 84, a very rich widow....
    Died in Georgetown, S. C. on the 9th inst., Capt. James Harvey, a number of year an inhabitant of that place.
    Died in New-York, suddenly on Sunday morning, the 31st ult. in the 55th year of his age, Dr. Jean Perrein, a native of France....

Issue of April 19, 1805

Married last evening, Mr. Hugh Campbell, to Miss Mary-Ann Jones, both of this city.
    Married on Tuesday evening, by the Rev. Dr. Furman, Capt. Clark Tingham, to Miss Susan Foffler, both of this city.

Issue of April 20, 1805

Married on Thursday evening, by the Rev. Mr. Munds, Mr. Robert Fisher, to Miss Sarah Byers, both of this city.

Married last evening, by the Rev. Mr. Munds, Capt. David Leslie, to Miss Martha Cunningham, both of this city.

Died, yesterday, Mrs. Wilson, wife of Leighton Wilson, esq. of Brunswick, state of Georgia.

Issue of April 23, 1805

Died on Friday last, the 19th inst., in the 38th year of his age, Mr. Norbert Vinro, a native of Newport (R.I.), for 15 years past a resident in this city...left widow and five small children.

Issue of April 24, 1805

Married, last evening, by the Rev. Mr. Munds, Mr. William John Bryer, to Miss Sarah Miller.

Died at Walden (Ter.) of the dropsy, Mrs. Elizabeth Filman, wife of Mr. Peter Filman....

Issue of April 25, 1805

Married, on the 10th instant, by the Rev. Mr. Waddell, the Rev. Benjamin R. Montgomery, of Pendleton to Miss Eliza Nichols, eldest daughter of Julius Nichols, esq. of Abbeville.

Married on Thursday the 14th March last, by the Rev. Mr. Kelley, Mr. William H. Day, to Miss Polly Izard, both of Laurens district.

Married at Portsmouth (N. C.) the 9th inst., Mr. John Egleston, to Miss Sarah Morton, of that place.

Issue of April 29, 1805

Married last evening, by the Rev. Dr. Keith, Mr. Samuel Parks, to Miss Maria Richardson, both of this place.

Died in London, in the 76th year of his age, Dr. William Buchan, author of Domestic Medicine and Mr. Banks, F. R. S. the celebrated sculptor.

Died in Dublin, Mr. Edwin, a Comedian of considerable merit.

Issue of May 1, 1805

Married on Sunday the 21st ult.,by the Rev. Joshua Lewis, Mr. LaurencePrince to Miss Charlotte Benton, daughter of Col. Samuel Benton, of Cheraw-hill, Pedee.

Married, on Monday last, Mr. Simon Levy, merchant to Miss Eliza Aarons, both of this city.

Married at Limerick (Ireland) Thomas Kelly, aged 89, to Bridget Maddigan, aged 14 years.

Died on the 22d March last, Miss Maria Joseph Feuvette Verrette, late an inhabitant of the Island of St. Domingo.

Issue of May 2, 1805

Married, last evening, by the Rev. Mr. Munds, Mr. John Boyd, to Miss Sarah Legare, both of this City.

Died, on Sunday last, at his plantation in St. Bartholomew's Parish, Joseph Whitmarsh Fuller, Esq. aged 36 years.

Issue of May 4, 1805

Married on Thursday evening last, by the Rev. Dr. Furman, Mr. William Webber, to Miss Martha Shingleton, both of this city.

Married, on Thursday evening, in St. Thomas's parish, by the Rev. Dr. Hollingshead, Mr. Jonathan Bryan, to Miss Sarah Latham, both of this city.

Issue of May 7, 1805

Married by the Rev. John Atkins, at Batavia, on the Congaree, on the 30th April last, Dr. Fortunatis Bryan, to Miss Elizabeth Geodbee Du Pont, daughter of the late Josiah Du Pont, Esq.

Died on the night of the 4th ult., the Rev. Dr. Robert Cooler, late Pastor of the Congregation of Middle Spring, Cumberland county, Pa.

Died in Portsmouth, New Hampshire, the Hon. John Pickering, Esq., L. L. D. aged 68....

Issue of May 8, 1805

Died on the 21st day of March last, at the U. S. garrison, near Vincennes, Capt. Cornelius Lyman, of the 1st regt. of infantry....

Issue of May 10, 1805

Died at New-Orleans, on the 13th of March, Captain Robinson, of the U. S. Artillery.

Issue of May 11, 1805

Died on Thursday last, Mrs. Grace Cain, aged 73; a respectable inhabitant of this city.

Died on the 11th of March, aged 60, Elizabeth Clayton, of Wells, in Somersetshire, England....

Issue of May 15, 1805

Married at Columbia, S. C. on the 28th ult., by the Rev. Mr. Nixon, Mr. Edward Wingate, to Miss Sophia Brown, daughter of Capt. Richard Brown, near M'Cords Ferry.

Issue of May 17, 1805

Married on Thursday evening last, by the Rev. Dr. Hollinshead, Mr. Robert Little, to Mrs. Mary Keen, both of this city.

Issue of May 18, 1805

Died, in England, on the 13th Nov. last, Jacob Bryant, Esq., in the 89th year of his age....

Issue of May 20, 1805

Died, on Thursday the 16th inst., Mrs. Elizabeth Kemble, aged 22 years and 6 months....

Issue of May 21, 1805

Married on Saturday evening last, by the Rev. Dr. Buist, Capt. Alexander Campbell to Mrs. Martha Cameron, both of this city.

Issue of May 23, 1805

Married, last evening, by the Rev. Mr. Bowen, Capt. Jacob R. Valk, to Miss Sarah Gyles, both of this city.

Issue of May 25, 1805

Married on Thursday the 11th inst., by the Rev. Dr. M'Calla, Mr. John White, to Mrs. Mary Bollough, both of Christ Church parish.
Married on Thursday evening last, by the Rev. Dr. Jenkins, Mr. Minead Griner, to Miss Mercy Palmer, both of this city.
Died on the 25th of Feb., the Dowager Queen of Prussia, in the 54th year of her age.
Died at Antrim Castle (Ireland) the Right Hon. Clothworthy, Earl of Masserenne, aged 62....

Issue of May 27, 1805

Died on Thursday last, in the 40th year of his age, William Hunter Torrans, Esq. Attorney at law...left wife and six children....
Died at Newport, Rhode-Island, on Thursday the 25th ult., aged 76 years, Christopher Champlin, Esq. President of the Bank of Rhode-Island.

Issue of May 31, 1805

Married, on Sunday evening last, by the Rev. Dr. Buist, Mr. Peter Johnston, Printer, to Mrs. Sarah Hughes, widow of the late James Hughes, house-carpenter.
Married last evening, at Hampstead, by the Rev. Dr. Hollinshead, Mr. Isaac Bouchonneau, to Miss Ann M. Henrichson, both of this city.
Died, yesterday, Mrs. Esther Azuby, in the 50th year of her age, relict of the late Rev. Mr. Abraham Azuby....

Issue of June 1, 1805

Married on Thursday evening last, by the Rev. Mr. Bowen, Dr. Moses Bradley to Miss Elizabeth Tiebout, both of this city.

Issue of June 5, 1805

Married, on Sunday the 2d inst., by the Rev. Dr. M'Calla, Mr. William Zylks, to Miss Ann Costain, both of this city.
Departed this life, on the 29th inst., Miss Elizabeth Ashe, daughter of Cato Ashe, aged 45 years.
Died in England, aged 86, Mr. William Parrington, formerly a mole catcher....

Issue of June 7, 1805

Died, last evening, Mr. Charles J. Lewis, late merchant of this city, in the 26th year of his age.

Issue of June 10, 1805

Died, yesterday morning, Mrs. Philah Moise, aged 18 years (eulogy).

Issue of June 11, 1805

    Died, on the 19th ult., at Camden, Captain William Rembert, aged 33 years....

Issue of June 13, 1805

    Married, on Tuesday evening, by the Rev. Dr. Keith, Mr. Kinsey Burden, to Miss Mary Legare, both of this city.
    Married the same evening, by the Rev. Dr. Hollinshead, Mr. Thomas Mills, to Miss Eliza Humphreys, both of this city.
    Died on the 28th ult., Dr. Alexander Hogg, a native of Scotland....
    Departed this life on Monday last, at Mr. Wait's plantation, in St. John's parish, Mr. Philip Vaughan, a native of Virginia, in the 55th year of his age....
    Died in Barnwell, on Thursday the 30th of May, in the 30th year of his age, Mr. John C. Wyld...left a wife and many relations....

Issue of June 14, 1805

    Married on the 6th inst., by the Rev. Mr. Caple, Mr. Ferdinand Muller, of this place, to Miss Sarah Bruton, of Barnwell District.
    Married in the parish of St. Luke's, on Thursday the 6th June, by the Rev. Mr. Hicks, Thomas Deveaux, Esq. Sheriff of Beaufort district, to Miss Jane Porteous, daughter of Robert Porteous, Esq. deceased.
    Died on the 25th ultimo, Mrs. Martha Inglesby, wife of Mr. William Inglesby, aged 40 years.
    Died at Glasgow, on the 21st of March, John Murray, esq. consul of the U. S.

Issue of June 17, 1805

    Married, last evening, by the Rev. Mr. Thompson, Mr. John Powell, to Miss Clarissa Maccho, both of this city.
    Married, on Thursday evening last, by the Rev. Mr. Mathews, Mr. George Smith to Miss Maria Wilkins, daughter of the late Mr. John Wilkins, both of this city.
    Died on the 26th ult., John Neufville, Esq. for many years past Register of the Court of Equity.
    Died on the 19th ult., in Mifflin county, Pa., the Rev. Mr. Logan....

Issue of June 19, 1805

    Married on Saturday evening, by the Rev. Mr. Munds, Captain Joshua Turner to Miss Eliza Wilson, both of this city.
    Married on Sunday evening last, by the Rev. Mr. Munds, Mr. John Jones, to Miss Frances Smith, both of this place.
    Died on Monday morning last, Mr. Kennedy M'Kenzie, butcher, of Charleston, aged 53 years...left widow and six children....
    Long account of John J. Murray, native of Charleston (see above)

Issue of June 20, 1805

    Married on Tuesday evening last, by the Rev. Dr. Buist, Mr. James Beggs, Merchant, to Miss Ann Eliza Liber, both of this city.

Issue of June 24, 1805

Married, at Beaufort, on Thursday last, by the Rev. Mr. Palmer, Mr. Robert Means, of this city, to Miss Mary Hutson Barnwell, eldest daughter of Gen. John Barnwell, decd.

Issue of June 25, 1805

Married on Tuesday last, Artemas B. Darby, Esq. to Miss Mary E. Thomson, daughter of Col. W. R. Thomson.
Departed this life, the 23d instant, Miss Martha White, aged 14 years and two months...left father and mother, sisters and brothers....
Died at Wilmington, N. C. on the 4th inst., Mrs. Sabina T. Walker, wife of Mr. Carleton Walker, and eldest daughter of Nathan Legare, Esq. of this state.

Issue of June 26, 1805

Died in Camden, on the 14th inst., Mr. Thomas Dinkins, in the 38th year of his age....

Issue of June 27, 1805

Died, on Wednesday evening, the 19th of June inst., in the 7th year of her age, Miss Anne Skirving, the only child of William Skirving, jun Esq....

Issue of July 1, 1805

Married on Saturday evening last, by the Rev. Mr. Munds, Mr. George Beal, to Miss Martha Davis, both of this city.
Married, last evening, by the Rev. Mr. Munds, Captain Robert Long, to Miss Mary Blackaller, both of this place.
Married, on Thursday evening last, by the Rev. Dr. Hollinshead, Mr. Philip Ling, to Miss Charlotte Black, both of this city.

Issue of July 2, 1805

Married on Monday evening, 1st inst.,John Ball, Esq. of St. John's Parish, to Miss Caroline Swinton, of this city.
Married on the 16th ult., at Henley, South-Carolina, the seat of Samuel T. Hall, Esq., Sinclaire D. Jervais, Esq. to Miss Catharine Olivia O'Keefe.

Issue of July 3, 1805

Married, last Sunday evening, by the Rev. Dr. Gallagher, Mr. James Moles, to Mrs. M. Shields, both of this city.

Issue of July 6, 1805

Died, at Mohegan, near New-London, Martha, aged 120. She was the widow of Zachariah, one of the Nobility of the Mohegan Tribe of Indians, many years an Agent from said Tribe to the General Assembly of Connecticut.

Issue of July 9, 1805

Married last evening, by the Rev. Mr. Hollinshead, Charles Baldwin, Esq. attorney at law, of the state of Georgia, to Mrs. Jane Culliatt, of this city.

Died on the 8th inst., Mr. James West, a native of England, aged 42 years, a once celebrated Comedian....

Issue of July 11, 1805

Married at East Hartford, Connecticut, on Sunday evening the 23d ult., Mr. Thaddeus Gale (Medico Electrician) aged 43 to Miss Harriet Bates, aged 11 years.

Issue of July 12, 1805

Married, at Savannah, on Thursday the 4th inst., Mr. John M'Nish, to Miss Ann Dupont, both of this state.

Issue of July 15, 1805

Married on Wednesday last, by the Rev. Dr. Furman, Captain Nathaniel Bingly, to Mrs. Lenox, both of this city.

Married, at New-Orleans, on the 4th of June, by the Rev. Father Walsh, Edward Livingston, Esq. to Madame Marie Louise Magdeleine Valentine Davezac Castra Moreau, widow of the late Louise Moreau de Laffy.

Died on Thursday evening last, at Hillsborough, the seat of Major Charles Lining, in the 63d year of his age, Major Thomas Bartholomew Bowen, a member of the society of the Cincinnati of this state, and a much respected officer of the Pa. line (long account)

Died on Thursday last, Arnold Wells, Esq. one of the Representatives of Christ Church Parish, in the legislature of this state...left a widow and five small children.

Died in this city on Saturday last, Mr. R. C. Porter, a native of England, and a Member of the City Guard.

Issue of July 16, 1805

Married on Sunday evening last, by the Rev. Mr. Munds, Mr. James L. Florence, to Miss Mary Miller, both of this place.

Died, on Sunday evening last, Mr. John Stewart, of this city.

Issue of July 17, 1805

Died, on the 12th inst., in the 56th year of her age, Mrs. Jane Robertson, wife of Alexander Robertson, of this city, merchant.

Died on the 15th inst., in the 41st year of her age, Mrs. Elizabeth Brownlee, wife of John Brownlee, esq. of this city, merchant, and eldest daughter of Gen. Robert Cunningham, formerly of this state.

Died on the 13th inst., at Cuthbertville, Miss Caroline Cuthbert, eldest daughter of Col. Cuthbert.

Issue of July 18, 1805

Married, last evening, by the Rev. Mr. Munds, Mr. John M. Cants, to Miss Mary E Owens.

Issue of July 19, 1805

Married, last evening, by the Rev. Mr. Munds, Mr. Alexander Coventry, to Mrs. Catharine O'Donald.

Died at Havana, on the 4th inst., Mr. Kelton, of this place.

Issue of July 20, 1805

Married on Thursday evening last, by the Rev. Dr. Hollinshead, Doctor William S. Stevens, to Mrs. Hannah Ashe, widow of Samuel Ashe, Esq. deceased.

Married in Europe the Rev. Thomas Coke, L. L. D., one of the Bishops of the Methodist Episcopal Church in the U. S.

Died on the 17th inst., Captain Moses Andrews, aged 48 years. He has left a wife and a number of friends to lament his loss.

Issue of July 23, 1805

Married on Sunday evening last, by the Rev. Mr. Munds, Mr. Robert S. Robinson, to Mrs. Ann Sutton, both of this city.

Departed this life on the morning of the 20th inst., Mr. Isaac Weatherly, Bricklayer, aged 23 years, he has left a wife, brother and sisters....

Died at Beaufort, on the 13th inst., Mr. Wm. M. Finley, Schoolmaster.

Issue of July 24, 1805

Died, last evening, after 8 hours illness, Miss Harriott Henrietta Bounetheau, youngest daughter of Mr. G. M. Bounetheau.

Issue of July 25, 1805

Died, in March last, at Cheltenham, near London, in the 67th year of her age, Mrs. Elizabeth Garden, relict of Dr. Alexander Garden, formerly of this ctiy.

Issue of July 26, 1805

Departed this life on the 21st inst., in the 49th year of her age, Mrs. Henrietta Wilhelmina Louisa Daly, a native of Holland. (long account)

Died this morning, of the country fever, Mr. John Williamson, aged 26 years, of the house of Thomas & John Williamson, merchants, of Savannah....

Died at Georgetown, on the 19th inst., Francis Shackelford, Esq. in the 35th year of his age....

Died at Brandon, Vermont, on the 2d May, Matilda Harris, aged 10 years; on the 4th, Nabby Harris, on the 17th year of her age; on the 9th, Lucinda Harris, in the 14th year of her age; on the 21st, Otis Harris, aged 19; children of Mr. Nathaniel Harris, of that town, in July 1803, they buried two daughters, of the dysentery.

Issue of July 27, 1805

Married in this city, on the 6th inst., by the Rev. Mr. Munds, Mr. Jeremiah Jackson, merchant, to Mrs. Ellen Fernald, daughter of the late Mr. Charles Crawley.

Died, in Russia, on the 20th of March, the Right Rev. Father Gabriel Gruber, Gen. of the Society of Jesuits...born in Vienna (long account)

Issue of July 29, 1805

Died, on Sullivan's-Island, on Sunday the 21st inst., Francis Shackelford, aged 31 years.

Issue of July 30, 1805

Died, yesterday morning, Miss Mary Jacks, youngest daughter of Mr. James Jacks, of this city.
Accidental death of Mrs. Harris, widow of the late Mr. Thomas Harris, of King-street. (account)

Issue of July 31, 1805

Died, in Savannah, on the 25th inst., in the 28th year of his age, Mr. Samuel Morse, a native of Connecticut, the Editor of the Georgia Republican.

Issue of August 1, 1805

Died on Monday evening, the 29th ult., in the 60th year of his age, Roger Smith, Esq.

Issue of August 2, 1805

Married last evening, by the Rev. Dr. Buist, Samuel W. Smith, Esq., Attorney at Law, to Miss Mary Crawley, youngest daughter of the late Mr. Charles Crawley, deceased.
Died at Wassamasaw, the place of his residence, on the 5th of May, Major Robert Thornley....an officer in the militia from the beginning of the rev. war...Senator for the Parish of St. James's Goose-creek. (eulogy and account)

Issue of August 3, 1805

Died yesterday, Mr. Solomon Pollock, aged 66 years, a native of Poland, and for many years a resident of this State.

Issue of August 5, 1805

Married, on Thursday evening last, by the Rev. Mr. Munds, Mr. David D. Salmon, of this city, to Miss Sarah M'Key, of Fayetteville, North Carolina.
Died a short time since, at his residence in Cheraw district, William Falconer, Esq. an eminent Attorney at Law, and for many years a highly respected and useful member of the House of Representatives of this State...left a wife and several children.
Died on Thursday evening last, Mr. John M'Kee, aged 30 years.
Shocking Murder! On Monday the 29th ult., about 4 o'clock in the afternoon, Mr. Thomas Maples was shot near his dwelling-house, on the High Hills of Santee, by his eldest son Richard Maples, aged about 23....

Issue of August 6, 1805

Last evening was led to the Altar of Hymen, Miss Charlotte Collins, by Mr. Jacob Henry Miller. The Rev. Dr. Gallagher performed the ceremony....
Departed this life on the 5th inst., after a short illness, Mrs. Catherine Cordes, aged 80 years and 9 months.
Augusta July 27.
On Monday night last, the 22d inst., the house of Mr. John Wise, living in South-Carolina, about seven miles from Augusta, was struck with lightning, and a Mr. Simon Cushman, a young man, 18 years of age, was killed in his bed...son of Mr. Simeon Cushman, of S. C., Edgefield district.

Issue of August 8, 1805

Died, on Sunday morning, the 4th of August, Mr. Daniel B. Timmings, in the 42d year of his age, a native of England, and for many years a respectable inhabitant of this city. He has left a widow....

Died at Beaufort (S.C.) on the 28th ult., in the 60th year of her age, Mrs. Jane Watts, of Dawfuskie Island.

Mr. John Perriclard, on the 19th ult., while walking in a field on Port Royal Island, was struck dead, by a flash of lightning.

Issue of August 12, 1805

Married, last evening, by the Rev. Mr. Munds, Mr. John Harvey, to Mrs. Eleanor Smith, both of this city.

Issue of August 13, 1805

Died on Saturday, the 10th inst., in the 40th year of her age, Mrs. Margaret Frances Fair, wife of Capt. William Fair....

Died at Savannah, on the 8th inst., Mrs. Harriet Barnwell Bulloch, wife of William B. Bulloch, esq. Attorney-General of the U. S. for that district, and eldest daughter of Jacob Deveaux, esq. of Charleston....

Died at Halifax, N. C., on the 3d inst., Mr. Abraham Hodge, proprietor of the North Carolina Journal.

Died at Salem, Mass., on the 23d ult., Mr. William Carlton, aged 33, proprietor of the Salem Register.

Issue of August 16, 1805

Died on the 12th inst., Mrs. Margaret Williams, aged 85 years.

Issue of August 17, 1805

Died, at Sullivan's Island, on Wednesday evening last, Mrs. Elizabeth Johnston, in the 63d year of her age.

Issue of August 19, 1805

Married on the 15th inst., by the Rev. Dr. Hollinshead, Mr. Clarence Morgan, to Miss Ann Wolfe, both of this city.

Married on Wednesday evening last, by Mr. E. D. L. Motta, Mr. Solomon Solomon to Miss Alice Abrahams, both of this city.

Married, on the 29th of July last, by the Rev. Mr. Munds, Mr. John Babcork, to Miss Ann Cooper, of St. Bartholomew's Parish.

Issue of August 21, 1805

Married on Saturday evening last, by the Rev. Mr. Munds, Mr. Thomas Smith of Philadelphia, to Mlle Clotilda Boudeaud, of St. Domingo.

Issue of August 22, 1805

Died, on Thursday the 15th inst., in the 76th year of his age, Mr. Laurence Carnes, a native of Ireland.

Departed this life, Mr. Gilbert Chalmers, aged 60 years, 4 months and 20 days....

Issue of August 24, 1805

Died, at Newport, R. I. on Friday evening the 26th ult., in the 46th year of his age, Joseph Wiseman, Esq. Vice-Consul from his Catholic Majesty, the King of Spain, to the State of Rhode-Island...a native of Ireland, but educated in Spain....

Issue of August 26, 1805

Died, on Saturday evening last, in the 26th year of his age, Mr. George Whalley, a native of England....(lines)
Died on Tuesday last, Captain Lewis Collet, aged 29 years; left a wife, mother, sisters and brothers....
Died at Augusta, on the 13th inst., Miss Sarah House, youngest daughter of Samuel House, Esq. of this city, aged 6 years.
Died on the 18th June last, near London, Arthur Murphy, Esq. an eminent barrister....

Issue of August 29, 1805

Died at Montpelier (France) aged 69, Baron Hompesch, formerly Grand Master of the Order of Malta.
Died in the Fleet Prison, London, aged 32, Miss E. F. Robinson, of swindling notoriety.
Died at Whitehaven (Eng.) William Woodburn....

Issue of August 30, 1805

Died at his house in this city, on Wednesday last, in the 82d year of his age, General Christopher Gadsden (long account)

Issue of August 31, 1805

Married on the 17th inst., by the Rev. Mr. Munds, Mr. Charles O'Neal, to Miss Mary Terrell.
Married on Thursday evening last, by the Rev. Mr. Munds, Capt. Joshua Anthony to Miss Charlotte Rowan.

Issue of September 2, 1805

Died suddenly, on the 29th ult., by the bursting of a blood vessel, at the house of Mr. Joseph J. Murray, on Eding's Bay, Miss Margaret Manners, only child of Mr. Archibald Manners, late of Charleston.

Issue of September 3, 1805

Died in Savannah, on Monday the 26th ult., in the 58th year of his age, Mr. Ebenezer Hills...native of Mass. and came to Savannah in 1784....

Issue of September 4, 1805

Departed this life on the 7th ult., at Baltimore, Mr. Humphrey Minchin, late of this city.
Died in Richmond Co., Ga., on the 24th ult., in the 40th year of his age, Col. Robert Watkins.
Died at Savannah, on the 27th ult., Mr. Elihu Potter, a native of Connecticut.

Issue of September 5, 1805

Died on the 20th of August last, John Wilson, mariner, a native of Scotland.

Issue of September 6, 1805

Died on Tuesday evening last, Mrs. Sarah Jones, aged 72 years, a native of London, and upwards of 60 years resident in this city.
Died at Baltimore, on the 22d ult., Jonathan Wilmer, Esq., a native of that state to which he had a few weeks since returned from Charleston, S. C....

Issue of September 9, 1805

Died, on Friday morning last, Mr. Alexander Barnard, a native of London, in the 25th year of his age....left a father.
Died on Saturday the 16th July, at his apartments at Chelsea (Eng.), Suet, the actor....

Issue of September 11, 1805

Died, on Sunday afternoon, Mrs. Wyatt, wife of Peter Wyatt, Esq.... left three children.
Departed this life, on Friday last, Mrs. Mary Ann Brown, eldest daughter of Mr. Charles Bouchonneau, decd., in the 22d year of her age...left a husband, three infant children....
Died at Columbia, S. C. Mr. Roger Crayton, Merchant, of Granby. Mr. David Lewis, carpenter.
Died at Augusta (Georgia), Mr. Thomas Moore, Merchant, aged 21. Mr. John Powell, aged 16, son of Dr. Powell, of Louisville.
Died at Savannah, on the 5th inst., Joseph Hutchinson Stevens, Esq., Attorney at Law, aged 25, a native of Connecticut.

Issue of September 12, 1805

Died, yesterday morning, in the 21st year of his age, Mr. Lewis Ogier, jun son of Mr. Lewis Ogier, factor, of this city....
Died on the 23d ult., Miss Carolina Maria Crowly, aged 7 years and 6 months; on the 25th of the same month Miss Louisa M. M. Crowly, aged 9 years 2 months and 17 days, daughters of Mr. Michael Crowly, Merchant, of this city, deceased.
Died on Tuesday the 10th inst., at his house, in St. Philip-street, Mr. Stephen Sherman, a native American, also Mr. Laurance France, a native of Germany....

Issue of September 14, 1805

Married, on the 5th inst., by the Rev. Mr. Smith, Mr. James Callahan, to Miss Elizabeth Ford, both of Kershaw District.
Died on the 7th inst., at Georgetown, Capt. John T. Young, of this city, in the 28th year of his age.
Died on the 16th of June, at his house in Norfolk-street, London, John Rose, Esq., aged 84 years.

Issue of September 16, 1805

Died, at Darlington College, on the 23d ult., Master Douglas Stark, son of Reuben Stark Esq. of Camden, aged 12 years and 2 months....
Died on Saturday last, at his place on John's Island, Mr. George Hix Freer....left a wife and five children.

Issue of September 17, 1805

Married on Saturday evening last, by the Rev. Mr. Munds, Mr. George Carroll, planter, of Virginia, to Miss Charlotte Allen, of New-York.
Died on Friday last, Miss Lucretia Berwicke, in the 50th year of her age.
Died in Savannah, on the 11th inst., Capt. John Snow, of Truro, Mass., aged 33 years...left an affectionate wife....
Augusta / September
Died on Friday, the 30th ult., at her father's the Rev. Thomas Daniel, in Green county, Mrs. Mary Fauche....
Died on Saturday last, in this city, Mr. Thomas Moore, merchant...
Died on Monday evening, Mr. John Powell, son of Dr. Powell, of Louisville....
Died on the 5th inst., Master Joseph Walton, eldest son of Mr. William Walton, aged near 12 years....
Died on Thursday last, the Rev. Mr. M'Night, minister of St. Paul's church, and Rector of Richmond Academy....

Issue of September 18, 1805

Died at Newburgh, state of New-York, on the 25th ult., Maj. Gen. John Skey Eustace, aged 45 years....

Issue of September 19, 1805

Married last evening, by the Rev. Mr. Hollinshead, Mr. Thomas Whitesides, to Miss Ann Jefferds, both of Christ Church Parish.
Died on the 16th inst., Mr. William Armstrong, aged 61 years, a native of Scotland, and for 18 years a respectable inhabitant of this city.
Died on the 10th inst., at the plantation of Mr. Joseph Fickling, Stono, Miss Maria W. Fickling, the only daughter of Mr. Samuel Fickling, late of Edisto planter, decd, in the 3d year of her age....

Issue of September 20, 1805

Died, on Wednesday last, Mr. William Hunter, a native of Ireland....
Died at Dorchee, St. John's Parish, Dennis Sweeney, Bricklayer, a native of Ireland.
Died on the 18th inst., Master John Wissinger, eldest son of Mr. John Wissinger.

Issue of September 21, 1805

Married on Thursday evening, on Sullivan's Island, by the Rev. Mr. Munds, Mr. Bernard Clarke, to Mrs. Gertrude Rockwell.
Died this morning, at Shell Hall, Christ Church parish, Hon. William Marshall, Judge in Equity.
Departed this life on the 17th inst., in the 43d year of his age, Mr. Charles Morgan, a native of Scotland....
Died on the 12th July, at Lyme Regis, Dorset, (England), Mrs. Ann Stuart, of America, and the wife of Rev. James Stuart, formerly Rector of Georgetown and All Saints, S. C.

Issue of September 24, 1805

Died on Sunday last, at James' Island, Capt. Benjamin Stiles, an old and respectable inhabitant of St. Andrew's Parish.

Died on Tuesday the 17th inst., Mr. John Pollock, a native of Ireland, aged 32 years.
Died at her house in London, on the 21st of June, Mrs. Mary Wells, the widow of the late Robert Wells, Esq. formerly of this city.
Died at Sapeio, Georgia, on the 11th inst., on board the sloop Nabby, Capt. John Edwards, of Philadelphia, aged 50 years.
Died at Darien, Georgia, on the 10th inst., Dr. L. Salmon, after a short illness.

Issue of September 26, 1805

Married last evening, by the Rev. Dr. Jenkins, Mr. Samuel Halman, of St. James, Santee, planter, to Miss Agnes Mitchell, of this city.
Died on the 18th inst., Jean Louis Polony, M. D. aged 62 years...a native of Bayonne in France....

Issue of September 27, 1805

Died at Georgetown on the 22d inst., in the 22d year of his age, Mr. David Blanche, of that town.
Died on Saturday the 14th inst., on Jeffers' Creek, Darlington district, Mrs. Ann Morgan- in the 91st year of her age... born and married in Virginia, had four children, and resided the last 30 years of her life in this state....

Issue of September 28, 1805

Died on the 26th inst., Miss Beadah C. P. Billings, aged 3 years, 2 months and 8 days, daughter of Samuel and Elizabeth Billings....
Yesterday morning, at half past 1 o'clock, departed this life in the 76th year of his age, Maj.-Gen. William Moultrie... (long account)

Issue of September 30, 1805

Died on Thursday last, on Charleston neck, Mrs. Ann Du Bois, aged 69 years.
Died at Newport, R. I., on the 30th ult., in the 33th year of his age, George Paddon Read, Esq. of Savannah.

Issue of October 1, 1805

Died on the 24th July last, on board the ship William Murdock, captain Thom, on his passage from London to Philadelphia, John Churchman, in the 53d year of his age....Philadelphia paper.

Issue of October 2, 1805

Died on Sunday last, in the 51st year of his age, Lt. Nathaniel Fanning...a native of Connecticut....
Died yesterday morning, Mr. Cade Gotbold of Pee Dee (N. C.)
Died on Monday the 16th ult. at New-York, Mr. Gysbert Newkerk, a native of Holland....

Issue of October 3, 1805

Married on Thursday evening, by the Rev. Dr. Gallagher, Augustau Follin, Esq. to Miss Mary Montama, both of Cape Nichola-Mole, Island of St. Domingo.

Issue of October 4, 1805

Died, at Savannah, on the 1st inst., Mr. Oliver Foster, merchant, a native of New-York.

Issue of October 5, 1805

Died on the 29th ult., Miss Mary Catherine Tofel, aged 7 months and 9 days, daughter of John & Catherine Tofel (lines)

Issue of October 7, 1805

Departed this life on Tuesday last, in the 31st year of his age, Mr. Thomas Hamett, Chair-Maker, a native of this city....
Died, near Camden, on the 2d inst., Mrs. Rebecca Boykin, the amiable consort of Mr. Stephen Boykin, in the 30th year of her age....

Issue of October 8, 1805

Died on Sunday evening last, Mrs. Lydia Roper, wife of Major Thomas Roper, in the 45th year of her age....buried at St. Philip's Church....
Died, yesterday, Mr. Benj. Childs, aged 26 years, a native of Massachusetts....
Died at Fort Johnson, on Sunday evening last, Serjeant Worcester Thompson, a native of Massachusetts....
Died at Columbia, on Wednesday evening last, Mr. John Lindsay.
Died at his residence in Chester district, on Friday the 20th ult., Mr. James Pagan, in the 56th year of his age...left wife and several children.
Died at Augusta, on Saturday the 14th ult., Miss Mary Ramsey aged 6 years, youngest daughter of the late Judge Ramsay, of this state.
Died at Augusta, on Sunday the 15th ult., Master Robert Martin Mims, aged 4 years, 10 motnsh and 19 days, eldest son of Capt. Briton Mims, of Martintown, in this state.
Died at Augusta on Friday, the 27th ult., Master John Macmurphy, aged 15 years, son of Daniel Macmurphy, of that city.

Issue of October 9, 1805

Died on Friday morning, last, William Henry Johnson, eldest son of the hon. William Johnson, aged 9 years.
Died on Thursday the 3d instant, at Camden, S. C. in the 34th year of her age, Mrs. Ann Louisa M'Ca, consort of Mr. John M'Ca, merchant....
Died on the 29th ult., at the plantation of John Bowen, Esq., Charleston Neck, Mrs. Frances Withers, wife of Mr. John Withers, Sen, of Laurens County, aged 50 years.

Issue of October 11, 1805

Died on the 28th ult., Miss Mary Strother, aged 17 years, daughter of Charles Strother, esq. of Cheraw.
Died at Savannah, on the 5th inst., Mrs. Mary Freeman, a native of Connecticut, and wife of Mr. Timothy Freeman, merchant, of Savannah.
Died at Savannah, on the 6th inst., Mr. Samuel Bullen, a native of Massachusetts.
Died at Frankfort, Germany, Pineus Levi Harwitz, aged 74, first Rabbi of the Synagogue, and of the highest rank in Germany.

Died on the 24th of August, at Mr. Thomas Griffiths in Moore county (state of N. C., Fayette district) John Hull, a youth 16 or 17 years of age; who said he was the son of Charles Hull, shoemaker of Franklin County, Virginia.... Raleigh Register.

Issue of October 12, 1805

Married on Thursday evening last, by the Rev. Dr. Hollinshead, Mr. John Dolles, to Miss Maria Bell, both of this city.

Departed this life on Wednesday evening last, Mrs. Jane Gamble, a native of Ireland, and for many years past a respectable inhabitant of this city. (lines)

Issue of October 14, 1805

Died on the evening of Saturday last, in the 30th year of her age, Mrs. Maria Haig, a native of England, and wife of Mr. David Haig, of this city...interred in the Presbyterian Church burying ground, discourse by Rev. Dr. Buist....

Died on Wednesday last, Master Benjamin Langstaff, aged 9 years, second son of Mr. Benjamin Langstaff, of this city.

Died at Jamesville, Santee, on Thursday the 3d inst., Dorcas Dow, in the 7th year of her age, daughter of Robert Dow and Dorcas his wife...they are bereft of their sixth child....

Died at Camden on the 7th Oct. last, in the 54th year of her age, Mrs. Elizabeth Adamson, wife of John Adamson, Esq.... married 38 years....

Died, on Monday the 22d July at his seat in Horry District, Samuel Foxworth Esq. Lt. Col. Commandant of the 25th Regt, aged 44 years and 3 months.... (lines)

Issue of October 15, 1805

Died on the 29th ult., at his father's place, near Augusta, by the bite of a Rattle Snake, Elias C. M'Coombs, aged 9 years and 7 months, son of Capt. R. M'Coombs....

Issue of October 16, 1805

Died on Sunday morning the 13th inst., Mr. Evean M'Lean, a native of North-Britain....

Departed this life on the 7th inst., Mrs. Sarah M'Donald, wife of Col. Adam M'Donald, of St. Mathew's parish...left husband and two small children.

Issue of October 17, 1805

Died in this city, on the 14th inst., Mr. John Bryson, late of Mecklenburg County, North Carolina.

Died on Sunday the 13th inst., Captain Jeremiah Tatem, a native of Bermuda....

death of Rev. Jas. Waddell, of the county of Albemarle....
Richmond Enquirer.

Issue of October 18, 1805

Died on Sunday last, Capt. Warren C. Foster, master of the schooner Hannah and Polly, of this port, a native of Connecticut.

Died in this city, on Saturday last, Mr. Charles Campbell, aged 24 years....

Died on the same day Master Henry Sims, aged 16 years, a native of this place....

Died a few days ago, at Louisville, Mrs. Fanny Forsyth, for many years a respectable inhabitant of this city. At the same place, also, the only child of John Forsyth, esq.

Died on the 24th ult., on his journey to the Warm Springs, Mr. George Miller, of Beach Island, S. C. aged 44....

Departed this life on the 3d ult., in her 40th year, Mrs. Sarah Anderson, wife of Mr. Elisha Anderson, of Burke County.

Issue of October 19, 1805

Died at Philadelphia, on Tuesday, the 1st inst., Mr. William Lancaster, Printer, formerly of this city.

Funeral for Mr. Loring Andrews, at the house of Miss Buford, No. 115 Queen-strret, tomorrow morning.

Issue of October 21, 1805

Died on Saturday last, Mr. Loring Andrews, one of the Proprietors and Editors of the Charleston Courier....born at Bingham, Mass...(long account)

Issue of October 22, 1805

Departed this life on the 15th inst., Mrs. Matilda Hayden, aged 45 years, wife of Mr. William Hayden, of this city.

Issue of October 24, 1805

Married, last evening, Thomas H. Deas, Esq. to Miss Caroline Hall, daughter of the late George Abbot Hall, Esq.

Issue of October 25, 1805

Departed this life on Tuesday the 8th inst., at his seat in Mecklenburg county (Virginia) Sir Peyton Skipwith, Bart. in the 72d year of his age.

Issue of October 26, 1805

Died, at St. Helena, on the 9th inst., Ann Caroline Edwards, aged 13 years, second daughter of James Edwards, late of Charleston.

On Thursday morning, the 24th inst.,departed this life Miss Anna Maria Adams, in the 22d year of her age...native of England, resided in this city about 10 years....

Issue of October 28, 1805

Married, on Saturday evening last, by the Rev. Dr. O'Gallagher, Mr. John Laffont, to the amiable Miss Maria Louisa Gonse, both of this city.

Died on Thursday the 17th inst., at Columbia, in the 53d year of his age, Major Joshua Benson, an old and respectable inhabitant of that place.

Died at Rocky-Mount, on the Catawba river, on the 6th ult., Francis Mentges...a native of Deaux-Ponts, in German Zweybrucker, now belonging to the French empire.

Departed this life, on the 3d inst., George Freaser, at New-Castle county, Delaware. Mrs. Fraser his widow, has brothers living in Charleston, S. C.

Died at Camp Claiborne, New-Orleans, Dr. Hall, a surgeon's mate.

Died at Leonard-Town (Md.) On Wed. the 9th inst., Samuel

Jameson Maginnis, the Puppett-shew man, in the 33d year of his age....

Issue of October 29, 1805

Died, at Savannah, on the 23d inst., Mr. John Bowmar, a native of England.

Issue of October 30, 1805

Died, on the 15th inst., at Town Creek Mills, S. C., Mr. William Williamson, aged 28 years, the youngest and only surviving son of the late Brig.-Gen. Andrew Williamson, of this state.

Died at Georgetown, on the 22d inst., Mr. William K. Clark, merchant, a native of Connecticut, but for several years past a resident of that town.

Died at Savannah on the 15th inst., Mr. James Johnston, Pilot, a native of Weathersfield, Conn.

Issue of October 31, 1805

Married this morning, by the Rev. Mr. Munds, Mr. Peter Lawrence Jumelle, to Miss Ann Margaret Eckhart, both of this city.

Married at Curracoa, on the 1st of Sept., Captain Thomas Jervey, of this city, to Miss Poligne Changuion, eldest daughter of the Gov. of that place.

Died on Monday evening, the 28th inst., Mr. Archibald Whaley, aged 21 years, son of the late Thomas Whaley, of this city, decd. ...

Issue of November 1, 1805

Died in Savannah, on the 23d ult., Mr. Gideon Seaman, aged 36 years...a native of Long Island, state of New-York.

Died in Savannah, on the 24th inst, Master Major L. Pryor, aged 16 years, son of Mrs. Delphia Wilson....

Died in Savannah, on the 26th inst., Mr. John Smith, a native of England.

Died in Savannah, on the 28th inst., Mr. Wm. Berniwez, a native of Russia. On the same day, Mr. Henry Carson.

Issue of November 2, 1805

Married on Thursday evening, by the Rev. Mr. M'Calla, Mr. N. Hamblin, to Miss Maria Anderson, both of Christ Church parish.

Issue of November 4, 1805

Married on Sunday evening last, by the Rev. Dr. Hollinshead, Mr. Benjamin Wilkins Ruberry, to Miss Elizabeth Rhoda Badger, daughter of Mr. James Badger, all of this city.

Married on Thursday evening, the 24th ult., at Beaufort, by the Rev. Mr. Hicks, D. Archibald Campbell, jun. to Miss Sarah Crawford.

Departed this life on Saturday last, the 2d inst., on Edisto Island, Mrs. Ann S. Clark, consort of James Clark, Esq. of that place....

Died in this city, on Wednesday last, Mrs. Hannah Moultrie, widow of the late William Moultrie, jun. esq.

Issue of November 5, 1805

Married on Thursday evening last, by the Rev. Mr. Munds, Mr. William Brown, to Mrs. Elizabeth Luscomb, both of this place.
Died, on Saturday the 2d inst., in the 67th year of her age, Mrs. Sarah Minott....

Issue of November 6, 1805

Married on Sunday evening last, by the Rev. Mr. Munds, Mr. John Sharp to Miss Sarah Maria Long, both of this city.

Issue of November 8, 1805

Died in Sidmouth (Eng.) Dr. James Corrie, late of Liverpool, physican and F. R. S.

Issue of November 9, 1805

Married at Orangeburgh, on Tuesday evening last, by the Rev. Mr. O'Farrel, George Washington Potter, Esq. Merchant, of this city, to Miss Louisa Ann Lestargette, daughter of Lewis Lestarjette, Esq. of Orangeburgh.

Issue of November 12, 1805

Died in this city, on Sunday last, in the 44th year of his age, Benjamin Perry, Esq. of St. Paul's Parish.

Issue of November 13, 1805

Died, on Sunday last, Miss Caroline Edwards, in the 14th year of her age....

Issue of November 14, 1805

Married on the 7th inst., in St. Stephen's, by the Rev. Mr. O'Farrel, Capt. Peter Gaillard, Sen. of St. John's, to Mrs. Ann Stevens, daughter of capt. John Palmer, of St. Stephen's.

Issue of November 15, 1805

Died, in the City of Washington, on the 26th ult., Mr. Charles D. Hopkin, Comedian....

Issue of November 18, 1805

Died, in Abbeville District, on the 25th ult., in the 81st year of his age, Mr. Jahn Maxwell, an old and respectable inhabitant of that place.

Issue of November 19, 1805

Married on the 16t inst., by the Rev. Dr. Buist, Mr. Robert F. Livingston, Merchant, to Miss Margaretta M'Lean, both of this city.
Died on the 23d ult., Mr. Anthony Butler, of Edgefield District, left a wife and seven small children....

Issue of November 26, 1805

Died on Wednesday morning the 20th inst., in the 42d year of his age, Mr. James Burges, a native of Linlithgow, Scotland...

leaving a wife and only son.
    Died in St. Paul's Parish, on Friday morning last, Henry M. Evans, esq.... (lines)

Issue of November 28, 1805

Extract of a letter from the Rev. Frederick Joseph Wallace (sic, for Wallern), to Judge Waties, dated Dutch Fork, November 11, 1805.
"On the third day of October last, I attended, in one of my congregations, the funeral of Mrs. Margaret Sheely, a native of Germany, and fifty-three years a resident of this place. She departed this life in the ninety-fifth year of her age; and had been a widow these thirty years past. She had in all nine children, and in the course of her good old age, the happiness of seeing fifty-nine grandchildren, one hundred and seventy-one great grandchildren, and three great great grandchildren, besides those she never did see; all of them the issue of her only son and five daughters."

Issue of November 30, 1805

Married on Thursday evening by the Rev. Mr. Jenkins, Daniel C. Webb, Esq. to Miss Eliza Ann Ladson, daughter of Thomas Ladson, Esq. deceased.
    Married on Thursday evening last, by the Rev. Dr. Buist, Mr. Josiah Taylor, to Miss Mary Stiles Rivers, both of this city.

Issue of December 2, 1805

Married on the 28th ultimo, at the Rocks, Saint Stephen's Parish, by the Rev. Mr. O'Farrell, Mr. John Stoney, merchant of this city, to Miss Elizabeth Gaillard, eldest daughter of captain Peter Gaillard, of said parish.

Issue of December 3, 1805

Died at Monk's Corner, on Sunday evening last, Mrs. Mary Ohiver, consort of Mr. Peter Ohiver.
    Died, at his plantation, near Statesburgh, on the 11th ult., in the 68th year of his age, Mr. Anthony Lee....
    Died on the 21st inst., at his house near Cambridge, John Dunlap, Esq. attorney at law, a native of Laurens District....
    On Friday evening, Mr. Isaac Cohen, aged 70 years, fell downstairs, and died immediately.

Issue of December 4, 1805

Married this morning by the Rev. Dr. Hollinshead, Thomas Mathews, Esq. of White-Hall, John's Island, to Miss Harriet Edwards, of this city.

Issue of December 5, 1805

Married on the 2d inst., by the Rev. Mr. Mattin Detargny, Mr. Bernard Litzs, to Mrs. Mary Russel, both of St. James's Parish, Goose-Creek.

Issue of December 6, 1805

Married on Wednesday evening last, by the Rev. N. Bowen, James Brown, Esq. planter, to Miss Martha Hall Jervey.

Married on Wednesday evening, by the Rev. Mr. Mills, Mr. John Dixon, to Miss Mary Wilkinson, both of this city.

Died at Savannah, on Sunday last, James Todd, Esq., Cashier of the Philadelphia Bank, in the 40th year of his age....

Died at Savannah, on Sunday last, Mr. Peter Michael Joseph Mirault, a native of St. Domingo....

Issue of December 9, 1805

Married on Saturday evening last, by the Rev. Dr. Buist, Mr. John Liddle, deputy-inspector of the customs, to Mrs. Roach, both of this city.

Issue of December 10, 1805

Married on the 7th inst., by the Rev. Mr. Munds, Mr. George Lusher, to Miss Sarah Mills, both of this city.

Died on the 3d inst., at Columbia, in the 69th year of his age, Capt. Benjamin Hicks, Messenger to the Senate of this State.

Issue of December 12, 1805

Married on Tuesday evening, by the Rev. Dr. Hollinshead, Wilmot S. Gibbes, Esq. to Miss Anna Frances Desaussure, daughter of Henry W. Desaussure, esq.

Married on Thursday evening last, by the Rev. H. Fraser, Mr. Henry B. Toomer, to Miss Elizabeth C. Shackelford, of Georgetown.

Issue of December 16, 1805

Married on Saturday evening last, by the Rev. Dr. Gallagher, Mr. James Decempt, late inhabitant of St. Domingo, to Miss Laura Prieur, youngest daughter of the late Mr. Prieur, respectable inhabitant of said Island.

Issue of December 17, 1805

Died on the 16th of October last, in Union District, Mr. William Williams, late of this city, house-carpenter.

Died in Savannah, on the 7th inst., Mr. Nathaniel Greene, planter, of S. C., aged 50 years. He was a native of Rhode-Island.

Issue of December 18, 1805

Married, last evening, by the Rev. Dr. Gallagher, Mr. T. Laimalbe Pezan, to Miss Sophie Hebert, both of Capt Nichola Mole, Island of St. Domingo.

Married last evening, by the Rev. Dr. Gallagher, Mr. Francois Cormier, to Miss Marie Gospard, both of Cape Nichola Mole, Island of St. Domingo.

Issue of December 20, 1805

Married last evening, by the Rev. Dr. Keith, Mr. E. S. Thomas, to Miss Ann Fonerden, youngest daughter of Adam Fonerden, Esq. of Baltimore.

Married last evening, by the Rev. Dr. Jenkins, Percival Edward Vaux, esq. planter, of Waccamaw, to Miss Richards, of this city.

Departed this life on the 16th inst., in the 9th year of his age, Master Robert Chambers. (lines)

Issue of December 21, 1805

Married on Thursday evening, by the Rev. Mr. Pogson, the Hon. William Loughton Smith, to Miss Charlotte Wragg, daughter of the late Wm. Wragg, Esq. of Ashley Barony.

Issue of December 23, 1805

Married on Saturday last, at the Grove, Christ Church parish, by the Rev. Mr. M'Calla, Mr. Thomas Rodick, to Miss Hamilton, both of the above parish.
Died at Chyhaw, St. Bartholomew's Parish, in the 32d year of his age, William Skirving, jun. Esq.

Issue of December 27, 1805

Died on the 29th Sept. last, in Petersborough, Northamphshire, (Eng.) Roger Pinckney, jun. in the 14th year of his age, eldest son of Roger Pinckney, Esq. planter, of St. Thomas's parish.
Married on Wednesday evening last, by the Rev. Dr. Jenkins, Dr. Frederick Dalcho, to Miss Mary Eliza Threadcraft.

Issue of December 31, 1805

Married in Prussia, Prince Ferdinand, aged 50, to the Princess, daughter of the late Margrave Charles De Schwedt.
Died, in Paris, M. Pleville Lepelly, Member of the Conservative Senate, aged 80....
Died, in Russia, Count N. Surow....
Died in Germany, the Baron De Bamlel....
Died in Gallicia, the Austrian General Weyrotter....

Issue of January 2, 1806

Married on Tuesday evening, by the Rev. Dr. Jenkins, John L. North, Esq. to Miss Eliza E. Drayton, eldest daughter of Glen Drayton, esq. deceased.
Married on James Island, on Tuesday evening, last by the Rev. Mr. Price, Mr. James Maguier, of this city, to Miss Emily Barrett, of James Island.
Died in this city, on the 28th ult., Mrs. Mary Cleapor, consort of Mr. Charles Cleapor, sail-maker, in the 30th year of her age...left a disconsolate husband and four daughters...buried in St. Philip's Churchyard....

Issue of January 3, 1806

Married, last evening, by the Rev. Mr. Hollinshead, Benjamin Smith, esq. to Miss North, youngest daughter of Edward North, Esq. deceased.
Died in October last, near Dublin, Dean Kirwan, a celebrated Preacher.

Issue of January 4, 1806

Married on Thursday last, by the Rev. Dr. Furman, the Rev. Mathew M'Cullers, of St. James' parish, Goose-creek, to Miss Jane Reddall, of the same place.

Issue of January 7, 1806

Died on the 21st ult., at his plantation in M'Intosh co., Georgia, in the 49th year of his age, Major Lachlan M'Intosh....

Issue of January 8, 1806

Married last evening, by the Rev. Dr. Furman, Mr. William James Berrie, of Combahee, to Miss Sarah Swindersine, of this city.

Issue of January 9, 1806

Married on Thursday the 26th of December last, at Hollow Creek, the upper part of Saluda, Mr. George Eberley Kelly, of this city, to Miss Mary Kelly, of Saluda.
Died, lately in Scotland, a man named Joice, aged 82....

Issue of January 10, 1806

Died at Long-Island (Bahamas), on the 18th ult., Mr. David Workman, of Nassau, N. P., merchant, aged 27 years.
Died, at Nassau, N. P., on the 27th ult., Capt. Robert Wilson, of the ship Diana.

Issue of January 11, 1806

Married on Thursday evening, by the Rev. Dr. Furman, Mr. Nathaniel Cohin, to Miss Christiana Browers, both of this city.
Married, last evening, by the Rev. Mr. Munds, Capt. Robert Fletcher, to Miss Hannah Macleod, both of this city.
Married, last evening, by the Rev. Mr. Munds, Mr. George Grant, to Miss Elizabeth Sinclair, both of this city.

Issue of January 13, 1806

Married, on Saturday evening last, by the Rev. Dr. Hollinshead, Mr. James Grantt, printer, to Miss Cynthia Loveless Snead, both of this city.

Issue of January 14, 1806

Died on Monday evening, the 30th ult., at his plantation near Augusta, in the 84th year of his age, Col. William Mead, for upwards of 20 years an inhabitant of that state. Col. Mead was a native of Virginia, and resided in Bedford county in that state (where he acted as High Sheriff, and commanded a regiment of militia) before his removal to Ga....

Issue of January 15, 1806

Married last evening, by the Rev. Dr. Hollinshead, Dr. Nathaniel H. Rhodes, to Miss Mary Hamilton, daughter of his Excellency Paul Hamilton.
Married, last evening, by the Rev. Le Mercier, of the Roman Catholic Church of this city, Mr. Pierre Dile', to Mrs. Eugenie Magniant Simonet, widow of the late Stephen Simoner, of this city.
Married on Tuesday, the 7th Jan., by the Rev. Dr. Furman, Mr. William Alstine, to Mrs. Rachel Cooper, both of this city.
Died, on the 20th ult., on board the sloop Frederick, on her passage from Norfolk to this port, the Rev. Joseph Washburn, of Farmington, Connecticut.

Issue of January 24, 1806

Died in this city, on the 21st inst., in the 23d year of his age, Peter Robert Witten, of St. John's Parish, Planter, and Lt.

in the 30th Regiment.
    Died at Jamesville, on the 10th inst., Mr. Samuel Moore, aged 27 years.

Issue of January 25, 1806

    Died, in this city, on Wednesday morning last, Mr. James Roddick aged 25 years.
    Died, at New-Orleans, on the 18th ult., Mrs. Lucy Brown, relict of Wm. Brown, Esq. Collector of that port.

Issue of January 27, 1806

    Married on Thursday evening last, by the Rev. Mr. Munds, Captain Joshua Rogers, to Miss Eliza Maria Ashman.
    Married on Friday evening, Mr. George Darley, to Mrs. Isabella Londay.
    Married on Saturday evening, Mr. Isaac Jones, to Miss Margaret Lowe.

Issue January 29, 1806

    Died, at Amherst (N. H.) widow Hannah Lovejoy, aged 101....

Issue of January 30, 1806

    Died at Goree (Africa) in December last, Mr. Hast. Handy, formerly of the Eastern shore of Maryland.

Issue of February 4, 1806

    Married on Wednesday the 29th ult., by the Rev. Dr. Hollinshead, Mr. Jeremiah Crowell, to Miss Sarah Dewers, both of this city.
    On Saturday the 1st inst., in her 40th year, Mrs. Eliza Gibbes, consort of William Hasell Gibbes, Esq....
    Died at Nassau, N. P., on the 9th ult., Mrs. Anne Lord, wife of Benjamin Lord, Esq. aged 66 years...married to Mr. Lord in this city in 1759 by the late bishop Smith, left a number of children and grandchildren.

Issue of February 5, 1806

    Married on Saturday evening last, by the Rev. Dr. Hollinshead, Mr. Jacob Gottfried Dieckert, of this city, to Mrs. Rebecca Whitesides, of Christ Church Parish.

Issue of February 6, 1806

    Died on the 5th of October last, in the Rio Pongus, Africa, Mr. John Watson, late Super-cargo of the schooner Doris, of this port, and a native of Carlise, in England....
    Died on Monday last, in the 18th year of her age, Miss Mary Ash Pearsons, of Boston.

Issue of February 10, 1806

    Married on Saturday evening last, by the Rev. Mr. Jenkins, Dr. William Burgoyne, to Miss Eliza Moser.
    Married last evening, on James Island by the Rev. Mr. Price, Mr. Thomas Rivers, to Miss Eliza M'Kinney.

Issue of February 11, 1806

Married on Saturday evening last, capt. John Warren, to Mrs. Elizabeth Hearkley, both of this city.
Married on Sunday evening last, by the Rev. Dr. Hollinshead, capt. William Newton, to Miss Ann Minott.
Died on Sunday evening, Mrs. Jane Parsons, aged 23 years.

Issue of February 13, 1806

Married on Tuesday evening, by the Rev. Mr. Bowen, Mr. James Fowler to Miss Mary Eliza Hart, both of this city.
Died, yesterday morning, Mrs. Bachelier, wife of Mr. Thomas Bachelier, senior, merchant....

Issue of February 14, 1806

Married on Tuesday the 28th ult., by the Rev. Mr. Hunter, William Edward Hayne, Esq. of York district, in this state, to Miss Eloisa Davidson Brevard, of Lincoln county, North-Carolina.
Died on the 9th of January last, Miss Ann Richards, aged 34 years, sister to Mr. William Richards, merchant, at his house in Pendleton district....
Died at his plantation on Combahee, in St. Bartholomew's parish, on the 24th of Jan. last, William Berrie, Sen. aged 73 years.
Died at his plantation near Savannah, on Saturday the 1st inst., Mr. Robert Dillon, at the advanced age of 74 years....a native of Ireland, formerly a resident of this city.

Issue of February 15, 1806

Died on the 5th inst., in St. John's Parish, Miss Ann Sample, in the 17th year of her age....(lines)

Issue of February 17, 1806

Died, on Thursday last, Mr. Peter N. G. Toutain, aged 44 years, a native of Rouen, in France....

Issue of February 18, 1806

Married last evening, by the Rev. Dr. Furman, Mr. Charles Lawrence, Factor, to Miss Sarah C. Yates, both of this city.
Married on Thursday last, by the Rev. Dr. Hollinshead, Mr. James Washington Brandt, to Miss Mary W. Pepper, of Christ Church Parish.
, Married on Saturday evening, by the Rev. Mr. Munds, Mr. Lewis Harper, to Miss Charlotte Chambers.
Married on Sunday evening, by the Rev. Mr. Munds, Mr. Peter Marley to Miss Laney Thompson.
Married on Sunday evening, by the Rev. Mr. Munds, Mr. George Scott, to Miss Mary Cook.

Issue of February 19, 1806

Married, last evening, by the Rev. Dr. Keith, Mr. William S. Bennet, to Miss Ann Theus, both of this city.

Issue of February 21, 1806

Married last evening, by the Rev. Mr. Johnson, Mr. Nathaniel Slawson, to Mrs. Dorothea M. Luscombe.

Married last evening, by the Rev. Dr. Jenkins, Mr. Timothy Sullivan, to Miss Mary Hamilton, both of this city.

Died in childbed, at her family residence on the river Pee Dee, in the 32d year of her age, on Wednesday the 5th inst., Mrs. Lucia Campbell, consort of Robert Campbell, esq....

Issue of February 22, 1806

Married on Monday evening last, by the Rev. Dr. Jenkins, Mr. Peter Artman, to Miss Margaret C. Hauser, both of this city.

Married, last evening, by the Rev. Mr. Caple, Mr. Daniel Benoist, to Miss Catharine Adams, both of this city.

Married last evening, by the Rev. Mr. Munds, Captain Joshua Irwin, to Miss Rosanna Mary Bland, both of this place.

Latedly died at an obscure lodging, at White Chapel, in England, aged 81, Richard Weston. His room had not been cleaned for 55 years!

Issue of February 24, 1806

Died on the 16th inst., at his plantation on the Horse Shoe Major William Clay Snipes, in the 64th year of his age...in the rev. war....

Issue of February 25, 1806

Died, in Savannah, on the 20th inst., Brig. General Lachlan M'Intosh, aged 80 years...one of the first settlers of Georgia, and an old revolutionary officer.

Issue of February 26, 1806

Married on Thursday last, Mr. Nathaniel Lee, aged 78 years (after being three times married, and having 11 children, 49 grandchildren, and 10 great grandchildren) to Miss Elizabeth Tucker, aged 25 years, both of Prince George County.
                                                    Virginia paper.

Issue of February 28, 1806

Married in Christ Church parish, on Wednesday last, by the Rev. Daniel M'Calla, Dr. David Jervey, to Miss Sarah Capers, daughter of Gabriel Capers, esq. deceased.

Married on Sunday evening last, by the Rev. Dr. Hollinshead, Mr. Barnard Farrol, to Miss Elizabeth Phillips.

Issue of March 1, 1806

Married, on Thursday evening, by the Rev. Mr. Bowen, Dr. George Hall, to Miss Ann Dawson, daughter of John Dawson, Esq.

Issue of March 3, 1806

Married on Sunday evening, by the Rev. Dr. Hollinshead, Mr. Magness Ohring, to Mrs. Catherine Louisa Brown, both of this city.

Married, at Savannah, on Monday evening, by the Rev. Mr. Clarkson, Mr. George Horlbeck, of this city, to Miss Catherine Bass, of the former place.

Issue of March 6, 1806

Married on Tuesday evening last, at colonel James Postell's, St. Luke's Parish, by the Rev. William B. Johnson, Mr. Othniel

John Giles, to Miss Rebecca Perry.

Issue of March 7, 1806

Married on Sunday evening last, by the Rev. Dr. Hollinshead, Mr. Christopher Jordon to Miss Eleanor Clark, both of this city.

Issue of March 8, 1806

Died, last night, capt. Rich. Harden Picket, formerly master of the ship Sisters, of this port.

Issue of March 11, 1806

Married on Wednesday evening last, the 5th instant, by the Rev. Mr. Le Mercier, Rector of the Roman Catholic Church of this city, Mr. Xavier Joseph Leroy, to Mrs. Julie Platon, widow of Lewis Mege.

Issue of March 13, 1806

Married on Tuesday evening last, by the Rev. Mr. Furman, Mr. John Porter, of Philadelphia, to Miss Eleanor Gray, daughter of Mr. Caleb Gray.

Died in London, in December last, in the 76th year of his age, Mr. King, a celebrated comedian.

Issue of March 17, 1806

Married on Saturday evening, by the Rev. Dr. Buist, Mr. Michael Kelly, to Miss Eliza Kennedy.

Died suddenly in Savannah, on Tuesday last, Madame Maria Pouyat, at the age of 21, consort of Monsieur John Francis Pouyat, both of St. Domingo.

Issue of March 19, 1806

Departed this life on the 9th inst., at his plantation in Fairfield district, Major Robert Ellison, in the 64th year of his age.

Issue of March 20, 1806

Married on Sunday evening last, on Edisto Island, Henry Bailey Esq. to Miss Sarah Beynard.

Died at Goose-Creek, on the 5th inst., in the 34th year of his age, Mr. Peter Tampley Fendin...left a wife and four small children....

Issue of March 21, 1806

Married, at Norfolk, by the Rev. Mr. Grigsby, Capt. Stephen Decatur Jun. of the U. S. Navy, to Miss Susan Wheeler, only daughter of Luke Wheeler, esq. Mayor of that borough.

Died in this city, on Tuesday the 18th inst., Capt. William Whitmarsh, of the ship Fame, of Wascasser...left a family in Charlestown, Mass.

Died on Wednesday last, Captain John Clastria, aged 56 years, a native of France....

Issue of March 22, 1806

Married on Tuesday evening, by the Rev. Mr. Pogson, Thomas P.

Chiffelle, Esq. to Miss Henrietta Ladson.
Died on Thursday the 13th inst., Mr. Eleazer Levi, aged 56 years...left a large family.

Issue of March 25, 1806

Married on Saturday the 22d inst., by the Rev. Dr. Jenkins, Capt. John Nervis, to Mrs. Ann Morriss.
Married in Georgetown, on Tuesday the 18th inst.,by the Rev. Mr. Hugh Fraser, Mr. Robert S. Hort, to Miss Sarah M. Vaux, daughter of William Vaux, Esq. deceased.

Issue of March 26, 1806

Died, yesterday morning, Mr. Cotton M. Stevens, aged 62 years.

Issue of March 29, 1806

Died on the 4th inst., in this city, Mr. John Barry, son of Mr. Thomas Barry, merchant of Albany, New-York.
Died at his house in Coosawhatchie, on the 16th inst., Mr. John Morgandollar, in the 55th year of his age.
Died at Georgetown, on Saturday last, Mrs. Mary Heriot, consort of William Heriot, Esq. in the 35th year of her age.
Died Mr. William Henry Lide, merchant, in the 38th year of his age.

Issue of March 31, 1806

Married on Saturday evening last, by the Rev. Dr. Hollinshead, John R. Mathews, Esq. to Mrs. Elizabeth Whaley.

Issue of April 1, 1806

Married on Thursday evening, the 6th of March last, in Wilmington, N. C. by Peter Maxwell, Esq. Mr. George Cross of that place, to Miss Rebecca Brookman, of this city.
Married on Sunday, the 30th of March, by the Rev. Phillip Matthews, Mr. David Dare, to Miss Ann Brookman, both of this city.
Died, at the City of Washington, on the 14th ult., John Pitman Lovell, Esq. master of the navy yard, and formerly commander of gun-boat Nora.

Issue of April 8, 1806

Married on Sunday evening last,by the Rev. Dr. Furman, Mr. Samuel J. Elliott, printer, to Mrs. Patience Wilcox, of Newport, R. I.
Married at Wadmalaw, on Thursday evening last, by the Rev. Dr. Mills, Mr. Thomas Richardson, merchant, to Miss Sarah Seabrook, daughter of John Seabrook, Esq.
Married at Cater Hall, in St. Peter's parish on Thursday, the 3d of April, by the Rev. Mr. Beck, James Jervis, Esq. Attorney at Law, to Miss Mary Postell, youngest daughter of capt. Andrew Postell, deceased, of Prince William's Parish.
Died in England, Sir Hyde Parker, and Alderman Skinner.

Issue of April 9, 1806

Married last evening, by the Rev. Dr. Furman, Mr. Julius Petsch, to Miss Jane Harriott Darby.

Died at Bermuda, on the 29th ult., Vice-Admiral Sir Andrew Mitchell, Bart.

Issue of April 10, 1806

Died on the 8th inst., at his Plantation, in Colleton District, in the 52d year of his age, Joseph Glover, Esq...left wife and six children. (lines)

Issue of April 11, 1806

Married on Wednesday evening last, by the Rev Mr. Mills, Major James Miles, to Miss Eliza Smith Miles, daughter of Robert Miles, Esq.

Savannah, April 9
Died at the city of Washington, on the 9th of March last, in the 50th year of his age, the Hon. James Jackson, a Senator from this State in the Senate of the U. S....(long account)

Issue of April 14, 1806

Married at Port Royal on the 2d of February last, by the Rev. Mr. Hadley, Mr. Felix M'Golrick, to Miss Eve C. Hauser, of this city.

Issue of April 15, 1806

Married on Sunday evening last, by the Rev. Mr. Bowen, Mr. William Milligan, ship-carpenter, to Miss Catherine M'Kenzie, both of this city.
Died at Frederick-town (Maryland) on the 26th ult., Mrs. Mary Humes, a native of Germany, aged 103 years....

Issue of April 16, 1806

Married, last evening, by the Rev. Mr. Mills, the Rev. Edmund Matthews of St. Andrew's Parish, to Miss Mary Ann Teasdale, eldest daughter of Isaac Teasdale, esq. of this city.
Died in Philadelphia, on the 29th ult., in the 57th year of his age, Jesse Waln, Esq. a respectable merchant....
At the same place, on the 31st ult., in the 42d year of his age, Mr. Elihu Palmer....

Issue of April 18, 1806

Died on Wednesday evening last, Mr. John Reid, aged 40 years, a native of Scotland, but had resided in this city upwards of 20 years....interred in the cemetery of the Presbyterian Church.

Issue of April 21, 1806

Married, last evening, by the Rev. Dr. Jenkins, Charles Lesesne, Esq. of Georgetown, to Miss Ann Eliza Sergeant, of this city.

Issue of April 22, 1806

Died on the 1st inst., Dr. William Dumont, about 61 years of age, a native of Mont Dasterac, province of Haute Guinne, in France, and resident in this state for about 12 years.
Died at Beaufort, on Thursday the 17th inst., Mrs. Sarah Grayson, widow of the late John Grayson, deceased, in the 73d year of her age....

Issue of April 23, 1806

Died at his plantation in Fairfield district, in this state, Mr. Turner Stark, aged 56 years, a native of Virginia...left wife and five children...in rev. war.

Issue of April 24, 1806

Married on Tuesday the 23d inst.,by the Rev. Dr. Keith, Doctor Thomas Stock, to Miss Jane Smith.

Issue of April 25, 1806

Died, yesterday morning, Mrs. Catharine West, aged 79 years, an old and respectable inhabitant of this city. This is the third member of the same family who has been summoned from hence within a month.
Died on Wednesday morning last, Mr. William Redlich, aged 42 years.
Died in the state of New-York, on the 10th inst., the Hon. Horatio Gates....

Issue of April 26, 1806

Departed this life, early this morning, John Duncan, jun., the youngest son of Mr. John Duncan, aged 23 years, 9 months, and 16 days....

Issue of April 28, 1806

Married, last evening, by the Rev. Mr. Bowen, Mr. Joseph Simmons, to Miss Elizabeth Morton, both of this city.
Died on Saturday last, the 26th inst., Mr. Thomas Carew, in the 38th year of his age...left widow and numerous relatives....
died on the 3d inst.,in the state of New-York, Richard Lee, Jun., proprietor of the celebrated Patent and Family medicines.
Died at Newburyport, Timothy Dexter, esq. commonly called Lord Dexter....

Issue of April 29, 1806

Died on the 22d inst., at Silk Hope Plantation, near Savannah, Mr. Robert Squibb, superintendant of the Botanic Garden near this city.
Died on Wednesday the 18th inst., at Newpost, the seat of Gen. Alexander Spotswood, in the state of Virginia, Capt. John A. Spotswood, late of the U. S. navy, aged 34 years.

Issue of April 30, 1806

Married on Monday evening, the 21st inst., by the Rev. Dr. Gallaghar, Monsieur Francois Tite Duboc, merchant from Havre de Grace, in France to Miss Sophie Leroy of St. Domingo.

Issue of May 1, 1806

Married, on Tuesday last, by the Rev. Dr. Hollinshead, Mr. William Clarkson, Jun. to Miss Esther Susannah Doar, both of this city.
died, at sea, on the 23d of Jan. last, on board the ship Diana, from this port for Africa, Capt. francis Elliott, formerly of the Schooner Belvidere, of this port...left a family in Portland, Mass.

Issue of May 2, 1806

Married yesterday morning, by the Rev. Dr. Keith, Mr. Sterling Edward Turner, to Miss Susan Ogier, eldest daughter of Lewis Ogier, esq.

Died, in Prince William's Parish, Beaufort district, on the 22d ult., Mr. John Harrison, long a resident in that parish, in the 53d year of his age...left wife and four children....

Died at Georgetown, on Monday last, Mrs. Mary Ann Lowson, consort of Captain John Lowson of that place.

Died at Philadelphia, on Tuesday the 15th ult., the Hon. Edward Shippen, in the 78th year of his age, late Chief Justice of the Supreme Court of Pa.

Issue of May 5, 1806

Married last evening, by the Rev. Mr. Faber, Mr. Christian Koehler, to Miss Margaret Riedfield, both of this city.

Married, at London, William Francis, Esq. of Charleston (South-Carolina) to Mrs. Richardson, widow of Long-Acre.

Issue of May 6, 1806

Married on Sunday evening last, by the Rev. Dr. Buist, Joseph Bellinger, Esq. to Miss Lucia Georgiana Bellinger, daughter of Dr. George Bellinger.

Issue of May 7, 1806

Married, last evening, by the Rev. Dr. Hollinshead, Langdon Cheves, Esq. to Miss Mary Elizabeth Bulles.

Died, this morning, Mr. Richard Wrainch, of the Carolina Coffee House....

Died on the 5th inst., at his plantation at Goose-Creek, Mr. Robert M'Kenzie Johnston.

Died at Washington on the 21st ult., Doctor Starling Archer, late of the navy, aged 24 years...duel on the 17th ult....

Died at Burlington (Ver.) Col. Ebenezer Allen, aged 64 years....Green Mountain Boys....

Issue of May 9, 1806

Married, at Camden, on Sunday evening last, by the Rev. Mr. Flin, Mr. James K. Douglas, merchant, to Miss Mary Martin, daughter of the late Dr. James Martin.

Married, at Camden on the same evening, by the Rev. Mr. Flin, Abraham Blanding, Esq. Attorney at Law, to Miss Elizabeth P. Martin, daughter of the late Dr. James Martin.

Issue of May 10, 1806

Married at Beaufort, on Thursday the 1st inst., by the Rev. Joseph E. Cook, Samuel Reed, Esq. merchant, formerly of Boston, to Miss Eliza Mary Dopson, of Beaufort.

Issue of May 13, 1806

Married at Orangeburgh, on Sunday evening, the 4th inst., by the Rev. Mr. O'Farrell, Mr. John Vinyard, to Miss Eliza Elliott Lestargette, daughter of Lewis Lestargette, Esq.

Married, on the 4th inst., William Nibbs, Esq. of Cambridge, Attorney at Law, to Miss Mary Mims, of Edgefield district.

Married in Newberry district, on Thursday the 1st May, Mr.

James Fifer (?), planter, to Miss Cary Glover, both of said district.
  Died on Sunday evening, the 11th inst., Mr. Nathaniel Cohen, a native of Pennsylvania, aged 23 years....
  Died on the 5th inst., on Santee, in the 44th year of her age, Mrs. Mary Patterson, consort of Mr. William Patterson....

Issue of May 14, 1806

  Married, on Saturday evening, by the Rev. Dr. Jenkins, Mr. John Whiting, to Miss Jane Willis, both of this city.

Issue of May 15, 1806

  Married on Tuesday evening last, Ralph Bailey, Esq. to Miss Sarah Jenkins, both of Edisto-island.

Issue of May 17, 1806

  Married on Thursday evening last, by the Rev. Dr. Jenkins, William Chaplin Fripp, Esq. to Miss Eliza Hann Edwards, eldest daughter of James Edwards, Esq. both of St. Helena Island.
  Married on Thursday evening last, by the Rev. Dr. Hollinshead, capt. Henry Leslie, to Miss Ann P. Bingley.
  Died in this city, on the morning of the 15th inst., Joseph Legare, Esq. of St. James's Santee, aged 64 years....
  Died at Islington, on Thursday the 8th inst., Mr. John Wershing, in the 32d year of his age...left father and mother....
  Drowned in Savannah River, opposite that city, on Sunday the 11th inst., Mr. Henry Jeffers, bricklayer, formerly of Billrica, Middlesix county, Mass.

Issue of May 19, 1806

  Married on Saturday evening last, by the Rev. Dr. Buist, Capt. John Thomas Crout, to Mrs. Susannah Woodall, both of this city.
  Married on Friday evening last, by the Rev. Dr. Jenkins, Richard W. Cogdell, Esq. to Miss Cecile Langlois, both of this city.
  Married on Saturday evening last, by the Rev. Mr. Munds, Captain Philip Drayton to Miss Catharine Moss.
  Married, last evening, by the Rev. Mr. Munds, Mr. Alexander Gregory, to Miss Henrietta Moore.

Issue of May 20, 1806

  Died on Saturday last, Capt. John Legare, in the 24th year of his age...left a mother....
  Died on Saturday night last, the 17th inst., at Beaufort, Mr. James Black, Ship-Wright, late of Charleston.

Issue of May 21, 1806

  Died on the 6th of Nov. last, at Stone-haven, in the North of Scotland, William Beattie, Esq. of Midseat, late merchant of Petersburgh, Virginia.

Issue of May 22, 1806

  Died on Tuesday the 20th inst., Mr. Ronald Anderson, late of Kingston, Jamaica.

Issue of May 23, 1806

Married at St. Andrew's Parish, on the 5th of Jan. last, by the Rev. Thomas Mills, Mr. Joseph Alexander, to Miss Sarah Findley, both of this city.

Died, at his plantation, in St. Bartholomew's parish, on the 19th inst., Jacob Walter, Esq. aged 56 years.

Died on Saturday the 10th inst., at Barnwell Court-House, in this state, Mr. George Latham. He was about 35 years of age, a native of Virginia, and for a number of years past an inhabitant of Barnwell district....

Died in Philadelphia, on Thursday the 8th inst., Robert Morris, Esq....in the rev. war.

Issue of May 24, 1806

Married on Friday evening last, by the Rev. Mr. Munds, Mr. Jeremiah Ross, to Miss Charlotte Maria Roberts.

Married last evening, by the Rev. Mr. Munds, Mr. John William Morton, to Mrs. Hannah M'Leod.

Issue of May 26, 1806

Died in New-York, on the 16th inst., James Watson, Esq. a patriot of the revolution.

Died at Havana, on the 23d ult., Nathaniel Fellows, Esq. of Boston....

Issue of May 28, 1806

Married on Thursday evening last, by the Rev. Mr. Bowen, John Stock, Esq. to Miss Ann Chiffell.

Married on Monday the 26th inst., by the Rev. Dr. Jenkins, Mr. Josiah Sturgis Lovell, to Miss Hannah Frances Poinsett, daughter of the late Mr. Joel Poinsett, of this place.

Issue of May 30, 1806

Married last evening, by the Rev. Dr. Hollinshead, Captain John Bonnell, to Miss Mary Ann Yates, both of this city.

Married last evening, by the Rev. Dr. Hollinshead, Mr. William Austin Jun. to Miss Susannah Ellsworth, both of this city.

Died on Tuesday last, in the 25th year of her age, Mrs. Marie Elizabeth Francoise Emerie Le Compte, wife of Jean Jacques Heulan, of St. Domingo.

Issue of May 31, 1806

Married on Thursday evening last, by the Rev. Mr. Munds, Capt. William Nelson, to Miss Catherine Darley.

Issue of June 3, 1806

Died on Friday last, Captain Joseph Doane, aged 45 years.

Issue of June 4, 1806

Married on Sunday evening last, by the Rev. Mr. Munds, Mr. John Steele(?) to Miss Sarah Holmes both of this city.

Died at Camden on Tuesday the 27th ult., Mrs. Margaret Alexander, wife of Dr. Isaac Alexander, in the 45th year of her age.

Issue of June 9, 1806

Married on Sunday evening last, by the Rev. Mr. Munds, Mr. Thomas Elswood, to Mrs. Susannah M'Niel, both of this city.

Issue of June 10, 1806

Departed this life on Sunday night last, Mrs. Martha Dorman, in the 35th year of her age.

Issue of June 16, 1806

Married on Sunday evening the 1st inst.,by the Rev. Samuel Marsh, Charles Martin, June. Esq. Attorney at Law, to Miss Joyse Jane Scott, both of Edgefield District.
Died on Wednesday last, at his plantation at Ashepoo, Benjamin Webb, Esq.

Issue of June 20, 1806

Died, yesterday morning, Mr. Joseph Hopkins Jones, aged 23 years and 6 months.
Departed this life on the 1st of April last, at Shark's Point, Congo River, African in the 34th year of his age, Captain Joseph Purcell....
Died at Richmond, on the 8th inst., George Wythe, Chancellor of Virginia....   Raleigh paper.

Issue of June 23, 1806

Died in Somers (Conn.) widow Mary Sexton, aged 91...midwife 55 years....
Died at New-Fairfield, Mass., on the 9th inst., Mr. John Cradshaw, who was born on Long Island, June 7, 1701. O. S. aged 104 years, 10 months and 20 days....

Issue of June 24, 1806

Married on Tuesday evening last, by the Rev. Dr. Gallagher, Mr. Andrew Modeste, to Miss Rosalie Bourg, both of St. Domingo.
Died at Parker's Ferry, on the 19th inst.,Mr. Samuel Byrd, in the 56th year of his age.
Died on the 18th inst., Mrs. Barbara M'Dowell, wife of John M'Dowell, merchant, aged 48 years.
Died at Wadmalaw, on Wednesday evening, the 18th inst., Mrs. Rachael Freeman, wife of Mr. James Freeman, aged 21 years and 9 months...left husband and two young children....

Issue of June 25, 1806

Married last evening, at the house of A. Motte, esq., by the Rev. Mr. Bowen, Abraham Crouch, Esq. of this city, to Miss Sophia Jane Withers, of Wilmington, N. C.
Married at Newport, R. I. on the 1st inst., by the Rev. Mr. Dehone, Dr. John P. Mann, to Mrs. Ann Robinson, widow of the late William R. Robinson.
Died yesterday, on Sullivan's Island, Mrs. Lydia Bradford, of this city.

Issue of June 26, 1806

Died at Sullivan's-Island, on Monday evening, the 23d inst., Mrs. Lydia Ann Bradford, a native of England...interred in the

Burial Ground of the Independent Church in Archdale-street....

Issue of June 27, 1806

Died in Savannah, on Wednesday the 18th inst., Mrs. Rebecca White, in the 59th year of her age, relict of Thomas White, of South-Carolina.

Issue of July 1, 1806

Died on Friday last, at Dorchester, St. George's Parish, Miss Susan Garner, daughter of Melcher Garner, esq. deceased.

Issue of July 2, 1806

Died on Sunday morning, at Mr. John Cape's plantation, Daniel's island, Mr. Thomas Cape....
Died in London the 3d of May, Sir Richard Ford, chief magistrate of the police.

Issue of July 3, 1806

Married on Sunday evening last, in this city, by the Rev. Mr. Faber, Mr. John Scwartz, to Miss Mary Staker, both of this place.
Died in this city, last night, in the 26th year of his age, Mr. Andrew M'Farlan, Printer, joint proprietor of the Georgetown Gazette.
Died on Monday last, Mrs. Eliza S. Schirer, aged 21 years, the wife of Mr. John Schirer, gunsmith.

Issue of July 5, 1806

Married on Thursday the 3d July by the Rev. Mr. Faber, Mr. Nathaniel Green Welsh, bricklayer, to Miss Margaret Maria Hook, both of this city.

Issue of July 7, 1806

Married at Baltimore, on the 24th ult., Mr. Thomas Parker, merchant, of this city to Miss Rachel Wilkinson, of Baltimore.
Died on Friday night last, Mr. Charles M. Pickion, aged 28 years, Serjeant-Major of the Ancient Battalion of Artillery.

Issue of July 8, 1806

Married last night, Mr. Leonard Summet, Shoemaker, to Mrs. Sarah Redman.
Married at Beach Island, S. C. on Tuesday the 1st inst., by Walter Taylor esq. Mr. Daniel Neal, Jun to Miss Mary Nail, daughter of Mr. Casper Nail, of that place.
Married at Augusta, on Tuesday evening, the 1st inst., by the Rev. Mr. Cloud, Captain John Beale Barnes, of the U. S. Artillery, to Miss Mary Ann Douglas Hammond, of Augusta.
Died on Thursday the 3d inst., Mr. James Norris, in the 37th year of his age.

Issue of July 9, 1806

Married at Norfolk, on Tuesday evening, the 24th ult., by the Rev. Mr. Grisby, Mr. Reuben Coffin, to Miss Polly Butt, both of Norfolk.

Issue of July 11, 1806

Married last evening, by the Rev. Mr. Bowen, William S. Hasell, Esq. attorney at law, to Miss Elizabeth G. Tart, both of this county.
Married last evening, by the Rev. Dr. Jenkins, Lieut. Robert Roberts, of the U. S. Artillery, to Miss Harriet K. Mercer.
Died on Monday evening last, in childbirth, Mrs. Mary Middleton, in the 28th year of her age....left husband and three children....
Died in Savannah, on the 4th inst., Mrs. Margaret P. Dawson, in the 24th year of her age, a native of S. C., wife of Mr. John Dawson....
Died at Somers, Mass., on the 27th of April, Mrs. Mary Sexton...born in New-London in 1716, married at 18 years of age...midwife at birth of 3500 children.

Issue of July 14, 1806

Married on Saturday evening last, by the Rev. Mr. Munds, Mr. George Thomas M'Leod, to Miss Henrietta Campbell.
Died in Middlebury, Vermont, on the morning of the 11th ultimo, John B. Brown, aged 11 years....

Issue of July 15, 1806

Died at Syracuse, in Feb. last, Lieut. Joseph Naxwell, of the U. S. Navy.

Issue of July 16, 1806

Married near Camden, on Sunday evening, the 6th inst., by the Rev. Mr. Roberts, Stark Hunter, Esq. planter, to Miss Elizabeth Boykin, daughter of Burwell Boykin, esq. planter.
Died on the 6th of June on board the U. S. bomb-ketch Vengeance, Mr. Simon Smith, midshipman....a native of Rhode-Island.
Died at Syracuse, in April last, Lt. Seth Cartee, commander of Gun-Boat No. 10, a native of Rhode-Island and Mr. Brent, Midshipman, on board the U. S. cutter Hornet.

Issue of July 17, 1806

Married on Tuesday the 8th inst., on Santee, by the Rev. Mr. Raame, Dr. Philip Carolan, to Mrs. Mary Davis, both of that place.
Died in Bordeaux, on the 20th of April last, Mr. John Frederick Lesesne, aged 24 years....

Issue of July 18, 1806

Died on Wednesday last, Mr. Nicholas Delone, aged 72...a native of France....
Died in Savannah, on Saturday evening last, Capt. Thomas allen, commander of the Revenue Cutter, aged 40 years....left a widow and orphans.

Issue of July 19, 1806

Died on Tuesday last, the 15th inst., Mr. John Blair, aged 30 years, 5 months and 24 days...a native of Paisley in Scotland, and arrived in this city early in the year 1794....

Issue of July 21, 1806

    Died on Tuesday last, on John's Island, Mr. Henry Mills, aged 29 years...left a widow and infant son....

Issue of July 23, 1806

    Departed this life at Dover, in the state of Delaware, on the 5th inst., the Rev. Richard Whotcoat, one of the Bishops of the Methodist Episcopal Church.

Issue of July 25, 1806

    Died, suddenly, last night, aged 62 years, Mrs. Mary-Ann Scrieber Hall....
    Departed from the terrestrial abode, Mr. Charles G. Corre, aged 47 years a native of Germany...left a wife....

Issue of July 26, 1806

    Died at new-Orleans, on the 19th March last, Mr. Thomas Harvey, sail-maker, formerly of this place.

Issue of July 28, 1806

    Died on the 14th inst., capt. W. Tobler, of Beach-Island, South-Carolina, aged 36 years.
    Died in Barnwell District, on the 14th inst., Miss Matilda Gillett, aged 7 years, daughter of Dr. E. Gillett. And on the 11th inst., Miss Evelina Gillett, daughter of the same, in the 5th year of her age.
    Died at New-Orleans, on the 11th ult., Mr. Hugh Pollock, of the house of Pollock and Morgan, merchants of that city.
    Same day, Mr. Wm. J. Bealert....

Issue of July 29, 1806

    Died on the 23d instant, in the 34th year of her age, Mrs. Catherine Johnson, wife of Jabez W. Johnson, of this city....
    Died, yesterday, on Sullivan's Island, James Duncan, Esq., Attorney at Law.
    Died on the 5th inst., at his place in the township of Germantown, Pa., in the 68th year of his age, Major John Nice, of the revolution army.
    Died at Nassau, on Thursday the 17th inst., Mr. Powell, Surgeon of H. M. brig Port Mahon...also death of Mr. Conrad Coakley, son of Dr. Coackley....   Royal Gazette.

Issue of July 31, 1806

    Married in Columbia, on Tuesday evening, the 25th inst., by the Rev. Dr. Maxey, Mr. E. Hammond, Professor of the South-Carolina College, to Miss Catharine Fox Spann.
    Died on Tuesday evening, Barnard Elliot, Esq. left mother, wife and children....

Issue of August 1, 1806

    Died, at Beaufort, on Thursday the 23d ult., Mrs. Mary Verdier, wife of Mr. Alexander Verdier, merchant....

Issue of August 2, 1806

Died at Darien (Geo.) on the 22d ultimo, Dr. Charles F. Bartlett, a native of Rhode-Island, aged 40 years....left widow and three children.

Issue of August 4, 1806

Married at Wilmington, N. C., on Sunday the 27th ult., Mr. Michael Delaney of this city, to Miss Fanny Williams, of North Carolina.
Died yesterday, in the 53d year of her age, Mrs.Rebecca Theus, wife of Simeon Theus, esq....

Issue of August 6, 1806

Died on Thursday the 24th ult., in Chester district, in the 47th year of his age, Mr. Abraham Patterson, a native of Ireland.

Issue of August 7, 1806

Died last night, Mr. Jones, of the Theatre.

Issue of August 8, 1806

Married, last evening, by the Rev. Dr. Keith, Dr. Daniel Legare, to Miss Elizabeth Martha Jones, both of this city.
Married on Tuesday evening last, by the Rev. Mr. Munds, Mr. George William Lewis, to Miss Charlotte Payton.
Married on Tuesday evening last, by the Rev. Mr. Munds, cap=tain John Sherlock, to Miss Mary Dunscombe.
Died, in Prince William's Parish, on the 4th inst., in childbed, Mrs. Amarinthia Lowndes Lockwood (wife of Mr. Joshua Lockwood) in the 32d year of her age.
Departed this life, yesterday morning, Mrs. Mary Gasser, aged 70 years.
Died, yesterday afternoon, Captain John Rollins, a native of England, aged 40 years....
Died, yesterday morning, Mr. Jones, late of the Charleston Theatre....
Died at his plantation in Edgefield district, South-Carolina, on Monday the 28th July, Mr. Mason Mosely....murdered by a Negro ...information to be sent to William Mosely, living at Deer Savannah, Edgefield district on the road leading from Long-Cane to Charleston, S. C. 16 miles distant from Augusta in Georgia....
Died at Staten Island (state of New-York) on the 18th ult., John Miller, Esq. in the 48th year of his age...a native of England, for many years resident at Nassau, New-Providence....left widow and four children

Issue of August 9, 1806

Departed this life on the 2d inst.,Mr. Joseph Latham, aged 55 years....
Departed this life at Cuthbert-ville on Monday, the 4th inst., Master James Maine, aged 12 years and 6 months, youngest son of James Maine, Esq. decd....

Issue of August 11, 1806

Died on Wednesday last, Mrs. Margaret Holmes, aged 42 years and 6 months, wife of William Holmes, Esq. of this city.

Issue of August 12, 1806

Departed this transitory life on the 8th inst., Mrs. Eliza Geyer, consort of capt. John Geyer...left a family of eight children....

Issue of August 13, 1806

Married in Baltimore, on the 31st ult., Jacob Myers, Esq. of Georgetown, S. C. to Miss Miriam Etting, daughter of Mr. Solomon Etting, merchant.
Died on Sunday, the 10th inst., on Edisto Island, Ralph Bailey, Esq. aged 22 years and 10 months.

Issue of August 14, 1806

Married, on Saturday evening last, by the Rev. Dr. Galagher, Mr. Hermin Follin, to Miss Victoria Hebert, both of Cape Nicola Mole, Island of St. Domingo.
Suicide of Ashur Bennet, a Carpenter....

Issue of August 16, 1806

Married on Thursday evening, by the Rev. Dr. Gallaghar, Mr. Salem Roe to Miss Mary Dempsey, both of this city.
Died early this morning, Master William Joor, only son of Dr. Joor.
Died at New-Orleans, on the 3d July, Lieut. Josiah Taylor, of the 2d U. S. Regiment of Infantry....

Issue of August 18, 1806

Drowned in D'Oyley's Dock, John Drunckmoller....

Issue of August 19, 1806

Died on the 17th inst., Mrs. Eliza Quin, aged 40 years... left a disconsolate husband and a number of friends and relations.
Died on Sunday morning last, at the age of 31 years, Francis Lacroix, a native of the Province of Champaigne, in France....

Issue of August 21, 1806

Died on the 19th inst., Mrs. Henrietta Nelson, aged 43.
Died on Thursday the 7th inst., at his plantation in Fairfield Distirct, Major Thomas Starke, in the 59th year of his age....

Issue of August 23, 1806

Died on the 22d inst., Mr. Charles Homassek, merchant of this place, in the 49th year of his age.

Issue of August 25, 1806

Died on Tuesday the 19th inst., in the 40th year of his age, Mr. Nicholas Sprith.
Died on the 23d inst., Mrs. Henrietta Kempton, in the prime of life....

Issue of August 26, 1806

Married, last evening, by the Rev. Mr. Munds, Mr. William Morgan to Miss Sarah Parker.

Departed this transitory life, at his plantation on Hilton=Head Island, on the 13th inst., John Leacraft, Esq....

Issue of August 27, 1806

Died on Thursday the 21st inst., Mrs. Elizabeth Farro, a native of this city.
Died, yesterday, Mr. John Sweeny, of the house of Simmons & Sweeny, of this city.
Died on Sunday evening, the 24th inst., Mrs. Mary Martin, in the 39th year of her age.
Died on Thursday last, in the 35th year of her age, Mrs. Ann Cross, wife of Mr. M. W. Cross, of this city....

Issue of August 29, 1806

Departed this life on Thursday the 14th inst., in Beaufort, S. C., Master Charles Wilson Smith aged 6 years and 3 months, and Master William Penn Smith, aged 3 months, son of William Smith, esq....
Died at Belvidere, on Monday last, in the bloom of life, Miss Hannah Heyward Shubrick, third daughter of Col. Shubrick, in the 15th year of her age....
from the Philadelphia Daily Advertiser of the 16th inst. Died in this city on Tuesday the 11th of August, in the 42d year of his age, Jacob Drayton Esq. of Charleston, S. C.

Issue of August 30, 1806

Married at Newport, R. I. on the 8th inst., Mr. William A. Alston, to Miss Mary Young, both of South-Carolina.
Died, on the 6th inst., in the 41st year of her age, Mrs. Mary S. Smith, consort of Aaron Smith, esq. of South-Carolina, Barnwell District.

Issue of September 1, 1806

Married by the Rev. Mr. Munds, Mr. Thomas Hennon to Miss Catherine Martin, both of this place.
Married last Saturday by the Rev. Mr. Munds, Mr. Thomas William Shaw, to Miss Sarah Young, both of this place.
Died on Sullivan's Island, on Friday morning, the 29th of August, Mrs. Anne Geddes, wife of John Geddes, Esq., in the 18th year of her age....
Died, at Columbia, on Monday last, John James Haig, esq.
Died on Thursday the 21st inst., near Jamesville, Miss Mary Matilda Manning, in the 22d year of her age, eldest daughter of the late col. Manning....

Issue of September 3, 1806

Died on the 29th ult., in the 58th year of his age, Mr. John Combe....left widow and four children.
Died on Sullivan's Island, on Monday last, in the 29th year of his age, Mr. George Kirk, a native of England.
Died at his seat in Rocky Mount, South-Carolina, on the 24th ult., Col. Christian Senf, Chief Engineer to the State of S. C. ...in rev. war.
Died at Columbia, on the 28th ult.,Mr. John Drennon.

Issue of September 4, 1806

Married at Falmouth (Mass.) on the 21st ult., by the Rev. Mr.

Lincoln, Mr. David W. Gillison of South Carolina, to Miss Emmaan Swiff of that place.

Issue of September 8, 1806

Died, at her residence, near Orangeburgh, on Saturday, the 23d of August, in the 20th year of her age, Miss Ann Williams, daughter of the late Mr. Philip Williams, of that place.

Issue of September 9, 1806

Died on the 27th ult., at Henley, S. C., Miss Sarah Hull.
Died on Wednesday the 27th of August, at North-Island, near Georgetown, in the 16th year of her age, Miss Sarah Eliza Ramsay....

Issue of September 10, 1806

Married in this city, by the Rev. Mr. Bowen, Mr. Thomas M'Millan, to Miss Elizabeth Godfrey.
Departed this life on Monday the 8th inst., in the 23d year of her age, Miss Margaret Nixon, of this city.
Departed this life at Bath, in Buncomb county, North Carolina, on the 29th ult., in the 49th year of his age, Major Thomas Pasteur, of the U. S. army....

Issue of September 12, 1806

Departed this life on the 8th inst., at his plantation in St. John's parish, James Theus, Esq...left widow and two daughters....

Issue of September 13, 1806

Married on Thursday evening last, by the Rev. Mr. Munds, Mr. Peter Bowman, to Miss Mary Halliday.
Married on Thursday evening last, by the Rev. Mr. Munds, Mr. John D. Kirk, to Miss Ruth Webberly.

Issue of September 15, 1806

Departed this life on the 6th inst., in the 29th year of his age, Mr. John S.Chinners...left a widow and child.
Died at White-hill, near Orangeburgh, on Monday the 8th inst., Van-da-Vastine Jamison, second son of Dr. V. D. V. Jamison, aged 2 years and 8 months....

Issue of September 16, 1806

Died on Sunday evening last, Mr. William Bampfield Geyer, eldest son of Captain John Geyer, of this city.
Died, at Georgetown, on Thursday last, Mr. William Cuttino, a native of that place, near the close of the 59th year of his age.

Issue of September 17, 1806

Departed this life on the 12th inst., Mrs. Esther Gilchrist, wife of Adam Gilchrist, Esq....

Issue of September 18, 1806

Died, on Monday the 15th inst., in the 66th year of his age,

Thomas Radcliffe, Esq....

Issue of September 19, 1806

Died on Tuesday evening last, Miss Martha Prioleau, daughter of Samuel Prioleau, esq. decd....

Issue of September 20, 1806

Died on the 5th inst., at Coburg (Germany), Prince Lewis Charles Frederic, of Saxe Coburg...in his 53d year.

Issue of September 22, 1806

Married on Friday evening last, by the Rev. Mr. Munds, Mr. John Cook, to Miss Sarah Clement, both of this city.
Died, at Camden, on the 16th inst., Mr. William Hutchinson, merchant, in the 25th year of his age, a native of this state....

Issue of September 23, 1806

Married in this city, on the 16th inst., by the Rev. Dr. Hollinshead, Mr. Horatio Lincoln, to Miss Elizabeth Ann Darr.
Died on Wednesday night last, a few miles from Columbia, Captain James Taylor, for many years a respectable inhabitant of that district.
Departed this life on Friday the 15th inst., aged 54 years, Mrs. Jane Anderson, consort of Gen. Anderson, of Pendleton district....

Issue of September 24, 1806

Died in August last, at St. Ann's Bay (Jam.), Mr. James Scot, Jun., son of Mr. James Scot of this city....
Died at Cayenne, on the 5th of August last, in the 33d year of her age, Louisa Charlotte Marie Anne Angelique Tacquin, spouse of Mr. Victor Hughes...French Guinea.

Issue of September 26, 1806

Departed this life on Wednesday evening last, Mrs. Martha Brown, the wife of James Brown, esq. of Capers-Island, in the 19th year of her age...(lines)
Died at Georgetown, on the 18th inst., Mr. Joseph Clinton, shipwright, a native of Philadelphia, for several years an inhabitant of this town. Also on the 18th inst., Master Henry William Blyth Toomer, aged 5 years and 6 months, eldest son of Anthony Toomer, Esq.

Issue of September 29, 1806

Married last evening, by the Rev. Mr. Furman, Mr. Lewis Groning, merchant, to Miss Hannah Corn, both of this city.
Died, at New-Orleans, on the 22d ult., the Rev. Father Walsh, Vigar-General of Louisiana.

Issue of September 30, 1806

Died this morning, Guilliam Airsten, Esq., Cashier of the State Bank.

Issue of October 1, 1806

    Died on Thursday, the 25th ult., aged 30 years, Mr. Andrew Henrey, a native of Perthshire, Scotland....

Issue of October 2, 1806

    Married on Tuesday evening last, by the Rev. Mr. Munds, Capt. Edward Walker, to Miss Eliza Teasdale, both of this city.
    Died on Tuesday the 30th ult., Guilliam Aertsen, Esq. Cashier of the State Bank, in the 47th year of his age...native of Island of Sabe in the West-Indies....

Issue of October 4, 1806

    Married on Wednesday evening last, by the Rev. Mr. Munds, Capt. Joshua Duncan, of Baltimore, to Miss Elizabeth Brown, of this city.

Issue of October 6, 1806

    Died on Thursday last, Capt. Thomas Balantine, a native of Scotland, aged 35 years...left a widow....

Issue of October 7, 1806

    Departed this life, on the 5th inst., George Drennis, Jun. only son of Mr. George Drennis, of this city....

Issue of October 8, 1806

    Died on Monday last, Mrs. Barbara Kreitner, aged 73 years.
    Died at New-Orleans, on the 14th day of May last, Col. Frederick H. Baron de Weisseneels, aged 78 years...(account)

Issue of October 10, 1806

    Died on the 8th inst., Mrs. Maria Somarsall, consort of Thomas Somarsall, merchant, and only daughter of Col. Daniel Stevens.

Issue of October 11, 1806

    Died at Beaufort, last week, Mrs. Elizabeth Farr, relict of Thomas Farr, Esq. formerly of this city.

Issue of October 13, 1806

    Died on Saturday last, in the 51st year of her age, Mrs. Sarah Vincent Johnston, a native of this city....

Issue of October 14, 1806

    Died, at Camden, on Saturday the 4th inst.,Mr. Daniel Carpenter, in the 40th year of his age, leaving a wife and seven small children....

Issue of October 15, 1806

    Died on the 12th inst., in Christ Church Parish, in the 28th year of his age, Thomas James Barksdale, Esq. a member of the Legislature from that Parish, and a captain in the 30th regt. of militia.

Issue of October 18, 1806

Married on the 2d inst., at New-York, Lt. Ralph Izard, of the U. S. Navy, to Miss Elizabeth Middleton, both of S. C.

Issue of October 21, 1806

Died on Sunday the 12th inst., in this city, Mr. John Howard, a native of Pennsylvania, in the 63d year of his age....resided in Charleston upwards of 20 years.

Issue of October 23, 1806

Married on Thursday the 9th inst., by Robert Hinchinsen, Esq., Mr. James Park, to Miss Rachel Brown, eldest daughter of Dr. James Brown, both of Laurens District.

Issue of October 24, 1806

Died on Wednesday last, the 22d inst., in the 38th year of his age, Mr. Samuel Ham...native of New Hampshire, came to this state 17 years ago....(eulogy)

Issue of October 25, 1806

Died at Bob Savannah, on the 22d ult., Philip Givhan, Esq. in the 59th year of his age.

Issue of October 27, 1806

Married on Saturday evening last, by Dr. Hollinshead, John Walton, Esq. to Miss Elizabeth Wyly, both of this city.

Issue of October 29, 1806

Married at Black Swamp on Thursday evening last, by the Rev. Mr. Alexander Scott, Mr. Grimball Robert, of thatplace, to Miss Eliza T. Cook, of Barnwell.
Died on Sunday morning last, Mrs. Margaret Welsh, wife of Nathaniel Greene Welsh, of this city....
Died on Friday last, at his house in Hampstead, Mr. Thomas Stewart, many years a respectable merchant of this city.

Issue of October 31, 1806

Married last evening by the Rev. Mr.Bowen, John S. Bee, to Miss Charlotte A. Ladson, daughter of Major J. Ladson.
Died at Augusta, Georgia, on the 25th Sept., while on a journey to the Upper Country, Ralph Emms Elliott, Esq. of Beaufort, S. C. in the 43d year of his age.
Died on the 28th ult., Mr. David Watson Turner, a native of England, aged 58 years.

Issue of November 1, 1806

Married on Thursday evening last, by the Rev. Mr. Bowen, William R. Theus, Esq. of Georgetown (S. C.) to Miss Eliza Love Lenud, of this city.

Issue of November 3, 1806

Married at Camden, on the 33th (sic) ult. by the Rev. Mr. Flinn, Mr. John M'Caa, merchant, to Mrs. Rebecca Brown, youngest daughter of Col. Joseph Kershaw, deceased.

Issue of November 4, 1806

Died, in Newburyport, Mr. Timothy Dexter, in the 60th year of his age--self-styled "Lord Dexter, first in the East."

Issue of November 6, 1806

Departed this life on Friday last, the 31st ult., in the 22d year of his age, Mr. Andrew Carman, cabinet-maker....

Issue of November 7, 1806

Married on Thursday evening last, by the Rev. Mr. Faber, Mr. William G. Faber, to Miss Catharine Clark, both of this city.
Married at Newport, R. I., on the 15th ult., Mr. Francis Marian, Jun. of South-Carolina, to Miss Maria Peirce, of Newport.
Died in this city on the 28th Oct. last, Mr. William M'Callister Turner, in the 31st year of his age...left an aged mother. interred in the Presbyterian burial ground, attended by the Charleston Light Infantry....
Died at Penobscot Bay, 1st September last, Mr. John Walton, aged 106....

Issue of November 8, 1806

Died on the 11th ult. at Albany, in the state of New-York (While of a journey for his health) Isaac Mazyck, Esq. late of this state.

Issue of November 11, 1806

Married on the 9th inst., by the Rev. Dr. Buist, Mr. Robert Swan, to Mrs. Hannah Johnson, both of this city.

Issue of November 12, 1806

Married on Monday evening last, by the Rev. Dr. Hollinshead, John S. Cogdell, Esq. to Miss Maria Gilchrist, daughter of Adam Gilchrist, Esq. both of this city.

Issue of November 13, 1806

Married on Tuesday evening last, by the Rev. Mr. Munds, Mr. George Hamilton to Miss Rachel Morgan, both of this place.
Married on Tuesday evening last, by the Rev. Mr. Munds, Capt. William Peter Lewis of Baltimore, to Miss Susannah Mary Mashaw, of this place.
Died on the 7th inst., Mrs. Martha Cameron, aged 60 years....
Died in this city, on Thurdsday last, Mrs. Elizabeth Thomas, wife of Edward Thomas, esq....

Issue of November 14, 1806

Died on the 6th inst., Mrs. Mary L. Hunter, widow of the late Capt. Thomas Hunter.
Died in this city on the 6th inst., at an advanced age, Mrs. Elizabeth Neyle, formerly of Exeter on Devon, England....
Died at the High Hills of Santee, on the 26th ult., Miss Elizabeth Caldwell, and on the 28th ult in Orangeburgh district, her elder sister Mrs. Harriot Jones....

Died at his seat in Rockingham County, Va., on the 18th ult., the venerable Gabriel Jones, Esq. in the 85th year of his age....

Issue of November 15, 1806

Died this morning Captain James Payne, Commander of the Revenue Cutter of this state.

Issue of November 17, 1806

Married on Saturday the 15th inst., by the Rev. Dr. Buist, Mr. John Fair, to Miss Catharine Miller.

Departed this transitory life on the 24th day of October last, Mrs. Mary Gunn, consort of Mr. Willaim Gunn, of this city, aged 48 years...born in the city of London, resided in this city 17 years....

Issue of November 18, 1806

Died on the 24th of September last, in Abbeville District, Timothy Parson, Esq. of Wiscasset, District of Maine, aged 58 years.

Died on the 27th of July last, at John's island, Miss Elizabeth Harriet Parsons, aged 6 months, and 23 days, only daughter of Mr. Joseph Parsons, of this city.

Issue of November 21, 1806

Married last evening, by the Rev. Mr. Munds, Mr. Thomas F. Quin, to Miss Mary Elizabeth Gready, both of this place.

Married last evening, by the Rev. Mr. Munds, Capt. Joseph Jones, of Wilmington, N. C. to Miss Henrietta Ann Parker, of this place.

Married last evening, by the Rev. Mr. Munds, Mr. Benjamin Johnston, to Mrs. Charlotte Dawson, both of this place.

Issue of November 22, 1806

Departed this life at St. Helena, on the 16th October last, Mrs. Rebecca Edwards, the consort of Mr. James Edwards, aged 47 years.

Issue of November 24, 1806

Married on Saturday evening last, by the Rev. Dr. Buist, Mr. Robert Eason, ship-wright, to Miss Isabella Jane Grassell, both of this city.

Issue of November 27, 1806

Departed this life Mrs. Ann Wilson, aged 63 years, consort of Dr. Robert Wilson, sen....

Died at New-York, on the 11th inst., Mrs. Jones, the actress ....

Issue of November 28, 1806

Died on Tuesday night, the 25th inst., in the 56th year of her age, Mrs. Ann Holland Skirving, wife of Col. William Skirving ....

Died yesterday evening, Mrs. Susanna Jenkins, consort of the Rev. Dr. Jenkins, Rector of St. Philip's Church (eulogy)

Issue of November 29, 1806

Departed this life on the 7th inst., at Newbern, N. C. on the 26th year of her age, Mrs. Margaret Nicholls, wife of George Nicholls....

Issue of December 1, 1806

Married on Saturday evening by the Rev. Dr. Buist, Mr. I. Charles Hentz, a native of Bremen, to Miss Margaretta C. Henry, of this city.
Married on Tuesday last, by the Rev. Mr. Bowen, Mr. Joseph Taylor, to Mrs. Mary Willis, both of this city.

Issue of December 4, 1806

Died in this city, on the 1st inst., Mrs. Hannah Wells, formerly the widow of Mr. John Tuke, a native of Middlesex, England, aged 73 years, a respectable inhabitant of this city upwards of 50 years.

Issue of December 5, 1806

Married last evening, by the Rev. Dr. Hollinshead, Mr. James Clark, to Miss Sarah Mikell, both of Edisto Island.
Died on Monday the 1st, Henry Evan Edwards, aged 14 years and 6 months, youngest son of Major Evan Edwards.
Died at Raleigh, N. C. on Thursday night, the 27th ult., Mr. Charles Story, Comedian, late of the Charleston and Virginia Theatres.

Issue of December 6, 1806

Married at Columbia, on Sunday evening last, by the Rev. Mr. Dubose, Mr. James H. Chappell, to Miss Margaret Goodwyn, eldest daughter of Col. William Goodwyn, deceased.

Issue of December 8, 1806

Married, last evening, by the Rev. Dr. Gallagher, Mr. Benjamin Fordham, to Miss Eleanor F. Vanderherchen, both of this city.
Married on Saturday evening, by the Rev. Mr. Munds, Capt. Robert Fisher, to Miss Hannah Ingraham, both of Philadelphia.
Died yesterday morning, Mr. Daniel Strobel Sen. a native of Germany, in the 73d year of his age, and the 55th year of his residence in South Carolina.
Died on Tuesday last, the 2d inst., in the 75th year of his age, Mr. Alexander Robertson, for many years a respectable inhabitant of this city.
Died on Tuesday last, Mrs. Margaret M. Green, aged 36 years ....

Issue of December 9, 1806

Married at Savannah, on Thursday evening, the 4th inst., Jacob Hartstene, Esq. of Savannah, to Miss Savage of South-Carolina.
Died on Monday the 1st inst., in the 44th year of her age, Mrs. Rosanna M'Lean, relict of the late Evan M'Lean, of this city.
Died at Nassau, Mr. Richard Curry, merchant. At Harbour Island, Mrs. Patience Curry, wife of Mr. Joseph Curry.

Issue of December 10, 1806

Married on Thursday evening, the 27th ult., at New-River, Georgia, by the Rev. Mr. Beck, Joseph Adams Scott, of Savannah, to Miss Mary M'Nish, of South-Carolina.

Departed this life on Friday last, in the 23d year of his age, Mr. Benjamin W. Ruberry....

Issue of December 11, 1806

Died, at New-Orleans, on Friday the 14th ult., Simon M'Intosh, Esq. of South-Carolina.

Issue of December 12, 1806

Departed this life on Monday last, in the 89th year of her age, Miss Mary Bacot, a native of this state, and upwards of 60 years a resident of this city....

Issue of December 13, 1806

Died yesterday morning, Lucius Bellinger, Esq. aged 21 years, 1 months and 3 days, second son of John Bellinger, esq. of Ashepoo.

Issue of December 15, 1806

Married on Wednesday evening last, the 10th inst., by the Rev. Mr. Bowen, Captain Charles Muir, to Miss Catherine Davis, both of this place.

Issue of December 16, 1806

Died on the 9th inst., at his plantation in Prince William's Parish, John Lightwood, Esq. in the 62d year of his age.
Died on the 12th inst., Mr. Lucius Bellinger....

Issue of December 17, 1806

Married on Tuesday the 9th inst., in the Fork of the Congaree, by the Rev. Mr. Thigpen, Dr. John Latargue of this city to Miss Ann Wood Hirons.

Married at Providence, R. I. on the 22d ult., Mr. Sylvanus Keith, merchant, to Miss Margaret Howard, both of Charleston, S. C.

Died at Columbia, on the 3d inst., Mr. David Baldwin, Tanner and Currier in the 52d year of his age. He was a native of Newark, N. J.

Issue of December 18, 1806

Married last evening, by the Rev. Mr. Munds, Mr. Alexander Sparks, merchant, of Miss Jennet M'Kearly, both of Cheraws.

Married at Georgetown, S. C. on Thursday evening the 11th inst., by the Rev. Mr. Lilly, Doctor _____ Wilkinson, to Miss Eleanora Withers.

Issue of December 22, 1806

Married, last evening, by the Rev. Dr. Jenkins, Captain William Flagg, to Miss Jane Imer, both of this city.

Issue of December 23, 1806

Died on Thursday night, Mrs. Mary Nowell, wife of John Nowell, Esq....
Died in the Rio Pongus, Africa, on the 17th Sept. last, Mr. John Homer Lane, mate of the schooner Edward & Edmund, a native of Boston, aged about 29 years.
On Friday evening, the 12th inst., one of the seamen, by the name of Samuel Burnham, fell from the main-chains and was drowned.

Issue of December 24, 1806

Married, last evening, by the Rev. Dr. Hollinshead, Mr. James Davidson, Merchant, to Miss Margaret Eliza Cambridge.

Issue of December 26, 1806

Died at Georgetown on Sunday evening last, Miss Eliza Tomplat, of said place, aged 21 years.

Issue of December 27, 1806

Married on Tuesday evening last, by the Rev. Dr. Percy, Mr. Samuel Haskett, Saddler, to Miss Frances Moore, both of this city.

Issue of December 29, 1806

Departed this life on the 20th Dec., Mrs. Hester Johnson, aged 74 years.

Issue of December 30, 1806

Married on Sunday evening last, at Saltcatcher, Mr. Henry Fickling, of Wadmalaw Island, to Miss Wilkie Frampton, of Saltcatcher.
Married at Winnsborough, on the 16th inst, by the Rev. Mr. Reid, Mr. Robert Bones, of Newberry district, to Miss Elizabeth P. Yongue, daughter of the Rev. S. W. Yongue, of Fairfield district.
Died on the 25th inst., Mr. Robert Allan, lately from Tobago. Died at the High Hills of Santee, on the 3d inst., Mrs. Frances Ioor, wife of George Ioor, esq...left husband and children....

Issue of January 2, 1807

Expired, suddenly, on the 31st ultimo, Miss Esther Ruddock, only daughter of Samuel A. Ruddock, aged 40 days. (lines)

Issue of January 3, 1807

Died, yesterday morning, Mr. Isaac Elizer, merchant, formerly of Newport, R. I. but latterly of this city, aged 86 years and upwards.
Died at Bordeaux, on the 4th of Nov. last, in the 24th year of his age, Mr. Charles Lawrence, of the house of Adams & Lawrence, of this city....

Issue of January 5, 1807

Died on the 18th ult., at his plantation in Fairfield, William Kirkland, Esq. in the 71st year of his age.

Issue of January 6, 1807

Married on Edisto-Island, on the 25th ult., by the Rev. Mr. M'Leod, Mr. Robert Eason, to Miss Martha Miot, both of this city.
Died on Friday evening, the 2d inst., in the 33d year of her age, Mrs. Mary Courty, wife of Mr. John Courty....
Died in Friday last, Mrs. Brailsford, widow of Samuel Brailsford, Esq....
Died on Saturday evening last, in this city in the 68th year of her age, Mrs. Mary Fraser, relict of the late Alexander Fraser, Esq.
Died on the 1st ult., in Kingston, Jamaica, Hugh Lexon, Esq., Consul of the U. S. in that island.

Issue of January 9, 1807

Married on Wednesday evening last, by the Rev. Mr. Munds, captain William Harper, to Miss Maria Ann M'Dowell.
Married on Wednesday evening last, by the Rev. Mr. Munds, Mr. George Brown, to Miss Sarah Aikman.

Issue of January 14, 1807

Married on Sunday evening last, by the Rev. Mr. Munds, Mr. James Watson, to Mrs. Mary Cameron.
Died in St. Andrew's Parish, on Monday last, Mr. Richard Woodcraft, in the 27th year of his age.

Issue of January 15, 1807

Died in this city on Friday morning last, Mr. Thomas Simmons, formerly of Boston.
Died on the 29th of Oct., at Topsham in Devonshire (Eng.), Gen. Simcoe. On the 5th of Nov., Lord Ponsonby.

Issue of January 16, 1807

Died at Savannah on the 8th inst., Miss Caroline Elizabeth Jacqueline Rossignol de Bellianse, a native of the Island of St. Domingo in the 30th year of her age.

Issue of January 19, 1807

Married at Glasgow, on the 17th Nov., Mr. H. M. Haig, of Charleston, S. C. to Miss Agnes Ritchie, daughter of Mr. Alexander Ritchie, merchant, Glasgow.
                    Nassau, January 6
Died, yesterday morning, Miss Mary Wells, eldest daughter of John Wells, Esq. formerly proprietor of the Bahama Gazette....

Issue of January 20, 1807

Married on Sunday evening last, by the Rev. Mr. Munds, Mr. Joshua Brown, to Miss Letitia Foster, both of this place.
Married, last evening, by the Rev. Mr. Munds, Captain Joseph Charles, to Miss Louisa M'Kenzie, both of this place.
Died at Edinburgh, on the 10th Nov., Sir William Forbes, of Pitiligo, Bart.

Issue of January 23, 1807

Died last evening, Mr. George Drennes, baker aged 63 years.

Died on the 15th Nov., last in Laurens distirct, Mrs. Ann Newby, at the advanced age of 112....She has left her husband, Mr. Robert Newby only 37 years of age....

Issue of January 24, 1807

Married in St. Philip's Church the 22d inst., by the Rev. Dr. Jenkins, the Rev. James Dewar Simons to Miss Harleston Corbett, daughter of Thomas Corbett, Esq.

Married, yesterday, by the Rev. Mr. Munds., Mr. John Williams Allan, to Miss Eliza Hibben, both of Christ Church Parish.

Issue of January 27, 1807

Married on Thursday evening last, by the Rev. Dr. Gallagher, Mr. Alexander M. Orr, to Miss Alician Purfield.

Died, on Friday evening last, Mr. Jacob Ulmer, aged 74 years, a native of Germany but a resident of this state for 56 years.

Issue of January 29, 1807

Died yesterday morning, in the 67th year of his age, Mr. Israel D'Lieben, a native of Prague in Bohemia. America has been his residence 36 years...left a wife and niece.

Issue of January 31, 1807

Married last evening, by the Rev. Mr. Mills, Mr. James H. Cambridge, to Miss Anne Seabrook.

Issue of February 2, 1807

On Monday morning, the 25th ult., at Vernerobre Plantation, in St. Peter's parish, departed this life, Miss Eliza Maria Cross....(lines)

Died suddenly, in this city, on the 23d ult., Mr. Solomon Peter June, aged 23 years...left an only sister....

Died on the 22d ult., in the vicinity of Orangeburgh, Mr. John Jennings sen. aged 59 years.

Died on Edisto Island, on the 26th ult., in the prime of life, Mr. Thomas B. Maxey.

Died on the 30th Dec. last, Capt. John C. Mack, of Beverly, Mass.

Died on the 19th Nov. last, at sea, off Cumberland Harbour, Cuba, Mr. William Robinson, of Hartford, Mass.

Died in the Rio Pongua, Africa, in Nov. last, capt. James Woodward, of the schooner Three Friends, of this port.

Issue of February 3, 1807

Died at Goree, on the 4th Nov. last, Mr. John Poullet, merchant.

Died on the 9th inst., at the house of John Floyd, Esq., in Camden county, Ga., Mrs. Anne Maxwell, aged 62 years, a native of South-Carolina.

Issue of February 4, 1807

Died at sea, on the 16th ult., on his passage from Montserat to this port, in the ship Fair American, Mr. Daniel Goodwin, of Hartford, Conn.

Issue of February 5, 1807

Married on Monday evening last, by the Rev. Mr. Munds, Mr. William Clark, to Mrs. Mary G. Marshall, both of the Theatre.

Issue of February 6, 1807

Married, last evening, by the Rev. Dr. Buist, Mr. William Walton, merchant, to Miss Justina Louisa Gennerick, both of this city.

Issue of February 7, 1807

Married on Sunday, the 18th ult., Mr. Charles Harris, merchant, to Miss Cynthia Beesly, both of Laurens District.

Issue of February 10, 1807

Died last Saturday night, Mr. John Fisther, School-master, to the Orphan-House, aged 55 years....
Died in London on the 21st Oct. last, in his 29th year, Mr. William Hopton Powell, only son of Col. Robert William Powell....

Issue of February 13, 1807

Married on Wednesday evening last, by the Rev. Mr. Phillips, pastor of Trinity Church, Captain William Fair, to Miss Margaret Boyd, both of this city.
Died at Nassau, on the 8th ult., aged 76 years, Benjamin Lord, Sen. esq. formerly of South-Carolina; afterwards Surveyor-General of East Florida, and for the last 21 years a resident of the Bahama Islands.

Issue of February 16, 1807

Married 1st Dec. last, at Thorpe Place, Middlesex (Eng.), John J. Pringle, jun Esq. to Miss Izard, daughter of Ralph Izard, Esq.
death of James Henry Hancock, late of this city, son of Henry Hancock, Esq...(lines)
Departed this life on Thursday last, Captain Thomas Ross, of this city...left widow and six children....

Issue of February 17, 1807

Died at Santee, on the 15th inst., Mr. John Peronneau, aged 49 years....

Issue of February 18, 1807

Married, at Georgetown, on Thursday evening last, by the Rev. Mr. Lilly, Mr. Elisha Woodward, to Miss Esther Lepear, both of that place.
Married by the Rev. Mr. Sweat, on Thursday, 15th ult., John Heard, Esq. to Miss Martha Wood, both of Barnwell district.
Married by the Rev. Mr. Sweat, on Thursday, the 22d ult., Jeremiah S. Fickling, Esq.to Miss Jane M. Leslie, both of Barnwell district.
Married by the Rev. Mr. Sweat, on Thursday the 5th inst., George R.Dunbar, Esq. to Miss Mary S. Fickling, daughter of Francis Fickling, esq. both of Barnwell.

Departed this life on Wednesday the 11th inst., in St. Bartholomew's Parish, Mrs. Mary Caveneau, late of Cannonsborough, in the 63d year of her age.

Departed this life on Saturday the 7th inst., at his plantation in St. Andrew's parish, William Miles, Esq. for several years a member of the Legislature for that parish.

Issue of February 19, 1807

Married, on Tuesday evening last, by the Rev. Dr. Gallagher, Mr. Auguste St. Martin to Miss Frances-Ninette Peire, both of the Island of St. Domingo.

Issue of February 20, 1807

Married on the 2d of Sept., by the Rev. Mr. Matthews, Mr. Samuel Roberts, of Bordeaux, to Miss Rachel Jamieson of this city.

Died in this city on the 18th inst., in the 38th year of her age, Mrs. Mary Anne Addison, wife of James Addison, esq. of St. Stephen's parish...left husband and five children.

Died in this city on the 5th inst., in the 63d year of his age, Mr. William Moer a native of Aberdeen, Scotland...an inhabitant of this place for 43 years.

Died at New-orleans, on the 21st ult.,Mr. Gulien M'Eves, of the city of New-York.

Issue of February 21, 1807

Departed this life, on the night of the 2d ult., Mr. William Wilson, sen. of Spartanburgh District, in the 67th year of his age.

Issue of February 23, 1807

Died, yesterday morning, Mrs. Jane Stent Strobel, wife of Capt. Lewis Strobel....

Departed this life, on the 18th inst., in the 43d year of her age, Mrs. Dorothy Allston, consort of Benjamin Allston, sen. esq. of All Saints Parish.

Died at Norwich (Eng.) Mrs. Sarah Rickwood, aged 49 years....

Issue of February 24, 1807

Married, last evening, by the Rev. Dr. Bowen, Mr. Henry O'Hara, to Miss Martha Woodcraft, both of this city.

Married, at Nassau, N. P., on the 3d inst., Robert Duncome, Esq. Collector of his Majesty's Customs, to Miss Eliza D. Kelsall.

Departed this life on Sunday last,in the 25th year of her age, Mrs. Jane Stent Strobel....(lines)

Died on the 17th inst., on his way fromthis city to his residence in St. James's, Goose-creek, capt. Hugh Strain Winter, aged about 48 years....left a widow and five small children....

Died on Sunday the 22d inst., Nathaniel Keantish, Esq. late of the Island of Jamaica.

Issue of February 25, 1807

Married at Camden, on the 12th inst., by the Rev. Mr. Flinn, Thomas Salmond Esq. attorney at Law, to Mrs. Margaret Brisbane, both of that place.

Married on the 6th inst., by the Rev. Philip Matthews, of St. James's Santee, Theodore Guerry, Esq. to Miss M. Dumay, both of

St. Stephen's Parish.

Issue of February 26, 1807

Died, last evening, Mr. John Martin, blacksmith, a native of Ireland, many years a resident in this city.

Issue of February 27, 1807

Married last evening, by the Rev. Dr. Jenkins, Benjamin D. Roper, Esq. to Miss Barbary C. Jenkins, daughter of Micah Jenkins, Esq. all of this city.
Married, last evening, by the Rev. Mr. Charles Faber, Mr. Christian Henry Faber, Factor, to Miss Mary Ann Desel, daughter of Mr. Charles Desel.
Married, last evening, by the Rev. Dr. Hollinshead, Mr. Joseph Parsons, of Abbeville, to Mrs. Esther Hook, of Hampstead.
Married, on Wednesday evening, by the Rev. Mr. Sauares, Mr. Phillips, of Georgetown, to Miss Caroline Lazarus, of this city.

Issue of February 28, 1807

Died on the 22d inst., Mr. Pierre Dabouville, aged 72 years, a native of Quebec, in Canada...a resident of this city for some years past, left widow and six children....

Issue of March 3, 1807

Died, yesterday morning, Mr. William M'Kimmy, in the 20th year of his age....
Died on the 28th ult., Mr. Matthew Clark, in the 35th year of his age, a native of this place, left a wife and numerous relatives and friends....

Issue of March 4, 1807

Departed this life in Barnwell District, on Sunday evening, 22d Feb., Mr. Jeremiah S. Fickling, in the 22d year of his age... left widow, father, mother, brother and sisters....

Issue of March 9, 1807

Married, at Ashepoo, on the 5th inst., by the Rev. Mr. Floyd, Mr. Thomas Boone, of Christ Church Parish, to Miss Mary S. Jones, daughter of William Jones, Esq.
Married, on Tuesday evening, the 3d inst., in the Parish of St. James's, Goose-creek, by the Rev. Mr. M'Cullah, Mr. Lewis F. Breaker, to Miss Martha Canty, both of said parish.
Died in Camden, on the 1st inst., Mr. Henry Cunningham, in the 32d year of his age.
Died in Abbeville District, on the 17th ult., captain John Gray, a soldier of '76.

Issue of March 10, 1807

Died on Sunday evening last, in the 32d year of his age, Mr. Samuel Gourlay, a native of this city....

Issue of March 11, 1807

Died, on Monday evening last, in the prime of life, Major Joseph Dickinson, Brigade Major of the 7th Brigade of the Militia of this State.

Died at Baltimore, on Friday the 30th of Jan., Mr. Samuel Campbell....

Issue of March 12, 1807

Died, in this city, on the 7th inst., John R. Thomas, Esq., late Planter of the Island of St. Domingo.

Issue of March 13, 1807

Died on Wednesday last, William Roberts, aged 18 years, an apprentice in the Times office....

Issue of March 14, 1807

Married on Thursday evening, by the Rev. Mr. Munds, Capt. Joshua Enfield, of New-York, to Miss Henrietta Harper, of this place.

Issue of March 16, 1807

Married on Thursday evening last, by the Rev. Dr. Hollinshead, Mr. John Cromer, to Miss Margaret Buckie(?), both of this city.
Married last evening, by the Rev. Dr. Buist, Mr. John Mushett, to Miss Margaret Flemming, both of this city.
Married last evening, by the Rev. Mr. Munds, Mr. Henry Williams, to Miss Mary Jones, both of this city.

Issue of March 18, 1807

Married on the 12th inst., in Prince William's Parish, by the Rev. Mr. Benjamin M. Palmer, of Beaufort district, Dr. Daniel D'Oyley, to Miss Elizabeth Maine, only daughter of James Maine, Esq. deceased.

Issue of March 20, 1807

Married last evening, by the Rev. Dr. Keith, Mr. Thomas A. Verdell, to Miss Susan Phillips, both of this city.
Married on Thursday the 12th inst., by the Rev. Philip Mathews, Mr. Peter Cuttino, to Georgetown, to Miss Elizabeth Mary Gaillard, daughter of Charles Gaillard, esq. of St. James's, Santee.
Married on Tuesday the 17th inst., by the Rev. Philip Matthews, William Gaillard, to Miss Esther Barton, both of St. James's, Santee.
Married last evening, by the Rev. Dr. Jenkins, Mr. Joseph Douterier, to Miss Emily Louisa Kirk, both of St. John's parish.
Married, on Tuesday the 17th inst., by the Rev. Mr. Munds, Mr. John Thomas, to Miss Jane Brooks, both of this city.
Married on Sunday the 22d ult., by the Rev. Thomas H. Price, Mr. Henry Sterling Rivers, to Mrs. Esther Rivers, widow of Mr. William Rivers, all of James Island.
Died on Saturday the 14th inst., Mrs. Ann Vieyra, aged 55 years....left orphan daughter.
Died at Deal (England) on the 6th Jan., Capt. Alexander Shaw, late master of the ship Ruby of this port.

Issue of March 21, 1807

Married last Thursday evening, by the Rev. Dr. Jenkins, James Reid Pringle, Esq. to Miss Eliza M. M'Pherson, daughter of the late Gen. John M'Pherson.

Married last evening, by the Rev. Mr. Munds, Mr. Joseph Gardner, to Miss Elizabeth Martin, both of this city.
Died at New-Orleans, on Monday the 23d ult., Mrs. Anne Wilkinson, consort of Gen. Wilkinson....

Issue of March 23, 1807

Married on Tuesday evening, by the Rev. Mr. Faber, Mr. Stephen Bulkley, to Mrs. Maria M. Fanning.

Issue of March 24, 1807

Died at Princeton, New-Jersey, on the 12th inst., the Rev. Anthony Schmit, a respectable Catholic Priest....

Issue of March 25, 1807

Departed this transitory life, on the 22d inst., in the 40th year of her age, Mrs. Elizabeth Deliesseline, consort of John T. Deliesseline, of Dewees's Island....left husband, and eight children.
Died, in this city, on the 13th inst., in the 32d year of her age, Mrs. Elizabeth Galloway, a native of Charleston...left husband and three children....

Issue of March 26, 1807

Married, last evening, Mr. S. M. Isaacks, of New-York, to Miss Catharine Cohen, daughter of the late Mr. Gershon Cohen, of this city.
Died on Saturday evening, the 21st inst., Mr. Samuel Mulligan, of Georgetown, S. C.
Departed this life on Wednesday morning, the 21st of Jan., Mrs. Mary Lilly, consort of Rev. David Lilly, of the vicinity of Cambridge....

Issue of March 27, 1807

Married on the 19th inst.,by the Rev. Mr. Hollinshead, Mr. John Munro, mariner, to Mrs. Eliza Curtlet.

Issue of March 28, 1807

Died in St. John's Parish, Santee, on Tuesday the 17th inst., Paul Warley, Esq. in the 56th year of his age.
Died in England, Feb. 5th Gen. Pascal Pagli, the Corsican Patriot, and God-father to Bonaparte.
Died in Boston, the Rev. Samuel Stillman, D. D., Pastor of the Baptist Church in that city.

Issue of March 31, 1807

Married on Sunday evening last, by the Rev. Dr. Buist, Mr. Peter Lanneau, to Miss Rebecca Armstrong, both of this city.
Died, last Wednesday morning, Mr. James Kay, Grocer, aged 40 years.

Issue of April 1, 1807

Married on Sunday evening last, by the Rev. Mr. Faber, Mr. John Burn, to Mrs. Christiana Brown, both of this city.
Died in this city on the 28th ult., Miss Sarah Butler, in the 81st year of her age....

Died in Barnwell district, on Saturday the 21st of March, in the 45th year of his age, Mr. James Bowie...left a widow and three children.
Died at Calcutta, Mr. James Murray Lillibridge, a native of Exeter, in Rhode-Island....

Issue of April 2, 1807

Married on Thursday the 26th ult., by the Rev. Mr. Clarkson, Charles Gabriel Capers, Esq. of St. Helena, to Miss Mary Y. Reynolds, daughter of Benjamin Reynolds, esq. of Wadmalaw.
Married on Saturday evening last, by the Rev. Mr. Marin Detargny, Mr. Thomas Smith, to Miss Charlotte Suder, both of this city.

Issue of April 3, 1807

Departed this life on the 30th ult., in the 55th year of his age, Mr. William Mikell, of Edisto Island....

Issue of April 7, 1807

Died, on Tuesday the 24th March, at the plantation of Richard Pearis, near St. Mary's, Nathaniel Munro, Esq. of the house of Messrs. Forbes, Munro & Forbes, of Nassau, N. P....

Issue of April 9, 1807

Died at his residence in Hampstead, on the 4th inst., David Maybank, Esq. of St. Thomas's Parish, aged 40 years.
Died on the 5th inst, Mr. Peter Bonneau, planter, in St. James's Santee, in the 34th year of his age.
Died at Norfolk, on the 20th ult., Mr. Patrick Burke at the age of 104; a native of Ireland....

Issue of April 10, 1807

Married on Tuesday evening last, by the Rev. Mr. Bowen, Frederick Kohne, Esq. to Miss Eliza Neufville.
Married last evening, by the Rev. Mr. Simons, Robert Gilmor, jun. Esq. of Baltimore, to Miss Sarah Reeve Ladson, daughter of Major James Ladson, of this city.
Married last evening, by the Rev. Dr. Buist, Archibald S. Johnston, Esq. to Miss Agnes Bolton Ewing, daughter of the late Adam Ewing, esq. all of this city.
Married last evening, by the Rev. Dr. Hollinshead, Mr. William B. Tucker, of this city, to Miss Ann Blake, daughter of Capt. John Blake, of St. James, Santee.
Married last evening, by the Rev. Dr. Hollinshead, Mr. Nathaniel Black, of this city to Miss Elizabeth Dewa, of Christ Church Parish.
Married last evening by the Rev. Mr. Munds, Mr. William Smith, to Miss Eliza Jones, both of this place.
Married in Beaufort, S. C. on the 25th ult., by the Rev. Joseph B. Cook, Mr. Robert L. Holcombe, of Savannah, to Miss Eliza Witter, of Beaufort.
Died on the 29th ult., at his seat at Curles (in Richmond, Va.) Col. William Heth....

Issue of April 11, 1807

Married on the 19th ult., in Laurens District by Robert Hutchinson, Esq., Mr. Joshua Hitch, to the amiable and accomplished Miss Elizabeth Compton, both of that district.

Issue of April 13, 1807

Married last evening, by Mr. Suares, Mr. H. M. Hertz, to Mrs. Bella Levy, widow of the late Mr. Hart Levy, of this city.

Married on Saturday evening, by the Rev. Mr. Munds, Mr. Isaac Grant, to Miss Mary Patterson, both of this place.

Married on Saturday evening, by the Rev. Mr. Munds, Mr. William Taylor, to Miss Martha Moore, both of this place.

Married at the city of Burlington, N. J., on Wednesday the 25th ult., by the Rev. Dr. Charles H. Wharton, Nathan W. Cole, M. D., to Miss Rebecca Peace, formerly of this city, now of that place.

Died on the 10th inst., at Mr. Darby's on Charleston Neck, Col. William T. Thomson, of Amelia....

Issue of April 15, 1807

Died, in this city on Sunday last, Miss Louisa Nott, aged 43 years.

Issue of April 16, 1807

Died in St. Stephen's, on the 8th inst., John Peyre, Esq., in the 57th year of his age....

Issue of April 17, 1807

Married, in St. Philip's Church, on Wednesday last, by the Rev. Dr. Jenkins, Mr. Samuel Patterson, to Miss Levingston Smith.

Died on the 18th ult.,Thos. Hasell, Esq. in the 56th year of his age; an old and respectable inhabitant of Georgetown.

Issue of April 18, 1807

Married on Tuesday evening, bythe Rev. Dr. Hollinshead, Mr. John C. Gilbert,of New-York, to Mrs. Frances Chinners, of this city.

Issue of April 20, 1807

Died at New-Orleans, on the 12th ult., Richard J. Avery, deputy collector of that port.

Died at Granville (N. Y.) on the 13th ult., Mr. Benjamin Greene...native of Rhode-Island and borther of Gen. Greene... nigh 70 years of age.

Issue of April 21, 1807

Died on Wadmalaw Island on Sunday evening last, John Seabrook, esq. leaving a wife and eight children....

Died at Savannah, on the 17th inst., Mr. Andrew M'Credie, a native of Scotland....

Issue of April 22, 1807

Married on the 27th ult., by the Rev. Marin Detargny, Mr. Peter Robin, Merchant, to Miss Antoinette Laroque, both formerly from the Island of St. Domingo. and now residents in this city.

Married on Tuesday the 7th inst., Edward Simkins, Esq., attorney at Law of Edgefield distrct, in this state, to Miss

Eliza H. Smith, daughter of Benjamin Smith, esq. of Milford, state of Georgia.

Died on the 29th ult., in Abbeville district, Mrs. Rose Bowie, wife of Major John Bowie, in the 63d year of her age, leaving a husband and six children....

Died at the City of Washington, on the 8th inst.,John Beckley, Esq. Clerk of the House of Representatives of the U. S.

Died at Beverly (Mass.) Capt. George Raymond, in the 100dth year of his age...pillar of the second church in that place.

Issue of April 23, 1807

Married last evening, by the Rev. Dr. Hollinshead, Mr. John Allin, to Miss Elizabeth Baker, both of this city.

Issue of April 24, 1807

Married, last evening, by the Rev. Dr. Hollinshead, Mr. John M. Wilson(?), to Miss Mary Oats, both of this city.

Issue of April 25, 1807

Married on Thursday evening last,by the Rev. Mr. Munds, Mr. John Bridehoop, to Mrs. Henrietta Frobus.

Married last evening, by the Rev. Mr. Munds, Mr. William Jones, to Miss Sarah Elizabeth Lewis, both of this place.

Died on the 18th inst., at his seat, near Orangeburgh, in the 66th year of his age, Lewis Lestargette, Esq. for many years Clerk of the Courts for that district.

Issue of April 27, 1807

Married on Friday, the 17th inst.,by the Rev. Dr. Gallagher, Mr. Joseph Perrault, to Mrs. Letitia Atkinson.

Married on the 19th inst., by the Rev. Mr. Roberts, Mr. James W. Murrell, to Miss Louisa Sumter, both of Statesburgh, S. C.

Married last evening by the Rev. Mr. Jackson, Mr. John Lloyd, to Mrs. Mary Pollock, both of this city.

Issue of April 28, 1807

Married, on Sunday evening last, by the Rev. Dr. Hollinshead, Mr. David Phillips, to Miss Celina Bradley, both of this city.

Married, on Sunday evening last, by the Rev. Mr. Charles Faber, Mr. John Lewis Linsee, to Miss Mary Leetz, both of this city.

Married on Saturday evening, by the Rev. Dr. Hollinshead, Mr. John Cashman, to Mrs. Ann Hoey, both of this city.

Married on Sunday evening last, by the Rev. Dr. Hollinshead, Mr. John Doudney to Miss Charlotte Arms, both of this city.

Married on Thursday last, by the Rev. Dr. Gallagher, Mr. John Courty, to Miss Mary Elizabeth Gauihs, both of this city.

Died at Nassau, N. P., on the 20th inst., Rawlins Lowndes Gervais, Esq. of this city.

Issue of May 1, 1807

Married last evening, by the Rev. Mr. Simons, Mr. Elias couturier, to Miss Henrietta Couturier, both of St. John's, Santee.

Married on Wednesday evening last, by the Rev. Mr. Munds, Capt. Joshua Miller, to Miss Elizabeth Wood.

Married on Wednesday evening last,by the Rev Mr. Munds, Mr. John Anderson, to Mrs. Elizabeth Patterson, both of this place.
Died on the 21st inst., Alexander Chovin, Esq. of Santee, planter, in the 64th year of his age....

Issue of May 2, 1807

Married in Orangeburgh, on Thursday the 22d ult.,by the Rev. Dr. Eccles, Mr. Donald Rowe, to Mrs. Ann Sabb.
Died in London on the 16th March, Admiral Sir Hyde Parker, aged 67.

Issue of May 4, 1807

Married on Tuesday evening last, by the Rev. Dr. Hollinshead, Capt. James Cooper, to Miss Mary Broeskey, both of this city.
Died, on Saturday the 25th ult., Mr. Roger Saunders Gough.

Issue of May 5, 1807

Married at Cow-Savannah, St. Paul's Parish, on the 23d ult., by the Rev. Mr. Floyd, Mr. Frederick Hamilton to Mrs. Frances Giveham, widow of the late Philip Giveham, decd.
Married on Tuesday evening, the 17th of Feb. last, by the Rev. Mr. Hand, Aaron Smith, Esq. of Barnwell district, South Carolina, to Mrs. Elizabeth Rutherford, of Screven Co., Ga.

Issue of May 6, 1807

Married on Monday evening last, by the Rev. Dr. Keith, the Rev. Mr. Benjamin M. Palmer, to Miss Mary Bunce.
Married on the 2d inst., by the Rev. Dr. Hollinshead, Mr. John Burk to Mrs. Ann Smith, widow both from Holland.
Married on Saturday evening last, by the Rev. Martin Detargny, Mr. James Haynes, to Miss Susannah Hoats, both of this city.

Issue of May 7, 1807

Married last evening, by the Rev. Dr. Hollinshead, Dr. E. P. Crocker, of Georgetown, S. C. to Miss Sarah M. Mackay, eldest daughter of Dr. John Mackay, of this city.
Married on Tuesday evening last, by the Rev. Mr. Munds, Capt. James Brown, to Miss Ann Mary Gibson.
Married last evening by the Rev. Mr. Munds, Mr. William Watson, to Miss Martha Turner.
Married this morning by the Rev. Mr. Munds, Mr. Daniel Francis Fisher, of Baltimore, to Miss Rosanna Berry, of this place.
Married on Saturday morning last, by the Rev. Mr. Simons, Mr. Isaac Couturier of St. John's Santee, to Miss Charlotte Hodgson White, of this city.
Died in this city, on the 23d ult., Peter Porcher, Esq. planter, of St. John's Parish, in the 43d year of his age.

Issue of May 9, 1807

Married last evening, by the Rev. Mr. Simons, Mr. John Marshall, to Miss Maria Medcalf, both of this city.

Issue of May 11, 1807

Married, last evening, by the Rev. Mr. Munds, Mr. John Scott, to Miss Sarah Peister, both of this city.

Issue of May 12, 1807

Married on Sunday evening last, by the Rev. Dr. Jenkins, Mr. John Gros, to Miss Elizabeth Catharine Love, both of this city.

Issue of May 16, 1807

Married on Wednesday evening last, by the Rev. Mr. Percy, Mr. Charles Newman, to Mrs. M. Moore, both of this city.

Issue of May 18, 1807

Married, last evening, by the Rev. Dr. Gallagher, Mr. Charles Spann, Jun. of Statesburgh, S. C. to Miss Eleanor Crowly, of this city.

Issue of May 20, 1807

Died on Monday night last, in the 31st year of his age, Capt. Josias Allston, of Georgetown, a respectable member of society.
Died at Savannah, on the 12th inst., Mr. William Cruvillier, formerly a merchant in St. Domingo, born in Provence, the south part of France, aged 42 years....reached America 12 years ago....

Issue of May 21, 1807

Married on Sunday evening last, by the Rev. Mr. Munds, Mr. John Christian Landershind, to Miss Catharine Mary Shum, both of this city.

Issue of May 22, 1807

Died in Savannah, on the 7th inst., Mr. Edward G. Malbone, of Newport, R. I.

Issue of May 25, 1807

Married in St. Peter's Parish, on the 12th inst., Mr. James Porcher, to Miss Mary J. Boswood.
Departed this life on the 20th inst., Madame Suzanne De Lezar(?) Thomas, aged 44 years, 3 months and a half....left husband and three children.

Issue of May 26, 1807

Married, last evening, by the Rev. Dr. Jenkins, Mr. Peter Gaillard, to Miss Rebecca Weyman Foster, only daughter of Mr. Thomas Foster.

Issue of May 27, 1807

Married at Fuller-Hall, on Monday evening last, by the Rev. James Simons, Mr. William Lee, merchant, to Lady Belhaven.
Married, on Tuesday evening last, by the Rev. Mr. Faber, Mr. John H. Deubell, merchant, to Miss Nancy Kircher, both of Savannah.
Married on Sunday evening last, by the Rev. Mr. Munds, Mr. Thomas Eustace, to Mrs. Sarah Wolfe, both of this place.
Married on Monday evening, by the Rev. Mr. Munds, Mr. Charles William Cummins, to Miss Mary Roach, both of this place.
Died on the 5th ult., at Mr. Grossland's, near Marlborough Court-House, state of North-Carolina, the Rev. Bennet Kendrick... native of Virginia (long account)...Methodist Episcopal Church.

Issue of May 28, 1807

Died on Tuesday evening last, Robert D. Lawrence, Esq. Attorney at Law.

Died on Tuesday evening last, Mr. George G. Bailey, merchant.

Issue of June 5, 1807

Died at Ashepoo, on the 26th ult., John H. Girardeau, Esq., in the 29th year of his age...left a widow and children.

Died on Saturday, the 30th ult., Mrs. Mary Gerley, wife of Mr. John Gerley, in the 77th year of her age....

Issue of June 6, 1807

Died, on Tuesday morning last, Joseph R. Purcell, surveyor...

Died yesterday, Mr. Elhanan Winchester Wheeler, merchant, of the house of Wheeler & Scott, of this city, aged 36 years, native of Grafton, Mass.

Issue of June 8, 1807

Married, last evening, by the Rev. Mr. Munds, Mr. Alexander Duncan, Blacksmith, to Miss Ann Catharine Disher, both of this city.

Married on the 28th ult., Mr. John Tweed, merchant and planter, to Miss Millia Studwant, both of Prince William's Parish.

Died, at Savannah, on the 2d inst., Mr. James Allison, cooper, late of this city.

Issue of June 9, 1807

Died, at Cambridge, Abbeville district, on the 29th ult., Mrs. Elizabeth Montgomery, consort of the Rev. Benjamin R. Montgomery.

Died on the 4th of May, Lt. Col. William Scott, of the 1st Regt. of the S. C. Line....rev. war.

Issue of June 10, 1807

Married on the 3d inst., in St. Andrew's Parish, by the Rev. Mr. Price, William Rivers, Esq. to Mrs. Elizabeth Mary Ainger.

Died at Southwest Point, in the state of Tennessee, on the 11th ult., William Peters, Esq. late a Major in the army of the U. S., aged 53 years....rev. war.

Issue of June 11, 1807

Died on the Coast of Africa, in Oct. last, Henry Duffy, Esq. late of this city, a native of Ireland.

Issue of June 15, 1807

Died on Friday the 12th inst., in the 50th year of his age, Mr. James Grierson, a native of Aberdeenshire, in Scotland....

Died on Saturday last, Mr. John Jones, in the 24th year of his age.

Issue of June 16, 1807

Married last Sunday evening, by the Rev. Dr. Furman, Mr. Robert Roulain, to Miss Sarah Gordon, both of this city.

Died on Friday last, Mr. James Carmichael, formerly of the house of Sutherland & Carmichael, merchants, in this city.

Issue of June 19, 1807

Married on Wednesday evening, by the Rev. Mr. Munds, Mr. John Chisam, to Miss Eliza Shields.

Married on the same evening, by the Rev. Mr. Munds, Mr. Robert Stewart, to Mrs. Letitia Glen, of this place.

Married on the same evening, by the Rev. Mr. Munds, Capt. Charles Gordon, of Boston, to Miss Elizabeth Mary Harper, of this place.

Issue of June 22, 1807

Died on Thursday evening last, Mr. John Shirer, sen, House Carpenter, in the 55th year of his age...native of Germany, and has been upwards of 40 years a resident in this state....

Issue of June 23, 1807

Married on Sunday evening, by the Rev. Mr. Bowen, Mr. John Zylstra, of this city, to Miss Charlotte Cordell, from England.

Issue of June 25, 1807

Married last evening, Mr. R. J. Recardo, to Miss Sarah Hyams, both of this city.

Issue of June 29, 1807

Married, last evening, by the Rev. Dr. Hollinshead, John Todd, Esq., of James-Island to Miss Savage, of this city.

Issue of June 30, 1807

Married, last evening, by the Rev. Mr. Charles Faber, Mr. John Frederick Cutler, to Miss Sally Lee, both of this city.

Married on Monday evening, the 10th inst., by the Rev. Samuel Marsh, Mr. James Scott, Merchant, of Campbellton (S. C.) to Miss Catharine Tomkins Key, daughter of Capt. Thomas Key.

Died on the Coast of Africa, on the 12th of March last, Mr. James Fisk of Framingham, Mass.

Issue of July 2, 1807

Married, on Tuesday evening last, in Christ Church Parish, by the Rev. Dr. M'Calla, Mr. Peter M. Ehney to Miss Hannah Jeffords, of said parish.

Issue of July 3, 1807

Died, yesterday morning, John Bowman, Esq. aged 61 years, an old and respectable inhabitant of this city.

Issue of July 6, 1807

Died in this city, on Friday last, the 3d inst., Miss Mary E. Singeltary in the 20th year of her age....
Died in Saturday last, Mr. John Callaghan, merchant, of this city.
Died on Saturday last, in the 29th year of her age, Mrs. Ann Stol Otis, wife of Mr. Joseph Otis...left husband and two children.
Departed this life on the 29th ult., at Georgetown, in the 34th year of her age, Mrs. Ann Doggett, wife of Mr. Henry Doggett, of this city.

Issue of July 10, 1807

Died, in St. Bartholomew's Parish, on the 7th inst., Dr. Peter Foissin.
Died on Tuesday last, at his plantation at Goose-creek, St. James's parish, in the 31st year of his age, Mr. John Poppenheim ...left widow and two infant children....

Issue of July 11, 1807

Died last night, Mr. James Keating, a native of Ireland, aged 25 years....
Died on Thursday the 2d inst., at his house in this city, John Bowman, Esq. in the 62d year of his age...(long account)

Issue of July 13, 1807

Married on Saturday evening last, by the Rev. Mr. Simons, Spencer John Man, Esq. to Mrs. Ann Barkesdale.
Died on the 7th inst., on Tucker's island, Mrs. Martha Rivers, consort of Mr. Stiles Rivers, in the 33d year of her age.
Died at Georgetown, on the 3d inst., the Rev. Samuel Lilly, in the 54th year of his age...a native of Great-Britain, and for some time rector of the Episcopal Church in that town....

Issue of July 14, 1807

Married last Thursday evening, by the Rev. Mr. Faber, Mr. John Pickenpack, to Mrs. Dorothea Schriner, both of this city.
Died on Saturday evening last, Mr. Isaac Teasdale, aged 61 years....
Departed this life on Wednesday evening, the 1st inst.,at the residence of Rev. Philip Matthews, St. James, Santee, Dr. Peter Foissin, aged 25 years...interred in the Echaw Church yard.

Issue of July 15, 1807

Died in New-York, Mr. Eli Ives, of the house of John P. White & Co., of this city, aged 25 years.

Issue of July 16, 1807

Married on Sunday evening last, by the Rev. Dr. Buist, Mr. Thomas Ley to Mrs. M'Lardy, both of this city.
Married, last evening, by Mr. Abraham Alexander, sen., Mr. M. L. Henry to Miss Miriam Solomons of Georgetown.
Died in Union District, on the 24th ult., Mr. William Hunt, aged about 35 years, who has left five children...his brother Mr. Harrison Hunt of Columbia.... Being engaged to be married

to a widow lady in the neighbourhood, they set out for that purpose and were overtaken by a violent thunder storm...shot by a son to the lady above mentioned....

Issue of July 18, 1807

Married on Thursday evening last, at Colleton District, by the Rev. Mr. Hailey, Mr. Hammond Grubbe of Charleston, to Miss Mary Crawford, of Colleton District.

Issue of July 22, 1807

Died on the 21st inst., Mr. John Mills Lahiffe...left a widow and child....

Issue of July 23, 1807

Died in Barnwell district, Lower Three Runs, in the 25th year of her age, Mrs. Elizabeth Bardon, consort of Mr. John J. Bardon of that place...left husband and three small children.

Died in Kershaw district, on the 17th ult., Mrs. Mary West, aged 29 years, consort of Capt. Simeon West....

Issue of July 24, 1807

Died on the 14th inst., Mr. David Razdel, aged 87 years, a native of Virginia and many years an inhabitant of this state. He has left an aged widow and a son to deplore his loss....

Died on the 9th inst., Jane Eliza Dunlap, in the 10th year of her age, eldest daughter of Samuel Dunlap, esq. of Lancasterville, S. C....left father, mother, three brothers and two sisters.

Issue of July 27, 1807

Married last evening, by the Rev. Dr. Gallagher, Mr. Thomas Duggan, to Miss Jane Cleyton, both of this city.

Issue of July 29, 1807

Married last evening by the Rev. Dr. Hollinshead, Mr. George A. Z. Smith, to Miss Ann Eliza Withers, daughter of Captain John Withers.

Married at Camden, on Wednesday evening, the 15th inst., by the Rev. Isaac Smith, Dr. Isaac Alexander, of the above place, to the amiable Miss Sarah Thompson, late of New-York.

Died on Thursday last, in the 18th year of her age, Susannah Broughton, youngest daughter of Alexander Broughton, Esq. deceased....

Died on the 12th inst., on his passage to New-York, on board the brig Huntress, capt. Breeze, James Gregorie, sen of this city.

Died at Havana, Mr. Joseph M. Bowles, merchant, of Providence, R. I.

Issue of July 31, 1807

Died on the 19th inst., at the City of Washington, Uriah Tracey, Esq. a Senator of Congress from Connecticut.

Died at Savannah, on the 23d inst., Mrs. Margaret Treutlan, aged 79 years, a native of Switzerland, and 67 years a resident of that place.

Died at Savannah, on the 25th inst., Mr. Cunningham Newall, a native of Scotland.

Died at Savannah, on the 26th inst., Mr. Thomas Williamson, merchant, a native of Great Britain.

Died, at Nassau on the 8th inst., in the 61st year of his age, Nathaniel Hall, Esq. Collector of his Majesty's Customs....

Issue of August 1, 1807

Died on the 28th inst., Col. Alexander Moultrie, in the 57th year of his age...patriot of '76....

Issue of August 4, 1807

Married last evening, by the Rev. Charles Faber, Mr. John Philip Happoldt, to Mrs. Ann Flauch, both of this city.

Died at Jacksonborough, in the 12th year of her age, Miss Eliza Oswald, only daughter of Mrs. Sarah Oswald....left three brothers.

Died in Martinico, on the 2d of June, Madame De Lapacerie, mother of the Queen of France and Italy, aged 71....

Issue of August 5, 1807

Married on the 13th ult., at the seat of Mrs. Izard, near Haerlem (New-York) by the Rev. Mr. Wilkins, Mr. Lewis Morris, Jr. of Charleston, S. C. to Miss Elizabeth Manigault, of the same place.

Married on the 28th ult., by the Rev. Andrew Flinn, Mr. Robert Mickle, merchant, to Miss Catharine Ervin, both of Camden.

Married at Savannah, on Sunday evening last, by the Rev. Mr. Cloud, Mr. James England, Merchant, to Miss Jane Gribbin, daughter of the late Capt. Gribbin.

Departed this life on the 17th ult., at Rippon Lodge, his seat in Virginia, Col. Thomas Blackburn....

Issue of August 7, 1807

Died in Savannah, on the 4th inst., in the 34th year of his age, Mr. Edward Courtney, a native of Ireland but for many years an inhabitant of S. C. and Ga.

Issue of August 8, 1807

Died last night, Mr. Thomas Sikes, a native of Ireland, in the 90th year of his age...resided in this city about 60 years.

Died on the 4th inst., James Michel, second son of Dr. D. L.' Homaca, aged 13 months and 21 days.

Issue of August 12, 1807

Died on Thursday morning last, Bryan Edmonson Hussey, son of Mr. Bryan Hussey, aged 18 months.

Died at his plantation in Edgefield district on the 13th ult., Dannitt Hill Jun. in the 34th year of his age.

Issue of August 14, 1807

Married, last evening, by the Rev. Dr. Hollinshead, Mr. John Streater Glen, of this city, planter, to Miss Sarah Ann Cole, of Christ Church parish.

Died in France, Gen. de Rochambeau...aged 82....

Issue of August 17, 1807

Married on Saturday evening last, by the Rev. Dr. Buist, Capt. John Caruth, to Miss Ann Louisa Marsh, both of this city.
Died on Saturday last, in the 46th year of his age, Daniel Ravenel, esq. of this city.
Died on Saturday last, in the 9th year of his age, Master Jonas Green, second son of Mr. Edmund Green, of this city....
Died in London, on the 13th of May last, Robert Livie, Esq. a native of this city.

Issue of August 18, 1807

Married on Sunday evening last, by the Rev. Dr. Hollinshead, Mr. Noah D. Baker, to Miss Martha Christian, both of this city.
Died at his residence on Goose Creek, on the 17th inst., Mr. Richard Berisford Keyler, in the 57th year of his age.
Died at Nassau (N.P.) Capt. John Slater, late of this city.

Issue of August 19, 1807

Married on Monday evening last, by the Rev. Mr. Munds, Capt. Joshua Campbell, of Boston, to Miss Elizabeth Mary Mashaw, of this place.
Married last evening, by the Rev. Mr. Munds, Mr. William Booth, to Mrs. Ann Little.
Married on Thursday evening 9th inst., by Mathew S. Moore, Mr. Richard Moore, of Manchester, to Miss Whittington of the same place.
Departed this life on Thursday the 30th ult., at his seat in Fairfield district, Major John Turner, late a member of the senate from the united districts of Chester, Fairfield and Richland....
Died on the 17th ult., at his residence in Lancaster Ville, in the 45th year of his age, Mr. David Dowser, a native of the county Armagh, in Ireland, and for a long time past, a merchant in this state...left a sister and niece....

Issue of August 20, 1807

Died on the 7th inst., Mrs. Mary Elizabeth Stroble, relict of Mr. Daniel Strobel sen. in the 61st year of her age.
Died on Monday morning the 17th inst., in the 24th year of his age, Mr. John Wheeler, a native of Providence, R. I....
Died on Tuesday the 18th inst., Mr. John Minola, a native of Comono, in Italy, of the firm of A. Tarone & Co. of this place.
Died on Wednesday the 19th inst., Joseph Ballarini, a native of Comona, in Italy....

Issue of August 24, 1807

Departed this life on Friday morning, last, in the 36th year of her age, Mrs. Ann Gordon, the wife of Mr. John Gordon of this city....(eulogy)

Issue of August 25, 1807

Departed this life on Monday evening last, Charles Williams, in the 41st year of his age, a native of Scotland, but for 16 years a citizen of this place.

Issue of August 26, 1807

Married on the 25th inst., by the Rev. Marin Detargny, Mr. Joseph Finch, to Miss Catherine Spencer, both of this place.
Died lately in England, Elizabeth Clayton, aged 60....

Issue of August 27, 1807

Married at New-York, on the 17th inst., Mr. William Smith, merchant, of Charleston, S. C. to Miss Mary M'Knight, daughter of the Rev. John M'Knight, of that city.

Issue of August 28, 1807

Died on the 23d inst., Mr. Jacob Ernest, Taylor, many years an inhabitant of this city.

Issue of August 29, 1807

Died on the 23d inst., Mr. Daniel Ewing, merchant, a native of Scotland.

Issue of August 31, 1807

Died on Saturday last, Mrs. Jane Lockless, aged 20 years, a native of England...resided in this city about 9 months...left a husband....

Issue of September 1, 1807

Departed this life on the 29th of August, Mr. John H. Rodman, a native of New-York, and a resident of this city about 3 years; aged 34 years and 2 days.

Issue of September 4, 1807

Married, on Wednesday evening last, by the Rev. Mr. M'Quain, Mr. Nathaniel Green Welch, to Miss Fanny Elizabeth Clastrier, both of this city.

Issue of September 5, 1807

Departed this life on the 3d inst., in the 35th year of her age, Miss Mary Isabella O'Brien, eldest daughter of B. O'Brien, Merchant of Dublin.
Died on the 3d inst., in the 29th year of his age, Mr. John Tillinghast, of the firm of Pearce & Tillinghast, Merchants of this city...a native of Rhode-Island, a Lt. in the newly-raised company of Riflemen.
Died on the 3d inst., in the 24th year of his age, Mr. James Neilson, Merchant of this city.
Died on the 3d inst., Mr. James Drew, a native of Scotland.

Issue of September 7, 1807

Died in this city on the 28th ult., Mr. Joel Baldwin, and on the 2d inst., Mr. James Newton--they were of the firm of Newton & Baldwin, Boot and Shoe Makers, from Philadelphia.
Died on the 2d inst., Mr. Augustus D. Jones, a native of Virginia, and a resident of this city upwards of 3 years, aged 26 years....
Died on the 2d inst., in the 28th year of his age, Mr. Alexander Gibson, a native of Massachusetts.

Died on the 3d inst., Mary Mary=Ann Lamb, aged 30 years, wife of Capt. James Lamb. She was a native of Edinburgh, and left a husband and five children....
Died on the 5th inst., Mr. Andrew Holmes, merchant of this city.

Issue of September 8, 1807

Died on Saturday the 5th inst., Miss Mary White Barksdale....
Died on Friday last, Mrs. Bridget Turnbull, aged 45 years, a native of Ireland...
Died on the 5th inst., Mr. James Park, a native of Ireland, in the 22d year of his age....
Died, yesterday morning, Mr. Wm. Adams, aged 19 years, brother of Mr. J. S. Adams, merchant, of this city.
Died, yesterday afternoon, Mr. Patrick M'Dowall, for many years, a respectable merchant in this city.
Died on the 4th inst., Mr. James Bates, a native of England, aged 18 years, son of William Bates, Comedian.
Died on Sullivan's Island, on the 7th inst., Mr. William Rose, aged 38 years, a native of Sweden....

Issue of September 9, 1807

Died on Saturday the 5th inst., Mrs. Mary Petrie, widow of the late Mr. Edmund Petrie, in the 68th year of her age....
Died on the 7th inst., in this city, Mr. Samuel H. Porter, in the 23d year of his age, son of the Rev. Mr. Porter, of Rye, New-Hampshire.
Died, yesterday, on Sullivan's-Island, Mr. Samuel Chapman, Merchant, aged 27 years.
Died on Sullivan's-Island, on the 7th inst., Mr. John Diedrich Peper, a native of Hamburg, aged 25 years.

Issue of September 10, 1807

Died on Tuesday night, the 8th inst., Mr. John Urquhart, nephew of Mr. Charles Banks, in the 24th year of his age.
Died on the 8th inst., Mr. Jonathan W. Coy, a native of Rhode-Island, aged 23 years.

Issue of September 11, 1807

Died on the 4th inst., Mr. Thomas Noble, a native of England.
Died in New-York, on the 27th ult., Mr. Andrew Gordon, of this city, in the 53d year of his age.
The gallant commodore Preble, departed this life on the 26th August, at Portland.

Issue of September 12, 1807

Died, early yesterday morning, Mrs. Agatha M'Dowall, aged 36 years, relict of Patrick M'Dowall, who died on Monday last... leaving six orphans....

Issue of September 14, 1807

Died on Saturday last, Mrs. Ann Teasdale, relict of the late Isaac Teasdale, esq. deceased.
Died on Saturday last, in the 29th year of his age, Mr. Thomas Kennard, Printer, a native of Portsmouth,New-Hampshire....
Died on Sullivan's-Island, on the 10th inst., Mr. Archibald Johnston, merchant, a native of Scotland.

Died on the 18th ult., at his plantation in this state, Mr. Philip Lamar...and on the same day, his consort Mrs. Ruth Lamar.

Issue of September 15, 1807

Departed this life on the 18th of June last, in the city of York (Eng.) Mr. William Abbott, late merchant of this city.

Issue of September 16, 1807

Married on Thursday the 20th ult., in Camden, Dr. Jesse Howard, to Miss Sarah Stewart, both of said place.

Died on his passage from hence for Liverpool, on board the ship George Augustus, capt. Jackson, Mr. Thomas Gyles, aged 28 years, late of this city.

Died on Sunday morning last, Miss Mary Haynes, aged 19 years and 6 months, a native of Albany, state of New-York.

Died on Saturday last, Mr. Isaac Bouchonneau, in the 27th year of his age.

Departed this life on the 10th inst., Capt. Christopher Whipple, in the 38th year of his age, a native of Rhode Island.

Died on the 14th inst., in the 29th year of his Mr. I. Charles Hentz, a native of Bremen.

Died on the 14th inst., in St. Thomas's Parish, Dr. Alexander Methwin, a native of Scotland.

Died on Friday the 28th ult. at Chester Court-House(S.C.), Clement A Thompson, a member of the Republic Artillery Company of said place.

Died in Savannah, on the 10th inst., Mr. John Dougherty, Printer...a native of Ireland and formerly an inhabitant of this city.

Issue of September 17, 1807

Married last evening, Mr. Hyam Abendanone, of the Island of St. Thomas, to Miss Grace Abendanone, of this city.

Married on the 13th ult., in Laurens district, by John A. Elmore, esq. Charles Ferguson, Esq. to Miss Elizabeth Baizley.

Died on the 14th inst., in the 22d year of his age, Mr. Edmond Walton, after a painful illness of 6 days.

Died on the 15th inst., Mr. John Norment, formerly a resident, near Newbern, N. C.

Died on Tuesday last, Mr. Argyle Williamson, gunsmith, a native of Richmond, Va.

Died on Sunday the 13th inst., in this city, in the 30th year of her age, Mrs. Elizabeth Lois Rivers, relict of Malory Rivers, jun. late of James-Island...left two small children....

Issue of September 18, 1807

Departed this life on the 12th ult., in the 37th year of her age, Mrs. Hedley, consort of the Rev. J. Hedley...left husband and five helpless children....

Issue of September 19, 1807

Married, Mr. Isaac Da Costa, to Miss Jane Samuel, both of this city.

Departed this life early in the morning of the 17th inst., Master John Buhanan, in the 16th year of his age....

Died on Thursday the 17th inst., Mr. Andrew Bell, co-partner, of the House of Wm. Marshall & Co., aged 32 years...native of Annan, in the county of Dumfries, Scotland....

Died at Baltimore, on the 6th inst., John Price, Esq. of this city, merchant, aged 44 years....

Issue of September 21, 1807

Beaufort (S.C.) September 16
Departed this life on Monday afternoon, Mr. Arthur Smith, and on Tuesday morning, Mr. Thomas Hutson....duel.

Issue of September 23, 1807

Died at Georgetown, district of Columbia, on the 11th inst., Mrs. Matilda Cox, wife of John Cox, Esq. brother of Mr. Cox of this Office.

Died on Sullivan's Island, on Saturday morning last, Mr. Jonathan Bird, Cabinet Maker, aged 80 years, a native of Yorkshire, England....

Died on Saturday last, in the 33d year of her age, Mrs. Christina Barnstein, wife of John Henry Barnstein, of this place.

Issue of September 24, 1807

Died at Washington Village, near this city, on the 1st inst., Charlotte, daughter of Mr. William R. Payne, aged 21 months, and on Tuesday the 22d inst., in the 24th year of her age, Mrs. Jane Payne, wife of Mr. William R. Payne...left two children.

Died on the 22d inst., in the 25th year of her age, Mrs. Catharine Douglas, a native of Greenock, Scotland.

Died yesterday morning, in the 25th year of his age, Mr. Jacob Corre, a native of Amsterdam.

Died yesterday morning, Master James P. Coy, in the 15th year of his age...native of Providence, R. I.

Issue of September 25, 1807

Married last evening, by the Rev. Dr. Hollinshead, Mr. Archibald Whitney, to Miss Mary Drennes, only daughter of the late Mr. George Drennas, deceased, both of this city.

Married on Tuesday morning, by the Rev. James D. Simons, Charles D. Simons, esq. to Miss Sarah Barksdale, youngest daughter of Thomas Barksdale, esq. deceased.

Died on the 9th inst., Mr. J. B. Bacquetty, one of the first performers on the Violin, in South-Carolina.

Died on the 2d inst., in St. James's, Santee, Mrs. Mary Steed Michaw, consort of Captain Abraham Michaw.

Died on Saturday last, Mr. Hugh Duncan, aged 19 years, recently from New-York, a native of Glasgow.

Died in Savannah, on Saturday last, aged 70 years, the Hon. Edward Telfair, a member of the Senate of that State from Chatham County, and President of that body--Judge of the Inferior Court, and formerly Gov. of the State of Ga.

Died at Nassau, N. P., on Thursday the 27th ult., in the 26th year of his age, Mr. Christopher H. Gilfert, a native of Hesse Cassell, but for these eight years past, a resident in the U. S.

Issue of September 26, 1807

Died on Saturday last, in the 20th year of her age, Mrs. Mary Ann Brown, wife of Alexander Brown, a native of Liverpool...left husband and two children....

Died on the 25th inst., Mr. Samuel Denny, aged 22 years, a native of Middleton (Con.)

Issue of September 28, 1807

Died on the 25th inst., in the 31st year of his age, Peter Simons, Esq. formerly of Georgetown.

Died on Saturday morning, the 26th inst., Mr. David Davis, aged about 25 years, a native of England...residence of three years in S. C....

Issue of September 29, 1807

Died on Friday morning the 25th inst., Mrs. Ann Jones, wife of Dr. Edward Jones, aged 32 years, and on the 26th inst., Master Edward Jones, their Son, aged 8 years.

Died on the 25th inst., in the 24th year of his age, Mr. Samuel M'Conchie, a native of Scotland, but for 2 years a resident of this city....

Died on Saturday morning, the 26th inst., Mr. John Comly, aged 28 years, a native of Philadelphia, and Mate of the sloop Friendship, George Binder, master.

Died at New Orleans, Captain David Patterson, of this port. Died in London on the 1st of August, aged 76, John Walker, Esq. author of the pronouncing Dictionary, &C.

Issue of September 30, 1807

Died on the 25th inst., Mr. John Tarlton, aged 36 years, a native of St. Mary's County, state of Maryland....

Died on the 28th inst., on Sullivan's Island, in the 18th year of his age, Mr. John Brown, a native of Glasgow, in Scotland ....

Issue of October 1, 1807

Died on the 24th ult., in the 16th year of his age, John J. De Berniere, son of Col. John De Bernier, of North-Carolina, much lamented.

Issue of October 2, 1807

Died on Monday the 28th ult., Mr. William Carver, aged 76 years, a native of England....

Died in Prince William's Parish, on the 27th ult., Mr. Charles Love, in the 20th year of his age....

Died on Friday, the 25th ult., John Ladson Freazer Bee, nine years and four months old.

Issue of October 3, 1807

Died, on Friday the 18th ult., Mrs. Mary Snell, consort of Adam Snell Esq. of St. Mathew's Parish, Orangeburgh District, in the 47th year of his age.

Issue of October 5, 1807

Married, by James Addison, esq., Mr. Joshua Ribault, to Miss Martha Bunch, of Broughton-Hall, St. John's Parish.

Died on the 21st ult., Mr. John Muncrieffe, Jun. in the 41st year of his age.

Died on the 26th ult., Mr. Philip Millar, a native of Pa., for some years past a respectable inhabitant of this place.

Issue of October 6, 1807

Married in England, Mr. William Meadows, aged 75 to Mary Lowe, aged 57, being his sixth wife....
Married, in England, his Grace the Duke of Newcastle, to Miss Mundy daughter of Edward Miller Mundy, Esq....
Died at his plantation near Coosawhatchie, in St. Luke's parish, on the morning of the 29th ult., John Kinney, in the 61st year of his age.

Issue of October 9, 1807

Died, yesterday afternoon, Mr. Meinrad Greiner, a native of Switzerland.
Died at Philadelphia, on Thursday the 1st inst., Gen. Peter Muhlenberg, Collector of the Port at that place.

Issue of October 10, 1807

Died on Monday the 5th inst., Mr. John Frederick Generick, in the 61st year of his age, a native of Germany, an old inhabitant of this city....

Issue of October 12, 1807

Married, at Savannah, on Wednesday evening last, Joshua Aydilott, of this city, to Miss Tabitha Bell Edwards of that place.
Died, on Saturday the 10th inst., Mr. Thomas M'Keil, aged 32 years, a native of Baltimore....

Issue of October 13, 1807

Married, at Parish, on the 27th of August, last, Mr. Benjamin Strobel, merchant of htis city to Miss Sarah Russell Church, of Boston.
Died at Parish, on the 25th August last, Mr. Portalis, aged 63 years....

Issue of October 15, 1807

Died in Georgetown, on the 6th inst., Miss Sarah Bossard Shackelford, aged 13 years and 7 months, youngest daughter of John Shackelford....

Issue of October 16, 1807

Married, last evening, by the Rev. Mr. Simons, Mr. John Gabeau, of this city, to Miss Susannah Hartman, of Christ Church Parish.
Died on the 13th inst., Mr. William Edward Scott, aged 27 years.
Died in Barnwell District on the 6th inst., Mr. Charles Steed, in the 40th year of his age....

Issue of October 17, 1807

Died on the 10th inst., on Charleston Neck, in the 74th year of his age, Mr. John White, a native of Europe, but resided in Boston, New England, nearly 40 years...left wife and daughter....
Died in this city, on the 5th inst., Miss Sarah Murrell....

Issue of October 19, 1807

Departed this life on the 14th inst., Mr. Benjamin Blake, in the 25th year of his age.

Issue of October 20, 1807

Died at Beaufort, on the 3d inst., Mrs. Jane Barnwell, relict of the late John B. Barnwell, esq. deceased.
Died at Mount Ararat, in Barnwell Dist., on the 28th ult., Miss Adeline Eliza Hagood, aged 3 years and 5 months, daughter of Major Gideon Hagood.

Issue of October 21, 1807

Died on Monday last, the 19th inst., Mrs. Ann Peyton, wife of Richard H. Peyton, Esq...left husband and four infant children.
Died, yesterday morning, Mr. Thomas H. Hatton, Comedian, formerly of Haymarket, London and late of the Charleston Theatre.
Died on the 18th inst., Mr. David Hoskins, a native of Hartford, Conn....
Died on the 19th inst., in the 22d year of his age, Mr. John Davis, a native of Blumingburg, in the state of New-York....
Died at his plantation in Edgefield, S. C. on the 23d ult., in the 25th year of his age, Mr. Michael Blocker, leaving a wife and four children....
Died at Adams (Berkshire county, Mass.) on the 19th ult., Mr. J. Peters, aged 107 years....
Died at Schenectady (N. J.) Mrs. Elizabeth Cowans, in the 104th year of her age....

Issue of October 22, 1807

Married on Saturday evening last, by the Rev. Dr. Hollinshead, Mr. Peter Guyon, to Mrs. Ann Paterson, both of this city.
Died on Sunday last, in the 27th year of her age, Mrs. Leveen, a native of London...left husband and 4 orphan children....
Died on the 19th inst., in the 16th year of her age, Miss Margaret Swinton Ward, daughter of Daniel Ward, of this city.
Died on the 16th inst., Miss Susannah Steedman Morison, youngest daughter of James Morison, merchant....
Died in Savannah on the 29th ult., Dr. Elijah P. Crocker, aged 33 years, a native of Mass., but for several years past an inhabitant of Georgetown, S. C.

Issue of October 23, 1807

Married last evening, by the Rev. Dr. Furman, Mr. John T. Lacey, to Miss Mary Hughes, both of this city.
Died on Sunday evening last, aged 4 years and 10 months, William Harris Clarkson, eldest son of Mr. William Clarkson, merchant....
Died on Wednesday morning last, in the 38th year of his age, Mr. John Gourlay....
Died on Tuesday the 13th inst., at his plantation on Black River, Mr. Thomas D. Porter, planter, in the 22d year of his age.
Died in Savannah on the 20th inst., Mr. Matthew Lyon Edwards, Printer, about 20 years of age, a native of Wales in England.
Died on the 14th inst.,on board the U. S. frigate Chesapeake, Lt. Benjamin Smith, first lt. of that frigate.

Issue of October 26, 1807

Died on Wednesday morning last, in this city, Mr. John Wilson, cabinet-maker, in the 55th year of his age...left a wife and seven small children....in Rev. War.

Died near Sumterville, on the 7th inst., Mrs. Rebecca Coppedge, in the 18th year of her age...left an infant about 10 months old....

Issue of October 27, 1807

Died on the 25th inst., in the 54th year of his age, Capt. Lewis Fogartie....left widow and infant son.

Died at Monk's Corner, on the 17th inst., in the 26th year of his age, Mr. Stephen St. John.

Departed this life in Barnwell Dist., S. C., Master George Galphin, aged 18 years, son of Thomas Galphin, Esq....

Issue of October 28, 1807

Died on the 24th inst., in the 58th year of his age, Mr. Charles Desel, an old and respectable inhabitant of this city....

Died on the 25th inst., Miss Sarah Carew, in the 38th year of her age....

Issue of October 29, 1807

Died on Tuesday last, Capt. Paul Rosse, in the 37th year of his age...interred in the Roman Catholic Church....

Died on Tuesday last, Mr. Samuel Brailsford, in the 19th year of his age....

Issue of October 30, 1807

Married last evening, by the Rev. Mr. Charles Faber, Mr. Frederick Naser, to Miss Ann Custer, daughter of Mr. James Custer, all of this city.

Died on the 27th inst., in the 79th year of her age, Mrs. Judith Lennox, widow of William Lennox, Esq. of this place.

Died in this city on the 20th inst., Benjamin Franklin Timothy, Esq. formerly Proprietor of the S. C. State Gazette, published in this city.

Died on the 26th inst., in the 72d year of his age, John Beale, Esq. the oldest wharf-owner in this city....

Died in Baltimore, on the 17th inst., in the 25th year of his age, Lieut. James S. Higinsbothom, of the American Navy.

Issue of November 2, 1807

Died on the Coast of Africa, Mr. John Sabb, and Mr. James Quin, both of this city.

Died at Cayenne, the wife of Victor Hughes, the Gen. himself is not dead, as stated.

Issue of November 3, 1807

Died on Sunday morning, the 25th ult., Mrs. Elizabeth Smith, consort of Capt. Peter Smith, in the 53d year of her age....

Issue of November 4, 1807

Married on Thursday evening the 22d ult.,by the Rev. Mr. Jones, Mr. Patrick Ardagh,to Miss Charlotte Richardson, daughter

of Mr. David Richardson, of Richardsonville, Edgefield district.
Died yesterday, Michael Kalteisen, Esq. Commandant of Ft. Johnson....
Died on the 2d inst., Mr. William Barker, aged 39 years, a native of Smyrna.

Issue of November 5, 1807

Died last evening, in this city, Mr. George Irving, merchant, late from Rio Pongus, aged 43 years....

Issue of November 6, 1807

Died, at Bellevue, on James Island, in the 76th year of her age, Mrs. Margaret Bennett...a native Carolinian, and lived about 60 years in this city....
Died at New-Orleans, on the 5th ult., Capt. William Berry, of the brig Armed Neutrality, of this port.

Issue of November 7, 1807

Died on the 3d inst., in the 38th year of his age, Mr. John Haslett, Sen. a native of Ireland...left widow....

Issue of November 9, 1807

Married on Friday evening last, by the Rev. Mr. Munds, Capt. Joseph Stevens, to Miss Mary Richardson, both of this place.
Married on Saturday evening last, by the Rev. Mr. Munds, Mr. Israel Read, to Miss Ann Fisher, both of this place.
Departed this life on the 26th Oct. last, in the 62d year of her age, Mrs. Sarah Mackie, widow of Dr. James Mackie, of Waccamaw....
Died on the 29th ult., in this city, Mrs. Anna Morgan, aged 84 years and 5 months....

Issue of November 10, 1807

Died in St. Luke's parish, on Wednesday morning, the 4th inst., in the 35th year of his age, Alexander Rose Porteous, Esq. He left wife and infant daughter....
Died on the 8th inst., Mr. Patrick Moon, in the 59th year of his age...a native of Newcastle-upon-Tyne, but had resided in this state 37 years.
Died on Friday evening last, Mr. Benjamin Green, a native of Holland, in the 56th year of his age.
Died on the 8th inst., Hon. John Lloyd, esq. in the 73d year of his age....

Issue of November 11, 1807

Married last evening by the Rev. Mr. Simons, Mr. Simson Williams, to Miss Catharine Devaull.
Departed this life on Saturday evening, the 7th inst., aged 25 years, Mrs. Martha Mary Raynal, wife of Mr. Lewis Raynal, and only daughter of Mr. William Rouse.
Departed this life on the 2d inst., Mrs. Ann Mary Faber, wife of Mr. Christian Henry Faber, and daughter of the late Mr. Charles Desel, aged 21 years and 5 months....

Issue of November 12, 1807

Married on Sunday evening last, by the Rev. Dr. Buist, Henry James Chalmers, Esq. to Miss Eliza Geddes, both of this city.

Married last evening, Mr. Josiah Moses, to Miss Rebecca Phillips.

Died on Saturday the 7th inst., in the 53th year of his age, Stephen Lee, Esq....

Issue of November 13, 1807

Married on Wednesday evening last, by the Rev. Mr. Gadsden, William Washington Jun. Esq. to Miss Martha Blake, daughter of John Blake, esq. all of this city.

Married last evening, by the Rev. Dr. Gallagher, Mr. James Riley, to Miss Maria Mayberry.

Issue of November 14, 1807

Died last evening, Mr. Amos Babcock, in the 26th year of his age, a native of Connecticut.

Issue of November 17, 1807

Married on Thursday evening, by the Rev. Dr. Hollinshead, Mr. Thomas G. Riggs, to Mrs. Maria Marlen.

Died at Beaufort, on Monday the 9th inst., Mrs. Mary Grayson, wife of Capt. Thomas Grayson, who has left a husband and five young children....

Issue of November 18, 1807

Died on the 6th inst.,in Bryan County, Ga., Simon Maxwell, Esq. Collector for the port of Hardwick.

Issue of November 19, 1807

Died on the 16th inst., at his plantation on Waccamaw, near Georgetown, Mr. John Cogdell, in the 79th year of his age, left a widow and numerous relatives.

Died at Matanzies on the 6th Nov., Capt. Moses G. Powers, of the schr. Laura, of Charleston.

Departed this life on the 9th inst., Mrs. Eleanor Witten, wife of Peter Witten, esq. and eldest daughter of capt. Robert Hails, of Santee....

Issue of November 20, 1807

Married on the 19th Oct., by William Clinton, Esq., Mr. E. J. Adickes, merchant of Chester district, to Miss Sarah Moore, eldest daughter of Alexander Moore, Esq. Ordinary of York Dist.

Issue of November 21, 1807

Married on Tuesday evening last, by the Rev. Dr. Gallagher, Mr. Peter Suau, merchant, to the amiable Miss Rose Antoinette Champy, daughter of Edme Champy, esq. attorney at law.

Died at the Cheraws, on the 3d inst., in the 19th year of her age, Mrs. Ann Eliza Davis, wife of Mr. John W. Davis, of Georgetown, and only daughter of the late Mr. John M'Iver, of this city.

Died on the 17th inst., at John's Island, Mr. John Ball, aged 29 years and 10 months.

Departed this life on Thursday the 13th inst., in St. Paul's Parish, Mr. Adam F. Gitsinger, in the 50th year of his age.
Died on the 3d inst., at his plantation on Saluda River, Newberry District, Mr. Elisha Brooks, in the 47th year of his age...left wife and eight children, two brothers and one sister. in Rev. war....

Issue of November 23, 1807

Died at his plantation near Orangeburgh, on the 7th inst., Capt. Christian Rumph, aged 43 years.

Issue of November 24, 1807

Married on Saturday evening last, by the Rev. Dr. Hollinshead, Mr. Henry D. Herron, to Miss Maria Buhanan, both of this city.
Died on Saturday morning, the 21st inst.,in the 64th year of her age, Mrs. Ann T. Wish, relict of the late Mr. Benjamin Wish....

Issue of November 25, 1807

Married on Sunday evening, by the Rev. Mr. Simons, Mr. James Welsman, to Miss Amelia Holwell, both of this city.
Died on Saturday last, in the 78th year of her age, Mrs. Ann Glover, relict of Col. J. Glover.

Issue of November 27, 1807

Died on the 23d inst., Miss Elizabeth Mouatt, of this city.
Died at Slann's Bridge, on the 19th inst., in the 48th year of his age, Mr. J. Chandless, a native of Surry, in England... left a wife and four children....

Issue of November 28, 1807

Married on Thursday evening by the Rev. Mr. Munds, Mr. John Harrison, to Miss Elizabeth Young, both of this place.
Married last evening, by the Rev. Mr. Munds, Capt. Thomas Williamson, to Miss Sarah Maria Bailey, both of this place.
Died on the 16th inst., at Potosi, in M'Intosh Co., Ga., Mrs. Elizabeth Wood, wife of Major Wood, and daughter of William Brailsford, Esq. of this state, in the 21st year of her age, and the first of her marriage...left infant son 6 days old....
Died at Georgetown, on the 20th inst., Mrs. Elizabeth Brodut, in the 57th year of her age....

Issue of December 1, 1807

Died on Tuesday last, aged 73, Mrs. Jane M'Whann, consort of Wm. M'Whann, esq.
Died on the 15th inst., in Amelia Township, Mr. Joseph M'Cord.
Departed this life in Columbia, in her 17th year, Mrs. C. Creyon, consort of Mr. John Creyon, Merchant of that place....

Issue of December 2, 1807

Departed this life, at John's-Island, on the 25th ult., Mrs. Elizabeth Elliott Holmes, consort of Isaac Holmes....
Died on the 28th ult., Mrs. Elizabeth Mitchell Shrewsbury, wife of Mr. Stephen Shrewsbury, of this city....
Died on the 13th ult., in the 71st year of his age, Mr. Adam Spidle...a native of Wirtemburg, in Germany, and emigrated to

South Carolina, about 1750....

Issue of December 3, 1807

Married on Sunday evening last, by the Rev. Mr. Gadsden, George Warren Cross, Esq. to Miss Mary Man Pawley, daughter of the late Anthony Pawley, esq. of Waccamaw.
Died at Georgetown (S.C.) on the 21st ult., in the 82d year of her age, Mrs. Hannah Murray, sister of Hugh Swinton, esq. of this city.

Issue of December 4, 1807

Married on Wednesday evening last, by the Rev. Thomas Price, Mr. John Rivers, planter, to Miss Susannah Love Rivers, youngest daughter of Mallory Rivers, esq. decd., all of St. Andrew's Parish.
Married on Wed. evening last, by the Rev. Mr. Jacob Suares, Mr. Aaron Moise, to Miss Sarah Cohen, daughter of the late Mr. Gershon Cohen, of this city.
Married on Wed. evening last, by the Rev. Jacob Suares, Mr. Hyam Moise, to Miss Cecilia Woolf, daughter of the late Mr. Solomon Woolf, of this city.
Married, last evening, by the Rev. Dr. Hollinshead, Mr. Robert Stent, to Miss Rebecca Wood, both of this city.
Married last evening, by the Rev. Mr. Gadsden, Mr. Philip P. Broughton, to Miss Mary Broughton, second daughter of Alexander Broughton, Esq. late of this city, decd.
Died on the 25th of Nov., in Fairfield District, Mrs. Charlotte Player, consort of Joshua Player, esq. and eldest daughter of the late Mr. James Hamden Thomson, of this city....
Died on Tuesday afternoon, Mr. Abraham Jones, aged 100 years and upwards...a native of Germany and came to this country about 1749 or 1750....

Issue of December 5, 1807

Married on Wed. evening last, by the Rev. Mr. Jacob Suares, Mr. Nathan Hart, Merchant, to Miss Rachel Hart, eldest daughter of Daniel Hart, Esq. of this city.
Died on the 17th ult., at his seat in Barnwell District, in the 28th year of his age, Captain Edward Kirkland, commander of the Republican Troop of Horse of said District.

Issue of December 7, 1807

Died on Friday the 13th ult., at his place near Cambridge, S. C., the Rev. David Lilly, aged about 39 years.
Died at Boston, on the 29th ult.,Mr. Samuel Hall, aged 67 ....

Issue of December 8, 1807

Died on his passage from Africa, to this port, capt. John Sabins, late master of the ship Charlotte.

Issue of December 9, 1807

Married on Wednesday evening last, by Mr. Alexander Solomons, Mr. Michael Simpson,merchant, to Miss Ann Cohen, daughter of the late Mr. Abraham Cohen, merchant of this city.
Died on the 24th ult., Mr. John English, of Kershaw District, inthe 23d year of his age.

Died, at Laurens Ville, on the 28th ult., in the 28th year of his age, Mr. John Hunter, eldest son of the late John Hunter, esq.

Issue of December 10, 1807

Died on the 2d inst., at Charley Wood Plantation, in St. Thomas' Parish, Mrs. Harriot Wigfall, consort of Thomas Wigfall, Esq...left husband and seven young children....

Issue of December 11, 1807

Married on Tuesday evening last, by the Rev. Dr. Gallagher, Capt. Cornelius O'Driscol to Miss Maria R. Ralvande, both of this city.
Died in London, at an advanced age, Sir Brook Watson....

Issue of December 12, 1807

Married on Wednesday evening last, by the Rev. Dr. Hollinshead, Mr. John Johnson, to Mrs. Elizabeth Granville.

Issue of December 19, 1807

Married on Wednesday evening last, by the Rev. Mr. Simons, Dr. James H. Fayssoux, to Miss Elizabeth Cripps, second daughter of John Splatt Cripps, esq.
Died lately in Beaufort, Mrs. Ann Mackie, relict of the late Dr. John Mackie....aged 63 years.

Issue of December 21, 1807

Married on Thursday the 17th inst., by the Rev. Dr. Buist, Mr. William Birnie, merchant, to Miss Mary Rout, both of this city.
Married last evening by the Rev. Dr. Buist, Mr. Nicol Bryce, to Miss Mary Elizabeth Scot, daughter of Mr. James Scot, all of this city.
Married last evening, by the Rev. Mr. Faber, Mr. John Michael Miller to Miss Sarah Armstrong, both of this city.
Died on Thursday the 17th inst., Mrs. Elizabeth Denniss, aged 53 years.

Issue of December 22, 1807

Married on Thursday last, by the Rev. Dr. M'Calla, Mr. John White to Miss Sarah Hamlin, second daughter of Thomas Hamlin, esq. all of Christ Church Parish.
Married on Sunday evening last, by the Rev. Dr. Buist, Mr. Samuel Smith Jun. to Miss Jane M'Cliesh, both of this city.
Married in Philadelphia, on the 10th inst., by the Right Rev. Bishop White, Mr. Condy Raguet, merchant to Miss Catharine S. Simmons, daughter of Mr. James Simmons, of Philadelphia.

Issue of December 23, 1807

Died on his passage from this port for Havana, Mr. John Main, of this city.
Died on Wednesday the 16th inst., Theodore Gaillard Marshall, second son of the late Chancellor Marshall.
Died at his place in Horry District on the 15th ult., Capt. William Snow, in the 70th year of his age.
Died on Saturday the 13th inst., at his residence on Sampit, Edward Thomas, Esq. aged 63 years.

Issue of December 28, 1807

Married in St. John's parish, on Thursday evening last, by the Rev. Mr. Thompson, James Addison, Esq. of St. Stephen's parish, to Miss Amelia L. June, of St. John's parish.

Issue of December 30, 1807

Died on the 19th inst., at his house in Cumming-street, Mr. Alexander Chollet, in the 50th year of his age...thirty years resided in this state.
Died on the 26th inst., John Ewing, merchant of this city, a native of Scotland.
Died at Nassau, N. P., on the 5th inst., Capt. Ezekiel Phillips, late master of the brig Ann, of this port.
Died at Jamaica, on the 17th of Oct., the Rev. Father William Lebun, Apostolic Prefect of St. Domingo....

Issue of December 31, 1807

Married on Tuesday evening, 22d inst., by the Rev. Dr. Furman, Capt. John Davis to Miss Jane Bruse Richardson, youngest daughter of Mr. James Richardson, of the Island of Bermuda.
Married in Orangeburgh District, on Thursday the 24th inst., by the Rev. Mr. Barr, Mr. Henry Patrick, to Miss Bertheny Berry, both of this place.
Died on Monday the 28th inst., in the 64th year of his age, Mr. John Webb, a resident of this city....
Died on the 28th inst., James Boyle, grocer, of this city....
Died in this city on the 28th inst., Dr. Cassillis Shaw, of Kingston, Jamaica.

Issue of January 2, 1808

Married on Thursday evening last, by the Rev. Dr. Hollinshead, Capt. George Preble, to Mrs. Mary Thomas, both of this city.

Issue of January 4, 1808

Married, on Saturday evening last, at Runnimede, on Ashley River, by the Rev. Mr. Mills, Robert Smith, Esq. son of the late Right Rev. Bishop Smith, to Miss Elizabeth Mary Pringle, daughter of John Julius Pringle, esq.

Issue of January 5, 1808

Married on Thursday evening last, by the Rev. Mr. Bowen, Edward Barnwell, jun. Esq. of Beaufort, to Miss Elizabeth Osborn, daughter of Thomas Osborn, Esq. of this place.

Issue of January 8, 1808

Married at Georgetown, on Thursday evening, the 31st ult., by the Rev. Mr. Botsford, Mr. Thomas Dowdney, to Miss Rebecca Villepontoux.

Issue of January 7, 1808

Married on Tuesday evening, by the Rev. John Phillips, Mr. Henry Bennett, of this city, to Mrs. Hannah Weles, of Christ Church Parish.
Married on Sunday evening sen'night, by the Rev. Dr. Buist, Mr. James Barkley, merchant, to Miss Sarah Flemming, both of this

city.

Issue of January 8, 1808

Married on Tuesday the 5th inst., by the Rev. Mr. Simons, Dr. Alexander Baron, jun. to Miss Elizabeth Ferguson Ladson, daughter of Major James Ladson.
Married, on Tuesday evening, by the Rev. Mr. Nankivel, Mr. Thomas Melrose, of Christ Church Parish, to Mrs. Mary Phelps, of St. Thomas's parish.

Issue of January 9, 1808

Married on Thursday evening last, by the Rev. Mr. Munds, Capt. James George Hall, to Miss Catharine Jane Lee.
Married last evening, by the Rev. Mr. Munds, Mr. Henry Seymour, to Miss Elizabeth Thomas, both of this place.
Departed this life on Monday the 28th ult., Mr. John Darzaugh, aged 34 years and 3 days.
Died on the 4th inst., Mr. Henry Ker, merchant, of the house of Henry and John Ker, of this city....
Died near Savannah, on the 23d ult.,Mrs. Mary Charlotte Jackson, relict of Major Gen. Jackson.

Issue of January 11, 1808

Departed this life on Monday evening, the 4th inst., George Wagner, Esq....left wife and family....

Issue of January 12, 1808

Died, yesterday morning, the Lady of Gen. Vanderhorst....
Died on the 7th inst., Mrs. Mary Ballantine, in the 87th year of her age, a resident in this city for near 70 years....
Died on the 9th inst., in the 40th year of her age, Mrs. Mary Futhey, wife of Mr. Heartly Futhey....
Died on the 8th inst., Mr. James Gotea, in the 27th year of his age....

Issue of January 13, 1808

Married last evening, by the Rev. Mr. Hollinshead, Mr. John Fraser, to Miss Ann Mathews, daughter of Wm. Mathews, Esq. all of this city.
Married on the 31st ult., by Thomas Palmer, esq. Mr. David Hinds, to Miss Margaret Hughes, daughter of Samuel Hughes, of Scuffle-Town, St. Stephen's Parish.
Departed this life on the 4th Oct. last, at Pocotaligo, in the 43d yearof her age, Mrs. Elizabeth Hauser, widow of the late Mr. Elias Hauser...left five children....

Issue of January 14, 1808

Married on Tuesday evening, by the Rev. Dr. Hollinshead, Mr. Joseph Dorrill of Christ Church Parish, to Miss Rachel Combee, of this city.
Departed this life on the 12th inst., Mrs. Elizabeth Keating, long an inhabitant of this city, aged 40 years.

Issue of January 15, 1808

Died on Monday evening last, Mr. Joseph Solomon, for many years a respectable inhabitant of this city.

Issue of January 16, 1808

Died in the State of Tennessee, on the 11th ult., John Dickey, formerly of this state.
Married on Thursday evening last, in St. Thomas's Parish, by the Rev. Mr. Phillips, Mr. John M. Hoff, to Miss Nancy Morgan, both of this place.
Departed this life on the 4th inst., at Branford, the seat of Paul Hamilton, Esq. Paul Hamilton Rhodes, son of Dr. Nathaniel Rhodes, aged 13 months and 20 days.
Died in Christ Church Parish, on the 12th inst., in the 31st year of his age, Mr. John Love, planter, a native of Fayetteville, N. C....left wife and child....

Issue of January 18, 1808

Married on Thursday evening the 31st Dec. last, by Robert Hutchinson, Mr. William Hutchinson, to Miss Jane Workman, both of Laurens District.

Issue of January 19, 1808

Married, at Black Swamp, S. C. on the 11th inst.,by the Rev. Mr. Crawford, Mr. John P. Haymon, to Miss Ann B. Winkler, both of the same place.

Issue of January 20, 1808

Died in this city, on Monday the 11th inst., Mrs. Ann Scott, relict of Mr. Thomas Scott, of James-Island, aged 62 years and 6 months.

Issue of January 21, 1808

Married on Tuesday evening, by the Rev. Dr. Hollinshead, Mr. William Patterson, of St. James's, Santee, to Mrs. Rebecca Ashworth, of this city.

Issue of January 22, 1808

Married last evening, by the Rev. Dr. Buist, the Hon. William Hasell Gibbes, Master in Equity, to Miss Mary Wilson, daughter of Dr. Robert Wilson, all of this city.

Issue of January 23, 1808

Married on Tuesday evening last, the 19th inst., by the Rev. Dr. M'Leod, Mr. Joseph Whaley, to Miss Louisa B. Seabrook, all of Edisto Island.
Married on Wednesday evening last, by the Rev. Dr. Hollinshead, Mr. Jacob Martin, of this city, to Miss Ann Gano, of Philadelphia.
Departed this life on the 20th inst., Mrs. Emilia Williamson, a native of this state and relict of the late Capt. Williamson, formerly of the S. C. line, in the American Rev. Army.
Died in Northumberland (Eng.), on the 15th of Nov., Gen. Charles Grey....

Issue of January 25, 1808

Died on Friday morning the 22d inst., Miss Jane Johnston, in the 57th year of her age, and for upwards of 30 years a resident in this place.
Died at the seat of his brother Col. William Boone Mitchell,

on Friday, the 15th inst., in the 41st year of his age, Dr. John Mitchell, a Representative from the Parish of St. Paul to the State Legislature....

Died on the 17th inst., in this city, Thomas Osborn, Esq. in the 64th year of his age....

Died near Franklin, Tenn., on the night of the 18th December last, John Dickey, Esq., formerly of Williamsburgh in this state....

Issue of January 26, 1808

Married on Thursday last, by the Rev. Mr. Simons, Mr. James Deveaux, to Mrs. Martha Garden, all of this city.

Died, on Saturday the 23d inst., Mr. William Haydon, an inspector of the Customs...a native of England.

Issue of January 27, 1808

Died some time in Dec. last, at St. Pierre's (Martinico) Mr. John O'Kelly, late a schoolmaster....

Issue of January 29, 1808

Married last evening in St. Bartholomew's Parish, by the Rev. Mr. Fowler, Mr. Richard Henry Fishbourne, to Miss Martha Eliza Postell, daughter of the late Col. Benjamin Postell.

Issue of January 30, 1808

Died at Kingston (Jam.) on Friday the 8th inst., in the 21st year of his age, Mr. Daniel O'Hara Jun. fifth son of Mr. Daniel O'Hara, of this city.

Issue of February 1, 1808

Married last evening, by the Rev. Dr. Buist, Mr. James Mackey, to Miss Margaret Munro, both of this city.

Died, at Beaufort, on the 15th ult., Robert G. Guerard, Esq. Collector of that port.

Issue of February 2, 1808

Married on Thursday evening last, by the Rev. Dr. Gallagher, Michael Nedligah, to Miss Judy Dempsey, both of this city.

Departed this life on Friday last, the 29th ult., Mrs. Harriot Simms, aged 23 years, wife of Mr. William Simms, merchant, of this city.

Issue of February 3, 1808

Died in Georgetown, on the 29th ult., Joseph Wragg, Esq. in the 53d year of his age.

Died at Augusta, on the 24th ult., Mr. Andrew Groshon, in the 27th year of his age, a native of New York...left wife and child....

Issue of February 6, 1808

Married on Thursday the 21st ult., at Salem (S.C.) by the Rev. James W. Stephenson, Robert Witherspoon, of Williamsburgh, to Miss Eliza M'Faddin, daughter of Col. Thomas M'Faddin.

Departed this life on the 24th ult., in the 68th year of his age, Mr. James Spears, a native of Fifeshire in Scotland....

Departed this life on the 30th ult., at his residence in York district, James M'Neal, in the 67th year of his age.

Died on the 4th inst. in this city, Mr. Robert Gordon, a native of Ireland....

Issue of February 9, 1808

Died on the 24th ult., in the 57th year of his age, Mr. John Glen of Goose-creek, planter....left a widow and four children...-

Issue of February 10, 1808

Died on Tuesday evening last, at Jacksonborough, in St. Bartholomews parish, Mr. Moses Simons, aged 40 years, a native of London.

Died in Abbeville district on the 26th ult., Capt. Andrew Bowie, of the Cavalry, in the 34th year of his age--son of Major John Bowie.

Died on the 7th ult., in the 53d year of his age, James Barry, Esq., Consul General from the Prince Regent of Portugal to the Eastern States.

Died at his residence in Frederick county, Md., the Rev. Henry Willis, a member of the Methodist Church....

Issue of February 12, 1808

Died suddenly in New-York, on the 15th ult., 'the Rev. William Linn, aged 55 years and 11 months, one of the Ministers of the Reformed Dutch Church in that city.

Issue of February 13, 1808

Married on Wednesday evening last, by the Rev. Mr. Simons, Mr. John Macnamara, merchant, to Mrs. Mary Donnill, both of this city.

Died on the 31st ult., Mrs. Mary Cole, a native of the state of New-York, and wife of Capt. John Cole, of this city.

Died at Washington, on the 28th ult., the Hon. Ezra Darby, in the 40th year of his age, member of the House of Representatives from New-Jersey....

Issue of February 15, 1808

Married, last evening, at the Village of Hampstead, on Charleston Neck, by the Rev. Mr. Simons, Mr. John Jarman, Jun. to Miss Harriett Clapperson, both of said place.

Married at Newberry District, on the 12th Nov. last, Mr. John Black, merchant, of Laurens District to Mrs. Sarah Conway Blair, relict of John Blair, deceased, late of the house of M'-Dowall & Blair, merchants, of this city.

Issue of February 16, 1808

Married at Beaufort, on the 28th ult., by the Rev. Joseph B. Cook, Mr. Thomas Gardner to Miss Rachell Radcliffe, both of that place.

Issue of February 17, 1808

Married on the 11th inst., by the Rev. Dr. M. Maddell, the Rev. Benjamin R. Montgomery, to Mrs. Ann Dunlap, both of Cambridge, S. C.

Issue of February 18, 1808 .

Married at Georgetown, S. C., on Thursday the 14th inst., by the Rev. Hugh Fraser, Mr. Henry Vernon, of this city, to Miss Florida Guerry, of Sampit.

Issue of February 22, 1808

Died in England, Dr. William Gordon, author of the History of the American Revolution.
Died at Martinico, on the 4th Jan., in the 43d year of his age, Major Ulrick Ravardi....

Issue of February 23, 1808

Married on Sunday evening last, by the Rev. Mr. Munds, Mr. Thomas Nevin, to Miss Elizabeth Devison, both of this place.
Married, last evening, by the Rev. Mr. Munds, Mr. James Clarke, to Miss Rosanna Harrison, both of this place.
Died at Sunbury, Georgia, on the 10th inst., in the 40th year of his age, M. Von Yeveren, Esq. formerly a merchant of this city....
Died in London, Rev. John Newton, aged 82....

Issue of February 24, 1808

Married last evening, by the Rev. Joseph Myers, Mr. Isaac Levy, to Mrs. Ridgeway.
Departed this life on the morning of the 21st inst., George W. Woodham, in the 26th year of his age, a native of England....

Issue of February 25, 1808

Married on the 14th inst., by the Rev. Mr. Munds, Mr. B. T. Stoops, to Mrs. Jones, both of this city.
Died on the 16th inst., Mrs. Rebecca Gilbert, in the 31st year of her age...left husband and children.
Died on the 15th inst., at Wilmington, Del., John Dickinson, Esq. formerly President of that Commonwealth....

Issue of February 26, 1808

Married, last evening, by the Rev. Dr. Hollinshead, Henry Tudor Farmer, Esq. to Miss Ann Coates.
Married, on the 18th inst., in St. Bartholomew's Parish, by the Rev. Mr. Johnston, Mr. John Fitts, to Miss Margaret Berrie, daughter of Mr. William Berrie, of said parish, decd.
Married on Thursday evening, the 18th inst., by the Rev. Mr. Munds, Capt. James Mooney, to Mrs. Ann Levy, all of this city.

Issue of February 27, 1808

Married on Sunday evening last, by the Rev. Charles Faber, Mr. John C. Martin, to Miss Ann Nauman, all of this city.
Died at the Grove, in Christ Church, Mrs. Jane H. Witherspoon, wife of Dr. John R. Witherspoon, and only child of the Rev. Dr. M'Calla, of that place...the 23d inst., in the 28th year of her age....
Died on Friday morning, Mr. Ferdinand Hillerd, in the 22d year of his age.
Died at his house in this city, on Wed. last, in the 86th year of his age, William Ancrum, Esq., formerly a most respectable merchant, of this city...a native of the North of England,

resided in this country for 60 years....

Issue of March 2, 1808

Died in Barnwell district, on the 23d ult., in the 47th year of his age, William Johnson, Esq. formerly of Wadmalaw Island... left widow and seven children....

Issue of March 3, 1808

Married at Georgetown, S. C. on Saturday evening last, by the Rev. Mr. Wayne, Mr. Clement Broquer, to Miss Harriet Carville, daughter of the late capt. Peter Carville, of that place.
Married at Georgetown, S. C. on Wednesday the 24th ult., by the Rev. G. G. M'Whorter, Mr. Samuel E. Fulton of Williamsburgh, to Miss Ann Witherspoon, of Salem.
Died, on Friday last, in the 29th year of his age, Mr. Alexander Johnston...left widow and two children....

Issue of March 4, 1808

Married last evening, by the Rev. Mr. Bowen, Capt. John F. Brooks, to Mrs. Jane Bishop, all of this city.
Married on James Island, on the 3d inst., by the Rev. Mr. Price, David Raburn, to Mrs. Martha Nelson, both of said Island.
Married on Monday evening last, by the Rev. Dr. Keith, Capt. John Cooper, to Miss Julia Ann Mumford, both of this city.

Issue of March 5, 1808

Married on Sunday the 14th Feb., by the Rev. John Yeoman, Reuben Roberds, Esq. to Miss Margaret Ball, daughter of Sampson Ball, Esq. both of Beaufort District.
Died at Savannah, on the 29th of last month, aged 30 years, Mrs. Susan Turnbull, wife of Nichol Turnbull, Esq. of that city.

Issue of March 7, 1808

Died on Friday last, George Meadows, a native of Italy, aged 31 years.
Departed this life on Friday evening, the 5th of Feb. last, Mr. Joshua Hitch, aged about 28 years, a native of Maryland, but a resident of S. C. for about 7 years....left wife and four brothers.

Issue of March 8, 1808

Died on Saturday evening last, the 5th inst., Mrs. Ann Anderson, in the 89th year of her age.

Issue of March 9, 1808

Married on the 8th inst., in St. Bartholomew's Parish, by the Rev. Mr. Fowler, Mr. John Miles of this city, to Miss Susan Alison Braly, of said parish.
Died on the 2d Feb. last, at sea, on his passage from the Coast of Africa, bound to this port, Capt. John Connelly, master of the ship Africa, aged 44 years....left widow and two children.

Issue of March 10, 1808

Married on Sunday last, by the Rev. Mr. Simons, Mr. Henry M'Kenzie of Charleston, to Miss Ann Maria Smith, of Europe.

Issue of March 11, 1808

Died at Havana, on the 18th ult., Mr. Abraham Douthwaite, a native of England, for many years a resident of this city.

Issue of March 12, 1808

Died from a fall from a ship's main-yard, yesterday evening, Mr. Charles Warsham Rivers, in the 23d year of his age.

Died on the 10th inst., in the 40th year of her age, Mrs. Hannah Jordan, a native of this state, but for many years a resident in Georgia...left three children....

Issue of March 13, 1808

Married on the 7th inst., in St. George's Parish, by the Rev. Dr. Fates, Mr. William Winter Simmons, Planter, of said Parish, to Miss Sarah Joyse M'Nellage, of Christ Church Parish.

Married on Thursday last, by the Rev. Mr. Bowen, Mr. John Jennings, of Maryland, to Mrs. Mary Ann Burges, of this city.

Married last evening, by the Rev. Mr. Munds, Capt. Edward Maxwell, to Miss Charlotte Mary Bland, both of this city.

Died in this city, on the 1st inst., Mr. William Bullock, of the house of Norvall, Wiatt & Bullock, of Richmond, Va.

Departed this life on Friday, March 11th, Miss Maria Ann King, only daughter of Benjamin and Peninnah King, aged 3 years and 4 months...(lines)

Issue of March 15, 1808

Married at Beaufort, on the 9th inst., by the Rev. B. M. Palmer, Mr. William Peden, to Miss Sarah Bell, both of that place.

Married, on Friday evening last, by the Rev. Mr. M'Quinn, Mr. Abel M'Kee, to Mrs. Mary Burr, both of this city.

Issue of March 18, 1808

Married last evening, by the Rev. Dr. Hollinshead, Capt. William Brow, to Miss Harriet Murphy, both of this place.

Died on Monday last, Mr. John Jacob Kaiser, for many years past an active officer in the militia of this city....

Issue of March 21, 1808

Died on Friday evening the 18th inst., Mrs. Susanna Lloyd, wife of John P. Lloyd....

Issue of March 22, 1808

Married on Thursday evening, by the Rev. Dr. Furman, Mr. Burges Webb, to Miss Catherine Taylor, both of this city.

Died on the 16th inst., Mrs. Mary Mills, of St. Thomas's parish, in the 69th year of her age.

Died on the 15th ult., at his seat in Pendleton district, S. C., the Rev. John Simpson, in the 68th year of his age...left an aged consort with a respectable family and two bereaved congregations....

Died in the river Gambia on the 12th Nov. last, Capt. John Vincent, master of the brig Leander, of this port; and on the 14th, Mr. Eschul Eschulson, mate of said brig. On the 17th Oct., Capt. James Donnald, late master of the schr. Friendship, of this port.

Issue of March 23, 1808

Died at Saltsburg (sic), N. C., on the 8th inst.,Nathaniel Alexander, Esq. in the 53d year of his age, late Gov. of N. C.

Issue of March 24, 1808

Married, last evening, by the Rev. Dr. Hollinshead, Mr. William Highton, to the amiable Miss M. P. Pearse, both of this city.
Departed this life on Friday, the 18th inst, in the 73d year of her age, Mrs. Hannah Hornby....native of Ireland, for many year inhabitant of this city.

Issue of March 25, 1808

Married in Christ Church parish, on Tuesday last, the 22d inst., by the Rev. Dr. M'Calla, Thomas Hinds, Esq. to Miss Sarah Hall.
Married last evening, by the Rev. Charles Faber, Capt. Lewis Strobel, of this city, to Miss Ann Statia Honeywell, of New-York.

Issue of March 26, 1808

Died on the 5th inst., at Medway, Ga., Mrs. Elizabeth Hargreaves, wife of Mr. Joseph Hargreaves....

Issue of March 30, 1808

Married on Monday last, in St. Thomas's Parish, by the Rev. Dr. Nankevil, Mr. Jacob Nathaniel Lord, of this city, to Miss Mary Elizabeth Tarbox, of said parish.
Died, on the 28th inst., in the 24th year of her age, Miss Sarah Elliott, eldest daughter of Thomas Elliott, Esq. (long eulogy)

Issue of April 2, 1808

Married last evening, by the Rev. Mr. Munds, Mr. J. G. Segerstrom, to Miss Denny(?) Glais, both of this city.
Died on Tuesday last, at Coosawhatchie, Mr. George Quinley... a native of Bristol Mass....

Issue of April 4, 1808

Married on Thursday evening last, by the Rev. Mr. Fowler, Mr. Samuel Jones, to Mrs. Sarah Byrd, all of St. Bartholomew's Parish.
Died on the 17th Feb., at his usual residence on Black Swamp, Beaufort district, Dr. George Mosse...a native of Ireland, but for about 40 years an inhabitant of this state....left widow and seven daughters.

Issue of April 5, 1808

Married on Friday evening last, by the Rev. Dr. Phoebus, Capt. Martin Blanck, to Mrs. Mary Ballard, both of this place.
Died, in Christ Church Parish, on Saturday the 26th ult., Mrs. Sarah Capers, relict of Gabriel Capers, Esq. of said Parish. And in this city, on Wed., 30th ult., Mrs. Catharine Paterson, wife of Mr. Hugh Paterson, merchant and eldest daughter of sd. Gabriel Capers.

Issue of April 6, 1808

Died, in St. John's Berkley, on the 20th ult., in the 64th year of her age, Mrs. Esther Moore....

Issue of April 7, 1808

Died, at sea, on the 16th ult., off the Island of Antigua, Capt. Christopher Grant, late master of the brig Washington, of this port.
Drowned at sea, on the 3d ult., Master Gordon M'Neal Murphy, aged 16 years....
Died at Philadelphia, on the 19th ult., Dr. John Redman, aged 87 years, one of the most respectable physicians in the U. S.

Issue of April 11, 1808

Died on the 6th inst., at the advanced age of 80 years and 11 months, Mrs. Margaret Young, a respectable inhabitant of this city, and relict of the late Thomas Young, esq. of Goose-creek.

Issue of April 14, 1808

Married last evening, by the Rev. Mr. Munds, Mr. Theodore Bissiere, to Mrs. Elizabeth Newton.

Issue of April 15, 1808

Died on the 10th inst., in the 44th year of his age, Mr. John Makky, a native of Ireland, but for about 24 years an inhabitant of this state....
Died on the 13th of March last, Mrs. Rachel Frierson, consort of Major John Frierson, of Santee, Sumter District....
Died at Philadelphia, on the 31st ult., in the 63d year of his age, Isaac Wharton, late a Director of the Bank of the U. S.
...
Died at Norfolk, on the 3d inst., James Bean, Esq. merchant, of the Island of Jamaica, but lately from this city.
Died at Baltimore, on the 1st inst., Gabriel Christie, esq. Collector of the Customs at that port.

Issue of April 19, 1808

Married at New-York, on the 4th inst., by the Rev. Mr. Willard, Henry Bedlow, Esq. only newphew to Col. Henry Rutgers, of New-York, to Miss Julia Halsey, adopted daughter of Dr. Samuel Fairchild, of South-Carolina.
Departed this life on Wednesday the 13th inst., Capt. John Dolles, in the 31st year of his age....
Died on Friday the 15th inst., in the 56th year of his age, Mr. Antonie Vigie, a native of France, near Boreaux, formerly a resident of the island of St. Domingo, but for the last 15 years resided in this city....
Died at Petersburg, (Vir.) on the 11th inst., John D. Burk, esq., a native of Ireland....

Issue of April 20, 1808

Died on Wednesday last, at his plantation in St. Bartholomew's Parish, in the 44th year of his age, John Minot, esq. of the house of John & Benjamin Minot, factors, of this city.
Mr. Charles J. Nixon, a native of Philadelphia, and Mr. Alfred Burrows were drowned.... Burrows left wife and eight children.

Issue of April 25, 1808

Died on the 20th inst., Mr. Joseph Grant, for many years a respectable inhabitant of this place...left a widow and two small children....

Issue of April 26, 1808

Departed this life on Friday the 22d inst., Mrs. Dorcas Fritts....brothers and sisters and aged parents.
Departed this life on the 18th of April at Newberry, the Rev. John Harper....

Issue of April 27, 1808

Married, at Beaufort, on the 13th inst., by the Rev. Mr. Hicks, Mr. George Logan, of St. Bartholomew's, to Miss Eliza Verdier, daughter of J. M. Verdier, Esq.

Issue of April 30, 1808

Died, at Beaufort, S. C. on Friday the 15th inst., Col. Edward Barnwell...left a wife and nine children...descendant of one of the most ancient families of this place, being one of the grandsons of Col. Matthew Barnwell, who commanded the first expedition against the Tuscorora Indians in the year 1712.

Issue of May 3, 1808

Married on Wednesday evening last, by the Rev. Dr. Gallaher, Mr. Benjamin Lasteu, to Miss Sophia Berard, from St. Domingo.
Married on Saturday evening last, by the Rev. Dr. Hollinshead, Mr. John M'Kenzie, to Miss Mary-Ann Schooler, both of this city.
Married last evening, by the Rev. Dr. Buist, Mr. Adam Hutchinson, of the house of Jackson and Hutchinson, merchants, Augusta, Ga. to Miss Elizabeth Anderson of this city.
Died on Charleston Neck, on the 21st ulst., Mrs. Keziah Barrett, in the 63d year of her age, for the last 25 of which she was a widow....
Died yesterday morning at Hampstead, Mrs. Eleanor Hill, aged 53 years.

Issue of May 4, 1808

Married in Barnwell district, on Wednesday evening the 13th ult., by the Rev. Mr. Yeomans, James Owens, Esq. of said district, to the agreeable Mrs. Harriett Steads, late of Wadmelaw island.
Died last night, aged 8 years, Robert Alexander Wilson, eldest son of Dr. Robert Wilson, jun. of this city.
Died in Barnwell district, on Friday evening, the 15th ult., Capt. Reddin Cannon...left wife, son and a daughter....

Issue of May 7, 1808

Married on Thursday evening last, by the Rev. Dr. Gallagher, Mr. John Fairbrother, to Miss Mary-Anne Keough, both of this city.

Issue of May 10, 1808

Married, at Camden, on Thursday evening last, by the Rev. Mr. Flinn, John D. Witherspoon, esq. Attorney at Law, to Miss Elizabeth Boykin.
Died at Bath (Eng.) Mr. Siddons, husband of the actress....

Issue of May 13, 1808

Married on Thursday the 5th inst., on South Island, by the Rev. Mr. Fraser, John C. Walter, Esq. of Jamesville, to Miss Magdaline Bonneau Taylor, daughter of Capt. Samuel Taylor, of South Island.

Died at Hilton Head on the 7th inst., William Elliott, Esq. of Beaufort (S.C.) left a widow with many children and relatives. (long eulogy)

Issue of May 16, 1808

Married last evening by the Rev. Thomas Mills, Henry Veitch, Esq. of St. Paul's Parish, to Miss Margaret Morrison, only daughter of capt. Joseph Morrison, of St. Bartholomew's Parish.

Issue of May 17, 1808

Married on the 10th inst., at Orangeburgh, by the Rev. Mr. O'Farrell, David Rumph, Esq. to Miss Elizabeth Carmichael, daughter of James Carmichael, esq.

Married on Saturday evening last, by the Rev. Dr. Hollinshead, Cornelius Hamlin, esq. of St. Thomas's Parish, to Miss Jane Gibson, of this city.

Issue of May 20, 1808

Died, on Wednesday the 4th inst., in the 66th year of his age, Mr. Edward Forshaw, of James Island, planter.

Issue of May 21, 1808

Departed this life, on the 15th inst., Mrs. Elizabeth Harvey, widow of the late Mr. Robert Harvey, of this city, in the 90th year of her age...born in England, resided in this city 85 years, left a numerous family....

Issue of May 25, 1808

Married at Orangeburgh, on the 17th inst., by the Rev. Mr. Porter, Mr. William H. Pooser, to Miss Margaret Stroman, daughter of Mr. Paul Stroman.

Married last evening, by the Rev. Mr. Phillips, Mr. Robert Scattarty, to Miss Rachel Hamilton, both of this city.

Died at Philadelphia, on Monday evening, the 9th inst., Mr. Jared Bunce, Jun. son of capt. J. Bunce, in the 19th year of his age.

Issue of May 26, 1808

Departed this life on the 22d inst., Mrs. Margaret Woolf, in the 80th year of her age.

Issue of May 27, 1808

Married on Wednesday the 18th inst., at Walnut Hill, near Beaufort, by the Rev. Mr. Hicks, Richard W. Habersham, Esq., Attorney at Law, of Savannah, to Miss Sarah H. Elliott, of the former place.

Issue of May 28, 1808

Married on Thursday evening, by the Rev. Dr. Keith, Mr. John M'Fie, to Mrs. Elizabeth Bruse, both of this city.

Issue of June 1, 1808

Married on Monday evening last, by the Rev. Mr. M'Quain, Mr. Samuel Chatburn, to Mrs. Frances Duett, widow of the late Mr. Duett, merchant, of this city.

Issue of June 2, 1808

Married in Leesburg, Virginia, by the Rev. J. Mines, capt. J. Slater, aged 82 years, to Mrs. Elizabeth Dorshtimer, about 75.
Married in Philadelphia, by the Rev. Bishop Wright, Mr. George Hill, formerly of Boston to Miss Mary Hudson, after a long and tedious courtship of--one night!!!

Issue of June 4, 1808

Married in Orangeburgh, by the Rev. Samuel Eccles, on Sunday evening the 29th ult., Mr. George E. Salley, to Miss Margaret Lockhart Jones, daughter of Mr. Samuel P. Jones.
Married, in Newberry District, on Sunday the 22d ult., by the Rev. D. Owens, Mr. John Patton, merchant, to Miss M. A. Brewer, of Santee.
Died at Salem, Mass. Mr. Alexander Smith, aged 31, a native of this city.

Issue of June 7, 1808

Married, on Monday the 2d ult., by the Rev. Mr. Philips, Dr. T. P. Cambridge, to Mrs. Eliza T. Motte, both of this city.
Married at Pimlico, on the 1st inst., by the Rev. Mr. M'Cullers, Mr. Sugar Edwards, to Miss Elizabeth Steele, both of St. John's Parish, Berkley County.

Issue of June 8, 1808

Married last evening by the Rev. Dr. Furman, Mr. Peter Larry, of this city, to Miss Ann Gibbons Chaplin, of St. Helena.
Died on the 5th inst., Mr. Samuel Cochran, youngest son of the late Thomas Cochran, esq. of this city....

Issue of June 10, 1808

Married, last evening, at Mount Pleasant Farm, on Charleston Neck, by the Rev. Mr. Faber, Martin Strobel, Esq., to Miss Eliza Martin, both of this city.
Married on Tuesday evening, by the Rev. Mr. Faber, Mr. C. F. Matthiessen, a native of Altona, to Mrs. I. F. Sandoz, of Marseilles.
Died at his plantation on Horse Creek, in Scriven county, state of Ga., Mr. Michael Dougherty, aged 135 years, and was one of the first settlers in that state....died 29th May 1808.

Issue of June 11, 1808

Married on Thursday evening last, by the Rev. Mr. Munds, Mr. George Williamson, to Miss Ann Maria Walton, both of this place.

Issue of June 14, 1808

Married in Barnwell District, on Wednesday the 8th inst., by the Rev. James Sweat, Dr. John S. Fowke, to Miss Sarah B. Johnson, daughter of Richard Johnson, esq. all of said District.
Died on the 5th inst., Mrs. Alice Legare, relict of Benjamin Legare, in the 50th year of her age....

Issue of June 15, 1808

Married on Thursday evening, the 2d inst., on Black Swamp, by the Rev. Alexander Scott, Mr. Robert G. Norton, to Miss Sarah Mosse, daughter of the late Dr. George Mosse, of that place.
Departed this life on Tuesday the 7th inst., in the 26th year of her age, Miss Mary Clement Conyers....

Issue of June 17, 1808

Died at Newport, R. I. Master William Horry, in the 10th year of his age, son of Elias Horry, Esq. of this city.
Married in Washington (Vir.) Mr. George Huson to Miss Seraphana-Matilda-Juliana-Sophia-Anna Mansfield. Only one lady, gentle reader.

Issue of June 21, 1808

Departed this life on the 20th ult.,Miss Catharine Elizabeth Fell, aged 12 months and 12 days.

Issue of June 22, 1808

Married at Pineville, St. Stephen's Parish, on Thursday the 9th ult., by the Rev. Mr. Gadsden, Mr. Samuel Dubose Jun. to Miss Eliza Marion, daughter of Theodore Samuel Marion, esq.

Issue of June 23, 1808

Died on the 19th inst., Master Daniel Russell, aged 6 years, 5 months and 24 days.
Departed this life on Sunday the 5th inst., Capt. Philip Gilder, of Newberry District by a fall from his horse the day before.

Issue of June 30, 1808

Died on Tuesday the 28th inst., Mr. John Cannon, in the 83d year of his age...a native of Maryland, but the last 60 years a citizen of S. C...supported his country in the late revolution. He resided greater part of his time in the Distrct of Orangeburg.

Issue of July 7, 1808

Married at St. John's Parish, on Thursday last, by the Rev. Mr. M'Allister, Mr. William Hutchison, to Miss Mary Pope.

Issue of July 8, 1808

Married on Thursday evening the 30th ult., at St. Mary's, Lt. Samuel Elbert, of gun-boat No. 2, to Miss Harriet A. Jackson, formerly of Savannah.

Issue of July 9, 1808

Married on Monday last, the 4th of July, by the Rev. Dr. Hollinshead, Doctor Presson Simpson of Virginia, to Mrs. Martha Latham, of this city.

Issue of July 12, 1808

Married last evening, by the Rev. Dr. Hollinshead, Mr. John Cignes, of Brosh in Flanders, to Mrs. Margaret Roller of this city.
Died, on Friday evening last, Mr. Isaac Levy, in the 37th year of his age.

Issue of July 13, 1808

Died at Baltimore, William Calhoun, esq. formerly a merchant in this city.

Issue of July 14, 1808

Married on the 8th inst., by the Rev. Mr. Philips, Mr. James M'Cleish, to Mrs. Mary Guy, both of this city.

Issue of July 18, 1808

Died on the 14th inst., at Mr. A. M'Kowen's plantation Goosecreek, on his way from St. James's Santee, Mr. William Jones, in the 45th year of his age, a native of King's county, Ireland.

Issue of July 20, 1808

Departed this life at Keiwah, on the 13th inst., Mrs. Mary Gibbes Shoolbred, esq....
Departed this life on the 18th inst., in the 33d year of his age, Mr. Robert B. Hislop...left wife and three children, two sisters, and an aged mother....
Died at his seat at Dedham, Mass., on the morning of the 4th inst., the Hon. Fisher Ames....

Issue of July 25, 1808

Married on the 14th inst., at Manchester, by the Rev. Mr. Roberts, Thomas Polk, Esq. to Miss Sarah I. Moore, all of Sumter district.
Married on the 17th inst., at Statesburg, by the Rev. Mr. Roberts, John B. Miller, Esq. attorney at law, of Sumterville, to Miss Mary E. Murrell, of Statesburg.

Issue of July 26, 1808

Died, in this city, on Saturday the 23d inst., Mr. David M'Dowell, a native of Ireland, in the 28th year of his age.

Issue of July 29, 1808

Married last evening, by the Rev. Mr. Munds, Capt. William Brown, to Miss Sarah Ann Jones.
Married last evening, by the Rev. Mr. Munds, Mr. Alexander Webb, to Miss Hannah M. Bailey, both of this place.
Capt. Jehu Hay, late master of the sloop Regulator, was drowned ...
Died, at Albany, Mr. John Barber, publisher of the Albany

Register....

Issue of August 1, 1808

Married last evening by the Rev. Dr. Furman, Mr. George Kimball, merchant, to Miss Eliza Gordon, both of this city.

Died at Camden, on the 26th of May last, Dr. J. D. Deveaux.

Died on the 21st ult., at his residence Hopewell Mills, Barnwell district, S. C. Mr. Duncan M'Lachlan, in the 25th year of his age.

Issue of August 2, 1808

Died in Jacksonborough, on Monday the 25th ult., Mrs. Mary Taylor, in the 40th year of her age.

Issue of August 3, 1808

Departed this life on the 10th ult., Mrs. Mary Prentice, in the 33d year of her age...left husband and two children....

Issue of August 4, 1808

Died on the 30th of last month, Mrs. Martha Stewart, relict of Robert Stewart, esq....

Issue of August 5, 1808

Married on Tuesday evening last, by the Rev. Dr. Furman, Mr. Robert Arthur Baird, to Mrs. Susanna Bunting, both of this city.

Issue of August 6, 1808

Married on Thursday evening, by the Rev. Dr. Hollinshead, John Hancock Woodward, esq. to Mrs. Esther S. Gantt, both of this place.

Issue of August 9, 1808

Drowned last evening, Mr. John Wardrop, of this city...body not yet found.

Died at his place of residence in Darlington District on the 12th ult., the Rev. Samuel Eccles of the Baptist Church, a native of Roscommon, Ireland.

Departed this life on Monday evening last, in the 34th year of his age, Mr. Michael Muckenfuss, cabinet maker of this city....

Issue of August 12, 1808

Married at Hampstead, on the 30th ult., by the Rev. Mr. M'Vain, Mr. John Brindley, of St. John's parish, to Mrs. Mary Campbell, of this city.

Married on Wednesday evening last, Mr. Mark Marks, to Miss Hetty Benzenken, both of this city.

Drowned on Monday evening last, Mr. John Wardrop, in the 21st year of his age, a native of Glasgow, and resided in this city about 3 years....

Issue of August 15, 1808

Married last evening, by the Rev. Mr. Munds, Mr. Thomas Ward, to Mrs. Norvel, both of this place.

Died, at Black Creek, St. Bartholomew's Parish, on the 7th inst., John Barton Ulmer, second son of John Ulmer, esq. of Prince William's Parish, aged 7 years and 11 months.

Died, near Coosawhatchie, in Prince William's Parish, Louis Francois Cauchoin, a native of Brittany, for many years an inhabitant of said Parish.

Issue of August 16, 1808

Died on the 25th ult., in Augusta, Ga.,Mrs. Priscilla Tully, late of Orangeburgh, S. C., aged 101 years.

Issue of August 17, 1808

Married on Sunday evening last, by the Rev. Dr. Furman, Mr. James Hayden Discombe, to Miss Eliza Clearey.

Issue of August 18, 1808

Married, last evening, by the Rev. Mr. M'Vain, Mr. George Cromer, to Miss Bulah Swain, both of this city.

Issue of August 24, 1808

Married last evening, by the Rev. Mr. Munds, Mr. Clinton Cregier, to Mrs. Elizabeth Wyatt, both of New-York.

Issue of August 25, 1808

Died on Sunday last, Miss Margaret Munro, second daughter of Mr. John Munro, in the 15th year of her age....

Issue of August 27, 1808

Married on Wednesday evening last, by the Rev. Dr. Hollinshead, Capt. John S. H. Cocks, to Mrs. Arabella Purcell, both of this city.

Issue of August 29, 1808

Departed this life on the 24th ult., Stephen Mazyck, Esq. in the 53d year of his age....left wife and several small children.

Issue of August 30, 1808

Departed this life on the 31st ult., in St. Mathew's parish, in the 57th year of her age, Mrs. R. E. Sabb....

Issue of August 31, 1808

Departed this life on the 31st ult.,in St. Mathew's Parish, in the 57th year of her age, Mrs. R. E. Sabb, relict of Major Morgan Sabb....

Issue of September 2, 1808

Married last evening, by the Rev. Mr. Gadsden, Mr. John H. Willis, to Miss Mary H. Gabeau, both of this city.

Issue of September 3, 1808

long account of life of Rev. George Buist, D. D. who died on the 31st ult., and left wife and six children and parents in Scotland....

Died on the 1st inst., Miss Mary Elizabeth Fordham, aged 8 months.

Issue of September, 5, 1808

Married last evening, by the Rev. Mr. Simons, Mr. Abraham Shoulters, of this city, to Miss Margaret Baker, of Philadelphia.

Married on Saturday last, by the Rev. Mr. Munds, Mr. George Durrett, to Miss Margaret Wallis, both of this city.

Departed this life on the 16th ult. in the 60th year of his age, Mr. Joseph Brunet, a native of Paris....

Issue of September 7, 1808

Departed this life in Prince William's Parish, on the 30th ult., Mr. William Veitch, in the 46th year of his age, leaving a wife and four children....

Died at Savannah, on the 29th ult., Capt. Madiso, late of the sloop Regulator.

Died at Newburyport, on the 13th ult., in the 75th year of his age, Benjamin Cotton....

Issue of September 8, 1808

Died on the 2d inst., in the 21st year of her age, Mrs. Mary Scott, wife of Mr. William Scott, merchant, and only daughter of the Hon. Benjamin Boyd, Esq., Intendant of this city....

Died on the 27th ult.,Mrs. Elizabeth Washington Matthews, aged 31 years, consort of Mr. R. Matthews, of Pimlico, St. John's.

Issue of September 9, 1808

Died on Monday last, in child birth, in the 21st year of her age, Mrs. Ann Tucker, consort of Mr. William B. Tucker....

Issue of September 10, 1808

Departed this life on the 9th inst., in the 25th year of his age, Mr. John Cooke, a native of Londonderry, in Ireland.

Issue of September 12, 1808

Married on Saturday evening by the Rev. Mr. Munds, Mr. William Clark, of Christ Church parish to Miss Eliza Vanderhoff, only daughter of Cornelius Vanderhoff, of this city.

Issue of September 13, 1808

Married at Ashepoo, on Thursday last, by M. B. Pinckney, esq. justice of the quorum, Mr. Willis Hall, to Miss Mary Channel, both of St. Bartholomew's Parish.

Married on Tuesday the 6th inst., by the Rev. Dr. Fowler, Mr. John Gray Green, of St. Andrew's parish, to Miss Ann Catherine Martin, of St. Paul's parish.

Married on Thursday the 8th inst., at Coosawhatchie, by the Rev. William B. Johnson, Mr. Benjamin H. Buckner, merchant, to Miss Susan Riley, both of that place.

Departed this life on the 7th inst., in the 80th year of her age, Mrs. Rachel Caw....

Died on the 7th inst., at North-Island, near Georgetown, Mr. William W. Sarjeant, in the 22d year of his age, formerly of this city.

Issue of September 16, 1808

Died on the 11th inst., in St. Bartholomew's Parish, Mr. Patrick Carns, of St. Paul's, aged about 20 years.

Died on Monday evening last, Master John Hamilton Potter, aged 4 years and 8 months, third son of John Potter....

Issue of September 19, 1808

Died on Friday last, in this city, Dr. James H. Air, aged 30 years.

Issue of September 20, 1808

Married in Barnwell District, S. C. on Wednesday the 7th inst., by the Rev. Mr. James Sweat, Lewis Scott Hay, esq. to Miss Harriet T. Johnson, daughter of William Johnson, esq. decd.

Died at Georgetown, on the 9th inst., in the 16th year of his age, William Richards Addison, third son of the late capt. John Addison.

Died at North-Santee, on the 12th inst., Miss Kezia Ann Lynn eldest daughter of Mr. John Lynn, aged 4 years and 10 months.

Issue of September 21, 1808

Married in Barnwell District on the 5th inst., by the Rev. Mr. Yeomens, Mr. William Lee, to Mrs. Elizabeth Aikin, both of that place.

Married in Barnwell District on the 4th inst., by the Rev. Mr. Wilson, Mr. Elijah Johnson, to Miss Ann Cook, all of the same place.

Died at Beaufort on Monday the 19th inst., Capt. Thomas Grayson, one of our Rev. Patriots, who was sent away from this his native State in 1780....

Departed this life on Saturday evening last, in St. John's parish, Berkley, Dr. Peter D. Ravenel, in the 30th year of his age....

Died, yesterday, Edward C. Lightwood, esq. of this city. (eulogy)

Died on the 14th inst., in St. Stephen's parish, in the 3d year of her age, Miss Margaret Scouler, daughter of Thomas Scouler....

Married at Baltimore, Mr. David Mewshaw, aged 81 years, to Miss Elizabeth Mitchell, aged 71 years, the mother of ten children!!! both of Anne Arundel county-

Issue of September 24, 1808

Departed this life on the 12th inst., in the 23d year of her age, Mrs. Margaret Martha Fitzgerald, wife of Mr. Edward C. Fitzgerald.

Died at Hopewell-Mills, Barnwell District on the 17th inst., Mr. Alexander Smith.

Issue of September 27, 1808

Died on Friday last, Mr. Tobias Cambridge, aged 53 years... left wife and eight children.

Departed this life on the 14th inst., Thomas Foster, Esq., aged 57 years and 11 months....

Died on the evening of the 20th inst., at his plantation, Sewee, Richard Shackelford, Esq. in the 36th year of his age....

Issue of September 28, 1808

Died on the 13th inst., at St. James' Goose-creek, Miss Mary Leadbetter, aged 11 years and 5 months.
Died, on the 25th inst., Mrs. Elizabeth Tarver, aged 34 years.
Departed this life on Black-River, Sumter District, on the 11th inst., Mr. Daniel M'Neil, of Robinson (sic) County, N. C.

Issue of September 29, 1808

Died on Sunday last, Master William Washington Simons, aged 14 years 8 months and 25 days, fourth son of Major Simons....
Died on Sunday morning, the 24th July at her brother's house, at Cranbrook, England, in the 68th year of her age, Mrs. Paine, wife of Tom Paine...daughter of Mr. Ollivo.....
Died on the 5th inst., Mr. James Harvey, carpenter a native of Scotland....

Issue of September 30, 1808

Died in St. John's parish, Berkley, on Wednesday morning, the 28th inst., aged 29 years, Mrs. Rebecca Chiffelle Gaillard, wife of Mr. Bartholomew Gaillard, and third daughter of William Doughty, esq....
Died in London, the 1st July last, in his 50th year, William Bullen(?), esq. laste of Bombay, East Indies.
Died at Savannah, on the morning of the 23d inst., Mrs. Emily W. Charlton, wife of Judge Charlton....

Issue of October 1, 1808

Died at Wilmington, N. C. on the 24th ult., Capt. William Mulloy, of the schr. Milly, of this port.

Issue of October 3, 1808

Died on Saturday last, in Christ Church Parish, Mr. Thomas Hall, Bricklayer, in the 27th year of his age....
Died on Friday morning, Mary Shaw, eldest daughter of Mr. Terrence Shaw, aged 10 years, and 8 months...(lines)

Issue of October 4, 1808

Died, at Clapton, Middlesex, Eng., on the 17th July last, Mrs. Catharine Ogier, aged 76 years, relict of the late Mr. Lewis Ogier, formerly merchant of this city.

Issue of October 6, 1808

Died at Perth Amboy, N. J., on the 13th ult., in the 23d year of his age, William Willis Duke, of this city....

Issue of October 7, 1808

Departed this life on Sunday night, the 2d inst., Mr. John Bryant, Gardener, and Clerk of the Markets, in the 49th year of his age...native of Norfolk, England, but had resided in America upwards of 20 years, 15 in Charleston...left widow and three young children.
Married on Wed., the 14th ult., by the Rev. Dr. Hollinshead, Mr. Joseph Siebert, to Mrs. Masey Greiner, both of this city.
Died in Savannah, on Sunday last, Thomas Mendenhall, Esq.,

Cashier of the U. S. Branch bank in that city.

Issue of October 10, 1808

Married on Thursday evening last, by the Rev. Dr. Hollinshead, Capt. Frederick Elsworth, to Miss Mary Elizabeth Burckmyer, both of this city.

Married at Philadelphia, on the 24th ult., by the Rev. Dr. Blackwell, Mr. Samuel Brooks, merchant, to Miss Eliza Inskeep, daughter of John Inskeep, esq.all of that city.

Died at Gluncullen, county of Dublin, Ireland, aged 109 years 3 months and 16 days, Valentine Welsh, farmer....

Issue of October 11, 1808

Married on Thursday last, on James-Island, by the Rev. Mr. Price, Mr. John W. Holmes, to Miss Susan Holmes, both of said Island.

Married on Wednesday evening last, by the Rev. Jacob Suares, Mr. Israel Solomons to Miss Esther Ottolegui, both of this city.

Died at May-River, at the plantation of Col. Daniel Stevens, on the 3d inst., Mr. Samuel M. Stevens, aged 20 years....

Issue of October 13, 1808

Married last evening, on Sullivan's Island, by the Rev. Dr. Furman, Mr. John Haynsworth, to Miss Mary M. H. Delorme, both of this city.

Issue of October 14, 1808

Died on the 8th inst., Major Tobias Bowles, a native of Nassau, in New-Providence, in the 37th year of his age....

Died on the 22d ult., at Makefield, in Bucks Co., Pa., within one month of the completion of his 81st year, William Hollinshead, esq. father of the Rev. Dr. Hollinshead, of this city....

Issue of October 15, 1808

Died in this city, on the 2d inst., Mrs. Jane E. M'Kewn, in the 50th year of her age....

Issue of October 18, 1808

Departed this life on the 8th inst., Major Tobias Bowles, in the 34th year of his age....

Died at Hampstead, on Friday last, Miss Caroline Hook, aged 12 years. (lines)

Died on Tuesday last, at his residence in Lexington District, Major John Hampton, an old and respectable inhabitant of that place.

Issue of October 20, 1808

Married last evening, by the Rev. Mr. Munds, Mr. Samuel Brown, a native of England, to Mrs. Rebecca Hopkins, of this city.

Died on Monday last, Master John Charles Rade, aged 9 months and 23 days, only son of Dr. Rade....

Issue of October 22, 1808

Died on the 5th inst., at her house in Franklin Court, Pa., aged 64 years, Mrs. Sarah Bache, wife of Richard Bache, esq., and only daughter of Dr. Benjamin Franklin.

Issue of October 25, 1808

Married on Sunday the 16th inst., by the Rev. Mr. Bernhard, Mr. Godfrey Drehr, to Miss Ann E. Saylor, both of Lexington Dist.
Died on Wednesday the 12th inst., at her plantation in St. Thomas's parish, in the 36th year of her age, Mrs. Elizabeth A. Addison, wife of Joseph Addison, esq. of said place...left husband and three children.

Issue of October 26, 1808

Married last evening, by the Rev. Dr. Hollinshead, Mr. John Ker, merchant, to Miss Ann B. Perrie, both of this city.

Issue of October 28, 1808

Married last evening, by the Rev. Mr. Munds, Capt. George Ryan, to Miss Susannah Fuller, of this place
Married last evening, by the Rev. Mr. Munds, Mr. William Harper, to Miss Sophia M'Key.
Died on Monday last, M. Jaque Marps Truelle, aged 46 years, a native of Normandy.
died on the 18th of August, in Louisiana, Thomas Hunt, Esq., Col. of the 1st Regt. U. S. Infantry.
Died on the 12th inst., at his residence in Germantown, near Mount Airy College (Penn.), J. H. C. Heinekin, Agent for the King of Holland....

Issue of October 31, 1808

Married on Thursday evening last, by the Rev. Mr. Munds, Mr. David Pemble, to Mrs. Catharine Spreth, both of this city.
Died near Monk's Corner, on the 23d inst.,Mr. William Staley, aged 26 years, a native of England.
Died, at Sandy Hill, on the 13th inst., on his way from Canada to New-York, Archibald M'Niel, esq....

Issue of November 1, 1808

Died at Islington, on Saturday the 29th ult., aged 2 years and 8 months, Master Horatio Nelson Macadam, second son of Mr. James Macadam, merchant.
Departed this life in Barnwell district, on the 17th ult., Mrs. Mary Brown, wife of Robert Brown, of said district.

Issue of November 3, 1808

Married on the 18th ult., by the Rev. Bishop White, Capt. James R. Callendee, of Philadelphia, to Miss Martha B. Ogle, of Wilmington, Delaware.

Issue of November 5, 1808

Married on the evening of Thursday last, by the Rev. Dr. Percy, Cornelius Dupont, M. D., of the Parish of St. Luke, to Miss Maria Hutchinson, daughter of Col. Mathias Hutchinson, of the parish of St. George, Dorchester.
Died at Pineville, on Monday last, in the 65th year of her age, Mrs. Eleanor Gaillard, relict of Theodore Gaillard, esq. late of this city....

Issue of November 7, 1808

Married last eveing by the Rev. Dr. Hollinshead, Mr. Caleb B. Duhadway, to Miss Catherine Hoburn, both of this city.
Married in Columbia, S. C. on the 6th Oct. last, John Hooker, Esq. Counsellor at Law, to Miss Mary-Ann Chapman.
Died on the 24th ult., William Keas, Esq. Collector of the Port of Washington, N. C.

Issue of November 8, 1808

Married on the 15th ult., at Winchester, Vir., Mr. Robert Mills of South-Carolina, to Miss Eliza Barnwell Smith, daughter of the Hon. John Smith, of Virginia.
Married last evening, by the Rev. Mr. Bowen, Mr. William Harth, to Miss Mary I'ans, both of this city.
Died at her place near Coosawhatchie, on the 31st ult., Mrs. Abigail Hubbird, aged 80 years.

Issue of November 9, 1808

Married on Saturday evening by the Rev. Mr. Munds, Mr. John Williams, to Miss Anne Henry, both of this city.
Died on the 18th ult., Mrs. Rebecca Mordica, wife of Mr. Goodman Mordica.
Died in Scotland, John Hume, Esq. aged 86 years, author of the Tragedy of Douglas.

Issue of November 10, 1808

Died on Sunday last, Mr. William Noel.
Died at Georgetown on Friday evening last, Capt. Thomas A. Addison, in the 21st year of his age, second son of the late Capt. John Addison of that place.

Issue of November 11, 1808

Married last evening, by the Rev. Dr. Hollinshead, John D. Heath, esq. Attorney at Law, to Miss Eliza Desel, both of this city.

Issue of November 12, 1808

Died on the 10th inst., Mrs. Deborah Parker, wife of Mr. Phineas Parker, dyer of this city.

Issue of November 14, 1808

Married at Orangeburgh on Tuesday evening the 8th inst., by the Rev. Mr. O'Farrell, Sanders Glover, Esq. to Miss Sophia Margaretta Lestargette, daughter of the late Lewis Lestargette, Esq.
Died at Wraggsborough, on the 9th inst., Mr. Robert Hislor, in the 49th year of his age...native of Dumfries, in Scotland....
Died at Baltimore, on the 2d inst., in the 30th year of his age, Mr. Lucas George, A. M. professor of Belles Lettres, in St. Mary's College.

Issue of November 15, 1808

Married at Camden, on Wed. evening the 9th inst., by the Rev. Mr. Flinn, James S. Deas, Esq. of this city to Miss Margaret E. Chesnut, daughter of Col. John Chesnut, of that place.

Married on Wednesday last, by Mr. Alexander Salomon, Mr. Gomez Mordecai, to Miss Jane Cohen, daughter of the late Mr. Abraham Cohen, of this city.

Issue of November 21, 1808

On Saturday last, departed this life in the 48th year of her age, Mrs. Catherine M'Kee, wife of Mr. John M'Kee...(eulogy)

Issue of November 23, 1808

Married last evening, by the Rev. Dr. Holinshead, Stephen Mazyck Jun. of St. John's Parish, to Miss Susan Waring, eldest daughter of Morton Waring, esq.

Issue of November 25, 1808

Married on Wednesday evening by the Rev. Mr. Simons, Philip Smith Postell, Esq. of St. Bartholomew's parish, to Miss Sarah Dewees, of this city.

Issue of November 30, 1808

Married on Thursday evening by the Rev. Mr. M'Vain, Mr. Dale Carr, to Mrs. Eliza Walker, both of this city.

Issue of December 2, 1808

Died on Friday evening last, Mr. Moses Alexander, in the 32d year of his age, for 25 years a respectable inhabitant of this city...

Issue of December 5, 1808

Departed this life on Tuesday the 29th ult., at Savannah, in the 63d year of his age, Mr. Denis Nicholas Cottineau, a native of Nantz in Brittany...capt of the Pallas in the American Revolution....
Died at Roseywards, near Ballymony (North of Ireland) the Rev. John Tennent, aged 82....

Issue of December 6, 1808

Married, at Camden, on Thursday evening last, by the Rev. Mr. Flinn, Mr. Henry Hinson Dickinson, merchant, to Miss Martha Brevard, both of that place.
Died, at Georgetown on Monday the 28th ult., in the 16th year of her age, Miss Mary Serjeant....

Issue of December 7, 1808

Married on Sunday evening last, by the Rev. Dr. Gallagher, Dr. James C. Moles, of this city to Miss Eleanor Jacob, late of New-York.

Issue of December 10, 1808

Died in this city on the 28th ult., in the 24th year of his age, Mr. William D. Lawrence...left an aged mother and a sister....

Issue of December 14, 1808

Died on Monday last, Mrs. Mary Man Cross, wife of George W.

Cross, Esq.

Issue of December 15, 1808

Departed this life on the 30th Nov., in the 76th year of her age, Mrs. Margaret Mann, an old and respectable inhabitant of this city.

Issue of December 17, 1808

Died on the 16th inst., in the 70th year of his age, Mr. Jacob Cohen, vendue master....

Issue of December 19, 1808

Married, last evening, by the Rev. Mr. Simons, Benjamin Allston, Esq. of Wacaamaw, to Miss Mary Coachman, of this city, daughter of the decd. James Coachman, Esq.
Married on Saturday last, by the Rev. Mr. Charles Faber, Mr. Christian Henry Faber, to Miss Ann Margaret Weissinger, both of this city.
Died on Saturday the 17th inst., Miss Margaret M'Kinzy....

Issue of December 21, 1808

Died at West-Ham, Middlesix, England, on the 15th of Oct., Dr. James Anderson....

Issue of December 23, 1808

Married, on Thursday the 22d inst., by the Rev. Dr. Hollinshead, Mr. George E. Hahnbaum, to Mrs. Eliza Rhoda Ruberry, both of this city.
Departed this life on the 7th inst., Mrs. Ann Greenwood, consort of Wm. Greenwood, Esq. aged 62 years, 7 months and 7 days.

Issue of December 24, 1808

Departed this life on Thursday last, Mr. Francis S. Lawson, in the 27th year of his age....
Departed this life on the 10th inst., at Black Swamp, Mrs. Eliza St. John Polhill, aged 19 years...left an infant a few days old, husband....

Issue of December 28, 1808

Married, on Saturday the 24th inst., by the Rev. Dr. M'Calla, Dr. L. N. Rees, of this city, to Miss Elizabeth Martha Player Legare, of Christ Church, only daughter of the late Isaac Legare, esq.

Issue of December 29, 1808

Married, at Whin Hall, near Glasgow, on the 20th Sept., John Nisbet, Esq. Merchant, of this city, to Miss Mary Anderson.
Married on the 24th inst., by the Rev. Dr. Hollinshead, Mr. Samuel Stine to Miss Barbara Wilson, daughter of the late John Wilson, cabinet-maker, of this city.
Married on Tuesday evening last, by the Rev. Mr. Munds, Capt. George L. Rushton, to Miss Catharine Mary Frazier, both of this place.
Married on Tuesday evening, last by the Rev. Mr. Munds, Mr. George Harper, of New-York, to Miss Charlotte M'Kenzie, of Ga.

Died on Sunday morning last, Edward Mood, the youngest son of Mr. P. Mood, aged 1 year, 9 months and 21 days.

Issue of December 30, 1808

Departed this life on the 19th inst., in the 45th year of her age, Mrs. Mary Custer, wife of the late Mr. James Custer, factor, of this city....

Issue of December 31, 1808

Departed this life on the 20th inst., in the 87th year of his age, Mr. Jean Baptiste Collas, born in the parish of Gournac, district de la Gironde, in France, a planter of Port-de-Paix, St. Domingo....

Died on Thursday last, in this city, Margaret Glen Drayton, youngest daughter of Glen Drayton, Esq. decd....

Issue of January 3, 1809

Married, on Saturday evening last, by the Rev. Dr. M'Vain, Mr. John Du Bois, to Mrs. Susannah Bannartine, both of this city.

Died at Coosawhatchie, on the 22d of Nov., in the 57th year of her age, Mrs. Morgandollar, relict of John Morgandollar, esq... left daughters....

Died in St. Stephen's parish, on the 30th ult., Mrs. Elizabeth Hardcastle, in the 67th year of his age....

Died, at Savannah, on Sunday, the 18th ult., Miss Elizabeth D. Horlbeck, and on Monday the 19th, Mrs. Maria Catherine Horlbeck, in the 23d year of her age, wife of Mr. George Horlbeck, late of this city.

Issue of January 4, 1809

Married on Sunday evening last, by the Rev. James D. Simmons, Mr. John Hederick, to Miss Ann Burks.

Died on the 31st ult., on Simmons' Island, Thomas Branford Smith, Esq....

Issue of January 5, 1809

Married, at Huntsville, Laurens District, on Wednesday the 14th ult., by the Rev. Dr. Montgomery, Captain John Caldwell, to Miss Eliza Hunter, daughter of the late John Hunter, esq.

Issue of January 7, 1809

Married on Tuesday evening last, by the Rev. Mr. Munds, Mr. Stephen Johnson, to Miss Rosanna Smith, both of this place.

Married on Tuesday evening last, by the Rev. Mr. Munds, Mr. William Campbell, to Miss Susannah Hall, both of this place.

Died yesterday morning, in the 72d year of his age, Mr. Samuel Jones, for many years a respectable inhabitant of this city....

Issue of January 9, 1809

Married, last eveing, by the Rev. James Dewar Simons, Mr. John Davis, to Miss Martha Moubray.

Married, on Saturday evening last, by the Rev. Dr. Furman, Mr. Robert Davis Eckert, of this city, to Mrs. Ann Vanbiber, of Goose Creek.

Died on Monday, the 2d inst., Mr. John M. Clement, in the

25th year of his age.

Issue of January 10, 1809

Obit. of Gov. James Sullivan from the New-England Palladium. (long account)

Married at Columbia, on Thursday evening, the 5th inst., by the Rev. Dr. Maxey, Mr. Serre Dubose of that town, to Miss Sarah Weston Goodwyn, of that district.

Issue of January 11, 1809

Died this morning, Mrs. Frances Remmington, wife of Mr. James Remmington, taylor, of this city.

Issue of January 13, 1809

Married last evening, by the Rev. Dr. Hollinshead, Mr. Foster Burnet, to Miss Abigail Elsworth, both of this city.

Married on the 31st of December last, by the Rev. Mr. M'Vean, Mr. Jacob Miller to Miss Sarah Clastries, both of this city.

Issue of January 14, 1809

Married on Tuesday evening last, at Mount Pleasant, on Charleston Neck, by the Rev. Charles Faber, Paul S. H. Lee, esq. of Miss Jane E. Martin, both of this city.

Issue of January 18, 1809

Married on Tuesday the 13th Dec., by the Rev. Dr. Montgomery, Mr. James Durret, to Miss Eliza Cunningham, both of Cambridge, S. C.

Married on Thursday 29d (sic) December, by the Rev. Dr. Montgomery, Telliafero Livingston, Esq. to Miss Martha Bostick, both of Cambridge, S. C.

Died in Williamsburgh district on the evening of the 12th inst., Hamilton Couturier Gourdin, youngest son of Theodore Gourdin, Esq. aged 6 years and 19 days.

Issue of January 19, 1809

Married on New Year evening, by the Rev. Philip Mathews, of St. James's Santee, Mr. Peter Vedeau Guerry, of Black River, to Miss Mary Elizabeth Guerry, daughter of Theodore Guerry, Esq. of Guerry-Town, St. Stephen's Parish.

Married on Wed. last, by the Rev. Mr. Simons, Mr. Henry Clifford, to Mrs. Frances Ann Slatter, both of this city.

Issue of January 20, 1809

Married last evening, by the Rev. Dr. Hollinshead, James Fisher Edwards, Esq. eldest son of the late John Edwards, esq. to Miss Sarah Barksdale M'Calla, only daughter of Dr. M'Calla, of this city.

Married, last evening at Hampstead, by the Rev. Charles Faber, Mr. B. Henrichsen, to Mrs. Lucy Grafft, both of the same place.

Married, on the 30th ult., on Charleston Neck, Mr. Lewis Poyas, to Miss Ann Ham.

Died on Saturday the 14th inst., at Oak Forest, near Dorchester, John Simmons, Esq. in the 55th year of his age....

Issue of January 21, 1809

Married on Tuesday evening last, by the Rev. Thomas Price, Mr. Thomas F. Hendlen, to Mrs. Sarah Rivers, both of James-Island, St. Andrew's parish.
Married on Wednesday last, by the Rev. Charles Faber, Mr. Philip Anderson, of St. James' Santee, to Miss Elizabeth Brown.
Died on the morning of the 19th inst., at the advanced age of 73 years, Hugh Swinton, sen. Esq. a native of this city....

Issue of January 24, 1809

Married on Sunday afternoon, by the Rev. Charles Faber, Mr. Christian Tameru, to Miss Fanny Moran.
Married at Beaufort, on Sunday evening, the 22d inst., by the Rev. Mr. Palmer, Mr. Charles Christian, of this city, to Miss Mary Lawson Saltus, of the former place.
Married on Saturday evening last, by the Rev. Mr. Munds, Capt. Joseph Potter, of New-York, to Miss Mary Jones, of this city.
Married on Sunday evening last, by the Rev. Mr. Munds, Mr. William Frazier, to Miss Eliza Charlotte Ward, both of this city.
Married on Sunday evening last, by the Rev. Mr. Munds, Mr. George William Miller to Mrs. Martha Cooper, both of this place.
Died, suddenly on Tuesday night last, in Augusta, George Steptoe Washington, esq. of Virginia, nephew of the late President, in the 37th year of his age....

Issue of January 25, 1809

Died on the 21st inst., Mrs. Mary Charlotte Truchelut....

Issue of January 27, 1809

Died on the evening of the 24th inst., Mrs. Amelia Casey Frances, in the 34th year of her age....

Issue of January 28, 1809

Died, at Winnsborough, on the 23d ult., Edwin Leroy M'Call, M. D. in the 27th year of his age.

Issue of January 30, 1809

Died at Savannah, on Thursday the 26th inst., Levi Sheftall, Esq., U. S. Agent for the State of Ga....

Issue of January 31, 1809

Married on Thursday morning last, by the Rev. Dr. Percy, Joseph Addison, esq. of St. Thomas's Parish, to Mrs. Sophia Taylor, of this city.

Issue of February 3, 1809

Died lately on Penouscot river, Madam Orono, aged 115 years, relict of Orono, late chief of the Penouscot Tribe of Indians, who died a few years since, aged 110.

Issue of February 4, 1809

Died on the 18th ult., at his plantation in St. Bartholomew's Parish, John Bellinger, Esq. in the 64th year of his age.

Departed this life in Kingston, Jamaica, on the 20th Oct., last, in the 35th year of his age, John O'Hara, Esq. second son of Daniel O'Hara, esq. of this city....

Issue of February 6, 1809

Married on the 5th Jan., by the Rev. Mr. Fowler, Capt. William Patterson, to Mrs. Mary Kling, all of St. Bartholomew's Parish.

Issue of February 8, 1809

Died on Saturday morning last, Mrs. Sarah Barksdale Edwards, wife of James F. Edwards, esq. the only child of Dr. Thomas H. M'Calla, aged 19 yeras and 3 months....(long eulogy)
Married last evening, by the Rev. Mr. Simons, John H. Dent, Esq. commander of the U. S. sloop Hornet, to Miss Ann Horry, daughter of Jonah Horry, Esq. of this city.
Departed this life on Wed. February 1st, in the 32d year of his age, Mr. Aaron Johnston, bricklayer, a native of Liverpool, in England....left an aged mother in Liverpool, and a sister in Charleston....

Issue of February 9, 1809

Married on Wednesday evening, the 1st inst., Mr. Levi Moses, to Miss Mary Joseph, both of this city.

Issue of February 11, 1809

Departed this life on the 8th inst., in the 29th year of her age, Mrs. Esther Raine, wife of Mr. Samuel Raine, and eldest daughter of the late Mr. James Nelson, merchant, of this city.

Issue of February 13, 1809

Married on Saturday night last, by the Rev. Dr. Furman, Mr. Hugh Macguire, to the amiable Mrs. Jane A. Hands, both of this city.

Issue of February 14, 1809

Married on Saturday evening last, by the Rev. Mr. Faber, Mr. James Perry, to Miss Mary Ann Kern, eldest daughter of Mr. John F. Kern, merchant, both of this city.
Died at Georgetown, on Thursday the 2d inst.,in the 56th year of her age, Mrs. Mary Serjeant, formerly of this city... left two daughters....

Issue of February 15, 1809

Married on Monday evening, by the Rev. Dr. Furman, Mr. Alexander B. Waugh, merchant, to Miss Margaret Christie, both of this city.
Died in Newberry district on the 1st inst., Mrs. Maria Claudia Donnan, in the 23d year of her age...left husband, three lovely infants....
Died at Philadelphia, on the 30th ult., Mr. John Craig, late of this city.
Died in Mercy County, Ky., Mrs. Hannah Higgins, aged 97 years, 3 months and 12 days...Robert Higgins, her husband died some years ago aged 110....

Issue of February 16, 1809

Married on Tuesday evening last, by the Rev. Dr. Gallagher, Mr. Peter Remondo, to Miss Simonette Lege, both of this city.

Issue of February 20, 1809

Married last evening, by the Rev. Dr. Keith, Lewis T. Raynall, Esq. to Miss Jane Holmes, daughter of the late John Holmes, esq. of John's Island.
Married on Saturday evening last, by the Rev. Mr. Mills, Mr. George Creitzburg, to Mrs. Mary Hislop, both of this city.
Died on the 1st of Feb., in the 31st year of her age, Mrs. Elizabeth Dunklin, consort of James Dunklin, Esq. of Laurens District....left five small children.

Issue of February 21, 1809

Died on Wednesday morning, the 15th inst., at Beaufort, S. C., Mrs. Margaret Knap, in the 64th year of her age....

Issue of February 23, 1809

Departed this life in this city, on the 19th inst., Eliza, late the wife of Walter Bourne, of New-York, and daughter of Robert Southgate, esq. of Scharborough (Maine) aged 25 years.

Issue of February 24, 1809

Died at Mulberry, St. John's, Berkeley, on the 6th inst., in the 58th year of his age, Thomas Broughton sen. esq....left two sons, a daughter....

Issue of February 25, 1809

Married, on Thursday evening last, by the Rev. Dr. Keith, Mr. Paul T. Jones, to Miss Mary L. Beach, both of this city.

Issue of February 28, 1809

Married, on Saturday the 25th inst., by the Rev. Dr. Furman, Mr. Thomas Logan, to Mrs. Susannah E. Clark, both of this city.
Departed this life at Newport, Rhode-Island, on the 13th inst., aged 39 years, Mrs. Sarah Read, consort of Doctor William Read, of this city....
Died at St. Mary's, on the 16th inst., in the 50th year of his age, Mr. Alexander Crawford, Painter, formerly of this city.

Issue of March 2, 1809

Married, on Tuesday evening last, by the Rev. Dr. Percy, Mr. Elias Coppley, of St. Marks, Santee, to Miss Dinah Young Brimner, of this city.
Married, on Tuesday, by the Rev. Dr. Hollinshead, James D. Mitchell, Esq. to Miss Amelia Waring, daughter of Thomas Waring, sen. Esq.
Married in Winnsborough, by the Rev. Mr. Reid, on Friday the 13th ult., Christian H. Bricthaupt, Esq. to Mrs. Gertrude J. Senf, relict of the late Col. Senf.
Died in Georgetown, on the morning of the 23d ult., Benjamin Allston, Jun. Esq. of Waccamaw, in the 43d year of his age.
Died at Exuma (Bahamas) on the 5th ult., Capt. Robert Monies, late Master of the ship Mississippi, of this port.

Issue of March 3, 1809

Married last evening by the Rev. Dr. Keith, Mr. Benjamin Russ, to Miss Sarah Mitchell, both of this city.
Married, last evening, by the Rev. Dr. Furman, Captain John Cole, to Miss Eliza L. Bennett, both of this city.

Issue of March 4, 1809

Married, on Thursday evening last, by the Rev. Dr. Furman, Mr. Peter Archer Green, of York district, to Miss Sarah Walton, of this city.
Died, on Monday the 20th ult., Mr. George Samuel Saltus, aged 21 years, a native of Bermuda.

Issue of March 6, 1809

Married last evening, by the Rev. Mr. Simons, Mr. John Prince, to Miss Elizabeth B. Bounetheau, daughter of the late Peter Bounetheau, esq.
Died on the 10th of Jan. last, on board the British schooner Polly, on her passage from this port to the Bahamas, Dr. John Shaw, a native of Annapolis, Maryland.

Issue of March 7, 1809

Married at Statesburg, S. C. on Wednesday 22d ult., by the Rev. Mr. Russell, Mr. James C. Postell, of the Hills, to Miss Tabitha M. Green, daughter of Francis Green, esq. of Georgetown.

Issue of March 9, 1809

Departed this life on Monday the 20th ult., at his place of residence in St. Luke's Parish, Beaufort District, Major Charles Pelot, in the 46th year of his age....

Issue of March 13, 1809

Married on Thursday evening last, by the Rev. J. D. Simons, Arthur Middleton Esq. to Miss Alicia Russell, daughter of Nathaniel Russell, esq.
Married on the 27th ult., at Smithville, N. C., Mr. Seth H. Gilbert, of this city, to Miss Catherine Davis, of that place.
Died on Tuesday last, in the bloom of life, Miss Mary Stevens, eldest daughter of W. S. Stevens. (lines)
Died, in Spartanburgh district in this state, on the 17th ult., Mr. John Herron, merchant, formerly of this city.

Issue of March 15, 1809

Married on Wednesday morning the 8th inst., by the Rev. Dr. Hollinshead, Capt. Nathaniel Green Hillard, of Connecticut, to Miss Ann Elizabeth Watt, of this city.
Married on Monday evening, by the Rev. Mr. Munds, Capt. George William Smith, to Miss Elizabeth Ward, both of this place.
Married last evening, by the Rev. Mr. Munds, Mr. George Kennedy, to Miss Hannah Mary M'Donald, both of this place.

Issue of March 17, 1809

Married last evening, by the Rev. Dr. Mills, Captain Alfred Galloway, to Miss Ann Sears, both of this city.

Issue of March 18, 1809

Married last evening, by the Rev. Dr. Hollinshead, Mr. Thomas Banks, of the house of Robinson & Banks, to Miss Margery Armstrong, both of this city.

Issue of March 22, 1809

Married on the 16th inst., by the Rev. Mr. Fowler, Richard B. Bedon, esq. of the Horse Shoe, to Miss Jane L. Perry, daughter of Dr. James Perry, of the Round O.
Married on Saturday evening last, by the Rev. Mr. Munds, Mr. Archibald M'Alpin, to Mrs. Mary Walling.
Married on Sunday evening last, by the Rev. Dr. Furman, Mr. Christian Gradick, to Miss Susannah North, both of this city.

Issue of March 23, 1809

Married, last Monday by the Rev. Mr. Faber, Mr. Christian Nagel, to Miss Jane Mathews, both of this city.

Issue of March 25, 1809

Married, at Hampstead, on Thursday evening, last, by the Rev. Dr. Hollinshead, Mr. George Curling, to Mrs. Ann M. Bouchoneau, both of this city.

Issue of March 28, 1809

Died at Beaufort, on the 24th inst.,Mr. James Doharty Talbird(?), aged 27 years....

Issue of March 29, 1809

Married, on Sunday evening last, by the Rev. Dr. Keith, Mr. Samuel Rain, to Mrs. Mary M'Lean, both of this city.

Issue of March 30, 1809

Departed this life in St. Luke's Parish, on the 23d inst., Mrs. Caroline Porteous, relict of Alexander R. Porteous, Esq. deceased, in the 27th year of her age.

Issue of March 31, 1809

Died on Tuesday the 21st inst., Mr. Isaac Prioleau, aged 29 years.
Died on the 28th inst., Captain Edward Ross, a native of Newport, Rhode Island, aged 48 years.
Died on Tuesday morning last, John Lewis James Gervias, Esq aged 20 years and 9 months. (eulogy)

Issue of April 1, 1809

Married last evening, by the Rev. Dr. Hollinshead, John N. Davis, Esq. of St. Mathew's Parish, to Miss Julia Lehre, daughter of Col. Thomas Lehre, of this city.
Married on Thursday evening last, by the Rev. Mr. Munds, Mr. Ezekiel Torrey to Miss Ann Lewis, both of this place.
Married on Thursday evening last, by the Rev. Mr. Munds, Mr. Stephen Harper, to Miss Susannah Moore, both of this place.
Married on Thursday the 16th ult., at Chester, by the Rev. Thomas Nuby, Mr. Alexander Cabeen, to Miss Margaret Anderson,

daughter of the Rev. John Anderson, deceased.

Issue of April 4, 1809

Married on Sunday evening last, by the Rev. Mr.Faber, Mr. Edward G. Sass, to Miss Mary S. Switzer, both of this city.

Married on Thursday evening last, by the Rev. Mr. Faber, Mr. Christian Pagels, to Miss Maria Adams, both of this city.

Died on Sunday the 19th ult.,at Richmond, on Cooper, River, the residence of Mr. Edward Rutledge, Aaron Thompson Esq. of the State of New-Jersey....

Issue of April 7, 1809

Married, on Sunday the 19th ult., on Wadmalaw Island, Mr. John Bates, planter, to Miss Sarah Duynmier, both of said Island.

Died on the 4th inst., John Pearis Cunningham, Esq., aged 24 years and 4 months....

Issue of April 12, 1809

Died on Monday night last, in the 31st year of his age, Thomas Sheppard, Esq. one of the Editors of the "Times."

Accident in Prince William's Parish, on the 3d inst...Major James Miles died by being thrown from his horse...in the 36th year of his age...represented in the Legislature of this state... left widow and children.

Died on the 6th inst., at the Grove, Christ Church parish, in the 61st year of his age, the Rev. Dr. M'Calla....

Died on Callawassi Island, in St. Luke's Parish, on the 5th inst., Capt. Thomas Rhodes, nephew to Mr. John Rhodes....

Died on Friday the 30th ult., in the 35th year of his age, Mr. Daniel Boyden...left an aged mother and a number of relations....

Issue of April 13, 1809

Married in Barnwell District on the 6th inst., by the Rev. James Wilson, Jennings O'Banon, Esq. to Miss Harriet C. Ford, both of the same place.

Married at Hampstead, on Sunday evening last, by the Rev. Dr. Faber, Mr. John Ditmore, to Miss Eliza Henrichsen, both of this city.

Issue of April 14, 1809

Died in Franklin Co., N. C., Mrs. Jane Bledso, at the advanced age of 92 years....

Issue of April 15, 1809

Died suddenly on the 11th inst., at White Hill, near Orangeburgh, Jacob Rumph Jamison, in the 8th year of his age, eldest son of Dr. V. D. V. Jamison....

Died on the 23d ult., in Orange Co., Va., Mr. John Madison, nephew to the President....

Issue of April 17, 1809

Died, in Charleston, on Friday evening, the 14th inst., Mrs. Milly Purdue, in the 36th year of her age....left husband and three children....

Issue of April 18, 1809

Died on the 6th inst., at the Grove, in Christ Church Parish, in the 61st year of his age, the Rev. Daniel M'Calla, D. D., for 21 years Pastor of the Independent or Congregational Church in that place....(long eulogy)

Died at Cheraw-Hill, on Wed., the 5th inst., Lt.-Col. Andrew Smith, in the 44th year of his age.

Died on Thursday morning the 13th inst., Master Washington Rendell, youngest son of Mr. George Rendell, of this city.

Issue of April 19, 1809

Died at his seat in Richmond Co., N. C. on the 31st ult., in the 62d year of his age, Gen. Henry W. Harrington....officer in the revolution....

Issue of April 20, 1809

Married on Tuesday evening, by the Rev. Mr. Munds, Capt. George William Buchanan, to Miss Eliza Webster, both of this place.

Married last evening by the Rev. Mr. Munds, Mr. Francis Joseph to Mrs. Winifred Wrand.

Died on Sunday the 16th inst., Mr. Archibald Brebner, Merchant Taylor, in the 39th year of his age...a native of Tarland, near Aberdeen, Scotland....left wife and child.

Issue of April 21, 1809

Married on Wednesday morning the 19th inst., in St. Philip's Church, by the Rev. J. D. Simons, Mr. Francis Cobia, to Miss Jane Lowrey, both of this city.

Died on the 17th inst., at his residence at White-Hall, St. Luke's Parish, Thomas Heyward, Esq. in the 63d year of his age.

Departed this life on Sunday the 16th inst., in the 26th year of his age, Mr. James Kirkpatrick....

Issue of April 24, 1809

Died in East-Florida, on the 9th inst., Alexander Dunn, a native of South Carolina, aged 25 years. He went to visit his relations in St. Mary's....

Issue of April 27, 1809

Died, on Wednesday, the 19th inst., in the 32d year of his age, Mr. William Conover, son of Peter Conover, Esq. of New-Jersey.

Issue of April 28, 1809

Married at Hampstead, last evening, by the Rev. Mr. Percy, Mr. James Moore, to Miss Elizabeth Belser.

Issue of May 2, 1809

Married in Orangeburgh, on Thursday the 22d ult., by the Rev. Dr. Eccles, Mr. Donald Rowe, to Mrs. Ann Sabb.

Died in London, the 16th March, Admiral Sir Hyde Parker, aged 67.

Issue of May 5, 1809

Married last evening, by the Rev. Mr. Bowen, George Fraser, Esq. to Miss Maria Boone.

Issue of May 6, 1809

Married on Thursday evening last, by the Rev. Dr. Hollinshead, Mr. John J. Evans, one of the Proprietors of the Savannah Republican, to Miss Mary M'Dow, of this city.
Married on Thursday evening last, by the Rev. Mr. Munds, Mr. George Kennedy, to Miss Martha Sprout, both of this place.

Issue of May 8, 1809

Married last evening, by the Rev. Dr. Percy, Mr. John Ling, to Miss Mary Jones, daughter of Mr. Joseph Jones, all of this city.
Married, last evening, by the Rev. Dr. Hollinshead, Mr. William H. Gilliland, to Miss Anne Eliza Elmore, both of this city.
Married this morning, in St. Philip's Church, by the Rev. Dr. Percy, Mr. William Fell, to Miss Elizabeth Macaulay Skrine, both of this city.
Died on Tuesday last, the 2d inst., Mrs. Martha DuVall, in the 36th year of her age...left relatives and friends.
Died at his plantation in Bourke county, Ga., about the 1st of March, Mr. John D. Dickinson, formerly of the house of Belcher & Dickinson, of Savannah.

Issue of May 10, 1809

Died on Sunday night last, Mr. Moise Abrahams, in the 73d year of his age...born at Strasburgh, in Germany....(account) left wife and nine children.

Issue of May 13, 1809

Died on the 4th inst., in Chester District, Mr. Archibald Pagan, late of this city, merchant.
On Sunday last, the 7th inst., departed this life, in the 62d year of her age, Mrs. Elizabeth M'Intosh....

Issue of May 15, 1809

Married last evening, by the Rev. Dr. Hollinshead, Capt. John M'Intosh, to Mrs. Rebecca Dieckert, of Christ Church Parish.
Departed this life at Beaufort, S. C. in the 33d year of her age, Mrs. Eliza C. Black of said place....left three infant children, and fond parents.

Issue of May 17, 1809

Married, in Christ Church Parish, late evening, by the Rev. Mr. Christopher Gadsden, Mr. William Lebby, to Miss Frances Sarah Scott, both of this place.

Issue of May 18, 1809

Departed this life the 3d inst., Marie Rose Jeanne Gabrielle Dugaric Celeste D'Uzech, only daughter of the late Count Dugaric D'Uzech, and consort of Dr. J. Dumaine, of this city....
Died at Savannah, on the 10th inst., Mrs. Elizabeth Smith, aged 78 years, a native of this state....

Issue of May 19, 1809

Married on Wednesday evening, the 10th inst., by the Rev. Mr. Gadsden, Mr. Paul Pritchard, sen. to Miss Lydia Glover, both of St. Thomas's Parish.

Issue of May 20, 1809

Died on the 19th inst., Mr. Stephen Dutch, a native of Ipswich, Mass., but a resident here upwards of 10 years.

Issue of May 22, 1809

Died on Cooper River, St. Thomas's Parish, the 9th inst., Mrs. Mary Feay, wife of Mr. Obadiah M. Feay, and left three small children with a disconsolate husband....

Issue of May 29, 1809

Died, at Williamsburg, on the 22d ult., in the 24th year of her age, Mrs. Mary Mouzon, consort of Mr. Samuel R. Mouzon, and eldest daughter of Capt. Shadrick Simons, decd...left husband, two brothers....

Issue of May 30, 1809

Died on the 12th inst.,Mr. John Miot, by accidental shooting. left wife and four children.

Issue of May 31, 1809

Died this morning the 12th year of her age, Susan Cox Young, youngest daughter of Mr. W. P. Young.
Married at Pelham, Mass., Mr. WilliamM'Fall, aged 100 years, to the widow Judith Perkins, aged 79, both paupers.

Issue of June 1, 1809

Married, yesterday by the Rev. Mr. Jacob Suares, Mr. Isaac Wolfe, to Miss Sarah Moses, youngest daughter of Mr. Solomon Moses, all of this city.

Issue of June 2, 1809

Departed this life on the 27th ult., in St. James' Parish, Santee Mrs. Elizabeth Percy, consort of Major John F. Percy....

Issue of June 3, 1809

Died at the Cantonment, Columbian Crping, near Fort Adams, Capt. Francis Johnson, of the U. S. Army.

Issue of June 5, 1809

Married, yesterday, at St. Michael's Church, by the Rev. Mr. Bowen, Mr. Thomas Higham, to Miss Frances C. Hubert, both of this city.

Issue of June 7, 1809

Died on Saturday last,in the 43d year of his age, Mr. Robert Forster, of this city.

Departed this life on Wednesday last, in the 3d year of his age, John Houston, youngest son of Mr. James Houston, of this city.

Issue of June 9, 1809

Departed this life on the 17th ult., at his residence in Greenville District, South Pacolet, Mr. Jeremiah Browne, aged 27 years....

Issue of June 15, 1809

Died at Philadelhpia, on Sunday afternoon, the 4th inst., in the 39th year of his age, Dr. James Woodhouse, late Prof. of Chemistry in the University of Pennsylvania.

Issue of June 16, 1809

Married, in New-York, on the 30th ult., by the Rev. James D. Simons, of this city, Paul Hamilton, esq. eldest son of the Secretary of the Navy, to Miss Rhodes, daughter of John Rhodes, esq. of Beaufort.

Issue of June 21, 1809

Married, last evening, by the Rev. Mr. Flinn, Mr. William Scott, jun. Merchant, to Miss Rebecca Eliza Bigelow, both of this city.

Died on Sunday evening last, in the 56th year of her age, Mrs. Mary Muncreef, relict of the late Robert Muncreef, Esq. of this city, Merchant.

Issue of June 22, 1709

Died in St. Thomas's Parish, on Monday last, in the 44th year of her age, Mrs.Priscilla Rembert, relict of Capt. Wm. Rembert, late of Camden.

Long obit of Mrs. Mary Muncreef....

Died on the 30th ult., in the city of New-Haven, Conn., Mr. Amos B. Doolittle, aged 23 years....

Issue of June 24, 1809

Died, at Baltimore, on the 11th inst., Mr. Joseph Barrymore, (formerly of the Charleston Theatre)...he was an officer in the U. S. Navy.

Issue of June 27, 1809

Died, in London, on the 28th April last, James Gadsden, Esq. in the 75th year of his age.

Issue of July 1, 1809

Departed this life on Thursday evening, in the 20th year of her age, Miss Zelie Laborde, a native of Cape Francois, in the Island of St. Domingo....

Issue of July 6, 1809

Died in St. George's Parish, on the 2d inst., Dr. William Morgan, in the 34th year of his age....

Issue of July 10, 1809

Died on Saturday the 8th inst., in the 21st year of her age, Mrs. Cynthia Loveless Grantt   (lines)

Issue of July 12, 1809

Departed this life on Monday evening, the 3d inst., Mrs. Mary Flagg, aged 36 years....

Issue of July 14, 1809

Died on the 9th inst., Mr. Nicholas Miller, aged 56 years....

Issue of July 18, 1809

Departed this life on Saturday morning last, Mr. Thomas Baas, in the 51st year of his age....
Died at Philadelphia, on the 30th ult., in the 109th year of her age, Susannah Warder, formerly the wife of Virgil Warder, who was one of the house servants of William Penn. This aged black woman was born at his mansion house in Pennsburg Manor, March 1701....

Issue of July 22, 1809

Departed this life on the 14th inst., John Cornelius Russell, Jun. aged 1 year and 18 days....

Issue of July 25, 1809

Departed this life on Sunday the 22d inst., in the 55th year of his age, Mr. William Stephen, a native of Aberdeen, Scotland, and for many years a respectable Merchant of this city.

Issue of July 27, 1809

Died on Sunday the 15th inst., at the seat of Major Haskell, on the Congaree, in the 76th year of her age, Mrs. Eugenia Thomson, relict of Col. William Thomson, late of BelleVille, in Amelia Township.....
Died on Sunday last, the 23d inst.,Mr. William Stephen, in the 55th year of his age, a native of Aberdeen in Scotland... (long account)

Issue of August 7, 1809

Married at Portsmouth, Rhode-Island, on the 16th ult., Capt. Isaac Burdick, of the ship Minerva, to Miss Eliza Brightman.

Issue of August 11, 1809

Died, on the 7th, Mr. Alexander M'Dowall, for many years a respectable merchant of this city.
Departed this life on the 7th inst., Mr. Elijah Velser, in the 23d year of his age...a native of Huntington, New-York, and has left there and aged father, mother, brothers and sisters....

Issue of August 12, 1809

Married last evening, by the Rev. Mr. Munds, Mr. Benjamin Hawes, to Miss Ann Frances Dupre.

Issue of August 16, 1809

Died on the 13th inst.,Mrs. Eliza Kimball, consort of Mr. George Kimball, Merchant of this city in the 17th year of her age. (lines)

Died, at the Cheraw Bluff, Mr. William Snipes, a native of Virginia, but for many years a resident of that place, in the 42d year ofhis age.

Died at Waccamaw, on the 31st ult., Mr. John Boone.

Issue of August 21, 1809

Died, at Combahee, on Monday evening, August 14th, John Whalley, esq. of the house of Whalley & Broadfoot, aged 31 years.

Died last evening, at Hibbins' Ferry, opposite this city, Capt. John Miles, of New-Haven, Conn.

Died on the 16th inst., at his plantation on James Island, Mr. John Hearne Stent, late of Charleston, bricklayer, in the 28th year of his age....

Issue of August 22, 1809

Died on Sunday the 13th inst., in the 50th year of his age, Samuel House, Esq. a native of Philadelphia....left daughter and two sons.

Issue of August 30, 1809

Died on Sunday afternoon, in the 26th year of his age, Mr. Thomas Banks, a native of Ireland, for three years past a resident of this city...left wife...interred in the burial ground of the Presbyterian Church...

Died on Thursday the 17th inst.,at his residence in the Dutch Fork, near Columbia, the Rev. Mr. Bernhard, Minister of the Lutheran Church.

Died in the District of Orangeburgh, on Wed., the 2d inst., in the 22d year of his age, Mr. Philip D. Williams....

Issue of September 1, 1809

Married, last evening, by the Rev. Mr. Simons, Mr. Frederick Nasted, to Mrs. Mary Hunter, both of this city.

Died on the 29th ult., Mrs. Sally Clemmons, wife of Capt. James Clemmons, of Marblehead, Mass., aged 24 years...left husband, two young children and a sister.

Died yesterday morning, the 31st ult., in the 27th year of his age, Mr. David Fleming, a native of Scotland, for several years past a resident of this place. (lines)

Departed this life on Monday the 28th ult., in the 21st year of his age, William Tweed Watson....

Issue of September 4, 1809

Married on Saturday last, by the Rev. Dr. Keith, Mr. William D. Shaw, to Miss Eliza Palmer, both of this city.

Died on the 9th ult., near Granby, after two days illness, Mrs. Ann Drehr, wife of Godfrey Drehr, jun. and daughter of the late Mr. Jacob Saylor, of the Congaree.

Died this morning, in the 3d year of her age, Elizabeth S. Righton, the youngest daughter of Joseph Righton.

Issue of September 8, 1809

Died on the 2d inst., on his passage from New-York to this place, Mr. Joseph Milligan, aged 63 years, a native of Ireland.
A Negro Fellow, named Cuffee, the property of Mrs. M'Cleish, fell into the river and drowned....

Issue of September 9, 1809

Departed this life at his residence in Richland district, on the 21st ult., Mr. John Griffin, aged 99 years and 6 months... he was born in America--and his widow who is upwards of 90 years of age, is now living.

Issue of September 12, 1809

Married at Freetown, Mass., on the 15th ult., Mr. John Hinds, formerly of this place, to Mrs. Anna Peirce.

Issue of September 13, 1809

Departed this transient existence on Sunday evening, the 10th inst., at St. John's Parish, Mr. John Hort M'Call, in the 27th year of his age....interred in the cemetery of St. Philip's Church.

Issue of September 15, 1809

Died on Monday evening last, Mr. Nathaniel Eels, a native of New-London, in the 25th year of his age...left mother and brother.

Issue of September 18, 1809

Died at his plantation, in St. George's Parish, on the 8th inst., Thomas Cantey, Esq., aged 37 years, 7 months, 12 days... left wife and six small children.
Died on the 14th inst., in the 37th year of his age, James Mair, gardener, a native of Scotland.
Departed this life on Thursday morning last, Josias Allston Deliesseline, son of Francis G. Deliesseline, aged 8 years 7 months and 10 days....
Died on Friday last, in the 25th year of his age, Capt. Justus Pierce, a native of New-London.

Issue of September 19, 1809

Departed this life on Sunday morning last, the 17th inst., Mr. John Healy, son of Major I. Healy, of Worcester, state of Mass., in the 26th year of his age...
Died at Columbia, on Sunday morning last, Mrs. Mary Brice, wife of Mr. John Brice, of that place.

Issue of September 23, 1809

Died at Camden, on Wed. the 6th inst.,Mrs. Susanna Blanding, consort of Dr. William Blanding, of that place...a native of Rehobath, Mass., and had resided nearly two years in Camden....

Issue of September 26, 1809

Died, on James Island, on Saturday morning last,Hannah Sarah Bennett, only child of Mr. John S. Bennett, in the 5th year of her age.

Departed this life on Sunday the 10th inst., Martha S. Jenkins, aged 42 years, 1 month, 8 days...relict of Mr. John Jenkins, deceased, of Edisto Island...(lines)

Issue of September 27, 1809

Died on Sunday the 10th inst.,in the 22d year of her age, Mrs. Sophia Jane Crouch, consort of Abraham Crouch. Esq. (lines)

Died on Friday night last, in the 76th year of her age, Mrs. Christiana Weaver, a native of Germany.

died on Monday afternoon, on Edisto Island, Mr. Abraham S. Abrahams, aged 20 years.

Issue of September 28, 1809

Died, this morning, Mrs. Martha Wallace, in the 20th year of her age...left a doating husband.

Issue of January 9, 1810

Died yesterday morning, the 8th inst., Joseph Yates, aged 11 years and 3 months, eldest son of Jeremiah and Elizabeth Yates.

Died on board the schooner Two Brothers, on her passage from Senegal to this port, Mr. Augustine Dumouline, one of her seamen.

Issue of January 29, 1810

Married on Saturday evening last, by the Rev. Mr. M'Leod, Mr. James Morrison, to Miss Jane Douglas Miller, both of this city.

Issue of April 3, 1810

Died at the plantation of Mr. Francis Peyre, on the 29th ult., Mr. Peter Robert, of St. Stephen's parish...left no family....

Died at his seat in Willtown, on Sunday evening the 25th ult., Capt. James Zuill, in the 51st year of his age...a native of Balfron, in Scotland, came to this country soon after the close of the rev. war....left widow, two infant children....

Issue of April 6, 1810

Departed this life on the 17th ult., Mrs. Elizabeth Anderson, wife of Mr. John Anderson, aged 27 years...left husband and two children....

Issue of April 9, 1810

Married on Saturday evening,the 7th inst., by the Rev. Dr. Hollinshead, Mr. Benjamin Singellton, Merchant, to Miss Eliza Haslett Douglass, both of this city.

Issue of April 12, 1810

Died, at Parker's Ferry, on the 9th inst., Mrs. Byrd....

Issue of April 14, 1810

Married on Thursday evening last, by the Rev. Dr. Furman, Mr. Joseph Otis, jun. Factor, to Miss Jane Munroe, daughter of Mr. John Munroe, all of this city.

Issue of April 17, 1810

Departed this life, the 29th ult., Mrs. Susannah North, in her 60th year...she was the oldest member of the Baptist Church.

Issue of April 19, 1810

Departed this life on Thursday morning last, Mrs. Mary Verree, in the 68th year of her age....

Issue of April 20, 1810

Died, at Georgetown, on Friday evening, the 13th inst., in the 24th year of his age, Lieut. Henry Laurens Lenud, of the U. S. light artillery.

Issue of April 21, 1810

Married, on Saturday evening last, by the Rev. Mr. Simons, Dr. William Warley, to Miss Mary Motte Wilson, daughter of the late Daniel Wilson, esq.

Issue of April 29, 1810

Married in the city of Augusta, Ga., on the 3d inst., by the Rev. Mr. Brantley, Robert Raymond Reid, Esq. Attorney at Law, late of South-Carolina, to Miss Anna Margaretta M'Laws.

Issue of April 25, 1810

Married on Thursday evening, by the Rev. Mr. Simons, Major Robert Howard, to Miss Harriet Lee, daughter of the late Col. William Lee.

Married, on Thursday last, by the Rev. Mr. Floyd, Mr. Samuel Perry, of St. Paul's Parish, to Miss Ann Jane Coburn, daughter of Capt. James Coburn, late of St. George's Parish.

Issue of April 26, 1810

Married on Thursday evening last, by the Rev. Dr. Hollinshead, Thomas Smith, Esq., planter, of St. Bartholomew's Parish, to Miss Elizabeth Mary Baker, eldest daughter of Mr. Joseph Baker, of this city.

Issue of April 27, 1810

Died on the 21st inst., in St. John's Parish, Mr. Samuel Bird, of Massachusetts, in the 25th year of his age....

Departed this transitory life at Belfast, Laurens district, on the 9th inst., in the 56th year of her age, Mrs. Mary Simpson, consort of Col. John Simpson...native of Burford, Oxfordshire, England, and removed to this place in the beginning of the year 1787....(lines)

Issue of May 5, 1810

Died last evening, at Sullivan's Island, Mr. John Clough, late of the Charleston Theatre.

Issue of May 7, 1810

　　Married on Wednesday evening the 2d inst., by the Rev. Mr. Simons, Capt. Jeremiah Connolly, to Mrs. Mary Halet Connolly, all of this city.
　　Departed this life on the 30th ult., Capt. Edward Walker, in the 34th year of his age....

Issue of May 8, 1810

　　Died on Sunday morning last, in St. Paul's Parish, Miss Elizabeth James, a native of England, for 44 years an inhabitant of this state.
　　Died on the morning of the 31st ult., Antoine Groscol, a native of Parish, aged about 57 years, having resided in Charleston about 13 years.

Issue of May 11, 1810

　　Died, yesterday morning, the Rev. Dr. Rattoone, principal of the Charleston College.

Issue of May 12, 1810

　　Married on Thursday evening by the Rev. Mr. Dehon, Mr. John Holmes, of John's Island, to Miss Ann Glover, daughter of Charles Glover, Esq.

Issue of May 17, 1810

　　Married on Sunday evening the 13th inst., by the Rev. C. Faber, Mr. Peter Wartenberg, to Miss Mary Catharine Bayer, daughter of Mr. J. Friederick Bayer, of this place.
　　Departed this life on Saturday the 5th inst., in Fairfield District, the Rev. William Rosborough, aged 45 years....a Presbyterian preacher.
　　Married last evening by the Rev. Mr. Wilson, Howell Cobb, esq. member of Congress from Ga., to Miss Martha J. Rootes, daughter of Thomas R. Rootes, esq. of this place Virginia Herald, May 9

Issue of May 19, 1810

　　Married on Monday last, 14th inst., by the Rev. Mr. Pogson, Mr. Thomas Pearce, to Miss Ann Lucas, daughter of Mr. Jonathan Lucas, of Christ Church Parish.

Issue of May 21, 1810

　　Departed this transitory life, at Beaufort, on the 17th inst., Miss Mary Rhodes, second daughter of J. Rhodes, Esq.

Issue of May 23, 1810

　　Married on Wednesday evening the 9th inst., by the Rev. Dr. Dehone, Mr. Charles H. Miott, to Miss Eleanor P. Bell, both of this city.
　　Married at Johnson County, N. C., on the 10th inst.,Mr. Charles Hood, to Miss Sally Ellington, sister of his former wife.

Issue of May 26, 1810

　　Married on Wednesday evening last, by the Rev. Thomas H. Price, of James-Island, Mr. Sandiford Holmes, to Miss Martha Hilyard, both of this city.

Issue of May 30, 1810

Married on Monday evening the 28th inst., by the Rev. C. Faber, Mr. John Schroder, to Miss Ann Dorothea Boyer, daughter of Mr. J. Frederick Boyer, of this place

Issue of May 31, 1810

Married on Tuesday evening last, by the Rev. Mr. Simons, Thomas Wright Bacot, Esq. to Miss Elizabeth Sarah Wainwright, daughter of Richard Wainwright, esq. deceased.

Issue of June 2, 1810

Departed this life on Sunday 27th ult., Mr. James Walker, aged 23 years and 11 months. (lines)

Issue of June 4, 1810

Married, on Thursday last, by the Rev. Dr. Keith, Dr. Alexander M. Edwards, to Miss Caroline Parker Scott.

Died on the 27th ult, Mr. Abraham Williamson, a native of Cumberland, England, about 23 years a resident of this place... left widow and three young children.

Issue of June 5, 1810

Departed this life on the 25th ult., at his seat in St. Thomas's Parish, Gen. John B. Caradeux, in the 70th year of his age...native of St. Domingo...arrived here in 1792....

Issue of June 12, 1810

Departed this life on the 15th ult. at his residence in York district, William Clinton, Esq...left consort with six children.

Issue of June 14, 1810

Died at Norfolk, on the 6th inst., Mrs. Margaret West, Proprietor of the Norfolk Theatre. Mrs. West was a Member of the Charleston Theatre about 14 years ago.

Issue of June 16, 1810

Married at Jamesville, on the 12th inst., by the Rev. Mr. Gadsden, the Hon. Col. William Boone Mitchell, of St. Paul's, to Miss Dorothy S. Richardson, eldest daughter to the Hon. Col. J. B. Richardson, formerly Governor of this State.

Issue of June 18, 1810

Departed this life on Saturday the 16th inst., in the 33d year of his age, Mr. John G. D. Meursett....

Issue of June 19, 1810

Married, on Thursday evening last, by the Rev. Mr. M'Leod, Robert A. Pringle, Esq. to Miss M. Sarah Maxwell, only daughter of James R. Maxwell, Esq. deceased.

Issue of June 25, 1810

Died, at her late residence in Wentworth street, on Thursday, the 21st inst., Mrs. Mary Hume, wife of John Hume, esq., and eldest daughter of the late Wm. Mazyck, Esq.

Issue of June 26, 1810

Died on the 19th inst., after a painful illness, in the 28th year of her age, Mrs. Charlotte Toomer, consort of Anthony Toomer, esq. of this place...left husband and five young children....
Georgetown Paper.

Issue of July 2, 1810

Married on Sunday evening, the 24th ult.,by the Rev. Dr. Hollinshead, Mr. John Casper, to Miss Ann Wingwood.

Issue of July 3, 1810

Married on Sunday evening the 24th ult., by the Rev. Dr. Hollinshead, Mr. John Caskin, to Miss Ann Wingood, both of this city.
Died suddenly on the 28th ult., at his residence on the High Hills of Santee, William Rees, Esq. in the 72d year of his age....

Issue of July 7, 1810

Died on the 2d inst., Capt. John Blake....
Departed this life on the 1st inst., in the 54th year of his age, Mr. John Rodolph Switzer, for many years a respectable inhabitant of this city....

Issue of July 11, 1810

Died on Sunday last, at his plantation in St. Paul's Parish, John Miles Sen....
Died on Friday last, the 6th inst., Mr. William Daverson, aged 32.

Issue of July 12, 1810

Departed this life, on Sunday last, Mrs. Rebecca Darby, aged 33 years and 7 months.
Died on Monday, the 25th ult., Mr. David M'Kelvy, a native of Ireland, in the 30th year of his age.

Issue of July 13, 1810

Married last evening, by the Rev. Dr. Percy, Mr. George Realey(?) to Miss ___ Armstrong, both of this city.
Died on the 26th ult., Mr. Jesse Vaughn, of this city, in his 56th year....left wife and three small children.

Issue of July 16, 1810

Married in this city, on Thursday evening last, by the Rev. Mr. Faber, Mr. William M'Nellage, of Christ Church Parish, to Miss Jane Matilda Perry, of St. Paul's Parish.

Issue of July 20, 1810

Died at Baltimore, on the 30th ult., Samuel T. Wright, Esq. Clerk of Queen-Ann's County, and Adjutant-General of Maryland.

Died at Baltimore, on the 8th inst., Thomas Dickson, Esq., President of the Franklin Bank, in that city.

Issue of July 24, 1810

Died on the 18th inst., in the 22d year of his age, Mr. Adam Ogilvie Aitchison, a native of Scotland....

Issue of July 28, 1810

Died at Georgetown, on the 9th inst., in the 29th year of his age, Mr. Richard M'Grath, a son of Evin....

Issue of July 30, 1810

Died on the 18th inst., in St. Bartholomew's Parish, in the 60th year of her age, Mrs. Ann Postell, consort of the late Major John Postell....

Issue of July 31, 1810

Died, on Friday the 25th May last, in Sumter District, at Mr. James B. Richardson's, near Jamesville, Thomas Glenn sen. an old and respectable inhabitant of the state of Virginia....

Died on Saturday the 30th of June last, in Sumter District, at the seat of Mr. John P. Richardson, Thomas Glenn Junr....

Issue of August 2, 1810

Died, in Pine Ville, St. Stephen's Parish, on the 24th ult., Miss H. A. Wiare, daughter of the late capt. James G. Wiare, of St. John's Parish.

Issue of August 3, 1810

Departed this life, John Brailsford, Jun, Esq., in the 38th year of his age....

Issue of August 4, 1810

Died on Thursday morning, Mr. Samuel Rodgers, a native of England, and long a resident in this city. He was employed as organist in St. Michael's Church, for nearly 20 years past....

Issue of August 6, 1810

Married at New-York, on Monday the 23d July, by the Rev. Dr. Romaine, Joseph De Jongh, Esq. of the house of Williamson, Worrall & Co. of Liverpool (England) to Miss Henrietta Williman, daughter of Christopher Williman, esq. of South-Carolina.

Issue of August 7, 1810

Died at Parkertown Vt., Capt. John Vincent, an Indian, aged 95....

Died in Edinburgh, Lieut. Angus M'Donnoll, aged 83. He served as an officer during Wolfe's American campaign....

Died, near Knaresborough, England, John Metcalf, commonly called Blind Jack, aged 94....

Issue of August 11, 1810

Departed this life on Wednesday evening, the 8th inst., Mrs. Mary Carr, in the 60th year of her age....
Died at St. Augustine, East-Florida, on the 1st ult., Mrs. Mary Magdalen Fatio, wife of Francis Philip Fatio, esq. of that place, aged 81 years....
Died at Philadelphia, on the 26th ult., Mr. John Glen Fleeson, Printer, aged 28 years, a native of South-Carolina.

Issue of August 17, 1810

Died, on the 3d inst. on board the schooner Ploughboy on her passage from Norfolk to Baltimore, Mr. William Wish, for a long time a respectable Merchant of this city.

Issue of August 18, 1810

Died at Beaufort, S. C., on the 11th inst., Mrs. Phoebe Sarah Campbell, wife of Dr. Archibald Campbell: the last of the children of the elder branch of Mr. John Barnwell.
Died at New-York, on the 8th inst., the Hon. John Broome, Lt.-Gov. of that State, aged 72 years.

Issue of August 20, 1810

Died on board the U. S. brig Vixen, on her passage from Havana to New-Orleans, Capt. Trippe, commander of said brig.

Issue of August 21, 1810

Died in Pendleton district, Mrs. Mary Dart, aged 24 years, consort of Dr. Thomas L. Dart. (eulogy)

Issue of August 23, 1810

Married on Wednesday evening the 8th inst., by the Rev. Samuel Marsh, John S. Glasgock, Esq. son of Gen Thomas Glascock, late of Augusta, Ga., to Miss Eliza Simkins, second daughter of John Simkins, esq. of Edgefield, South-Carolina.
Died at Baltimore, on the 13th inst., Thorowgood Smith, Esq., in the 67th year of his age, President of the Baltimore Insurance Co., and late Mayor of Baltimore.

Issue of August 24, 1810

Died at Novogooe, Russia, Miss Praskowoa Lupolow....

Issue of August 25, 1810

Married in New-Orleans, Mr. Alexander Philip Socrates Aemilius Caesar Hannibal Marcellus George Washington Treadwell, to Miss Carolina Sophia Margaretta Maria Julienne Wortley Montague Joan of Arc Williams.
Died at Dorchester, on the 26th ult., Mr. John David Thomas, aged 67 years, leaving no relatives...but an only son.

Issue of August 28, 1810

Married on the 18th inst., by the Rev. Dr. Hollinshead, Mr. George Smith, to Miss Margaret Morgan, both of this city.

Issue of August 29, 1810

Married on Sunday the 8th July by the Rev. Mr. Helfenstem, Capt. Joseph Weaver, to Miss Kitty Spinner, daughter of David Spinner, Esq. all of Milford township, Bucks Co., Pa.

Married in Norfolk, England, Mr. Joseph Handford, aged 85, to Miss Narcissa P. Weston, aged 18!!

Issue of August 30, 1810

Died at Nassau, N. P., on the 11th inst., R. Davis, Esq. from South-Carolina, the North side of Santee.

Issue of August 31, 1810

Departed this life on Wednesday the 22d inst., Mr. Francis Ley, a native of Aberdeenshire, Scotland, in the 69th year of his age, for many years a respectable merchant of this city.

Issue of September 3, 1810

Departed this life on Monday the 27th ult., Mr. Peter Zylstra, a native of Holland in the 51st year of his age, for 26 years, a merchant of this city...left a widow and son....

Issue of September 4, 1810

Died on Sunday the 26th ult., at James-Island, John Todd, Esq., in the 52d year of his age...left widow and three orphan children.

Issue of September 5, 1810

Died at Addersey Lodge, near Stoke Goldington, Bucks, England, on Saturday the 9th of June, at an advanced age, Col. Philip Skene, formerly of Skenesborough...left a son and two daughters (long account)

Issue of September 6, 1810

Married last evening, by the Rev. Dr. Furman, Capt. Antoine D'Bonnefons, to Miss Anna Snowden, both of this place.

Issue of September 14, 1810

Married on Wednesday evening by the Rev. Mr. Saures, Mr. Jacob Hertz, to Miss Rebecca Mordecai, eldest daughter of Mr. Joseph Mordecai, of this city.

Departed this life on Friday the 7th inst., Mrs. Catharine Finch, consort of Mr. Jos. Finch, of this city...left husband and infant daughter....

Died near Statesburg, on the 24th ult., Mrs. Jemima Lee, relict of the late Mr. Anthony Lee, a respectable and pious lady.

in the same neighborhood, on the 5th inst., Master Wood Haynesworth, youngest son of Mr. Henry Haynesworth.

Died in Washington City, on the 4th inst., Col. John Whiting, of the 5th reg. U. S. infantry.

Issue of September 21, 1810

Married on Tuesday evening last, by the Rev. Mr. Simons, William Crafts, Esq. to Mrs. Harriet B. Poaug, both of this city.

Issue of September 24, 1810

Married at Edinburg, on the 1st day of May, by the Rev. Mr. J. Robertson, John Bentley, Esq. of Mousebank, to Miss Jane Abernethie.

Departed this life on Friday the 21st, at the plantation of Dr. Montague Jackson, St. James, Goose-Creek, Sarah Whitlock, alias Sarah Jackson, aged 35 years 8 months and 21 days, consort of Dr. Jackson.

Issue of September 27, 1810

Departed this life, Mr. Thomas Potter, aged 23 years, a native of Manchester, in England.

Died at Scituate, Mass., on the 12th inst., the Hon. William Cushing, Esq. aged 77 years, one of the Associate Justices of the Supreme Court of the U. S.

Issue of September 28, 1810

Married on Thursday evening last, by the Rev. Dr. Gallagher, Mr. Lewis Maheo to Mrs. Lucia Maria Anna Daudier, Widow Cheramy, both inhabitants of St. Domingo.

Issue of September 29, 1810

Died at New-York, on the 19th inst., James Cheetham, Esq. Editor of the "American Citizen."

Issue of October 3, 1810

Died on Monday the 25th ult., in the 58th year of her age, Mrs. Mary Moses, wife of Mr. Solomon Moses, of this city...a native of Holland, for 16 years resident of Charleston...left a large family.

Died on the day after, Levi Wolf, an infant son of Mr. Isaac Wolf, of this city, and grandson to the above deceased.

Issue of October 4, 1810

Departed this life on Tuesday the 2d inst., Mrs. Tomlins, aged 19 years, wife of Mr. James Tomlins....left husband, two children, and near relatives....

Issue of October 5, 1810

Died on the 19th ult., at the house of Mrs. Benoist, in Natchez, Mississippi Territory, in the 12th year of his age, Caesar Rodney, eldest son of Caesar A. Rodney, esq. attorney-general of the U. S.

Issue of October 15, 1810

Died on the 9th inst., Captain Benjamin Risher, of the 34th Regiment in the bloom of life...one of the candidates at the late election in St. Bartholomew's Parish, for the House of Representatives....

Issue of October 18, 1810

Died, at Georgetown, (Col.) William Augustine Washington, in the 53d year of his age.

Issue of October 19, 1810

Died on Monday the 8th inst., Mr. Luke Bourreux, in the 27th year of his age, leaving a wife and an infant child....

Issue of October 23, 1810

Horrid Murder! Mr. Abner Tapp, a farmer of Orange County, was murdered on Saturday night the 29th ult., while attending to his still...left wife and nine children.
Raleigh Star, October 18.

Issue of October 25, 1810

Died on the 15th inst., Mrs. Mary Axson, aged 66 years.

Issue of October 27, 1810

Married at New-York, on Monday evening, the 15th inst., Mr. Michael Magrath, of the house of Megrath & Jones, of this city, to Miss Emily Jones, daughter of Perez Jones, merchant, of New-York.

Issue of October 29, 1810

Died, aged 55, at Belfon, the seat of Major Waddell, in Bladen County, on the 15th inst., the Hon. Alfred Moore, Esq. late an Associate Justice in the Supreme Court of the U. S. (long account) Wilmington Gazette, October 23
Died on the 14th inst., at the residence of her son, near Wilmington, Mrs. Eliza Clitherall, of this place, in the 66th year of her age....
Yesterday morning, the body of Barnard Jacobs (formerly of Charleston) was found on the eastern part of Fort Wayne....
Savannah Republican, Oct. 25

Issue of October 30, 1810

Married, last evening, by the Rev. Dr. Furman, Capt. George N. Reynolds, to Miss Martha Sims, eldest daughter of Capt. Wm. Sims.

Issue of November 8, 1810
Norfolk, October 31
Died on Sunday last, in Hampton, Commodore Samuel Barron, of the U. S. Navy...(long account)

Issue of November 10, 1810

Died on Saturday morning, the 3d inst., Mr. Seth Yates, Shipwright, aged 59 years, a native of the Island of Bermuda, but a resident of this his adopted country for 40 years....

Issue of November 12, 1810

Married on Thursday evening last, by the Rev. Dr. Bucham, Doctor Isaac Mazyck Wilson, to Miss Ann Mazyck.

Issue of November 13, 1810

Died on the 8th inst., Thomas T. Fell, aged 1 year and 11 months and 28 days, only son of Thomas and Mary Fell....

Issue of November 14, 1810

Married on Sunday evening last, by the Rev. Dr. Hollinshed, Isaac L. Holmes (?) Esq. of John's Island, to Mrs. Harriet ___, of this city.
Died on the 3d inst., Mr. Jacob Motte, son of the brave Major Charles Motte, who in 1779 was killed....

Issue of November 16, 1810

Died on the 29th ult., at Laurens Court-House, where he was prosecuting (sic) the study of law, George Davis...received the honors of the S. Carolina College....

Issue of November 21, 1810

Departed this life on Sunday the 11th inst., in the 24th year of her age, Mrs. Mary Anderson, wife of capt. W. C. Anderson.
Departed this life on Sunday the 18th inst., Mr. Bigoe Darrel Henzy, of Beaufort, aged 22 years and 7 months...an affectionate nephew....

Issue of November 23, 1810

Married last evening, by the Rev. Mr. Simons, Isaac Ball, Esq. of St. John's Parish, to Miss Elizabeth C. Poyas, of this city.
Married on Wednesday evening last, by the Rev. Mr. Kennedy, Mr. Robert Will, to Miss Margaret Wesner, both of this city.
Died, at Beaufort, on the 11th inst., Mr. William Eddington, son of Capt. Edward Eddington, of Newport, R. I. in the 25th year of his age....

Issue of November 26, 1810

Married on Saturday evening the 24th inst., by the Rev. Dr. Buchan, Mr. Justus Angel, of this city, to Miss Martha Waight, daughter of the late Isaac Waight, esq. of St. Helena Island.
Married last evening, by the Rev. Mr. Flinn, Mr. Henry C. Gefkin, Jun. to Miss Eliza Calwell, both of this city.

Issue of November 27, 1810

Died at Georgetown, on Thursday last, Mr. Jotham Williams, a native of Newark, N. J., and a resident of Charleston.

Issue of November 30, 1810

Married on Wednesday morning, by the Rev. Dr. Keith, John Bryan, Esq. of St. Thomas's Parish, to Miss Eliza C. Legare, of John's Island.

Issue of December 1, 1810

Died on the 24th ult., James Ladson, Jun. Esq. of St. Bartholomew's Parish, in the 37th year of his age.
Died on Wednesday last, Capt. John Manly, in the 43d year of his age....

Issue of December 3, 1810

Died at St. Helena, on the 25th ult., Mr. Benjamin F. Pritchard, late of this city.

Issue of December 4, 1810

Married on Tuesday evening last, by the Rev. Mr. Simons, Edward Simons, Esq. to Miss Mary Read Simons, daughter of the late Thomas Simons, esq.

Married on Saturday evening last, by the Rev. Dr. Hollinshead, Mr. Richard Stiff, to Miss Mary Mitchell, both of this city.

Married on Sunday evening last, by the Rev. Mr. C. Faber, Mr. Christian Adam Berz, to Miss Barbara Margaret Kahnle, eldest daughter of Mr. John Harman Kahnle, of this city.

Died on the 28th ult., Mr. Samuel Heron (of the house of Mortimer & Heron, merchant) in the 30th year of his age...left wife and infant child.

Issue of December 7, 1810

Married, on Wednesday evening last, by the Rev. Jacob Suares, Mr. Isaac Harby, of this city, to Miss Rachel Mordecai, of Savannah.

Issue of December 8, 1810

Died on the 4th inst., Alexander Chisolm, aged 72 years....

Issue of December 14, 1810

Married on Tuesday evening last, by the Rev. James Simons, Alexander Broughton, esq. to Miss Carolina Bullard Harris, daughter of Dr. Tucker Harris.

Issue of December 22, 1810

Died on the 8th inst., at Leesburg, Va., Edward Carter Stanard, Esq. late Editor and Proprietor of the "Spritis of '76."

Issue of December 28, 1810

Married on Tuesday evening last, by the Rev. Dr. Buchan, Mr. Charles Edmonston, to Miss Mary Pratt, daughter of Capt. John Pratt, all of this city.

Married last evening, by the Rev. Mr. Faber, Mr. John Hoffman, of this place, to Miss Jane Massey, of Philadelphia.

Issue of December 29, 1810

Married on Thursday evening last, by the Rev. Mr. Simons, Mr. Thomas Bolker, to Miss Hester Lloyd, both of this city.

Issue of January 10, 1811

Died at Spartanburgh, in October last, at her son's plantation, in the 42d year of her age, Mrs. Rebecca Laval, of Charleston, wife of Major Laval, of the U. S. army.

Issue of January 11, 1811

Married on Tuesday evening last, by the Rev. Dr. Dehon, the Hon. John C. Calhoun, to Miss Florida Calhoun, daughter of the late John Ewing Calhoun.

Issue of January 12, 1811

Died on the 5th inst., Mr. Michael Samuel De Bruhl, Watchmaker and Jeweller, of this city.

Issue of January 17, 1811

Married on Tuesday evening last, by the Rev. Dr. Buchan, Mr. William A. Caldwell, merchant, to Miss Dinah Williamson, both of this city.

Issue of January 18, 1811

Married, last evening, by the Rev. Dr. Furman, Mr. John Hudson, to Miss Ann Catherine Wish, both of this city.

Issue of January 19, 1811

Married on Thursday evening last, by the Rev. Dr. Keith, Francis Yonge Legare, Esq. of St. Paul's Parish, to Miss Martha Ward Motte, eldest daughter of Francis Motte, esq. of this city.

Issue of January 21, 1811

Departed this life, at his place of residence in York district, on the 5th ult.,Mr. David Gordon, in the 64th year of his age....
On the 29th of the same month, died, his son, Irvin Gordon, of this city, in his 37th year....
Died in Havana, on the 21st Dec. last, Mrs. Eliza Lincoln, in her 39th year, wife of Capt. Luther Lincoln.

Issue of January 23, 1811

Married last evening, by the Rev. Mr. Gadsden, John Wilson, Esq. to Miss Eliza Gibbes, eldest daughter of William Hasell Gibbes, esq. of this city.

Issue of January 24, 1811

Died at New-York, on the 10th inst., Capt. James Henery, formerly Commander of the Aurora East-Indianan, a native of Londonderry, Ireland....
Died at Boston, on the 11th inst, the Rev. Joseph Clay, aged 46, pastor of the First Baptist Church, in that town.

Issue of January 30, 1811

Died on Saturday evening last, in the Poor-House in this city, James Barry, a young man, a native of Albany, state of New York... lately a student in Columbia College, New-York.

Issue of January 31, 1811

Departed this life, yesterday morning, at St. James's Santee, William Read, Esq., late of New-York....

Issue of February 4, 1811

Married, last evening, by the Rev. Dr. Gallagher, Peter Fitzpatrick, to Miss Henoria Swedny, both of this city.
Departed this life, on Thursday evening last, Mr. James Evans. (lines)

240

Issue of February 5, 1811

Died at Jamesville, on the 30th ult., in the prime of life, J. P. Richardson, Esq...left widow and family....

Issue of February 11, 1811

Died on Thursday the 7th inst., in the 51st year of her age, Mrs. Susannah Stevens, wife of Jervis Henry Stevens, Esq....
Died on Sunday the 3d inst., Mrs. Jane M'Kenzie, in the 71st year of her age...a native of London....

Issue of February 12, 1811

Married on Tuesday evening last, by the Rev. Mr. Flinn, John Russell, Esq. to Miss Rachael Milligan, both of this city.

Issue of February 13, 1811

Died, on Sunday the 20th ult., Benjamin Boyd, Esq. in the 58th year of his age....

Issue of February 18, 1811

Married, last Thursday at Turkey-Hill, St. Paul's Parish, by the Rev. Dr. Mills, John Boyle, Esq. to Miss Sarah Wilson, eldest daughter of Jehu Wilson, Esq. deceased.

Issue of February 20, 1811

Died at Georgetown, on the 13th inst., Mrs. Elizabeth Trapier, aged 77 years.

Issue of February 21, 1811

Married at Washington City, on the 7th inst., by the Rev. A. T. M'Cormick, Lieut. R. D. Wainwright, of the Marin Corps, to Miss Juliana B. Scott, youngest daughter of Gustavus Scott, Esq. of that city.

Issue of February 25, 1811

Married on Saturday the 23d inst., by the Rev. Dr. Buchan, Mitchell King, Esq. to Miss Susanna Campbell, daughter of M'Millan Campbell, esq. all of this city.

Issue of February 27, 1811

Died this morning, Mr. Joseph Harper, of the Charleston Theatre, aged 52 years...a native of Norwich, Esq....
Died in St. Paul's Parish, on the 17th Feb., Henry Veitch, Esq., Planter....(lines)

Issue of February 28, 1811

Departed this life on the 5th Feb., in Chester District, S. C., and in the 93d year of her age, Mrs. Frances Timms, consort of Mr. Amos Timms, sen, whom with ten children she has left....

Issue of March 1, 1811

Married on Tuesday the 26th ult., by the Rev. James D. Simons, Mr. Simeon Theus, Jun. to Miss Harriet Poyas, both of this city.
Departed this life at Orangeburgh, on Saturday night, the 23d ult., Mrs. Ann Parsons, in the 65th year of her age....

Issue of March 5, 1811

Married, last evening, by the Rev. Dr. Hollinshead, the Rev. Andrew Flinn, to Mrs. Eliza B. Grimball.

Issue of March 13, 1811

Married, yesterday morning, the 12th inst.,by the Rev. Dr. Buchan, John Samuel Peake, Esq. to Miss Jane Ewing, eldest daughter of the late Adam Ewing, esq. of this city.
Died on the 5th inst., Mrs. Eliza Dodsworth, wife of Mr. Ralph Dodsworth, formerly merchant of this city.

Issue of March 15, 1811

Departed this life on Wednesday morning, in the 35th year of his age, Mr. David Johnston....Deputy Collector of this port....

Issue of March 18, 1811

Lately died at his plantation, in Barnwell district, S. C., Capt. Joseph Vince...in the rev. war.   **Augusta Chronicle**

Issue of March 19, 1811

Married on Tuesday evening, the 5th inst., at Washington, by the Rev. David Wiley, Gen. Thomas Moore, member of Congress from S.C., to Miss Mary Reagan, of George-Town (Potk.)
Married in January last, at Leith, Thomas Moffat, Esq., late of this city, to Miss Marion Moffat, daughter of the deceased Dr. James Moffat, Minister of the Gospel at Newlands, Peebleshire, Scotland.
Died on the 17th inst., Mr. George Welsh, a distinsuished revolutionary Soldier. (long account)

Issue of March 21, 1811

Married on the 19th inst., at the Hose-shoe, by the Rev. Mr. Fowler, Thomas Perkins Lockwood, Esq. of Prince Williams Parish, to Miss Mary Sophia Postell, youngest daughter of the late Col. Benjamin Postell, of St. Bartholomew's Parish.

Issue of March 22, 1811

Died, yesterday morning, in the 40th year of his age, Mr. John Paton, a native of Glasgow, and resident in this city for upwards of 20 years....

Issue of March 25, 1811

Departed this life on the 16th inst.,Mr. Samuel H. Pratt, a native of Massachusetts, and for a number of years past a respectable merchant of this city....
Died at Murfreesborough, N. C.,on Friday, the 15th inst., Mrs. Elizabeth Hichborn, wife of Mr. JohnHichborn, late a resident of this city.

Died on Sunday morning last, in his 49th year, Mr. D. Driscol, late Editor of this paper...left widow and acquaintances....
Augusta Chronicle

Issue of March 30, 1811

Died on Monday the 25th inst., Mr. Christian Booner, in the 47th year of his age, 45 of which he had resided in this city....

Issue of April 1, 1811

Married on Tuesday evening last, by the Rev. Dr. Furman, Mr. Archibald M'Quiston, to Mrs. Mary Murdock, both of this city.
Died on Saturday the 30th inst., Miss Elizabeth Johnston, in the 38th year of her age....left a mother.

Issue of April 3, 1811

Died on the 22d inst., at his plantation in St. Stephen's parish, in the 46th year of his age, the Hon. Robert Marion, late member of Congress from Charleston District.
Married at Dumfries, Scotland, the Lady Auchterfardle, to David Cushnie, Esq. of Overdumfifidling, in the County of Dumfries.

Issue of April 8, 1811

Married last evening, by the Rev. Benjamin M. Palmer, Mr. John C. Pillans, to Miss Eliza Palmer.

Issue of April 11, 1811

Died on the 6th inst., Daniel Hall, Esq. aged 61 years, a native of England, many years a respectable inhabitant of this city....

Issue of April 12, 1811

Married last evening by the Rev. Mr. Faber, Mr. Anthony A. Pelzer, to Miss Hannah Maria Clark, all of this city.
Died at Savannah, on the 11th ulst., Mr. Norman M'Lean, printer, aged 28 years, a native of Connecticut.

Issue of April 13, 1811

Married on Thursday evening last, by the Rev. Dr. Buchan, Mr. Robert Munro, to Miss Janet Perry, youngest daughter of the late Joseph Perry, Esq. of St. Paul's Parish.

Issue of April 19, 1811

Died at Edenton, N. C. on the 24th ult., Mr. John Gibbons, house-carpenter.

Issue of April 20, 1811

Died in London, on Friday the 25th of Jan., Mrs. Coke, wife of the Rev. Doctor Coke, Gen. superintendant of the Irish, West-India, Nova-Scotia, and Newfoundland Missions in the Methodist Connexion....

Issue of April 22, 1811

Died in England, Henry Hope, Esq., a native of Boston, born in 1736, died worth 27 million guilders.
Died on the 22d of Jan., Mary Sutton of Bladen County, N. C., aged 116 years...a native of Culpepper Co., Va., and had five sons and daughters, all now living, Her descendants amount to 1402....

Issue of May 6, 1811

Married on Sunday evening last, by the Rev. Thomas Mason, Mr. William M'Kewn, to Miss Mary Ann Shepherd, both of this city.

Issue of May 8, 1811

Died on the 19th ult., in the 91st year of her age, Mrs. Ann Fitzpatrick, a native of Ireland, and mother of the late Mr. John Fitzpatrick, of this city....resided in this city 20 years.
Died on Sunday the 28th ult at his house in Church-street, in this city, Major O'Brian Smith, aged 55....

Issue of May 11, 1811

Died, on the 27th ult., at his late residence in Church-street, Mr. Robert D. Eckert, Grocer, in the 33d year of his age, a native of New York...left a widow....

Issue of May 15, 1811

Died on Sunday evening last, Mr. Daniel Hart, merchant, of this city....left widow and seven orphans....

Issue of May 16, 1811

Died on the 12th inst., in the 38th year of his age, Mr. Stephen Sayre, a native of New-York, and for fifteen years a resident of this city.

Issue of May 17, 1811

Married on Wednesday evening last, by the Rev. Dr. Dehon, Richard Cunningham Esq. to Miss Ann Miller, daughter of James Miller, Sen. Esq.

Issue of May 20, 1811

Married on Monday evening the 18th inst., by the Rev. William Capers, the Rev. Thomas Mason, of the Methodist Episcopal Church, to Miss Elizabeth M. M'Farlane, of this city.
Married in Chester Co., Penn., on the 13th March, Mr. Jacob Wortman to Miss Catharine Moonshire....
Died at New-York, on the evening of the 7th inst., the aged Rev. Dr. Rogers, late Pastor of the First Presbyterian Church in that city.

Issue of May 21, 1811

On Wednesday the 15th inst., departed this life, in the 47th year of his age, Mr. Matthew William Cross....

Issue of May 22, 1811

Married in Raleigh, N. C. on the 9th inst., Chisley Daniel, Esq., of South-Carolina, attorney at Law, to Miss Eliza Pugh Weightman, of Alexandria, D. C.

Issue of May 24, 1811

Married on the 11th inst.,by the Rev. Dr. Harman, Mr. Josiah Phenney, pilot, to Miss Elizabeth Scott, both of this place.

Issue of May 27, 1811

Married on Wednesday last, at the plantation of Christopher Fuller, Esq., by the Rev. Mr. Mills, Mr. Joshua Collins, of Philadelphia, to Miss Elizabeth Letitia Field, of England.
Died on the 11th inst., Mrs. A. Elizabeth Ross, aged 50 years, left a sister and five daughters....

Issue of May 28, 1811

Died on the 22d inst., Mr. Lewis Mareo...left a wife and son. came from St. Domingo....

Issue of May 30, 1811

Married in St. Paul's Parish, on Tuesday the 21st inst., by the Rev. Mr. Gadsden, Mr. Henry Smith Poyas, of this city to Miss Elizabeth Ann Scott, of St. Paul's.
Married on Thursday evening the 23d inst., by the Rev. Mr. Mallard, Samuel Felder, esq. to Miss Elizabeth Stroman, both of Orangeburgh District.

Issue of May 31, 1811

Died, at his mother's house in this city, in the 41st year of his age, Mr. Jacob Ehney....
Died in the afternoon of the 29th inst., Dr. Robert Pringle, much lamented by his relatives and friends.
Died in his bed on the morning of the 30th inst., at the house of Mr. Barksdale, Dr. Alexander Edwards, of Christ Church Parish, in the 23d year of his age....(lines)

Issue of June 3, 1811

Married last evening, by the Rev. Dr. Buchan, Capt. Thomas Windsor, to Mrs. Elizabeth Mann, both of this city.

Issue of June 7, 1811

Married last evening, by the Rev. Mr. Simons, Mr. Robert Aldrich, to Miss Ann Hawkins Lebby, both of this city.

Issue of June 11, 1811

Married on Sunday evening last, at St. Philip's Church, by the Rev. James D. Simons, Lionel H. Kennedy, Esq. to Miss Mary-Ann Jane Stevens, daughter of Jervis Henry Stevens, esq.
Married last evening, by the Rev. Dr. Furman, Lt. William Peters, of the U. S. Navy, to Miss Rebecca P. Swaine, youngest daughter of Capt. Luke Swaine, deceased.

Issue of June 12, 1811

Died on the 10th inst., in this city, the Hon. Joshua G. Wright, of Wilmington, N. C., one of the Judges of the Superior Courts of this state...in the 43d year of his age....body will be removed to Wilmington, for interment.

Died on the 22d ult., at the house of her son, the Hon. David R. Williams, Esq., in the 71st year of her age, Mrs. Anne Brown, a native of England, but for more than 60 years in this state....

Issue of June 17, 1811

Married on Thursday the 13th inst., at Camden, Mr. Lewis Ciples, to Miss Sarah Adamson, daughter of John Adamson, esq.

Issue of June 18, 1811

Died on the 10th inst., Mrs. Martha Laurens Ramsay, consort of Dr. David Ramsay....daughter of the late Hon. Henry Laurens, and sister to Col. John Laurens (long account)

Died on the 8th inst., the Rev. Samuel Miles, Minister of the Methodist Church, at Camden....

Issue of June 19, 1811

Died on Monday evening, in the 70th year of her age, Mrs. Susanna Dill, widow of the late Mr. Joseph Dill sen. of this city.

Issue of June 20, 1811

On Friday morning the 7th inst., a most horrid act of Suicide was commited in Edgefield district, by Joseph Hightower, Esq., one of the Representatives in the Legislature from that district....
       Columbia State Gazette

Issue of June 21, 1811

Married last evening, by the Rev. Emanuel Nunes Carvalho, Mr. Solomon Hyams, to Mrs. Catharine Jacobs, both of this city.

Died at his residence, in Darlington district, on the 6th inst., Lt. Col. John Smith, of the 3d Regt. U. S. Infantry, and Lt. Col. Cor andant of S. C.

Died at Brimfield, Mass., on Saturday evening, the 1st inst., Gen. William Eaton....

Issue of June 24, 1811

Married on Tuesday evening the 18th inst., by the Rev. Dr. Hollinshead, Samuel Yates, Jun. Esq., to Miss Jane Eliza Righton, daughter of Joseph Righton, Esq.

Issue of July 1, 1811

Died on the 18th ult., on his passage from this port to Philadelphia, Major C. M. F. Bert....

Died at Baltimore, in the night of the 17th ult.,Hon. Samuel Chase, a Judge of the Circuit Court of the U. S.

Issue of July 5, 1811

Died on the 26th ult., Mrs. Mary Ann Caldwell, aged 38 years and 9 months.

Issue of July 12, 1811

Married last evening, by the Rev. Dr. Hollinshead, Capt. Robert A. Darby, to Miss Maria S. Taylor, all of this city.

Issue of July 13, 1811

Died on the 10th inst., at Mr. Grooms's plantation, Goosecreek, Mr. Alexander Middleton, in the 20th year of his age, a native of Yorkshire, in England.

Issue of July 15, 1811

Died on Friday last, at noon, Miss Ann Judith Miller, aged 23 years and 6 months, eldest daughter of Major John David Miller.

Issue of July 17, 1811

Died on the 30th of last month, at the Havana, James Miller, Esq., for many years a respectable Merchant of this city....

Issue of July 18, 1811

Died on Tuesday the 9th inst., Capt. William Collins, in the 33d year of his age...left wife and one child.
Departed this life on the 7th inst., Mr. Joseph Gladding, aged 27 years, a native of Rhode-Island. He has left a wife and three children to lament his loss.

Issue of July 19, 1811

Died, on the 11th inst., Miss Margaret Smith, daughter of Morton Smith, deceaed, aged 24 years.

Issue of July 20, 1811

Died on Sunday evening, the 14th inst., Louis Claude Henry De Montmain, ancient Knight of St. Louis, aged about 70 years. He was born in Tennerre, Dept. of Yonne, and was a planter of St. Domingo, but has resided 15 years in this city.
Departed this life on Friday the 29th ult., at Salem, Mr. Haven Pool, one of the editors and proprietors of the Essex Register, aged 29.

Issue of July 22, 1811

Married at Elizabeth-Town, New-Jersey, on Monday the 8th July, by the Rev. Mr. Rudd, John Harleton Read, Esq. of this city, to Miss Mary W. Withers, of Georgetown, S. C.
Died on the 11th inst., Mrs. Janet Munro, consort of Mr. Robert Munro, aged 18 years and 4 months...left a husband....

Issue of July 25, 1811

Died on the 17th inst., in St. Matthew's Parish, Santee, Henry Haynesworth Monk, son of John Monk, Esq. aged 4 years.
Died on the 16th inst., in Christ Church, Horatio Lincoln, only child of Horatio and Elizabeth Lincoln, aged 1 year and 6 months.
Died at Elizabethtown, New-Jersey, on the 20th ult., Miss Keturah Cox, a native of this city.

Issue of July 30, 1811

Died, on Monday the 22d inst., Mrs. Sarah Hatfield, aged 76 years.
Died, at Richmond, England, on the 27th May, Richard Penn, Esq., in the 76th year of his age, grandson of William Penn....

Issue of July 31, 1811

Married on the 6th of June, in St. Luke's Parish, by the Rev. Mr. Sweat, Dr. Francis Y. Porcher, to Miss Sarah Julia Pelot, eldest daughter of Major Charles Pelot, deceased.
Married on the 23d inst., in St. Luk's Parish, by the Rev. Mr. Sweat, Col. James Postell, to Mrs. Rachel Kenney.
Died on Monday last the 29th inst., Miss Margaret Reid, aged 30 years, she was a native of the State of New-Jersey, but has been a resident of Charleston 10 or 11 years.

Issue of August 2, 1811

Departed this life on Monday the 29th ult., aged 72 years, the wife of George Macauly, Esq., Mrs. Lydia Macaulay, a native of England....

Issue of August 6, 1811

Died in St. Augustine, East-Florida, on the 2d of July, Francis Philip Fatio, Esq. an old and respectable inhabitant of that Province.

Issue of August 7, 1811

Died at Beaufort, S. C. on the 31st of July, Middleton Fuller, second son of Mr. Thomas Fuller, aged 19 years and 11 months....
Died at New York, on the 20th ult., Mrs. Sarah Cave, consort of Mr. Thomas Cave, and a native of this place.

Issue of August 14, 1811

On the morning of Monday the 29th of July, 1811, in the 74th year of his age, died Richard Bache, of Settle, in the County of Bucks, Pa. (long account)

Issue of August 15, 1811

Departed this life on the 8th inst., Alexander Edwards, Esq., late Recorded of the city, in the 44th year of his age....left widow and children.

Issue of August 20, 1811

Died on the 4th inst., Mrs. Ann Middleton, widow of the late Thomas Middleton esq. and eldest daughter of the late Peter Manigault, esq....

Issue of August 23, 1811

Departed this life on the 17th inst., in the 28th year of his age, Mr. George Smith, a native of London...left wife and one child.

Issue of August 26, 1811

Married on the 25th of July, by the Rev. Mr. Sweat, Thomas H. Dixon, Esq. to Miss Mary Miller, both of Prince William's Parish, Beaufort District.
Died near Kings-tree, in this State on the 16th inst., Mrs. Martha Scott, consort of Thomas Scott, Esq.
Died in Indian-town, in this state, on the 18th inst., Mrs. Jane James, mother of the Hon. Judge James.
Died at Georgetown, S. C. on the 22d inst., Mr. William B. Murray, in the 26th year of his age.
Died at Columbia, on the 7th of Oct. last, Mr. Peter Le Poole, in the 82d year of his age...native of City of Leyden, in Holland....

Issue of August 27, 1811

Departed this life on the 24th inst., in the 33d year of his age, Mr. William Hopwood, a native of Virginia....

Issue of August 30, 1811

Died, at Waccamaw, on the 19th inst., Master Benjamin Tucker, aged 4 years and 10 months, and on the 23d inst., Master George Heriot Tucker, aged 3 years, both sons of Benjamin Tucker, Esq.

Issue of September 2, 1811

Died on the 29th ult., at Woodville, S. C. in the 33d year of his age, William Anslie Moultrie, Esq.
Departed this life on the 2d Aug., Mrs. Maria Lucy Ley, relict of Mr. Francis Ley, in the 61st year of her age....left two surviving sons.
Died on the 2d ult. at Montgomery, Orange Co., N. Y., in the 71st year of his age, Col. John Nicholson, a Rev. Officer....
Died at Kingston, Jam., on the 1st ult., Thomas Dancer, Esq., M. D....

Issue of September 3, 1811

Murder of Mr. William Chambers, who kept an extensive Grocery Store....

Issue of September 4, 1811

Died on the 24th ult., at Mount Pleasant, Mrs. Hannah Hamlin, aged 60, long a member of the Congregational Church....

Issue of September 6, 1811

Departed this life on the 4th inst., in the 64th year of his age, Mr. Charles Nicholas Hubert, a native of Holland, left three children....
Departed this life at St. Mary's, Ga., on the 20th of July last, Charles Baldwin, Esq. in the 36 year of his age...left a widow....
Died at Philadelphia, on the morning of the 27th ult.,Joseph Clay, Esq. formerly Member of Congress for the first district of Pa....

Issue of September 9, 1811

Died at Philadelphia, on the 26th ult., in the 70th year of his age, Thomas Fitzsimons, Esq....

Issue of September 10, 1811

Married at Chillicothe, on the 8th of July, John Shook, recently from Germany, to Miss Ann Wilson, late from Ireland, both of Ohio.

Issue of September 13, 1811

death of Robert Quash...

Issue of September 16, 1811

Married last evening, by the Rev. Dr. Furman, Mr. Charles George Shaffer, to Miss Elizabeth Slowman, both of this city.
Departed this life on the evening of the 2d inst., Mr. William Chambers, in the 38th year of his age...a native of Ireland.

Issue of September 20, 1811

Died on the 17th inst., Mrs. Mary Augustine Vanderherchen, in the 57th year of her age...left husband and five children....
Departed this life at Hampstead, on Thursday evening, the 12th inst., Miss Susannah Dickson Ham, fourth daughter of Mr. Thomas Ham, of said place.

Issue of September 21, 1811

Married on Thursday evening last, by the Rev. Dr. Furman, Mr. George Washington Rivers, to Miss Eliza Tucker, both of this city.
Married lately at Montreal, by the Rev. Dr. Mountain, Mr. G. Greatwood, to Miss Mary Oakes....
Died at Cadiz, on the 5th of July last, Mr. Charles Augustine Washington, of Virginia, aged 20 years.
Died at the Havana, on the 10th of August, in the 23d year of his age, Mr. S. J. Gardette, Dentist, son of James Gardette, Dentist of Philadelphia....

Issue of September 23, 1811

Died, at Boston, while on a visit for the benefit of her health, Mrs. Dinah Adams, late of Camden, in this State, widow of the late Rev. Thomas Adams, aged 33.

Issue of September 25, 1811

Died on the 18th inst., at Georgetown, Mr. James Rembert, in the 24th year of his age.

Issue of September 26, 1811

Died in the Village of Washington, on Wed. evening, the 25th inst., Mr. Henry Caloff, in the 51st year of his age....funeral at the house of Mrs. George, his mother.
Died at Philadelphia, on Monday the 9th inst., Rev. Jacob Cohen, aged 70 years, reader for the Hebrew Congregation of that city.

Issue of September 27, 1811

Married on Saturday last, by the Rev. Dr. Furman, Mr. Thomas Wright, Merchant, to Mrs. Eliza M'Cormick, both of this place

Issue of September 28, 1811

Married on Tuesday evening last, by the Rev. Mr. Gervais, Mr. Philip Patrick to Miss Sarah Branford Cambridge, daughter of the late Mr. Tobias Cambridge, both of this city.

Issue of September 30, 1811

Died in this city on the 26th inst., in the 37th year of her age, Mrs. Mary Long, wife of Mr. John Long....
Departed this life on Sunday morning last, Master Thomas B. Bennett, in the 9th year of his age, eldest son of Thomas Bennett, jun. esq. of this city (lines).
Died at Georgetown, on Tuesday morning last, Mrs. Susannah M'Daniel, aged 63 years, consort of Mr. Daniel M'Daniel.
Died, at Georgetown, on Friday morning, last, Mr. Francis Elliott, watchmaker, a native of Ireland. He has left a disconsolate widow and an infant son....
Died at Morristown, Penn., Miss Lavinia Roulstone, aged 20, killed by lightning....
Died at Staffordshire, England, about 20th July last, Mrs. Anne Moore....

Issue of October 1, 1811

Died, at Orangeburgh District on the 9th ult., Miss Mildred A. C. Muncreef, daughter of Richard Muncreef, of Wadmelaw Island, esq. deceased, aged 14 years and 6 months....

Issue of October 2, 1811

Married last evening, by the Rev. Dr. Furman, Mr. Thomas Napier, to Miss Eliza Jane Hillman, both of this city.

Issue of October 5, 1811

Died on the 2d inst., in the 47th year of her age, Mrs. Elizabeth Smith, wife of George Smith, esq....

Issue of October 7, 1811

Married, at Burlington (Mass.) by the Rev. Mr. Marret, Mr. Thomas Jones Horsey, of this city, to Miss Floranthe Reed, of the former place.
death of John S. Cripps, Esq., who departed this life on Saturday morning last....
Died at Georgetown, S. C. on Saturday evening, the 28th ult., in the 27th year of his age, John Grant, Esq. attorney at law.
On Tuesday the 1st inst., Mrs. Catherine Blanch, aged 44 years.

Issue of October 8, 1811

Died yesterday in the 11th year of her age, Miss Eliza Cohen, daughter of Mr. Mord. Cohen....(lines)

Issue of October 10, 1811

Died on Sunday morning last, Miss Eliza Gibbes Boone, in the 25th year of her age....

Issue of October 11, 1811

Died on the 26th ult., Miss Lord, daughter of Andrew Lord, esq. deceased, in the 41st year of her age.
Died at Georgetown, on the 3d inst., in the 25th year of her age, Mrs. Lovey M. Greaves, consort of Mr. Thomas B. Greaves.
Died at Georgetown, on the 7th inst., Mr. Moses Sarzedar, aged 43 years.
Died at North-Inlet, near Georgetown, on the 3d inst., Miss Eleanor Taylor, daughter of John Taylor, sen. esq. aged 4 years and 7 months.

Issue of October 14, 1811

Died at his plantation near Congaree, on the 7th inst., in the 60th year of his age, James Mis-Campbell, Esq. Lt. Col. of the 22d Regt. of Militis of this state, and a Senator in the Legislature from St. Mathew's Parish...born in County of Down, in Ireland....

Issue of October 16, 1811

Departed this life on Monday the 14th inst.,Master Milton Flud, aged 5 years and 16 days, son of Daniel Flud, esq. of this city....
Departed this life, on the 6th inst., at the house of Dr. Jamieson, of Orangeburgh district, the Rev. Thomas Dickerson, one of the itinerant preachers belonging to the Methodist connexion....
Died at Columbia, on Tuesday the 8th inst., Capt. Benjamin Waring, in the 70th year of his age....(lines)
Died at Columbia, on the 6th inst., Mr. John Carew, a native of Ireland....

Issue of October 17, 1811

Departed this life at M'Cord's Ferry, on the 5th inst., Mr. Joseph Wingate....
Died on the 12th inst., in the 45th year of his age, Mr. Jacob Yoer, a native of this state....

Issue of October 18, 1811

Married on the 6th inst., in the City of New-York, by the Rev. Mr. Geissenhainer, Minister of the Lutheran Church, the Rev. Mr. Charles Faber, of Charleston, S. C. to Miss Maria Christina Faber, daughter of J. C. Faber, esq.

Issue of October 21, 1811

Departed this life on Friday the 18th inst., Miss Sarah Harriot Bollough, aged 18 years 8 months and 8 days...(lines)

Issue of October 23, 1811

Married last evening, by the Rev. Dr. Gallagher, Mr. Louis Boudo, to Miss Louise Simonette.
Married at Germantown, Pa., on the 20th ult., Mr. Peter

Fayssoux, youngest son of the late Dr. Peter Fayssoux, of this city, to Miss Rebecca A. Irvine, youngest daughter of the late Gen. Irvine, of Philadelphia.

Issue of October 26, 1811

Died on Sullivan's Island, on the 27th Sept., Mrs. Eliza Wheeler, in the 30th year of her age....

Died on Monday last, in the 33d year of his age, Mr. David Loathridge, a native of Ireland...left widow and sister....

Died at New-Orleans, on the 20th of August, Mr. E. A. Hutchinson, aged 28 years...a native of Lebanon, Conn...left a widow.

Issue of October 28, 1811

Died at Beaufort, on the 21st inst., Dr. John Smith, Principal of Beaufort College.

Issue of October 29, 1811

Married on the 11th inst., by the Rev. Mr. Phillips, Mr. James Calder, to Miss Mary-Ann Wallace, both of this city.

Died on the 20th inst., Mrs. Mary B. Desel, relict of Dr. Charles Desel, in the 48th year of her age....

Issue of October 30, 1811

Departed this life on Tuesday evening the 15th inst., Mrs. Elizabeth Legare, relict of Daniel Legare, jun. esq in the 79th year of her age...leaving three children, grandchildren....

Departed this life on the 17th inst., Miss Eleanor Davies, aged 26 years, a native of England....

Departed this life at Beaufort on the 21st inst., Mr. William Cormick, for many years a respectable inhabitant of this place.... left widow and two children.

Departed this life on the 11th inst., at his estate on Naushan Island, Pa., the Hon. James Bowdoin, formerly U. S. Ambassador to Spain.

Issue of October 31, 1811

Married on Tuesday evening, by the Rev. Mr. Flinn, Mr. William Aitchison, merchant, to Miss Mary Murray.

Departed this life on Saturday the 26th inst., Mr. Alexander Shirras, a native of Aberdeenshire, in Scotland, upwards of 30 years a respectable Merchant in this city....

Issue of November 1, 1811

Died at Georgetown, S. C. on Sunday morning last, Mr. Daniel M'Daniel, aged 76 years.

Died at Georgetown, S. C., on Monday last, Samuel Smith, Esq. aged 69 years, Ordinary for Georgetown district.

Issue of November 5, 1811

Died, on Tuesday last, in Prince William's Parish, the Rev. Robert M. Adams, Pastor of the Presbyterian Church in that place.

Issue of November 9, 1811

Died on the 29th ult., David M'Credie, a native of the shire of Galloway, in Scotland....

Issue of November 11, 1811

Died on Friday the 1st inst., at the house of Mr. Charles K. Lesesne, at Georgetown, S. C., Mrs. Jane Sheppard, of this city, aged 60 years, mother of the late Thomas Sheppard, esq. formerly one of the Editors of the "Times."
Died at Philadelphia, on the 29th ult., in the 41st year of his age, John Paul Thomson, Esq. of Belleville, in this State....

Issue of November 14, 1811

Died at East-Granby, on Friday night, the 1st inst., Capt. William Goodwyn, of Richland District.

Issue of November 16, 1811

Died on Tuesday the 12th inst., in the 30th year of his age, Mr. John Prioleau, of this city....

Issue of November 18, 1811

Died on the 16th inst., Miss Ann Saunders Legge, only daughter of Edward Legge, decd.
Married at Canton, China, in May last, Mr. James M'Comb, of the ship Triton, of New-York, to Miss Chraltangi Hoam, youngest daughter of Altangi Hoam....

Issue of November 20, 1811

Married this morning by the Rev. Mr. Munds, Mr. Swan J. Brown, to Miss Emiline A. J. Woodson, both of Virginia.
Married, in St. John's Church, at Providence (R. I.), on Sunday morning, the 3d inst., Mr. John B. Chase, merchant, of that place, to Mrs. Harriet F. Jones, daughter of Mr. Alexander Jones, formerly of this city.
Died, at the Village of Washington, on the 10th inst., Mr. James Davidson, aged 36 years, a nativeof Scotland....

Issue of November 21, 1811

Departed this life on the 6th inst., in the 48th year of his age, Mr. Edward M'Grath, a native of Ireland. He has left a wife and one child....

Issue of November 25, 1811

Died at his seat in Kershaw District on the morning of the 30th ult., Capt. Thomas Hopkins, in the 36th year of his age.

Issue of November 26, 1811

Departed this life on the 31st of Oct., at Fort-Johnson, N. C., in the 32d year of his age, Capt. Robert Roberts, of the U. S. Artillery, a native of Virginia...left widow with two children....
Departed this life, on the 17th inst., at Oakland, near Augusta, Ga., Mrs. Mary Hornby, aged 36 years, wife of Mr. Thomas Hornby, late of this city.

Issue of December 9, 1811

Married at Georgetown, S. C. on Wednesday evening last, by the Rev. Mr. Norton, Capt. John Addison, to Miss Frances Ann Dunnam, both of that place.

Died on Friday evening the 29th ult., John Elias Moore, Esq. in the 49th year of his age.

Died on Black River, on the 1st inst., Mrs. Elizabeth Henderson, in the 54th year of her age....

Died on the Light-House Island, on the 4th inst., occasioned by being thrown from a horse, Master Edward Calhoun, aged 10 years, eldest son of Mr. John Calhoun, keeper of the Light-House.

Issue of December 10, 1811

Died at New-York, on Sunday evening, the 24th ult., Mr. Charles Watts, in the 55th year of his age....

Issue of December 14, 1811

Married last evening, Manuel Somersett, Esq. Planter of the Island of St. Domingo, to Miss Henrietta Bacon Vibert, of Philadelphia.

Died at Baltimore, on the morning of the 3d of Dec., Mr. George Dobbin, one of the Proprietors of the "Baltimore American," aged about 35 years...left wife and three children.

Issue of December 16, 1811

Married, on Thursday last, in St. Philip's Church, by the Rev. Mr. Gadsden, Mr. Thomas Townsend, Jun. of Christ Church Parish, to Miss Mary Magdalene Grimball Miller, second daughter of Major John D. Miller.

Issue of December 19, 1811

Departed this life on the 19th ult., at his Plantation in Orangeburgh District, Mr. Henry Jones in the 65th year of his age, left wife and seven children....

Issue of December 21, 1811

Died on the 3d inst., Mr. Daniel Jaudon, of St. Thomas's parish, aged 21 years and 6 months...left widow, one child....

Departed this life on the 13th inst., at Mount Pleasant Village, Mrs. Mary Bonneau, consort of Capt. Bonneau....

Issue of December 26, 1811

Married on Tuesday evening last, by the Rev. Mr. Francis Ward, Mr. Simeon Luther, to Miss Mary E. Mood, both of this city.

Married last evening, by the Rev. Dr. Hollinshead, Mr. Samuel J. Wagner, to Mrs. Margaret Wood, both of this city.

Issue of December 28, 1811

Died at his plantation, in Amelia Township, Orangeburgh District, on Wed. the 4th inst., aged 65 years, Mr. Robert Crab, an old and respectable inhabitant of this city...native of Dundee in Scotland....

Departed this life in West-Florida, William Henry Mayer, of this city, a Midshipman in the Navy of the U. S.

Issue of December 20, 1811

Departed this life on the 12th inst., at his Farm on Charleston Neck, John Bowen, Esq. aged 43 years.
Departed this life on the 28th inst., Sarah Pearse, aged 56 years, 6 months and 24 days....

Issue of January 2, 1812

Married last evening, by the Rev. Dr. Furman, Mr. Samuel Berbant, to Miss Eliza Gordon.

Issue of January 6, 1812

Melancholy Accident. Mrs. Eliza Smith, wife of Capt. Smith, of the schooner Blake, of this port, who resided in Wall-street, Gadsden's Green..burned to death....
Married on Thursday evening last, by the Rev. Dr. O'Belan, Mr. Andrew Talvande, Merchant, to Miss Ann Marsan, both of this city.

Issue of January 8, 1812

Died at half past 4 o'clock, on the 4th of Jan. 1812, Mary Pinckney, wife of Major-General Charles Cotesworth Pinckney, aged 60 years.

Issue of January 11, 1812

Died at Belle Terre, near Statesburg, on the 3d inst., Mrs. Sarah Theus, aged 68 years and 8 months...left an only son....
Died at Boston, where he had lately arrived from France, Mr. J. J. Himely, for many years a resident of this city.

Issue of January 13, 1812

Died at Charlestown, Mass., on Sunday evening, the 29th ult., Commodore Samuel Nicholson, senior office in the navy of the U. S., aged 69 years.

Issue of January 14, 1812

Died yesterday morning, in this city, Mr. Moses Northrop, aged 34 years, of the house of Northrop, Wolcott & Abbe, merchants of Montreal, Canada.
Died in Christ Church Parish, on the 30th Dec. last, Mrs. Ann White, in the 54th year of his age.

Issue of January 16, 1812

Married at Beaufort, on the 9th inst., by the Rev. Mr. Campbell, John Habersham, Esq. of Savannah, to Miss Ann Middleton Barnwell, daughter of the late Gen. Barnwell, of S. C.
Died at Savannah, on Thursday the 9th inst., Major Edward White, aged 50 years, a patriot of the Revolution.

Issue of January 20, 1812

Died on the 7th inst., at Philadelphia, Joseph Dennie, Esq. Editor of the Port Folio, in the 45th year of his age.

Issue of January 21, 1812

Married on Thursday evening last, by the Rev. Dr. Dehon, William Lance Esq. to Miss Maria Fraser.
Died on Wednesday the 15th inst., Mr. David Lopez, in the 63d year of his age...
Died on Saturday evening last, Master William Pollock, aged 11 years and 10 months...left mother and three small sisters....

Issue of January 22, 1812

Died on the 16th inst., Mrs. Elizabeth Gains, wife of George W. Gains, sail-maker, in this city, aged 37 years, a native of New-York, leaving a husband and aged parents....

Issue of January 23, 1812

Married on the 15th inst, on Edisto Island, by the Rev. Mr. Warren, Dr. Edward Mitchell, late of Georgetown, to Miss Eliza G. Beynard, daughter of William Beynard, esq. of Edisto.
Died on Monday the 13th ult., Mr. Benjamin Langstaff, in the 39th year of his age, late Merchant of this city...left widow and seven small children.

Issue of January 24, 1812

Departed this life on Friday evening, the 10th inst., in St. Thomas's Parish, Daniel's Island, Marshall Glen, in the 29th year of his age....left mother, brother, and sisters....

Issue of January 25, 1812

Died at Columbia, on Friday the 10th inst., David Riddlespurger, Esq....
Died at Camden, on Monday the 13th inst., Dr. Isaac Alexander, aged about 65 years, an old and respectable inhabitant of that place.

Issue of January 27, 1812

Departed this life on Wed., 22d inst., in the 50th year of his age, Mr. James Cox, Partner of the House of Messrs Tunno & Cox of this city...
Departed this life on the 20th inst., in the 25th year of her age, Mrs. Elizabeth Ruberry, consort of Mr. John Ruberry....

Issue of January 28, 1812

death of Charles Dewar Simons, Esq. late of this city....
Departed this life on the 2d inst., Mr. John Reid, in the 53d year of his age, a native of Fifeshire, Scotland....left widow and six children.

Issue of January 31, 1812

Died at the plantation of Mr. James Brown, Christ Church Parish, in the 22d year of her age, Mrs. Eliza Brown, wife of William Brown, M. D. of Philadelphia....left husband and two children....

Issue of February 1, 1812

Departed this life on the 21st inst., in the 26th year of his age, Charles Dewar Simons, Esq. Professor of Chymistry (sic) and Natural Philosophy in the College of S. C....(long eulogy)
Departed this life on the 28th inst., Major Samuel Beekman, in the 62d year of his age

Issue of February 5, 1812

Died on the 27th ult., in Prince William's Parish, in the 94th year of his age, James Love, Esq...native of Tyrone in Ireland...

Issue of February 7, 1812

Departed this life on Tuesday morning last, at his Plantation, in the Parish of St. James, Santee, Thomas Satur Jerman, Esq., in the 38th year of his age.

Issue of February 10, 1812

Died at his plantation on the Santee, on the 21st ult., Major James Ladson, in the 58th year of his age...in the War of the Revolution....

Issue of February 14, 1812

Died at Conway Borough, in Horry District, on the 28th of Nov. last, Mrs. Juliana Conway, consort of Gen. Robert Conway.

Issue of February 15, 1812

Married on the 6th inst., by the Rev. Dr. Flinn, Mr. James Harrison, to Miss Mehetable Pilsbury, both of this city.
Married on Sunday evening, the 9th inst., by the Rev. Dr. Buchan, Mr. Robert Walker, to Miss Margaret Murdoor, both of this city.

Issue of February 16, 1812

Departed this life on Friday the 14th inst., Mrs. Catharine Postell...leaves two young children....

Issue of February 20, 1812

Died on his passage from Wilmington, N. C., Capt. Benjamin Cartwright, master of the sloop Charlotte....

Issue of February 22, 1812

on Tuesday morning, the 18th inst., died Thomas Bee, Esq., one of the oldest inhabitant of this city, and Judge of the Federal District, appointed by Washington in 1790. (long account)
Died on Saturday the 15th inst., aged 17 years and 5 months, Mrs. Juliana B. Wainwright, consort of Lieut. Wainwright....

Issue of February 24, 1812

Died on the 9th inst., Mrs. Eliza Jane Napier, consort of Mr. Thomas Napier, merchant of this city, aged 17 years and 7 months ....

Died at Philadelphia, on Sunday the 9th inst., in the 51st year of his age, Brig. Gen. Michael Bright....
death of Lieut. Lee Massey.... Norfolk paper, Feb. 6

Issue of February 28, 1812

Married last evening, by the Rev. Mr. Gervais, Mr. Tacitus G. Skrine, to Miss Christiana Brailsford, both of this city.

Issue of February 29, 1812

Married on Thursday evening last, by the Rev. Dr. Hollinshead, Mr. John Taylor, to Miss Eliza Ann Hill, both of this city.
Died at North Kingston, State of Rhode-Island, on the 29th of Jan. last, Mrs. Sarah Chisolm, relict of Alexander Chisolm, Esq. decd.

Issue of March 4, 1812

Departed this life on Friday evening, the 28th ult., Miss Mary Ann Banks, aged 2 years and a few days, only child of Mr. Thomas Banks, decd, and his surviving widow, Mrs. Margery Banks, both natives of the Kingdom of Ireland....

Issue of March 5, 1812

Married on Tuesday evening last, by the Rev. Dr. Keith, Mr. William Bell, to Miss Susannah Eliza Taylor, all of this city.

Issue of March 9, 1812

Died at Nassau, N. P., on the 2d ult., Mr. Robert Wilson, late Editor of the Royal Gazette and Bahama Advertiser.

Issue of March 19, 1812

Married, on Tuesday morning, the 10th inst., by the Rev. Mr. Mills, Daniel Ravenel, Esq. to Miss Caroline Cripps, fourth daughter of John S. Cripps, Esq. decd.

Issue of March 23, 1812

Died on Thursday the 27th ult., aged 86 years, Mrs. Mary Linguard, a native of this State....
Died in Newberry District on the 6th inst., Mr. Isaac Mitchell, in the 86th year of his age--an honest man.

Issue of March 28, 1812

Departed this life on the 7th inst., Mrs. Elizabeth Spidle, in the 76th year of her age....

Issue of April 1, 1812

Died on the 6th inst., in the City of Williamsburg, in the 63d year of his age, the Right Rev. James Madison, D. D.,first and only Bishop of the Episcopal Church of Virg....
Norfolk Ledger

Issue of April 3, 1812

Married on Wednesday last, by the Rev. Dr. Dehon, Lawrence M. Dawson, Esq. to Miss Jane Vanderhorst.

Issue of April 6, 1812

Departed this life on the 3d inst., Mr. Christian Belzer, aged 59 years, for many years a respectable inhabitant of this place.
Departed this life on Saturday the 28th of March, Miss Elizabeth Hauser, in the 14th year of her age...daughter of the late Mr. Elias and Elizabeth Hauser, deceased...(lines)

Issue of April 7, 1812

Departed this life on the 24th ult., in the 19th year of her age, Mrs. Elizabeth M. Mason, consort of Rev. Thomas Mason....(lines)
Died on the 1st inst., at Amelia-Township, Mr. Arthur A. de Bendeleben, aged 22 years and 6 months. (see below)

Issue of April 8, 1812

Died on the 17th ult., at his Plantation in Abbeville District, Mr. Donald Fraser, a native of Inverness, Scotland.
Died on the 1st inst., at Amelia-Township, Mr. Arthur A. de Bardeleben, aged 23 years and 6 months.
Married on Sunday evening the 28th ult., at the residence of the President of the U. S., at Washington, by the Rev. Mr. M'Cormick, Thomas Todd, Esq., on of the Supreme Judges of the U. S., to Mrs. Lucy Washington, sister of Mrs. Madison.

Issue of April 11, 1812

Departed this life on the 1st inst., Mr. John Horlbeck, Sen., a native of Leipsic in Saxony, and arrived in this city in 1764.
Died lately, at St. Mary's, Camden County, Ga., Mrs. Judith Best, wife of the Rev. Dr. Best, Minister of the Protestant Episcopal Church....　　　　　　　Savannah, April 9

Issue of April 13, 1812

Mr. Alexander M'Clure (late of the firm of Alexander & John M'Clure in this city) was drowned a few days past...from a letter 7 Feb.

Issue of April 14, 1812

Died at Augusta, on Tuesday evening, the 7th inst., Mr. Matthew Sully Jun., formerly of the Charleston Theatre, for a few weeks resident of this city.
Married on Saturday evening last, by the Rev. Dr. Buchan, Mr. John Magrath, merchant, to Miss Maria Gordon, both of this city.

Issue of April 15, 1812

Died, near Wilmington (Del.), on Monday the 30th ult., the Hon. Gunning Bedford, Judge of the District Court for the District of Delaware.

Issue of April 17, 1812

Married at Kensington, near Georgetown, on Saturday evening, the 11th inst., by the Rev. Dr. Halling, Keating L. Simons, Esq., of Charleston, to Miss Ann Kinloch, daughter of Francis Kinloch, Esq.

Issue of April 25, 1812

Died on Tuesday last, in the 21st year of his age, Mr. Joseph Elliott, third son of Thomas Elliott, esq.

Issue of April 27, 1812

Married on Thursday evening, the 16th inst., in St. Stephen's Parish, by the Rev. Mr. Rschudy, the Rev. Mr. Charles B. Snowden, to Miss Maria L. Drake.

Died at the City of Washington, on the morning of the 20th inst., General George Clinton, late Vice-President of the U. S.

Issue of April 28, 1812

Died on the 25th inst., in the 47th year of his age, Mr. Andrew Charles, a native of Pennsylvania, and for upwards of 20 years a respectable Merchant in this city. (lines)

Died at the Horse-Shoe, on the 23d inst., Mrs. Sarah Postell, aged 62 years. (eulogy)

Issue of April 30, 1812

Departed this life on the morning of the 24th inst., in the 42d year of his age, Dr. Moses Bradley....

Issue of May 2, 1812

Married, last evening, by the Rev. Dr. Buchan, John Heger, Esq. to Miss Ann Herron, all of this city.

Issue of May 4, 1812

Married on Thursday evening last, by the Rev. Mr. Emanuel Nuares Carvalho, Mr. Abraham Ottolengue, to Miss Sarah Jacobs, both natives of this city.

Issue of May 7, 1812

Married on the 1st inst., by the Right Rev. Dr. Dehon, Mr. Francis J. Lee, to Miss Ann Lee Beekman, daughter of Major Sam. Beekman, decd.

Issue of May 11, 1812

Departed this life on the 5th inst., Mrs. Elizabeth Roupell, one of the oldest inhabitants of this city, in the 86th year of her age....

Died on Friday the 3d ult., Isaac Holmes, Esq. aged 53 years and 11 months.

Issue of May 13, 1812

Departed this life on Thursday the 23d ult., Mr. David Kinmont, aged 50 years, a native of Aberdeen, Scotland, but upwards of 20 years a resident of this city....

Issue of May 16, 1812

Married on Tuesday evening the 12th inst., by the Rev. Dr. Hollinshead, Thomas Barksdale, Esq. to Miss Serena Maria Payne, daughter of William Payne, esq.

Issue of May 19, 1812

Married, a short time since, in the Woods, near Pittsborough, Chatham County, N. C., Mr. John Rickets, aged 18, to Mrs. Ann Aitman, aged 77. The moment after the knot was tied, the Bridegroom mounted his horse, rode off, and has not since been heard of, leaving the Bride to the lone enjoyment of the honey moon. (N. B. Mr. R. was a hired substitute in this business, for which he received sixty dollars and a pair of spurs.)

Issue of May 22, 1812

Married, on Wednesday last, by the Rev. Dr. Hollinshead, Mr. Theodore Powers, Merchant, of this city, to Miss Carolina E. F. Peronne, only daughter of Capt. Caesar Peronne, of this city.

Issue of May 27, 1812

Married last evening, by the Rev. Dr. Hollinshead, Mr. Grandison Guerry, to Miss Louisa Gefkin, both of this city.

Issue of May 28, 1812

Died in this city, on Sunday the 17th inst., in the 56th year of his age, Mr. William Stewart, a native of the County of Antrim, in Ireland, but for upwards of 20 years a resident in this city....

Issue of May 29, 1812

Married on Wednesday evening last, by the Rev. Dr. Hollinshead, Mr. Joseph Oliver, to Miss Esther Ann Ellis.

Issue of June 2, 1812

Married in Scriven County, Ga., on the 7th ult., by the Rev. Mr. Hand, Samuel R. Gillison, Esq. of Beaufort District, S. C., to Miss Elizabeth Ann Smith, daughter of Aaron Smith, esq.

Issue of June 4, 1812

Married at Portsmouth, N.H., by the Rev. Mr. Ballon, Mr. Thomas Batchelder, to Miss Martha Muchmore.
Died on Wednesday the 27th ult., in the 48th year of his age, Mr. John Burckmyer, a native of this place...interred in the burial ground of the German Lutheran Church....
Died at New-Brunswick, N. J., Mrs. Melmoth, a celebrated actress....
Died at Alexandria, on Wed. monring, the 20th ult., Capt. Henry Washington, in the 49th year of his age.
Died at New Haven, Conn., Mr. Thomas Green, Printer, aged 77, formerly Editor of the Connecticut Journal.

Issue of June 11, 1812

Died on the 28th ult., Emeline Jenkins, fifth daughter of Elias and Elizabeth Jenkins, aged 2 years 9 months and 23 days.

Issue of June 13, 1812

Departed this life on Sunday the 10th of May, in the 68th year of his age, Col. John De Berniere, late of His Britannic Majesty's 60th Regiment.

Issue of June 18, 1812

Married, on Monday evening last, by the Rev. Mr. Gadsden, James Hartley Hext, Esq. of St. Paul's Parish, Planter, to Miss Mary Brailsford, daughter of John Brailsford, Esq. of said Parish.

Issue of June 20, 1812

Died at the plantation of Capt. Francis Saltus, in Prince William's Parish, on the 10th inst., Mr. William Clarke, Shipwright, in the 83d year of his age, a native of the Island of Bermuda, and a resident of Georgia and this State, for 46 years past.

Died on the 6th inst., Mr. Henry Jones, Merchant, late of the House of Crockat & Jones, London...In this city resided about 15 years...aged 54. (long account)

Issue of June 22, 1812

Married on Saturday evening, the 20th inst.,by the Rev. Dr. Buchan, Mr. Alexander Kire, to Miss Eliza Denoon, both of this city.

Issue of June 23, 1812

Died on the 19th inst., Mr. Benjamin Russell, aged 68 years, a native of this State, and 50 years a resident in this city.

Issue of June 25, 1812

Died on Sullivan's Island, on the 20th inst., Mr. Lawrence Leduc, of the House of Leduc & Danjou, of this city, in the 65th year of his age, a native of St. Maloes, France, and a resident of the U. S. upwards of 50 years, 6 in this city.

Issue of June 27, 1812

Married at New-York, on the 11th inst., by the Rev. Dr. Rowen, Thomas C.Cooper, Esq. Tragedian, to Miss Mary Fairlie.

Departed this life on Thursday evening last, in the 19th year of her age, Miss Martha Doughty Gaillard, eldest daughter of Theodore Gaillard, jun. esq. (lines)

Issue of June 29, 1812

Died in England, the Right Hon. Spencer Perceval, Chancellor of the Exchequer, and Prime Minister of England....

Issue of July 1, 1812

Departed this life on the 11th ult., in the 73d year of her age, Mrs. Jane Mylne, a native of this State...(lines)

Issue of July 14, 1812

Death by Lightning! Messrs Roma and Midy were sitting in a room after dinner, when a sudden stroke of lightning drove in the north-east corner of the house, injured the chimney materially and laid the two gentlemen senseless on the floor. Mr. Roma Recovered his senses in a short time; but Mr. Midy, unfortunately did not survive the shock. Mr. Midy has left behind him a disconsolate widow, and a large number of friends....
Savannah Republican, June 11

Issue of July 15, 1812

Married on Sunday evening last, by the Rev. Dr. Flinn, Capt. Thomas Davis, of North-Carolina, to Miss Ann Oats, of this place.

Issue of July 18, 1812

Died on Thursday the 9th instant, in Richland District, Capt. Gale Hampton.
Died at Chatham (Eng.) on the 6th of May, Capt. Henry Whitby, of His Brittanic Majesty's ship Briton (formerly of the Leander 50 gun ship) aged 30 years.

Issue of July 20, 1812

Married at St. Mary's, on the 9th inst., Mr. Robert Ripley, Merchant, to Miss Mary Matilda Rudulph, both of that place.

Issue of July 23, 1812

Died on Friday last, in the 22d year of her age, Mrs. Ann Gibbon Larry, wife of Mr. Peter Larry, of this city. (eulogy)
Departed this life on the 29th ultimo, James Rembert, of Black River, an old resident and respectable inhabitant of that part of the country, in the 74th year of his age....
Departed this life at his late residence in Montego Bay (Jamaica) on the 20th May last, Clement Crooke Blake Stevens, Esq., formerly of Charleston; where his immediate relatives, a brother and sister, reside....

Issue of July 28, 1812

Married last Sunday evening, by the Rev. Dr. Best, Mr. Henry Drewes, to Mrs. M. Wilson.
Died on the 23d July aged 13 months and 23 days, Miss Eleanor Reilly, daughter of Mr. James Reilly, of this city....(lines)

Issue of July 30, 1812

Married last evening, by the Rev. Mr. Munds, Mr. John Michel, son of Ignace de Michel, inhabitant of St. Domingo, to the amiable Miss Bethia S. Price, daughter of Thomas W. Price, esq. of this place.

Issue of August 1, 1812

Married on Sunday evening, by the Rev. Dr. Flinn, Mr. William Symons, of this city, to Miss Eliza Jackson, of St. John's Parish.

Issue of August 3, 1812

Departed this life on the 2d inst., Frances Lavinia Curtis Billing, youngest daughter of Mrs. Elizabeth Billing, of this city, a most endearing child, aged 2 years, 4 months and 18 days.

Issue of August 4, 1812

Married on Sunday evening last, by the Rev. Mr. Mills, Mr. George Gladden, to the amiable Miss Susan Syfan, eldest daughter of John Syfan, both of this city.

Issue of August 14, 1812

Departed this life on the 11th inst., Mr. John M'Carthy, a native of Ireland, but upwards of 40 years a resident of this place, and during thirty years of that period, a constable....

Issue of August 17, 1812

Died on Thursday evening the 6th inst., at his summer retreat in Sumter District, William Grant, Esq., Attorney at Law, aged 38 years. He was a native of Massachusetts, and for the last 16 years of his life a respectable citizen of this place. (eulogy).   Georgetown Gazette.

Issue of August 18, 1812

FROM A BOMBAY PAPER. Died on Friday, November 15th, 1811, at Mr. Falcona's house, on Coloba, in the 29th year of his age, Lieutenant William Percy, of the Grenadier Battalion, eldest son of the Rev. Dr. Percy. (eulogy)

Issue of August 19, 1812

Departed this life on the 9th inst., in the 27th year of his age, at his residence in Liberty County (Georgia), David Galphin Holms, Esq....left a widow and two infant children. This premature dispensation of Divine Providence was brought on by exposure to the inclemency of the weather, whilst performing his duty in the detachment of Citizens who had volunteered their service for the protection of Sunbury, in that State....

Issue of August 21, 1812

Married, on Saturday evening the 15th inst., by the Rev. Mr. Munds, Lieut. E. R. Davis, of the U. S. Navy, to Miss Martha E. M. Mitchell, daughter of Col. John Mitchell, of this place.

Issue of August 24, 1812

Died, at the High Hills of Santee, on the 19th inst., Mrs. Amelia Adamson, consort of Mr. Wm. Adamson, of Camden.

Issue of August 25, 1812

Departed this life on the 18th inst., Mr. Oliver Cromwell, in the 27th year of his age.... He has left an aged mother, wife, and six young children....

Issue of August 26, 1812

Died at Mecklenburgh (North-Carolina) on the 7th inst., after a lingering and distressing confinement of near six weeks, Col. Charles Polk, of Statesburgh, South-Carolina. Col. Polk was a native and for many years a resident of North Carolina. He entered the army at the early age of 14, and served until the termination of the contest that ushered us into independence....
Raleigh Star.

Issue of August 31, 1812

Departed this life at the residence of Mr. Thomas Hornby, near Augusta, Georgia, in the 47th year of her age, Miss Hannah Hornby, late of this city.

Issue of September 1, 1812

Departed this life on Friday last, the 28th ult., Captain Christopher Gadsden, of the U. S. brig Vixen, in the 32d year of his age. (lines)

Issue of September 2, 1812

Married last evening, by the Rev. Mr. Munds, Chevalier Daymand De Villeman, a son of Marquis Antoine Guillaume Francois Jean Garquille De Daymard de Villeman Chevalier of the Orders of St. Louis and Malia, &c. &c., planter, of the Island of Marinco (West-Indies) of the City of St. Pierres, to Mrs. Eliza Billings, of this city.

Issue of September 7, 1812

Died in Christ Church Parish, on Wednesday night, the 2d inst., Mrs. Sarah Hinds, aged 43 years, consort of Thomas Hinds, esq. (lines)
Departed this life, Mrs. Catherine Henry, wife of Mr. Jacob Henry...left a husband and three children. (lines)
Died in this city, on the 3d inst., Mrs. Marie Francoise Merceron, widow Petit Bois, formerly an inhabitant of the Island of St. Domingo. (eulogy)
Died on Sunday, the 30th ult., at Pineville, St. Stephen's Parish, Master George Verree, in the 9th year of his age....
Died at Augusta, Georgia, on the 30th ult., General George Mathews, late General for the U. S. in the affairs relative to East-Florida.

Issue of September 11, 1812

Died in this city on the 9th inst., the Rev. Mr. Charles Faber, a native of Rosenfeld, in the German Kingdom of Wirtemberg, aged 30 years and 10 months....

Issue of September 15, 1812

Married, this morning, by the Rev. Mr. Gadsden, Mr. William P. Dove, to Miss Sarah P. Flint, daughter of Mr. Joseph Flint, all of this city.
Died, on Saturday last, in the 35th year of his age, Lieutenant Samuel Parks, of the 2d Battalion, Regiment of Artillery, of this city.

Departed this life, at Haddrell's Point (near Charleston), on the 12th inst., Mr. John Alexander Placide (second son of Mr. A. Placide, late of the Theatre, deceased) in the 18th year of his age....

Issue of September 16, 1812

Died, in Granby, on the 23d ult., in the 14th year of her age, Miss Elizabeth Coram Mortimer, only daughter of Wm. Mortimer, deceased. She has left a disconsolate mother to lament her irreparable loss.

Departed this life at his farm on Liberty Hill, Edgefield District, South-Carolina, on the morning of the 20th ult., in the 57th year of his age, Mr. Joseph Maria Lequinio Kerblay.... Mr. K. emigrated to the U. S. in search of that political freedom which he had the mortification of seeing denied in his native land... He arrived at Newport, Rhode-Island, in the year 1800, where he resided in the capacity of "French Consul." He has left an amiable wife, who is one of the most disconsolate of beings: She has probably no relative in the United States. He has left no children. (long account) **Augusta Chronicle**

Issue of September 17, 1812

Departed this life on Tuesday last, Mrs. Maria Ramsay, wife of Dr. John Ramsay....(eulogy)

Died, on Friday last, Benjamin Smith Carns, Esq. aged 27 years and one month.

Died at his plantation in Pendleton District, on the 25th ult., in the 37th year of his age, Dudley Hammond, Esq., Member of the State Legislature.

Issue of September 18, 1812

Married, last evening, by the Rev. Mr. Munds, Mr. Henry W. Byrne, to Miss Mary Smith, all of this city.

Departed this life on the 7th inst., Master Mathias Christopher, aged 15 years and 6 months. This youth was a native of New-York, and had resided in this city but four months....(lines)

Issue of September 19, 1812

Departed this life on the 16th inst., in the 39th year of his age, Mr. Martin Scott, a native of Bennington, in the State of Vermont...left a consort and 4 children...at Middlebury, near Canada.

Died on the 5th inst., at St. Mary's, State of Georgia, Thomas N. Best, Attorney at Law, son of the Rev. Dr. Best, of this city.

Died in D'Etroit, on Sunday the 16th ult., Dr. James Reynolds, surgeon's mate in Col. Cass's regiment of Ohio volunteers, and only brother to Major John Reynolds, of this county--aged 24 years.... **Zanesville (Ohio) paper, Sept. 3**

Issue of September 21, 1812

Married on Thursday evening last, by the Rev. Dr. Hollinshead, Mr. Joseph Cox, planter, of John's Island, to Miss Eliza Ann Weatherford, of this city.

Issue of September 22, 1812

Departed this life on the 15th inst., at Debordieu's-Island, contiguous to Georgetown, Mrs. Mary Boone, relict of Thos Boone, Esq. of Prince George, Winyaw. (eulogy)

Departed this life on the 9th inst., Mr. John Muncreef, in the 70th year of his age, an old and respectable inhabitant of this city.

Issue of September 28, 1812

Departed this life on Monday last, after three weeks illness, in the 53d year of his age, Mr. Thomas Townsend, Sen. of Christ Church Parish, much lamented by Friends and Relatives.

Issue of September 29, 1812

Departed this life on the 24th inst., in the 80th year of her age, Mrs. Mary Parry, widow of the late John Parry, Esq. of Gray's Inn, London, a native of South-Carolina, and many years a resident of Charleston.

Issue of October 1, 1812

Died on the 16th ult. at his father's house in Hampstead, Mr. Jacob Henrichsen, in the 18th year of his age....

Issue of October 2, 1812

Married, last evening, by the Rev. Dr. Keith, Mr. Hugh Smith, to Miss Eliza C. Martin, both of this city.

Issue of October 5, 1812

Died on Saturday morning the 3d inst., Mr. J. Legras, in the 54th year of his age. He has left a widow and 7 children.

Died at Sunbury, Georgia, on the 7th ult., Mr. Thomas G. Riggs, a native of Massachusetts, and late Captain of U. S. Barge No 2. He has left a wife and two children, and a large circle of acquaintances....

Issue of October 6, 1812

Departed this life on Sunday morning last, aged 12 years and 14 days, Margaret, the only child of Patrick and Eliza Murphy, of this city. (eulogy)

Died yesterday, Mr. John Will, aged 28 years, a native of New-York. Mr. Will lately returned from the service at Haddrell's Point, and fell a victim to the prevailing fever.

Issue of October 7, 1812

Married at Augusta, by John Antignac, esq. Mr. Thomas Burke, to Miss Cornelia Thomas, both of the Charleston Theatre.

Issue of October 12, 1812

Departed this life, on the 6th inst., at his summer residence at Woodville, in St. John's Parish, Berkeley, Doctor Thomas Winstanley Mazyck, M. D. only son of Daniel Mazyck, Esq. aged 25 years...left wife, three infant children, three sisters (long eulogy and account)

Died, in this city, on Wednesday morning last, Mr. Samuel Seabury Stilwell, aged 25 years, of the firm of Stillwell and Everett, of Providence (R. I.)....
Departed this life on the 4th inst., M. Ellis Sutcliff, in the 36th year of his age. (eulogy)

Issue of October 14, 1812

Died on Sunday the 11th inst., Miss Mary-Ann Alexander, youngest daughter of the late Mr. Alex. Alexander, of this city.

Issue of October 20, 1812

Died on Saturday night last, in the 35th year of his age, Mr. Samuel Cole, a native of Rhode-Island, but for many years a resident of this city.
Died on Sullivan's Island, on the 16th October, Mr. Samuel James, aged 45 years, 9 months and 11 days.

Issue of October 21, 1812

Died on Saturday last, Mr. Henry Geddes, Jun. aged 31 years and 7 months.
Died in this city on Saturday the 17th inst., Mr. Knox, late of the Charleston Theatre, aged 32 years. Mr. Knox was a native of England....(lines)

Issue of October 23, 1812

Married on Tuesday evening last, by the Rev. Mr. Gadsden, Mr. Wm. V. Howard, to Miss Hannah Elfe, both of this city.
Departed this life on the 5th inst., Mr. Samuel Smith, Jun. in the 36th year of his age; a native of Massachusetts, but for many years a resident of this city.
Died on Sunday Morning, the 18th inst., in the 38th year of his age, Mr. James M. Heath, a native of Rhode-Island, of the firm of Heath & Byrne, Sail Makers of this city.
Departed this life on the night of the 19th inst., in the 40th year of his age...Mr. Amos Pilsbury. He has left a widow and six small children.
Died at Georgetown, S. C. on Saturday the 17th inst., Capt. William E. Cheesborough, aged 27 years and 9 months. He has left an aged mother, a loving wife, two small children and a number of relatives and friends....

Issue of October 24, 1812

Married on Thursday evening last, by the Rev. Dr. Hollinshead, Mr. John J. Jeannerett to Miss Mary T. Tucker.

Issue of October 26, 1812

Married, on Thursday evening last, by the Rev. Mr. Simons, Mr. William Waller, to Miss Maria Thomson Maybury.
Died on the 10th inst., at his plantation near Orangeburgh, Brig. Gen. Jacob Rumph, in the 63d year of his age. (eulogy)

Issue of October 28, 1812

Married last evening, by the Rev. Dr. Furman, Robert Wilson Mazyck, Esq. to Miss Helen Wilson.
Died, at Statesburg (S. C.) on Tuesday evening the 20th inst., John C. Walter, Esq. in the 32d year of his age...He has

left a wife and child....

Issue of October 29, 1812

Married on Tuesday evening last, by the Rev. Dr. Hollinshead, Mr. James Roddey, Merchant, to Miss Mary Latham, daughter of Mr. Daniel Latham, of this city.

Issue of October 30, 1812

Married last evening, by the Rev. Dr. Buchan, Mr. Abraham Jones to Miss Jane Walker, both of this city.

Died on the 27th inst., Mr. William Miner, a native of New-London, in Connecticut, and for a few years, resident in this city...(lines)

Issue of October 31, 1812

Died at Haddrell's Point, on the 15th inst., Sergeant Tilman Goodrich... in the 22d year of his age. (eulogy) while performing his duty in the armies of his country.

Died at Savannah on the 23d inst., whither she had gone on a visit to some of her relations, Miss Catharine Dickinson, daughter of the late Capt. Jeremiah Dickinson, of this city.

Issue of November 2, 1812

Obit. of Mrs. Ann Mitchell who last Tuesday night took a final farewell....

Issue of November 4, 1812

Married at Providence, R. I. on the evening of the 19th ult., in St. John's Church, by the Rev. Mr. Crocker, George Warren Cross, Esq. of this City, to Miss Frances Maria Halsey, daughter of Thomas Lloyd Halsey, of Providence.

Died on Thursday evening the 22d ult., in the 5th year of her age, Eliza Harrison Porter, daughter of John Porter, of this city.

Issue of November 6, 1812

Died in Richmond, Vir. on the 28th ult., Skelton Jones, Esq. a young Virginian of the first grad of talents--some years since he was Editor of the Richmond "Examiner," and was subsequently engaged in completing the History of Virginia, commenced by Mr. Buck....

Issue of November 7, 1812

Died at Columbia, S. C. on the 24th ult., Lieutenant Henry Raushner, of the U. S. Army, and a native of Germany.

Issue of November 10, 1812

Departed this life on the 21st ult., Miss Mary Capers, of this city, in the 39th year of her age, after a long and lingering illness.

Issue of November 12, 1812

Died, at Sullivan's-Island, on the 21st ult., Elizabeth Haig, daughter of Maham Haig.

Died, last evening, Mellisscent Colcock, Jun. in the 44th year of her age.

Issue of November 13, 1812

Died on the morning of the 9th inst., in the 51st year of his age, Daniel Ward....

Issue of November 14, 1812

Married on Thursday evening, the 12th inst., by the Rev. Dr. Gallagher, John M. Creyon, Esq. of Columbia, to Miss Louisa A. Reigne, only daughter of John Reigne, esq. of this city.

Issue of November 16, 1812

Married, on Sunday evening, by the Rev. Dr. Hollinshead, Captain Elijah Phelps, of the State of Massachusetts, to Miss Mary Elizabeth Russell, of this City.

Issue of November 17, 1812

Married on Wednesday morning last, by the Rev. Mr. Gervais, John Huger, Esq. to Miss Ann Heyward Glover, daughter of Wilson Glover, Esq.

Married, on the 11th inst., by the Rev. Mr. Dunwoody, Mr. George Hancock, to Miss Sarah M. Lewis, both of this city.

Issue of November 18, 1812

Died, in Christ Church Parish, on Monday morning last, Mr. James Bollough, sen. in the 52d year of his age.

Died on Sunday the 8th ult., Mrs. Sally Smith, in the 30th year of her age, a native of this city.

Issue of November 19, 1812

Died at St. Mary's, on the 3d inst., in the 27th year of his age, Lieutenant William Peters, of the U. S. Navy. Descended from a respectable family in Maryland, to whom he was deservedly dear....

Died on the 6th inst., at Laurel View, in Liberty County, Mrs. Esther Dunwody, in the 66th year of her age (eulogy)
                                            Savannah Museum.

Issue of November 20, 1812

Married last evening, by the Right Rev. Bishop Dehon, William S. Harvey, Esq. of Georgetown, to Miss Sarah A. Murrell, of this City.

Issue of November 25, 1812

Married last evening, by the Rev. Mr. Leland, William Boyd, Esq. Merchant to Miss Susan J. Wilson, youngest daughter of Doctor Robert Wilson.

Issue of November 26, 1812

Married on the 19th inst., by the Rev. Dr. Keith, Dr. Isaac A. Johnson, to Miss Jane H. Dupont, both of this city.
Married on Sunday evening last, by the Rev. Dr. Best, Mr. Andrew Kippenberg, to Miss Mariana Guyot.
Married on Tuesday evening last, by the Rev. Dr. Keith, Samuel Ashe, Esq. to Miss Mary Elizabeth Pinckney, daughter of the late Hopson Pinckney, Esq.

Issue of November 27, 1812

Married on Wednesday evening the 25th inst., by the Rev. Dr. Keith, Mr. Andrew Manson, Merchant, of Georgia, to Miss Mary Hutchins, of this city.
Died in Wilmington, N. C. on the 28th September last, where she had gone on a visit, Mrs. Susannah Quince, aged 60 years. Mrs. Quince was the great grand daughter of the very respectable Col. Rhett, formerly of this then Province, by his lady, afterwards the eminent and venerable Madame Trott....

Issue of November 30, 1812

Died at Georgetown, S. C. on Thursday morning last, Mr. Peter Cooper, Cabinet-Maker. He has left a wife and child. On Thursday evening, Mr. Philip Elliot, a native of Scotland.
Obituary. Col. Jeremiah Olney, late Collector of Customs of the port and district of Providence....(long account)
New-York Gazette

Issue of December 1, 1812

Died on Wednesday the 30th Sept. last, the Rev. John D. Murphy, one of the Pastors of the Presbyterian Congregation, Hopewell, Pendleton District. (eulogy)
And, on Sunday the 4th of October, the Rev. James M'Elhenney, the other Pastor of the Congregation at Hopewell...left a family....

Issue of December 2, 1812

Departed this life, on Tuesday the 24th ult., Dr. Ralph Depass, above 80 years of age; for the last 25 years, an inhabitant of this city.

Issue of December 4, 1812

Married, on Wednesday evening last, by the Rev. Dr. Andrew Flinn, Captain John H. Silliman, to Miss Eliza Milligan, both of this city.

Issue of December 7, 1812

Married on the 26th last month, at Runnimede, on Ashley River, by the Rev. Mr. Mills, Rector of St. Andrew's Parish, William M. Smith, Esq. to Miss Susan Pringle, daughter of John J. Pringle, esq.

Issue of December 9, 1812

Departed this life in Greene County, near Greeneborough, in the State of Georgia, on the night of the 12th Sept. last, Mrs. Mary Haughton, consort of Col. Joshua Haughton....

Issue of December 11, 1812

Died, at Savannah, on Saturday the 5th inst., Mrs. Mary Genovley, a native of South-Carolina, but for many years past a resident of that place, aged 61 years.

Died at Bermuda, John Christopher Baker, aged 24 years, a midshipman on board the U. S. ship of war Wasp, and son of George A. Baker, esq. of Philadelphia....

Died at Plattsburgh, Dr. Peter Turner, Surgeon's Mate in the U. S. Regiment of Flying Artillery.

Died in Montreal (Lower Canada) Colonel Edward M'Donnell, Quarter-Master-General, late Aid to Gen. Brock, aged 45.

Issue of December 14, 1812

Married last evening, by the Rev. Dr. Hollinshead, Captain Jonathan Emery, of Saco (Massachusetts) to Miss Eliza Moore, of this City.

Issue of December 18, 1812

Murder and Suicide. A man by the name of Jesse Hoxey, who resided near Beaufort, in this state, on Sunday last, committed a most brutal murder...his Wife. He afterwards cut his own throat.... Mr. H. was a native of Massachusetts; and his wife was in possession of a very handsome property. They have left no children. Courier

Married on Thursday morning, by the Rev. Dr. Hollinshead, John W. Payne, Esq. to Mrs. Sabina Bonneau.

Issue of December 24, 1812

Obituary of Dr. William Burke...fell a victim to a fever which prevailed at Kingston, (Jam.) on the 3d of October last, aged about 35 years....

Died on the 13th ult., on his passage from Bermuda to the U. S., John C. Holcomb, late a Midshipman, and one of the victors of the Wasp....

Issue of December 26, 1812

Married on Thursday evening last, by the Rev. Dr. Keith, Mr. John Reed, of this City, to Miss Margaret Mason Tew, of Newport, Rhode-Island.

Married by the Rev. Dr. Best, Mr. Moriarty, to Jane, relict of the late Mr. Brady, merchant, of this City, and sister to the High Sheriff of the County of Longford, Ireland.

Issue of December 28, 1812

Died in this city on Friday evening, the 18th inst., Mr. Gibbes Rodman, son of Gilbert Rodman, esq. of Bucks County, Pennsylvania...just entered his 21st year. (eulogy) remains were interred in the Friends burial ground....

Issue of December 30, 1812

Married, last evening, by the Rev. Mr. Cloriviere, Mr. Frederick Michel, son of Ignace de Michel, to Miss Mary Louise Cournand, daughter of Peter De Cournand, both of this city.

Died on Saturday, 19th inst., Mr. James Fowler, aged 36 years.

Issue of January 2, 1813

Married, last evening, by the Rev. Dr. Furman, Mr. Robert Anderson to Miss Naomi Euphan Blair, daughter of James Blair, esq., all of this city.

Died on Friday the 11th ult., in the 47th year of his age, Daniel Lesesne, Esq. of St. Thomas's Parish.

Issue of January 4, 1813

Married on Thursday the 24th ult., by the Rev. Dr. Buchan, Mr. M. Mahar, to Mrs. Mary Fiddy, relict of the late Mr. Fiddy, of this city.

Died on Thursday morning the 17th Dec. last, Mr. William Shirtliff, a native of Ireland, and for many years past a respectable merchant in this city.

Died, at his Country Seat, on Saturday morning, the 19th inst., in the 54th year of his age, William Loughton Smith. (eulogy)

Issue of January 7, 1813

Married on Thursday evening 31st ult. by the Rev. Dr. Furman, Mr. Oliver O'Hara, to Miss Amelia Deborah Yates, both of this city.

Married, on Tuesday evening, by the Rev. James D. Simons, Mr. Richard Pearce, Merchant, late of Rhode-Island, to Miss Harriett Petsch, of this city.

Issue of January 8, 1813

Died in this city (Washington) at 2 o'clock yesterday afternoon, the venerable John Smilie, a Representative in Congress from Pennsylvania, aged about 74 years. He was a native of Ireland....

Married last evening, by the Rev. Dr. Dehon, Mr. John Gyles, to Miss Mary Richards Crooks, both of this city.

Issue of January 11, 1813

Married in St. Paul's Parish, on Thursday last, by the Rev. Dr. Keith, Hext M'Call, Esq. of this city, to Miss Susan B. Hayne, eldest daughter of Wm. Hayne, Esq. of St. Paul's Parish, Planter.

Issue of January 13, 1813

Died in this city, Lewis Du Pre, of Charleston, S. C. Author of several Tracts against Slavery and the use of Animal Food...
                                                    Raleigh Star

Issue of January 14, 1813

Died on the 7th of December, at his plantation in Sumter District, Major William Capers, an active officer in the Revolution. (long account and eulogy)   City Gazette

Issue of January 18, 1813

Married at New-York, on Sunday evening, the 3d inst., by the Rev. Dr. Romeyn, Mr. Charles B. Mease, merchant, of this City, to Miss Sarah M. Graham, of New-York.

Issue of January 20, 1813

Died in Savannah on the 15th inst., Mr. John Joseph Evans, the Editor of the Savannah Republican.

Died at St. John's, Florida, on the 22d ult., Lieut. Samuel Elbert, of the U. S. Navy.

Issue of January 22, 1813

Married last evening, by the Rev. Dr. Hollinshead, Mr. Alexander Phillips, of this City, to Miss Margaret Murrell, of Christ Church Parish.

Issue of January 23, 1813

Died on the night of the 25th ult., at his Plantation, Seneca, in Pendleton District, Brig. Gen. Robert Anderson, aged 70 years. He was an officer in the Revolutionary War' and for many years Brig. Gen. of the 4th Brigade of the Militia of this State.

Died at the plantation of Col. Benjamin Long, in Newberry District, on Wednesday the 30th ult., Mrs. Elizabeth Turner in the 93d year of her age. She together with her husband Capt. Wm. Turner, were the first settlers above Rawl's Ferry, on Saluda River. The young may die, but the aged must.

Issue of February 1, 1813

Died on the 27th ult., at Dean-Hall, St. John's, Alexander Nisbett, Esq. in the 42d year of his age.

Issue of February 3, 1813

Died on the 29th ult., in the 38th year of her age, Mrs. Mary Ward, wife of Col. John Ward, and only daughter of William Somarsall, Esq.

Issue of February 4, 1813

Departed this life on the 9th of January, in the 67th year of her age, Mrs. Susannah Johnston, relict of Robert Johnston, esq. deceased; much regretted by all who knew her.

Issue of February 11, 1813

Married, last evening, by the Right Rev. Dr. Dehon, Alexander Hinckley M'Gillivray, Esq. to Miss Eliza Bampfield Geyer.

Died on Saturday evening last, at 10 o'clock, at the residence of his son, in Morrisville, Bucks County, George Clymer, Esq., President of the Bank of Philadelphia....Phildelphia Register, Jan. 25

Issue of February 13, 1813

Died on the evening of the 8th inst., Major William Murray, in the 50th year of his age.... Georgetown Gazette

Issue of February 15, 1813

Died on the 1st inst., at his residence on Black River, James S. Dick, Esq. in the 38th year of his age. He has left several small children to lament the loss....

Issue of February 16, 1813

Departed this life on Tuesday the 9th inst., Mrs. Mary Highton, in the 23d year of her age....

Issue of February 18, 1813

Died on the 3d inst., in St. John's Berkley, Miss Sarah Barton, after a lingering illness.
Died at Spanish-Town (Jamaica) on the 4th ult., Captain Reed, late of the U. S. brig Vixon.

Issue of February 20, 1813

Died, at Fort Moultire, on the night of the 10th Feb., Capt. Adison Bowles Armistead, of the 1st Regt. U. S. Artillery. He had served 18 years in the army of his country. His remains were interred at Fort Johnson, on the 13th inst.
Died at his residence in Fairfield District, on Thursday the 11th inst., Mr. John Crow, late of this city.

Issue of February 23, 1813

Married on the 2d inst., at Baltimore, Dr. Horatio S. Waring, of Charleston, S. C. to Miss Henrietta Higinbotham, of Baltimore, daughter of Ralph Higinbotham, esq. of Annapolis.
Married on Wednesday evening last, by the Rev. Mr. Carvalho, Mr. M. H. De Leon, to Miss Rebecca Lopez, both of this city.

Issue of February 24, 1813

Departed this life yesterday morning Mrs. Dorothy Bommer, aged 96 years and 7 months; a native of Germany, but has resided in this City upwards of seventy years.

Issue of February 27, 1813

Married on Tuesday evening the 16th inst., by the Rev. Mr. Gadsden, Mr. John Langton, to Mrs. Susannah Eliza Hilldrup, all of this city.

Issue of March 2, 1813

Married on Sunday evening last, by the Rev. Dr. Hollinshead, Mr. Richard Fairweather, to Mrs. Ann Patton, both of this city.
Died at Canajohary (state of New-York) on the 24th Jan., Mr. Daniel M'Donald, aged 102 years and 3 months. He was a native of Ireland, born in the Reign of Queen Anne....

Issue of March 6, 1813

Married on Thursday evening the 4th inst.,by the Right Rev. Dr. Dehon, Mr. Henry Cowing, Merchant, to Providence, R. I. to Miss Ann Wagner, eldest daughter of the late George Wagner, esq. of this city.

Issue of March 11, 1813

Married, yesterday, by the Rev. Dr. Furman, Mr. John P. Burn, to Miss Catherine Prizgar, both residents of this city.

Issue of March 15, 1813

Death of Joel Barlow...our Minister Plenipotentiary and Envoy Extraordinary in France.... National Intelligencer, March 2

Issue of March 16, 1813

Died at Savannah, on the 6th inst., Mr. John H. Woodward, a native of Connecticut, but for some years past a resident of Charleston. He left Charleston in December last, and went to St. Mary's for the benefit of his health....

Issue of March 18, 1813

Died at Clermont, N. Y. on Thursday the 25th ult., the Hon. Robert R. Livingston, Esq. late Chancellor of the State of New-York and formerly Minister at the Court of Bonaparte.
Died at sea, January 28th, on board the U. S. frigate Constitution, of wounds received in the action with the Java, Lieut. John Cushing Aylwin, of the U. S. navy....

Issue of March 19, 1813

Departed this life, on the 9th of January last, on John's Island, Mr. Henry C. Gefken, in the 65th year of his age....

Issue of March 20, 1813

Married, on Thursday evening last, by the Rev. Dr. Hollinshead, Isaac Couturier Jun. Esq. of St. John's Parish, to Mrs. Eliza Maria Lawrence, of this city.

Issue of March 23, 1813

Died on the 23d ult, in the 71st year of his age, Samuel Prioleau, Esquire, an old and respectable inhabitant, and native of this City. In the contest for our Independence, he took an early and an active part. (eulogy)
Married on Sunday evening last, by the Rev. Mr. Hanckell, Mr. Edward Power, Merchant, to Miss Eliza Catherine Wolf, all of this city.

Issue of March 25, 1813

Died at Kingston (Jam.) in February last, of four days illness, Capt. George Dutchman, late of the British ship, Grenada.

Issue of March 26, 1813

Died, on the 18th instant, at his residence in Mazyckborough, in the 66th year of his age, Capt. Daniel Mazyck...(eulogy)

Issue of March 29, 1813

Married last evening, by the Rev. Dr. Furman, Mr. James M'Cleish, to Miss Ann Williams, all of this place.
Departed this life on Sunday the 21st inst., Mrs. Sarah Bingley, aged 57 years and 2 months; a native of Virginia, but for a number of years a respectable inhabitant of this city....
Died at Nassau, N. P. on the 9th ult., in the 75th year of his age, General Robert Cunningham--formerly of this state.

Issue of March 31, 1813

Died in Champlain (N. Y.) Mr. Louis Harney, 103; he had 34 children by one wife.

Issue of April 1, 1813

Married on Tuesday evening, by the Rev. Dr. Gallagher, Mr. P. Bulet, to Miss Mary Jane Rose Dastas, both of this city.

Issue of April 3, 1813

Married on Sunday evening last, by the Rev. Dr. Flinn, Mr. Henry Livingston, to Miss Jane Moore, both of this city.

Issue of April 6, 1813

Married on Saturday evening last, by the Rev. Dr. Buchan, Mr. William Young, merchant, to Miss Sarah Marshall, both of this city.
Married on Sunday evening, by the Rev. Dr. Flinn, Mr. James Galloway, to Miss Ann Eliza Syfan, both of this city.

Issue of April 7, 1813

Married, on Wednesday evening, the 10th ult., by the Rev. Mr. Gadsden, Mr. William Frampton, merchant, of Pocotaligo, to Miss Violetta Lingard Wyatt, of this city.

Issue of April 8, 1813

Married on Tuesday evening last, in St. Thomas's Parish, by the Rev. Dr. Furman, Mr. John R. Rogers, to Miss Mary B. Threadcraft, daughter of Mr. Bethel Threadcraft, all of Charleston.
Married on Sunday evening last, by the Rev. Dr. Buchan, Solomon Tift, Esq. to Miss Mary M'Leod, both of this city.

Issue of April 10, 1813

Died at Albany (N. Y.), Mr. Bates, aged 52, Comedian, formerly of the Charleston Theatre.

Issue of April 12, 1813

Died on the 1st inst., Mr. Wm. F. Ehney, in the 44th year of his age...left mother and affectionate sisters.
Died last evening, suddenly, Mr. David Tarbox, printer AE. 21. During the last eight years, he had been employed in this office.... Georgetown Gazette, April 10.

Issue of April 13, 1813

Departed this life on Wednesday the 7th inst., Mrs. Hannah Smiser, aged 87 years 4 months and 13 days, a native of Germany, but for 68 years a resident of this state....(eulogy)

Issue of April 14, 1813

Married, last Monday evening, by the Rev. Mr. Simons, Thomas Bampfield, Esq. to Miss Sarah Hawie, all of this city.

Issue of April 17, 1813

Married on Thursday evening last, by the Rev. Dr. Buchan, Mr. Robert Tennant, to Mrs. Mary Ann Aitcheson, both of this city.

Issue of April 20, 1813

Married on the 10th inst., by the Rev. Mr. Leland, Mr. James Thomson, to Miss Mary Hudson, second daughter of Capt. Joseph Hudson, all of this city.

Died, suddenly, on Wednesday the 14th inst., Mrs. Ann Olsey Harleston, the truly amiable wife of Nicholas Harleston, Esq.

Died at Porto Rico, on the 7th of December, 1812, James Rannie, the celebrated Ventriloquist, aged 39 years.

Issue of April 24, 1813

Died on Wednesday the 21st inst., in the 32d year of her age, Mrs. Margaret Phelp Deas. wife of Dr. Robert Deas.

Issue of April 30, 1813

Died in Lynn (Mass.) on the 9th inst., the much celebrated and far famed widow Mary Pitcher, aged 75 years....

Issue of May 5, 1813

Married, last evening, by the Rev. Dr. Hollinshead, Mr. John Watkinson, to Mrs. Frances White, widow of the late Capt. Henry White--both of this city.

Issue of May 6, 1813

death of Miss Mary H. Butman, a native of Chelsea, Massachusetts. (long account and eulogy)...left brother and sister.

Issue of May 8, 1813

Married on Wednesday evening last, by the Rev. Mr. Henckell, Mr. Alfred Augustus Lovely, to Miss Eliza Henry, both of this city.

Departed this life, on the 2d inst., in the 59th year of her age, Mrs. Marie Duvevier Remoussin, consort of Mr. Paul Dan. Remoussin, formerly Planter of the Island of St. Domingo. This lady belonged to one of the most ancient and respectable families of that Island....

Departed this life on Tuesday the 4th May, in this city, Mrs. Mary Bennett, aged 78 years.

Died on the 21st ult., at Annapolis, Maryland, the Rev. Ralph Higginbotham, long the Vice Principal of St. John's College of that state and a Minister of the English Episcopal Church.

Died on the 22d ult., between the hours of 9 and 10 o'clock, at Alexandria (Vir.) the Rev. Lastly Matthews, aged 57 years, the last 27 of which were spent as a travelling minister in the Methodist connection....

Issue of May 10, 1813

Married on Tuesday evening last, by the Rev. Mr. Henckell, Mr. John Schirer, to Miss Charlotte Peigne, both of this city.

Issue of May 12, 1813

Married, last evening, by the Rev. Dr. Hollinshead, Mr. James C. Martindale, Merchant, to Miss Louisa O'Neale, both of this city.

Issue of May 13, 1813

Died yesterday, Mr. Henry Allen, of Boston (Mass.) AE 47. He arrived here a few days since in the cartel from Jamaica, at which place he had been a prisoner 10 months.
                    Georgetown (S. C.) Gazette, May 12

Issue of May 17, 1813

Married, on Thursday evening, by the Rev. Mr. Fowler, Wm. Manigault Heyward esq. to Miss Susan Pinckney Simmons.

Issue of May 20, 1813

Married last evening by the Rev. Nicholas Powers, the Rev. Dr. Samuel M. Meek, of Abbeville District, to Miss Ann A. M'Dowell of this city.
Married on Tuesday evening last, by the Rev. Dr. Hollinshead, Captain Benjamin R. Waring, of Columbia, to Miss Hess M. Waring, daughter of the late Dr. Thomas Waring.
Married on Monday evening, the 10th inst., by the Rev. Mr. C. Gadsden, William Ellison, Esq. of Edgefield District, Attorney at Law, to Miss Ann C. Thomson, of this city.

Issue of May 24, 1813

Died at his Plantation in St. Thomas's Parish, on the 22d inst., in the 45th year of his age, Ezekiel Pickens, Esq....
Died, at Philadelphia, on the 10th inst., Mr. Anthony Toomer, aged 36; many years a reputable merchant of Georgetown.

Issue of May 25, 1813

long account of the death of Mr. Wm. Jackson, who departed this life on 19th May 1813, in the 50th year of his age. (1½ columns.)

Issue of May 28, 1813

Married on Wednesday the 26th inst., by the Rev. Mr.Simons, Rector of St. Philip's, John Hinckley Mitchell, Esq. to Miss Eliza Chanler, of this city.

Issue of May 29, 1813

Married on the 25th ult., by the Rev. Mr. Floyd, Captain John C. Logan, to Miss Eliza Cambridge, both of St. Bartholomew's Parish.
Died on the 5th inst., at his residence near Columbia Co., Ga., Col. Hugh Blair, a member of the Legislature from that County.

Issue of June 2, 1813

Married on the 27th ult. at Cain Acre, by the Rev. Mr. Parks, Mr. Francis F. Gist, of Union District, to Mrs. Ann Tonge, of St. Paul's Parish.

Died at Lorraine, near Sackett's Harbor, on the 10th ult., Capt. John Nickels, of Boston, aged 34; late Sailing-Master of the U. S. Frigate Constitution.

Issue of June 3, 1813

Died on Monday last, the 31st ult., Master Charles Cleary, son of John R. Cleary, Esq. of this city, and brother of Col. Nathaniel Greene Cleary, Sheriff of Charleston District...aged 13 years, one month and 19 days. (long account)

Issue of June 5, 1813

Died at his Plantation, in St. John's Berkley, on the 25th ult., Alexander Broughton Motte, Esq. aged 33 years....
Died on the 31st ult., at his Plantation in St. Bartholomew's Parish, Major Paul Walter, in the 56th year of his age...left widow and child....

Issue of June 9, 1813

Departed this life on the 25th ult., Mr. Joseph Smith, in the 60th year of his age...for many years Master of one of the Sullivan's Island Packets.
Died on the 5th inst., in this city, Mrs. Mary Coffin, wife of Capt. E. Coffin, of St. Helena, aged 39.

Issue of June 12, 1813

Died at the plantation of John Pyne, in St. Bartholomew's Parish, on the 17th ultimo, Thomas H. Hutchinson, Esq. aged 28 years. And in this city, on Monday the 7th inst., John Pyne, Esq. aged 47 years.
Died on Tuesday morning the 8th inst., Mr. John Johnston, aged 40 years....

Issue of June 15, 1813

Married, on the evening of the 17th of February ult. at the Chateau of his Excellency John Quincy Adams, Minister Plenipotentiary from the U. S. to the Court of St. Petersburg, William Steuben Smith, Esq. Secretary of Legation, to Miss Catherine Johnson, Sister of Mrs. Adams, the Minister's Lady.

Issue of June 30, 1813

Obituary of Mr. John Davidson, late Librarian of the Charleston Library Society. (long account and eulogy).

Issue of July 1, 1813

Died, on board the U. S. Frigate Chesapeake, the 4th inst., Captain James Lawrence, fighting in defence of "Free Trade and Sailors' Rights," AE 30.... Phil Dem. Press, June 22.

Issue of July 8, 1813

From the Boston Gazette. Died at Halifax, on the 13th June, Lieut. Augustus C. Ludlow, second in command on abord the Chesapeake frigate, aged 21...(lines)
Died on board the frigate Chesapeake, during the action with the Shannon, on the 1st June, Wm. Augustus White, aged 26, a native of Rutland, Mass. (lines)

Issue of July 9, 1813

Married near Harrisburg, Mr. John Pancake, to Miss Harriet Fries....   Salem Gazette

Issue of July 10, 1813

Departed this life, on the 4th inst., Mr. William Eason, aged 42 years.... (lines)

Died at New-York, on the 29th ult., Silas Talbot, Esq., late Captain in the U. S. Navy, and formerly Commander of the Frigate Constitution.

Issue of July 13, 1813

Died on Friday the 2d inst., in the 27th year of his age, Paul T. Jones, Esq. (eulogy)

Died on board the U. S. frigate Chesapeake, on the 1st June, during her engagement with His Britannic Majesty's ship Shannon, Midshipman John Evans, of the City of Washington. Also, on the same day, in consequence of a wound received in the action, Midshipman Pollard Hopewell, of Mary's County, Md....

Issue of July 17, 1813

Married on Thursday evening last, by the Rev. Mr. John Capers, Mr. John Manno, to Miss Ann DeBow, both of this city.

Issue of July 26, 1813

Died, at Buntzlaw, in Prussia, the 28th April, the celebrated Russian Prince Kutusoff Smolensro, aged 70.

Died in Berlin (Pruss.) May 3, His Royal Highness Prince Augustus Ferdinand, aged 83. He was the youngest son of Frederick William I, brother of Frederick II, and great uncle to the present reigning Monarch.

Killed, in the battle of Lutzen, the hereditary Prince of Meclenburg Strelitz, brother in law to the King of Prussia, and nephew to the Queen of England.

Issue of July 28, 1813

Died on the 23d inst., Mrs. Frances Jones, aged 47 years and 9 months and 23 days....

Issue of August 4, 1813

Died at Philadelphia, on Tuesday evening, 20th ult., Mr. J. B. Dumoutet, a native of the Department of Cher, in France, aged 52--for many years a respectable inhabitant of Philadelphia.

Died in Augusta (Maine) on the 6th inst., Mr. John Gilly, at the advanced age of 124 years. He was born in the west of Ireland, a few miles from Cork--migrated to America about 70 years ago....He has left a large family; his youngest child is in his 25th year.

Issue of August 5, 1813

Died, on Tuesday, the 27th July, Major Edward Weyman, aged 44 years and 10 months, late Surveyor of the Customs of the Port of Charleston.... left wife and four children.

Issue of August 6, 1813

Married, in England, Sir William Scott, Judge of the High Court of Admiralty, to the Marchioness of Sligo, only surviving daughter of the celebrated Admiral Lord Howe and mother of the Marquis of Sligo, lately find and imprisoned for receiving some deserters from a ship of war.

Issue of August 12, 1813

Died in Georgetown on the 31st ult., Ensign Robert Logan, of the 10th Regiment of U. S. Infantry, a native of Rutherford Co., N. C. The correctness of his deportment while stationed at Fort Winyaw secured the esteem of the inhabitants of Georgetown and its vicinity. He was interred with military honors.

Issue of August 19, 1813

Departed this life, on Saturday the 7th inst., Miss Anna Claudia Bennett, youngest daughter of Thomas Bennet, sen. of this city. (eulogy)
Died, last month, at Wilmington, N. C., Mrs. E. Wright, relict of Mr. Thomas Wright, lately deceased of Hydrophobia--formerly of Charleston.

Issue of August 23, 1813

Died, at Yorkville, in this state, on Monday the 16th inst., in the 27th year of his age, Captain John H. Negge, of the Cadet Company of the Charleston Regiment of Artillery.

Issue of August 31, 1813

Departed this transitory life on the 9th inst., (on Sullivan's Island, at the residence of Major-General Thomas Pinckney) Mrs. Mary Foster, aged 64 years and 6 months....

Issue of September 1, 1813

Died on the 26th of August, Dr. John Bernard Houseal, resident of Prince Williams Parish, South Carolina....

Issue of September 6, 1813

Died, at Amelia Township, aged 40 years, Mr. Isaac Pool, a native of Germany, and for many years a resident in this city....

Issue of September 8, 1813

Married at New-York, on Sunday evening, the 29th ult., by the Rev. Benjamin Mortimer, Mr. Jacob Bininger, of the house of Abraham Bininger & Son, of that place, to Miss Harriet Burger, daughter of the late Mr. David Burger, of this city.
Departed this life on the 28th of August last, Mrs. Jane Makky, relict of Mr. John Makky, formerly of this city.
Died on Sunday the 29th ult., Mrs. Catherine Cudworth, wife of Benjamin Cudworth, esq. of this city, in the 60th year of her age... (eulogy)

Issue of September 10, 1813

Died, on the 5th inst., at the Summer Retreat, near Pocotaligo, Prince William's Parish, Miss Elizabeth Maine D'Oyley, aged

3 years, 8 months and a few days, the only daughter of Dr. Daniel D'Oyley....

Issue of September 14, 1813

Died in England, Dr. Anthony Fothergill, formerly Physician of Bath....

Issue of September 20, 1813

Departed this life on Wednesday the 8th inst., in Lexington County (in the State of South-Carolina) after a short illness of eight days, Mr. Jacob Kelly, of the City of Charleston, aged 29 years--much regretted by his relatives and friends....

Issue of September 23, 1813

Died at St. James, Goose-creek, on the morning of the 19th inst., Mr. John Filbin, aged 46 years.

Issue of September 24, 1813

Died on Wednesday, the 8th inst., Mr. Montague Simons, aged 50 years, a native of London, but for the last 35 of his life, resident of this state, upwards of 25 he lived at Jacksonborough ....

Died at Hazzard Hill, St. Luke's Parish, on the night of the 13th inst., Miss Delia Augusta Hazzard, aged 7 years and 6 months, second daughter of Major William Hazzard....

Issue of September 25, 1813

Died, at Liberty Hall, Amelia Township, on the 3d inst., Mrs. Judith Davis, in the 45th year of her age, relict of the late Mr. Israel Davis, of this city. This amiable Lady was a resident of Charleston, for the last 23 years of his life. (eulogy) Left son and a daughter.

Departed this life on the 30th ult.,Mr. John S. Hepburn, aged 30 years, a native of the State of New-Jersey, and for 3 years past a respectable inhabitant of this city....(eulogy)

Issue of September 27, 1813

Died, on the 20th inst., Mr. Michel Follin, native of Buachan, in Normandy (France) and late of St. Domingo, and for these 10 years past a resident in this city, Aged 82 years, 11 months and 2 days.

Issue of September 29, 1813

Died on Sullivan's Island, on Monday the 20th inst., Mrs. Ann Horry, wife of Elias Lynch Horry, Esq. (eulogy)

Issue of September 30, 1813

Died on the 4th inst., in the 51st year of his age, Mr. Edmund Green, a native of Boston, Mass. and for upwards of 12 years a worth and respectable inhabitant of this city. (eulogy)

Issue of October 5, 1813

Married, last evening, by the Rev. Dr. Gallagher, Mr. Benjamin Colman, to Miss Olei Couyo Costal, both of this city.

Died on the 30th of August last, Thomas Lesesne, Esq., aged 38 years.

Departed this life on Friday the 1st inst., Mrs. Mary Miller, an old and respectable inhabitant of this city, in the 66th year of her age....

Died at his residence near Cranburg, in Middlesex County, New-Jersey, Charles Barclay, in the 80th(?) year of his age. He was descended from the ancient and honorable family of the Barclay of Ury in Scotland. He was the Grandson of John Barclay one of the proprietors and first Governor of East-Jersey, who came to this country in the year 1682. Mr. Charles Barclay was fourteenth in descent from Theobald De Berkeley (as as the name is since spelled Barclay) who lived in the reign in the year of David the 1st, King of Scotland, who began to reign in the year 1124....

Issue of October 7, 1813

Married, on Sunday evening last, by the Rev. Mr. Meek, Mr. John H. Flemming, to Miss Margaret E. Lewis, both of this city.

Issue of October 9, 1813

Columbia (S. C.) October 5

Died in this town on Thursday evening last, James H. Cuthbert, Esq. a member of the Legislature of this state, from the election district of St. Helena...body of the deceased was interred in the State-House yard.

Issue of October 11, 1813

Departed this life in the 62d year of her age, Mrs. Helen Perry. (eulogy) on the morning of the 6th....

Departed this life on Sunday the 3d inst., Master John B. Horlbeck, eldest son of Henry Horlbeck, Esq, in the 15th year of his age (lines)

Died, at St. Mary's, Georgia, on the 26th ult., Wm. M'Clure, Esq. for many years a respectable Merchant of this place....

Died in Russia, Miers Fisher, of the house of Miers Fisher & Co. St. Petersburg, formerly of Philadelphia.

Died in Philadelphia, in the 72d year of his age, Nicholas Waln, formerly a distinguished member of the Philadelphia Bar, and latterly an eminent Minister of the Gospel among Friends.... (lines)

Issue of October 12, 1813

Died, on Friday evening last, of Hydrophobia, Master Gabriel B. Brown, aged 15 years, eldest son of Mr. Joshua Brown, of this city....

Issue of October 13, 1813

Died on the morning of Sunday, the 10th inst., in the 17th year of his age, Master William, son of Mr. Robert Shand...left parents, brothers, sisters....

Issue of October 15, 1813

Died on Wednesday morning last, Mrs. Mary King, in the 32d year of her age....
Died in Beaufort (S. C.) James D. West, M. D. aged 55. (poem)

Issue of October 16, 1813

Died, at Newberry court-house, South-Carolina, on Friday evening, the 17th inst., Doctor Freeborn Adams, a native of Byfield, a parish of Newburyport, in the state of Massachusetts.

Issue of October 19, 1813

Died at Beaufort, S. C. onthe morning of the 13th(?) inst., Prentiss Willard, Esq. Captain in the Corps of Engineers in the U. S. service....

Issue of October 21, 1813

Departed this life on Sunday the 17th inst., Mrs. Malinda Disher, wife of Wm. Disher, of this city, in the 22d year of her age. She has left a husband and a tender infant....
Died on the 8th inst., at Smithville, North-Carolina, Wm. H. Tillinghast, of Fayetteville, about 19 years of age...in defence of his country.
Died lately in the Havana, Capt. J. Mairs Levy, late of the U. S. Flotilla of Wilmington, N. C.

Issue of October 24, 1813

Married in New-York, on Thursday evening the 14th inst., by the Rev. Mr. Bowen, Francis Jeffrey, Esq. of Edinburgh, Editor of the Edinburgh Review, to Miss Charlotte Wilkes, daughter of Charles Wilkes, Esq. Cashier of the Bank of New-York.
Died at Orangeburgh, on the 24th July last, Mr. Jonathan Anderson, eldest son of the late Rev. John Anderson, in the 25th year of his age....left brothers and sisters.

Issue of October 27, 1813

Married on Wednesday last, in St. Philip's Church, by the Rev. Mr. Simons, Beekman M'Call, Esq. to Miss Anna Berresford Ferguson, both of this city.

Issue of October 28, 1813

Died at Society-Hill, Cheraws, on Wednesday the 13th inst., Mrs. Elizabeth D. Cuttino, aged 45--a lady pre-eminent in piety and virtue.
Died at Matthew Allen's, near Georgetown, South Carolina, Hannah Gordon about 6 years old a native of New-Haven, Connecticut. Her parenst are supposed to be in Savannah, as they were travelling for that place in the year 1812, and being destitute left this child with Mr. Allen.
Died on Black River, near Statesburg, on the   inst., Master William R. Theus, in the fourth year of his age, second son of William R. Theus, esq. formerly of Georgetown, S. C.
Died on Thursday the 7th inst., in the 42d year of his age, at the residence of Travers Daniel, esq, in Stafford Co., Va., Doctor John Moncure Daniel, Senior Hospital Surgeon in the Military service of the U. S.

Died at New-Brunswick, New-Jersey, on Sunday the 10th inst., Miss Lucy Lawrence, sister of the late gallant and lamented commander of the Chesapeake frigate....

Issue of October 29, 1813

Death of Mr. Frederick W. Dalton, formerly a Student of Columbia College in this State, and son of Dr. James Dalton. (long eulogy)

Died at St. Mary's Georgia, the 13th inst., Captain Joseph Green Stevens, second son of Robert Stevens, Esq. of Newport, Rhode-Island....parents, sisters and brothers left.

Issue of November 1, 1813

Departed this life on the afternoon of the 30th September, at the Marine Hospital, Robert Christian, for many years past an inhabitant of this city....

Issue of November 3, 1813

Departed this life on the 15th ult., on St. Helena, John Jenkins, Sen. Esq. in the 64th year of his age, leaving a disconsolate widow, with six sons and daughters, a number of grand children...a native of St. Helena.

Issue of November 4, 1813

Married last evening, by the Rev. Dr. Hollinshead, Robert Y. Hayne, Esq. to Miss Frances Henrietta Pinckney, daughter of Charles Pinckney, esq.

Issue of November 5, 1813

Died in Fairfield district, on Thursday the 7th ult., Nicholas Peay, Esq. in the 60th year of his age. He was an active patriot during the Revolution; he left a widow a son and a grandson....

Issue of November 6, 1813

Died on the 6th ult., aged about 33 years, Samuel B. Jones, leaving a wife, seven children, an aged father and mother, an only sister....

Departed this life, on the 3d inst., Mrs. Margaret Coslett, the hightly respected consort of Charles Grimke Coslett, esq. of this city. a native of Ireland, and at an early age was sent to France to receive her education....

Issue of November 9, 1813

Married, on Thursday the 4th Nov., by the Rev. Mr. Gadsden, Bartholomew Gaillard, Esq. of St. John's Parish, Berkley, to Miss Sarah Donnom, daughter of Joseph Donnom, Esq. deceased.

Issue of November 10, 1813

Died on Friday the 5th inst., Mrs. Jane Rembert, in the 41st year of her age.

Issue of November 12, 1813

Died, on Tuesday morning last, 9th inst., in the 23d year of her age, Mrs. Hannah Hughes, consort of Mr. Henry Hughes, of this city. She was a native of Bloomingdale, New-York....(eulogy)
death of Miss Eliza Ann Brenan, who died on the 9th of Nov., aged 7 years and 11 months...
Died on the 9th inst., at his residence in George-street, Peter Freneau, Esq., aged 57 years (long eulogy)
City Gazette

Issue of November 13, 1813

Died, on Tuesday evening last, at 5 o'clock, in the bloom of youth, Mrs. Hess M. Waring, wife of Capt. B. R. Waring, of Columbia, and daughter of the late Dr. Thomas Waring, of Waccamaw.

Issue of November 15, 1813

Death of Miss Sarah Blackwood, third daughter of Thomas Blackwood, Esq. merchant of this city, on Friday morning last, after 6 days severe illness, aged 8 years and 3 months....
Departed from this transitory stage of existence, Miss Mary M'Leod, in the 15th year of her age, eldest daughter of the Rev. Donald M'Leod, of Edisto Island....

Issue of November 17, 1813

Departed this life on the 13th inst., James Wilson, Esq. son of Dr. Wilson Sen. of this city, aged 25 years....
Died on the 7th of Sept. last, at his residence in Tradd street, Doctor George Carter, in the 76th(?) year of his age. This gentleman was a native of Ireland, and had adopted this country as his own. In the year 1776 he came to this Country... (account)
Died on Thursday the 11th inst., Mr. John Kelly, for many years past a Branch Pilot of this city, aged 35 years and 6 months. He was a native of Waxford, in Ireland. He has left an affectionate wife and three small children....

Issue of November 19, 1813

Married on Tuesday evening last, by the Right Rev. Bishop Dehon, Nathaniel Farr, Esq. of St. Paul's Parish, to Miss Katharine Blacklock, eldest daughter of Wm. Blacklock, esq. of this city.

Issue of November 20, 1813

Married in Fairfield district, on Thursday last, Dr. Benjamin F. Harris, of this town, to Miss Mary Ann Milling, daughter of Captain Milling, of that district. Columbia paper, Nov. 16

Issue of November 29, 1813

Married on Thursday evening last, by the Rev. Mr. Gadsden, Mr. Frederick Kohler, to Miss Josephine Durbec, both of this place.
Married on Sunday evening, August 1st, by the Rev. Thomas Durant, at Socaster, Horry District (S. C.), Mr. John Buxton, of New-York, to Miss Rebecca Brown, of Fayetteville (N. C.)

Issue of November 30, 1813

Married on Tuesday evening last, by the Rev. Dr. Flinn, Capt. J. C. Anthony, to Miss Jane Brown, both of this city.
Died on the 3d ult., in the 34th year of his age, Mr. Robert Eason, a native of Greenock, in Scotland, and for many years a resident of this city.

Issue of December 2, 1813

death of Master William Sanders Badger....

Issue of December 4, 1813

Died, on the 29th ult., in the 45th year of his age, Mr. Andrew Nathony Charles Lechais, a native of the river Dores, in the parish of Marmelade, in the Island of St. Domingo, and for the last 20 years a resident of this city. (long account)

Issue of December 8, 1813

Married in Boston, on the 25th ult., by the Rev. J. S. J. Gardiner, Charles Stewart Esquire, Commander of the U. S. Frigate Constitution, to Miss Delia Tudor, daughter of the Hon. William Tudor.

Issue of December 11, 1813

death of Miss Ann Maria Lee, youngest daughter of Stephen Lee, Esq. deceased on the 6th inst, in the 25th year of her age (eulogy)   Collins.
Departed this life on Monday last, in the 20th year of his age, Mr. James Armstrong Spierin, son of the late Rev. George Heartwell Spierin. (poem)

Issue of December 15, 1813

Departed this life on Sunday night last, Mrs. Susan Mason Cox, in the 30th year of her age, consort of Thomas Campbell Cox, Editor of "The Times." (eulogy)

Issue of December 16, 1813

Departed this life on the 11th inst., Miss Lydia Elsworth, a native of Albany (State of New-York), aged 30 years....

Issue of December 18, 1813

Departed this life on the 14th December, the Rev. Isaac Stockton Keith, in the 59th year of his age. For upwards of 25 years he officiated as one of the Pastors of the Independent Church of this city. (eulogy)

Issue of December 24, 1813

Married, last evening, by the Rev. Mr. Simons, Mr. Charles Burger, of this city, to Miss Lavinia Perran Lestargette, daughter of Lewis Lestargette, Esq. of Orangeburgh, deceased.
Died, at New-York, on the 13th inst., Mrs. Elizabeth Twaits, wife of Mr. Wm. Twaits, of the Broadway Theatre, in the 27th year of her age.

Issue of December 28, 1813

    Married, on Saturday evening the 18th inst.,by the Rev. Mr. Leland, Mr. Josiah Wheeler, to Miss Susan H. Gibson, second daughter of Mr. James Gibson, all of this city.
    death of Midshipman Rousseau, of New-Orleans, attached to the U. S. Schr. Caroline....

Issue of December 30, 1813

    Departed this life on the 25th inst., Mrs. Ann Shaw, daughter of Mr. George Fardo, formerly of this city. She has left two distressed female children....
    Died on the 19th inst., at his seat in Bladensburg, Maryland, Benjamin Stoddard, Esq...Secretary of the Navy, during the administration of Mr. Adams.
    Died on the 16th November 1813, at his farm in Fairfax Co., Va., Mr. Philip Chull (commonly called Shoals) in the 115th year of his age; born in Germany, in 1699, emigarted to America in 1721. His wife Elizabeth, by whom he had nine children, lived to the advanced age of 101 years. his youngest son Menassa is now in his 53d year....
    Married at Woodville, near Winchester, Vir., on the 14th inst., by the Rev. A. Balmain, Mr. Joseph Gales Jun. one of the Editors of the National Intelligencer to Miss S. Juliana M. Lee, daughter of Theodorick Lee, Esq.

Issue of December 31, 1813

    Married on the evening of the 23d inst., by the Rev. Mr. Leland, Thomas Napier, Esq. to Miss Hannah Hibben, daughter of James Hibben, esq.

Issue of May 27, 1814

    Married on Tuesday evening last, by the Rev. E. N. Carvalho, Mr. D. N. Carvalho, to Miss Sarah Cohen D'Azevedo.
    Departed this life on the 19th inst., at the residence of Joseph Koger, sen. at St. Bartholomew's Parish, the Rev. James M. Sharp, in the 43d year of his age.

Issue of January 16, 1815

    Departed this life on Monday the 9th inst., Mrs. Ann Johnson, aged 37 years 5 months and 24 days.

Issue of January 20, 1815

    Married, on Thursday the 12th inst., at Tivoll, in Chester district, by the Rev. Dr. Montgomery, William F. Desaussure, esq. second son of the hon. Henry W. Desaussure, to Miss Sarah Jones Davie, second daughter of Major Gen. William R. Davie.

Issue of February 4, 1815

    Died on the 10th of January, Mrs. Ann E. Dennison, consort of Mr. James Dennison, in the 60th year of her age...left husband and three daughters. (eulogy)

Issue of February 10, 1815

    Married on Sunday last, Mr. Timothy Rieves, aged 80 years, to Mrs. Sally Finch, aged 75, both of Prince George county.

previous notice from Petersburg (Va.) pap. 3d inst.
Married last evening by the Right Rev. Dr. Dehon, William Howlet Joyner, Esq. of Beaufort, to Miss Eliza Mary Hartley, of this city.

Issue of February 11, 1815

Died on Thursday the 9th inst., in this city, to which place he had come for the benefit of his health, Mr. Curtis R. Burritt, son of Dr. Ely Burrit, of Troy, New-York.

Issue of February 17, 1815

Married last evening, by the Rev. Mr. Gadsden, Major Alexander Sevier, of the U. S. Marine Corps, to Miss Jane Bacot, daughter of Thomas W. Bacot, Esq. of this city.

Issue of February 24, 1815

Died on the 13th inst., Mrs. Mary Mazyck, relict of Isaac Mazyck, in the 72d year of her age.
Departed this life on the 24th day of December last, Mr. Joseph Maxcy, in the 39th year of his age, a native of John's Island....

Issue of February 27, 1815

Married, last evening, by the Rev. Dr. Flinn, Mr. James Badger, Jun. to Miss Mary Blaylock Bell, both of this city.

Issue of March 1, 1815

Departed this life on the 19th ult., Zachariah Villepontoux, in the 25th year of his age. He was a dutiful son, a kind master, and an affectionate friend.

Issue of March 2, 1815

Departed this life on the 21st ult. in the 67th year of her age, Mrs. Ann Askew, a native of London (and relict of Mr. James Askew, jeweller) but for many years resident in this city... Her remains were deposited in St. Michae's Church yard, near to where her deceased husband had been buried some years before.
Died lately in the City of New-York, Quashee, an African, at the advanced aged of 117 years. He had resided with the family of Mrs. Rachel Arden for upwards of 70 years. N. Y. paper

Issue of March 3, 1815

Died, at New-York, on Sunday the 19th ult., Mr. Alexander Forbes, a native of Scotland, and one of the oldest Printers in America.

Issue of March 7, 1815

Died at New-York, on Thursday morning the 23d ult., Robert Fulton, Esq...his name will not be forgotten so long as the Hudson and the Mississippi continue to flow.

Issue of March 11, 1815

Married on Wednesday evening by the Rev. Mr. Gadsden, Mr. Samuel J. Morris of Virginia, to Miss Elizabeth Reilly, of this City.

Issue of March 16, 1815

Married on Saturday last, by the Rev. Dr. Buchan, Dr. Stephen H. Woolley, of His Britannic Majesty's Navy, to Miss Frances Louisa H. Well, daughter of John Wells, Esq. late of Nassau, N. P.

Issue of March 29, 1815

Married on Thursday the 16th inst., in Maryland, Thomas P. Grosvenor, Esq. a Representative in Congress, from the State of New York, to Miss Mary L. Hanson.

Issue of March 31, 1815

Departed this life on the 26th inst., at his Plantation in the Parish of St. Bartholomew's, Jacob H. Alison, Esq. in the 42d year of his age.
Died on the 19th ult., Henry Daingerfield, Esq. Secretary of the Mississippi Territory, and Register of the Land Office west of the Pearl River.
Died at New-Orleans, on the 20th ult., Gen. Byrd Smith. Gen. Smith was an early settler in Tennessee, had been for several years a Member of the Legislature, and at the day of his death commanded the West Tennessee brigade of Militia, which acted so conspicuous a part in the several battles below New-Orleans.

Issue of May 13, 1815

Died in Brighton, England, in December last, Mr. James Blair, of the house of Blair Nahier & Co. of this city.

Issue of May 19, 1815

Married, on Wednesday last, by the Rev. Dr. Buchan, Alexander Gibson, Esq. to Miss Elizabeth Ewing, youngest daughter of the late Adam Ewing, Esq.

Issue of August 2, 1815

Departed this life on the 25th ult., Mrs. Susanna Nelson, aged 64 years and 5 months, relict of the late Mr. Isaac Nelson....

Issue of January 3, 1816

Departed this life on the 25th ult., in the 77th year of her age, Mrs. Mary Desaussure, relict of the late Daniel Desaussure, Esq.
Died at Nassau, New Providence on the 22d ult., Thomas Starr, Esq. of the house of Carter & Starr, Liverpool.

Issue of January 4, 1816

Died yesterday morning, in the 49th year of his age, Dr. Benjamin Smith Barton, Professor of the Theory and Practice of Medicine and of Natural History and Botany, in the University of Pennsylvania.

Issue of January 6, 1816

Married on Thursday the 28th ult., by the Rev. Robert B. Walker, Mr. Alex'r Cabean, to the amiable Miss Mary Ann Patterson, both of Chester District.   Columbia S. C. State Gazette
Died in Granby on the night of Thursday last, Mr. James M'Gowen, an old and respectable inhabitant of that village.
Died in Granby, on Saturday night last, Mr. David Kelly, merchant of that place.

Issue of January 9, 1816

On Saturday morning, the 30th of December 1815, departed this transitory state of being, Major James Simons, in the 55th year of his age. (long eulogy)

Issue of January 13, 1816

Married on the 20th November by the Rev. Jacob Cooke, Mr. George West of Giles, Virginia, aged 106 years, to Mrs. Mary Gardner, of Monroe, aged 80 years.
Died at Pittsburg on the 13th ult., Col. Stephen Bayard, in the 67th year of his age--a respectable soldier of the Revolution. He had resided in Pittsburg since the year 1783.
Died in London, Nov. 1, the celebrated Dr. Lettsom, aged 70. He introduced in England the root called Mangle Wurkell....

Issue of January 17, 1816

Died at Boston, on the evening of the 4th inst., the Rev. John Lathrop, D. D. aged 76. The venerable Pastor of the Second Church in that town.

Issue of January 18, 1816

Died, at Georgetown, S. C., on Tuesday morning last, Mr. Moses G. Crosby, aged 47 years, a native of Vermont, but for many years a resident of that place.

Issue of January 19, 1816

Married in Edgefield District, on the 2d last, Dr. Alexander B. M'Whorter, to Miss Eleanor Youngblood, both of said district.
Died on the 1st instant, at his residence in Newberry District, Captain John Henderson, in the 50th year of his age....
Died Feb. 9, at Broxbourne, Herts, where he was superintending an edition of the Scriptures for the use of the Syrian Christians, Rev. Claudius Buchanan, D. D. (of Queen's college, Cambridge, M. A. 1796) (long account).

Issue of January 20, 1816

Departed this life in Santee district on the 5th inst., in the 75th year of his age, Mr. Cason Scott. He has left an aged widow, seven sons and two daughters. Two of his sons fought under Jackson at New Orleans... Mr. Scott was a member of the Baptist Society for more than 50 years....

Issue of January 25, 1816

Married at Mount Pleasant, on Tuesday evening last, by the Rev. Dr. Leland, the Rev. John Bachman to Miss Harriet Martin.

Died, lately in Washington-city, Mr. Joseph Maguire, Printer, for many years a reporter of the proceedings of congress....
Raleigh Minerva

Issue of January 27, 1816

Died at Amelia-Island, on the 6th inst., William Muir, Esq., Merchant of this place, a native of Kukcudbright, in Scotland, in the forty eighth year of his age. (eulogy)

Died also at Amelia Island, the 28th ult., John M'Clure, Esq. late of the house of Alexander & John M'Clure, of this place....

Issue of February 2, 1816

Married, in Camden, Col. Francis A. Deliesseline, of Georgetown, to Miss Amelia Adamson, daughter of Mr. John Adamson.

Issue of February 7, 1816

death notice of William Muire...left widow and six children. Departed this life on the 18th ult., at his father's seat, in Bedford, Va., Major John Reid, of the U. S. army, the well known aid of General Jackson in his transactions against the Creeks and British.

Issue of February 13, 1816

Married on Sunday evening last, by the Rev. Dr. Palmer, Mr. William B. Cross, to Miss Anne Bythewood Hutson, both of this city.

Issue of February 14, 1816

Departed this life on the 13th ult., Miss Frances Jones, daughter of Mr. Joseph Jones, of this city, aged 21 years and 3 months....

Issue of February 15, 1816

Classical Marriage. Married in Hector, N. Y., Dr. Thomas, of Ulysses, to Miss Harriet Wheeler, of Ovid.

Issue of February 17, 1816

Married on Sunday evening last, by the Rev. Dr. Flinn, Mr. Henry P. Wesner, to Miss Ann M. Brindlay, both of this City.

Married at Baltimore, on the evening of the 8th inst., by the Rev. Dr. Inglis, Capt. John A. Webster (late of the U. S. Navy) to Miss Rachel Biays, daughter of Col. Joseph Biays, all of that city.

Issue of February 19, 1816

Married in Wilmington, N. C. on the 4th inst., Mr. John Brown, of North Carolina, to Mrs. Rebecca P. Peters, of this City.

death of Rev. Avery Williams, the late Pastor of the Church in Lexington, Mass....

Issue of February 23, 1816

Departed this life on Saturday the 17th inst., Mrs. Eliza Elliot Vinyard, wife of Mr. John Vinyard, of this city, and daughter of the late Lewis Lestargette, Esq. of Orangeburgh, aged 35 years and 7 months. (eulogy)...left husband and three children.

Issue of February 27, 1816

Departed this life on the 11th inst., Miss Mary Ann Campbell, in the 63d year of her age. (eulogy)

Issue of March 7, 1816

Departed this life on Wednesday the 14th inst., Doctor Daniel D'Oyley, aged 31 years. He left his native land, South-Carolina, to seek health in this hospital clime....

Royal (Bahama) Gazette, 17th Feb.

Died in Amsterdam, aged 107, Moses Gomez Carvaldo, a Jew, born in Portugal in 1706, and who emigrated from thence in 1729. He was twice married and had many children, of whom the eldest died when 78 years of age, the youngest is only 22 years. His second wife was delivered in 1798 of a son, who died shortly after. ...

Issue of March 8, 1816

Married on Sunday evening, the 25th Feb. by the Rev. W. Phoebus, Mr. Samuel E. Bennom, Collector for this office, to the amiable Miss Ann Reeves, all of this city.

Died on the 1st inst., Gavin Turnbull, late Comedian....

Issue of March 12, 1816

Died on the 3d inst., Mrs. Kinloch, the wife of Francis Kinloch, Esq. and eldest daughter of the Hon. John Rutledge, deceased. (eulogy)

Died on the 4th inst., at his late residence in St. Mathew's Parish, in the 63d year of his age, the Rev. James O'Farrell, a native of Ireland.

Issue of March 16, 1816

It is our duty to announce to the public, the death of John London, Esq. late President of the Bank of Cape-Fear. He died on the 1st inst., in the 70th year of his age, in this town, where he has resided about 50 years.

Wilmington (N. C.) Gazette, March 9

Issue of March 19, 1816

Married on Sunday evening last, by the Rev. Dr. Hollinshead, Captain John Whitney to Mrs. Mary Hammond, both of this city.

Issue of March 20, 1816

Departed this life on Friday the 15th inst., Mr. William Burger, second son of the late David Burger, of this city, aged 30 years, 11 months and 12 days....

Died in London, on the 29th of December last, Phineas Bond, Esq. for many years Consul General of his Britanick Majesty for the Middle and Southern States of America.

Died, in England, in January last, Lieut. Gen. George Prevost, Bart., late commander in chief in Canada, aged 49. He was son of Major Gen. Prevost, who was severely wounded on the plains of Abraham, under Gen. Wolfe....

Issue of March 21, 1816

Murder! Early last week a Mr. Kerton of Pee Dee, who was on his return home from Georgetown, was cruelly murdered by a young man (Jones).... Mr. Kerton was old and infirm, and had passed the 50th year of his age.   Georgetown S. C. Gazette, March 20

Issue of March 23, 1816

Married, on Thursday evening last, by the Rev. Mr. Lee, Mr. Geo. Henry Smith, of St. George, Dorchester, to Miss Maria Day, of St. Paul's parish.

Issue of March 25, 1816

Departed this life on the 18th inst., in the city of Raleigh, the Rev. James W. Thomson, a clergyman of the Presbyterian order and late of Newbern.

Issue of April 4, 1816

Died on the 24th inst., at his residence in Suffolk, John Barber, for many years a respectable member of the bar, and long attorney for the Commonwealth, for this district....During the late war, he was a Quarter Master in the 3d Regt Virginia Militia ...   Norfolk American Beacon, 27th ult.

Issue of April 5, 1816

Died on his passage from Hamburg to Boston, Nov. 17th, Capt. Wingat H. Pilsburg, aged 25, late master of the ship Salus....

Issue of April 8, 1816

Died, at Georgetown, on the morning of the 3d inst., Mrs. Jennet Smart (of Charleston) in the 58th year of her age. Mrs. Smart had arrived at that place from Charleston on a visit, but a few days before her death.

Issue of April 10, 1816

Departed this transitory life on the 2d inst., Miss Rebecca Cook Geyer, second daughter of Capt. John Geyer....
Died in Bronklin, N. H., a child of Mr. Luther Rockwood...
Another Patriot of the Revolution is no more. Departed this life on the 30th ult., in the 73d year of his age, Capt. Edward Pegram, of Dinwiddie county....   Petersburg Intelligencer

Issue of April 11, 1816

Departed this transitory life on the 2d inst., Miss Rebecca Geyer, of this city, aged 21 years, 2 months and 18 days....

Issue of April 12, 1816

The venerable Francis Asbury, Superintendant of the Methodist Episcopal Church, closed a valuable and useful life at the house of Mr. George Arnold in this county.   Fredericksburg Va. Herald

Issue of April 13, 1816

Married on Tuesday evening last, by the Rev. Dr. Palmer, Mr. Abraham D. Reeves, to Miss Hannah Keith Palmer, both of this city.

Issue of April 16, 1816

Died at his lodgings in Georgetown, yesterday, the Hon. Richard Stanford, a Representative in Congress from the state of North Carolina, aged about 47 years.... National Intelligencer, 10th inst.

Issue of April 22, 1816

Married in Boston, Lt. Col. Nathan Towson, of the U. S. Light Artillery, to Miss Sophia Bingham, daughter of Caleb Bingham, Esq.
Departed this life the 17th inst., in the 31st year of his age, Mr. Thomas Warnock. He has left a wife and three children, together with an aged mother.... (lines)

Issue of April 23, 1816

Died on the 18th ult., in Tennessee, of wounds received in a rencontre with Col. Simpson, Gen. Thomas K. Harris, lately a Member of Congress from that State.

Issue of April 25, 1816

Departed this life 17th inst., Thomas Jefferson, son of Puckshun Cubbe, a principal chief of the Choctaw nation of Indians ....

Issue of April 26, 1816

Married on Tuesday the 23d inst., by the Rev. Dr. Gadsden, Dr. John Grimke, to Miss Sophia Ladson, both of this city.

Issue of May 2, 1816

Died on Monday morning last, the Rev'd John Garvin of this place, in the 54th year of his age--he was a native of Windsor in England, and was a preacher of the Methodist connection 24 years....   Augusta Herald, 24th ult.

Issue of May 4, 1816

Married on Wednesday evening last, by the Rev. Mr. Lance, Thomas L. S. Fraser, Esq. to Miss Isabella Wakefield, both of this city.

Issue of May 7, 1816

Died on the 6th inst., Samuel Frazier, late Master of the British brigantine Amelia, of Kingston (Jam.)

Issue of May 10, 1816

Died, on Monday the 6th inst., aged 74 years, Mrs. Abigail Johnson, wife of John Johnson, esq. a native of the state of New-York, but for upwards of 38 years, a resident of this city... remains carried to the second Presbyterian Church....

Issue of May 11, 1816

Died in Abbeville district on the 28th ult., Mr. James W. Cotten, aged 47. left an affection wife, eight children, and numerous relatives and friends. He was a native of this city, and was well known for a number of years as the keeper of the thirty two mile house establishment, between Charleston and Georgetown. (eulogy)

Issue of May 15, 1816

Departed this life at Mobile on the 8th of Feb. last, Capt. John A. Watson, lateof the 3d Regt. U. S. Infantry....
Died in England, Lieut. General Sir W. P. Acland, K. C. B.

Issue of May 23, 1816

Married at Savannah, on Wednesday evening 15th inst., by the Rev. Mr. Hill, Mr. John King, to Miss Jane Achord, both of that place. (poem) Savannah Republican.

Issue of May 31, 1816

Married, on Wednesday evening last, by the Right Rev. Bishop Dehon, Peter Thomas Ryan, Esq. to Miss Elizabeth Hall Mortimer, daughter of Edward Mortimer, Esq. both of this city.

Issue of June 1, 1816

Columbia (S. C.) May 28
Died on Tuesday evening the 7th inst., Mr. Jeremiah Shannon of Orangeburgh district, in the 18th year of his age.
Died on the 17th of last month, Mrs. Nancy Hannah, wife of James Hannah, post-master of Huntington post-office, after a short illness of the epidemic disease.

Issue of June 10, 1816

Married on Saturday Evening by the Rev. Dr. Gallagher, A. D. Torre, Esq. to Miss Margaret Ryan, both of this city.

Issue of June 21, 1816

death of Mrs. Catharine Ravenel, wife of Dr. Henry Ravenel, who died at Pineville, St. Stephen's Parish, on the 12th inst. (eulogy)

Issue of June 24, 1816

Died in Georgetown, S. C. on Wednesday morning last, Mr. John N. Taylor.
On Friday evening, in Philadelphia, James Fennell, Teacher of Elocution &c. departed this life....
Balt. paper of the 17th inst.

Issue of June 27, 1816

Married in Savannah on the 22d inst., by the Rev. B. Scriven, Mr. John Howlen, to Miss Harriot Chaplin, of St. Helena Island, Beaufort District, South-Carolina.

Issue of June 29, 1816

Died at his residence in Union district on Monday the 17th inst., John Haile, Esq. in the 70th year of his age--he was a parent to a numerous offspring. (eulogy)

Died at Russelsville (Ky) on the 20th ult., Mrs. Abigail Morgan, aged 73, widow of the celebrated General Morgan.

Issue of July 1, 1816

From the Fayetteville American. Married at the Court-House in Lumberton, on the 28th day of May, Mr. Isaac Medling, aged about 50, to Miss Mary King, in the 54th year of her age. (long account.) Robeson County, June 1, 1816

Issue of July 4, 1816

Married, last evening, by the Rev. Dr. Palmer, Mr. Adam Ker, to Miss Mary Martha Sanders, both of this place.

Married, on Sunday evening last, by the Rt. Rev. Dr. Dehon, William Patton, Esq. Merchant, to Miss Elizabeth Ker, daughter of Andrew Ker, Esq. all of this city.

Married in Columbia, on Thursday evening, the 18th ult., by the Rev. Mr. Mercer, David P. Hillhouse, Esq. Editor of the "Carolina Telegraph," to Miss Lucy Lipham, only daughter of Major Aaron Lipham, of Washington, Wilkes County, Georgia.

Departed this life in Savannah, on Monday the 17th ult., Mrs. Eliza Wyatt, a native of Charleston, aged 22 years 7 months and 28 days....

Died at Ashepoo, St. Bartholomew's Parish, S. C., Mrs. Elizabeth Girardeau, late consort of Col. Peter B. Girardeau, of said place.

Died in Columbia, on Wednesday morning, the 26th ult., Mrs. Sarah Faust, wife of Mr. Daniel Faust.

Issue of July 6, 1816

Married in Prince William's Parish, on the 3d inst., by the Rev. Mr. Parks, John Lingard Hunter, Esquire of this city, attorney at law, to Miss Sarah Elizabeth Bowler, of the former place, daughter of James Henry Bowler, esq. dec.

Married on Wednesday evening, by the Rev. Dr. Bachman, Mr. George Gruber to Miss Elizabeth Carpenter, both of this city.

Issue of July 10, 1816

Married, last evening, by the Rev. Dr. Palmer, Mr. John Smith, to Miss Mary Corrie, eldest daughter of Mr. Samuel Corrie, all of this city.

Issue of July 11, 1816

Departed this life on Monday last, the 8th inst., Mr. Henry Hughes, aged 33 years, a native of this city. He has left an infant daughter and a number of relatives and friends to mourn the prematurity of his death.

Issue of July 12, 1816

Departed this life on the morning of the 10th inst., Mr. Washington Gibbes, son of William Hasell Gibbes, Esq. (eulogy) in the 22d year of his age....

Issue of July 15, 1816

Departed this life on the 22d ult., in the 44th year of his age, the Rev. Thomas Price, Minister of the Church on James Island...left a widow and daughter to lament his loss.

Issue of July 16, 1816

Died at Major Wm. Gholson's, in Brunswick Co., Va. on Thursday, Hon. Thomas Gholson, a Representative in Congress from the State of Virginia....

Issue of July 17, 1816

Married, May 8, at Edinburgh, James Pemberton Morris, Esq., of the U. S., to Rosa, daughter of the Rev. Dr. Gardiner.
Died at Sullivan's Island, on the morning of the 15th inst., Miss Mary-Ann Kerr, in the 20th year of her age....(lines)
Died on the 14th inst., Mr. Peter Greffin, aged 52 years, a native of France, but has been a resident of the U. S. for the last 20 years....

Issue of July 20, 1816

Married at New York on the evening of the 10th inst., Mr. Alexander Marks, merchant of Charleston, S. C. to Miss Hetty Hart, daughter of Mr. Jacob Hart, of that city.

Issue of July 26, 1816

Removed from this to a better world, on the 22d ult., in the 44th year of his age, the Rev. Thomas Price, Pastor of the Church on James Island, St. Andrew's Parish. (eulogy)

Issue of July 30, 1816

Died on Saturday the 27th inst., Captain George Cross, an old and respectable inhabitant of this city.
Departed this life on Saturday the 27th inst., John C. Folker, Esq., aged 64 years...in the Council of our City and the Legislature of our State, where he served many years....

Issue of July 31, 1816

Died on Saturday last, the 27th inst., Mrs. Mary M. Warley, consort of Dr. Wm. Warley, aged 23 years. (eulogy)

Issue of August 1, 1816

In the death of Gen. Jacob Read (who departed this life on Tuesday the 17th ult., in the 65th year of his age) has another of those worthies, who bore arms in the defence of his country in her infant struggles for liberty and self government....left a family (eulogy).

Issue of August 2, 1816

Departed this life on the 25th ult., aged 65 years, Miss Mary Bee....

Issue of August 5, 1816

Departed this life on Saturday the 27th ult., at his residence, on James Island, Mr. John Stent, Sen. in the 62d year of his age (eulogy)

Issue of August 10, 1816

Departed this life on the 3d inst., Mrs. Isabel Susannah Boyd, in the 31st year of her age, relict of Wm. Boyd, Esq., deceased. (eulogy)

Issue of August 14, 1816

Married at Halfway Tree Church in St. Andrew's, on Tuesday, by the Rev. Alexander Campbell, Oliver O'Hara, Esq. of Charleston, S. C. to Miss Matilda Blair, eldest daughter of John Blair, Esq. Knight of the Royal and Military Order of St. Louis, and a Captain in his Majesty's Service. Kingston, Jamaica paper, June 22.

Issue of August 16, 1816

Died this morning after a lingering illness in the 48th year of her age, Mrs. Martha Cook, formerly of St. Luke's parish, S. C., and lately a resident of Savannah, Geo., from whence she came to this city a few weeks since in pursuit of lost health. New York Commercial Advertiser, 7th inst.

Issue of August 17, 1816

Died, in Onondago, New-York, on the 18th inst., Benjamin Ketchum, aged 101 years, the 19th of February last. His wife, with whom he had lived nearly 80 years, died 4 years ago the 3d of April last, wanting but three days of 102 years of age. They lived to see their fifth generation....

Issue of August 24, 1816

Married in Lexington District, on Sunday last, by the Rev. John H. Winkhouse, Mr. Thomas Frick, of Lexington District, aged 70 years, to Mrs. Susannah Cromer, relict of Michael Cromer, late of Newberry District, aged 55 years. Columbia paper.

Issue of August 30, 1816

Died, on the 29th inst., at Islington, Mr. Joseph Dickinson, of this city, house carpenter, aged 46 years.

Issue of September 4, 1816

Died on Friday the 16th inst. (August), Daniel Pulsar(?), about 10 years of age, son of Mr. Martin Pulsar(?) of Liberty-street.... New York Gazette
Died at the State Prison, Charlestown, Mass., Elijah Stone, one of the convicts who attempted to escape in the late insurrection.

Issue of September 5, 1816

    Married, in the vicinity of Philadelphia, by Parson on Monday the 19th inst., Mr. Wm. B. Gregory, Merchant, of Suffolk, Va., to Mrs. Nancy Tull, from the same place.

Issue of September 7, 1816

    Died in Wheelock, Dr. James Huse, killed by falling from a load of hay, on the prong of a pitch-fork.

Issue of September 9, 1816

    Died at the village of Haddrid's Point, on Sunday evening the 1st inst., Miss Mary Egleston, in the 23d year of her age, daughter of Azariah Egleston, Esq. of Lenox, Mass., and niece of Mr. John Egleston, of this city...burial in St. Philip's Church. (eulogy)

Issue of September 11, 1816

    Died at Georgetown, S. C. on the 19th of August, Mr. Nathan Bates, a native of Boston, formerly of the house of Bates & Perkins, of this city.

Issue of September 12, 1816

    Died, on the 22d ult., in Burke County, Georgia, where she had gone for some time, Mrs. Sarah B. Norton, of Beaufort, in this state, leaving an affectionate husband and many children.... (lines)
    Died at his father's house, in King-street, on the 10th inst., Gen. Joseph Alston, aged 38 years, formerly Governor of S. C.

Issue of September 13, 1816

    Married on Thursday evening by the Rev. Dr. Leland, Mr. Peter Ehney, of Christ Church Parish, to Mrs. Susannah Gabeau, of this city.
    Died on the 1st inst., near Pocotaligo, Mrs. Martha Hutson, the wife of Richard H. Hutson, Esq. in the 21st year of her age.

Issue of September 14, 1816

    Departed this life on the 4th inst., Mrs. Ann Bowles, in the 56th year of her age. (eulogy)

Issue of September 16, 1816

    long obituary of Gen. Joseph Alston, who died 10th inst., in the 38th year of his age.

Issue of September 21, 1816

    Departed this life on Wednesday morning the 18th inst., in the 24th year of his age, Mr. John Gribbin, printer, of Savannah. He was one of the unhappy sufferers that was in the Steam Boat, and was supposed to be the least burnt.

Issue of September 23, 1816

Died on the 19th inst., Mr. Lewis Bryer, Printer, aged 29 years, a native of London, but for the last two or three years a resident of this city.

Died, at Columbia, S. C. on the 10th inst., Mr. Jeremiah Miles, of St. Paul's Parish, left a wife and three children....

---- lately, Col. William Gill, of Granville, N. C., an old Revolutionary officer.

Died at his residence in Virginia, on the 11th inst., the Hon. John Clopton, for more than 20 years a Representative in Congress from the State of Virginia....

Issue of September 26, 1816

Married last evening, by the Rev. Bishop Dehon, Mr. George Wagner, to Miss Charlotte Ogier Martin, both of this city.

Died, on Tuesday last, Eliza Spierin Duke, an infant of John Grand H. Duke.

Departed this life, at Cordesville, St. Stephen's Parish, on the 30th of last month, in the 33d year of her age, Miss Theresa J. Detolanaire. (eulogy)

Issue of September 28, 1816

Departed this transitory life, on the 12th inst., at Hillsborough, on the Eastern Shore of Maryland, in the 59th year of his age, the Rev. Jesse Lee, late Chaplain to Congress, and for 33 years a respectable itinerant preacher among the Methodists... corpse carried to Baltimore, and deposited in the Methodist Grave-yard.

Died at Baltimore, on the 1st inst., Hugh Priestley Belles, of Sunbury, Penn., aged seven years and a half.

Issue of September 30, 1816

Married on Sunday evening, in this town, Mr. Solomon Canada, to Miss Susannah Britain. Wilmington, N. C. Recorder, 23d inst.

Died, suddenly, on the morning of the 19th inst., at New-York, Col. John Ward, of this city.

Issue of October 4, 1816

Married, on Wednesday evening last, by the Rev. Mr. Forster, Mr. Charles Banks, to Miss Harriet Edwards, daughter of the late Major Evan Edwards.

Issue of October 8, 1816

Married, on Saturday evening last, by the Rev. Dr. Buchan, Mr. John Rose, merchant, to Miss Margaret Crawford Hunter, both of this city.

Died on the 8th ult., in the 25th year of her age, Mrs. Jane Smith, widow of the late Samuel Smith, junr., principal teacher of the South-Carolina Society School.

Departed this life on the 15th ult., in the 55th year of his age, Isaac Griggs, Esq., Attorney at Law; a native of Connecticut, but for nearly thirty years a much respected inhabitant of this city.

Died, at sea, on the 22d July last, Burridge Purvis, Esq., in the 46th year of his age, a native of Scotland, and many years a respectable inhabitant of Columbia, S. C....left widow and eight children. (eulogy).

Issue of October 10, 1816

    Died, suddenly at Frankfort, on the 30th ult., Harry Innis, Esq., Judge of the U. S. Court, for the District of Kentucky.

Issue of October 11, 1816

    Died, in Hannah's Town, on Tuesday night, at a very advanced age, John Reeder, a well known black man, as having been many years Captain of the Charles Town Maroons. He is the person who in the year 1781 killed the noted and desperate robber Three Fingered Jack... He did not know his exact age, but said only a few days ago that he was a stout boy at the first peace with the Maroons in the year 1739. Kingston (Jam.) paper, 3d ult.

Issue of October 12, 1816

    Married, on Wednesday evening, 9th inst., by the Rev. Mr. Bachman, Mr. Laurent Dursse, to Miss Eliza Parker, both of this city.

Issue of October 15, 1816

    Died, suddenly on his passage from this port to South America, Lieutenant Loring Palmer, late of the U. S. army.
    Died yesterday, at half past one o'clock, in the 62d year of his age, Col. Nicholas Buxton Moore, late a Member of Congress and commandant of a Cavalry Regiment attached to the 3d division M. M.
                                Baltimore pap. 8th inst.

Issue of October 16, 1816

    death of Capt. Robert Mackay in the city of New York....
                               Savannah Museum, 14th inst.

Issue of October 17, 1816

    Died, at Willtown, on Thursday last, of the small pox, previously contracted in Charleston, Mr. Lewis Fitzgerald, a native of Virginia, but for many years past a resident of this place.
                                Georgetown Gazette, Oct. 16

Issue of October 18, 1816

    Died, in Washington City, on the 11th inst., Col. Tobias Lear, Accountant of the Department of War. (eulogy)

Issue of October 21, 1816

    Departed this life on the morning of the 17th inst., Mrs. Elizabeth Harvey, aged 85 years, 8 months and 19 days, relict of Mr. Thomas Harvey, formerly of this city (vintner) She was a native of this state...interred in the family burial ground of St. Philip's Church....

Issue of October 24, 1816

    Died at Smithville, N. C., on the 17th inst., Mr. Henry Long, aged 39 years, a native of that place, and for near 20 years past a Branch pilot of this port....

Issue of October 26, 1816

Died on Tuesday the 22d inst., Samuel Robertson, Esq., Merchant, of this city. (eulogy and lines)

Issue of October 31, 1816

Died in Franklin County, Penn. in the 102d year of her age, Mrs. Elizabeth Elder, wife of Mr. J. Elder, who is now in his 102d year. This couple was married when about 21 years of age.

Issue of November 2, 1816

Married at SummerVille, on Thursday Evening last, by the Rev. Mr. States Lee, Benjamin Singellton, Merchant, of this city, to Mrs. Elizabeth Ladson, of St. Pauls Parish.

Issue of November 9, 1816

Married in Columbia, S. C. on Thursday Evening the 31st ult., by the Rev. Mr. Capers, the Rev. William Capers, of Sumter District, to Miss Susan M'Gill, of that place.

Issue of November 14, 1816

Departed this life on the morning of the 2d instant, Miss Carolina Glover, aged 21 years and 10 months.

Issue of November 22, 1816

Departed this life at Gettysburg, on the morning of the 8th inst., in the 26th year of his age, Mr. Robert Harper, editor and proprietor of the "Adams Centinel" left a widow and two children.
                                                Chambersburg Repository

Issue of November 27, 1816

Suicide. Emanuel Levy, widower, and a man much respected put a period to his life this morning.... He has left four children, and many relatives....

Issue of November 29, 1816

Married last evening, by the Rev. Mr. Frost, Mr. John Camidge Surr, to Mrs. Lydia Pritchard, all of this city.

Issue of December 4, 1816

Died on Saturday the 30th ult., in the 27th year of his age, Mr. Charles Row.

Issue of December 7, 1816

Married on Thursday evening last, by the Rev. Mr. Frost, Thomas Parker Jun. Esq. to Miss Eleanor Legare Frost, both of this city.

Issue of December 12, 1816

Married at Workington, England, Mr. Wm. Bennet, of Senton, to Mrs. Sarah Twentyman, being the fifth time the happy couple have entered into the state of matrimony, the bridegroom is 73 years of age, and the bride 68.

Married at Savannah, on Tuesday evening the 3d inst., by the Rev. Doctor Henry Kollock, Mr. G. W. Prescott, merchant of Charleston, to Miss Ann B. Bacon, eldest daughter of Mr. Joseph Bacon, merchant, of that place.

Issue of December 13, 1816

Died on the 25th ult., Mrs. Eleanor Sarah Bonneau.... (eulogy)

Died, at Savannah, on the 4th inst., Captain George Haig, late of the U. S. Light Dragoons, an officer as highly distinguished for his gallantry, as revered for his virtues.

Issue of December 19, 1816

Married, at Augusta, on Thursday evening, the 5th inst., by the Rev. Mr. Waddle, Mr. Wm. H. Blackwell, of Columbia county, to Miss Eliza Collier, daughter of James Collier, Esq. of Abbeville District, South-Carolina.

Issue of December 21, 1816

Departed this life on Thursday the 19th inst., Mrs. Sarah Sarzedas, in the 49th year of her age. Mrs. S. was born in this city, and has left many relatives and friends....

Issue of December 24, 1816

Died on the 4th inst., Miss Elizabeth Steel, aged 21 years, a native of Ireland....

Departed from the world on the 21st inst., Mrs. Caroline Deas, wife of Thomas H. Deas, Esq. of this city. (eulogy)

Issue of December 27, 1816

Died, at Havana, about 4 weeks since, Mr. Ebenezer Stocker, Merchant, of Boston.

Issue of December 28, 1816

Married, in New-Jersey, on the 16th inst., by the Rev. Mr. Crose, Mr. John Hammel, Merchant, of New-York, to Miss Helena D. Freneau, daughter of Philip Freneau, Esq.

Issue of January 4, 1817

Married, at Columbia, on Tuesday evening, the 14th ult., the Rev. Mr. Stanley, of the Methodist Episcopal Church, to Miss Ellen Ramsay, of that place.

Issue of January 9, 1817

Died, at Wilmington (N. C.) on the 21st ult., Samuel Russell Jocelyn, Esq. of that town.

Issue of January 10, 1817

Died on Tuesday evening last, Mrs. Moore of Boston (formerly Mrs. Woodham, of the Theatre)....

Died in Philadelphia, on the 23d ult., Thomas MacDonough, Student of Medicine, cousin to the gallant Commodore of the same name.

Died at Hartford, Connecticut, on the 25th ult., the Rev. Nathan Strong, D. D., Pastor of the first Ecclesiastical Society in that town, in the 69th year of his age.

Issue of January 11, 1817

Married in Columbia, on Thursday evening the 2d inst., by the Rev. B. Montgomery, Doctor David Means to Miss Francis Coalter.

Married, in Lexington District, on the 1st inst., by the Rev. Jas. Mellard, Henry Seables, Esq. of Granby, to Miss Lavinia Baker, of Sandy Run.

Another Revolutionary patriot gone! Died at his residence in York District, on the 1st December, Col. William Hill, in the 76th year of his age.

Issue of January 13, 1817

Married, at Philadelphia, on Thursday evening, the 3d inst., Mr. Samuel Guirey, merchant, of Columbia, S. C. to Miss Eliza Venneman, of the former place.

Died at the residence of Mr. William Wilkinson, in Brunswick County, Va. Gen. John Woods, of Pittsburg, Pennsylvania, a member from that State in the Congress of the U. S.

Issue of January 15, 1817

Died, in this city, on the 7th inst., in the 35th year of her age, Mrs. Mary Moore, wife of Col. Abraham Moore, of Massachusetts...Her remains were entered (sic, for interred) in the Church Yard of St. Michaels, on the morning of the 9th inst. Left three children. (eulogy)

Died in New-Bedford, Mass. on Tuesday afternoon, the 31st of December, Elisha Thornton, aged 70--an eminent Minister in the Society of Friends.

Died, suddenly, at West-Point, on the 1st inst., Cadet Vincent M. Lowe, aged 18 years....

Issue of January 16, 1817

Died, at Philadelphia, on Sunday the 5th inst., Mrs. Elizabeth Febiger, relict of the late Col. Christian Febiger, in the 63d year of her age.

Died at Phila. on Sunday the 5th inst., in the 66th year of her age, Mrs. Anna Maria Hemsley, widow of the late William Hemsley, Esq. of the state of Maryland, and sister of Chief Justice Tilghman.

Died, on Saturday the 23d ult., at his residence at Hamilton College, in the State of New-York, the Rev. Doctor Backus, President of that Institution.

Issue of January 18, 1817

Married, at Chateaugay, Deacon Andrew Blackman, aged 77, to widow Relief Alvore, aged 71.

Married at New-York, on the 6th inst., Mr. Azor S. Marvin, of Georgetown, S. C. to Miss Delia Maria Penny, daughter of Mr. Samuel Penny, of that city.

Married, on the 18th ult., under the Painted Rock, in Buncombe County, N. C. by a Magistrate, Mr. Lewis Sawyers, Sen. aged eighty years, to Mrs. Hannah Poston, aged ninety, both of Greene county, Tennessee. The lady who waited on the bride was one hundred years old.

Died, at Cayuga, Major Peter Hughes, aged 66....
Died on the 9th inst., at his seat, in Mecklenburg county, (Va.) Presley Hinton, Esq. Merchant.

Issue of January 20, 1817

Married, at New-York, Major John Marshal Gamble, of the U. S. Marine Corps, to Miss Hannah Laetitia Lang, eldest daughter of Mr. John Lang.
Died in Schenectady, N. Y. on the 28th ult., Mr. Andrew Rynex, aged about 70 years. He was an active, valuable soldier of the revolution....
Died, in Albany, on the 1st inst., Mrs. Catalina Wendell, consort of General John H. Wendell, in the 56th year of her age.

Issue of January 21, 1817

Died on Saturday evening last, Mr. James Elsinore, aged 31 years, a native of this city.
Died at New-Haven, Conn., on Saturday the 11th inst., the Rev. Dr. Timothy Dwight, in the 65th year of his age, President of Yale College....

Issue of January 23, 1817

Died on the 20th inst., Mr. John Cripps. (eulogy)

Issue of January 24, 1817

Departed this life on the morning of the 19th inst., Miss Elizabeth Clara Prioleau, eldest child of John Cordes Prioleau, Esq. of this city. (eulogy)

Issue of January 25, 1817

Death of Mr. Alexander J. Dallas. (eulogy)
                    Phila. True American, 17th inst.

Issue of January 27, 1817

It is our painful duty to announce the death of the Rev. and venerable Dr. William Hollinshead, for many years Pastor of the Congregational Church of this city.
Departed this life on the 22d inst., Miss Mary Eliza Glen, aged 18 years 5 months and 12 days, only daughter of Mrs.Glen, widow of John Glen, Esq. Planter, of St. James, Goose-creek....

Issue of January 29, 1817

Died, in Liverpool, England, on the first of November last, Jacob Aemilius Irving, Esq. formerly of this City.
Died in Rutland, Vt., the Rev. Samuel Williams, L. L. D., Edinburg and New-Haven....
Died in New-York, on the 19th inst., Mr. William Miller, aged 72 years, an old and respectable inhabitant of that city.
     in Philadelphia, on the 20th inst., Mr. James Fullen... left widow and four small children.
     at the same place, on the 18th inst., at the advanced age of 97, Mr. Martin Rowe, late a respectable inhabitant of that city.

Issue of January 31, 1817

Married last evening, by the Rev. Mr. A. W. Leland, Mr. Gabriel W. Wayne, to Miss Mary Lane, all of this city.

Issue of February 3, 1817

Married, on the 28th ult., at Rosemont, by the Rev. Mr. Fowler, James L. Gibbes, Esq. to Miss Adelaide Gibbes Elliott, eldest daughter of the late Barnard Elliott, Esquire.

Issue of February 4, 1817

Departed this life on the 12th day of January, the Rev. Clarke Brown, Rector of William and Mary Parish, Charles County, Maryalnd....
Died at New-York, on the 25th ult., in the 77th year of his age, Jotham Post, Sen.
_____ in the island of Jamaica, on the 22d Nov. last, Mr. James R. Savage...received his education in the state of Mass., and was graduated at Harvard College, in the year 1812.

Issue of February 6, 1817

Died, at Voluntown, Conn. on the 19th ult., Miss Dolly Stanton, formerly of Guilford....

Issue of February 7, 1817

Died on the 22d ult., Anna Maria Lewis, in the 21st year of her age. (eulogy)

Issue of February 10, 1817

Married, in New-York, on the 30th ult., by the Rev. Mr. Clarke, Col. Charles K. Gardner, Adj. General of the Northern Division of the U. S. Army, to Ann Eliza M'Lean, daughter of John M'Lean, Esq. Quarter Master General of the State of New-York.

Issue of February 11, 1817

Married, on Saturday evening last, by the Rev. Mr. Frost, Mr. Edward Crow, one of the Editors of the Savannah Daily Gazette, to Miss Eliza Hislop.
Departed this sublunary state of existence, on the 7th inst., Mr. James Bulkley, in the 49th year of his age (a native of Wethersfield, Conn.) but for several years past a respectable merchant of this City....
Died on the 31st ult., aged 13 years and 5 months, Master J. B. Carey Duplat, eldest child of Mr. J. B. Duplay, merchant of this city.

Issue of February 17, 1817

Died, last evening, in this city, Mr. George Hatch, Printer, aged about 26 years, a native of Boston, Mass. Mr. Hatch's father, mother, brothers and sisters, all died of the same complaint, except one brother who was drowned.

Issue of February 20, 1817

Obituary of George A. Baker, Esq....born in Germantown, county of Philadelphia, on the 27th July 1756. (long account of Rev. service)

Issue of February 25, 1817

Married, on Sunday evening last, ghe 23d inst., by the Rev. Dr. Gadsden, Joseph George Holman, Esquire, Manager of the Charleston Theatre, to Miss Mary Latimer.
death of Edmund B. Jenkins, Esq. Surveyor General of this state, inhabitant of Milledgeville.
Milledgeville Journal.

Issue of February 28, 1817

At St. Philip's Church last evening, Major James T. Dent, of the U. S. Army, was married by the Rev. Mr. Gadsden, to Miss Catharine Ann Cooper, daughter of Major Samuel Cooper, of New-York.

Issue of March 1, 1817

Departed this life on the 15th ult., aged 23 years, Mrs. Sarah Arthur Harvey, wife of Mr. Wm. S. Harvey. This young lady was educated and protected, during her minority, by the Miss Stewards. (eulogy)

Issue of March 3, 1817

Married on Sunday evening, last, by the Rev. Mr. Cooper, Mr. Charles Henry to Miss Martha Ann Cantey, both of this city.
Married last evening, by the Rev. Mr. Schaeffer, Philip Jacobs, esq. aged 80, to Miss Eliza Brown, aged 18, all of this city.
Died in Stokes county, N. C. on the 23d ult.,Mr. Wm. Barrow, father of the Rev. David Barrow. He was 89 years of age, had been a member of the Baptist Church for near fifty years....
Died at Belmont, his seat in Wayne County, Penn., on the 10th inst., Samuel Meredith, Esq. formerly Treasurer of the U. S., aged 76 years.
Died at Pomfret, on the 4th inst., the Hon. Sylvanus Backus, member of Congress elect, aged 48.
Departed this life at Philadelphia on Monday after, 17th inst., in the 47th year of his age, Mr. George Booth, for many years an eminent Teacher, in that city.
Died in Medford, Mass., Benjamin Hall, Esq., aged 87 years. In the winter preceding the 19th of April 1775, Mr. H. then a Member of the Provincial Congress, was chosen a Member of the Committee of General Safety....
Died at Ward's Bridge, Montgomery, Orange county, N. Y., on the 10th ult., the Rev. Moses Fraeligh, Minister of the Reformed Presbyterian Dutch Church, at that place, aged 54 years.
Died in the beginning of November last, at Cape Nichola Mole, St. Domingo, in the 33d year of his age, Capt. Wm. Nicholas, late of the corps of artillery of the army of the U. S.
Died at Greenbush, N. Y. on the 6th inst., J. C. Alexander, late a Sergeant in the army...from the neighborhood of Carlisle, Penn....

Issue of March 4, 1817

Married on the 25th ult., at St. Paul's Church, by the Rev. Mr. Campbell, Edward Blake, Esq. to Miss Catharine L. Deveaux, both of this city.

Issue of March 6, 1817

Died in Georgetown, S. C. on Sunday morning last, Mr. John D. Skrine, in the 20th year of his age, eldest son of Thomas Skrine, Esq. of that town.

Issue of March 7, 1817

Married last evening, by the Rev. Dr. Gadsden, O'Brien Smith Price, Esq. planter, to Miss Elizabeth Hamilton M'Call, daughter of James M'Call, Esq. all of this city.

Issue of March 11, 1817

Married on the 24th February, by the Rev. Dr. Flinn, Thomas Hayne Simmons, Esq. of John's Island, to Miss Mary Jones Read, of Newport, R. I.

Issue of March 13, 1817

Mr. Eleazer Read, late a grocer in this place, was brought to an instant death on the 22d ult by the fall of a spar on board the schooner Hiram, when on her passage to New York. He had been absent from his family near 6 months and had taken passage in the above vessel for the purpose of visiting them.
             Georgetown S. C. Gazette, 12th inst.

Issue of March 15, 1817

Died in Worcester, Mass. on the 23d ult., the Hon. Francis Blake, aged 43, late an eminent Counsellor at Law, a distinguished Advocate at the Bar....
Died on Tuesday the 3th inst., at Baltimore, the Hon Joseph Hopper Nicholson, aged 47, Chief Judge of the sixth Judicial District, and a Judge of the Court of Appeals in Maryland.
Died in England the Rt. Hon. Charles Earl Stanhope, a conspicuous opposition member of the British house of peers.

Issue of March 18, 1817

Married, in this city, on Tuesday 11th inst.,by the Rev. Dr. Flinn, Robert Hazlehurst, Jun. Esq. to Miss Elizabeth Pettingal Wilson, only daughter of Leighten Wilson, Esq. of Brunswick, Georgia.
Died, at St. Simon's Island, at the residence of C. S. Wylly, Esq., on Wednesday, the 5th inst., Dr. George V. Proctor, health officer of the port of Savannah, aged 35 years, a native of South-Carolina. (eulogy)   Savannah Republican.

Issue of March 20, 1817

Married, on Wednesday evening, the 19th inst., by the Rt. Rev. Bishop Dehon, Mr. William Budd, to Miss Jane Videaux Miller, eldest daughter of the late William Miller, all of this city.

Issue of March 24, 1817

Departed this life, on Friday the 21st inst., Mrs. Elizabeth Prince, in the 38th year of her age...left husband and five children. (eulogy)

Died, in this city, on the 19th inst., Mr. James Gordon, aged 81 years, a native of Scotland, for upwards of 60 years a respectable merchant of this state.

Issue of March 26, 1817

Died, at Lancaster, Pa., on Friday the 14th inst., at an advanced age, the Hon. Jasper Yeates, one of the Judges of the Supreme Court of that State.

At Lexington, Mass., on Tuesday March 4th, were interred with Masonic honors, the remains of Col. John Chandler.

Issue of March 28, 1817

Married, last evening, by the Rev. Mr. Gadsden, Mr. James Poyas, to Miss Charlotte Bryer Bentham; and on the same evening also by the Rev. Mr. Gadsden, Mr. Joseph Fitch, Merchant, to Miss Caroline Hardy Bentham, all of this city.

Issue of April 2, 1817

Married last evening, by the Right Rev. Bishop Dehon, Mr. Chales Tew, to Miss Eleanor Carr, both of this city.

Issue of April 3, 1817

Married in Springfield, by the Rev. Mr. Osgood, T. Dickman, Editor of this paper, to Miss Sarah Brewer, daughter of Dr. Chauncey Brewer.

At Goshen, Maj. Ozias Humphreys, aged 60, to Miss Margaret Lish, aged 23, being the Major's fifth wife.
Hampton (Mass.) Federalist

Issue of April 4, 1817

Died on the 23d of March, at his residence on Savannah river, Barnwell District, S. C., Aaron Smith, Esq.,in the 59th year of his age. He was one of those worthies who bore the toils and difficulties of the Revolutionary war... His father, mother, a brother and sister were killed by the Indians; three brothers, one sister and himself made their escape...(long account)

Issue of April 9, 1817

Married, on the 10th ult., at Ainwell, N. J. by the Rev. Mr. Kirkpatrick, Commodore Thomas Tingey, of the Navy, to Miss Anne Evelina Craven.

Issue of April 11, 1817

Married on Thursday evening last, by the Rev. Dr. Gadsden, Major G. H. Manigault, of the U. S. Army, to Miss Ann Heyward, all of this city.

Issue of April 15, 1817

Married in Boston, on the 2d inst., in the Stone Chapel, by the Rev. Dr. Freeman, the Hon. Jonathan Russell, late Ambassador to the Court of Sweden, to Miss Lydia Smith, daughter of Barney Smith, Esq.

Issue of April 17, 1817

Died at his residence in Anson-street, on the 25th ult., Mr. Isaac Neufville, of this city, in the 50th year of his age... left an affectionate partner and six children. (eulogy)

Issue of April 18, 1817

Married, last night, by the Rev. Dr. Dalcho, Mr. Samuel Jeffords, to Miss Eliza Marsh, both of this city.
Died on the 7th inst., in the 47th year of his age, Mr. William M'Credie, a native of Scotland...left wife and four children.

Issue of April 21, 1817

Died on Monday the 14th inst.,Mrs. Eliza Gardenia Gibbs, consort of G. Gibbs, Esq. and only child of Major Alexander Garden. (eulogy)

Issue of April 22, 1817

Married, at Norfolk, on the 8th inst., by the Rev. Mr. Hall, Capt. Ethan A. Allen, of the U. S. Artillery, commanding at Craney Island, to Miss Mary Susan Johnston, second daughter of Capt. John Johnston, at Lebanon, on Tanners' Creek, Norfolk Co.
Died at Fort-Hawkins, on the 22d ult., in the 26th year of his age, Capt. Philip Hawkins, formerly an officer of the U. S. army, and late Assistant Agent for Indian Affairs....
Died in England, Thomas Taylor, the eldest preacher in the Methodist communion, aged 77....

Issue of April 24, 1817

Married in Northumberland, England, Mr. Peter Percy, aged 80, to the widow Hannah Godfrey, aged 80....

Issue of April 25, 1817

Died, on Wednesday the 16th inst., at the residence of his father, in Baltimore, Lieut. Thomas W. Magruder, of the U. S. Navy, in the 27th year of his age.

Issue of April 28, 1817

Died, at Georgetown, on Thursday morning last,in the 35th year of his age, Francis Marion Baxyer, Esq. Proprietor of the Georgetown Gazette.

Issue of April 29, 1817

Died on Friday the 11th of April, John Wheelock, L. L. D., President of Dartmouth University, aged 63 years....
Died, at his residence at Cat-Island, near Georgetown, on Thursday last, Robert Smith, Esq., in the 53d year of his age.

Departed this life on the 15th inst., Mr. Joseph Hagey, late Papermaker of Lower Merion, Montgomery county, Pa., in the 33d year of his age.

Issue of May 1, 1817

Married, in Montgomery county, K. on the 12th ult., by the Rev. W. Ray, Mr. Jesse Johnson, 18 or 19 years of age, 4 feet 1 inch high, weighing 75 pounds, to Miss Nancy Fowler, about 26 or 27 years of age, 6 feet 3 inches high, weighing about 250 lbs.

Issue of May 2, 1817

Married in Boston, on Tuesday the 15th ult., by the Rev. Dr. Freeman, Samuel M'Kay, Esq. aid de camp to Maj. Gen. Brown, to Miss Katharine Gordon Dexter, daughter of the late Hon. Samuel Dexter.

Died at the seat of the hon. Judge Hanson, Maryland, on the 25th ult. in the 38th year of his age, the Hon. Thomas P. Grosvenor, Member of Congress, from the state of New York.

Issue of May 7, 1817

Married, on Monday evening, by the Right Rev. Bishop Dehon, Mr. William Webb, late of New-York, to Miss Caroline I'ans Thorne, youngest daughter of John G. Thorne, Esq. of this city.

Died in Philadelphia, on the 26th ult., in the 73d year of his age, Mr. Frederick Heiz, for many years a respectable inhabitant of this city.

Died on the evening of the 28th ult., after a tedious illness, Mr. Joseph Williamson, an old and respectable inhabitant of the district of Southward, Penn., in the 75th year of his age.

Issue of May 8, 1817

Married on Thursday evening, the 1st inst., by the Rev. Dr. Roberts, Mr. John Frierson, of North Santee, only son of Major John Frierson, to Miss Julia Vaughan, of the High-Hills, eldest daughter of Henry Vaughan, deceased.

Issue of May 9, 1817

Died on the 25th ult., Mrs. Mary L. Thomas, relict of the Rev. John Thomas, in the 72d year of her age....(eulogy)

Issue of May 16, 1817

Married at Nottingham, England, Mr. Samuel Mabbot, aged 72, to widow Thornton aged 76... At Hudworth, Eng., Mr. Thomas Richmond, 81, to Miss Dinah Wood, 20! At Wilton, England, Mr. John Cuckton, 70 to Miss Ann Cowley, 30!

Issue of May 17, 1817

Married on Wednesday evening last, by the Rev. Dr. Palmer, Mr. James Streater Glen, to Miss Anna Sommerset Curtis, daughter of Mr. Francis S. Curtis, all of this city.

Issue of May 19, 1817

Married at New-York, on the 7th inst., by the Rev. Bishop Hobard, Leiut. Col. Croghan, to Miss Serena Livingston, daughter of John R. Livingston, Esq.

Issue of May 24, 1817

Married, on Thursday evening, the 22d inst., by the Rev. Dr. Gallagher, William Flack, Esq. of St. Paul's Parish, to Miss Julia Gallagher, of Charleston, S. C.

Issue of May 26, 1817

Married at Georgetown, S. C. on Thursday evening last, 22d inst., by the Rev. Samuel K. Hodges, Elder Anthony Senter, of the Methodist Episcopal Church, to Mrs. Elizabeth Shackelford, of that place.

Issue of May 28, 1817

Departed this life on the 9th inst., at Dr. Read's residence, on Cooper river, Mrs. Mary W. Read, wife of John Harleston Read, Esq. (eulogy)

Issue of May 29, 1817

Died at the residence of John Porter, Esq., Sampit, S. C., on Sunday the 18th inst., Mrs. Mahettaba Chapman, aged 55 years.
Died in Tewksbury, M., Deacon Ezra Kendall, aged 97 years. In Connecticut, Deacon Timothy Stanley, aged 90.

Issue of May 30, 1817

Died, on the 26th inst., in the 22d year of his age, Mr. James Rogers Harvey, a native of Boston, Mass.... (eulogy)

Issue of June 3, 1817

Died, at Savannah, on the 30th ult., Capt. John Smith, in the 32d year of his age--a native of Virginia, but for many years a respectable resident of this city....
Drowned in Savannah River, on the 24th inst., Capt. Stephen Williams, a native of the state of New York.

Issue of June 5, 1817

Married last evening, by the Rev. Dr. Gadsden, Thomas C. Mitchell, Esq. to Miss Sarah Anderson.

Issue of June 7, 1817

Married on Thursday evening last, by the Rev. Dr. Percy, Daniel Jennings Waring, Esq. to Miss Constantia Wigfall, eldest daughter of Thomas Wigfall, Esq.
Married last evening, by the Rev. Dr. Palmer, David Ramsay, Esq. to Miss Mary E. L. Pinckney, second daughter of Charles Pinckney, Esq.

Issue of June 10, 1817

Died, at Pineville, St. Stephen's Parish, on the 5th of June, Philip Porcher, Sen. aged 55 years and 2 months. (long eulogy)

Issue of June 11, 1817

Married, at Boston, on the 28th ult., by the Rev. Mr. Holley, Major Alexander S. Brooks, of the U. S. regiment of Light Artillery, to Miss Sarah Turner, of that place.

Died, at Boston, on the 30th ult., Mr. William Burdick, late Editor of the Boston Evening Gazette.

Issue of June 14, 1817

Married, on the 20th of May, 1817, near the Warm Springs (N. C.) by the Rev. Dr. Coffin, Mr. Archibald D. Nelson, to Miss Eliza M. Lines, late of St. John's Parish, Berkley (S. C.)

Issue of June 17, 1817

Married in Ontario county, N. Y. on the 16th ult., Mr. Ezekial Folsom, aged 13 years, to Miss Lucy Fitch, aged 16, daughter of Rev. Ebenezer Fitch, D. D., late President of Williams College.

Issue of June 18, 1817

Married, at Philadelphia, on the evening of the 9th inst., Francis Otway Byrd, Esq. of the U. S. Army to Miss Elizabeth R. Pleasants, of Philadelphia.

Issue of June 21, 1817

Married, at Savannah, on Saturday morning last, by John Lillibridge, Esq., Mr. John H. Clark (a native of Ireland, but a resident of this city) to Miss Susannah Harrison, daughter of Mr. John Harrison, of that place.

Married, at Augusta, on Thursday evening, the 12th inst., by the Rev. Mr. Carsin, Mr. William M'Hay, of that place, to Miss Ann Harker, of Edgefield District, in this state.

Died in the town of Greenbush, New-York, on the 8th of this month, Mr. Adam Cook, aged 96 years, who wife aged 94 years, performed for him the last pious office of closing his eyes....

Issue of June 25, 1817

Died in Philadelphia, on Saturday morning, the 14th inst., Miss Carolina Manigault, daughter of the late Gabriel Manigault, Esq., who had just completed her 14th year. (eulogy)

Died in Baltimore, the 18th inst., between the hours of one and two, in the 71st year of his age, the Most Rev. Leonard Neale, Archbishop of Baltimore....

Died, in Germany, Dr. Jung Stilling....

Issue of June 26, 1817

Died, in Marborough, Mass., Capt. John Parker at the advanced age (according to the best information) of 120 years.

Issue of July 2, 1817

Died, suddenly, on the 25th of June, Capt. James Levins, in the 30th year of his age, a native of the Isle of Wight (Eng.). He arrived in America at the age of 14...left a widow and child.

Issue of July 3, 1817

Died, in Savannah on the 12th ult., in the 46th year of his age, Jacob Deveaux, Esq. a native of this City.

Issue of July 5, 1817

Married in Wilkes County, Georgia, on the 26th ult., William C. Lyman, Esq. of the U. S. Army, to Miss Euphemia Talbot, daughter of the Hon. Matthew Talbot, Esq.

Issue of July 7, 1817

Married on the 5th inst in St. Philip's Church, by the Rev. Dr. Gadsden, Mr. Charles P. Gordon, to Miss Margaret Elizabeth Campbell, daughter of Laurence Campbell, deceased.

Issue of July 8, 1817

Raleigh, N. C. July 4
On Tuesday the 24th June last, the Rev. Mr. John Hyde Saunders, a Minister of the Gospel of the Church of England, and late Rector of the Parish of Southam, in Virginia... lived to the advanced age of 77 years.

Issue of July 10, 1817

Married at Richmond, on Saturday the 7th inst., by the Rev. David Jones, Thomas Broadway, Esq., aged 66, to Miss Maria Bowler, just turner of 15--both of Amelia County.

Issue of July 15, 1817

Died, in Philadelphia, on Saturday evening, the 5th inst., in the 76th year of his age, Adam Kuhn, M. D.

Issue of July 19, 1817

Departed this life on the 14th inst., in the 55th year of her age, Mrs. Mary Switzer, lamented by an aged Mother, a Son, and numerous relations....

Issue of July 23, 1817

death of Captain Robinson Crocker, at the port of Havana, on the 14th inst....
Called from this transitory world, on the 18th inst., in the 14th year of her age, Harriet Amanda Ward, daughter of Maj. James Ward. (lines)
Departed this life on the 18th inst., Mr. Joseph Lloyd, a native of this city in the 57th year of his age. (eulogy)

Issue of July 25, 1817

Died, on the 25th ult., at his seat in Lenoir, N. C., Gen. Bryan Whitfield, a gentleman of great wealth and respectability.

Issue of July 29, 1817

Departed this life on the 24th inst., in the 57th year of his age, Mr. James Browne, a native of England, but for 40 years a respectable resident of this place.

Issue of July 30, 1817

Departed this life on the 21st inst., Capt. William Laidler, aged 40 years and 4 months, a naive of St. Augustine, East-Florida, and 32 years a resident of this city. He has left an aged mother and three orphan children....

Issue of July 31, 1817

Departed this life on the 26th inst., Mr. Peter Wartenberg, aged 40 years and 9 months, a native of Germany, but a resident of Charleston 14 years. He has left a wife and two children. (lines)

Issue of August 1, 1817

Married, on Thursday evening, the 24th ult., by the Rev. Mr. Bachman, Mr. R. Post Johnson, to Miss Martha S. Jenkins.
Suicide. Died in this city, on the 15th inst., Mr. John Pittenger, in the 29th year of his age.... New-Brunswick paper, 17th inst.
Died at his residence in the county of Powhatan, Va., on the 24th June, the Rev. John H. Saunders, in the 76th year of his age.

Issue of August 7, 1817

death of Right Rev. Bishop Dehon on the evening of yesterday.

Issue of August 9, 1817

Married, in Cambridge, Mass., on the 24th ult., by the Rev. Dr. Gardiner, Mr. Ebenezer Flagg, to Miss Margaret P. Belin, both of this city.

Issue of August 15, 1817

Long obituary of Bishop Theodore Dehon.

Issue of August 16, 1817

Departed this life on Sunday the 18th ult., Thos. Hutchison, son of Mr. John Hutchison, of Fairfield District, S. C., in the 19th year of his age. (eulogy)

Issue of August 22, 1817

Married, last evening, by the Rev. Dr. Gadsden, Mr. Christopher Kelly, to Miss Eliza M'Devett, both of this city.

Issue of August 29, 1817

Departed this life on the Coast of Africa, in the 21st year of his age, Capt. William Murphy, a native of this place. (eulogy)

Issue of August 30, 1817

Departed this life on the 27th inst., Mr. George Griffin, son of Susannah Griffin, a native of this place, but resided in Beaufort for seven years. He has left a mother and two sisters.

Issue of September 1, 1817

Departed this life on the 29th ult., Mr. John Parrish, aged 22 years and 6 months, a native of North-Carolina...resident of this city for the last 2 years. He has left relatives in North-Carolina....

Issue of September 2, 1817

Died, on Monday morning, in the 28th year of his age, Mr. Addison Melvin, of the firm of Butler Melvin & Co., a native of Massachusetts....
Departed this life on the 29th ult., Mr. Daniel Parker, many years a resident in this city, a native of Boston, Mas., aged about 31 years. left father, mother, brother and sister in the state of Mass. His father was of the Revolutionary school...

Issue of September 3, 1817

Died at Rockaway (Long-Island) in the State of New-York, on Saturday evening, 23d ult., Joseph George Holman, Esqr., Tragedian, and Manager of the Theatre in this city.

Issue of September 4, 1817

Died at Camden, S. C., on the 25th ult., Mrs. Mary H. Johnston, wife of Mr. P. W. Johnston, former printer of the "Camden Gazette."
Died on the 2d inst., William Hunt, aged 26 years, a native of Edinburg, and resident in this city 3 months....
Departed this life on the 25th ult in the 30th year of his age, Lieut. Thomas W. Legge, of the Marine Corps of the U. S.
Died at Watering Place, Rockaway, Long Island, on Sunday morning, the 24th of August, Joseph George Holman, Esq. in the 53d year of his age. a native of England, and a descendant of Sir John Holman, Bart. of Wakeworth Castle, Banbury. (account)

Issue of September 5, 1817

Death of Richard Brashers, an officer in the Navy....
Departed this life at the General Hospital, on James Island, Mr. Mathew Quigley, a soldier of the U. S. corps of Artillery.
Died on the 13th August, Mr. John Lee Thornhill, aged 45 years, a native of England, but a resident of this city 30 years.

Issue of September 6, 1817

Died, on Saturday the 30th ult., in St. Stephen's Parish, Mrs. Mary-Ann June, consort of Mr. John Stephen June.

Issue of September 8, 1817

Departed this life on the 4th inst., Miss Margaret E. Curtis, in the 13th year of her age....
Died on Sunday morning, Miss Martha Elizabeth Bounetheau, aged 8 years, 6 months and 18 days; second daughter of Mr. Edward Weyman Bounetheau.
Died at Haddrill's Point, on Friday, the 5th inst., Mr. Henry Hunt, a native of New-Orleans....

Issue of September 9, 1817

Died, on the 4th inst., in the 15th year of his age, Miss Ann E. Nichols, a native of Vermont. (eulogy)

Died, on Saturday morning, Master Edwin C. Folker, son of Mr. Joseph Folker.

Issue of September 10, 1817

Died in this city, on the 30th ult., in the 21st year of his age, Mr. Nathan Gile, a native of Boston, Mass.

Issue of September 13, 1817

On death of Miss Mary Kandal, a native of England, who departed this life on the 5th inst., AE 21. (lines)

Died in St. Paul's Parish, on the 9th inst., John F. N. Farr, in the 23d year of his age. (eulogy)

Died, at Sullivan's Island, on the night of the 10th inst., Mr. Richard Chapman Goodwin, aged 30 years, son of Capt. Ozias Goodwin, of Boston, and late of the firm of Greenleaf & Goodwin, merchants, of this city.

Died on the 5th instant, James D. Windsor, in the 5th year of his age, eldest son of Capt. Thomas Windsor.

Issue of September 15, 1817

Died, on the 13th inst., at the house of his afflicted parents, in Archdale-street, in the 21st year of his age, Isaac Mazyck, the third son of William Mazyck, of this city.

Issue of September 17, 1817

Died, at Savannah, on the 9th inst., Mrs. Elizabeth S. Mork, aged 21 years and 7 months, daughter of Isaac Course, Esq., merchant of that city, and wife of Lieut. James Mork....

Departed this life on the evening of the 10th inst., in the 14th year of her age, Miss Harriet Prince Course, youngest daughter of Isaac Course, Esq. of Savannah. (eulogy)

Issue of September 18, 1817

Died, at Savannah, on the 11th inst., in the 76th year of her age, Mrs. Agnes M'Cleish, a native of Scotland, but for upwards of 40 years past a resident of this city.

Issue of September 19, 1817

Died, in the village of Cannonborough, adjoining Charleston, on Wednesday last, Daniel Webb Logan, youngest child of Mr. William Logan, of that place.

Issue of September 20, 1817

Died on the 13th inst., in the 6th year of her age, Sarah Arrabella Withers Read, only daughter of J. H. Read, Esq....

Issue of September 25, 1817

Died on Sunday morning, the 21st inst., Elizabeth L. L. Hutchinson, aged 3 years and 10 months, only daughter of the late Leger Hutchinson, esq. (eulogy)

Died on the 21st day of Sept inst., Wiley Gresham, Esq., in the 24th year of his age...a native of Green County, Ga., and had come to this State, to reside as a Merchant. (eulogy)

Died on the 20th in the 23d year of his age, Mr. Richard Tunis, a native of Philadelphia, and partner in the house of Coates, West & Tunis, of this place....

On Sunday last, died in this city, Thomas Mellichamp, Esq. of St. Paul's Parish, eldest son of Saint Lo Mellichamp, Esq of the same place....

Died, at Wilmington, N. C. on the 17th inst., in the 29th year of his age, Col. Thornton A Posey, late of the U. S. Army. Col. Posey was a native of Virginia, and the son of Gov. Posey, a distinguished veteran of the Revolution.

Issue of September 26, 1817

Died on Wednesday morning the 24th inst., Elizabeth Ann Browne, aged 5 years, only daughter of the late James Browne, Esq.

Died on the 8th inst., in the 21st year of his age, Mr. Christian H. Schwartz, a native of Bremen....

Issue of September 27, 1817

Died, on the 17th inst., Mr. John Walton, late Treasurer of the Lower Division of this State. (eulogy)

Died at Augusta, Ga., on Thursday evening, the 18th inst., Capt. Samuel W. Miller, aged 27 years, a native of this city....

Died at Mount Vernon, on the 17th inst., Richard Henry Lee Washington, grand nephew of the illustrious Gen. Washington.

Issue of September 29, 1817

Long obituary of Dr. James Macbride.

Issue of September 30, 1817

Departed this life on the 20th inst., Mrs. Eliza L. Brailsford, wife of Capt. Robert Brailsford, of Clarendon County, Sumter District.

Issue of October 1, 1817

Died on the 23d ult., William Trescott, Esq. in the 34th year of his age. (eulogy)

Died on the 26th of September, Mr. Mordecai Hyams, aged 30 years, a native of England, and a resident of this city 7 years. He has left a wife and three children....

Issue of October 2, 1817

Death of Mrs. Susanna Elsworth, wife of Theophilus Elsworth, Esq. of this city, who departed this life on Saturday the 21st day of September, aged 59 years and 4 months....

Died at Newar, Miss Mary Beach, aged 16, and on Thursday, Alfred (about 7 years old) son of Mr. William Peck...
New York Gaz.24th ult.

Departed this life at the house of Mr. Forester in Richmond Co., Va., the Rev. Henry Padget, a circuit rider in the Methodist connexion. Lately, at Farnham Church, Richmond County, Mr. Francis A. Mongar, formerly a Minister in the Methodist connexion.
Georgetown D. C. Messenger

Issue of October 6, 1817

Departed this life on the 12th ult., Mr. David Cochran, a native of New-Hampshire....
Died in this city on the 30th ult., aged about 23 years, Mr. Alexander M'Innes, a native of Richmond County, N. C.
Died on the night of the 22d ult., at the Plantation of Capt. William Humphreys, near Jamesville, Sumter District, S. C., Capt. Francis Noble, late from Boston, Mass.
Died in Columbia, S. C., on the 26th ult., Mr. William Chapman, of that place, Coachmaker, aged 28 years...two years' residence in Columbia....
Died in Columbia, S. C., on the 28th ult., aged 26 years, Mr. Jacob Daten, Carpenter,or a Sailor. He was a native of New-York, and had been but a few days from Charleston.

Issue of October 7, 1817

Departed this life on the 30th of September, Mrs. Mary Gouldsmith, aged 63 years and 8 months, a native of England, and a resident of New-York, for 14 years...left husband and son....

Issue of October 8, 1817

Died, on Thursday, the 2d inst., Miss Ann Bailey, in the 16th year of her age....

Issue of October 10, 1817

Death of Urban Cooper, the humble and faithful Divine. (eulogy)
Died on the 3d of this month, Miss Angelina Mary Eliza Heath, in the 6th year of her age.
Died, in New-York, on the 30th ult., Mrs. Mary Sutton, wife of Capt. George Sutton.
Died, at Middlebury, Vt., Mr. Solomon M. Allen, Professor of Langauges in Middlebury College....

Issue of October 11, 1817

Died on the morning of the 8th inst., the Rev. Urban Cooper, aged 27 years 3 months and 4 days, a minister of the Methodist Episcopal church. (eulogy)
Died in Augusta, on Monday night, the 27th ult., Captain Kenneath Mackenzie, of the 4th Battallion U. S. Artillery, in the 51st year of his age.
Died, in Savannah, on the 7th inst., Michael Keating, a native of Ireland, for many years a resident of this city, and lately a lieutenant in the patriot service.
Died at his residence near M'Cords Ferry, on Tuesday the 30th ult., in the 75th year of his age, Captain Richard Brown.

Issue of October 14, 1817

Married, on Saturday evening last, by the Rev. Dr. Furman, Mr. Godfrey Humbert, to Mrs. Elizabeth Patterson, both of this city.

Issue of October 16, 1817

Died, at Stroud, in the County of Gloucester, England, in July last, Henry Wyatt, Esq. in the 80th year of his age, brother of Peter Wyatt, Esq. of this city.

Issue of October 18, 1817

Died, in Edgefield District, on the 3d inst., at the house of Col. C. Breigthaupt, Benjamin C. Yancey, Esq. Attorney at Law, aged 34 years.

Issue of October 21, 1817

Died on the 15th inst., in the 12th year of his age, Master Oliver Utt, formerly attached to the Theatre....His parents have been left childless.

Issue of October 22, 1817

Departed this life on the 5th inst., at his father's residence in Marlborough District, in the 19th year of his age, Mr. Lewis Pledger, second son of Major Wm. Pledger....(eulogy)

Issue of October 23, 1817

Died, on the 14th inst., William Mathewes, Sen., Esq., in the 62d year of his age. He has left a widow, children, and many relatives to mourn this sad bereavement. (lines)

Issue of October 24, 1817

Married, last evening, in St. Michael's Church, by the Rev. Dr. Dalcho, Elias Horry, Esq., late intendant of this city, to Miss Mary Rutledge Shubrick, of Belvedere.

Issue of October 28, 1817

Married on Tuesday evening, the 16th inst., by the Rev. Dr. Furman, Mr. John P. Young, to Miss Mary Emeline Shecut, eldest daughter of Dr. J. L. E. W. Shecut, all of this city.
Died, at Dickson's Island, on the 21st inst., Mrs. Susannah Rivers, consort of Francis Rivers, and daughter of the late John Holmes, of John's Island, deceased...left husband, a tender infant, and brothers and sisters.

Issue of November 3, 1817

Died, on Friday morning last, at Cordesville, St. John's, Berkley, Dr. James Ravenel...(eulogy)

Issue of November 8, 1817

Died on Wednesday, the 29th of October, John Ball, Esq. of St. John's, Berkley. (eulogy)

Issue of November 12, 1817

Married on Saturday afternoon, at St. Philip's Church, by the Rev. Dr. Gadsden, James Holmes, Esq. to Miss Sarah Freer, both of this city.
Departed this life on Wednesday evening, the 5th inst., Mrs. Elizabeth Gardiner, a native of Rathfriland, County of Down, Ire-

land; this lady came with her Husband and children, accompanied by her sister, sailed from Newry, on board the Indian Hunter, for Norfolk Vir. with the intention of settling at Richmond....left husband and four small children. (eulogy)

Died at Beaufort, S. C. on the 24th of October last, Mrs. Ann Barnwell, relict of Major Gen. Barnwell, aged 63 years.

Died at Savannah, on the 5th inst., in the 66th year of his age, Capt. Thomas Rice....

Issue of November 14, 1817

Died, at Hampstead, on the 7th of this month, Master Henry Doddridge Bennett, eldest son of Henry Bennett, aged 7 years and 4 months.

Issue of November 22, 1817

Married on Tuesday the 18th inst.,by the Rev. Mr. Galluchat, Mr. Huria B. Clark to Miss Mary Forshaw, both of this city.

Issue of November 26, 1817

Married, last evening, the 25th inst., by the Rev. Dr. Gadsden, Edward P. Simons, Esq. to Miss Catharine Paterson, youngest daughter of Hugh Paterson, Esq.

Issue of November 27, 1817

Death of Dr. Joseph Kirkland...born in Fairfield District, S. C., on the 21st of March 1770, and commenced the study of Medicine at Columbia...in 1795 removed to Charleston. (long account)

Issue of November 28, 1817

death of Master Chas. Samuel Faber, eldest son of Mr. Christian Henry Faber, who died on the 18th inst....(eulogy)

Issue of December 2, 1817

Died on the 26th ult., Mr. John Brown, a native of Portgleone, Ireland, and lately arrived in this country. He was only 21 years old....

Issue of December 3, 1817

Married last evening, by the Rev. Mr. Forster, Mr. James M. Spears, to Miss Margaret Belcher, both of this city.

Issue of December 4, 1817

Married, last evening, Dec. 3d, by the Rev. Dr. Flinn, Mr. William Steel, Merchant, to Miss Eliza Holmes, all of this place.

Departed this life on the morning of the 26th November, in the 33d year of her age, Mrs. Charlotte A. Wilson, consort of John L. Wilson, Esq., of this town....

Winyaw (S. C.) Intelligencer, 3d inst.

Issue of December 12, 1817

Married, on Wednesday Evening last, by the Rev. Dr. Flinn, Mr. S. H. Skinner, one of the Editors of the City Gazette, to Miss Annette Haines, of New-York

Issue of December 13, 1817

Married, on Thursday evening last, by the Rev. Dr. Dalcho, Jacob Axson Jun. Esq. to Miss Sarah B. Bryan, all of this city.

Issue of December 15, 1817

Married, on Thursday the 11th inst., at St. Andrew's Church, by the Rev. Dr. Buchan, James Calder, Esq. to Miss Jane Elizabeth Mitchell.
Died on the 26th Nov., Mr. Jacob Boyer, aged 63 years and 10 months. He was a native of Germany, but a resident of this city 35 years....

Issue of December 17, 1817

Died, on the 9th inst., Mrs. Ann Neufville, Sen. of this city, in the 75th year of her age. (eulogy)

Issue of December 18, 1817

Married on Tuesday the 2d of December, by the Rev. Dr. Campbell, Miss Caroline Matilda Deveaux, to Mr. Andrew Ashe, both of this place.

Issue of December 20, 1817

Married on Saturday last, by the Rev. Mr. Rater, Mr. Jonathan Caldwell, Printer, of this city, to Miss Rebecca Storts, of Delaware. (lines) Phila Demo Press

Issue of December 23, 1817

Married, last evening, by the Rev. Dr. Furman, Mr. William Given, to Mrs. Barbara Stine, both of this city.

Issue of December 26, 1817

Died in Georgetown, S. C., on Tuesday evening, the Rev. Anthony Senter, of the Methodist Church. He preached in almost every part of our state, and in much of North-Carolina. (eulogy)
Died on Pee Dee, on Wednesday last, Mrs. Martha Grier, aged 55 years....
Died at New-Orleans, a few weeks ago, Charles G. Roerstler, late a Lt. Col. in the Army of the U. S.
Died on the 23d November, at New-Orleans, William G. C. Claiborne, late Gov. of Louisiana and recently chosen Senator of the U. S. from that state.

Issue of December 27, 1817

Married at Black River, on Thursday evening, the 18th inst., by the Rev. Mr. Cousar, Mr. Benjamin Hammet, of this city, to Miss Isabella Eliza Nelson, eldest daughter of Mr. James Nelson, of the former place.
Married on Wednesday evening last, by the Rev. Dr. Gadsden, Mr. Daniel Miller, to Miss Elizabeth Love, of this city.

Issue of December 31, 1817

    Married on Tuesday evening, the 23d inst., by the Rev. Dr. Flinn, Mr. Felix Long, to Miss Maria Bennett, both of this city.
    Departed this life on the 11th inst.,Mrs. Elizabeth B. Hatter, born in the city of New-York, and third daughter of the Hon. Judge Wm. Smith, of that city, who was one of His Majesty's Privy Council before the Revolution, and also one of the founders of the Wall-street Presbyterian Church. This lady married Mr. John Torrans, and settled in this city, where she has been a resident sixty odd years, and at the advanced age of 82 years.... (eulogy)

Issue of January 3, 1818

    On the 20th ult., departed this life, Mr. John Jennings Jeannerett, in the 29th year of his age...left wife and two small children...remains depostied in the Burial Ground of the Circular Church.

Issue of January 30, 1818

    It is our painful duty to announce the death of Dr. Wistar...
                                            Phil. Daily Advertiser

Issue of February 16, 1818

    Died, on the 18th inst., near Orangeburg, Mr. Alexander Christie Jun. aged 30 years

Issue of March 6, 1818

    Married last evening, by the Right Rev. Nathaniel Bowen, D. D., John M. Ogier, Esq. to Miss Providence Grimball Jenkins, both of this city.
    Married on Thursday last, by the Right Rev. Nathaniel Bowen, D. D., Henry W. Peronneau, Esq. to Miss Mary S. Coffin, eldest daughter of Ebenezer Coffin, deceased.

Issue of March 7, 1818

    Married on Wednesday the 4th inst., by the Rev. Dr. Gadsden, J. E. Holmes, Esq. to Miss Mary Holmes, daughter of Wm. Holmes, Esqr.

Issue of March 11, 1818

    Died at Havana, on the 25th ult., James Roddey, Esq. a native of Virginia, and for many years past a respectable merchant....
    Died at the place of his usual residence in York District, on the 19th ult., William Pettus, Esq. a native of Virginia, but for many years a respectable and useful citizen of this State; held a seat in the Legislature...left wife and large family of children...member of the Baptist Church.
    Died, June last, in Augusta, Geo., Mr. John M. Castens, a native of Bremen, Germany.

Issue of April 25, 1818

    Married on Wednesday evening last, by the Rev. Dr. Furman, Joseph Paine, Esq. of the House of Lovell & Paine, to Miss Harriet, daughter of the late Morton Brailsford, Esq. all of this city.

Issue of May 6, 1818

Died in St. Paul's Parish, on the 21st ult., Robert Mackewn Haig, M. D., in the 41st year of his age. (eulogy)

Issue of May 9, 1818

Married, on Wednesday May 6th, by the Rev. R. De Clorivere, Mr. W. H. Brown, to Mrs. C. Grady, both of this city.

Issue of May 11, 1818

Married on Thursday, the 7th inst., by the Rev. Dr. Gadsden, Dr. Alexander W. Garden, of Clarendon County, Sumter District, to Miss Anna Maria Brailsford, of Charleston, S. C.

Issue of May 25, 1818

Married last evening, by the Rev. Mr. Fowler, Mr. Edmund Horatio Jermyn, of Ipswich (England) to Miss Millisent Carlton Abbott, of this City.

Issue of May 28, 1818

Departed this transitory life on Saturday the 16th of May 1818, by the upsetting of a boat on Wando River, opposite Cat Island about 17 miles from this city, on his way to a Camp Meeting, Capt. Joseph Quinby, a native of Newburyport, in the state of Massachusetts, for about 30 years a resident of this city, 20 of which he hald a commission in the 29th Regt....born 16th May 1764.

Issue of June 8, 1818

Married on Saturday evening last, by the Rev. Dr. Furman, Capt. Joseph Callender, of Boston, to Miss Ann Catharine Hippius, of this City.
Death of Mrs. Mary Ann Robinson, who died 31st of May, 1818, aged 55 years 1 month and 19 days. (eulogy)
Died, aged 62, at Kalorama, on the evening of the 30th of May, Mrs. Ruth Barlow, relict of the late Joel Barlow...a native of Connecticut. (eulogy)

Issue of September 7, 1818

Married in Belfast, Ireland, the Rev. John Worthington Fea, Rector of St. George's Church, to Miss Anna Maria Lynn, daughter of Robert Lynn, Sen. esq. of that place.

Issue of September 9, 1818

Died in Cedar Street, in the City of New-York, on the 31st ult., Gabriel M. Bounetheau, Esq. for upwards of 20 years a public officer of the City of Charleston....

Issue of September 15, 1818

Married on Sunday evening last, by the Rev. Mr. Bachman, Mr. Augustus D. Gaffarbelly, to Miss Eliza Ann Sanders, both of this place.

Issue of September 17, 1818

Departed this life on the 6th inst., Jeffrey Otis Prentiss, Esq. of St. Helena Island, in the 25th year of his age...left widow, three children, a mother and two sisters....

Died at Georgetown, S. C., on Saturday the 12th inst., Jacob Motte Alston, Esq. in his 21st year.

Monday morning, the 7th inst., terminated the probation of Mrs. Martha Shackleford, consort of John Shackelford, Esq. Cashier of the Branch Bank in this town, in the 58th year of her age, and the 35th of her residence where she in early life removed from Bermuda, the place of her nativity. *Winyaw Intelligencer*

Issue of September 23, 1818

Died on the 13th inst., in the 56th year of his age, George Smith, Esq. (eulogy)

Issue of October 12, 1818

Departed this life on the 8th inst., Mrs. Frances Henrietta Hayne, wife of Robert Hayne, esq., in the 28th year of her age. (eulogy)

Died, on board the ship Diana, on the 23d August, on her passage from Liverpool to his port, Mr. James Broadfoot, formerly a respectable merchant of this city.

Issue of October 28, 1818

Departed this life on Sunday the 31 inst., in the 41st year of her age, Mrs. Rebecca E. Frink, relict of Mr. Thomas Frink, for many years a respectable merchant of this city....

Departed this life on the 15th inst., in the 34th year of his age, William B. Tucker, Esq., Register of Mesne Conveyance, for Charleston District. (eulogy)...left widow, mother, brother, sister....

Issue of October 29, 1818

Departed this life on Saturday the 7th inst., Mrs. Anna Heyward, the wife of Capt. Josias Heyward, of Prince William's Parish...husband and children are left....

Issue of November 16, 1818

Married on Tuesday evening last, by the Rev. Dr. Gadsden, Edward D. Perry, Esq. to Miss Rachel C. Carroll, eldest daughter of Bartholomew Carroll, Esq. of this city.

Died on the 24th ult., on his way home from the Warm Springs, in North-Carolina, Doctor John P. Gough, aged about 40 years....

Died on Tuesday the 10th inst., Mr. Benjamin Minott, aged 26 years, a native of this city. (eulogy)

Died near Camden, S. C., on he 20th ult., Major Greene M. Duke, in the 45th year of his age.

Issue of November 25, 1818

Married on Thursday evening last, by the Rev. Dr. Flinn, Mr. Gardner Haford, of Providence, R. I. to Miss Ann Goodwin Williamson, youngest daughter of the late Mr. Benjamin Williamson, of Georgetown, S. C.

Issue of December 4, 1818

Married on Wednesday last, December 2, 1818, by the Rev. Dr. Gadsden, Mr. John T. Wightman, to Miss Eliza Stoll, both of this city.

Issue of February 5, 1819

Married on Tuesday evening last, by the Rev. Mr. Foster, William Smith, Esq. of the house of Low, Wallace & Co., Savannah, to Miss Kitty F. Righton, daughter of Mr. Joseph Righton, of this city.
Died in Prince William's Parish, on the 31st ult., Miss Amariathea Perkins Lockwood, in the 24th year of her age, daughter of Joshua Lockwood, Esq.
Died at Milledgeville, Geo., Mr. Flemming Grantland, one of the Editors of the Georgia Journal...left wife and two children.

Issue of February 10, 1819

Departed this life on the morning of the 5th inst., in the 41st year of her age, Miss Elizabeth Prioleau, daughter of Samuel Prioleau, Esq. deceased....

Issue of April 23, 1819

Married, in this City, on Thursday evening, the 22d April, by the Rev. R. Simmes, D. D., Gov. Morris Wilkins, Esq. of New York, to Miss Mary Somarsall Ward, eldest daughter of the late Col. John Ward, of this City.

Issue of April 29, 1819

Died, of a bullet wound, on the 10th inst., on the Florida side of St. Mary's River, opposite Trader's Hill in this state, Lt. Wm. H. Belton, of the 4th Regiment U. S. Infantry...in a duel.   Darien Gaz. 26th inst.

Issue of May 1, 1819

Married in Philadelphia, on Monday the 5th ult., by the Rev. Mr. Kemper, Mr. Samfs L. Freer, of Charleston, S. C. to Miss Elizabeth W. Tillton, of that city.
Died on the 23d ult., at Belmont, in the 33d year of his age, the Hon. Alexander C. Manson, Senator of the U. S. from Maryland.
Died at Sacket's Harbor, on the 14th ult., Lt. Lewis German, of the U. S. Navy, and son of Gen. Obadiah German, of Chenango... left widow and two children.

Issue of May 3, 1819

Died on Friday last at the residence of General Youngblood, St. Bartholomew's Parish, Mr. Thomas Singleton, in the 27th year of his age. (eulogy)

Issue of May 7, 1819

Departed this life on Monday morning 3d inst., Mrs. Anna Catharine Horlbeck, widow of the late Mr. Peter Horlbeck, in the 66th year of her age.
Died on the 29th ult. at his seat in Kent co., Md., Thomas S. Smith, Esq. in the 89th year of his age...he was among the last of the survivors...of the convention that formed the con-

stitution of Maryland, in 1776, and a member of the Council of Safety of the state during the Revolutionary War.
Died lately in Marblehead, Capt. Nathan Bartlett, aged 70. He was on the pension list and the only remaining officer on that list in Marblehead...(long account)

Issue of May 13, 1819

Died, on Wednesday the 5th inst., Mr. William V. Howard, in the 52d year of his age....left widow and three children.

Issue of May 29, 1819

Married here yesterday, by the Rev. Dr. Buchan, Henry Molin(?) of Savannah, to Miss Helen, only daughter of Mr. Joseph M'Innes of this city.

Issue of June 2, 1819

Departed this mortal life on the 21st ult., at his plantation on the Island of St. Helena, Capt. Benjamin Jenkins, in the 41st year of his age...left a wife and four small children....
Died, in New-York, on Saturday the 22d of May, in the 84th year of his age, Hugh Williamson, M. D., L. L. D. Fellow of the American Philosophical society.

Issue of June 23, 1819

Died, in this city, on the 17th inst., in the 39th year of his age, Mr. Thomas H. Whitney.

Issue of July 12, 1819

Married in Baltimore, Lt. Commander Alexander Clanton, of the U. S. Navy, to Miss Rodolphe Lavall.
death of James O'Connor, Esq. Senior Editor of the "Norfolk and Portsmouth Herald"...

Issue of July 28, 1819

Died on Wednesday last, Mr. David Langston, a respectable merchant of this city....
death of Doctor Allen, a young Physician and lately from the Medical Institution of Philadelphia... Augusta Herald, 23d inst.

Issue of September 6, 1819

Died on Friday morning, the 27th ult., Mr. Michael B. Latimer of Vermont, Superintendant of the Sabbath School No. 1. of this city...left a mother and two sisters....
Departed this life on the 1st inst., Mr. James Epilwraith(?), aged __ years, Printer.

Issue of September 10, 1819

Died on Wednesday afternoon, aged 53 years, Gen. John Rutledge, of South Carolina...son of the late Gov. Rutledge....
Phila Adv. 3d inst.

Issue of November 26, 1819

Married, on Tuesday evening last, at the house of Wm. Aiken, Esq. in King street, by the Rev. Mr. Gadsden, William K. Pledger, of Marlborough District, to Miss Mary Ann Dalton, of this city.

(The only issue extant from 1820 has no notices pertinent to this volume.)

Issue of January 2, 1821

Married in Kingwood township, Hunterdon county, N. Jersey, on the 2d ult., by the Rev. Mr. D. Bateman, Master Nathaniel Rittenhouse, aged seventeen, to Miss Sarah Taylor, aged thirteen, both of the above mentioned place.

Issue of January 3, 1821

Died on board the Catharine, on her passage from Havana to this port, on the 29th ult., Mr. George Munro, of yellow fever. Mr. Munro had been for some time residing in Cuba, and was his way to visit his family at Bristol, R. I.

Issue of January 9, 1821

Married, on Sunday evening last, by the Rev. Dr. Gadsden, Mr. James P. Seaward, of New-York, to Miss Elizabeth Bering, daughter of Mr. John Bering, of this city.
Married at Boston, Mr. John Milk, to Miss Eliza Waters. (lines)

Issue of January 12, 1821

Married in this city, last evening, by the Rev. Dr. Buchan, Mr. Virgil Maxcy, formerly of Boston, to Miss Elizabeth Ann Maxcy, of Edisto Island.
Died on the 19th ult., Christopher Wotton, a native of Brunswick, N. C. but for many years a Pilot for the bar and harbor of Charleston....

Issue of January 13, 1821

Died, at Nassau, N. P., 23d October last, the Hon. James Moss, aged 61 years.

Issue of January 17, 1821

Married, at Edisto Island, on Wednesday evening, the 3d inst., by the Rev. Dr. Buchan, Mr. John Hanahan, to Miss Martha Mary Murray; and Mr. William Clarke, to Miss Abigail Jenkins Murray, daughters of the late Joseph J. Murray, Esq., Planter, of Edisto Island.

Issue of January 22, 1821

Died, on the 19th inst., Mrs. M. Hyams, aged 41, wife of Mr. Samuel Hyams, of this city....

Issue of January 24, 1821

Died, on the Coast of Africa, on board the U. S. ship John Adams, Midshipman James M. Freeman, of Sandwich, in the state of Massachusetts. In the action of the 11th Sept 1814, on Lake Champlain, he was associated with the gallant officers who achieved that distinguished victory....
Died on the Coast of Africa, on board the U. S. Ship John Adams, Midshipman, Henry E. Turner, of Newport, R. I....

Issue of January 25, 1821

death of Mr. Levi Maxcy, Jun. eldest son of Levi Maxcy, Esq. formerly of Boston, who departed this life on Tuesday night, Jan. 17, 1821....

Issue of January 30, 1821

Died on the 16th inst., Mr. James S. Fraser, Printer, aged 31 years, son of Hugh Fraser, deceased, formerly of this city. left a brother and other relatives.
Died at New-York, on Saturday the 20th inst., the Rev. Solomon Allen, in the 70th year of his age, formerly of Northampton, Mass. father of Messrs. S. & M. Allen.

Issue of January 31, 1821

Died in this city, yesterday, Capt. Abiel Wardwell, aged about 45, commander of the brig Elizabeth, of Salem, of which place Capt. W. was a native.

Issue of February 1, 1821

The Rev. the Clergy, and the Friends of the Rev. Dr. Donald M'Leod are invited to attend his Funeral This Afternoon...from the house of Mrs. Munro, No. 36 Church-street.

Issue of February 3, 1821

Married, on Thursday evening last, by the Rev. Mr. Boice, Mr. A. M'Neill Burke, to Miss Caroline M'Lean.
Died, at New-Orleans, on the 8th Jan. last, John R. Cleary, Esq. late Sheriff of Charleston District, in the 69th year of his age.

Issue of February 7, 1821

Died, on Sunday, the 28th ult., Mr. John Horry Ferguson, aged 57 years, and on the Thursday following, his relict Mrs. Rebecca Ferguson, ceased to be among the living, in the 52d year of her age.

Issue of February 15, 1821

Married on the evening of the 8th inst., by the Rev. James H. Mellard, Col. William Mellard, to Miss Mary Elizabeth Shingler, of St. James Goose-creek Parish.

Issue of February 17, 1821

Departed this life on the 5th inst., Mr. James George Bowles, in the 24th year of his age. (eulogy)

Issue of February 26, 1821

Died, in Philadelphia, on the 13th inst., Mrs. Martha Gadsden, of Charleston, South-Carolina, relict of the late Thomas Gadsden, Esq.

Issue of March 1, 1821

Died, at Waterloo (N. Y.) 30th ult., Mr. David Milner, a native of England, and an old resident of Geneva, aged 57... (lines)

Issue of March 3, 1821

Died in Pendleton District on the 8th ult., in the 24th year of his age, Mr. William Lee, late of this city.
Died, at Nice (in France), on the 12th November last, Mrs. Eliza C. Turnbull, consort of William Turnbull, and daughter of the late Rev. Dr. Percy, of this city.

Issue of March 7, 1821

Died, on Sunday the 11th February, in the 85th year of his age, Capt. John Johnson, a native of the city of New York, but for upwards of 43 years last past a resident of this city. (long account). Rev. War soldier.

Issue of March 10, 1821

Married, on Thursday evening, by the Rev. Mr. Bachman, Mr. Jno. H. Jenkins, of Beaufort, S. C. to Miss Maria E. Casey, of this place.

Issue of March 14, 1821

Departed this life on Sunday the 18th February in the 48th year of her age, Anna Maria Graeser, consort of C. I. Graeser, of this city. (eulogy)

Issue of March 16, 1821

Departed this life on the 11th inst., Robert Wilson, M. D., in the 51st year of his age....(eulogy)

Issue of March 17, 1821

Died on the 9th inst., Mary Drinker Hort, wife of Benjamin S. Hort, of this city, in the 30th year of her age.
Died on Tuesday 13th inst., Mr. Samuel Stilwill, aged 38 years, a native of New-Brunswick, State of New-Jersey, but for the greatest part of his life a resident of New-York...on a visit to this city in search of health.

Issue of March 22, 1821

Died, at the Matanzas (Cuba) on the 22d ult., Major O. Burton, late of the U. S. Army. He had left his residence at West Point, last December....

Issue of March 23, 1821

Married on Thursday the 22d inst., by the Rev. Mr. Honour, Mr. Joshua Plair Legare, to Miss Rebecca E. R. Chinners, all of this city.
Died at Columbia, on the 18th inst.,Mr. Francis W. Donlevy, Merchant, aged 34 years. Mr. D. was a former resident of this city....a native of the county of Sligo, Ireland.

Issue of March 29, 1821

Departed this life on Wednesday the 12th ult., Mr. Charles Frish, aged 78 years and two days, Mr. Frish was a native of Germany, but for near half a century an inhabitant of this city. (eulogy)

Issue of April 6, 1821

Died on Friday last, in the 63d year of his age, Mr. Samuel Herron, Merchant of Columbia. Mr. Herron, was a native of the county Down, Ireland, and emigrated to this country about 30 years ago, nearly twenty of which he has been a resident of this place.... Colum. Telescope

Issue of April 7, 1821

Died, at Prospect-Hill, near Stateburg, on the 15th ult., Martha A. F. Roberts, the consort of the Rev. John M. Roberts.

Issue of April 11, 1821

Died at Providence, R. I.,on the 27th ult., Gardner Daggett, Esq. aged 39.

Issue of April 13, 1821

Married, last evening, by the Rev. Mr. Dalcho, James Creighton, Esq. of Baltimore, Md., to Ann, daughter of the late Gen. John M'Pherson, of this city.
Drowned, on the 25th of March last, as he was going to Georgetown, from North Island, in a sail boat, Mr. Eli S. Bostwick, aged about 39 years...a native of Connecticut, a carpenter and a house-joiner....
Died at Aberdeen, in Scotland, on the 18th of September last, in the 45th year of his age, Mr. James Ogilvie, the Orator....
In Chanceford, Penn., Mr. Charles Bradshaw, aged 100. He was a soldier in Braddock's defeat, and wounded in regaining the loss sustained by that defeat.

Issue of April 19, 1821

Died, at Hartford, Conn., on the 7th inst., Elisha Babcock, Esq., 37 years proprietor and publisher of the American Mercury. ....
Died at Waterford, Ireland, on the 7th Sept. last, Mr. Alexander Hammet (brother of the late Rev. Wm. Hammet) aged 65 years, leaving a numerous and respectable circle of relatives and friends.
Died on the 25th ult., at the plantation of her son, Mrs. Sarah Wigfall, a member of the Methodist Church....

Issue of April 28, 1821

Married, on Thursday evening last, by the Rev. Dr. Furman, Mr. Otis Bishop, of this city, to Miss Eliza B. Vidall, of New-York.
Died on the 19th inst., in the 73d year of his age, James Miller, Sen. Esq. for many years a respectable merchant of this city. He was born in the County of Antrim, North of Ireland, but had resided in the U. S. since 1783. (eulogy)
Died on the 20th inst., Mr. Lyon Moses, a native of Amsterdam, but for many years a respectable citizen of this place.

Died on the 12th inst.,near Columbia, Mr. John Wyche...left a numerous family.

Issue of April 30, 1821

Married on Saturday evening the 28th inst., by the Rev. Mr. Boice, Capt. Jos. S. Munro, of Providence, R. I. to Miss Louisa Henderson, daughter of the late Capt. John Henderson, of New-York.

Issue of May 7, 1821

Departed this life on Thursday last, the 3d inst., Mr. Eleazer Reed, aged 29 years, a native of Massachusetts....

Issue of May 12, 1821

Departed this life on the 4th inst., Mr. Charles Bradley, Printer, aged 43 years and 6 months, a native of Ireland.... (eulogy)

Issue of May 21, 1821

Married in New-York, on Thursday last, by the Rev. Mr. Baldwin, Mr. Jacob Bell, to Miss Phoebe Clock.
Died in Philadelphia, on Saturday__, Arthur Hughes, Esq., late of St. Bartholomew's Parish, S. C.

Issue of May 23, 1821

Married on Tuesday the 22d inst., by the Rev. Mr. Morgan, Mr. William Fraser, to Miss Maria Purdy, both of this city.
Married at Baton Rouge, Louisiana, on the 15th ult., Hon. Thomas Bolling Robertson, Gov. of the State of Louisiana, to Miss Skipwith, eldest daughter of Fulwar Skipwith, Esq.

Issue of June 2, 1821

Married in Boston, 3d ult., Mr. Geo. Dodd, merchant of this city, to Mrs. Sarah Gerry, of the former place.
Married, at Hartford, Dr. Augustus Fitch, of Columbia, S. C., to Miss Abigail Putnam, of the former place.

Issue of June 4, 1821

Married in Southbury, Conn., Mr. Marcus Van Knap, aged 65, to Miss Polly Ferry, aged 22.

Issue of June 5, 1821

Married, on Saturday evening last, by the Rev. Mr. Munds, Mr. John Stoney Lynn, to Miss Maria Julianna Miller, youngest daughter of the late Major John David Miller, all of this city.

Issue of June 9, 1821

Died on the 28th ult., Augustus C. Miller, in the 8th year of his age....

Issue of June 12, 1821

Married, on the 4th Feb. last, by the Rev. Dr. Dalcho, Mr. Thomas Annely, to Miss Jennet G. Smith, all of this city.

Issue of June 13, 1821

Remarkable Longevity. Died on the 17th May 1821 in the county of Campbell, Mr. Charles Layne, Sen. at the remarkable age of 121 years. He was born in Albermale (sic) near Buckingham county, in the year 1700... He has left a widow aged 110, and a numerous family down to the third and fourth generations.
Rich. Enq.

Issue of June 15, 1821

Died at Shenton, Jacob Taylor, aged 103. At Libblits, Lincolnshire, Thos Spalding, farmer aged 107.
Died in East Greenwich, R. I., Thomas Arnold, Esq., in the 78th year of his age...in Col. Greene's regiment in the Rev. War.

Issue of June 16, 1821

Married on the 14th inst., by the Rev. Samuel Gilman, J. B. Whitridge, M. D. to Miss Sarah B. M'Leod, daughter of the late Rev. Donald M'Leod, D. D. of Edisto Island.

Issue of June 27, 1821

Departed this life on Friday the 22d inst., Mrs. Margaret Coils, in the 77th year of her age, a native of Ireland, but for near 50 years an inhabitant of this place. For 30 years she was a member of the Methodist Church....

Issue of July 9, 1821

Friday Afternoon the 6th inst., closed the life of Tucker H Harris, M. D...in the 74th year of his age. (eulogy) born in Charleston, his father was a native of Scotland, and his mother of the Island of Bermuda....

Issue of July 14, 1821

Died at his father's residence, Marlboro' District, S. C. on the 10th May last, Mr. John M'Call, for many years a respectable inhabitant of this city.

Issue of July 23, 1821

Departed this life on Sunday morning the 8th inst., in the 22d year of his age, Mr. Washington Breed, a native of this place. (eulogy)
Camden Gazette

Issue of July 24, 1821

Married on the 5th inst., by the Rev. Mr. M'Cabe, Mr. Ahasuerus Van Antwerp, to Miss Hannah Potter, all of Milton. (lines)

Addenda:

Issue of January 8, 1803

Married at Edinburgh, on the 20th September, Mr. George P. B. Hasell, of this city, to Miss Penelope Bentley.
The same morning, Mr. Paul Weston, of this city, to Miss ____ Bently.

Issue of January 10, 1803

Departed this life on Sunday morning, Mr. Thomas Harris, in the 66th year of his age, upwards of 30 years a resident of this city....
Died on Wednesday morning, in the 24th year of her age, Mrs. Harriet Geddes, wife of John Geddes, esq...left husband and two young children, her father, mother, brothers, and sister....
died, lately, in the island of Trinidad, at the seat of John Shaw, Esq., near Saint Juans, whither she had retired for the benefit of her health, Mrs. Juliana Petre Workman (for some time residence in this city)wife of James Workman, Esq. of the Middle Temple and daughter of the late John Wright, Esq. of Mosely Hall, Warwickshire....

Issue of January 12, 1803

Died, at Huntsville, in Laurens district, on the 30th of December last, John Hunter, Esq. for many years past a member of the Legislature of this state, and sometime a Senator of the U. S. from this state. Mr. Hunter was born in Ireland, and came to this country at an early age. He has left a widow and several children, chiefly grown up, and some married.

Issue of January 17, 1803

Married last evening, by the Rev. Dr. Isaac Keith, Mr. Charles W. Bulow, merchant, to Miss Abigail Fowler Johnson, youngest daughter of John Johnson, esq. both of this city.

Issue of February 15, 1803

Died on the 24th January last, in the 70th year of his age, the Rev. James Gourlay, Minister of the Presbyterian Church of Prince William's Parish....

Issue of March 7, 1803

Married on Thursday evening last, by the Rev. Edward Jenkins, Mr. George Williman, to Miss E. Robertson, both of this city.

Issue of March 17, 1803

Married, at Augusta, on the 3d inst., Mr. John S. Adams, merchant, of this city, to Miss Sarah Eve, daughter of Captain Oswell Eve, of Augusta.

Issue of April 19, 1803

Married, on Saturday the 16th inst., by the Rev. Doctor Frost, Mr. John Parks, of this city, to Mrs. Sarah Morgan, of St. James's Parish.

Issue of May 9, 1803

Died, on Sunday the 1st inst., Mrs. Martha Wilkins, in the 40th year of her age. (eulogy)

Issue of May 13, 1803

Died on the 16th of January last, at Camsbarren, near Stirling, James Hosier, aged 104 years. (long account)
London paper

Issue of May 28, 1803

Married, near Georgetown, S. C., at Rural Hall, the 15th inst., by the Rev. Hugh Frazer, Major William Capers, of Waccamaw, to Mrs. Hannah Postell, of Black river, relict of the late colonel Jehu Postell.
Josiah Smith (not the Cashier of the Branch Bank) who died on the 4th ult., has left a wife and eight children....

Issue of June 29, 1803

Died, in the East Indies, John Bristow, esq. sen. member of the board of trade at Fort William....

Issue of July 16, 1803

Died on the 14th inst., in the 40th year of her age Mrs. Harriot Colcock, consort of the late Job Colcock, auctioneer, of this city.

Issue of October 8, 1803

Died at Port Royal (Jam.) Capt. Solomon Ferris, commander of L'Hercule, of 74 guns, in the British navy, aged 55....
Died at Suffield, county of Trumbull, and state of Ohio, on the 25th June last, Mr. Orestes Hale, son of Samuel Hale, of Suffield (Con.) aged 23. Hartford pap.

Issue of October 31, 1803

On Thursday October 6th, at Newport, Rhode-Island, died Mrs. Elizabeth Pickens, wife of Ezekiel Pickens, esq. of this state. (eulogy)

Issue of December 17, 1803

Married on Thursday evening, by the Rev. Mr. Frost, Mr. William F. Shackelford, of Georgetown, to Miss Eliza Ashby, youngest daughter of Thomas Ashby, esq. of St. Thomas' Parish.
Married on Tuesday the 6th inst., by the Rev. Joseph Cook, capt. John F. Bythewood, to Mrs. Ann Bowman.
Married on Wednesday evening last, by the Rev. Mr. Furman, Mr. W. W. Moore jun. to Miss Eleanor S. Gilbert, both of this city.

Index prepared by Mary Elizabeth Phillips, Fort Worth, Texas

Aarons, Eliza 109
Abbe, ___ 256
Abbott, Mellisent Carlton 327
  William 177
Abendanone, Grace 177
  Hyam 177
Abercrombie, Rev. Mr. 96
Abernathie, Jane 236
Abrahams, Abraham S. 228
  Alice 117
  Anna 30
  Moise 222
Achord, Jane 298
Adams, Anna Maria 124
  Barnard 73
  Bernard 65
  Catharine 133
  David 98
  Dinah 250
  Eliza Aleanor 98
  Dr. Freeborn 285
  J. 104
  J.S. 176
  James S. 32
  John 19
  John Quincy 281
  John S. 337
  Maria 220
  Martha 6
  Mary 70
  Mary P. 14
  Nathaniel 17
  Rev. Mr. 38
  Rev. Robert M. 253
  Samuel 70,71
  Sarah 65
  Thankful 104
  Rev. Thomas 250
  William 80,176
Adamson, Amelia 265,294
  Elizabeth 15, 123
  John 2,15,40,123,246,294
  Sarah 246
  William 2,265
Addison, Elizabeth A. 209
  James 160,179,188
  Capt. John 87,206,210,255
  Joseph 209,215
  Mary Anne 160
  Capt. Thomas A. 210
  William Richards 206
Adely, Frances Ann 2
Adickes, E.J. 184
Aiken, William 330
Aikin, Elizabeth 206
  see also Akin
Aikman, Charles 1
  Sarah 157
Ainger, Elizabeth Mary 169
Airsten, Guilliam 149,150
Airs, Charles James 26
  Elizabeth 24
  Dr. James H. 206
  Dr. James Henry 32
Aitcheson, Mary Ann 279
Aitchison, Adam Ogilvie 233
  William 253
Aitman, Ann 262
Akin, William 26
  see aksi Aiken, Aikin
Aldrich, Robert 245
Alexander, Abraham Sr. 171
  Adam 35
  Alexander 65,73,269

Alexander,(contd.)
  Amelia 2
  Annis 33
  Dr. Isaac 2,140,172,257
  J.C. 310
  Joseph 140
  Margaret 140
  Mary Ann 269
  Moses 211
  Nathaniel 196
  Rachel 65,102
  Solomon 25
  William 8
Alison, Jacob H. 292
  see also Allison
Allan, John Williams 158
  Mary Ann 24
  Robert 156
  Robert 156
  William 13
Allen, Charlotte 120
  Dr. ___ 330
  Col. Ebenezer 138
  Capt. Ethan A. 313
  Henry 280
  M. 332
  Matthew 286
  Richard M.L. 42
  S. 332
  Rev. Solomon 332
  Solomon M. 322
  Capt. Thomas 143
Allin, John 166
Allison, James 169
  Susannah 100
  William 100
  see also Alison
Allman, John 102
Allston, Benjamin 212
  Benjamin Jr. 217
  Benjamin Sr. 23,56,160
  Dorothy 160
  Eliza 107
  Capt. Josias 168
  see also Alston
Allwood, James 94
Allwrong, Elizabeth 94
Alstine, William 130
Alston, ___ 12
  Jacob Motte 328
  Joseph 10
  General Joseph 302(2)
  William 12
  William A. 147
  see also Allston
Alvore, Relief 307
Ames, Fisher 202
Ancrum, James H. 27
  William 45,193
Anderson, Ann 194
  Anne 33
  Archibald 22
  Atcheson 41
  Daniel 87
  Elisha 124
  Elizabeth 49,198,228
  Gen. ___ 49,57,103,149
  Capt. George 40
  Harriet Ann 30
  Dr. James 212
  Jane 149
  John 63,167,228
  Rev. John 76,220,286
  Jonathan 286

Anderson, (cont'd)
  Lydia 57
  Margaret 219
  Maria 76,125
  Mary 212,238
  Philip 215
  Robert 80,108,274
  Gen. Robert 33,275
  Ronald 139
  Sarah 124,315
  Capt. W. C. 238
  William 87
Andrews, Elizabeth 71
  James 29
  Loring 124(2)
  Mitchell 29
  Capt. Moses 115
  Sarah 29
Angel, Justus 238
Annely, Thomas 336
Annesley, Thomas 47
Anson, Capt. ___ 53
Anthony, Capt. J.C. 289
  Capt. Joshua 118
  Capt. Stephen 14
Antignac, John 268
Appleton, Thomas 28
Archer, Dr. Starling 138
Ardagh, Patrick 182
Arden, Rachel 291
Armistead, Capt. Adison Bowles 276
Arms, Charlotte 166
  Mary 79
  Sylvester 3
Armstrong, Miss ___ 232
  Margery 219
  Rebecca 163
  Sarah 187
  William 120
Arnold, Capt. ___ 22
  George 296
  Thomas 336
Arthur, George 25
Artman, Peter 133
Asbury, Francis 296
Ashby, Catharine 47
  Eliza 338
  Thomas 338
Ashe, Andrew 325
  Cato 111
  Elizabeth 111
  Hanah 115
  Samuel 115,272
Ashman, Eliza Maria 131
Ashworth, Rebecca 190
Askew, Ann 291
  James 291
Assalit, Joseph 67
Atkins, Rev. John 110
Atkinson, Harriet 32
  John 90
  Joseph 32
  Letitia 166
Atmar, Ralph 6
Attiner, Ann Margaret 58
Attwood, Ruth 78
  Sheffield 78
Auchterfardle, Lady ___ 243
Austin, Jane Stent 7
  Margaret 10
  Mary Susanna 94
  William Jr. 140
Avery, Isabella 9

Avery (cont'd)
  Park 7,93
  Richard J. 165
Axson, Jacob Jr. 325
  Mary 237
  William 18
Aydilott, Joshua 180
Aylwin, Lt. John Cushing 277
Azevado, Isaac 100
  Sarah 84
Azuby, Rev. Mr. Abraham 111
  Rev. Mr. Abraham (officiate) 24,25,104
  Esther 111
  Rev. Mr. (officiate) 50,52 55,62,84

Baas, Thomas 225
Babbs, Jesse 25
Babcock, Amos 184
  Elisha 334
Babcork, John 117
Bache, Sarah 208
  Richard 208,248
Bachelier, Thomas 132
  Mrs. Thomas 132
Bachman, Rev. Dr. (officiate) 299
  Rev. John 293
  Rev. Mr. (officiate) 304, 318,327,333
Backus, Rev. Dr. 307
  Sylvanus 310
Bacon, Ann B. 306
  Joseph 306
Bacot, Jane 98,291
  Mary 155
  Thomas W. 98,291
  Thomas Wright 231
Bacquetty, J.B. 178
Badger, James 125
  James Jr. 291
  William Sanders 289
Bailey, Ann 322
  Eliza 97
  George G. 169
  Hannah M. 202
  Henry 134
  Ralph 139,146
  Sarah Maria 185
Baird, Capt. James 8
  Robert Arthur 203
Baizley, Elizabeth 177
Baker, ___ 89
  Elizabeth 166
  Elizabeth Mary 229
  George A. 273,310
  John Christopher 273
  John J. 48
  Joseph 229
  Lavinia 307
  Margaret 205
  Mary 61
  Mary Caroline 48
  Noah D. 174
  William Bohun 32
Baldwin, Charles 113,249
  David 155
  Joel 175
  Rev. Mr. 335
Balantine
  Mary 189
  Thomas 150
Ball, Elizabeth 91
  Isaac 238
  Jane 94
  John 94,113,184,323
  Margaret 194

Ball (cont'd)
  Sampson 194
Ballard, Mary 196
Ballarini, Joseph 174
Ballon, Rev. Mr. 262
Balmain, Rev. A. 290
Bampfield, Thomas 278
Banks, ___ 109
  Charles 176,303
  Margery 259
  Mary Ann 259
  Thomas 219,226,259
Bannartine, Susannah 213
Bannatyne, Thomas 14
Barber, John 202,296
Barclay, Charles 285
  John 285
Bardon, Elizabeth 172
  John J. 172
Barker, William 183
Barkley, James 188
Barksdale, ___ 245
  Ann 171
  Elizabeth 16
  Mary Ann 40,176
  Richard 40
  Sarah 178
  Thomas 16,178,262
  Thomas James 150
Barlett, ___ 14
Barlow, Joel 277,327
  Ruth 327
Barnard, Alexander 119
Barnes, Capt. John Beale 142
Barnstein, Christiana 178
  John Henry 178
Barnstine, Henry 93
Barnwell, Ann 324
  Ann Middleton 256
  Col. Edward 198
  Edward Jr. 188
  General ___ 256
  Jane 181
  John 234
  General John 113
  John B. 88,181
  Maj. Gen. ___ 324
  Mary 28
  Mary Hutson 113
  Col. Matthew 198
  Nathaniel 28
Baron, Dr. Alexander Jr. 189
Barr, James 42
  Nathan 42,46
  Nathan Jr. 46
  Rev. Mr. (officiate) 188
Barrett, Emily 129
  Keziah 198
Barron, James 71
  Samuel 237
Barrow, Rev. David 310
  William 310
Barry, James 192,240
  John 135
  Commodore John 70(2)
  Thomas 135
  see also Berry
Barrymoore, Joseph 224
Bartlett, Dr. Charles F. 145
  Capt. Nathan 330
Barton, Dr. Benjamin Smith 292
  Esther 162
  Sarah 276
Bass, Catherine 133
  William 61
Batchelder, Thomas 262
Bateman, Rev. Mr. D. 331
Bates, ___ 278

Bates (cont'd)
  Harriet 114
  James 176
  John 220
  Nathan 302
  William 176
Bauman, Col. Sebastian 72
Baxyer, Francis Marion 313
Bay, Emily 40
Bayard, Col. Stephen 293
Bayer, J. Friederick 230
  Mary Catharine 230
Beach, Mary 321
  Mary L. 217
Beale, George 113
  John 182
Bealert, William J. 144
Bean, James 197
  William 22
Beard, Catharine 83
  Col. Jonas 83
Beattie, Edward 94
  William 139
Beauchamp, Mary 31
Bechen, George Phillippi 95
Beck, Rev. Mr. 135,155
Beckford, Lydia 78
Beckley, John 166
Bedford, Gunning 260
  William 33
Bedlow, Henry 197
Bedon, Richard B. 219
Bee, Eliza 102
  John 73
  John S. 151
  John Ladson Freazer 179
  Joseph 102
  Judge ___ 65
  Mary 73,300
  Susanna Bulleine 65
  Thomas 258
Beekman, Annie Lee 261
  Maj. Samuel 258,261
Beesley, Cynthia 159
Begelow, Martha 26
Beggs, James 112
Belcher, ___ 222
  Margaret 324
Belhaven, Lady 168
Belin, Margaret P. 318
Bell, Andrew 177
  Eleanor P. 230
  Jacob 335
  James 44
  Maria 123
  Mary Blaylock 291
  Sarah 195
  Susannah Louise 50
  William 259
Bellenger, Edward 77
  Mary C. 77
Belles, Hugh Priestley 303
Bellinger, B.B. 74
  Barnaby B. 23
  Barnaby Bull 23
  John 155, 215
  Joseph 23,138
  Lucia Georgiana 138
  Lucius 155(2)
  Mrs. ___ 23
  Sarah C. 74
Belser, Catharine Ann 74
  Elizabeth 221
  Jacob 59
Belton, Lt. William H. 329
Belzer, Christian 260
Belzons, Jane 32
Bennett, Anna Claudia 283

Bennett (cont'd)
  Ashur 146
  Charles 85
  Eliza L. 218
  Francis Marion 106
  Hannah Sarah 227
  Henry 188,324
  Henry Doddridge 324
  John S. 99,227
  Margaret 183
  Maria 326
  Mary 38,279
  Susannah 56
  Thomas Jr. 10,251
  Thomas Sr. 283
  Thomas B. 251
  William 305
  William S. 132
Bennom, Samuel E. 295
Benoist, Charles 79
  Daniel 76,95,133
  Elizabeth 95
  Mrs. ___ 236
Benoitte, Theresa Victoria du Mouchel 11
Benson, Maj. Joshua 124
  Lawrence 75
  Mary Ann 90
Bentham, Caroline Hardy 312
  Charlotte Bryer 312
  Harriet Sophia 6
  James 6, 69
  Jane Boswell 69
Bentley, ___ 337
  John 236
  Penelope 337
Benton, Charlotte 109
  Capt. John Augustus 2
  Col. Lamuel 2
  Col. Samuel 109
Benzenken, Hetty 203
Berard, Sophia 198
Berbant, Samuel 256
Beresford, Richard 57
Bering, Elizabeth 331
  John 331
Bernard, Rene 38
Bernhard, Rev. Mr. 208,226
Berniwez, William 125
Berry, Bertheny 188
  Margaret 193
  Rosanna 167
  Sarah 33
  William 193
  Capt. William 183
  William Sr. 132
  William James 130
  see also Barry
Bert, Maj. C.M.F. 246
Berwicke, Lucretia 120
Berz, Christian Adam 239
Besselleu, Charles 29
  Martha Catherine 81
  Mary 29
Besselieu, Philip A. 85
Best, Rev. Dr. 260,267
  Rev. Dr. (officiate) 264, 272,273
  Rev. Mr. (officiate) 29
  Judith 260
  Thomas N. 267
  Rev. William 94
Bethune, Angus 7
Bevans, Simeon 96
Beynard, Eliza G. 257
  Sarah 134
  William 257

Biays, Col. Joseph 294
  Rachel 294
Bickley, Lucy 17
Bigelow, Sarah 97
  Rebecca Eliza 224
Bignall, Mrs. 103
Bilgin, James 71
Billings, Beadah C.P. 121
  Eliza 266
  Elizabeth 121,265
  Frances Lavinia Curtis 265
  Samuel 121
Binder, George 179
Bingham, Caleb 297
  Mrs. ___ 16
  Sophia 297
  William 16
Bingly, Ann P. 139
  Capt. Nathaniel 114
  Sarah 277
Bininger, Abraham 283
  Jacob 283
Bird, Jonathan 178
  Samuel 29
  see also Byrd
Birnie, William 187
Bishop, Capt. Charles 32
  Jane 194
  Otis 334
  Samuel 68
Bissiere, Theodore 197
Bixby, N. 96
Black, Ann 80
  Charlotte 113
  Eliza C. 222
  James 139
  John 192
  Nathaniel 27,164
  William 41
Blackaller, Mary 113
Blackburn, Col. Thomas 173
Blacklock, Katherine 288
  William 38,288
Blackman, Deacon Andrew 307
Blackwell, Rev. Dr. 208
  William H. 306
Blackwood, Sarah 288
  Thomas 13,288
Bladen, Rev. Mr. 11,12,19,23, 28,40,63,69
  Rev. T. D. 77
  Rev. Thomas D. 46,47,81
Blair, Col. Hugh 280
  Rev. Hugh 12
  James 274,292
  John 100,143,192,301
  Matilda 301
  Mrs. ___ 70
  Naomi Euphan 274
  Sarah Conway 192
Blake, Ann 164
  Benjamin 181
  Edward 311
  Francis 311
  John 103,184
  Capt. John 75,164,232
  Margaret 103
  Martha 184
  Mary 75
  William 68
Blakeley, Francis 68
Blakely, Robert 68
Blan, Richard 71
Blanch, Catherine 251
  David 121
Blanck, Capt. Martin 196
Bland, Charlotte Mary 195

Bland (cont'd)
  Rosanna Mary 133
Blanding, Abraham 138
  Susanna 227
  Dr. William 227
Bledso, Jane 220
Blocker, Michael 181
Bogle, Capt. Jonathan 22
Boice, Rev. Mr. 332,335
Boineau, Esther 93
Bolds, Eliza 76
  John 87
Bolker, Thomas 239
Bollard, Susannah 78
Bollough, James Sr. 271
  Sarah Harriot 252
  see also Bullough
Bolter, Joseph 91
Bommer, Dorothy 276
Bonaparte, Jerome 76
Bond, Phineas 295
Bones, Robert 156
Bonneau, Capt. ___ 255
  Eleanor Sarah 306
  Francis 34
  Mary 255
  Miss ___ 48
  Peter 164
  Sabina 273
  William 80
Bonnell, John 140
Bonner, Margaret 8
Bonnor, George 95
Boone, Eliza Gibbes 252
  John 226
  Maria 222
  Mary 268
  Mary Ford 61
  Robert 61
  Thomas 61,68,161,268
Booner, Christian 243
Booth, George 310
  William 174
Borohay, Joseph 32
Borrow, John 51
  Margaret 99
Borton, Ebenezer 21
Bostick, Martha 214
Bostwick, Eli S. 334
Boswood, Mary J. 168
Botsford, Rev. Mr. 81,101,188
Bouchell, Dr. Jesse C. 40
Bouchonneau, Ann M. 219
  Charles 77,119
  Isaac 111,177
  Mary Ann 32
Boudeaud, Clotilda 117
Boudet, ___ 31
Boudo, Louis 252
Bouguier, ___ 83
Boulger, Ann Elizabeth 35
Bounetheau, Edward Weyman 319
  Edward W. 36
  Elizabeth B. 218
  G.M. 115
  Gabriel M. 327
  Harriott Henrietta 115
  Martha Elizabeth 319
  Peter 218
Bourdieu, James 104
Bourg, Rosalie 141
Bourke, Thomas 57
Bourne, Eliza 217
  Walter 217
Bourreux, Luke 237
Bowdoin, James 253
Bowen, Charles B. 86

Bowen (cont'd)
  Ephraim 32
  John 84,90,122,256
  Mary 84
  Rev. N. (officiate) 104, 127
  Rev. Nathaniel 103
  Rt. Rev. Nathaniel (officiate) 326
  Rev. Dr. (officiate) 104, 160
  Rev. Mr. (officiate) 56(2) 58,74,79,95,102,103,105, 111(2),132,133,136,137,140, 141,143,148,151(2),154,155, 164,170,188,194,195,210, 222,223,286
  Maj. Thomas Bartholomew 114
Bowering, Henry 6
Bowers, Capt. David 5
  Hanan 5
Bowie, Capt. Andrew 192
  James 164
  Maj. John 166,192
  Rose 166
Bowler, James Henry 90,299
  Maria 317
  Sarah Elizabeth 299
Bowles, Ann 302
  Elisha 64
  James George 332
  Joseph M. 172
  Maj. Tobias 208(2)
Bowman, Ann 338
  John 170,171
  Peter 148
  Zachariah 21
Bowmar, John 125
Boya, Samuel 55
Boyd, Benjamin 205,241
  Isabel Susannah 301
  John 109
  Margaret 159
  William 271,301
Boyden, Daniel 93,220
Boyer, Ann Dorothea 231
  J. Frederick 231
  Jacob 325
Boykin, Burwell 143
  Elizabeth 143,198
  Frederick 90
  Rebecca 122
  Stephen 122
Boyle, Daniel 3
  James 188
  John 241
Bracey, Ephatha M. 85
  Mr. Merry 79
  William 85
Bradbury, Smith 21
Bradford, Lydia 141(2)
  Sarah 95
Bradley, Celina 166
  Charles 41,335
  Dr. Moses 111,261
Bradshaw, Charles 334
Bradson, Laurence 103
Brady, ___ 273
  Jane 273
Brailsford, Anna Maria 327
  Christiana 259
  Edward 36
  Eliza L. 321
  Harriet 326
  John 263
  John Jr. 233
  Mrs. ___ 157
  Mary 263

Brailsford (cont'd)
  Morton 71,326
  Samuel 157,182
  William 185
Braly, Susan Alison 194
Brandon, Gen. Thomas 33
Brandt, J.W. 54
  James Washington 132
Branford, Elizabeth 12
Brantley, Rev. Mr. 229
Brashers, Richard 319
Brazier Rev. Mr. 70,80,81
Breaker, Lewis F. 161
Brebner, Archibald 100,221
Breed, Washington 336
Breedlove, Mary 75
Breeze, Capt. ___ 172
Breigthaupt, Col. C. 323
Brenan, Eliza Ann 288
  Richard 81
Brent, ___ 143
Brett, Mrs. ___ 91
Brevard, Eloisa Davidson 132
  Judge ___ 40
  Martha 211
  Rebecca 40
Brewer, Dr. Chauncey 312
  Sarah 312
Brice, John 227
  Mary 227
Brichthaupt, Christian H. 217
Bridehoop, John 166
Briggs, Joseph 96
Bright, John 13
  Brig. Gen. Michael 259
Brightman, Eliza 225
Brimner, Dinah Young 217
Brindley, Ann M. 294
  John 203
Brisbane, Col. ___ 45
  Elizabeth 45
  Margaret 160
  Robert 86
Bristow, John 338
Britain, Susannah 303
Broadfoot, ___ 226
  James 328
Broadway, Thomas 317
Brock, Gen. ___ 273
Brockinton, Capt. ___ 81
  Mary 81
Brodut, Elizabeth 185
Broeskey, Charlotte Henrietta 86
  Mary 167
Broker, George 35
Brookman, Ann 135
  Rebecca 135
Brooks, Maj. Alexander S. 316
  Elisha 185
  Jane 162
  Capt. John F. 194
  Samuel 208
Broome, John 234
Broquer, Clement 194
Broughton, Alexander 172,186, 239
  Catharine 89
  Mary 186
  Mary Eliza 7
  Philip P. 186
  Richard 89
  Susannah 172
  Thomas Sr. 217
Broun, Ann 94
Brow, Capt. William 195
Browers, Christiana 130
  Jeremiah 86

Brown, Alexander 178
  Anne 246
  Anne Elizabeth 106
  Catherine Louisa 133
  Christiana 163
  Rev. Clarke 309
  Elijah 71
  Eliza 257,310
  Elizabeth 150,215
  Elizabeth Ann 321
  Gabriel B. 285
  George 157
  George W. 32
  Gustavus R. 94
  James 127,149,257,317,321
  Capt. James 167
  Dr. James 167
  Jane 289
  Jeremiah 224
  John 21,27,70,71,76,179, 294,325
  John B. 143
  Joshua 157,285
  Lucy 131
  Maj. Gen. ___ 314
  Margaret 106
  Martha 149
  Mary 209
  Mary Ann 119,178
  Patience 71
  Rachel 151
  Rebecca 151,288
  Rev. Dr. (officiate)33
  Richard 21, 110
  Capt. Richard 322
  Robert 82,209
  Capt. Roger 11
  Samuel 28,101,208
  Sophia 110
  Swan J. 254
  W.H. 327
  William 126,131,257
  Capt. William 202
  William B. 8
Brownlee, Elizabeth 114
  John 114
Bruce, Sarah 24
  see also Bruse
Brune, D.I. 65
  Mary 65
Brunet, Joseph 205
Bruse, Elizabeth 200
  see also Bruce
Bruton, Sarah 112
Bryan, Dr. Fortunatis 110
  John 238
  Jonathan 110
  Sarah B. 325
Bryant, Jacob 110
  John 207
Bryce, Nicol 187
Bryer, Lewis 303
  William John 109
Bryson, John 123
Buchan, Dr. William 109
  Rev. Dr. (officiate) 237, 238,239,240,241,242,243, 245,258,260,261,263,270, 274,278(2),279,292(2),303, 325,330,331(2)
Buchanan, Rev. Claudius 293
  George William 221
  John 177
  Dr. John 55
  Mary 55
Buck, ___ 270
Buckie, Margaret 162
Buckle, Margaret 20(2)

Buckle (cont'd)
  Capt. Thomas 20(2)
Buckner, Benjamin H. 205
Budd, Dr. John 84
  William 311
Budden, Richard 25
  Susannah 25
Buford, Ann 79
  Miss ___ 124
Buhanan, Maria 185
Buist, Rev. George 204
  Rev. George (officiate) 75
  Rev. Dr. (officiate) 1,2,3,
    6,7,8(2),10,11,13,14,21,
    26(2),33,37,38,40,41,42,
    44,47,48,52,55,58,66,67,
    76,82,85,94,99,100,103,107,
    110,111,112,116,123,126,127
    128,134,138,139,152,153(2),
    154,159,162,163,164,171,
    174,184,187(3),188,190,191,
    198
  Rev. Dr. George (officate)
    4,8,21
Bulet, P. 278
Bulkley, James 309
  Stephen 163
Bull, John 44
Bullen, Samuel 122
  William 207
Bulles, Mary Elizabeth 138
Bulloch, Harriet Barnwell 117
  William 195
  William B. 117
Bullough, Mary 111
  see also Bollough
Bulow, Charles W. 337
Bunce, Capt. J. 199
  Jared 29
  Mared Jr. 199
  Mary 167
Bunch, Ephraim 81
  Martha 179
Buntin, William 53
Bunting, Susanna 203
Burch, John 3
Burchall, Martha S. 43
Burchell, Lois 8
  Thomas 8
Burckmyer, John 262
  Mary Elizabeth 208
Burd, John 25
Burden, Kinsey 112
Burdick, Capt. Isaac 225
  William 316
Burger, David 52.92,283,295
  David D. 41
  Harriet 283
  Jane 41
  Mary 52
  William 295
Burgess, Charles 289
  James 126
  John 71
  Mary Ann 195
Burgoyne, Dr. William 131
Burke, Aedamus 36
  Ann 213
  A. McNeill 332
  John 167
  John D. 197
  Patrick 164
  Thomas 268
  Dr. William 273
Burn, John 163
  John P. 276
Burnet, Andrew 5
  Foster 214

Burnham, Samuel 156
  Thomas 38
Burr, ___ 10
  Mary 195
  Theodosia 10
Burritt, Curtis R. 291
  Dr. Ely 291
Burrows, Alfred 197
  Col. ___ 65
  Miss ___ 65
  William W. 106
Burton, John 8
  Maj. O. 333
Butler, Anthony 126
  Capt. Edward 65
  Sarah 163
Butman, Mary H. 279
Butt, Polly 142
Buxton, John 288
Buyck, Peter 56
Byers, Sarah 109
Byrd, Francis Otway 316
  Mrs. ___ 228
  Samuel 141
  Sarah 196
  see also Bird
Byrne, ___ 269
  Henry W. 267
  Mary 59
  P. 59
Bythewood, Capt. John F. 338

Cabean, Alexander 293
Cabeen, Alexander 219
Cahill, Daniel 38
  Michael 91
Cain, Grace 110
Calder, James 253,325
Caldwell, Elizabeth 152
  Capt. John 213
  Jonathan 325
  Mary Ann 246
  William A. 240
Calhoun, Edward 255
  Florida 239
  John 14,255
  John C. 239
  John Ewing 239
  Mrs. ___ 55
  William 202
  see also Colhoun
Callaghan, John 171
Callahan, James 119
Callendee, Capt. James R. 209
Callender, Capt. Joseph 327
Caloff, Henry 250
Calqohoun, Margaret 85
Calvert, John 74
  John James 50
Calwell, Eliza 238
Cambridge, Eliza 280
  James H. 158
  Margaret Eliza 156
  Sarah Branford 251
  Dr. T. P. 200
  Tobias 206,251
Cameron, David 71
  Martha 110,152
  Mary 157
Cammel, Elizabeth 11
Campbell, Alexander 110
  Rev. Alexander (officate) 301
  Dr. Archibald 234
  Charles 123
  D. Archibald Jr. 125
  Gen. Donald 61
  Edward Delegall 18

Campbell (cont'd)
  Henrietta 143
  Hugh 108
  Jane 106
  Joshua 79,174
  Laurence 72,317
  Lucia 133
  Margaret Elizabeth 317
  Mary 203
  Mary Ann 295
  McMillan 241
  Phoebe Sarah 234
  Rev. Dr. (officiate) 325
  Rev. Mr. (officiate) 256, 311
  Robert 133
  Samuel 79,162
  Sarah 100
  Susanna 241
  William 213
Canada, Solomon 303
Cannon, Daniel 14,48
  John. 201
  Capt. Reddin 198
Canter, Charlotte 55
Cantey, Ann S. 84
  Elizabeth B. 6
  James 6
  John 17
  Martha 161
  Martha Ann 310
  Polley 17
  Sarah Flud 99
  Thomas 227
Cants, John M. 114
Capes, Brian 21,63,77
  John 142
  Jonathan 31,63
  Letitia 92
  Mary 17,21
  Thomas 17,142
Capers, Charles Gabriel 164
  Elizabeth 57
  Gabriel 48,133,196(2)
  Rev. Mr. John (officate) 282
  Mary 9,270
  Rev. Mr. (officiate) 305
  Sarah 133,196
  William 9
  Major William 274,338
  Rev. William 305
  Rev. William (officiate)244
Caple, Rev. Mr. 112,133
Caradeux, Gen. John B. 231
Cardose, David 42
  Leah 42
Carew, Eleanor 6
  John 252
  Sarah 182
  Thomas 137
Carey, James 10
  John D. 96
Carlton, Eliza 35
  William 117
Carman, Andrew 152
Carmand, Margherite 57
  Peter 57
Carmichael, Elizabeth 199
  James, 103,170,199
Carnes, Laurence 117
Carns, Benjamin Smith 267
  Patrick 206
Carolan, Dr. Philip 143
Carpenter, Daniel 150
  Elizabeth 299
Carr, Dale 211
  Eleanor 312

343

Carr (cont'd)
  Jane 60
  Mary 234
Carrell, Charles 15
  Miss ___ 15
Carroll, Bartholomew 328
  George 120
  Rachel C. 328
  Rev. Bishop 76
Carsin, Rev. Mr. 316
Carson, Henry 125
  Rebecca 96
  William 96
Cartee, Lt. Seth 143
Carter, Dr. George 288
  Moses 44
Cartwright, Capt. Benjamin 258
  Thomas 76
Caruth, Capt. John 174
Carvaldo, Moses Gomez 295
Carvalho, D. M. 290
  Rev. E.M. (Officiate) 290
  Rev. Emanuel Nuares (officiate) 261
  Rev. Emanuel Nunes (officiate) 246
  Rev. Mr. (officiate) 276
Carver, William 179
Carville, Harriet 194
  Capt. Peter 194
Casey, Maria E. 333
Cashman, John 166
Caskin, John 232
Casper, John 232
Castens, John M. 326
Catlet, Elisha 98
Cattell, William 72
Cauchoin, Louis Francois 204
Cave, Sarah 248
  Thomas 248
Caveneau, Mary 160
Caw, Rachel 205
Chalmers, Ann 107
  David 72
  Gilbert 117
  Henry James 184
  Dr. Lionel 66
Chambers, Charlotte 132
  Rebecca 96
  Robert 128
  William 249,250
  Col. William 102
Champlin, Christopher 111
  Joseph 60
Champneys, John 4
  Roger 26
Champy, Edme 184
  Rose Antoinette 184
Chancognie, Simon Jude 66
Chandler, Col. John 312
  Mary 95
Chandless, J. 185
Changuion, Poligne 125
Chanler, Dr. ___ 19
  Eliza 280
  Isaac 5,36
  Dr. Isaac 56
  Isaac B. 19
  Sarah White
Channel, Mary 205
Channer, Benjamin 10
  Ester 10
Chaplin, Ann Gibbons 200
  Harriot 298
Chapman, Joseph 63
  Mahettaba 315
  Mary 12
  Mary Ann 210

Chapman (cont'd)
  Samuel 176
  William 62,322
Chappell, James H. 154
Charles, Andrew 261
  Elizabeth 46
  Capt. Joseph 157
  Susannah 49
Charlton, Emily W. 207
  Judge ___ 207
Chartier, Jean Jaque 17
Chase, John B. 254
  Samuel 246
Chatburn, Samuel 200
Cheesborough, Capt. William E. 269
Cheetham, James 236
Cheevers, Richard Holmes 55
Cheramy, Widow ___ 236
Chesnut, Col. John 210
  Margaret E. 210
Chevard, Peter Desiree 16
Chevers, Ann 60
  Richard Holmes 60
Cheves, Langdon 138
  Susanna 67
Chew, Capt. Henry 96
Chiffelle, Ann 140
  Thomas P. 134-135
Childs, Ann 61
  Benjamin 122
Chinners, Frances 165
  George Washington 100
  John S. 148
  Rebecca E.R. 333
  Sarah Ann Elizabeth 100
Chisam, John 170
Chisolm, Alexander 71,239,259
  Sarah 259
Chollet, Alexander 188
ChouJer, Dr. ___ 32,89
  Dr. Joseph 65,89
  Mary 32
Chovin, Alexander 167
Christian, Charles 215
  Lucinda 82
  Martha 174
  Mary 39
  Robert 287
Christie, Alexander Jr. 326
  Gabriel 197
  Margaret 216
Christopher Mathias 267
Chull, Elizabeth 290
  Menassa 290
  Philip 290
Church, Sarah Russell 180
Churchman, John 121
Cignes, John 202
Ciples, Lewis 246
Claiborne, Wm. G.C. 325
Clanton, Lt. Comm. Alexander 330
Clapperson, Harriett 192
Clark(e), Ann S. 125
  Bernard 120
  Catharine 152
  Eleanor 134
  Elizabeth S. 63
  Hannah Maria 243
  Huria B. 324
  James 125,154,193
  Jane 3
  Jeremiah 43
  John 7
  John H. 316
  Joshua 6,22
  Martha 59

Clark(e) (cont'd)
  Matthew 161
  Rev. Mr. 19,309
  Robert 67
  Susannah E. 217
  William 159,205,263,331
  William K. 125
Clarkson, Rev. Mr. 74
  Rev. Mr. (officiate) 133,164
  William 181
  William Jr. 137
  William Harrison 181
Clastria, Capt. John 134
Clastrier, Fanny Elizabeth 175
Clastries, Sarah 214
Clay, Joseph 98,249
  Rev. Joseph 240
Clayton, Elizabeth 110,175
  Morris 37
  see Cleyton
Cleapor, Charles 129
  Mary 129
Cleark, Elizabeth C. 43
Cleary, Charles 281
  Eliza 204
  John R. 281,332
  Col. Nathaniel Greene 281
  Robert Washington 102
Clement, Eleanor 5
  John 5,24
  John M. 213
  Sarah 149
Clemmons, Capt. James 226
  Sally 226
Cleyton, Jane 172
  see also Clayton
Clifford, Charles 73
  Hnery 214
Clinton, Gen. George 261
  Joseph 149
  William 184,231
Clitherall, Eliza 237
  Dr. James 15
Clock, Phoebe 335
Clois, Bigrel de Grand 39
  Henrietta Claude Bigrel de Grand 39
Clopton, John 303
Cloriviere, Rev. Mr. 273
Clothworthy, Rt. Hon. 111
Cloud, Rev. Mr. 142,173
Clough, John 229
Clymer, George 275
Coachman, James 212
  Mary 212
  Thomas 27
Coakley, Conrad 144
  Dr. ___ 144
Coalfoard, Mary Ann 82
Coalter, Francis 307
Coates, ___ 321
  Ann 193
  Christiana 100
Cobb, Ebenezer 31(2)
  Howell 230
Cobia, Francis 221
Coburn, Ann Jane 229
  Eliza 38
  James 38
  Capt. James 229
  John 1
  Mary 9
Cochran, Alexander 11
  David 322
  Samuel 200
  Thomas 72,200
Cock, Rev. Mr. 59

Cocke, Joseph 38
Cocks, Capt. John S.H. 204
Coffin, Capt. E. 281
　Ebenezer 326
　Mary 281
　Mary S. 326
　Peleg 107
　Reuben 142
　Rev. Dr. (officiate) 316
Cogell, John 184
　John S. 152
　Richard W. 139
Cohen, Abraham 25,186,211
　Ann 186
　Catharine 163
　Celice 25
　Eliza 251
　Gershon, 32,63,163,186
　Hetty 62
　Isaac 127
　Rev. J. 73
　Jacob 212
　Rev. Jacob 250
　Jane 211
　Nathaniel 130,139
　Mord. 251
　Philah 107
　Rina 55
　Sarah 186
Coils, Margaret 336
Coke, Mrs. ___ 243
　Rev. Dr. ___ 243
　Rev. Thomas 115
Colclough, Agnes 5
　Col. Alexander 5
　Col. ___ 28
Colcock, Harriot 338
　Job 338
　Mellisscent Jr. 271
Coles, Capt. John 192,218
　Kendall 79
　Mary 93,192
　Nathan W., M.D. 165
　Samuel 269
　Sarah Ann 173
Coleclough, James 22
　see also Colclough
Coleman, Nancy 41
　see also Colman
Colhoun, James Jr. 41
　John Ewing 51
　Col. Joseph 40,41
　Samuel 77
　see also Calhoun
Collas, Jean Baptiste 213
Collet, Capt. Lewis 118
Collier, Eliza 306
　James 306
Collins, Charlotte 116
　Daniel 13
　Israel G. 24
　Joshua 245
　Capt. William 247
Colman, Benjamin 285
　see also Coleman
Colwell, Henry Jr. 23
Combe, John 14,147
　Mary Magdalene 101
　Samuel 45
Combee, Rachel 189
Comly, John 179
Compton, Elizabeth 165
Conneau, Miss C. 48
Connelly, Capt. John 194
Connolly, Mary Halet 230
Connor, Rev. James 67
　Rev. William 67
Conover, Peter 221

Conover (cont'd)
　William 221
Conway, Juliana 258
　Gen. Robert 258
Conyers, Mary Clement 201
Cook, Adam 316
　Ann 206
　Eliza T. 151
　Rev. J.B. 50
　Jacob 293
　Jane 4
　John 149,205
　Joseph 56(2)
　Rev. Joseph (officate) 338
　Rev. Joseph B. (officiate) 164,192
　Rev. Joseph E. (officiate) 138
　Martha 301
　Mary 132
　Rev. Dr. (officiate) 8,39
　Rev. Mr. (officiate) 6,8,53
Cooler, Rev. Dr. Robert 110
Cooper, Rev. Mr. 310
　Ann 117
　Catharine Ann 310
　Capt. James 167
　Capt. John 194
　Martha 215
　Peter 272
　Rachel 130
　Maj. Samuel 310
　Thomas 1
　Thomas C. 263
　Rev. Urban 322(2)
Coppedge, Rebecca 182
Coppley, Elias 217
Corbet, Harleston 158
　Thomas 158
Cordell, Charlotte 170
Cordes, Catharine 99,116
Cordray, Thomas 82
Cormick, Eleanor 89
　Thomas 41,89
　William 253
Cormier, Francois 128
Corn, Hannah 149
Corre, Charles G. 144
　Jacob 178
Corrie, Mary 299
　Samuel 299
Corroll, Bishop 15
　see also Carrell
Corry, John 37
Coslett, Charles Grimke 287
　Margaret 287
Costain, Ann 111
Costal, Olei Couyo 285
Cotten, James W. 298
　see also Cotton
Cottineau, Denis Nicholas 211
Cotton, Benjamin 205
　see also Cotten
Course, Harriet Prince 320
　Isaac 320(2)
　John 53
Courtney, Edward 173
　Eliza M. 92
　Humphry 92
　James 92
Courty, John 157,166
　Mary 157
Cousar, Rev. Mr. 325
Couturier, Elias 166
　Henrietta 166
　Isaac 167
　Isaac Jr. 277

Coventry, Alexander 114
Cowans, Elizabeth 181
Cowen, Frances 52
Cowing, Henry 276
Cowley, Ann 314
Cowsar, James 25
Cox, James 48,257
　John 37,178
　John C.W. 5
　Joseph 267
　Keturah 247
　Mr. ___ 178
　Matilda 178
　Susan Mason 289
　Susannah 69
　Thomas Campbell 289
Coys, James P. 178
　Jonathan W. 176
Crab, Robert 255
Cradshaw, John 141
Crafts, William 235
Craig, John 216
Craven, Anne Evelina 312
Crawford, Alexander 217
　James 45
　Mary 172
　Rev. Mr. (officiate) 190
　Sarah 125
　William 35,36
　William H. 44
Crawley, Charles 115,116
　Mary 116
　see also Crowley
Crayton, Roger 119
Cregier, Clinton 204
Creighton, James 334
Creitzburg, George 217
Creyon, John 185
　John M. 271
　Mrs. C. 185
Cripps, Caroline 259
　Elizabeth 187
　John 308
　John S. 251,259
　John Splatt 187
Critchfield, Benjamin 20
Critesburg, Mary 58
Crockat, ___ 263
Crocker, Dr. E. P. 167
　Dr. Elijah P. 181
　Rev. Mr. (officiate) 270
　Capt. Robinson 317
Croft, Edward 51
　Rev. Mr.·(officiate) 85
Croghan, Lt. Col. ___ 314
Croll, John 30
Cromer, George 204
　John 162
　Michael 301
　Susannah 301
Cromwell, Oliver 265
Crooks, Mary Richards 274
Crosby, Moses G. 293
Crose, Rev. Mr. 306
Cross, Ann 147
　Eliza Maria 158
　George 135
　Capt. George 30
　George W. 211-212
　George Warren 186,270
　James 30
　John Jr. 35
　M.W. 147
　Mary Man 211
　Matthew William 244
　William B. 294
Crouch, Abraham 141,228
　Sophia Jane 228

Crout, Capt. John Thomas 139
Crow, Edward 309
  John 276
Crowell, Jeremiah 131
Crowley, Carolina Maria 119
  Charles 31
  Eleaner 31,168
  Eliza 38
  Louisa M.M. 119
  Michael 119
  see also Crawley
Crowther, Rev. Mr. 71
Cruger, David 88
Cruvillier, William 168
Cubbe, Puckshun 297
Cockow, ___ 76
Cuckton, John 314
Cudworth, Benjamin 283
  Catherine 283
  Eliza 28
  Nathaniel 27
Cuigno, Louis 91
Culiatt, Adam 1
  David 8
Culliatt, Ann 19
  Avery 23
  James L. 96
  Jane 113
Cummings, John 24
Cummins, Charles William 168
  Rev. Francis 40
  Rebecca Catharine 40
Cunningham, Eliza 214
  Henry 161
  John 66
  John Pearis 220
  Martha 109
  Richard 244
  Gen. Robert 62,114,277
Curling, George 219
Curry, Joseph 154
  Patience 154
  Richard 154
Curtis, Anna Sommerset 314
  Francis S. 314
  Margaret E. 319
  Mary 96
Curtlet, Eliza 163
Cushing, William 236
Cushman, Simeon 116
  Simon 116
Cushnie, David 243
Custer, Ann 182
  Elizabeth 51
  James 34,51,182,213
  Mary 213
Cuthbert, Caroline 114
  Col. ___ 114
  James H. 285
Cutler, John Frederick 170
Cuttino, Elizabeth D. 286
  Peter 162
  William 148

Dabouville, Pierre 161
Dacosta, Isaac 43,177
Daggett, Gardner 334
Daingerfield, Henry 292
Dalcho, Dr. Frederick 129
  Rev. Dr. (officiate) 313, 323,325,336
  Rev. Mr. (officiate) 334
Dallas, Alexander J. 308
Dalton, Frederick W. 287
  Dr. James 287
  Mary Ann 331
Daly, Henrietta Wilhelmina Louisa 115

Dancer, Thomas, M.D. 249
Danford, Mary 64
Daniel, Chisley 245
  Dr. John Moncure 286
  Rev. Thomas 120
  Travers 286
Danjou, ___ 263
Darby, Artemus B. 113
  Elizabeth 102
  Ezra 192
  Jane Harriott 135
  Rebecca 232
  Capt. Robert A. 247
  William 102
D'Arcey, Charles 91
Dare, David 135
Darke, Sardo 45
Darley, Chaterine 140
  Georgs 131
  Rev. Mr. (officiate) 99
Darr, Elizabeth Ann 149
Darrell, Edward 26,59
  Martha 59
  Nathaniel 63
  Thomas 4
Dart, Amelia 57
  Benjamin Sr. 57
  Mary 234
  Dr. Thomas L. 234
  Thomas Lynch 35
Darwin, Dr. ___ 41
Darzaugh, John 189
Dasta, Mary Jane Rose 278
Daten, Jacob 322
Datley, Rev. Mr. 70
Daudier, Lucia Maria Anna 236
Daverson, William 232
Davidson, Elizabeth 66
  George H. 74
  Gilbert 6
  James 3,156,254
  Jenny 94
  John 281
  Statira 80
  Susannah 16
  William 37
  Capt. William 80
Davies, Eleanor 253
  Mrs. ___ 37
  Sarah Jones 290
  Gen. Wm. Richardson 37,290
Davis, Ann Eliza 184
  Catherine 155,218
  David 179
  Dorothy 101
  Lt. E.R. 265
  Eleanor 50
  Elizabeth 58
  George 238
  Capt. Harman 101
  Henry 102
  Herman 73
  Israel 284
  John 181,213
  Capt. John 188
  John N. 219
  John W. 184
  Judith 284
  Margaret 4
  Martha 113
  Mary 143
  R. 235
  Thomas 90,91,104
  Capt. Thomas 264
Davison, James 4
  Mary 73
  Sarah 56
  see also Devison

Da Wega, Rev. Mr. 30
Dawes, Margaret 108
Dawson, Ann 133
  Charlotte 153
  Mrs. Christian 31
  John 133,143
  Lawrence M. 260
  Margaret P. 143
  William 31, 55
Day, Elizabeth 46
  James 25
  Maria 296
  William H. 109
  Capt. William 46
D'Azevedo, Sarah Cohen 290
Dealy, James 22
  Mary 68
Deas, Caroline 306
  David 1
  Elizabeth 33
  James S. 210
  John 33
  Margaret Phelp 279
  Dr. Robert 279
  Thomas H. 124,306
DeBardeleben, Arthur A. 260
  see also de Berdeleben
DeBellianse, Caroline Elizabeth Jacqueline Rossignol 157
DeBendeleben, Arthur A. 260
  see also de Bardeleben
DeBernier, Col. John 179,263
  John J. 179
  Miss ___ 64
Deblots, James S. 80
D'Bonnefons, Capt. Antoine 235
DeBow, Ann 782
  Garret 53
  Dr. William 1
DeBruhl, Michael Samuel 240
Decatur, Capt. Stephen Jr. 134
Decempt, James 128
Decker, Frederick 75
  Garret 103
DeClorivere, Rev. R. 237
DeCottes, Madam ___ 47
  Maria Louisa Victoria 47
DeCournand, Mary Louise 273
  Peter 273
Deering, Maria 13
DeGrasse, Adelle 10
  Count ___ 10
Dehon, Bishop Theodore 318
  Rev. Dr. (officiate) 239, 244,256,260,261,274,275, 276,291
  Rev. Mr. 70
  Rev. Mr. (officiate) 141, 230(2)
  Rt. Rev. Bishop 318
  Rt. Rev. Bishop (officiate) 271,288,298,303,311,312,314
  Rt. Rev. Dr. (officiate) 299
DeJongh, Joseph 233
Delacroix, Madame Anville 37
DeLaffy, Louise Moreau 114
  Marie Louise Magdeleine Valentine Davezac Castra Moreau 114
DeLaGorce, Paul Jacinthe Perrault 44
DeLaire, James 66
  Maria Susannah 66
Delany, Michael 77,145
  Sarah 77
DeLeon, M.H. 276
Delezay, Lise Emeline 44

Deliesseline, Elizabeth 163
  Col. Francis A. 294
  Francis G. 227
  John T. 163
  Josia Allston 227
Delone, Nicholas 143
Delorme, Magdeline Antoinette
  Dupont 67
  Mary M.H. 208
Delozeuir, Asa 86
  Rachel 86
DeMichel, Frederick 273
  Ignace 264,273
  John 264
  John Baptiste Ignace 16
  Maria Rose Antoinette 16
DeMontmain, Louis Claude
  Henry 247
Dempsey, Judy 191
  Mary 146
Dennie,Joseph 256
Dennison, Ann E. 290
  James 290
Denniss, Elizabeth 187
Denny, Capt. Orlando 61
  Samuel 178
  Dr. Thomas 73
Denoon, Ann 8
  David 102
  Eliza 263
Dent, Maj. James T. 310
  John H. 216
Depass, Abraham 45
  Ralph 45
  Dr. Ralph 272
DePetiot, John Philip 35
Depont, John 53
Desaussure, Anna Frances 128
  William F. 290
  Daniel 292
  Eliza Washington 5
  Henry 98
  Henry W. 128,290
  Mary 292
Desbeaux, Ann 99
  John 93
Desel, Catharine 19
  Charles 19,161,182,183
  Dr. Charles 253
  Eliza 210
  Mary Ann 161
  Mary B. 253
DesJardin, John Adrian 57
DeStack, Frances Paulin Josephine 35
Detargny, Rev. Mr. Mattin 127,164,165,167,175
DeTolanaire, Theresa J. 303
DeTollenare, Charles 16
  Sarah 16
DeTreville, Harriott L. 6
  Capt. John L. 6
  Robert 6
Deubell, John H. 168
Devaull, Catherine 183
Deveaux, Caroline Matilda 325
  Catharine L. 311
  Dr. J.D. 203
  Jacob 117,317
  James 191
  Thomas 112
DeVilleman, Antoine Guillaume Francois Jean Garquille de
  Daymord 266
  Daymand 266
DeVison, Elizabeth 193
Dewa, Elizabeth 164
Dewees, Sarah 211

DeWeisseneeis, Frederick H. Baron 150
Dewers, Sarah 131
Dexter, Katharine Gordon 314
  Samuel 314
  Timothy 137,152
Dick, James S. 275
Dickerson, Rev. Thomas 252
Dickey, John 190,191
  Sarah 3
Dickinson, Catharine 27,270
  Henry Hinson 211
  Capt. Jeremiah 87,270
  John 193
  John D. 222
  Joseph 27,301
  Maj. Joseph 161
  Mary Ann 29
Dickman, T. 312
Dickson, Thomas 233
Dieckert, Jacob Gottfried 131
  Rebecca 222
Dile, Pierre 130
Dilgar, Joseph 81
Dill, Joseph 20
  Joseph Sr. 246
  Sarah 72
  Susanna 246
Dillon, Robert 132
Dimes, Ann 44
Dinkins, Thomas 113
Discombe, James Hayden 204
Disher, Ann Catharine 169
  Malinda 286
  William 286
Ditmore, John 220
Dixon, John 128
  Sterling 24
  Thomas H. 249
D'Lieben, Israel 159
Doane, Capt. Joseph 140
Doar, Esther Susannah 137
  Capt. John 76
Dobbin, George 255
Dobel, Sarah 21
Dodd, George 335
Dodsworth, Eliza 242
  Ralph 242
Doggett, Ann 171
  Henry 171
Doll, Alexander 73
Dolles, John 123
  Capt. John 197
Donavon, Isaac 60
Donlevy, Francis W. 333
Donnald, Capt. James 195
Donnan, Maria Claudia 216
Donnavan, Henrietta 106
Donnill, Mary 192
Donnom, Joseph 287
  Sarah 287
Donnon, James C. 31
Doolittle, Amos B. 224
Doorobee, Dems 103
  see also Goorobee
Dopson, Eliza Mary 138
Dorman, Martha 141
Dorrell, Rebecca 66
  see also Dorrill
Dorrey, Elizabeth 79
Dorrill, Ann 59
  James 59
  Joseph 189
  see also Dorrell
Dorshtimer, Elizabeth 200
Doudney, John 166
Dougherty, John 99,177
  Michael 200

Doughty, Mary Ann 51
  Thomas Jr. 101
  William 101,207
  William Jr. 26,51
Douglass, Alexander 6
  Catharine 178
  Eliza Haslett 228
  James K. 138
  Capt. Stephen 45
Douterier, Joseph 162
Douthwaite, Abraham 195
Dove, William P. 266
Dow, Dorcas 123
  Robert 123
Dowdney, Thomas 188
Dowser, David 174
D'Oyley, Dr. Daniel 162,284, 295
  Elizabeth Maine 283
Drake, Maria L. 261
Drath, Sarah 35
Drayton, Eliza E. 129
  Glen 129,213
  Jacob 147
  Margaret Glen 213
  Capt. Philip 139
  William 74
Dregs, Polly 45
Drehr, Ann 226
  Godfrey 209
  Godfrey Jr. 226
Drennes, George 150, 157,178
  George Jr. 150
  Mary 178
Drennon, John 147
Drew, James 175
Drewes, Henry 264
Driscol, D. 243
Drummond, John 88
  Capt. William 97
Drunckmoller, John 146
Dubbert,Elizabeth R. 3
  Godfrey 9
  Rev. Mr. 3
Duboc, Francois Tite 137
DuBois, Ann 121
  Carlisle 87
  John 213
Dubose, David 57
  John 84
  Mary 8
  Rev. Mr. (officiate) 154
  Samuel 8,28
  Samuel Jr. 201
  Serre 24
Duddel, James 13
Duett, Frances 200
  Mr. ___ 200
Duffy, Henry 169
Duggan, Thomas 172
Duhadway, Caleb B. 210
Duke, Eliza Spierin 303
  Maj. Greene M. 328
  John Grand ___ H. 303
  William Willis 207
Dumaine, Dr. J. 222
Dumay, Miss M. 160
Dumont, Dr. William 136
DuMouline, Augustine 228
Dumoutet, J.B. 282
Dunbar, George R. 159
Duncan, Alexander 169
  Ann 58
  Archibald 79
  Dr. ___ 6
  Hugh 178
  James 144
  John 58,137

Duncan (cont'd)
    John Jr. 137
    Joshua 150
Duncome, Robert 160
Dunklin, Elizabeth 217
    James 217
Dunlap, Ann 192
    Rev. David E. 91
    Esther 43
    Jane Eliza 172
    John 127
    Rev. Mr. ___ 67
    Rev. Mr. (officiate) 41,68
    Dr. Robert 43
    Samuel 172
    Susannah 91
Dunlop, Esther 43
    Dr. Robert 43,81
Dunn, Alexander 221
Dunnam, Frances Ann 255
Dunscomb, Charlotte 5
    George 100
    Mary 145
Dunwoody, Esther 271
    Rev. Mr. (officiate) 270
Duplat, J.B. 309
    J.B. Carey 309
Dupont, Ann 114
    Benjamin 21
    Cornelius, M.D. 209
    Elizabeth Goodbee 110
    Jane H. 272
    Josiah 110
Dupre, Ann Frances 225
    Lewis 274
    Mary S. 30
Durant, Levi 37
    Rev. Thomas (officiate) 288
Durbec, Josephine 288
Durrett, George 205
    James 214
Dursse, Laurent 304
Dutch, Stephen 223
Dutchman, Capt. George 277
DuVall, Martha 222
Duynmier, Sarah 220
D'Uzech, Count Dugaric 222
    Marie Rose Jeanne Gabrielle
    Dugaric Celeste 222
Dwight, Rev. Dr. Timothy 308
Dwyer, Rev. Dr. 68

Early, William 103
Eason, Robert 153,157,289
    William 282
Easter, Mary 22
Eaton, General Wm. 246
Eccles, Rev. Dr. (officiate) 167,221
    Rev. Samuel 203
    Rev. Samuel (officiate)203
Eckely, Elizabeth D. 32
    William 32
Eckert, Robert D. 244
    Robert David 213
Eckhart, Ann Margaret 125
Eddington, Capt. Edward 238
    Eliza 66
    William 238
Eddy, John 10,58
    Rev. Mr. 78
Eden, Eleanor 66
Edings, Eliza B. 55
Edmonston, Charles 239
Edwards, Alexander 248
    Dr. Alexander 245
    Dr. Alexander M. 231
    Ann Caroline 124

Edwards (cont'd)
    Caroline 126
    Eliza Hann 139
    Elizabeth 74
    Maj. Evan 154,303
    George 16
    Harriet 127,303
    George 16
    Harriet 127,303
    Henry Evan 154
    James 124,139,153
    James F. 216
    James Fisher 214
    John 74,86,121,214
    John 74,86,121,214
    Matthew Lyon 181
    Rebecca 153
    Sarah Barksdale 216
    Sugar 200
    Tabitha Bell 180
Edwin, Mr. ___ 109
Eels, Nathaniel 227
Egleston, Azariah 302
    Elizabeth 102
    George 88
    John 109,302
    Mary 302
Ehney, Jacob 28,245
    Mary 28
    Peter 302
    Peter M. 170
    Sarah 38
    William 38,93
    William F. 278
Elbert, Lt. Samuel 201,275
Elder, Elizabeth 305
    J. 305
Elfe, Hannah 269
    Mary 62
Elizer, Isaac 156
Ellington, Sally 230
Elliott, Adelaide Gibbes 309
    Ann 76
    Barnard 144,309
    Francis 251
    Capt. Francis 137
    Capt. John 69
    Joseph 261
    Mary 69
    Philip 272
    Ralph Emons 151
    Samuel J. 135
    Sarah 196
    Sarah H. 199
    Thomas 196,261
    William 199
Ellis, Esther Ann 262
    Nancy 10
    Richard 6,96
    Sarah 6
Ellison, Henry 22,91
    Maj. Robert 134
    William 280
Elmore, Anne Eliza 222
    John A. 177
Elsinore, James 308
Elswood, Thomas 141
Elsworth, Abigail 214
    Capt. Frederick 208
    John Theophilus 35
    Lydia 289
    Susannah 140,321
    Theophilus 321
Emery, Capt. Jonathan 273
Enfield, Capt. Joshua 162
Engevin, Peter 104
England, James 173
English, Ann 74

English (cont'd)
    John 186
    Joshua 7
    Mary 7
Epilwraith, James 330
Ernest, Jacob 175
Ervin, Catharine 173
Eschulson, Eschul 195
Estel, Bordman 5
Etting, Miriam 146
    Solomon 146
Eustace, Gen. John Skey 120
    Thomas 168
Evans, Ann B. 76
    Henry M. 127
    James 13,240
    John 92,282
    John J. 222
    John Joseph 275
    Jonathan 57
    Sarah 75
    William 42
Eve, Capt. Oswell 337
    Sarah 337
Ewell, James 100
    Sarah C. 100
Ewing, Adam 164,242,292
    Agnes Bolton 164
    Daniel 175
    Elizabeth 292
    Jane 242
    John 188

Faber, Ann Mary 183
    Rev. C. (officiate) 230, 231,239
    Catharine 95
    Rev. Charles 252,266
    Rev. Charles (officiate) 161,166,170,173,182,193, 196,212,214(2),215(2)
    Charles Samuel 324
    Christian Henry 72,95,161, 183,212,324
    Rev. D. (officiate) 33
    J.C. 252
    Rev. J.C. (officiate) 2,3, 9,35,59,60
    Rev. John C. (officiate) 66
    Maria Christina 252
    Rev. Mr. (officiate) 7(2), 27,37,50,51,55,72,138,142 (2),152,163(2),168,171,187, 200(2),216,219,220(3),232, 239,243
    William G. 152
Fabre, Rev. J.C. 16
Fair, Harriet 100
    John 153
    Margaret Frances 117
    Capt. William 117,159
Fairbrother, John 198
Fairchild, Dr. Samuel 197
Fairfax, Rev. Brian Lord 44
Fairley, Rosanna 107
Fairlie, Mary 263
Fairweather, Richard 276
Falconer, William 116
Fallon, John 92
Fanning, L. Nathaniel 121
    Maria M. 163
Fardo, George 290
Fare, Isaac 96
Farmer, Henry Tudor 193
Farr, Elizabeth 150
    John F.N. 320
    Nathaniel 288
    Thomas 150

Farro, Elizabeth 147
Farrol, Barnard 133
Fasbender, J.H. 105
   John H. 105
Fasthender, Mr. ___ 62
Fates, Rev. Dr. 195
Fatio, Francis Philip 234,248
   Lewis 25
   Mary 25
   Mary Magdalen 234
Fauche, Marie Elizabeth 71
   Mary 120
Faust, Daniel 299
   Lewis 70
   Sarah 299
Fayssoux, Ann 90
   James H. 187
   Mary B. 90
   Miss ___ 58
   Peter 252-253
   Dr. Peter 58,253
Fea, Rev. John Worthington 327
Feay, Mary 223
   Obadiah M. 223
Febiger, Col. Christian 307
   Elizabeth 307
Felder, Samuel 245
Fell, Catharine Elizabeth 201
   Isabella 27
   Mary 237
   Thomas 237
   Thomas T. 237
   William 222
Fellows, Nathaniel 140
Fendin, Peter Tampley 134
Fennell, James 298
Feraud, Claudius Alexander 93
Ferguson, Anna Berresford 286
   Charles 177
   John Horry 332
   Margaret 45
   Rebecca 332
Fernald, Benjamin 31,35
   Ellen 115
Ferris, Capt. Solomon 258
Ferry, Polly 335
Fickling, Ann Eliza 68
   Francis 159
   Henry 156
   Jeremiah S. 159,161
   Joseph 120
   Maria W. 120
   Mary S. 159
   Samuel 27,120
   Samuel Jr. 68
Fiddy, ___ 274
   Mary 274
Fields, Elizabeth Letitia 245
   Sarah 23
   William Brown 108
   Zebulon 20
Fifer, James 139
Filbin, John 284
Filley, John 12
Filman, Elizabeth 109
   Peter 109
Finch, Catharine 235
   Joseph 175,235
   Sally 290
Findley, Sarah 140
Finley, William M. 115
Fisher, Ann 183
   Daniel Francis 167
   Capt. Joshua 107
   Miers 285
   Robert 109,154
Fishbourne, Richard Henry 191

Fisburne, Francis 77
   Col. William 104,105
Fisk, James 170
Fisther, John 159
Fitch, Dr. Augustus 335
   Rev. Ebenezer 316
   Joseph 312
   Lucy 316
Fitts, John 193
   John Sr. 46
Fitzgerald, Edward C. 206
   Lewis 304
   Margaret Martha 206
Fitzpatrick, Ann 244
   John 244
   Nicholas 6,15
   Peter 240
Fitzsimons, Thomas 250
Flack, William 56,315
Flagg, Ebenezer 318
   Mary 225
   Thomas Collins 12
   Capt. William 155
Flannery, Rev. Mr. 11
Flauch, Ann 173
Fleeson, John Glen 234
Fleming, David 226
Flemming, Jane 63
   John H. 285
   Margaret 162
   Nancy 82
   Sarah 188
Fletcher, Capt. Robert 130
Flinn, Rev. Andrew 242
   Rev. Andrew (officiate)173
   Rev. Dr. (officiate 258, 264(2),278(2),289,291,294, 311(2),324(2),326,328
   Rev. Dr. Andrew (officiate) 272
   Rev. Mr. (officiate) 138(2) 151,160,198,210,211,224, 238,241,253
Flint, Joseph 266
Florence, James L. 114
Floriutiu, Catherine 82
Floyd, Charlotte 40
   John 158
   Rev. Mr. 100,161,167,229, 280
Flud, Daniel 59,73,252
   Elizabeth Stanyarne 59
   Milton 252
Foffler, Susan 108
Fogartie, Lewis 182
Foissin, Elizabeth 11
   Dr. ___ 58
   Miss ___ 96
   Dr. Peter 171(2)
Folker, Edwin C. 320
   Elizabeth 96
   John C. 300
   Joseph 320
   Sarah 19
Follin, Augustan 121
   Hermin 146
   Michel 284
Folsom, Ezekiel 316
Fonerden, Adam 128
   Ann 128
Forbes, Alexander 291
   William 157
Ford, Elizabeth 119
   Harriet C. 220
   Richard 142
   Timothy 3
Fordham, Benjamin 154

Fordham (con'td)
   Mary Elizabeth 205
Fordyce, Elizabeth 30
Forgartie, Capt. Lewis 77
Fornew, John 46
Forrester, Bailey 85
   Mr. ___ 321
Forshaw, Edward 77,199
   James Edward 77
   Mary 324
Forster, Rev. Mr. (officiate) 303,324
   Robert 223
Forsyth, Fanny 124
   James 90
   John 124
   Walter 90
Foster, Frederick 50
   John B. 39
   Letitia 157
   Mary 283
   Moses 39
   Oliver 122
   Rebecca Weyman 168
   Rev. Mr. (officiate) 329
   Robert 27,69
   Thomas 18,168,206
   Thomas Edward 18
   Capt. Warren C. 123
Fothergill, Dr. Anthony 284
Foutain, Jane 13
Fowke, Dr. John S. 201
Fowler, Ann 88
   James 132,273
   Nancy 314
   Rev. James 34
   Rev. Mr. (officiate) 191, 194,196,205,216,219,242, 280,309,327
   Richard 54
Foxworth, Samuel 123
Fraeligh, Rev. Moses 310
Frampton, John 105
   Margaret 105
   Wilkie 156
   William 278
France, Amelia Casey 215
   Laurance 119
Francis, William 138
Franklin, Dr. Benjamin 209
Fraser, Alexander 157
   Catharine Mary 212
   Donald 210
   George 97,222
   Rev. H. (officiate) 128
   Hugh 97,332
   Rev. Hugh (officiate) 135, 193,338
   James 25
   Dr. James 68
   James S. 332
   John 189
   John Ladson 70
   Maria 257
   Mary 25,157
   Mrs. ___ 124
   Philip 81
   Rev. Dr. (officiate) 30
   Rev. Mr. (officiate) 56,75, 79,107,199
   Thomas L.S. 297
   William 215,335
Frazier, Samuel 297
Fray, John 89
Freazer, George
   John Ladson
   Mary 107
   Sarah 73

Freeman, James 104,141
  James M. 331
  Mary 122
  Rachel 141
  Rev. Dr. (officate) 313,314
  Timothy 122
  William 101
Freer, George Hix 119
  Mary 38
  Samfs L. 329
  Sarah 323
Freneau, Helena D. 306
  Peter 288
  Philip 306
Frick, Thomas 301
Fricre, T.C. 83
Frierson, John 48,314
  Maj. John 197,314
  Mary 48
  Rachel 197
Fries, Harriet 282
Frink, Rebecca E. 328
  Thomas 328
Fripp, Mrs. ___ 39
  Thomas 39
  William Chaplin 139
Frish, Catherine 50
Frish, Charles 334
Fritts, Dorcas 198
Frobus, Henrietta 166
Frost, Eleanor Legare 305
  Rev. Dr. (officiate) 13(2),
  26,31,33,34(2),43,55,57,
  72,82(2),337
  Rev. Mr. (officiate) 3(2),
  5(2),9,28,32(2),41,43,46(2)
  48,49,54,56,60,61,63(2),
  64(4),65,66,72,73,74(2),
  75(2),77,305(2),309,338
  Rev. Thomas (officiate) 87
Fuchey, Eliza 101
Fullen, James 308
Fuller, Christopher 245
  Joseph Whitmarsh 109
  Martha 53
  Middleton 248
  Susannah 209
  Thomas 248
  Col. Thomas 53
Fulton, Samuel E. 194
  Robert 291
Furchane, John 70
Furman, Rev. Dr. (officiate)
  6,13,30,45,75,76,80,81,82,
  91,92,99,107,108,110,114,
  129,130(3),132,135(2),170,
  181,188,195,200,203(2),204,
  208,213,216(2),217,218(2),
  219,228,235,237,240,243,
  245,250(2),251(2),256,269,
  274(2),276,277,278,322,323,
  325,326,327,334
  Rev. Mr. (officiate) 2,5(3)
  10,14,29,31,54,57,60,134,
  149,338
  Wood 5
Furse, James 22
Futhey, Heartly 189
  Mary 189

Gabeau, James 54
  John 180
  Mary H. 204
  Susannah 302
Gadsden, Ann 74
  Capt. Christopher 266
  Gen. Christopher 118
  Rev. Mr. C. (officiate) 280

Gadsden (cont'd)
  Rev. Mr. Christopher (officiate) 222
  James 224
  Martha 332
  Rev. Dr. (officiate) 297,
  310,311,312,315,317,318,
  323,324,325,326,327,328,
  329,331
  Rev. Mr. (officiate) 184,
  186(2),201,204,223,231,
  240,255,263,266,269,276,
  278,287,288,291,292,310,
  312,330
  T. 74
  Thomas 332
Gaffarbelly, Augustus D. 327
Gaillard, Bartholomew 207,287
  Charles 162
  David 18
  Eleanor 209
  Elizabeth 127
  Elizabeth Mary 162
  Florida Lydia 51
  John 51,58,100
  Miss ___ 100
  Mr. ___ 59
  Martha Doughty 263
  Mary 58
  Peter 168
  Peter Jr. 101
  Capt. Peter Sr.126,127
  Rebecca Chiffelle 207
  Theodore 209
  Theodore Jr. 263
  Theodore Sr. 18
  William 162
Gains, Elizabeth 257
  George W. 257
Gale, Joseph Jr. 290
  Thaddeus 114
Gallaghar, Julia 315
  Rev. Dr. (officiate) 6,
  10,11,16,17,27,35,38,41,
  51,56,57,75,76,99,113,116,
  121,128(3),137,141,146(2),
  154,158,160,166(2),168,172,
  184(2),187,191,198(2),211,
  217,236,240,252,271,278,
  285,298,315
  Rev. Mr. (officiate) 44
Galler, Eliza 105
Galloway, Capt. Alfred 218
  Elizabeth 163
  James 278
Galluchat, Rev. Mr. 324
Galphin, George 182
  Thomas 182
Gamble, Jane 123
  Maj. John Marshall 308
  Martha 45
Gander, Prater 64
Gano, Ann 190
  Rev. Dr. (officiate) 26
Gantt, Esther S. 203
Garden, Dr. Alexander 115,327
  Maj. Alexander 313
  Elizabeth 115
  Martha 191
Gardenhouse,Eliza 103
Gardette, James 250
  S.J. 250
Gardiner, Elizabeth 323
  Rev. Dr. 300
  Rev. Dr. (officiate) 318
  Rev. J.S.J. (officate)289
  Rosa 300
Gardner, Col. Charles K. 309

Gardner (cont'd)
  Joseph 163
  Mary 293
  Thomas 103,192
Garner, Melcher 142
  Susan 142
Garrett, Thomas 97
Garvin, Rev. John 297
  Rev. John (officiate) 31
Gasser, Mary 145
Gates, Horatio 137
Gauihs, Elizabeth 166
Gauvin, Jane Celest 91
Gaven, John 90
Geddes, Ann 147
  Eliza 184
  Harriet 337
  Henry Jr. 269
  John 107,147
  John Sr. 337
Gefkin, Henry C. 277
  Henry C. Jr. 238
  Louisa 262
Geiger, Jacob 30
Geissenhainer, Rev. Mr. 252
Gell, Rebecca 48
Generick, John Frederick 180
  Justina Louisa 159
  Rev. Mr. 76
Genovley, Mary 273
George, Capt. James 108
  Lucas 210
  Mrs. ___ 250
  Sophia 108
Gerley, John 14,169
  Mary 169
German, Lt. Lewis 329
  Gen. Obadiah 329
Gerry, Sarah 335
Gervais, Henry Laurens 72
  John Lewis 72
  John Lewis James 219
  Rawlins Lowndes 166
  Rev. Mr. (officiate) 251,
  259,271
  see also Jervais
Geyer, Eliza 146
  Eliza Bampfield 275
  Capt. John 146,148,296
  Capt. Peter 77
  Rebecca Cook 296(2)
  Wm. Bampfield 148
Gharnock, Charles 49
Gholson, Thomas 300
  Maj. William 300
Gibbes, Eliza 131,240
  James L. 309
  John 49
  Mrs. ___ 49
  Robert 8
  Sarah R. 8
  Washington 299
  Wm. Hasell 131,190,240,299
  Wilmot S. 128
  see also Gibbs
Gibbons, John 243
Gibbs, Eliza Gardenia 313
  G. 313
  John Walter 80
  Maria Ann 2
  see also Gibbes
Gibson, Alexander 175,292
  Ann Mary 167
  James 290
  Jane 199
  Susan H. 290
  William 25
Gilben, Archibald 4

Gilbert, Eleanor S. 338
  John C. 165
  Rebecca 193
  Seth H. 218
Gilbo, Peter 53
Gilchrist, Adam 148,152
  Esther 148
  Maria 152
Gilder, Capt. Philip 201
Giles, Col. Hugh 37
  Nathan 320
  Othniel John 133-134
  see also Gyles
Gilfert, Christopher H. 178
Gill, Isaac 76
  Col. William 303
Gillespie, Col. James 102
Gillespy, John 22
Gillett, Dr. E. 144
  Evelina 144
  Matilda 144
Gilliland, William H. 222
Gillison, Anna Maria 12
  David W. 148
  Derry 13
  Samuel R. 262
Gillman, Louisa 27
Gillon, Archibald 72
Gilly, John 282
Gilman, Rev. Samuel 336
Gilmor, Robert Jr. 164
Gingiliatt, Ann H. 42
  Gabriel 60
Girardeau, Elizabeth 299
  John H. 40, 169
  Col. Peter B. 299
Girdeer, Jonas 72
Giroy, Maria Louisa 38
Gist, Francis F. 280
  John 84
  Joseph 8
  William 50
Gitsinger, Adam F. 185
Giveham, Frances 167
  Philip 167
  see also Givhan
Givens, Elizabeth 8
  John 8
  William 325
Givhan, Mary 85
  Philip 85,151
  see also Giveham
Gladden, George 265
Gladding, Joseph 11,247
Glais, Miss Denny 196
Glascock, John S. 234
  Gen. Thomas 234
Glenn, James Streator 314
  John 192,308
  John Streater 173
  Letitia 170
  Marshall 257
  Martha 36
  Mary Eliza 308
  Thomas Jr. 233
  Thomas Sr. 233
Glover, Ann 185,230
  Ann Heyward 271
  Caroline 305
  Cary 139
  Charles 230
  Eliza 82
  Col. J. 185
  Joseph 91,136
  Lydia 223
  Sanders 82
  Wilson 271
Godber, William 105

Goddfrey, Mary 75
  Thomas 75
Godfrey, Ann 3
  Elizabeth 62,78,148
  Hannah 313
  Thomas 78
Goldsmith, Morriss 52
Gonse, Maria Louisa 124
Goodlet, Jesse 47
Goodman, Nancy 21
Goodrich, Sgt. Tilman 270
Goodwin, Daniel 158
  Maj. James 39
  Margaret 154
  Capt. Ozias 320
  Richard Chapman 320
  Sarah Weston 214
  Col. William 30,154,254
Goorobee, Dems 106
  see also Doorobee
Goose, Susannah 64
Gordon, Andrew 176
  Ann 174
  Capt. Charles 170
  Charles P. 317
  David 240
  Eliza 203,256
  Elizabeth 34
  Hannah 286
  Irvin 240
  James 7,312
  John 174
  Maria 260
  Margaret 7
  Robert 82,192
  Sarah 170
  Stephen 63
  Dr. William 193
  William Edward 74
Goring, Ann Elizabeth 60
Gospard, Marie 128
Gosselin, Magdalen 67
Gotbold, Cade 121
Gotea, James 189
Gourand, Antcine 51
Gough, Dr. J.P. 56
  Dr. John P. 328
  Roger Saunders 167
  Thomas 51
Gould, Thomas 75
Gouldsmith, Mary 322
Gourdin, Elizabeth 101
  Hamilton Couturier 214
  Theodore 101,214
Gourlay, Rev. James (officiate) 12,337
  John 181
  Rev. Mr. (officiate) 3(3),7,41
  Samuel 161
Gouvernuer, Nicholas 43
Gow, Mrs. Andrew 83
Gowdey, Mary Lee 73
Graaf, Peter C. 44
Gradick, Christian 219
Grado, Maron 35
Grady, Mrs. C. 327
Graeser, Anna Maria 333
  C.I. 333
  Lewis A. 60
Grafft, Lucy 214
Graham, Ann 3
  Martha 101
  Mary 82
  Sarah M. 274
  Rev. W.E. 3
  Rev. William E. 101
Grame, Hans 83

Grant, Capt. Christopher 197
  Cynthia Loveless 225
  George 130
  Hugh 90
  Isaac 165
  James 130
  John 29,251
  Joseph 198
  William 265
Grantland, Flemming 329
Granville, Elizabeth 187
Grassell, Isabella Jane 153
Gratten, Elizabeth 34
Graves, James 98
Gray, Ann 54
  Caleb 134
  Eleanor 134
  Capt. John 161
  William 60
Grayson, John 36
  Mary 184
  Sarah 36
  Capt. Thomas 184,206
Gready, Mary Elizabeth 153
Greatwood, G. 250
Greaves, Lovey M. 252
  Thomas B. 252
Green, Benjamin 183
  Edmund 174,284
  Francis 218
  James C. 63
  Jane 39
  John 39
  John Gray 94,205
  Jonas 174
  Margaret M. 154
  Peter Archer 218
  Tabitha M. 218
  Thomas 262
Greene, Benjamin 165
  Cornelia L. 38
  Gen. ___ 165
  Maj. Gen. ___ 38
  Nathaniel 128
Greenwood, Ann 212
  William 212
Greffin, Peter 300
  see also Griffin
Gregg, Capt. Aaron 98
Gregorie, Alexander 139
  James Jr. 9
  James Sr. 172
  William B. 302
Greiner, Mrs. Masey 207
  Meinrad 180
Gren, Charles 33
Gresham, Wiley 321
Grey, Gen. Charles 190
Gribbin, Capt. ___ 173
  Jane 173
  John 302
Grier, James M. 45
  Martha 325
Grierson, James 169
Griffin, Charles 94
  George 318
  John 227
  Lewis 16
  Susannah 318
  see also Greffin
Griffith, Dr. ___ 70
  Thomas 123
Griggs, Isaac 303
Grigsby, Rev. Mr. 134,142
Grigson, Mrs. D. 37
Grimball, Eliza B. 242
Grimke, Dr. John 297
Griner, Minead 111

351

Groning, Lewis 149
Grooms, ___ 247
Gros, Catherine 62
   John 168
Groscol, Antoine 230
Groshon, Andrew 191
Grossland, ___ 168
Grosvenor, Thomas P. 292,314
Grubbe, Hammond 172
Gruber, George 299
   Rt. Rev. Father Gabriel 115
Gudirow, Margaret 65
Guerard, Robert G. 191
Guerin, Henrietta 4
   Madame ___ 1
   Mons. ___ 1
Guerry, Florida 193
   Grandison 262
   Mary Elizabeth 214
   Theodore 160,214
Guignard, James S. 7
Guirey, Samuel 307
Gulick, Patience 17
Gunn, Mary 153
   William 153
Guy, James 24,56
   Mary 202
   Sarah 24
Guyon, Peter 181
Guyot, Mariana 272
Gyles, John 274
   Sarah 111
   Thomas 177
   see also Giles

Habersham, John 256
   Richard W. 199
Hadley, Rev. Mr. 136
Haford, Gardner 328
Hagan, Effey 54
   see also Hagen
Hageman, Ellen 99
   Jacob 99
Hagen, Richard 106
   see also Hagan
Hagety, Charles 54
Hagey, Joseph 314
Hagood, Adeline Eliza 181
   Maj. Gideon 181
   Johnson 105
   Tirza 45
Hahnbaum, Catharine 17
   Dr. Christian 7
   Eliza 7
   Dr. G. F. 7
   George 17
   George E. 212
   Mary 7
Haig, David 123
   Dr. ___ 79
   Elizabeth 271
   Capt. George 306
   Dr. George 13
   H.M. 157
   John James 147
   Maham 271
   Maria 123
   Dr. Robert Mackewn 327
   Sarah 13
Haile, John 299
Hailey, Rev. Mr. 172
Hails, Capt. Robert 184
Haines, Annette 324
Hale, Orestes 338
   Samuel 338
Hall, Anna Maria 37
   Benjamin 310
   Caroline 124

Hall (cont'd)
   Daniel 243
   Dr. ___ 124
   Dr. George 133
   George Abbot 124
   Henry 89
   Capt. James George 189
   Joseph 17
   Margaret 60
   Mary Ann Schrieber 144
   Nathaniel 173
   Rev. Mr. (officient) 313
   Samuel 186
   Samuel T. 113
   Sarah 196
   Susannah 213
   Thomas 40,43,207
   Thomas Jr. 28
   Capt. W. 28
   William 40
   Capt. William 37,40
   Willis 205
Hallard, Susanna 103
Halliday, Mary 148
Halling, Rev. Dr. 261
Halman, Samuel 121
Halsall, John Burford 104
Halsey, Frances Maria 270
   Julia 197
   Thomas Lloyd 270
Haly, Eleanor 6
Ham, Ann 214
   Susannah Dickson 250
   Samuel 151
   Thomas 250
Hamblin, N. 125
Hamett, Thomas 61,122
   see also Hammet
Hamilton, Cahterine 57
   Frederick 167
   George 45,152
   Mary 129,132
   Paul 104,130,190,224
   Rachel 199
   Rebecca 104
   William 61
   Sir William 64
Hamlin, Cornelius 199
   Hannah 249
   Sarah 187
   Thomas 187
Hammel, John 306
Hammet, Alexander 334
   Benjamin 325
   Rev. Mr. (officiate) 37,39,44,50,63
   Rev. William 334
   see also Hamett
Hammond, Dudley 267
   Mr. E. 144
   Mary 295
   Mary Ann Douglas 142
Hampton, Ann 58
   Capt. Gale 264
   Maj. John 208
   Col. Wade 17
Hanahan, Ann 30
   John 331
   John Jr. 3
   Rippon Sams Hamilton 22
   William 22
Hanckell, Rev. Mr. 277
Hancock, George 271
   Henry 159
   James Henry 159
   Richard 61
Hand, Jane A. 216
   Rev. Mr. (officient)167,262

Handford, Joseph 235
Handy, Hast. 131
Hannah, James 298
   Nancy 298
Hanson, Judge ___ 314
   Mary L. 292
Happoldt, John G. 32
   John Philip 173
Harby, Isaac 239
   Solomon 106
Hardcastle, Elizabeth 213
Hardwick, John 60
Hargreaves, Elizabeth 196
   Joseph 6,196
   Joshua 59
Harker, Ann 316
Harkness, James 86
Harleston, Ann Olsey 279
   Elizabeth 100
   Col. John 100
   Nicholas 279
Harman, Rev. Dr. 245
Harney, Louis 277
Harp, William 67
Harper, Charlotte 6
   Elizabeth Mary 170
   George 62,212
   Capt. George 70
   Henrietta 162
   Rev. John 198
   Joseph 241
   Lewis 132
   Lewis J. 27
   Rev. Mr. (officiate) 13
   Robert 305
   Robert G. 15
   Stephen 219
   William 157,209
Harrell, Mary 45
   Thomas 59
Harriett, Eliza 62
Harrington, Gen. Henry W. 221
Harris, Dr. Benjamin P.283
   Carolina Bullard 239
   Charles 159
   Lucinda 115
   Matilda 115
   Miss ___ 56
   Mrs. ___ 116
   Nabby 115
   Nathaniel 115
   Nehemiah 97
   Otis 115
   Sarah Tucker 6
   Thomas 116,337
   Gen. Thomas K. 297
   Dr. Tucker 6,239,336
Harrison, Frances 44
   James 258
   John 138,185,316
   Mrs. M. 43
   Rosanna 193
   Susannah 316
Hart, Daniel 186,244
   Hettie 300
   Jacob 300
   Mary Eliza 132
   Nathan 186
   Rachel 186
   Samuel 46
   Rev. Mr. Solomon 83
Harth, Maria 79
   William 210
Hartley, Eliza Mary 291
Hartman, Susannah 180
Hartstene, Jacob 154
Hartwell, Dr. Benjamin 103
Harvey, Capt. Benjamin 100

Harvey (cont'd)
  Catharine Frances 54
  Dorcas 34
  Elizabeth 41,199,304
  Eliza Margaret 100
  James 207
  Capt. James 108
  John 117
  John Rogers 315
  Maurice 34
  Robert 199
  Sarah 26
  Sarah Arthur 310
  Thomas 144,304
  William S. 271,310
Harwitz, Pineus Levi 122
Hasell, George P.B. 337
  James 108
  John 13
  Sarah 99
  Thomas 165
  William S. 143
Haskell, Major 225
Haskett, Samuel 156
Haslett, John Sr. 183
Hatch, George 309
Hatfield, Sarah 248
Hatter, Elizabeth B. 326
Hatton, Thomas H. 181
Haughton, Col. Joshua 272
  Mary 272
  William 1
  see also Houghton
Hauser, Elias 189,260
  Elizabeth 189,260
  Eve C. 136
  Margaret C. 133
Hawes, Benjamin 225
Hawie, Sarah 278
Hawkins, Capt. Philip 313
Hawthorn, Ann 46
Hay, Bernard 74
  Capt. Jehu 202
  Lewis Scott 206
  Samuel 82
Hayden, Matilda 124
  William 124
Haydon, William 191
Hayes, Jane 63
Haymon, John P. 190
Haynes, Frances Henrietta 328
  James 167
  Mary 177
  Robert 328
  Robert Y. 287
  Susan B. 274
  William 274
  Wm. Edward 132
Haynsworth, Henry 56,235
  John 208
  Rachel 56
  Wood 235
Hazlehurst, Robert Jr. 311
Hazlewood, Joseph 67
Hazzard, Delia Augusta 284
  Maj. William 284
Healy, Major I. 227
  John 227
Heard, John 159
Hearkley, Elizabeth 132
Hearn, John 78
  Margaret 78
  Maurice 71
Heartman, Sarah 102
Heath, Angelina Mary Eliza 322
  James M. 269
  John D. 210

Heatly, William 30
Hebert, Sophie 128
  Victoria 146
Hedley, Mrs. ___ 177
  Rev. J. 177
Hederick, John 213
Heileger, Susannah 56
Heinekin, J.H.C. 209
Heinrichs, Wilhemina Christiana 81
Heiz, Frederick 314
Helfenstem, Rev. Mr. 235
Hemsley, Anna Maria 307
  William 307
Henckell, Rev. Mr. 279(2)
Henderson, Daniel 74
  Elizabeth 255
  Capt. John 293,335
  Louisa 335
  Margaret M'La 105
Hendlen, Thomas F. 215
Henery, Capt. James 240
  see also Henry
Henley, Sarah 95
Henneguin, John Baptiste 46
Hennon, Thomas 147
Henrichson, Ann M. 111
  G. 214
  Eliza 220
  Jacob 268
Henry, Andrew 150
  Anne 210
  Catherine 266
  Charles 310
  Eliza 279
  Jacob 266
  Julien 9
  M.L. 171
  Major M. 56
  Margaretta C. 154
  Mary 93
  see also Henery
Hentz, I. Charles 154,177
Henwood, Samuel 27
Henzy, Bigoe Darrel 238
Hepburn, John S. 284
Herior, Robert 48
Heriot, George Washington 101
  Mary 135
  Sarah Caroline 48
  William 135
Hermon, Samuel 239
Herron, Henry D. 185
  John 218
  Samuel 334
Herschel, Dr. ___13
Hertz, H.M. 164
  Jacob 235
Heth, Col. William 164
Heulen, Jean Jacques 140
  Marie Elizabeth Francoise Emerie le Compte 140
Hext, James Hartley 263
Heyward, Ann 312
  Anna 327
  Hannah Shubrick 55
  James 101
  Josias 42,328
  Manigault 280
  Thomas 221
  William 55,101
Hibben, Eliza 158
  Hannah 290
  James 290
Hichborn, Elizabeth 242
  Isaac Barre 48
  John 242
Hicks, Capt. Benjamin 128

Hicks (cont'd)
  Rev. Mr. (officiate)112,
    125,198,199
  William 2
Higginbotham, Rev. Ralph 279
  see also Higinbotham,
    Higinsbothom
Higgins, Hannah 216
  Robert 216
Higham, Thomas 223
Highton, Mary 276
  William 196
Hightower, Joseph 246
Higinbotham, Henrietta 276
  Ralph 276
Higinsbothom, Lt. James S. 182
  see also Higginbotham
Hill, Acey 15
  Dannitt Jr. 173
  Edmund 21
  Eleanor 198
  Eliza Ann 259
  George 200
  Capt. John 79
  Rev. Mr. (officiate) 298
  Col. William 307
  see also Hills
Hillard, Capt. Nathaniel
    Green 218
  see also Hillerd
Hilldrup, Susannah Eliza 276
Hillegas, Catharine 95
Hillerd, Ferdinand 193
  see also Hillard
Hillhouse, David P. 299
Hills, Ebenezer 118
  see also Hill
Hilton, Eliza 67
  Jess 67
Hilyard, Martha 230
Himely, J.J. 256
Hinchinsen, Robert 151
Hinds, David 189
  John 227
  Sarah 265
  Thomas 196,266
Hinson, Martha 105
  Thomas 66
Hinton, James 5
  Presley 308
Hipp, George 52
Hippers, Mary 75
Hippius, Ann Catharine 327
Hirons, Ann Wood 155
Hislop, Eliza 309
  Mary 217
  Robert B. 202
Hislor, Robert 210
Hitch, Joshua 164,194
Hoam, Altangi 254
  Caraltangi 254
Hoare, Dr. ___ 45
Hoats, Susannah 167
Hobard, Rev. Bishop 314
Hobbs, John L. 75
Hoburn, Catherine 210
Hodges, Abraham 117
  Rev. Samuel K. (officiate)
    315
Hodgson, Mary 79
Hoey, Ann 166
  Bernard 91
Hoff, John M. 190
Hoffman, John 239
Hogg, Dr. Alexander 112
Holcombe, Rev. Mr. (officiate)
    64
  John C. 273

Holcombe (cont'd)
  Robert L. 164
Holland, Rev. Mr. 97
Holley, Rev. Mr. 316
Hollinshead, Rev. ___ 59
  Rev. Dr. 208
  Rev. Dr. (officiate) 5,6,
    9,10,14,24,26(2),27,30,33
    35,36(2),38,41,43,51,54,
    56,61(2),63(2),72,73(2),
    75(3),77,79,85,86,87,88,
    92,95,96,97,99,100,102,
    104(2),105,107(2),108,
    110(2),111,112,113,115,117
    123,125,127,128,130(2),
    131(2),132(2),133(2),134,
    135,137,138,139,140(2),
    149,151,152,154,156,161,
    162,164(2),165,166(5),167
    (3),170,172,173,174,178,
    181,184,185,186,187,188,
    189(2),190(2),193,195,196,
    198,199,202(2),203,204,
    207,208,209,210(2),211,212,
    214(2),217,218,219(3),222
    (3),228,229,232(2),234,238,
    239,242,246,247,255,259,
    262(4),267,269,270,271,272
    (2),275,276,277,279,280(2)
    287,295
  Rev. Mr. (officiate) 27,28,
    30(2),31,38,56,74,113,120,
    129,163
  William 208
  Rev. Dr. William 308
Holman, Joseph George 310,319
    (2),
Holmes, Andrew 176
  Charles 100
  Charlotte 37
  David Galphin 265
  Eliza 324
  Elizabeth Elliott 185
  Frances 8
  Isaac 185,261
  Isaac L. 238
  J.E. 326
  James 323
  Jane 217
  John 217,230,323
  John Bee 333
  John W. 208
  Margaret 145
  Mary 326
  Rebecca 33,50
  Sandiford 230
  Sarah 140
  Thomas 81
  William 145,326
Holwell, Amelia 185
  Thomas 53
Homaca, Dr. D. L. 173
  James Michel 173
Homasser, Charles 146
Hompesch, Baron 118
Honeywell, Ann Statia 196
Honour, Rev. Mr. 333
Honoteau, Peter Benoitte 11
Honywood, Arthur 65
Hood, Charles 230
Hook, Caroline 208
  Conrad 106
  Esther 161
  Margaret Maria 142
Hooker, John 210
Hope, Henry 244
Hopewell, Pollard 282
Hopkins, Charles D. 126

Hopkins (cont'd)
  Capt. Ebenezer 54
  Henry 50
  Rebecca 208
  Capt. Thomas 254
Hopson, George Jr. 83
Hopton, Sarah 24
Hopwood, William 249
Horlbeck, Anna Catharine 329
  Elizabeth 51,59
  Elizabeth D. 213
  George 213
  Henry 285
  John 51
  John Jr. 59
  John Sr. 260
  John B. 285
  Maria Catherine 213
  Peter 329
Hornby, Claudia K. 37
  Hannah 196,266
  Henrietta 74
  Mary 254
  Thomas 254,266
Horne, James 29
Horry, Ann 216,284
  Elias 201,323
  Elias Lynch 284
  Jonah 216
  William 201
Horsey, Thomas Jones 251
Hort, Benjamin S. 333
  Mary Drinker 333
  Robert S. 135
Hosier, James 338
Hoskins, David 181
Hosley, John 9
Houghton, Major Joshua 95
  see also Haughton
House, Eliza 90
  Samuel 18,90,118,226
  Sarah 18,118
Houseal, Dr. John Bernard 283
Houser, Elias 78
Houston, James 224
  John 224
Howard, James 19
  Jesse 177
  John 62,151
  Margaret 155
  Richard F. 34
  Maj. Robert 229
  Sarah 43
  William V. 269,330
Howell, Richard 39
Howlen, John 298
Hoxey, Jesse 273
Hoyt, Capt. Moses 10
Hrabowski, John S. 2
  Margaret Ann 2
Hubbard, Abigail 210
  Capt. Zenas 100
Hubble, Seats 86
Hubert, Charles Nicholas 249
  Frances C. 223
Hudson, John 240
  Capt. Joseph 279
  Mary 200,279
Hueston, Samuel 94
  Selina 94
Huff, Sarah 5
Huger, Ann 60
  Daniel 79
  Francis 26
  General ___ 60
  John 77,271
Hugg, Hope 103
Huggins, Joseph 60

Hughes, Arthur 335
　Hannah 288
　Henry 288,299
　James 101,111
　John 8,47
　Louisa Charlotte Marie Anne
　　Angelique Tacquin 149
　Margaret 189
　Mary 69,181
　Maj. Peter 308
　Samuel 189
　Sarah 111
　Susannah 47
　Victor 149,182
Huguinan, Abraham 12
Hull, Charles 123
　John 123
　Rev. Mr. (officiate) 39
　Sarah 148
Humbert, Godfrey 322
Humes, John 34,210,232
　Mary 34,136,232
Humphreys, Eliza 112
　Jane 41
　Mrs. ___ 26
　Maj. Ozias 312
　Rebecca 99
　Capt. William 322
Hunham, Jane 85
Hunt, Mrs. Hannah 1
　Harrison 171
　Henry 319
　Thomas 100,209
　William 171,319
Hunter, Ellen 52
　James 62
　John 17,187,213,337
　John Lingard 299
　Margaret Crawford 303
　Mary 226
　Mary L. 152
　Rev. Mr. (officiate) 132
　Stark 143
　Capt. Thomas 152
　William 38,120
　Dr. William 33
Huse, Dr. James 302
Huseey, Margaret 99
Huson, George 201
Hussey, Bryan 173
　Bryan Edmonson 173
Hutchins, Capt. ___ 21
　Mary 272
Hutchinson, Adam 198
　Ann 9
　E.A. 253
　Elizabeth 63
　Elizabeth L.L. 320
　Esther 43
　John 43
　Leger 320
　Maria 209
　Mary 21
　Col. Matthias 209
　Robert 164,190
　Thomas 21(2)
　Thomas H. 281
　William 9,149,190
Hutchison, John 318
　Thomas 318
　William 201
Hutson, Anne Bythewood 294
　Martha 302
　Richard H. 302
　Thomas 178
　William 3
Huxham, Mary 98
Hyams, Catherine 108

Hyams (cont'd)
　Mrs. M. 331
　Mordecai 321
　Samuel 331
　Sarah 170
　Solomon 108,246

I'ans, Mary 210
Imer, Jane 155
Inglesby, Martha 112
　William 112
Inglis, Rev. Dr. 294
Ingraham, Hannah 154
　Maria 92
　Mary Ann 75
Ingram, Grace 56
Innis, Harry 304
Inskeep, Eliza 208
　John 208
Ioor, Frances 156
　George 156
　Dr. William 54
Irvine, Gen. ___ 253
　Rebecca A. 253
　Maj. Gen. William 89
Irving, George 183
　Jacob Aemilius 308
Irwin, Capt. Joshua 133
Isaacks, Jacob 49(2)
　Johebed 49
　Judith 47
　Rachael 69
　Rebecca 49
　S.M. 163
Ives, Eli 171
Ivey, Elizabeth 64
Izard, Charlotte 19
　Eliza 75
　George 65
　Henry 19
　Miss ___ 159
　Mrs. ___ 173
　Polly 109
　Ralph 83,151,159
　Ralph Jr. 75

Jacks, Hannah 40
　James 116
　Mary 116
Jackson, ___ 198
　Capt. ___ 177
　Eliza 264
　James 136
　Jeremiah 115
　Maj. Gen. ___ 189
　Mary Charlotte 189
　Mary S. 11
　Dr. Montague 236
　Rev. Mr. (officiate)166
　Sarah 236
　William 280
Jacobs, Abraham 78
　Barnard 237
　Catharine 246
　Eleanor 211
　Philip 310
　Mrs. S. 78
　Samuel 108
　Sarah 261
Jacques, Ann 73
　William 73
Jahan, Joseph 17
James, Clarissa 57
　Elizabeth 75,230
　Jane 249
　Col. John 57
　Judge ___ 249
　Samuel 269

Jamieson, Dr. ___ 252
　Rachel 160
Jamison, Jacob Rumph 220
　Dr. V.D.V. 148,220
　Van-da-Vastine 148
Jarman, Charlotte 32
　John Jr. 192
Jaundon, Daniel 255
Jeannerett, John J. 269
　John Jennings 326
Jefferds, Ann 120
Jeffers, Henry 139
Jefferson, Thomas 297
Jefferys, Mary Ann 67
Jeffords, Hannah 170
　Samuel 313
Jeffrey, Francis 286
Jenkins, Ann 102
　Barbary C. 161
　Capt. Benjamin 330
　Maj. Daniel 11
　Edmund B. 310
　Rev. Edward (officiate)8,331
　Elias 262
　Elizabeth 262
　Emeline 262
　Isaac 56
　John 228,287
　Jno. H. 333
　Col. Joseph 102
　Martha S. 228,318
　Micah 161
　Providence 56
　Providence Grimball 326
　Rev. Dr. (officiate) 6,15,
　　25,51(2),78,81,92,95,96(2),
　　97,99,100(2),105,106,107,
　　111,121,128,129(2),133(2),
　　135,136,139(3),140,143,155,
　　158,161,162(2),165,168(2)
　Rev. Dr. 153
　Rev. Mr. (officiate) 1,3,
　　4(2),7(2),10,13,16,21,25,
　　27(2),32(2),33,36,37,38(2),
　　43,48,50(2),52(2),54,55,
　　58(2),62,72,79,108,127,131
　Sarah 139
　Susannah 153
Jennings, John 195
　John Sr. 158
　Margaret 98
Jerman, Edward 57
　Rebecca 57
　Thomas Satur 258
Jermyn, Edmund Horatio 327
Jervais, James 135
　Sinclaire D. 113
　see also Gervais
Jervey, Dr. David 133
　Florida 50
　Capt. Thomas H. 38,50,125
　Martha Hall 127
Jessop, Eliza 94
Jocelin, Henry 75
Jocelyn, Samuel Russell 306
Johnson, Abigail 297
　Abigail Fowler 337
　Ann 290
　Catherine 144,281
　Elijah 206
　Elizabeth 47
　Capt. Francis 223
　Hannah 152
　Harriet T. 206
　Hester 156
　Dr. Isaac A. 272
　Jabez W. 144
　Capt. James 8

Johnson (cont'd)
  Jesse 314
  John 49,187,297,337
  Capt. John 333
  John Jr. 64
  Dr. Joseph 48
  Joshua 38
  Lawyer 47
  Nicholas 50
  Rev. Mr. (officiate) 152
  Richard 201
  R. Pope 318
  Sarah B. 201
  Stephen 213
  Tabitha 43
  Thomas N. 51
  William 122,194,206
  Rev. Wm. B. (officiate) 133,205
  William Henry 122
Johnston, Aaron 216
  Alexander 194
  Archibald 176
  Archibald S. 164
  Benjamin 153
  Charles 77
  David 5,242
  Elizabeth 177,243
  Eliza Evans 103
  James 125
  Jane 190
  John 102,281
  Capt. John 313
  Mary H. 319
  Mary Susan 313
  P.W. 319
  Peter 111
  Rev. Mr. (officiate) 193
  Richard 83
  Robert 275
  Robert McKenzie 138
  Sarah Vincent 150
  Susannah 275
Joice, ___ 130
Jones, ___ 145(2),296
  Abraham 186,270
  Alexander 254
  Ann 179
  Augustus D. 175
  Rev. David (officiate) 317
  Edward 179
  Dr. Edward 179
  Elias 43
  Eliza 164
  Elizabeth Martha 145
  Emily 237
  Frances 282,294
  Gabriel 153
  George 98
  Hannah 48
  Harriet F. 254
  Henry 255,263
  Henry John 103
  Isaac 131
  James 8,73
  John 46,112,169
  Joseph 22,294
  Capt. Joseph 153
  Joseph Hopkins 141
  Joshua 2
  Mrs. ___ 153,193
  Margaret Lockhart 200
  Mary 162,215,222
  Mary Ann 108
  Mary S. 161
  Nuble Wimberly 101
  Parul T. 217,282
  Perez 237

Jones (cont'd)
  Rev. Mr. (officiate) 106 182
  Samuel 14,196,213
  Samuel B. 287
  Samuel P. 200
  Sarah 78,119
  Sarah Ann 202
  Skelton 270
  Rev. Thomas 78
  Vinson 47
  William 61,161,166,202
  Joor, Dr. ___ 146
  William 146
  see also Ioor
Jordain, Michael 4
Jordan, Christopher 134
  Hannah 195
  James 84
Joseph, Francis 221
  Israel 84
  Mary 216
Jouve, George 96
Joy, Abraham 48
Joyeux, John Charles 5
Joyner, J. 8
  Sarah Oliver 8
  William Howlet 291
June, Amelia L. 188
  John Stephen 319
  Mary Ann 319
  Solomon Peter 158

Kahnle, Barbara Margaret 239
  John Harman 239
Kaiser, John Jacob 195
Kalteisen, Michael 183
Kandal, Mary 320
Kay, Hester 44
  James 163
Keagg, Ann Catharine 103
Keanon, William 23
Keantish, Nathaniel 160
Keas, William 210
Keating, Elizabeth 189
  James 171
  Michael 322
  William 38
Keckeley, William 81
Keeling, William 76
Keen, Mary 102,110
  Capt. Thomas 81,102
Keily, Anne 11
  James 11
Keith, Ann B. 99
  Rev. Dr. Isaac S. (officiate) 8,11,81,337
  Rev. Dr. Isaac S. 85
  Rev. Dr. Isaac Stockton 289
  Rev. Dr. (officiate) 6,9, 11,16,26,29(3),31,34,40, 55,65,66(3),73(2),77,85, 90(2),91,95,98,99,109,112, 128,132,137,138,145,162, 167,194,200,217(2),218,219, 226,231,238,240,259,268, 272(3),273,274
  Rev. Mr. (officiate) 3(2), 5,98
  Sylvanus 155
Kelley, Rev. Mr. 109
Kelly, Christopher 318
  David 293
  Eliza 53
  George Eberley 130
  Jacob 284
  John 42,288
  Mary 130

Kelly (cont'd)
  Michael 134
  Thomas 109
Kelsall, Eliza D. 160
Kelsey,William 33
Kelton, Mr. ___ 114
Kemble, Elizabeth 110
Kemper, Rev. Mr. 329
Kempton, Henrietta 146
  Penelope Ann 67
Kenan, George 14,41
  Henry 93
  Thomas 44
Kendall, Ezra 315
Kendrick, Rev. Bennet 168
Kennard, Thomas 176
Kennedy, Andrew 47
  Ann Bensley 66
  Edward 63
  Eliza 134
  George 218,222
  Capt. James 66,82
  John 9,10,63
  Lionel H. 245
  Rev. Dr. (officiate) 90
  Rev. Mr. (officiate) 238
  Susannah 48
Kenney, Rachel 248
  see also Kenny
Kennon, Henry 85
Kenny, John 35
  see also Kenney
Kenrick, Rev. Mr. 89
Keough, Mary Anne 198
Kerr, Adam 299
  Andrew 299
  Anna 66
  Eliza 47
  Elizabeth 299
  Henry 189
  John 189,209
  Mary Ann 300
  Samuel 43
Kerblay, Joseph Maria Lequinio 267
Kern, Daniel 44
  Frederick 44
  J.F. 44
  John F. 216
  Mary Ann 216
Kerrison, Samuel 26
Kershaw, Col. Joseph 152
Kerton, ___ 296
Ketchum, Benjamin 301
Kettleband, David 99
Key, Catharine Tomkins 170
  Capt. Thomas 170
Keyler, Richard Berisford 174
Kiddell, Charles 102
Killan, James
Kimball, Eliza 226
  George 203,226
  John 62
Kimmel, Rachel 36
Kincaid, Alexander 88
  James 25
King, Benjamin 195
  James 107
  John 298
  Maria Ann 195
  Mary 286,299
  Mitchell 241
  Peninnah 195
Kinloch, Ann 261
  Ann Isabella 53
  Francis 53,261,295
  Mrs. ___ 295
Kirmont, David 33,261

Kinney, John 180
Kippenberg, Andrew 272
Kircher, Nancy 168
Kirkland, Dr. Joseph 324
Kirkpatrick, Rev. Mr. 312
Kire, Alexander 263
Kirk, Emily Louisa 162
   George 147
   John D. 148
   Rupert 75
Kirkland, Capt. Edward 186
   Dr. Joseph 66
   Joseph Jr. 66
   William 156
Kirkpatrick, James 221
Kirkwood, John 74
   Widow ___ 74
Kissick, Margaret 71
Kling, Mary 216
Knap, Margaret 217
Knox, ___ 269
   Matthew 78
   Rev. William 39
Koehler, Christian 138
   see also Kohler
Koger, Capt. Joseph 99
   Joseph Sr. 290
   Mary 99
Kohler, Frederick 288
   see also Koehler
Kohne, Frederick 164
Kollock, Rev. Dr. Henry 306
Kreitner, Barbara 150
Kuhn, Adam, M.D. 317

Laborde, Zelie 224
Lacey, John T. 181
   see also Lacy
Lacroix, Francis 146
Lacy, Mary 33
   see also Lacey
Ladson, Ann 9
   Charlotte 151
   Eliza Ann 127
   Elizabeth 305
   Elizabeth Ferguson 189
   Henrietta 134
   Maj. J. 151
   Maj. James 9,164,189,258
   James Jr. 46,238
   Major ___ 72
   Mary 72
   Sarah Reeve 164
   Sophia 297
   Thomas 127
Laffont, John 124
Lahiffe, John 15
   John Mills 172
Laidler, Capt. William 318
Lamar, Philip 177
   Ruth 177
Lamb, Capt. James 176
   Mary 83
   Mary Ann 176
Lampkin, Lt. Peter 68
Lamont, Capt. James 52
Lancaster, William 124
Lance, Lambert 18,79
   Major ___ 18
   Rev. Mr. (officiate) 297
   Sarah L. 79
   William 257
Landauer, Catharine 72
Landershind, John Christian 168
Lane, John Homer 156
   Mr. ___ 4
   Mrs. ___ 4

Lane (cont'd)
   Mary Jane 309
Lang, Hannah Laetitia 308
   James Wilson 74
   John 308
Langfitt, Thomas 102
Langley, William 25
Langlois, Cecile 139
Langstaff, Benjamin 123,257
   John Matthew 67
Langton, David 330
   John 276
Lanneau, Peter 163
L'Ans, Dorothea M. 51
Laroque, Antoinette 165
Larrabee, William 46
Larry, Ann Gibbon 264
   Peter 200,264
Lasteu, Benjamin 198
Latargue, Dr. John 155
Latham, Catharine 3
   Daniel 3,28,270
   Eliza 28
   George 140
   Joseph 145
   Martha 202
   Mary 270
   Sarah 110
Lathrop, Rev. John 293
Latimer, Mary 310
   Michael B. 330
Latta, Rev. Mr. 103
Laughton, Capt. William 11
Laurens, Henry 246
   Col. Henry 246
Laval, Jacint 95
   Major ___ 239
   Rebecca 239
   Rodolphe 330
Lawrence, Charles 132,156
   Edward 22
   Eliza Maria 277
   Ettsel 73
   Capt. James 281
   Lucy 286
   Peter 125
   Robert D. 169
   Samuel 8
   William D. 211
Lawson, Francis S. 212
   John 64
   Robert 108
   see also Lowson
Lawton, Bulah 8
   Winborn Jr. 105
Layne, Charles Sr. 336
Layten, William 2
Lazarus, Aaron 62
   Caroline 161
   Hannah 50
Leacraft, John 147
Leadbetter, Mary 207
Lear, Col. Tobias 304
Lebby, Ann Hawkins 245
   Nathaniel 72
   Nathaniel Sr. 36
   Robert 4
   William 22
Lebun, Rev. Father William 188
Lechais, Andrew Anthony Charles 289
Lechmire, Richard N. 92
Ledbetter, Henry 71
Leduc, Lawrence 263
Lee, Ann Maria 289
   Anthony 127,235
   Caroline Dorothea 72
   Catharine Jane 189

Lee (cont'd)
   Francis J. 261
   Harriett 57,58,229
   Jemima 235
   Rev. Jesse 303
   Joshua 87
   Mary 73
   Nathaniel 133
   Paul S.H. 214
   Rev. Mr. (officiate) 296
   Richard Jr. 137
   Sally 170
   S. Juliana 290
   Rev. Mr. States 305
   Stephen 184,289
   Maj. Stephen 72
   Susannah Martha 77
   Theodorick 290
   William 57,58,73,74,77,168 206,333
   William Jr. 58
   Col. William 229
Leefe, Benjamin 6
Lees, Catharine Ecklin 4
Leetz, Mary 166
Legare, Alice 201
   Benjamin 201
   Daniel Jr. 92,253
   Dr. Daniel 145
   Eliza C. 238
   Elizabeth 253
   Elizabeth Martha Player 212
   Francis Yonge 240
   Hannah A. 54
   Isaac 212
   John 139
   Joseph 14,139
   Joshua Plair 333
   Mary 14,112
   Nathan 80,113
   Nathaniel 30
   Sabina T. 80
   Sarah 109
Lege, Simonette 217
Leger, Elizabeth 62
Legge, Ann Saunders 254
   Edward 254
   Edward Bonneau 84
   Thomas W. 319
Legras, J. 268
Lehre, Julia 219
   Col. Thomas 219
Leith, Alexander 92
Leland, Rev. Dr. 293,302
   Rev. Mr. 271,279,290(2)
   Rev. Mr. A.W. 309
Lenox, Judith 182
   Mrs. ___ 114
   William 64,69,182
Lenud, Eliza Love 151
   Lt. Henry Laurens 229
   Louis 82
LeMercier, Rev. 130,134
Leonvalle, Andrew 51
Lepear, Esther 159
Lepelly, M. Pleville 129
LePoole, Peter 249
LePortevine, Jane 99
Lequeux, John 59
LeRoy, Mr. ___ 32
   Sophie 137
   Xavier Joseph 134
Lesesne, Charles 136
   Charles K. 254
   Daniel 274
   Eliza 82
   John Frederick 143
   Joseph 88

Lesesne (cont'd)
  Thomas 94,285
Leslie, Capt. David 109
  Capt. Henry 139
  Jane M. 159
  Mary 1
Lestargette, Eliza Elliott 138
  Lavinia Perran 289
  Lewis 126,138,166,210,289, 295
  Louisa Ann 126
  Sophia Margaretta 210
Letant, Gilleron 79
  Louise Francois Judet 79
Lettsom, Dr. ___ 293
Leveen, Mrs. ___ 181
Levi, Eleazer 135
  see also Levy
Levins, Capt. James 316
Levrier, Rev. Mr. 82
  Rev. Mr. (officiate) 105
Levy, Ann 193
  Bella 165
  Elizer 30
  Emanuel 305
  Hannah 83
  Hart 165
  Isaac 193,202
  Capt. J. Mairs 286
  John 26
  Samuel 44,83
  Sarah 40,52
  Simon 109
  Solomon 83
Lewis, Ann 219
  Anna Maria 309
  Charles J. 111
  D. 103
  David 119
  George William 145
  Rev. Joshua(officiate) 109
  Mrs. ___ 103
  Margaret E. 285
  Capt. Richard 76
  Sarah Elizabeth 166
  Sarah M. 271
  William 106
  Capt. Wm. Peter 152
Lexon, Hugn 157
Ley, Francis 235,249
  Maria Lucy 249
  Thomas 171
Liber, Ann Eliza 112
  John 73
Libert, Elizabeth 50
Liddle, John 128
Lide, William Henry 135
Lightbourn, Francis Stiles 55
Lightburn, Mary 43
Lightwood, E. 56
  Edward C. 206
  John 155
Lillibridge, James Murray 164
  John 316
Lilly, Rev. David 163,186
  Mary 163
  Rev. Mr. (officiate) 45, 155,159
  Rev. Samuel 171
Limehouse, Eliza 26
Lincoln, Elizabeth 240,247
  Horatio 149,247
  Capt. Luther 240
  Rev. Mr. 147-148
Lindo, William 100
Lindsay, John 122
Lindsey, Esther 51
  Capt. Samuel 51

Lines, Eliza M. 316
Ling, John 222
  Philip 113
Linguard, Mary 259
Lining, Maj. Charles 114
Linn, Rev. Mr. (officiate) 52
  Rev. William 192
  see also Lynn
Linsee, John Lewis 166
Linton, Samuel 36
Lipham, Maj. Aaron 299
  Lucy 299
Lippincott, Jacob 52
Lish, Margaret 312
Lithgow, Robert 49
Little, Ann 174
  Robert 110
  see also Liddle
Littlefield, Benjamin 21
Littlejohn, Duncan 97
Litz, Bernard 127
Livie, Robert 174
Livingston, Christian 92
  Edward 114
  Henry 278
  John R. 314
  Joseph H. 53
  Robert F. 126
  Robert R. 277
  Serena 314
  Telliafero 214
  Capt. William 92
Lloyd, Hester 239
  John 166,183
  John P. 195
  Joseph 317
  Susanna 195
Loathridge, David 253
Lockless, Jane 175
Lockwood, Amariathea Perkins 329
  Amarinthia Lowndes 145
  Joshua 145,329
  Joshua Jr. 72
  Thomas Perkins 242
Logan, Christian M. 56
  Daniel Webb 320
  George 40,51,198
  John 20,58
  John C. 280
  Mary 38
  Rev. Mr. 112
  Ensign Robert 283
  Thomas 217
  William 40,320
Londay, Isabella 131
London, John 295
Long, Col. Benjamin 275
  Felix 326
  Henry 304
  John 251
  Mary 251
  Capt. Robert 113
  William 4
Loper, Daniel 39
Lopez, David 257
  Rebecca 276
Lord, ___ 131
  Andrew 252
  Anne 131
  Benjamin 131
  Benjamin Sr. 159
  Jacob Nathaniel 196
  Miss ___ 252
  Richard 69
  Thomas 21
L'Orient, Lewis 89
Lorton, Thomas 96

Love, Charles 179
  Duncan 96,107
  Elizabeth 325
  Elizabeth Catharine 168
  James 258
  John 66,190
  Mrs. Rase 107
Loveday, John 86
Lovejoy, Hannah 131
Lovell, ___ 326
  John Pitman 135
  Josiah Sturgis 140
Lovely, Alfred Augustus 279
Lowe, ___ 329
  John 49
  Margaret 131
  Mary 180
  Vincent M. 307
Lowndes, Rawlins 4
  William 46
Lowrey, Jane 221
Lowson, Capt. John 138
  Mary Ann 138
  see Lawson
Lucas, Ann 230
  Jonathan 230
Ludlow, Lt. Augustuc C. 281
Lumberton, Miss ___ 99
Lupolow, Praskowoa 234
Luscombe, Dorothea M. 132
  Elizabeth 126
  Capt. George 70
  Capt. John 51
Lusher, George 128
Luther, Simeon 255
Lyman, Capt. Cornelius 110
  William C. 317
Lynch, Charles A. 85
Lynn, Anna Maria 327
  John 206
  John Stoney 335
  Kezia Ann 206
  Robert 327
  see also Linn
Lyons, John 12

McAllister, Rev. Mr. 201
McAlpin, Angus 87
  Archibald 219
McBride, Alexander 22
  James 63
  Margaret 48
  Rebecca 101
  see also Macbride
McCa, Ann Louisa 122
  John 122,151
  see also McKay
McCabe, Rev. Mr. 336
McCall, Beekman 286
  Dr. Edwin Leroy 215
  Elizabeth Hamilton 311
  Hext 274
  James 311
  John 3,336
  John Hort 38,227
McCalla, Rev. Daniel (officiate) 14,16,80,133
  Rev. Dr. Daniel 54,221
  Dr. ___ 214
  Jane Harrison 54
  Rev. Dr. 193,220
  Rev. Dr. (officiate) 66,93, 111(2),170,187,196,212
  Rev. Mr. (officiate) 38, 125,129
  Sarah Barksdale 214
  Dr. Thomas H. 216
McCants, John Croskey 23

358

McCants (cont'd)
  William 23
McCarthy, John 264
McClain, John 54
McClalen, Susannah 39
McClaren, Mary Ann 75
McCleish, Agnes 320
  James 202,277
  Mrs. ___ 227
  see also McCliesh
McClellan, Ann R. 87
McCliesh, Jane 187
  see also McCleish
McClure, Alexander 260,294
  John 260,294
  William 285
  William Jr. 91
McComb, James 254
McConchie, Samuel 179
McCoombs, Elias C. 123
  Capt. R. 123
McCord, Catharine 5
  Joseph 185
  William 5
McCormick, Rev. A. T. (officiate) 241
  Arthur 23
  Eliza 81,251
  Rev. Mr. (officiate) 260
McCreless, Lewis 77
McCrackan, James 98
McCrady, John 65
McCredie, Andrew 165
  David 254
  James 90
  William 313
McCullah, Rev. Mr. 161
McCuller, Rev. Matthew 129
  Rev. Mr. 100,200
McCulley, Rev. Andrew 35
McCulloch, John 26
  Rev. Mr. (officiate) 98
McDaniel, Daniel 251,253
  Susannah 251
McDevett, Eliza 318
McDonald, Col. Adam 123
  Daniel 276
  Hannah Mary 218
  Sarah 123
McDonnell, Col. Edward 273
McDonnoll, Lt. Angus 233
McDow, Mary 222
McDowall, ___ 192
  Alexander 225
McDowell, Agatha 176
  Ann A. 280
  Barbara 141
  David 202
  John 141
  Gen. Joseph 20
  Maria Ann 157
  Patrick 176(2)
McElhenney, Rev. James 272
MacErrocher, John 22
McEves, Julien 160
McFaddin, Eliza 191
  Col. Thomas 191
McFall, William 223
McFarlan, ___ 26
  Alexander 80
  Andrew 142
  Elizabeth M. 244
McFie, John 200
McGain, James 89
McGill, Margaret 31
  Susan 305
McGillivray, Alexander Hinckley 275

McGillivray (cont'd)
  Mary 79
  William 79
McGinney, Richard 7
McGiveran, Elizabeth 26
McGolrick, Felix 136
McGowen, James 293
McGrath, Edward 254
  Richard 233
McGregor, Neal 55
McGuerton, Daniel 62
McGuire, Elizabeth 103
  see also Macguire
McHay, William 316
McHeath, James 5
McHerron, Anne 5
McHugh, Francis 76
McHugo, Jane 25
McIlhenny, John 59
  Capt. John 92
McInnes, Alexander 322
  Helen 330
  Joseph 37,330
McIntire, Thomas 38
McIntosh, Elizabeth 222
  Capt. John 222
  Lachlan 129,133
  Simon 155
McIver, John 14(2), 184
McKay, Adam 101
  Ann 71
  George 67
  Mr. M. 71
  Samuel 314
  see also McCa, Mackay
McKearly, Jennet 155
McKee, Abel 195
  Catherine 211
  John 116,211
  see also McKey, McKie
McKeever, John 22
McKeil, Thomas 180
McKelvy, David 232
McKenzie, Alexander 51
  Catherine 136
  Charlotte 212
  Henry 194
  Jane 241
  John 198
  Kennedy 112
  Louisa 157
McKewn, Jane E. 208
  William 244
McKey, Sarah 116
  Sophia 209
  see also McKee, McKie
McKie, Brice 89
McKiernan, James 99
McKimmy, William 161
McKinney, Eliza 131
McKinzy, Margaret 212
McKnight, Rev. John 175
  Mary 175
  Rev. Mr. (officiate) 83
McKowen, A. 202
McLachlan, Duncan 203
McLardy, Mrs. ___ 171
McLaws, Anna Margaretta 229
McLean, Caroline 332
  Eliza 309
  Evan 154
  Evean 123
  Gilbert 91
  John 309
  Margaretta 126
  Mary 219
  Michael 87
  Norman 243

McLean (cont'd)
  Rosanna 154
McLeod, Rev. Donald 288,332, 336
  Rev. Donald (officiate) 52, 101,102
  George Thomas 143
  Hannah 140
  Mary 278,288
  Rev. Dr. (officiate) 190
  Rev. Mr. (officiate) 56, 103,157,228,231
  Sarah B. 336
  see also Macleod
McMahon, Owen 65
McMillan, Thomas 148
McMurrich, Donald 94
McNair, ___ 50
McNeal, James 192
  John 100
McNeil, Archibald 209
  Capt. ___ 43
  Daniel 207
  Susannah 141
McNellage, Sarah Joyse 195
  William 232
McNight, Rev. Mr. ___ 120
McNish, John 114
  Mary 155
McPherson, ___ 12
  Ann 334
  Eliza M. 162
  Gen. John 162,334
McQuain, Rev. Mr. 175,200
McQuinn, Rev. Mr. 195
McQuiston, Archibald 243
McVain, Rev. Dr. 213
  Rev. Mr. 203,204,211
McVean, Rev. Mr. 214
McVere, Catharine 70
McWhann, Jane 185
  William 185
McWhorter, Dr. Alexander B. 293
  Rev. G. G. 194
  Rev. Mr. 101

M___, Mrs. S. 53
Mabbot, Samuel 314
Macadam, Horatio Nelson 209
  James 82,209
Macauly, George 248
  Lydia 248
Macbride, Dr. James 321
  see also McBride
Maccho, Clarissa 112
MacDonough, Commodore ___ 306
  Thomas 104,306
Macguire, Hugh 216
  see also McGuire
Mack, Capt. John C. 158
Mackay, Dr. John 167
  Robert 304
  Sarah M. 167
  see also McKay
Mackenzie, H. 18
  Capt. Kenneath 322
Mackey, Crafts 93
  Dr. ___ 84
  Harriet 84
  James 191
  see also Mackie, Makky
Mackgivrin, Ann 93
Mackie,Ann 187
  Dr. James 183
  Dr. John 187
  Sarah 183
  see also Mackey,Makky

Macleod, Hannah 130
  see also McLeod
Macmurphy, Daniel 122
  John 122
Macnamara, John 192
Macomb, James 7
  Mary 7
Maddell, Rev. Dr. M. 192
Maddigan, Bridget 109
Maddon, Mary 83
Madiso, Capt. ___ 205
Madison, Rt. Rev. James
  (officiate) 259
  John 220
  Mrs. ___ 260
Maginnis, Samuel Jameson 124-125
Magrath, John 260
  Michael 237
Magruder, Lt. Thomas W. 313
Maguier, James 129
Maguire, Joseph 294
  see also McGuire
Mahar, M. 274
Maheo, Lewis 236
Maine, Elizabeth 162
  James 145,162
  John 187
Mair, Ann 37
  James 3,37,101,227
  Martha 62
  Patrick 26,62,106
  Rev. Mr. ___ 69
Makahaly, Michael 47
Makky, Jane 283
  John 197,283
  see also Mackey
Malbone, Edward G. 168
  Francis 70
  Freelove Sophia 70
Malcomson, Rev. James 92
  Rev. Mr. 82,84,87
Mallard, Rev. Mr. 245
Mallison, Sarah 99
Malone, John 32
Mann, Eleanor 72
  Elizabeth 245
  George James 93
  Dr. John P. 141
  Margaret 212
  Spencer John 171
Manigault, Carolina 316
  Elizabeth 173
  Maj. G.H. 312
  Gabriel 316
  Peter 248
Manly, Capt. John 238
Manners, Archibald 118
  Margaret 118
Manning, Col. ___ 147
  Laurence 99
  Mary Matilda 147
Manno, John 282
Mansfield, Seraphana Matilda
  Juliana Sophia Anna 201
Manson, Alexander C. 329
  Andrew 272
  Ebenezer 108
Maples, Richard 116
  Thomas 116
Mareo, Lewis 245
Margart, John Henry 79
Marian, Francis Jr. 152
Marion, Eliza 201
  Robert 243
  Theodore Samuel 201
Markley, Abraham 58
  Abraham Jr. 32

Markley (cont'd)
  Elizabeth 58
  Henry 60
  Peter 132
Marks, Alexander 300
  Mark 203
Marlen, Maria 184
  William C. 4
Maromet, Ann 63
Marret, Rev. Mr. 251
Marsan, Ann 256
Marsh, Ann Louisa 174
  Eliza 313
  Rev. Samuel (officiate)
  141,170,234
Marshall, Chancellor 187
  John 167
  Mary G. 159
  Robert 77
  Sarah 278
  Theodore Gaillard 187
  Dr. Thomas 17
  William 120,177
Martain, Philip B. 19
Martin, Ann Catherine 205
  Auguste 160
  Catherine 147
  Charles Jr. 141
  Charlotte Ogier 303
  Eliza 200
  Eliza C. 260
  Elizabeth 16,163
  Elizabeth P. 138
  Dr. George 86
  Harriet 293
  Jacob 190
  Dr. James 138(2)
  Jane E. 214
  John 161
  Gen. John 40
  John C. 61,193
  John Christian 16
  Mary 138,147
  Sarah C. 41
  Sarah G. 86
Martindale, James C. 280
Marvin, Azor S. 307
Mashaw, Elizabeth Mary 174
  Susannah Mary 152
Mason, Elizabeth M. 260
  Gen. Stephens Thomson 63
  Susan 48
  Rev. Thomas 244,260
  Rev. Thomas (officiate)244
  William 46,48,104
Massey, Jane 239
  Lt. Lee 259
  Miss ___ 33
Mathewes, Ann 54
  Eliza 47
  Rev. Edmund 47
  George 54
Mathews, Ann 189
  Benjamin 10
  Rev. Edmond 65
  Gen. George 266
  Jane 219
  John 50
  John R. 135
  Mary 47
  Rev. P. (officiate) 102
  Rev. Philip (officiate)
  106,162,214
  Rev. Dr. (officiate) 83
  Rev. Mr. (officiate) 1,3,
  4(4),5,14,21,25,29,94,100,
  102,112
  Thomas 47,127

Mathews (cont'd)
  William 189
  William Sr. 323
Matthews, Elizabeth Washington 205
  Rev. Edmund (officiate) 7,
  33,136
  Rev. Lastly 279
  Rev. Philip 171
  Rev. Philip (officiate) 54,
  55,135,160,162
  R. 205
  Rev. Dr. (officiate) 34
  Rev. Mr. (officiate) 160
Matthiessen, C.F. 200
Maull, James 85
Maverick, Samuel 49
Maxcy, Elizabeth Ann 331
  Joseph 291
  Levi Jr. 332
  Levi Sr. 332
  Virgil 331
Maxey, Rev. Dr. (officiate)
  144,214
  Thomas 52
  Thomas B. 158
Maxwell, Capt. Edward 195
  James R. 231
  John 126
  Joseph 143
  M. Sarah 231
  Peter 135
  Robert 98
  Simon 184
May, Robert 60
  Rose Ann 107
Maybank, David 164
Mayberry, Eliza Hayward 29
  Maria 184
  Maria Thomson 269
Mayer, Charlotte D. 21
  William Henry 255
Maylie, Charles 19
Mazyck, Ann 105,237
  Benjamin 4
  Catharine 4
  Daniel 268
  Capt. Daniel 277
  Daniel B. 56
  Isaac 152,291,320
  Mary 291
  Robert Wilson 269
  Stephen 105,204
  Stephen Jr. 211
  Dr. Thomas Winstanley 268
  William 4,232,320
Mead, Col. William 130
Meadows, Ann 13
  George 194
  Williams 180
  see also Medowes
Means, Dr. David 307
  Robert 113
Mease, Charles B. 274
Mecomb, Jane 20
  Robert 20
Medcalf, Maria 167
Medowes, George 58
  see also Meadows
Meek, Margaret 30
  Rev. Mr. (officiate) 285
  Rev. Dr. Samuel M. 280
Mege, Francis 85
  Julie Platon 134
  Lewis 134
Melding, Isaac 299
Mellard, Rev. James H. (officiate) 103,307,332

Mellard (cont'd)
  Col. William 332
Mellichamp, St. Lo 321
  Thomas 321
Melmoth, Mrs. ___ 262
Melrose, Thomas 189
Melvin, Addison 319
Mendenhall, Thomas 207
Mentges, Francis 124
Mercer, Harriet K. 143
Mercer, Rev. Mr. 299
Merceron, Marie Francoise 266
Meredith, Samuel 310
Merry, Catharine 25
  Maria 75
Messroom, Capt. James 48
Metcalf, John 233
Methwin, Dr. Alexander 177
Meursett, John G.D. 231
Mewshaw, David 206
Meyer, Joseph 98
Michau, Abraham 30
Michau, Capt. Abraham 178
  Mary Steed 178
Mickle, Robert 173
  see also Mikell
Middleton, Alexander 247
  Ann 248
  Arthur 218
  Elizabeth 151
  Mary 143
  Thomas 248
Midy, ___ 264
Mikel, John 97
  Josiah 71
  Sarah 154
  William 164
  see also Mickle
Miles, Eliza Smith 136
  James 136
  Capt. John 226
  Maj. James 220
  Jeremiah 303
  John 194
  John Sr. 232
  Robert 136
  Rev. Samuel 246
Milhouse, Daniel 71
  Frances 71
Milk, John 331
Millar, Philip 179
  William 44
Millen, Capt. ___ 26
Miller, Ann 244
  Ann Judith 247
  Augustus C. 335
  Capt. ___ 84
  Catharine 153
  Daniel 325
  David 106
  Frances 40
  George 124
  George William 215
  Jacob 214
  Jacob Henry 116
  James 247
  James Sr. 244,334
  Jane Douglas 228
  Jane Videaux 311
  John 87,101,102,145
  John B. 202
  Maj. John David 247,255,335
  John Michael 187
  Joshua 166
  Mrs. ___ 84
  Maria Julianna 335
  Martha A. 90
  Martha A.G. 50

Miller (cont'd)
  Mary 114,249,285
  Mary Ann 3
  Mary Magdalene Grimball 255
  Mathew 107
  Nicholas 225
  Rev. Mr. (officiate) 99
  Samuel W. 321
  Sarah 109
  Thomas Harvey 11
  William 39,87,308,311
Milligan, Eliza 272
  Joseph 227
  Rachel 241
  William 18,136
  see also Mulligan
Miling, Capt. ___ 288
  Mary Ann 288
Mills, Henry 52(2),144
  Honoria 24,82
  Hopewell 203
  Leonora 1
  Mary 195
  Rebecca 108
  Rev. Dr. (officiate) 72, 218,241
  Rev. Dr. 82
  Rev. Mr. (officiate) 53,65, 70,74,75,79,93,106,128,135, 136(2),158,188,217,245,259, 265,272
  Robert 210
  Sarah 128
  Susannah 65
  Thomas 112
  Rev. Thomas 24,65
  Rev. Thomas (officiate) 37, 140,199
  William 36
Milner, David 333
Mims, Capt. Briton 122
  Mary 138
  Robert Martin 122
Minchen, Humphrey 65,118
Miner, William 270
Mines, Rev. J. 200
Minola, John 174
Minot, Ann 132
  Benjamin 197,328
  John 197
  Sarah 98,126
  William Butler 29
Mintzeng, Ann Maria 27
  John P. 27
Miot, Charles 223
  John 223
  Martha 157
  Mary Ann 103
Mirault, Peter Michael Joseph 128
Mis-Campbell, James 99,252
  Mary 99
Mitchell, Agnes 121
  Andrew 73,136
  Ann 270
  Anna E. 32
  Charlotte 64
  Edward 32
  Dr. Edward 257
  Elizabeth 206
  Ephraim 55
  Isaac 259
  James D. 217
  Jane Elizabeth 325
  Col. John 265
  Dr. John 191
  John Hinckley 280

Mitchell (cont'd)
  Martha E.M. 265
  Mary 239
  Rev. Mr. (officiate) 86
  Sarah 218
  Thames 64
  Thomas C. 315
  Col. William Boone 190,231
Modeste, Andrew 141
Moer, William 160
Moffat, David 76
  Dr. James 242
  Thomas 242
Moise, Aaron 107,186
  Cherry 24
  Hyam 186
  Philah 111
Moles, Elizabeth 31
  James 31,113
  Dr. James C. 211
Molin, Henry 330
Moncrieffe, John 83
Mongar, Francis A. 321
Monies, Capt. Robert 217
Monk, Henry Haynesworth 247
  James 8,106
  John 56,247
  Rachel 8
Monpoey, Henry 106
Montague, Susannah 36
Montama, Mary 121
Montgomery, Rev. B. (officiate) 307
  Rev. Benjamin R. 109,169,192
  Elizabeth 169
  General ___ 96
  Miss ___ 14
  Rev. Dr. (officiate) 213, 214(2),290
  Dr. William 72
Monuar, Lewis 30
Mood, Edward 213
  Mary E. 255
  P. 213
Moody, William 20,21
Moon, Frances 60
  Patrick 183
  William 94
Mooney, Capt. James 193
  P. 70
Moonshire, Catharine 244
Moore, Col. Abraham 307
  Alexander 184
  Alfred 237
  Anne 251
  Charles 105
  Eliza 273
  Elsey 79
  Esther 197
  Frances 156
  General ___ 105
  Hannah 41
  Henrietta 139
  Isham 62
  James 221
  Jane 278
  John 39
  Maj. John 15
  John Elias 255
  Mrs. ___ 306
  Mrs. M. 168
  Martha 165
  Mary 307
  Mathew S. 174
  Col. Nicholas Buxton 304
  Richard 174
  Samuel 131
  Sarah 184

361

Moore (cont'd)
  Sarah I. 202
  Susannah 219
  Thomas 119,120
  Gen. Thomas 242
  W.W. Jr. 338
Moran, Fanny 215
Morang, Mr. ___ 4
Mordecai, David 55
  Gomez 211
  Joseph 235
  Rachel 239
  Rebecca 235
Mordica, Goodman 210
  Rebecca 210
Morel, Henrietta 64
  John 64
Morgan, Abigail 299
  Ann 121
  Anna 183
  Charles 34,120
  Clarence 117
  Elizabeth 34
  General ___ 299
  Isaac 73
  Margaret 234
  Nancy 190
  Rachel 152
  Rev. Mr. (officiate) 335
  Sarah 337
  William 146
  Dr. William 224
Morgandollar, John 14,135,213
  Mrs. ___ 213
  Susan 14
Moriarty, ___ 273
Morison, James 181
  Susannah Steedman 181
  see also Morrison
Mork, Elizabeth S. 320
  Lt. James 320
Morphey, Don Diego 97
  Thomas Manuel Julius 97
  see also Murphy
Morrel, Mrs. ___ 87
Morrill, Mary 83
Morris, James Pemberton 300
  Lewis 173
  Robert 140
  Samuel J. 292
Morrison, James 4,228
  John 17,76
  Capt. Joseph 199
  Margaret 199
  see also Morison
Morse, Mrs. ___ 17
  Rev. Dr. 17
  Samuel 116
Mortimer, ___ 239
  Rev. Benjamin (officiate) 283
  Edward 298
  Elizabeth Coram 267
  Elizabeth Hall 298
  William 267
Morton, Elizabeth 137
  John William 140
  Sarah 109
Moseley, Mason 145
  Patsey 40,41
  William 41,145
Moser, Eliza 131
Moses, Esther 24
  Isaac C. 50
  Israel 74
  Josiah 184
  Levi 216
  Mary 236

Moses,(cont'd)
  Meyer 50
  Myer 24,73,74
  Sarah 223
  Solomon 223,236
  Lyon 334
Moss, Catharine 139
  James 331
Mosse, Dr. George 196,201
  Sarah 201
Motta, E.D.L. 107,117
  Harris 84
  Isaac 41
Motte, A. 141
  Alexander Broughton 281
  Anne 58
  Maj. Charles 238
  Eliza T. 200
  Francis 240
  Jacob 58,238
  Martha Ward 240
  William 66
Mouatt, Elizabeth 185
Moubray, Martha 213
Moulson, Edward 87
Moultrie, Col. Alexander 173
  Eliza Charlotte 36
  Hannah 125
  William 36,121,125
  William Anslie 249
Mountain, Rev. Dr. 250
Mouzon, Charles 39
  Mary 223
  Samuel R. 223
Muchmore, Elizabeth 42
  Martha 262
Muckinfuss, Barbara 42
  Mr. ___ 63
  Michael 51,203
Muhlenberg, Frederick Augustus 17
  Gen. Peter 180
Muir, Capt. Charles 155
  William 294(2)
Muirhead, James 6
Muller, Ferdinand 112
  Isaac 46
Mulligan, B. 75
  John 25
  Joseph 99
  Samuel 163
  see also Milligan
Mulloy, Capt. William 207
Mumford, Julia Ann 194
Muncreef, John 16,268
  Mary 35,224(?)
  Mildred A.C. 251
  Richard 28,35,251
  Robert 224
Muncrieffe, John Jr. 179
  see also Moncrieffe
Mund, Rev. Mr. 2,43
Munds, Rev. Dr. (officiate) 37,94
  Rev. Israel (officiate) 21,91,105,106
  Rev. Mr. (officiate) 1(2),5,6,9,15,22,23,25,_,27(2),28,30(2),32,33,35(2),38,40(2),42,44(2),45,46(2),48(2),49,50(2),53(2),54(2)55,61,62(2),66,70(2),61,74 79(2),81,82(2),88,98(2),99 100(2),107(2),109(4),112(2) 113(2),114(3),115(2),116, 117(3),118(2),120(2),125, 126(2),128,130(2),131,132 (3),133,139(2),140(4),141,

Munds (cont'd)
  143,145(2),146,147(2),148 (2),149,150(2),152(2),153 (3),154,155,157(5),158,159, 162(3),163,164,165(2),166 (3),167(5),168(3),169,170 (3),174(2),183(2),185(2), 189(2),193(4),195,196,197, 200,202(2),203,204,205(2), 208,209(3),210,212(2),213 (2),215(3),218(2),219(3) 221(2),222,225,254,264,265, 266,267,335
  Rev. Mr. J. (officiate) 82
Mundy, Edward Miller 180
  Miss ___ 180
Munro, Amelia 41
  George 331
  Jane 228
  Janet 247
  John 163,204,228
  Capt. Joseph S. 335
  Mrs. ___ 332
  Margaret 191,204
  Nathaniel 164
  Robert 243,247
Muns, Rev. Mr. 14
Murdoch, Archibald 33
  Elizabeth 98
  Jannet 33
  Mary 243
  Robert 89
Murdoor, Margaret 258
Murphy, Arthur 118
  Eliza 268
  Gordon McNeal 197
  Harriet 195
  Rev. John D. 272
  Margaret 268
  Patrick 268
  Capt. William 318
  see also Morphey
Murray, Abigail Jenkins 331
  Elizabeth Hughes 74
  Hannah 186
  John 74,112
  John J. 112
  Joseph J. 118,331
  Martha Mary 331
  Mary 253
  Col. Thomas 44
  Maj. William 275
  William B. 249
Murrel, James W. 166
  John Jonah 22
  Margaret 275
  Mary E. 202
  Sarah 180
  Sarah A. 271
Mushett, John 162
Myers, Anna 95
  Charles 92
  George 45
  Rev. Joseph (officiate) 193
  Moses 95
Mylne, Elizabeth 27
  James 27.107
  Jane 263

Nagel, Christian 219
Nail, Casper 142
  Mary 142
Nankivel, Rev. Dr. 196
  Rev. Mr. 189
Napier, Eliza Jane 258
  Thomas 251,258,290
Naser, Frederick 182
Nasted, Frederick 226

Nauman, Ann 193
Neal, Daniel Jr. 142
  Most Rev. Leonard 316
  see also Neil, Niel
Nedligah, Michael 191
Negge, Capt. John H. 283
Negrin, Elizabeth 47
Neil, Peter A.R. 58
  see also Neal, Niel
Neilson, James 175
Neinerichs, Margareta Magdalena 105
Nelson, Archibald D. 316
  Rev. E. 42
  Henrietta 146
  Hester 29
  Isaac 292
  Isabella Eliza 325
  James 216,325
  Martha 194
  Susanna 292
  Lord Viscount 42
  Capt. William 140
Nesbit, Rev. Charles 78
Nevin, Thomas 193
Neufville, Ann 325
  Eliza 164
  Isaac 313
  John 88,112
Newall, Cunningham 172
Newby, Ann 158
  Jane 75
  John S. 17
  Robert 158
Newkerk, Gysbert 121
Newman, Charles 168
  Mary 43
Newton, ___ 51
  Elizabeth 197
  James 175
  Rev. John 193
  Capt. William 132
Neyle, Elizabeth 152
  William 54
Nibbs, William 138
Nice, Maj. John 144
Nicholas, William 310
Nichols, Ann E. 320
  Eliza 109
  George 154
  Margaret 154
  see also Nickels
Nicholson, Col. John 249
  Commodore John 91
  Joseph Hopper 311
  Commodore Samuel 256
Nickels, Capt. John 281
  see also Nichols
Niderburgh, Dr. S.N. 107
Niel, Melanie 64
  see also Neal, Neil
Nietheimer, Elizabeth 79
Nisbet, Alexander 275
  John 212
Nivison, John 62
Nixon, Charles J. 197
  Margaret 148
  Rev. Mr. (officiate) 110
Noble, Elizabeth 93
  Capt. Francis 322
  Hannah 39
  Mary Ann 24
  Thomas 176
Noel, William 65,210
Norman, Margaret 42
  Robert 42
Norment, John 177
Norris, Andrew 64

Norris (cont'd)
  James 142
North, Edward 35,51,129
  Elizabeth 5
  John L. 129
  Miss ___ 129
  Sarah 51
  Susannah 219,229
Northrop, Moses 256
Norton, Mary 53
  Rev. Mr. (officiate) 255
  Robert G. 201
  Sarah B. 302
  William 53
  William W. 88
Norvall, ___ 195
Norvel, Mrs. ___ 203
Nott, Louisa 165
Nowell, Edward B. 23
  John 156
  Mrs. Mary 156
  Thomas Smith 78
Nuby, Rev. Thomas 219

Oakford, Capt. Aaron 79
Oakes, Mary 250
Oats, Ann 264
  Mary 166
O'Banon, Jennings 220
O'Belan, Rev. Dr. 256
O'Brien, B. 175
  Mary Isabella 175
O'Connor, Daniel 47
  James 330
  Mrs. ___ 47
  Thomas 47
O'Daniel, Rev. Mr. 55
O'Donald, Catharine 114
O'Driscol, Capt. Cornelius 187
O'Farrell, Rev. Dr. (officiate) 99
  Rev. James 295
  Rev. Mr. (officiate) 40, 126(2),127,138,199,210
O'Gallagher, Rev. Dr. 124
Ogier, Catharine 207
  John M. 326
  Lewis 119,138,207
  Lewis Jr. 119
  Susan 138
  Thomas 95
Ogilvie, James 334
Ogle, Martha B. 209
Oglethorpe, General ___ 101
O'Hara, Daniel 191,216
  Daniel Jr. 191
  Henry 160
  John 216
  Oliver 274,300
O'Hear, Eliza 55
  Gates 105
  James 55,105
Ohring, Magness 133
O'Keefe, Catharine Oliwia 113
O'Kelly, John 191
Oldfield, Margaret 93
  R.P. 93
O'Leary, John 90
Oliphant, Elizabeth 13
  James 19
  Jane 19
Oliver, Elizabeth 3
  James 26
  Joseph 262
  Mary 127
  Peter 127
Ollivo, Mr. ___ 207
Olman, Joseph 46

Olman (cont'd)
  Mrs. ___ 46
Olney, Col. Jeremiah 272
O'Neal, Charles 118
  Louisa 280
  William 90
Ormond, Arabella 80
  Capt. William 46
Orr, Alexander R. 158
  William 65
Osborn, Elizabeth 188
  Thomas 188,191
Osgood, Rev. Mr. 312
Oswald, David 13
  Eliza 173
  John 18
  Dr. John 100
  Mary 3
  Sarah 173
Otis, Ann Stol 171
  Arthur 20
  Joseph 20,171
  Joseph Jr. 228
  Thomas 69
Otto, John 57
Ottolegui, Esther 208
Ottolengue, Abraham 261
Owens, James 198
  Mary E. 114
  Rev. D. (officiate) 200

Padget, Rev. Henry 321
Pagan, Archibald 222
  James 122
Pagels, Christian 220
Paine, Joseph 326
  Mrs. ___ 207
  Tom 207
  Seth 23
Palmer, Rev. B.M. (officiate) 195
  Rev. Benjamin M. 167
  Rev. Benjamin M. (officiate) 162,243
  Elihu 136
  Eliza 226,243
  Hannah Keith 297
  Capt. John 126
  Lt. Loring 304
  Mercy 111
  Rev. Dr. (officiate) 294, 297,299(2),314,315
  Rev. Mr. (officiate) 85,113 215
  Thomas 189
Pancake, John 282
Pardue, Lucilla 96
Parinchief, Mary 56
Parks, Elizabeth 53
  James 151,176
  John 91(2),337
  Rev. Mr. (officiate) 280, 299
  Samuel 109
  Lt. Samuel 266
  Sarah 91
Parker, Daniel 319
  Deborah 210
  Eliza 304
  Ferguson 35
  Henrietta Ann 153
  Sir Hyde 135,221
  Isaac 49
  John 34(2),78
  Capt. John 316
  John Wesley 81
  Mrs. ___ 35
  Nelly 71

Parker (cont'd)
  Phineas 210
  Rev. Dr. (officiate) 15,28
  Rev. Mr. (officiate) 39
  Rt. Rev. Samuel (officiate) 99
  Sarah 146
  Sophia 103
  Thomas 71,142
  Thomas Jr. 305
  Thomas C. 81
  Wm. McKenzie 35
Parkison, George 33,194
Parmele, Phineas 20
Parrington, William 111
Parrish, John 319
Parry, John 268
  Mary 268
Parsons, Ann 242
  Elizabeth Harriet 153
  Jane 132
  Joseph 153,161
  Timothy 153
Pasteur, Maj. Thomas 148
Paterson, Ann 181
  Catharine 196,324
  Eliza 2
  Hugh 196,324
  Robert 58
  see also Patterson
Paton, John 21,242
Patrick, Henry 188
  Philip 251
Patterson, Abraham 145
  Capt. David 179
  Elizabeth 76,167,322
  James 85
  Mary 139,165
  Mary Ann 293
  Capt. S. 56
  Samuel 165
  William 76,139,190
  Capt. William 216
  see also Paterson
Patton, Ann 276
  John 200
  William 299
  see also Paton
Paul, George 45,46
Pawley, Anthony 186
  Mary Man 186
Paxton, Henry W. 29
Payne, Charlotte 178
  Capt. James 153
  Jane 178
  John W. 273
  Serena Maria 262
  William 262
  William R. 178(2)
Payton, Charlotte 145
Peace, Rebecca 165
Pearce, Richard 274
  Thomas 230
  see also Pearse, Pierce
Peake, John Samuel 242
Pearis, Margaret 62
  Richard 62,164
Perase, M.P. 196
  Sarah 256
  see also Pearce, Pierce
Pearson, Capt. Benjamin 2
  Mary Ash 131
Peay, Austin F. 7
  Nicholas 287
Peck, Alfred 321
  William 321
Peden, William 195
Pegram, Capt. Edward 296

Peigne, Charlotte 279
Peire, Frances-Ninette 160
Peister, Sarah 167
Pellew, Sir Edward 85
Pelot, Maj. Charles 218,248
  Samuel 55
  Sarah Julia 248
Pelzer, Anthony A. 243
Pemble, David 209
Pendall, ___ 13
Pendarvis, Ann 1
Pendleton, Catharine 97
Penington, Edward 60
Penn, Richard 248
  William 248
Pennall, James 107
Penny, Delia Maria 307
  Samuel 307
Peper, John Diedrich 176
Pepper, Mary W. 132
Percy, Eliza Catharine 104
  Elizabeth 223
  Maj. John F. 223
  Peter 313
  Rev. Dr. 265,333
  Rev. Dr. (officiate) 104, 156,209,215,217,222(2)
  Rev. Mr. (officiate) 168 221
  William 265
Peries, M. 104
Perkins, Judith 223
Perman, George 27
Peronne, Capt. Caesar 262
  Carolina E.F. 262
Peronneau, Henry W. 326
  John 159
Perrault, Joseph 166
Perrein, Dr. Jean 108
Perriclard, John 117
Perrie, Ann B. 209
Perritt, Abraham 38
  Sarah 38
Perry, Benjamin 126
  Edward D. 328
  Eleanor 45
  Helen 285
  James 216
  Dr. James 59,219
  Jane L. 219
  Jane Matilda 232
  Janet 243
  Joseph 243
  Mary 27
  Rebecca 134
  Samuel 229
Perye, Mary 27
  see Peyre
Peters, J. 181
  Rebecca P. 294
  William 169
  Lt. William 245,271
Petre, G. 30
Petrie, Edmund 176
  Mary 176
Petsch, Harriett 274
  Julius 135
Pettus, William 326
Peyre, Francis 228
  John 27,165
  see also Perye
Peyton, Ann 181
  Richard 181
Pezan, T. Laimalbe 128
Phelps, Capt. Elijah 271
  Mary 52,189
Phenney, Josiah 245
Phillips, Alexander 275

Phillips (cont'd)
  Benjamin Hammett 64
  David 166
  Elizabeth 133
  Capt. Ezekiel 188
  Rev. John (officiate) 188
  Jonas 73
  Mary Philip 52
  Miss ___ 73
  Mr. ___ 161
  Rebecca 188
  Rev. Mr. (officiate) 159, 190,199,200,202,253
  Samuel 34
  Susan 162
Phipps, Jane 55
Phoebus, Rev. Dr. 196
  Rev. W. 256
Phoelon, Edward 43
Pickam, Margaret 4
Pickenpack, John 171
Pickens, Elizabeth 338
  Ezekiel 280,338
Pickering, John 110
Picket, Richard Harden 134
Pickion, Charles M. 142
Pierce, Anna 227
  Capt. Justus 227
  Maria 152
  see also Pearce, Pearse
Piercey, William 70
Piercy, Mary 28
Pike, Nathaniel 100
Pillans, John C. 243
Pilmore, Rev. Mr. 103
Pilsburg, William 23
  Capt. Wingat H. 296
Pilsbury, Amos 269
  Mehetable 258
  Samuel 23
Pinckney, Charles 287,315
  Maj. Gen. Charles Cotesworth 256
  Frances Henrietta 287
  Hopson 89,272
  M.B. 205
  Miss ___ 46
  Mary 89,256
  Mary E.L. 315
  Mary Elizabeth 272
  Roger 129
  Roger Jr. 129
  Thomas 46
  Thomas Jr. 75
  Maj. Gen. Thomas 283
Pinkerton, David 72
  Margaretta 72
Pintard, John Marsden 62
Pitcher, Mary 279
Pittman, Mrs. Ave 82
  Hardy 23
Pittenger, John 318
Placide, A. 267
  John Alexander 267
Platt, Ebenezer 3
Player, Charlotte 186
  Elizabeth 13
  Joshua 30,186
  Thomas 13
Pleasants, Elizabeth R. 316
Pledger, Lewis 323
  Maj. William 323
  William K. 330
Poaug, Harriet B. 25
Poalk, Margaret White 51
Pogson, Rev. Milward 104
  Rev. Mr. (officiate) 63,82, 84,99,129,134,230

364

Poincignon, Jane 49
Peter Anthony 49
Poindexter, Eliza 36
Poinsett, Dr. E. 55
  Dr. Elisha 70,88
  Hannah Frances 140
  Joel 140
  Susan 88
  Susannah 55
Polhill, Eliza St. John 212
Polk, Col. Charles 266
  Thomas 202
Pollock, Hugh 144
  John 121
  Mary 166
  Solomon 116
  William 257
Polony, Jean Louise, M.D. 121
Pon, Mary Ashby 10
Pool, Haven 247
  Isaac 283
Pooser, Elizabeth 96
  William H. 199
Pope, Mary 201
Poppenheim, Catherine 56
  John 171
  Lewis 56
Porcher, Dr. Francis Y. 248
  Isaac 38
  James 168
  Peter 167
  Philip Sr. 315
Portalis, Mr. ___ 180
Porteous, Alexander R. 219
  Alexander Rose 183
  Caroline 219
  Jane 112
  Caroline 219
  Jane 112
Porter, Rev. Mr. 199
Porter, Eliza Harrison 270
  John 134,270,315
  Rev. M. 176
  R.C. 114
  Samuel H. 176
  Thomas D. 181
Posey, Col. Thornton A. 321
Post, Jothan Sr. 309
Posson, Rev. Mr. Milward 67
Postel, Capt. Andrew 135
  Ann 25,233
  Col. Benjamin 5,191,242
  Catherine 258
  Eliza 191
  Hannah 338
  Col. James 133,248
  James C. 218
  Col. Jehu 338
  John 28
  Maj. John 233
  June Eliza 28
  Mary 135
  Mary Sophia 242
  Philip Smith 211
  Sarah 261
Poston, Hannah 307
Potter, Elihu 118
  George Washington 126
  Hannah 336
  John 206
  John Hamilton 206
  Joseph 215
  Thomas 236
Poullet, John 158
Pouyat, John Francis 134
  Maria 134
Powell, Dr. ___ 119,120
  Mr. ___ 144

Powell (cont'd)
  John 112,119,120
  Lt. John Floyd 97
  Col. Robert William 159
  William Hopton 159
Powers, Edward 277
  Mary 15
  Capt. Moses G. 184
  Capt. Nicholas 26
  Rev. Nicholas (officiate) 280
  Nicholes 19,57
  Rebecca 26
  Theodore 262
Poyas, Elizabeth C. 238
  Harriet 242
  Henry Smith 245
  James 312
  John L. 91
  John Lewis 46
  Lewis 214
  Mary Magdalen 46
Poyer, Rev. Mr. 71
Pratt, Capt. John 239
  Mary 239
  Samuel H. 242
Preble, Capt. George 188
  Commodore ___ 176
Prebble, Edward 13
Prentice, Jeffrey Otis 328
  Mary 203
Prescott, G.W. 306
Presley, John 81
  William 98
Pressley, John 88
Presstman, Frances 104
  George 104
Prevost, Lt. Gen. George 296
  Maj. Gen. 296
Price, Bethia S. 264
  Rev. G.H. (officiate) 8(2)
  John 178
  O'Brien Smith 311
  Rev. Dr. (officiate) 95
  Rev. Mr. (officiate) 43,46, 50,53,100,129,131,169,194, 108
  Rev. Thomas 300(2)
  Rev. Thomas (officiate) 186
  215
  Thomas H. 264
  Rev. Thomas H. (officiate) 162,230
Prieur, Laura 128
  Mr. ___ 128
Prince, Capt. Charles 87
  Elizabeth 312
  John 218
  Joseph 28
  Laurence 109
Pringle, Elizabeth Mary 188
  James Reid 162
  John J. 272
  John J. Jr. 159
  John Julius 188
  Judith 52
  Mary 21
  Robert 52
  Dr. Robert 245
  Robert A. 231
  Susan 272
Prioleau, Caroline 55
  Elizabeth 329
  Elizabeth Clara 308
  Isaac 219
  John 254
  John Cordes 308
  Mary 3

Prioleau (cont'd)
  Martha 149
  Dr. Philip G. 99
  Samuel 55,149,277,329
Prior, Samuel 32
Pritchard, Benjamin F. 238
  Joseph Price 37
  Lydia 305
  Mary 15,75
  Paul 75,223
  Paul Jr. 57
  Thomas 57
  William Sr. 28
Prizgar, Catherine 276
Proctor, Dr. George V. 311
Prosser, William 9
Provost, Louisa 62
Provoux, Capt. Adrian 100
Pryor, Major L. 125
Pugh, Rev. Evan 55
Pugson, Rev. Mr. (officiate)95
  see also Pogson
Pulsar(?), Daniel 301
  Mary 301
Puppo, Daniel C. 69
Purcell, Arabella 204
  Rev. Dr. Henry (officiate) 36
  Capt. Joseph 80,141
  Joseph R. 169
  Rev. Dr. (officiate) 7,13, 19,26,28,31
  see also Pursell
Purdie, Johannes M. 85
  Maria 335
Purdue, Milly 220
Purfield, Alician 158
Pursell, Rev. Dr. 17
  see also Purcell
Purvis, Burridge 303
Putnam, Abigail 335
  Elizabeth 97
  William 97
Pyeatt, Elizabeth 74
  Peter 74
Pyne, John 281

Quackinbush, Laurence 21
Quash, Robert 250
Quelch, Harriot 13
Query, John 82
Quigley, Mathew 319
Quimlan, Mary 76
Quin, Eliza 146
  James 75,182
  Thomas F. 153
  Thomas Fitzgerald 82
Quinby, Capt. Joseph 327
Quince, Susannah 272
Quinley, George 196

Raburn, David 194
Radcliffe, Rachel 192
  Thomas 149
  Thomas Jr. 82
Rade, Dr. ___ 208
  John Charles 208
Raguet, Condy 187
Raiford, William P. 36
Raine, Esther 216
  Samuel 29,216,219
  Sarah Ann 65
Ralvande, Maria R. 187
Ramadge, Mrs. ___ 10
  Samuel Smith 10
Rambert, Rachel 89
  see also Rembert
Ramsay, David 315

365

Ramsay (cont'd)
  Dr. David 246
  Ellen 306
  Dr. John 267
  Dr. Joseph Hall 73
  Judge ___ 122
  Maria 267
  Martha Laurens 246
  Mary 122
  Sarah Eliza 148
Ramsdy, Ephraim 28
Randal, Esther 30
Ranelagh, Lord Viscount 96
Rankin, Mary Ann 54
Rannie, James 279
Rater, Rev. Mr. 325
Rattoone, Rev. Dr. ___ 230
  Rev. Mr. ___ 65
Raushner, Lt. Henry 270
Ravardi, Maj. Ulrick 193
Ravell, John 105
  Rachael E. 104
Ravenel, Catherine 58
  Daniel 174,259
  Dr. Henry 298
  Dr. James 323
  Dr. Peter D. 206
  Stephen 4,58
Ray, Rev. W. 314
Raymond, Capt. George 166
Raynal, Lewis 183
  Lewis T. 42,217
  Martha Mary 183
Raynoldes, Caroline 27
  see also Reynolds
Razdel, David 271
Read, Dr. ___ 315
  Eleazer 311
  George Paddon 121
  Israel 183
  J.H. 320
  Gen. Jacob 300
  John Harleston 247,315
  Mary Jone 311
  Mary W. 315
  Sarah 217
  Sarah Arrabella Withers 320
  William 240
  Dr. William 217
  see also Reed, Reid
Reader, Catherine 2
Reagan, Mary 242
Realey, George 232
Reame, Rev. Mr. ___ 143
Recardo, R.J. 170
Redcliffe, Thomas Jr. 19
Reddall, Jane 129
Redlich, William 137
Redman, James 76
  Dr. John 197
  Samuel 29
  Sarah 142
Reed, Capt. ___ 276
  Eleazer 335
  Floranthe 251
  John 273,304
  Samuel 138
  see also Read, Reid
Rees, Elizabeth 40
  Dr. L.M. 212
  William 232
  William Jr. 40
Reese, ___ 15
Reeves, Abraham D. 297
  Amey 92
  Ann 295
  Capt. Enos 92
  see also Rieves

Reid, Eliza Hardy 81
  George 81
  Jane 11
  John 136,257
  Maj. John 294
  Joseph 11
  Margaret 248
  Rev. Mr. (officiate) 217
  Robert 41
  Robert Raymond 229
  Sarah H. 41
  see also Read, Reed
Reigne, John 271
  Louisa A. 271
Reilly, Eleanor 264
  Elizabeth 292
  James 264
  Robert 95
  Dr. T. 29
  Dr. Thomas 72
  see also Riley
Rembert, James 250,264
  Jane 287
  Priscilla 224
  Capt. William 112,224
  see also Rambert
Remmington, Frances 214
  James 214
Remondo, Peter 217
Remoussin, Daniel 27
  Marie Duvevier 279
  Paul Dan. 279
Rendell, George 221
  Washington 221
Reside, Elizabeth 41
Revel, George 61
  John 36,55
Rhett, Col. 272
Reynolds, Benjamin 164
  Carthew 85
  Elizabeth 33
  George N. 237
  Dr. James 267
  Maj. John 267
  Mary 107
  Mary Y. 164
  William 65
  see also Raynolds
Rhind, David 6
  Sarah Bruce 6
Rhodes, J. 230
  John 220,224
  Miss ___ 224
  Mary 230
  Dr. Nathaniel 190
  Dr. Nathaniel H. 130
  Paul Hamilton 190
  Thomas 220
Rhodus, Josiah 99
Ribault, Joshua 179
Rice, Capt. Thomas 324
Rich, Silvanus 102
Richards, Ann 132
  Mary 95
  Miss ___ 128
  Peggy 95
  Samuel 28
  William 95,132
  Capt. William 54
Richardson, Caroline 7
  Charlotte 40,183
  Cornelia Emerentia 18
  David 183
  Dorothy S. 231
  Gov. ___ 96
  Harriot 79
  Dr. Henry 25
  Col. J.B. 231

Richardson (cont'd)
  J. P. 241
  James 188
  James B. 233
  James Burchill 96
  Jane Bruse 188
  John P. 233
  Mrs. ___ 138
  Maria 109
  Thomas 135
  William G. 79
Richmond, Thomas 314
Rickets, John 262
Rickwood, Sarah 160
Riddlespurger, David 257
Rider, Capt. Matthias 106
Ridgeway, Mrs. ___ 193
Riedfield, Margaret 138
Rieves, Timothy 290
  see also Reeves
Riggs, Thomas G. 184,268
Righton, Elizabeth S. 226
  Jane Eliza 246
  Joseph 226,246,329
  Kitty F. 329
Riley, James 184
  John Sr. 29,79
  Nathan 106
  Susan 205
  Terence 84
  see also Reilly
Ripley, Robert 264
Risher, Benjamin 99
  Capt. Benjamin 236
Ritchie, Agnes 157
  Alexander 157
Rittenhouse, Nathaniel 331
Rivers, Charles Warsham 195
  Elizabeth 17
  Elizabeth Lois 177
  Esther 162
  Frances Susannah 95
  Francis 87,323
  George Washington 250
  Henry Sterling 162
  John 17,186
  Jonah 76
  Joseph 95
  Mallory 8,58,186
  Malory Jr. 177
  Martha 171
  Mary 68,87
  Mary Allson 95
  Mary Stiles 127
  Stiles 171
  Susannah 523
  Susannah Love 186
  Thomas 131
  William 169
Rivington, James 42
Roach, Mrs. ___ 128
  Mary 168
Roberds, Reuben 194
Roberts, Ann 100
  Charlotte Maria 140
  Col. ___ 100
  Grimball 151
  Capt. H. 39
  Rev. I.M. (officiate) 28
  Rev. J.M. (officiate) 15, 50,56
  John 10
  Rev. John 334
  Rev. John M. (Officiate) 57,79,85
  Rev. Mr. M. (officiate) 61
  Martha A.F. 334
  Peter 228

Roberts (cont'd)
 Rev. Dr. (officiate) 314
 Rev. Mr. (officiate) 7,143, 166,202(2)
 Capt. Robert 254
 Lt. Robert 143
 Samuel 160
 Sarah 81
 William 162
 William Henry 39
Robertson, Alexander 114,154
 Miss E. 337
 George 99
 Rev. Mr. J. (officiate)236
 James 114
 Samuel 76,305
 Thomas Bolling 335
Robin, Peter 165
Robinson, ___ 219
 Ann 81,141
 Capt. ___ 110
 Miss E.F. 118
 Elizabeth 107
 John 13,97
 Mary Ann 327
 Perdita 12
 Rachel 86
 Robert S. 115
 Samuel 107
 Septimus 86
 Susannah Fowler 82
 William 158
 William R. 141
Robiou, Charles 64
Rowland, Margaret D. 100
Ruberry, Benjamin W. 155
 Benjamin Wilkins 125
 Elizabeth 257
 Eliza Rhoda 212
 John 38,58,80,257
 Martha 58
 Sarah 38
Rudd,Rev. Mr. 247
Rockwell, Gertrude 120
Rockwood, Luther 296
Roddick, James 131
Roddom, Mary 70
Roddey, James 270,326
Rodgamon, Frances 107
Rodgers, Samuel 233
 see also Rogers
Rodick, Thomas 129
Rodman, Gibbes 273
 Gilbert 273
 John H. 175
 Sarah 10
Rodney, Caesar 236
 Caesar A. 236
Roe, Rev. Dr. (officiate) 93
 Salem 146
 see also Row, Rowe
Roerstler, Charles G. 325
Rogers, Isabella 77
 Rev. James 68
 Jane Wilson 68
 John R. 278
 Capt. Joshua 131
 Mary 25
 Rev. Dr. 244
 Sampson 16
 see also Rodgers
Roller, Margaret 202
Rollins, Capt. John 145
Roma, ___ 264
Romaine, Rev. Dr. ___ 233
Romeyn, Rev. Dr. 274
Roope, Catherine 40
Rootes, Martha J. 230

Rootes (cont'd)
 Thomas R. 230
Roper, Benjamin D. 161
 Elizabeth Harvey 102
 Lydia 122
 Maj. Thomas 102,122
Rosborough, Rev. William 230
Rose, Francis 53
 George Edward Charles Frederick Meredith 99
 Jeremiah 9,59
 John 119,303
 Susannah 9,14
 William 176
Ross, A. Elizabeth 245
 David 82
 Capt. Edward 219
 Elizabeth 84
 Jane 24
 Jeremiah 140
 John 89
 Capt. Thomas 159
Rosse, Capt. Paul 182
Roulain, Daniel 31
 Letitia 31
 Robert 170
Roulstone, Lavinia 251
Roupell, Elizabeth 261
Rouse, Martha M. 42
 William 183
Rousseau, Midshipman 289
Rout, George 52,86
 James 86
 Mary 187
Row, John Michael 49
 see also Roe, Rowe
Rowan, Charlotte 118
 see also Rowen
Rowand, Mary 37
 Robert 37
Rowe, Charles 305
 Donald 167,221
 Martin 308
 Samuel 35
 see also Roe, Row
Rowen, Rev. Dr. 263
 see also Rowan
Ruddock, Esther 156
 Samuel A. 156
Rudolph, Mary Matilda 264
Ruffhead, Sarah 45
Rugan, John 20
Rumph, Capt. Christian 185
 David 199
Rush, Dr. ___ 76
 Mary Ruth 76
Rushton, George L. 212
Russ, Benjamin 218
 Mary Coon 63
Russell, Alicia 218
 Benjamin 263
 Daniel 201
 John 241
 John Cornelius Jr. 225
 Jonathan 313
 Maria 14
 Mary 127
 Mary Elizabeth 271
 Nathaniel 218
 Rev. Mr. (officiate) 218
Rutgers, Col. Henry 197
Rutherford, Elizabeth 167
Rutledge, Edward 220
 John 295,330
Ryan, Capt. George 209
 Margaret 298
 Peter Thomas 298
Rynex, Andrew 308

Sabb, Ann 167,221
 John 182
 Maj. Morgan 204
 Mrs. R. E. 204(2)
Sabins, Capt. John 186
Sailor, Elizabeth A. 37
 Esau 73
 see also Saylor
St. John, Stephen 182
Salley, George E. 200
Salmon, David D. 116
 Dr. L. 120
 Thomas 160
Salomon, Alexander 211
 see Solomon
Salter, Mary 88
Saltus, Col. Francis 263
 George Samuel 218
 Mary Lawson 215
 Susannah 86
Samory, Claudius Nicolas 67
Sample, Ann 132
Sams, Catharine 59
Samuel, Jane 177
Sancry, Polly 77
Sanders, Eliza Ann 327
 John 55
 Margaret 94
 Mary Martha 299
 Roger 95
 Samuel 78
Sandford, Moses 87
Sandison, Donald 85
Sandoz, Mrs. I.F. 200
Sansom, Susanna 2
Santi, Angelo 79
Sargeant, Elizabeth 13
 John P. 13
Sarjeant,Mary 211
 William W. 205
 see also Sergeant,Serjeant
Sarzedar, Moses 252
 Sarah 306
Sasportas, Abraham 55
Sass, Edward G. 220
Sauares, Rev. Mr. 161
 see Suares
Saunders, Amarintha 4
 Rev. Mr. John Hyde 317,318
 Prisgy 46
 Roger Parker 4
Savage, George 6
 J. 94
 James R. 309
 Miss ___ 154,170
Sawyers, Lewis Sr. 307
Saylor, Ann E. 209
 Jacob 226
 see also Sailor
Sayre, Stephen 244
Scattarty, Robert 199
Schaeffer, Rev. Mr. 310
Schepeler, George 16
 Sarah Clarke 16
Schirer, Eliza S. 142
 John 105,142,279
Schmidt, Rev. Anthony 163
 John Frederick 85
 Rachel 35
Scholfied, Mrs. ___ 108
Schooler, Mary Ann 198
Schriner, Dorothea 171
Schroder, John 231
Schudy, Rev. Mr. 261
Schultz, John C. 99
 see Shultz
Schutt, Caspar C. 64,96
 Susanna D. 96

Schwartz, Christian H. 321
Scott, Rev. Mr. Alexander
  (officiate) 151,201
  Ann 190
  Ann Mary 25
  Archibald 31
  Archibald Henry 54
  Caroline Parker 231
  Cason 293
  Elizabeth 245
  Elizabeth Ann 245
  Frances Sarah 222
  George 132
  Gustavus 241
  James 58,149,170,186
  James Jr. 149
  John 167
  Joseph Adams 155
  Joyse Jane 141
  Juliana B. 241
  Martha 249
  Mary 205,267
  Mary Elizabeth 187
  Thomas 190,249
  Thomas D. 20
  Thomas G. 3
  William 20,205
  William Jr. 224
  Lt. Col. William 169
Scottowe, Amelia 23
  Samuel 93
  Susannah 93
Scouler, Margaret 206
  Thomas 206
Screven, Eleanor 5
  John 22
  Col. Thomas 83
  Rev. William 83
Scrimzeour, Charles 14,75
Scriven, Rev. B. 298
Scroter, J.J. 3
Schwartz, John 142
Seables, Henry 307
Seabrook, Anne 158
  Henry Hailey 19
  John 135,165
  Joseph 19
  Joseph B. 10
  Louisa B. 190
  Sarah 135
Seaman, Gideon 125
Sears, Ann 218
Seaver, Peter Johonot 91
Seaward, James P. 331
Sebbin, Sebbe 58
Secut, Dr. John L.E.W. 92
  Sarah 92
Segerstrom, J.G. 196
Seibels, Charlotte Caroline 68
  Jacob 68
Seiger, Dr. Charles L. 61
  M.M. 61
Seiller, Daniel 59
Senf, Col. ___ 217
  Col. Christian 147
  Gertrude J. 217
Senter, Anthony 315
  Rev. Anthony 325
Sergeant, Ann Eliza 136
Serjeant, Mary 216
  see also Sargeant,Sarjeant
Sevier, Maj. Alexander 291
Sewall, John 49
  Stephen 89
Sewell, Charles S. 103
  Samuel 43
Sexton, Mary 141,143
Seyle, Samuel 35

Seymour, Henry 189
  Capt. Isaac Sr. 77
  Mary 77
Shackelford, Elizabeth 315
  Elizabeth C. 128
  Francis 115(2)
  John 180,328
  Martha 328
  Richard 206
  Sarah Bossard 180
  William F. 338
Shaffer, Charles George 250
Shand, Robert 285
  William 285
Shannon, Jeremiah 298
Sharp, Elizabeth 98
  Rev. James M. 290
  John 98
  Joseph 23
Shaw, Capt. Alexander 162
  Ann 290
  Capt- ___ 97
  Dr. Cassillis 188
  David 101
  James 94
  Jane 44,103
  John 37
  Dr. John 218
  John A. 42
  Mary 207
  Sebellow 47
  Terrence 207
  Thomas P. 14
  Thomas William 147
  William 47,103
  William D. 226
  Zachariah 94
Shecut, Dr. John L.E.W. 103
  323
  Mary Emeline 323
  see also Secut
Shedden, Robert 8
Sheed, William 13
Sheely, Margaret 127
Sheftall, Levi 215
Shelback, Charles 26
  Mary 13
Shepherd, Mary Ann 244
Sheppard, Jane 254
  Thomas 100,220,254
Sherlock, Capt. John 145
  Capt. Robert 15
Sherman, ___ 43
  Michael 36
  Simon T. 51
  Stephen 119
Shields, Eliza 170
  Mrs. M. 113
Shingler, Mary Elizabeth 332
Shingleton, Martha 110
  see also Singleton
Shippen, Edward 138
  Elizabeth Carter 64
Shirer, John 170
Shirras, Alexander 253
Shirtliff, William 274
Shite, William 63
Shivas, Alexander 20
Shook, John 250
Shoolbred, Mary Gibbes 202
Shoulters, Abraham 205
Shrewsbury, Elizabeth Mitchell 185
  Stephen 185
Shrine, Ann 22
Shubrick, Col. ___ 31,147
  Hannah Heyward 147
  Mary Rutledge 323

Shubrick (cont'd)
  Sarah 31
Shultze, Frederick S. 98
  see also Schultz
Shum, Catharine Mary 168
Siebert, Joseph 207
Sikes, Jane Ann 52
  Thomas 173
Silbery, Nicholas 30
Simcoe, Gen. ___ 157
Sillman, Capt. John H. 272
Simkins, Arthur 33
  Edward 165
  Eliza 234
  John 234
  Capt. William 33
Simmes, Rev. R. 329
Simmons, Catharine S. 187
  Hayne 311
  James 187
  Rev. James D. (officiate) 213
  John 214
  Joseph 137
  Susan Pinckney 280
  Thomas 157
  William 11
Simms, Harriot 191
  Henry 123
  Jane 99
  William 84,191
  see also Sims
Simonet, Eugenie Magniant 130
  Louise 252
  Stephen 130
Simons, Ann 72
  Benjamin 38
  Dr. Benjamin B. 50
  Charles D. 178
  Charles Dewar 257,258
  Edward P. 324
  Elizabeth 45
  Rev. J.D. (officiate) 218
  221
  Maj. James 6,293
  Rev. James (officiate) 178,224,239
  Rev. James D. (officiate) 178,224,239,242,245,274
  Rev. James Dewar 158
  Rev. James Dewar (officiate) 213
  Keating 72
  Keating L. 261
  Maj. ___ 207
  Mary Read 239
  Montague 284
  Moses 192
  Peter 179
  Rev. Mr. (officiate) 164, 166,167(2),171,180,183,185, 187,189,191,192(2),194,205, 211,212,214,216,245,269,278 280,286,289
  Capt. Shadrick 223
  Thomas 42,45,72,239
  William Washington 207
  see also Symons
Simpson, James 63,68
  John 275
  Col. John 229,297
  Rev. John 195
  Mary 229
  Michael 186
  Dr. Presson 202
Sims, Martha 237
  Capt. William 237
  see also Simms

Sinclair, Daniel 19
  Elizabeth 130
Singeltary, Mary E. 171
Singleton, Benjamin 228,305
  Caroline Myrtilda 61
  Daniel 28
  Elizabeth 3
  Harriet 82,84
  John 82
  Mary 28
  Mrs. ___ 56
  Capt. Richard 99
  Richard Jr. 28
  Thomas 329
  see also Shingleton
Sinklin, James 88
Skene, Col. Philip 235
Skinner, Alderman 135
  S.H. 324
Skipwith, Fulwar 335
  Miss ___ 335
  Sir Peyton 38,124
  Peyton Jr. 38
Skirving, Ann Holland 153
  Anne 113
  Col. William 153
  William Jr. 113,129
Skrine, Elizabeth Macaulay 222
  John D. 311
  Mary 62
  Susanna 64
  Tacitus G. 259
  Thomas 311
  William 60
Slade, Laben 82
Slann, Mrs. Jane 3
Slater, Capt. J. 200
  Capt. John 174
Slatter, Frances Ann 214
Slawson, Nathaniel 132
Slowman, Elizabeth 250
  Mary 70
Smart, Jennet 296
  John Thomas 95
Smilie, John 46,274
  see also Smylie
Smindersine, Andrew 52
Smiser, Hannah 278
Smith, Aaron 147,167,262,312
  Alexander 200,206
  Andrew 107
  Lt. Col. Andrew 221
  Ann 102,167
  Ann Maria 195
  Archibald Jr. 60,94,102
  Arthur 178
  Barney 312
  Benjamin 129,166,181
  Bishop ___ 131
  Ben. Byrd 292
  Caleb 52
  Capt. ___ 256
  Catherine Eliza 107
  Charles Wilson 147
  Christian 94
  Dorothy 54
  Edward C. 50
  Dr. Edward D. 51
  Eliza 4,62,256
  Eliza Barnwell 210
  Eliza H. 166
  Elizabeth 70,182,222,251
  Elizabeth Ann 262
  Fanny 96
  Frances 112
  Frederick 47 328
  George 10,112,234,248,251,

Smith (cont'd)
  George A.Z. 172
  George Henry 296
  George William 218
  Mrs. H. 58
  Hugh 268
  Rev. Isaac (orriciate) 172
  James 48,56
  Jane 137,303
  Jane Field 28
  Jennet G. 336
  John 33,45,125,210,299
  Capt. John 315
  Dr. John 253
  Lt. Col. John 246
  John Christian 27
  Joseph 281
  Joseph Spencer 87
  Landgrave 83
  Levingston 165
  Lydia 313
  Margaret 98,247
  Mary 30,54,267
  Mary S. 147
  Michael 96
  Morton 247
  N. 89
  Maj. O'Brian 244
  Capt. Peter 54,182
  Rev. Bishop (officiate) 3, 4,6,10,24
  Rt. Rev. Bishop 188
  Rev. Dr. 62
  Rev. Mr. (officiate) 2,119
  Rt. Rev. Robert (officiate) 25
  Robert 53,188,313
  Roger 116
  Rosanna 213
  Sally 271
  Samuel 253
  Samuel Jr. 187,269,303
  Samuel W. 116
  Sarah 44
  Simon 143
  Thomas 29,55,117,164,229
  Thomas Branford 213
  Thomas S. 239
  Thorowgood 234
  Capt. W. 58
  William 66,98,147,164,174, 326,329
  Lt. William 19
  William Jr. 87
  William Loughton 129,274
  William M. 272
  William Penn 147
  William Steuben
Smithart, John 52
Smylie, Andrew 24
  see Smilie
Smyth, Bartlee 45
Snead, Cynthia Loveless 130
Snell, Adam 179
  Mary 179
Snetter, Charles 38
Snipes, Benjamin 63
  Catharine 94
  Eliza 11
  Mary 27
  Mary C. 104,105
  William 226
  Maj. William Clay 133
Snow, Capt. John 120
  Capt. William 187
Snowden, Anna 235
  Rev. Charles B. 261
Solan, Margaret E. 28

Solomon, Alexander 186
  Israel 208
  Joseph 189
  Miriam 171
  Solomon 117
  see also Salomon
Somarsall, Maria 150
  Thomas 150
  William 275
Somersett, Manuel 255
Sommers, John 24
  Martha 24
  Mary 1
Southgate, Robert 217
Spalding, Thomas 336
Spann, Catharine Fox 144
  Charles Jr. 168
Sparks, Alexander 155
Spears, James 191
  James M. 324
Speirin, George H. 90
  Rev. Mr. 70,90
  see also Spierin
Speissegger, John 81
Spencer, Catharine 175
Spidel, Eberhart 14
  Mary 14
Spidle, Adam 185
  Elizabeth 259
Spierin, Rev. Mr. 24
  Elizabeth 80
  Rev. George Heartwell 289
  James Armstrong 289
  Thomas P. 80
  see also Speirin
Spiesseger, Daniel 12
  see also Speisseger
Spinner, David 235
  Kitty 235
Spotswood, Gen. Alexander 137
  Capt. John A. 137
Spreth, Catharine 209
  see also Sprith
Spring, John 2
Sprith, Nicholas 146
  see also Spreth
Sprout, Martha 222
Squibb, Robert 137
Stack, Polly 61
Stafford, James 64
Staker, Mary 142
Staley, William 209
Stanard, Edward Carter 239
Stanford, Richard 297
Stanhope, Charles Earl 311
Stanley, ___ 85
  Rev. Mr. 306
  Timothy 315
Stannought, Martha 103
Stanton, Dolly 309
Stanyarne, Mary 73
Starr, Mary 94
  Thomas 292
Starke, Douglass 24,119
  Elizabeth 24
  Lucy 24
  Reuben 119
  Thomas 146
  Turner 40,137
Steads, Harriett 198
Steed, Charles 180
Steedman, Charles John 75
Steele, Elizabeth 200,306
  John 140
  William 324
Stent, John 5
  John Sr. 301
  John Hearne 33,226

Stent (cont'd)
  Mary 53
  Mary C. 53
  Robert 186
Stephens, John 21
  Miss ___ 96
  Sir Philip 96
  William 225(2)
  see also Stevens
Stephenson, Rev. James W. 191
  see also Stevenson
Stevens, Ann 126
  Ann Jane 245
  Clement Crooke Blake 264
  Cotton M. 135
  Daniel 150
  Col. Danil 208
  Jervis Henry 241,245
  John 20
  Capt. Joseph 183
  Capt. Joseph Green 287
  Joseph Hutchinson 119
  Mary 3,218
  O'Neal Gough 27
  Robert 287
  Samuel M. 208
  Sarah 14
  Susannah 241
  Dr. William S. 115
  see also Stephens
Stephenson, Jane 12
  John G. 82
  see also Stevenson
Stewards, Miss ___ 310
Stewart, Agnew 53
  Alexander 53
  Charles 289
  Daniel 99
  Eliza 45
  George 53
  Jane 32
  John 80,114
  Martha 203
  Robert 170,203
  Sarah 177
  Thomas 151
  William 268
  see also Stuart
Stiff, Richard 239
Stiles, Benjamin 33,120
  Benjamin Jr. 81,101
  Isaiah 74
Stilling, Dr. Jung 316
Stillman, Rev. Samuel 163
Stilwell, Samuel 333
  Samuel Seabury 269
Stine, Barbara 325
  Samuel 212
Stock, John 140
  Dr. Thomas 137
Stocker, Ebenezer 306
Stoddard, Benjamin 290
Stoddert, Maj. Benjamin 34
  Rebecca 34
Stoll, Eliza 329
  Jacob 48
  Sarah 47
Stone, Capt. Benjamin 10,31
  Elijah 301
  Elizabeth Rivers 31
  Mary Lightbourn 10
  William 8
Stoney, Harriet E. 65
  John 12,65,127
Stoops, B.T. 193
Storts, Rebecca 325
Story, Charles 154
  Eliza 43

Strobel, Benjamin 180
  Daniel Sr. 61,154,174
  Jacob 30
  Jane Stent 160(2)
  Lewis 7,160
  Capt. Lewis 196
  Martin 200
  Mary Elizabeth 32,174
Stroman, Elizabeth 245
  Margaret 199
  Paul 199
Strong, Rev. Nathan 307
Strother, Charles 122
  Mary 122
Strowman, Elizabeth 69
Stuart, Ann 120
  Rev. James 120
  Richard 101
  see also Stewart
Studwant, Millia 169
Suares, Mr. ___ 165
  Rev. Jacob (officiate) 186 (3),208,223,239
  Rev. Mr. (officiate) 235
  see also Sauares
Suau, Peter 184
Suder, Charlotte 164
Sullivan, James 214
  Timothy 133
Sully, Matthew Jr. 260
Summet, Leonard 142
Sumter, Louisa 166
Surr, John Cambidge 305
Sutherland, Alexander 92
  James 85
Sutliff, M. Ellis 269
Sutton, Ann 115
  Capt. George 322
  Mary 35,244,322
Swaine, Bulah 204
  Elizabeth 88
  Capt. Frederick 57
  Capt. Joseph 88
  Luke 26
  Capt. Luke 245
  Mary 82
  Rebecca P. 245
Swan, Robert 152
Sweat, Rev. James (officiate) 201,206
  Rev. Mr. 159(3),248(2),249
Swedny, Henoria 240
Sweeney, Dennis 120
  John 147
Swiff, Emmaan 148
Swigard, Capt. John 69
Swindersine, Sarah 130
Swinton, Caroline 113
  Hugh 186
  Hugh Sr. 215
  James 97
Switzer, John R. 7
  John Rodolph 232
  Mary 317
  Mary S. 220
Syfan, Ann Eliza 278
  John 265
  Susan 265
Symons, William 264
  see also Simons

Tait, George 21
  Thomas 93
Talbird, James Doharty 219
  Col. Thomas 69
Talbot, Euphemia 317
  Matthew 317
  Silas 282

Talpier, Tagek 95
Talvande, Andrew 256
Tameru, Christian 215
Tanois, M.F. 105
Tapp, Abner 237
Tapper, Thomas 51
Tarbox, David 278
  Mary Elizabeth 196
Tardieu, Ceserea 73
  Louis 73
Tardue, Antoinette 6
  Louis 6
Tarlton, John 179
Tarone, A. 174
Tart, Elizabeth G. 143
Tarver, Elizabeth 207
Tatem, Capt. Jeremiah 123
Tattnall, Mrs. H. 54
  Josiah Jr. 54
Taylor, Anne 34
  Bernhard 93
  Catherine 194
  Charles 108
  Eleanor 252
  Floride 38
  George 1
  Jacob 336
  Capt. James 149
  John 98,252,259
  John N. 298
  Joseph 154
  Joseph G. 71
  Josiah 127,146
  Magdaline Bonneau 199
  Maria S. 247
  Mary 203
  Capt. Samuel 199
  Sarah 331
  Sophia 215
  Susannah Eliza 259
  Thomas 69,313
  Walter 142
  William 30,165
Teasdale, Ann 176
  Eliza 150
  Elizabeth 86
  Isaac 86,136,171,176
  Mary Ann 136
Telfair, Edward 178
Tennant, Robert 279
Tennent, Rev. John 211
Terasson, Mary 17
Terrell, Mary 118
Tew, Charles 312
  Margaret Mason 273
Theus, Ann 132
  Caroline 15
  James 148
  Rebecca 81,145
  Sarah 256
  Simeon Jr. 242
  William R. 151,186
Thigpen, Rev. Mr. 155
Thomas, Ann 76
  Cornelia 268
  Dr. ___ 294
  E.S. 128
  Edward 152,187
  Edward G. 97
  Elizabeth 152,189
  George 108
  James 95
  John 162
  Rev. John 314
  John David 234
  Maria 108
  Mary 188
  Mary L. 314

Thomas (cont'd)
  Dr. Samuel 58
  Stephen 76
  Suzanne DeLezar 168
Thompson, Aaron 220
  Alexander 9
  Barbara Amelia 106
  Charlotte Elizabeth 30
  Clement A. 177
  Eliza 50(2)
  James 65,107
  James H. 30,50
  Rev. John (officiate) 73, 84
  John Paul 15
  Laney 132
  Rev. Mr. (officiate) 7,12, 17,35,112,188
  Sarah 172
  Worcester 122
Thomson, Ann C. 280
  Eugenia 225
  James 47,279
  James Hamden 186
  Rev. James W. 296
  John Paul 254
  Mary E. 113
  Col. W. R. 113
  Col. William 225
  Col. William T. 165
Thorne, Caroline I'ans 314
  John G. 314
Thorney, Jane 15
  William 15
Thornhill, John Lee 319
Thornley, Maj. Robert 116
  Thornton, Elisha 307
  Widow ___ 314
Threadcraft, Bethel 77,278
  Mary Eliza 129
Thursting, Sarah 16
Thwing, Edward 43
Thynnes, William 36
Tiebout, Elizabeth 111
Tift, Solomon 278
Tilghman, Chief Justice 307
Tillinghast, John 175
  Sally 67
  William H. 286
Tillton, Elizabeth W. 329
Timmings, Daniel B. 117
Timmons, Lewis 62
  Margaret 61
Timms, Amos Sr. 241
  Frances 241
  see also Tims
Timothy, Benjamin Franklin 38, 182
  Elizabeth 38
  Peter 34
  Robert Smith 34
Tims, Thomas 11
  see also Timms
Tinch, Ann 50
  Edward 50
Tingey, Commodore Thomas 312
Tingham, Capt. Clark 108
Tison, Rev. Aaron 108
  see also Tyson
Tobin, Miss ___ 41
Tobler, Capt. W. 144
Tock, Mary Ann 26
Todd, Elizabeth 70
  James 128
  John 170,235
  Thomas 33,260
Tofel, Catherine 122
  John 122

Tofel (cont'd)
  Mary Catherine 122
Tofet, John 50
Tomlins, James 92, 236
  Mrs. ___ 236
Tomplat, Eliza 156
Tonge, Ann 280
Tool, John 20
Toomer, Anthony 232,280
  Maj. Anthony 26,149
  Charlotte 232
  Henrietta Raven 26
  Henry B. 128
  Henry William Blyth 149
Torrence, Elizabeth 100
Torrans, John 326
  John Fordon 36
  Capt. William Hunter 39,111
Torre, A.D. 298
Torrey, Ezekiel 219
Tousset, Capt. ___ 66
Toutain, Peter N.G. 132
Townsend, Thomas Jr. 255
  Thomas Sr. 268
Townshend, Sarah 90
  Stephen 90
Towson, Lt. Col. Nathan 297
Tracey, Col. ___ 19
  Mrs. ___ 36
  Uriah 172
  Miss W. F. 19
Trair, Anna Barbary 10
Trapier, Benjamin Foissin 55
  Elizabeth 241
  Paul 31
Travers, John 21
Treadwell, Alexander Philip Socrates Aemilius Caesar Hannibal Marcellus George Washington 234
Tredwell, Joanna 49
Treutlan, Margaret 172
Trescott, William 321
Trezevant, Judge ___ 64
  Theodore 15
Trippe, Capt. ___ 234
Trist, H.B. 94
Trott, Madame ___ 272
Truchelut, Mary Charlotte 215
Truelle, Jaque Marps 209
Tucker, Ann 205
  Benjamin 249
  Eliza 250
  Elizabeth 133
  George Heriot 249
  Mary T. 269
  William B. 164,205,328
Tudor, Delia 289
  William 289
Tufts, Capt. Simon 100
Tuke, John 154
Tull, Nancy 302
Tully, Priscilla 204
Tunis, Richard 321
Tunno, ___ 257
  George 53
  Mrs. ___ 44
  Mrs. T. 33
Turnbull, Bridget 176
  Eliza C. 333
  Gavin 295
  James 3
  John 4
  Nichol 194
  Susan 194
  William 104,333
Turner, David Watson 151
  Elizabeth 275

Turner (cont'd)
  Henry E. 331
  Maj. John 174
  Capt. Joshua 112
  Martha 167
  Mary 100
  Dr. Peter 273
  Sarah 316
  Sterling Edward 138
  William 43
  Capt. William 275
  William McCallister 152
Twaits, Elizabeth 289
  William 289
Tweed, Capt. Alexander 58
  John 169
Twentyman, Sarah 305
Tyrall, ___ 99
Tyson, Rev. Mr. 105
  see also Tison

Ulmer, Jacob 158
  John 204
  John Barton 204
Urquhart, John 176
Utt, Oliver 323

Valk, Harriet 19
  Jacob 58
  Jacob R. 111
Van Allen, Peter L. 44
Van Alstyne, Charlotte 90
Van Antwerp, Ahasuerus 336
Vanbiber, Ann 213
Vanderherchen, Andrew 66
  Eleanor F. 154
  Mary Augustine 250
  Mary Sicile 66
Vanderhoff, Cornelius 205
  Eliza 205
Vanderhorst, Gen. ___ 50,189
  Jane 260
  Maria 50
Van Knap, Marcus 335
Vardell, Thomas A. 90
Vaughan, Henry 314
  Julia 314
  Philip 112
  Rosetta 48
Vaughn, Jesse 232
Vaux, Percival Edward 128
  Sarah M. 135
  William 135
Veitch, Henry 199,241
  William 205
Velser, Elijah 225
Venneman, Eliza 307
Verdell, Thomas A. 162
Verdier, Alexander 144
  Eliza 198
  J.M. 198
  Mary 144
Vernon, Henry 193
  Thomas 4
Verree, Elizabeth 16
  George 57,106,266
  Mary 229
  William 103
Verrette, Maria Joseph Feuvette 109
Vervier, Madenoselle 83
Vesey, John 83
  Capt. Joseph 70
Vibert, Henrietta Bacon 255
Vidall, Eliza B. 334
Vidler, John 40
Vieyra, Ann 162

Vigie, Antonie 197
Vigree, Rose 51
Villepontoux, Rebecca 188
  Zachariah 291
Villiers, Thomas Clarendon 69
Vince, Capt. Joseph 242
Vincent, Capt. John 194,233
Vinro, Norbert 109
Vinyard, Eliza Elliot 295
  John 138,295
Vionnay, Mary 34
Von Yeveren, M. 193
Vos, Andrew 78

Waddle, Major ___ 237
  Rev. James (officiate) 123
  Rev. Moses (officiate) 17,
    21,24,25,40,41(2),42
  Rev. Mr. (officiate) 109,
    306
Wadsworth, Susannah 105
  Thomas 105
Wagner, Ann 276
  George 189,276,303
  Samuel J. 255
Wagoner, Christopher 58
Waight, Isaac 238
  Martha 238
  see also Weight
Wainwright, Elizabeth Sarah
    231
  Juliana B. 258
  Lt. ___ 258
  Lt. R.D. 241
  Richard 45,231
Waits, Mr. ___ 112
Wakefield, Isabella 297
  Emma Martha 97
Waldo, Elisha H. 18
Waldrop, Isaac 94
Walker, Carleton 80,113
  Edward 150
  Col. Edward 230
  Eliza 211
  Elizabeth 80
  James 231
  Jane 270
  John 52,179
  Rev. Mr. (officiate) 98
  Robert 258
  Rev. Robert B. (officiate)
    293
  Sabina T. 113
  William 111
Wall, Mary 31
  Richard Gilbert 31
Wallace, ___ 329
  Rev. Frederick Joseph 127
  Martha 228
  Mary Ann 253
  Rev. Mr. (officiate) 51
Waller, William 269
Walliace, John 92
Walling, Mary 219
Wallis, John 46
  Margaret 205
Waln, Jesse 136
  Nicholas 285
Walsh, Rev. Father 149
  Rev. Father (officiate) 114
Walter, Jacob 100,140
  John C. 199,269
  Keziah 100
  Paul 24
  Maj. Paul 24,281
Walton, Ann Maria 200
  Edmond 177
  George 78

Walton (cont'd)
  John 151,152,321
  Joseph 120
  Sarah 218
  William 120,159
Ward, Ann 27
  Daniel 181,271
  Eliza 7
  Eliza Charlotte 215
  Elizabeth 218
  Rev. Mr. Francis 255
  Harriet Amanda 317
  Henry Dana 41
  Maj. James 317
  Col. John 275,303,329
  Joshua 7
  Margaret Swinton 181
  Mary Eliza 41
  Thomas 203
Warder, Susannah 225
  Virgil 225
Wardrop, John 203(2)
Wardwell, Capt. Abiel 332
Waring, Amelia 217
  Capt. B.R. 288
  Capt. Benjamin 252
  Capt. Benjamin R. 280
  Daniel Jennings 315
  Dr. Edmond T. 70
  Hess M. 280,288
  Dr. Horatio S. 276
  Joseph 71
  Mary 71
  Morton 211
  Col. Morton A. 104
  Susan 211
  Dr. Thomas 280,288
  Thomas Sr. 217
Warley, Christiana 35
  Mary M. 300
  Melchor 35
  Paul 163
  Dr. William 229,300
Warnock, Elizabeth 97
  Joseph N. 26
  Judith 73
  Thomas 297
Warren, Capt. John 132
  Capt. Peter 22
  Rev. Mr. 257
Wartenberg, Peter 230,318
Washburn, Rev. Joseph 130
Washington, Charles Augustine
    250
  General ___ 27,321
  Gen. George 40
  George Steptoe 215
  Capt. Henry 262
  Jane 27
  Lucy 260
  Martha 40
  Richard Henry Lee 321
  William Jr. 184
  Col. Wm. Augustine 236
Wasson, Jane 7
Waters, Eliza 331
  Rev. Mr. 80
  Rev. Nicholson 88
Waties, Judge ___ 127
Watkins, Sarah 26
  Col. Robert 118
Watkinson, John 279
Watson, Ann 35
  Sir Brook 187
  Elizabeth 17
  James 140,157
  John 131
  Capt. John A. 298

Watson (cont'd)
  Mary 17
  Rachel 78
  William 167
  William Tweed 226
Watt, Ann Elizabeth 218
Watter, Jane 54
Watts, Charles 255
  Jane 117
Waugh, Alexander B. 216
Way, Thomas 42
Wayne, Elizabeth 65
  Gabriel W. 309
  Richard 65
  Rev. Mr. (officiate) 194
Weatherby, Daniel 29
Weatherford, Eliza Ann 267
Weatherley, Isaac 89,115
  Capt. Isaac 81
  Sarah C. 81
Weaver, Christiana 228
  Capt. Joseph 235
  Margaret 48(2)
Webb, Alexander 202
  Benjamin 141
  Burges 195
  Daniel C. 127
  John 188
  Margaret D. 90
  Mary 53
  William 314
Webber, William 110
Webberly, Ruth 148
Webley, Benjamin 101
Webster, Eliza 221
  John A. 294
Weight, Elisa Pugh 245
  see also Waight
Weissinger, Ann Margaret 212
Welch, Eliza 93
  Nathaniel G. 50
  Samuel 34
Welles, Arnold 45
  Hannah 188
Wells, Arnold 114
  Edgar 31,61
  Frances Louisa H. 292
  Hannah 154
  Harriet E. 12
  Phoebe 61
  Robert 121
Wellser, Godfrey Sr. 60
Welsh, George 94,242
  Margaret 87,151
  Nathaniel Green 142,151,175
  Valentine 208
Welsman, James 185
Wendell, Cataline 308
  Gen. John A. 308
Wershing, John 139
Wesner, Henry P. 294
  Margaret 238
  Mary Susanna 35
West, ___ 321
  Catharine 137
  George 293
  James 114
  Dr. James D. 286
  Margaret 231
  Mary 172
  Mrs. ___ Jr. 103
  Rev. Dr. 77
  Capt. Simeon 172
Weston, Mary Jennett 38
  Narcissa P. 235
  Paul 337
  Plowden 38
Weyman, Maj. Edward 282

Whaley, Archibald 125
　Eliza R. 23
　Elizabeth 135
　John Calder 59(2)
　Joseph 190
　Thomas 23,59,125
Whalley, George 118
　John 226
Wharton, Rev. Dr. Charles H.
　(officiate) 165
　Isaac 197
Wheeler, Elhanan Winchester
　169
　Eliza 253
　Harriet 294
　John 174
　Josiah 290
　Luke 134
　Susan 134
　Zachariah 50
Wheelock, John 313
Whipple, Capt. Christopher
　177
Whitaker, Emma 3
Whitby, Capt. Henry 264
White, Ann 256
　Charlotte Hodgson
　Naj. Edward 256
　Francis 279
　George K. 96
　Capt. Henry 279
　Jane Pogson 55
　John 55,111,180,187
　John B. 107
　John P. 171
　Martha 28,113
　Peregrine 89
　Rebecca 142
　Rt. Rev. Bishop (officiate)
　76,187,209
　Dr. Sims 61
　Thomas 142
　William Augustus 281
Whitehead, Ann 45
　Rev. James 89
Whitesides, Charles 66
　John 30
　Rebecca 131
　Thomas 41,120
Whitfield, Gen. Bryan 317
Whiting, John 139
　Col. John 235
Whitlock, Edward 89
　Sarah 236
Whitmarsh, Capt. William 134
Whitmore, Tabitha 46
　see also Whittimore
Whitney, Archibald 178
　Capt. John 295
　Thomas H. 330
Whitridge, Dr. J.B. 336
Whitter, Martha 46
Whittimore, Rettier 54
　see also Whitmore
Whittington, Miss ___ 174
　Thomas 99
Whorry, Jane 78
Whotcoat, Rev. Richard 144
Wiare, H.A. 233
　James Gray 29
　Capt. James G. 233
Wiatt, ___ 195
　see also Wyatt
Wigfall, Constantia 315
　Harriot 187
　Levi Durand 50
　Samuel 108
　Sarah 334

Wigfall (cont'd)
　Thomas 187,315
Wigg, Maj. ___ 87
　William Hudson 86
Wightman, John T. 329
Wilcox, Patience 135
Wilkes, Charles 286
　Charlotte 286
Wiley, Rev. David 242
Wilkie, Ann Eliza 27
　Maj. ___ 27
Wilkins, John 7,11-
　Maria 112
　Martha 11,338
　Marh S. 74
　Morris 329
　Rev. Mr. (officiate) 173
　Capt. Thomas 74
Wilkinson, Abraham 89
　Anne 163
　Dr. ___ 155
　General ___ 163
　Capt. Joseph 97
　Mary 128
　Rachel 142
　Sarah D. 97
　William 307
Will, John 8,268
Willard, Prentiss 286
　Rev. Mr. (officiate) 197
Williams, Ann 148,277
　Rev. Avery 294
　Caroline Sophie Margaretta
　Maria Julienne Wortley
　Montague Joan of Arc 234
　Charles 174
　David R. 57,246
　Fanny 145
　Henry 162
　John 12(2),47,210
　John Mortimer 4
　Jotham 238
　Margaret 117
　Philip 148
　Philip D. 226
　Rev. Samuel 308
　Samuel Jr. 66
　Sarah 4,57
　Simson, 183
　Capt. Stephen 315
　William 63,128
Williamson, Abraham 231
　Andrew 125
　Ann Goodwin 328
　Argyle 177
　Benjamin 328
　Capt. ___ 190
　Charles 41
　Dinah 240
　Emelia 190
　George 200
　Dr. Hugh 330
　J.B. 49
　John 115
　John Brown 36
　Joseph 314
　Mary 49,70
　Thomas 115,173
　Capt. Thomas 185
　William 125
Williman, Christopher 7,84,91,
　233
　George 337
　Henrietta 233
　Dr. Jacob 91
　Margaret 7
　Mary 84
Willingham, Debora 73

Willington, Robert
Willis, Rev. Henry 192
　Jane 139
　John H. 204
　Mary 154
Will, Robert 238
Wilmer, Jonathan 119
　T.R. 8
Wilson, Ann 153,250
　Charlotte A. 324
　Daniel 229
　Delphia 125
　Eliza 112
　Elizabeth 98
　Elizabeth Pettingal 311
　Helen 269
　Hugh Jr. 102
　Dr. Isaac Mazyck 237
　James 98,288
　Dr. James 108
　Rev. James 220
　Dr. James Sr. 288
　Jehu 241
　John 9,119,182,212,240
　John L. 324
　John M. 166
　Leighton 109
　Mrs. ___ 109
　Mrs. M. 264
　Mary 16,92,190
　Mary Motte 229
　Rev. Mr. (officiate) 206,
　230
　Robert 9,259
　Capt. Robert 3,30
　Dr. Robert 105,153,190,271,
　333
　Dr. Robert Jr. 198
　Rev. Robert (officiate) 40
　Robert Alexander 198
　Samuel 16
　Sarah 241
　Susan J. 271
　William 160
Windsor, James D. 320
　Capt. Thomas 245,320
Wingate, Edward 110
　Hugh Strain 160
　Joseph 252
Wingood, Ann 232
Wingwood, Ann 232
Winkhouse, Rev. John H. 301
Winkler, Ann B. 190
Winn, Lettice 42
　Maj. Gen. ___ 35
　Minor Jr. 35
　Thomas 42
Winters, Charles 95
　Jane 49
　John Goerge 21
Wise, John 116
Wiseman, Joseph 118
Wish, Ann Catherine 240
　Ann T. 185
　Benjamin 185
　William 234
Wissinger, John 120
Wistar, Dr. ___ 326
Withers, Ann Eliza 172
　Eleanora 155
　Frances 122
　John 90,122
　John 90,122
　Capt. John 172
　John Jr. 84
　Mary W. 247
　Rebeca 90
　Sophia Jane 141

373

Witherspoon, Ann 194
  Jane H. 193
  John D. 198
  Dr. John R. 54,193
  Robert 191
Witsell, John 3
Witten, Eleanor 184
  Peter 184
  Peter Robert 130
Witter, Benjamin 87
  Eliza 164
  Mary 8
  Thomas 106
Wolcott, ___ 256
Wolf, Ann 117
  Eliza Catherine 277
  Isaac 223,236
  Levi 236
  Margaret 43
  Sarah 168
  see also Woolfe
Woods, Dinah 314
  Elizabeth 166,185
  James 72
  Gen. John 307
  Major 185
  Margaret 255
  Martha 159
  Rebecca 186
  Stephen 82
Woodall, Susannah 139
Woodburn, William 118
Woodcraft, Martha 160
  Richard 157
Woodham, George W. 193
  Mrs. ___ 306
Woodhouse, Dr. James 224
Woodill, John Anthony 105
Woodle, John Anthony 2
Woodman, John 91
Woodrouffe, Edward L. 67
Woodson, Emiline A.J. 254
Woodward, Elisha 159
  Capt. James 158
  John H. 277
  John Hancock 203
  Warham 86
Woodworth, Clarissa 61
Woolcock, William 34
Woolfe, Cecilia 186
  Margaret 199
  Mathias 106
  Solomon 186
see also Wolf
Woolley, Dr. Stephen H. 292
Workman, David 130
  James 337
  Jane 190
  Juliana Petre 337
Wortman, Jacob 244
Wotton, Christopher 331
Wragg, Charlotte 129
  Henrietta 32,104
  Joseph 191
  Samuel 10
  William 32,68,104,129
Wrainch, Ann Eliza 64
  Judith 34
  John 34
  Richardson 138
Wrand, Winifred 221
Wright, Alexander 5
  Mrs. E. 283
  Elizabeth 28
  Jack 53
  James Alexander 5
  John 337

Wright (cont'd)
  Joshua G. 246
  L. 50
  Rev. Bishop (officiate) 200
  Samuel T. 233
  Thomas 283
Wurkell, Mangle 293
Wyal, Martha 22
Wyatt, Mrs. C. 93
  Eliza 299
  Elizabeth 204
  Henrietta 26
  Henry 323
  Mrs. ___ 119
  Peter 119,322
  Violetta Lingard 278
Wyche, John 335
Wyld, John C. 112
Wylie, Eli abeth 151
  Jane 37
Wylly, C.S. 311
Wythe, George 141

Yancey, Benjamin C. 323
Yates, Amelia Deborah 274
  Elizabeth 228
  Jeremiah 228
  Joseph 37,228
  Mary Ann 140
  Samuel 30
  Samuel Jr. 246
  Sarah 77
  Sarah C. 132
  Seth 237
Yeadon, Eliza Ann 29
Yeates, Jasper 312
Yeoman, Rev. John 194
  Rev. Mr. 198,206
Yoer, Jacob 252
Yonge, Eliza 91
  Francis 11
  Sarah 11
Yongue, Elizabeth P. 156
  Rev. S.W. 156
You, John 6
Young, Ann 46
  Capt. Charles 48
  Elizabeth 185
  Grace 39
  John P. 323
  Capt. John T. 119
  Joseph 40
  Margaret 197
  Mary 147
  Capt. Richard 53
  Sarah 147
  Susan Cox 223
  Thomas 80,197
  W.P. 223
  William 79,278
Youngblood, Eleanor 293
  General ___ 329
  William 3

Zuill, Capt. James 228
  William 75
Zylks, William 111
Zylstra, John 170
  Peter 235

INDIANS
  Madame Orno 215
  Martha 113
  Zachariah 113

SLAVES
  Buck 86
  Cuffee 227
  Jack 102

www.ingramcontent.com/pod-product-compliance
Lightning Source LLC
Chambersburg PA
CBHW052140300426
44115CB00011B/1452